Guide to
Health Claims Examining

Includes Honors Certification™

ICDC Publishing, Inc.

Chapter 1, 5, 6

PUBLISHING, INC.

Los Angeles

Publisher: ICDC Publishing, Inc.
Editor-in-Chief: Sharon E. Brown
Editor: Caitlind L. Alexander
Assistant Editor: Anita M. Garcia
Assistant Editor: Shavon Z. Fletcher

Fifth Edition

Copyright © 2003 by ICDC Publishing, Inc.

Printed in the United States of America

ICDC Publishing, Inc.
4123 Lankershim Blvd.
North Hollywood, CA 91602
Phone: (818) 487-1199
Fax: (818) 769-3100
www.ICDCPublishing.com

International Standard Book Number 1-881159-16-7

Disclaimer

This text is a guide for learning the health claims examining field. Decisions should not be based solely on information within this guide. Decisions impacting the practice of medical billing and health claims examining must be based on individual circumstances including legal/ethical considerations, local conditions and payor policies.

The information contained in this text is based upon experience and research. However, in the complex, rapidly changing medical and insurance environments, this information may not always prove correct. The data used is widely variable and can change at any time. Readers should follow current coding regulations as outlined by official coding organizations.

Any five-digit numeric *Physicians' Current Procedural Terminology*, (CPT) codes, services descriptions, instructions and/or guidelines are copyright 2003 (or such other date of publication of CPT as defined in the federal copyright laws) American Medical Association. All Rights Reserved.

CPT is a listing of descriptive terms and five-digit numeric identifying codes and modifiers for reporting medical services performed by physicians. This presentation includes only CPT descriptive terms, numeric identifying codes and modifiers for reporting medical services and procedures that were selected by ICDC Publishing, Inc. for inclusion in this Publication.

The most current CPT is available from the American Medical Association.

No fee schedules, basic unit values, relative value guides, conversion factors or scales or components thereof are included in the CPT.

ICDC Publishing, Inc. has selected certain CPT codes and service/procedure descriptions and assigned them to various specialty groups. The listing of a CPT service or procedure description and its code number in this Publication does not restrict its use to a particular specialty group. Any procedure or service in this Publication may be used to designate the services rendered by any qualified physician.

The American Medical Association assumes no responsibility for the consequences attributable to or related to any use or interpretation of any information or views contained in or not contained in this Publication.

All codes contained in the dental services section of this text are copyright © 2003 American Dental Association. All Rights Reserved. Licensed for use under license # ADA 9192011.

The publisher and author do not accept responsibility for any adverse outcome from undetected errors, opinion and analysis contained in this manual that may prove inaccurate or incorrect, or from the reader's misunderstanding of an extremely complex topic. All names used in this book are completely fictitious. Any resemblance to persons or companies, current or no longer existing, is purely coincidental.

Acknowledgements

Many people have contributed to the development and success of *Guide to health Claims Examining*. We extend our thanks and deep appreciation to the many students and classroom instructors who have provided us with helpful suggestions for this edition of the text.

We would like to express our thanks to the following individuals who believed in the program in its initial stages and helped us work through the glitches associated with any new product:

Linda Jepson
Janet Grossfeld, Adelante Career Institute, Van Nuys, CA
Hollis Anglin and Michael Coffin, Dawn Training Institute, New Castle, DE
Michael Williams, 4-D Success Academy, Colton, CA
Anna McCracken, Lynn Russell, American Career College, Los Angeles, CA
Evelyn S. Wyskiel, CPC of Branford Hall Career Institute, Southington, CT
Annie Rackley, Western Technical Institute

We would like to thank those ICDC Publishing consultants who helped with this manual, especially **Caitlind L. Alexander, Anita M. Garcia** and **Shavon Z. Fletcher** for their loyalty and commitment, which was instrumental in bringing this edition to successful completion.

Thanks to the CPA firm of Miller, Kaplan, Arase and Company, LLP. To **Mannon Kaplan,** C.P.A., thank you for believing in and supporting ICDC, and for all of your knowledge and wisdom. A special thank you to **George Nadel Rivin,** C.P.A., and **Joseph C. Cahn,** C.P.A., for their valued consultation. For having the faith and commitment to see it through, we truly appreciate you and your partners; **Edwin Kanemaru,** C.P.A., **Kenneth R. Holmer,** C.P.A., **Douglas S. Waite,** C.P.A., **Charles Schnaid,** C.P.A., **Donald G. Garrett,** C.P.A., **Catherine C. Gardner,** C.P.A., and **Jeffrey L. Goss,** C.P.A.

And finally to **Sean Adams** and **Sydney Adams,** thank you for allowing me to spend the time and energy required to concentrate on this project. To **Floree Brown,** thank you for all of your love and support. I would like to dedicate this book to the memory of my father, **Nathaniel Brown Sr.**

Sharon E. Brown, Esq.
President
ICDC Publishing, Inc.

Preface

Health claims examining and medical billing are two of the fastest-growing employment opportunities in the United States today. Insurance companies, medical offices, hospitals and other health care providers are in great need of trained personnel to create and process medical billing claims.

With the aid of this textbook, you can learn the skills necessary to become a successful health claims biller or examiner. The material has been designed to be comprehensive, yet user-friendly. The text follows a logical learning format by beginning with a broad base of information and then, step by step, following the course of a health claim from billing to examining.

This text may be used with ICDC Publishing's *Guide to Medical Billing* and the Medical Biller/Health Claims Examiner Curriculum Program. The curriculum is developed in easy to understand, stand alone modules.

Special Features

The following special features of the text enhance understanding and retention of the material covered:

Each chapter begins with **learning objectives** to focus the student on the most pertinent topics covered in that chapter. **Key words and concepts** introduce the student to new terminology and processes. The straightforward, **easy-to-understand writing style** presents information clearly and concisely. **Questions for Review** at the end of each chapter reinforce key concepts. Answering questions without looking back into the chapter will help readers determine if they have grasped the main principles within the chapter or if there is a need for further study. They also serve to prepare students for exams. **Exercises** provided with most chapters give students the opportunity to put their knowledge into practice. These hands-on, real-life exercises will ensure competence in medical billing and claims examining. **Honors Certification**™ challenges encourage students to learn the material in order to graduate from a course "with honors."

Answers for all Questions for Review and Exercises are contained in the instructor materials for the course, along with the Honors Certification™ tests and answers. This material is available to schools.

The most important ingredient to success in this course is the desire to learn, without which the learning process is ineffective. The desire to learn can lead you to a rewarding career in the medical billing or health claims examining fields.

Table of Contents

x

Introduction to Insurance

In this chapter you will learn:

- The role of insurance companies in the U.S. economy.
- To recognize the different departments in an insurance company and discuss their functions.
- To identify the responsibilities of the Department of Insurance.

Key words and concepts you will learn in this chapter:

Actuarial Statistics – Studies that an insurance company uses. For a carrier which covers health insurance, these can include statistics covering average life span, number of days in hospital per year for each age group, number of doctor visits, costs of all medical services, etc.

Administrator – Someone who administers or handles the administrative duties of an insurance carrier.

Beneficiary – The person who receives payment on a claim, often the person who receives the benefit in the case of a deceased member.

Benefit – An item covered by an insurance policy, or something paid to or on behalf of a recipient.

Claim – A written request by the insured individual for payment by the insurance company of covered expenses under the insurance policy.

Covered Expense – Any expense for which complete or partial payment is provided under the insurance policy.

Co-payment – A provision requiring the member to pay a set or fixed dollar amount (i.e., $5, $10, or $25) each time a particular medical service is used. Co-payment provisions are frequently found in PPO and HMO plans.

Deductible – The initial portion of a covered expense that must be paid by the insured person before the insurance policy pays its part of the expense.

Department of Insurance – Is the legal entity that oversees the operations of all insurance companies.

Employee Benefit – Anything other than wages offered to an employee. This can include insurance coverage, vacation time, pension or retirement plans, sick pay, etc.

Group Insurance – Is insurance that covers more than one person or item under a policy.

Individual Insurance – Is an insurance policy for coverage of one person or item.

In-network – Are those providers approved by the plan.

Insurance – An agreement whereby an insurance carrier agrees to cover certain benefits in exchange for premium payments.

Insurance Carrier – The company which offers the health insurance policy. A corporation or association whose business is to make contracts of insurance.

Insurance Company – Often used to refer to companies that sell policies offered by insurance carriers.

Insurance Policy – A written contract defining the insurance plan, its coverage, exclusions, eligibility requirements, and all benefits and conditions that apply to individuals insured under the plan.

Insurance Premium – The amount of money required for coverage under a specific insurance policy for a given period of time. Depending on the policy agreement, the premium may be paid monthly, quarterly, semiannually, or annually.

Insured (also called **Member**) – The person who obtains or is otherwise covered by insurance on his health, life or property insurance.

Lapse in coverage – A break in continuous insurance coverage, usually resulting from nonpayment of premium.

Out-of-Network – Are those providers that have not been approved by the plan.

Products – Items or services offered for sale by a company. In the case of insurance carriers, the products are the various policies they offer.

Providers of Service (often just **Providers**) – The physician, chiropractor, dentist or other health care professional or establishment (hospital, nursing home, etc.) that provides health care services.

Reinsurance Carrier – An insurance carrier that offers to cover expenses when the benefit payments on a self-funded plan exceed a certain amount.

Renewal – Paying a premium in order to continue coverage after the initial policy period has expired.

Self-funded Plan – When the total and ultimate responsibility for providing all plan benefit payments rests solely with the employer, group or association.

Solvency – Ability to pay debts or obligations.

Stop-Loss Insurance – Insurance that covers plans when their benefit payments exceed a certain amount.

Third-Party Administrator (TPA) – A plan administration firm that deals solely with administering the eligibility and claim payment services (along with various other administrative services) for self-funded plans.

Because of the rising costs of health care and replacement of personal property, it is virtually impossible for each person to have the necessary funds available to cover his or her expenses in a disaster, whether it is a large-scale disaster or a personal one. For this reason, insurance has become a necessary part of life in American society.

Essentially, **insurance** is an agreement whereby insurance companies collect fees or "**premiums**" from individuals or companies on a regular basis. In return, they agree to pay for specific benefits. These benefits can be the payment of health care expenses, the replacement or repair of personal property, or the payment for expenses of others who may have been injured by you or your property.

A person does not have insurance until they complete an insurance application, pay the premium, and have their application accepted by the insurance company. Some policies specify a waiting period before coverage begins. All policies have an effective date of coverage and most have a termination date. To have the coverage continue premiums must be paid and eligibility qualifications must be maintained. Also the insured must renew their insurance before the coverage expires in order to remain insured. **Renewal** means paying a premium in order to continue coverage after the initial policy period has expired.

If the insured does not do so, they may have a lapse in coverage, and in some cases will not be able to purchase insurance, even by paying the premium. A **lapse in coverage** is a break in continuous insurance coverage. It is best to pay premiums as agreed to avoid complications ranging from having no coverage at all, to a large increase in premium.

After enrolling in an insurance plan, the insurance company will send the member an insurance identification card or policy. The card or policy remains valid only as long as the member continues to pay their insurance premiums.

The member must file a claim to be reimbursed for any benefits available under his or her insurance policy. A **claim** is a written request by the insured individual for payment by the insurance company of expenses that are covered under the insurance policy. Filing a claim notifies the insurance company of the member's loss and/or entitlement to reimbursement for any losses incurred. Failure to notify the insurance carrier in a timely manner could result in denial or a reduction of benefits. Therefore, it is wise to file a claim as soon as possible.

Insurance companies operate on the principal that most of those who pay premiums will not need services, or that the services they need will cost less than the premiums paid. As you can see, it becomes very important for an insurance company to place restrictions on the amount and type of benefits that will be paid. These restrictions can include eligibility requirements, deductibles, maximum benefits, exclusions to a policy, and many other policy provisions. The health claims examiner is responsible for ensuring that each claim or request for payment is within the guidelines set by the company or the policy.

The Rising Cost of Health Care

The inflation that has affected so many areas of the American economy has probably most severely impacted the cost of health care. Between 1983 and 2000, the cost of health care in the United States rose from $355.4 billion per year to more than $1.3 trillion per year. According to the Agency for Healthcare Research and Quality, national health expenditures are expected to reach $2.8 trillion in 2011, with an average annual growth rate of 7.3 percent from 2001 to 2011.

This astronomical figure has prompted the federal government to introduce major changes in the health care system in an effort to control costs and to help insure a higher percentage of Americans.

There are a number of reasons for the enormous increase in the cost of health care. The eight most significant factors are:

1. More people are seeking health care now compared with 20 years ago.
2. Medical treatments are more extensive and sophisticated than ever before. In addition, the equipment required for many treatments is extremely expensive. For example, one MRI unit can easily cost $1 million or more.
3. The cost of training health care professionals, such as physicians, nurses, and laboratory technicians is much greater than ever before.
4. The price that health care professionals pay for malpractice insurance has increased dramatically because of the increase in lawsuits.
5. When a significant part of a person's medical expenses are paid for by a health plan, neither

the patient nor the health care provider has much incentive to control costs or limit the utilization of services.

6. There is little competition among health care providers. Consequently, the marketplace does not place restraints on costs.
7. As people live longer, they require more health care, thus, prolonging the need for care and increasing costs.
8. Fraud by both providers and members (insured persons) is increasing.
9. The cost of drug research and development broke the $30 billion mark in 2001, reflecting an almost 11 percent increase over 2000.

For these reasons and many others, the cost of health care has been rising steadily and quickly for the past few decades. Unless major steps are taken to curb this increase, many Americans will find themselves unable to afford health care, and many companies will no longer be able to afford to insure their employees.

Employee Benefits

Auto, home and most other personal property insurance is purchased by individuals however, health care insurance is often supplied (partly or fully) by a person's employer. The supplying of health care insurance comes under the heading of an employee benefit. Health care benefits are an extremely important part of almost everyone's economic security. These benefits were once considered to be a fringe benefit by employers. Today, many employees consider the benefits to be a major consideration when seeking a job.

Benefits account for almost 40% of an employee's total compensation. In actuality, there are many definitions of employee benefits. In the broadest view, **employee benefits** are virtually any form of compensation other than direct wages paid or given to an employee. Other benefits include paid vacations, sick leave, pension plans, tuition reimbursement or payment plans, yearly bonuses, and many other perks that employers offer to attract employees.

Types of Insurance

There are various types of insurance coverage. The following list includes some of the most common:

- **Accidental Death and Dismemberment Insurance** pays a benefit to the beneficiary in the event of the insured person's death by accidental means. It also pays a benefit to the insured when an accident causes the loss of a limb.
- **Disability Insurance** covers an employee's salary, or a percentage of it, while the

employee is on disability leave. There is short-term disability insurance, usually up to 12 weeks, and long-term.

- **Health Insurance** covers medical and hospital services. Such policies are sold as individual policies or group policies.
- **Life Insurance** is coverage on a person's life. In the event of the insured person's death, a benefit is paid to the named beneficiary.
- **Medicaid** is a federal program established under Title XIX of the Social Security Act of 1965. Its purpose is to provide the needy with access to medical care.
- **Medicare** is the Federal Health Insurance Benefit Plan for the Aged and Disabled under Title XVIII of Public Law 89-97 of the Social Security Act. This program is for people 65 years of age and older and certain individuals who are totally disabled.
- **Property and Casualty Insurance** covers material items. It pays for repair or replacement of the item.
- **Workers' Compensation** is a medical and disability reimbursement program that provides 100% medical coverage and a scheduled weekly disability benefit for job-related injuries, illnesses, or conditions arising out of or in the course of employment.

Numerous other types of coverages may be purchased from insurance companies. It is possible to be insured against almost any loss if you are willing to pay the premium.

In addition, the term insurance is often incorrectly used to refer to all types of health coverage. In reality, insurance is only one type of health coverage. As part of this course, you will be expected to learn the correct terminology for referring to the various benefit plans.

Individual vs. Group Insurance

Insurance coverage is categorized as being either individual or group. **Individual insurance coverage** covers one person or item. That means premiums are usually higher because of the higher risks associated with insuring individuals on a case-by-case basis. With individual insurance, there is nowhere to spread risks, and the chance that losses may exceed the premiums collected is greater than in group insurance.

Group insurance covers more than one person or item. A group consists of any number of people who have a common purpose other than obtaining insurance coverage. Under this definition, members of unions, trade associations, and other organizations are able to purchase insurance as a group.

Example: Group Insurance: A company purchases insurance for all its employees, or a club or organization offers insurance to its members, through a specified insurance company. All members of the group or organization may buy the policy which the organization has chosen.

Individual Insurance: A person purchases an insurance policy from an insurance carrier that is customized based on their specifications (i.e., auto insurance where the insured may choose the amount of coverage, deductible and other factors).

Often individuals only purchase insurance when they feel there is a reasonable chance of needing the benefits. Therefore, there is often a greater risk to the insurance carrier since healthy people will tend not to purchase coverage.

However, there is less risk for the insurance carrier in a group coverage situation since an employer will purchase coverage for all the employees, not just those likely to be ill. Thus, the premiums for the well employees help cover the costs of those employees who need benefits.

Conventional Insurance

In a conventional insurance arrangement, an employer or individual purchases an insurance plan and agrees to pay premiums to the insurance company. In return, the insurance company agrees to pay specific benefits. The premium cost is based on the "experience" of the plan, which includes the actuarial statistics, inflation, and administrative expenses of the company.

In the past few years, the rise in health care costs has affected the increase in premiums. As a result, it has become almost prohibitively expensive for small employers and individuals to purchase coverage. For many larger employers, benefits have been decreased, the portion paid by the employee has been increased, or the plan has become self-funded.

Self-Funded Plans

In a **self-funded plan**, the total and ultimate responsibility for providing all plan benefit payments rests solely with the employer, group or association. Because of this economic risk, it is not uncommon for portions of the benefits to be self-funded, whereas other portions are insured. For example, the medical benefits may be self-funded, whereas the dental benefits may be insured. In self-funding, there are no insurance premiums because there is no associated insurance company. In addition, the plan is not governed by the Department of Insurance. The risk of loss is assumed by the employer. This potential risk may be decreased by the employer purchasing **reinsurance or stop-loss insurance**. Such insurance would reimburse the employer when losses exceed a specific amount agreed on by the employer and the reinsurance carrier.

In this book, the term "plan benefits" is used to refer to coverages – medical and/or dental – with no distinction made as to whether those benefits are insured or self-funded. Such a distinction is irrelevant

for our purposes, because handling and processing of claims within both arrangements are nearly identical.

Example: The Giant-Mega Corporation has 10,000 employees. The company determines that the yearly insurance premiums for all its employees would be approximately $10 million. However, the company does not expect the employees to receive $10 million in benefits during the year. Thus, the company chooses to become self-funded. The $10 million is placed in an account, and the company pays the benefits to the employees directly.

Third-Party Administrators

A **Third-Party Administrator (TPA)** is a plan administration firm that deals solely with administering the eligibility and claim payment services (along with various other administrative services) for self-funded plans. The administrator provides all the equipment and personnel required to meet the client's needs. In turn, the client supplies the funds or monies needed for payment of the administrator's services and for amounts paid out for claims. In contrast, the insurance company handles all plan administration along with providing all the equipment and personnel required, and funds for claim payments.

In response to the increase in the number of self-funded plans, many insurance companies now offer what are known as Administrative Services Only (ASO) contracts. These contracts basically work the same as a TPA insofar as all of the funding is provided by the client, and the expertise, equipment, and personnel are provided by the insurance company. As with all areas of the benefit industry, a multitude of variations are possible on both of these concepts.

Example: The Giant-Mega Corporation has decided that it takes too much time and effort for their claims department to process the claims submitted by its employees. They hire a TPA to process the claims and pay the benefits out of the account they have set up.

Types of Health Benefit Plans

There are many different types of insurance health plans which provide medical benefits. However, most people in the United States are insured under one of the following systems:

1. **Indemnity Plan** – Traditional indemnity plans are almost nonexistent today, but they used to be the most common type of benefit plan. Under an indemnity insurance plan, the member pays an insurance premium, and the insurance pays a fixed percentage of covered expenses. The policy would require the member to pay deductibles and co-payments (a portion of the payment), however the member can choose their own physician, other

health care providers, and specialists, and can otherwise make independent decisions about what type of care to seek.

2. **Preferred Provider Organization (PPO)** – A preferred provider organization operates much like an indemnity plan, except the plan provides incentives for insured individuals to seek care from providers who are on a list provided by the insurance company. A PPO plan is one type of managed care plan. Under a PPO plan, the insurance company will generally cover a higher percentage of the cost, and sometimes require the member to pay a lower deductible, if a preferred provider is chosen. However, a PPO lets the member seek services from providers outside the network if the member is willing to pay a larger portion of the cost.

3. **Health Maintenance Organization (open access)** – A Health Maintenance Organization (HMO) with open access provides coverage for many services but requires that the member seek care first from one selected physician ("primary care provider" [PCP]) before they go to any other physicians or health facilities. The HMO will provide the member with a list of physicians from which to select a primary care provider. The insurance will provide coverage for visits to the primary care provider and for most services that the PCP recommends. Services that are sought independently (without consulting the PCP) are generally not covered. If the member needs to see a specialist, be hospitalized or have lab or x-ray work, the member's PCP must refer them to a provider or facility. The member's PCP must give authorization for these services to be covered by the HMO.

4. **Health Maintenance Organization (closed panel)** – An HMO with closed panel is one in which the physicians and other practitioners work directly for the HMO. All services must be provided directly by the HMO and its staff. Services which are sought by the member outside the HMO are generally not covered.

5. **Point-Of-Service (POS)** – These plans combine characteristics of HMOs and PPOs. The member chooses a PCP who controls all aspects of care, including referrals to specialists. All care received under that physician's guidance (including referrals) is fully covered. Care received by out-of-network providers is reimbursed, but the member must pay a significant co-payment or deductible. So basically, the member decides each time they need medical care whether they want to use their plan as an HMO or a PPO.

6. **Dental Plan** – Dental insurance covers preventive and therapeutic services of the teeth and gums. Dental plans come in almost as many forms as health coverage. This coverage can be included as a benefit under an indemnity, PPO, or HMO plan, or can be an entirely separate plan. Some HMOs have dental practices associated with them. Other companies provide the same kind of in-network low-pay and out-of-network/higher-pay options as they do with their healthcare. Sill others opt for a traditional indemnity approach allowing members to go to the dentist of their choice, pay up front, and wait for reimbursement. Basic dental coverage in managed care plans usually includes 100% payment for annual checkups, with the member being responsible for a percentage of other necessary treatments (x-rays, surgeries, etc.).

7. **Vision Coverage** – This coverage can be included as a benefit under an indemnity, PPO, or HMO plan, or can be an entirely separate plan. Some plans offer coverage for annual eye exams and a percentage of the frame and prescription lens or contact lens costs every 24 months. HMOs usually have eye care professionals on site; other types of plans may have in-network and out-of-network restrictions.

8. **Prescription Drug Plan** – This coverage can be included as a benefit under an indemnity, PPO, or HMO plan, or can be an entirely separate plan. One of the highest costs of healthcare today is prescription drugs. Some health plans do not cover prescription drugs at all. HMOs generally have pharmacies on site that fill prescriptions from doctors in the network. Other plans cover a specific list of approved medications for a small co-payment, while still others reimburse the member for a percentage of the costs after they have purchased the prescription drug.

Departments in an Insurance Company

Within each insurance company there are a number of departments with varying responsibilities. Depending on the size of the company, a department may consist of a number of people or only one person. In fact, one person may perform the functions of several departments. However, each department is represented in each company, including the Human Resources, Marketing, Actuarial, New Business, Premium Services, Underwriting, Accounting, Claims, and Legal Departments.

The ***Human Resources Department***, also called the Personnel Department, is responsible for matters relating to the company's employees. The Human Resources Department formulates company policy with respect to hiring, training, compensation, and ensuring company compliance with federal, state and local employment laws and regulations. It also administers employee benefit plans, such as group insurance, tuition refund plans, and employee pensions.

Example: Innocuous Insurers, Inc. sells health and life insurance coverage. The personnel department makes sure that there are enough people working in each department to meet the needs of the company, and they handle all matters relating to hiring, termination, payroll and benefits for the employees.

The ***Marketing Department*** is responsible for presenting insurance products to the company's customers. "**Products**" within the insurance industry refers to various benefit plans. This department normally conducts market research, works with other departments in the company to develop new products and revise current ones to meet the changing needs of the company's customers, prepares advertising campaigns, designs promotional materials, and establishes and maintains distribution systems for the company's products. Marketing is also in charge of selling the products.

Example: Innocuous Insurers, Inc. decides to offer a policy which covers 20% of medical costs, up to their limits. Their research has shown that there are a lot of people who do not have health insurance coverage and they want to create a health insurance plan to sell to these people.

The ***Actuarial Department*** is responsible for ensuring that the company's operations are conducted on a mathematically sound basis. In conjunction with other departments, it designs and revises the company's products. The Actuarial Department is also chiefly responsible for establishing premium rates based on research performed to predict the profitability of the company's products. Research includes the use of a number of studies such as morbidity rates, life expectancy studies, cost of service studies, and others. These studies can help companies to determine the cost of premiums according to how long a person is expected to live, the types of services the average person will need as they grow older, and the cost of these services.

Example: The Innocuous Insurers Actuarial Department determines whether or not the company can afford to offer a new health insurance coverage. They use reports to determine the amount that can reasonably be expected to be paid out on the new health insurance policy the marketing department wants to sell. Together the Actuarial Department and the Underwriting Department determine the premium amount for the new policy.

The ***New Business Department*** does just what its name states: it processes new business acquired by the company. This department's primary responsibilities are to determine and verify that all information and forms submitted by the sales agents are complete and accurate. The New Business Department also schedules physical examinations for policies that require evidence of insurability.

Example: The New Business Department checks over all the forms submitted by people who want to purchase the new health insurance to make sure they are accurate and complete. It then sends out the complete information on the policy and any policy cards or identification needed by policyholders.

All policies issued require premium payments to be made to keep the policy in force. The ***Premium Services Department*** handles and processes all premium payments received. This department handles the billing of premium notices and overdue statements to policyholders.

Example: The Premium Services Department keeps track of all the people who have signed up for the new health insurance policy and makes sure that they are paying their premiums each month. If someone misses a premium payment, they cancel the policy and make sure that the claims department stops paying benefits to those people who have not paid their premiums.

The ***Underwriting Department*** is responsible for making sure that the premium rates are accurate and that claim payments do not exceed the amount assumed when the premium rates were calculated. The Underwriting Department makes determinations as to the insurability of applicants, both individuals and employer groups, based on their present experience and medical status.

Example: The Underwriting Department keeps a close eye on how much money the new health insurance policy is bringing in, and how much it is paying out. If they determine that too much is being paid out, or that too many people with extended illnesses are signing up for the policy, they may change the rules of who is eligible. They may also decide that the policy is only available to people who are under a certain age and who are well or require a physical before they allow coverage.

The ***Accounting Department*** maintains the records to show if the company is being run in a profitable manner. This department is responsible for maintaining the company's general accounting records, preparing financial statements, controlling receipts and disbursements, overseeing the budgeting process, administering the payroll program, and working with the Legal Department to ensure that the company is complying with government regulations and tax laws.

Example: The Accounting Department keeps track of all the money coming in and going out. They also create all the reports needed for tax filings each year. If they determine that the company does not have enough money, or is paying out too much in relation to what is coming in, they will discuss it with the Underwriting Department and suggest that the premium amount for all policies be raised to bring in more money.

The primary responsibility of the *Claims Department* is the processing of claims in a correct and timely manner. The claims examiner reviews the claims submitted by members or providers of service for the correct application of plan benefits. This area also includes a support staff of clerical and customer service personnel and often includes nurses and physicians for the administration of cost-containment programs.

Example: The Claims Department looks at each claim (bill) sent in for people covered under the new health insurance policy. They look at the contract and determine how much to pay after subtracting amounts for unreasonable fees, deductibles, non-covered services, items over a limit, and the portion the insured person is supposed to cover (i.e., if the policy covers 80% of reasonable fees, the insured is responsible for 20%). Once they determine the proper amount to pay on each claim, they will issue payment.

The *Legal Department* makes sure that the company's operations comply with federal, state, and local laws and with the Department of Insurance regulations. It studies current and proposed legislation to determine the effects on future operations and advises the Claims Department when claim disputes are received. This department also works with the Accounting Department in determining tax liabilities and represents the company in legal matters.

Claims Examiner's Responsibilities

The conduct of all claims personnel is extremely important. Claims personnel are more visible because most of the public interfaces with either the customer service representative or directly with claims processing personnel. The public's opinion of the payor is based primarily on their contacts with claims personnel. Therefore, it is important for claims examining personnel to establish and adhere to basic principals. The claims examiner's guiding philosophy should be to provide timely, competent, fair, and friendly claims

service to all members. A proposed workflow model is illustrated in **Figure 1 – 1**. Reviewing this model periodically will ensure that you have taken the basic steps toward proper claims processing. Keep in mind that this is a basic outline, and the specifics may vary from company to company.

When mail comes in it is opened, sorted, and stamped with the receipt date. If the mail is a response to a pended claim, the letter is matched with the original claim. The claims examiner then enters the claims and processes them, pends them, or refers them for review.

If the claim is to be processed (column one), it is either paid or denied, according to the terms of the contract. A check or statement is then generated. The claim is stored in a daily batch with the file copy. The clerk then mails out the check or statement and files the file copy.

If additional information is needed, the claim is pended (column two). A letter is generated by the system or the claims examiner manually fills out a form letter identifying the additional information needed. The pended claim is stored in the pended file for 30 days. If a response has not been received within 30 days, a follow-up letter is sent. A maximum of two follow-up letters should be sent. If the reply has not been received within 30 days of the last follow-up letter, the pended claim should be denied for lack of information.

If the claims examiner is unable to make a decision based on his or her own expertise, the claim is referred for review (column three). Many insurance companies have a listing of certain types of claims that should be referred for review. These claims are then reviewed by the consultant for appropriateness. The reviewer will inform the claims examiner of the action to be taken, and the claim is processed accordingly. Reviewing the consultant's decision helps the claims examiner to improve their claims processing abilities.

Since the examiner's main responsibility is to determine the payor's obligation in accordance with policy provisions and to discharge those obligations fairly and promptly, each examiner is expected to have exemplary integrity and to demonstrate forthrightness in dealings with the public. The following is a list of nine guiding principals to assist the examiner in adopting a professional claims philosophy:

1. Know the plan provisions of the contracts you are responsible for handling.
2. Be sure you understand the application of the provisions. If you are not sure, ask before processing claims
3. Conduct claim investigations that reflect a prompt and diligent search for the facts.
4. If additional information or clarification is required, review the claim and ask for all information needed at one time. Re-pending

claims and asking for additional information is extremely irritating to members and providers.

5. Conclude each claim, large or small, on the basis of its own merits, in light of the facts, the law, and the coverage afforded.

6. Give a prompt, courteous, and forthright explanation to each claimant about the company's position with respect to the claim.

7. Respond promptly when a response is indicated to all communications from policyholders, claimants, attorneys, and other involved persons. (Or refer the claim promptly to the designated person responsible for responding in those situations.)

8. Seek and support new methods designed to provide improved claims service.

9. Suggest or help establish procedures and practices to:
   a. Prevent misrepresentation of the pertinent facts or policy provisions.
   b. Avoid unfair advantage by reason of superior knowledge.
   c. Maintain accurate claim records as privileged and confidential.

Proposed Workflow Model

Figure 1 – 1: Sample Workflow Model

The Department of Insurance

The entire insurance industry is overseen by a larger body called the **Department of Insurance**. The Department of Insurance for each state holds the primary legal authority over the operations of all insurance companies within that state. Therefore, it has influence over insured benefit plans but generally does not have authority over self-funded plans. The many responsibilities of the Department of Insurance are:

- Issues certificates and licenses authorizing insurance companies and insured products to operate or be sold in the state.
- Licenses agents to sell insurance and revokes licenses when warranted.
- Reviews the annual statements of insurance companies for verification of solvency.
- Ensures that policy forms include the required provisions and are printed in the proper format.
- Performs on-site inspections of insurance companies.
- Maintains an office for receiving and acting on consumer complaints.
- Ensures that insurance companies observe the rules affecting policy reserve maintenance and investment activities.

Summary

There are several types of insurance companies, and each provides benefits in exchange for premium payments from its members. Insurance companies are overseen by the Department of Insurance, which holds the primary legal authority over the operations of insurance companies within that state.

We will be concentrating on the functions of the Claims Department. As a health claims examiner, you need to understand the principals that underlie the Claims Department's primary objective, which is to deliver timely, competent, fair, and friendly claim service. When conscientiously and consistently applied, these principals enable a company to build and maintain a respectable image with its customers and the general public. The maintenance of strong customer good will and the creation of a favorable public position are vital to the progress of a company as well as to each individual employee.

Assignments

Complete the Questions for Review.

Questions for Review

Directions: Answer the following questions without looking back into the material just covered. Write your answers in the space provided.

1. What is insurance? _____

   _____

2. What are the two types of insurance plans and how do they differ? _____

   _____

   _____

3. What does TPA stand for and what do these companies do? _____

   _____

4. What are employee benefits? _____

   _____

5. Give five reasons for the rising cost of health care.

   1. _____

      _____

2. _____
   _____

3. _____
   _____

4. _____
   _____

5. _____
   _____

6. List five responsibilities of the Department of Insurance.

   1. _____
      _____

   2. _____
      _____

   3. _____
      _____

   4. _____
      _____

   5. _____
      _____

7. What studies does the Actuarial Department of an insurance company use to help determine premiums? _____
   _____

8. What work does the Underwriting Department of an insurance company do? _____
   _____

9. What is the primary responsibility of the Claims Department? _____
   _____

10. What other types of professionals will the Claims Department use as support staff and why? _____
    _____

If you were unable to answer any of the questions, refer back to the section and then complete the answers.

Honors Certification™

The Honors Certification™ challenge for this chapter is a written test of the information contained within this chapter. Each incorrect answer will result in a deduction of between 1% and 5% from your grade. You must achieve a score of 85% or higher to pass this test. If you fail the test on your first attempt you may retake the test one additional time. The items included in the second test may be different from those in the first test.

2 Legal Issues

In this chapter you will learn:

- To understand what disclaimers are and how to use them appropriately.
- To understand HIPAA guidelines and privacy issues.
- To understand what constitutes fraud and the procedures to follow when fraud is suspected.

Key words and concepts you will learn in this chapter:

Compensatory Damages – Damages designed to compensate an insured for all of the actual losses or damages to make that person whole again.

Disclaimer – A denial or renunciation, as of responsibility.

Embezzlement – The act of an employee illegally taking funds from a company they work for.

Fraud – Deception to cause a person to give up property or something of lawful right.

Insurance Speculation – A person or entity buying insurance or maintaining coverage for the purpose of making a profit.

Legal Damages – Monetary awards that a plan member may attempt to recover, which are above and beyond the benefits provided by the group plan.

Malice – Intentional conduct to cause injury, or conduct that is carried on with the conscious disregard of the rights of others.

Oppression – Putting a person through cruel and unjust hardships with the conscious disregard of rights.

Punitive Damages – Damages which are intended primarily to punish a wrongdoing defendant and set them up as an example to help deter such actions in the future.

Subpoena – A written legal order directing a person or document to appear in court to testify.

There are several legal issues that affect the health claims examiner on a daily basis. The most common of these include the use of disclaimers, privacy regulations, and fraud.

Disclaimers

Insurance companies are in the business of providing health care benefits to their members. However, there are times when a health claims examiner may quote benefits to a provider or member, but based on changes in circumstances the benefits quoted may not be available when the claim is received (i.e., it is found that the member's coverage has terminated since the benefits were quoted, the group has not paid their premiums, or some other extenuating circumstance). Because of this it is highly advised that the health claims examiner use a disclaimer when giving benefit information.

A **disclaimer** is defined as a denial or renunciation, as of responsibility. In the health claims examiners world, it means to use words and phrases that refuse to promise an outcome.

Disclaimers are one of the best ways to protect yourself from possible legal action. Disclaimers use words such as "It appears that", or "This may be ... ." These words allow a general answer to a question without making any type of promise. If the examiner makes a statement that is later found to be in error, it can cause numerous problems both in customer satisfaction and in possible legal issues.

Example: Ms. Smith called the claims examiner in charge of her claim and was told, "Yes, you are covered for a hysterectomy." It was later discovered that there was no medical reason to perform the hysterectomy, Ms. Smith wanted it as a form of foolproof contraception. Since contraceptive devices and procedures were not covered by the contract, the claim was later denied. Ms. Smith insisted that she had been told that the procedure would be covered, and therefore the insurance carrier must pay, regardless of what it said in the contract. She insisted she had a verbal agreement from the insurance carrier that they would pay for the procedure.

All claims examiners should practice using disclaimers in their conversations. When confirming a member's eligibility and benefits, disclaimers should always be included. The following are disclaimers that may be used in your verbal and written responses:

Eligibility----We show that _____ is currently effective on group_____. To receive benefits, he or she must be eligible at the time services are rendered.

Benefits----These are the benefits now in effect for this contract. To receive benefits, your membership must be in good standing on the dates services are rendered.

Remember that your main purpose when using disclaimers is to clarify an issue or answer a customer's question without making a promise that the company may be held to later. This does not mean that you want to mislead the customer in any way, or neglect to answer their questions. It simply means that disclaimers should be used to insure that you are not making any promises the company will be held to later.

Privacy Guidelines

The very nature of health benefits administration requires a great deal of personal information to be gathered and maintained about many individuals. Therefore, the needs of the company must be carefully weighed against the person's right to privacy so as to avoid unwarranted invasions of that right.

In particular, claims information is considered to be privileged and confidential in the context of the administrator-member relationship, and unauthorized disclosure of information may represent a violation of that confidentiality.

The confidentiality of claims records has assumed a new importance for several reasons:

1. People are becoming more litigation-minded.
2. Health plans are reimbursing for more sensitive services that were excluded in the past, for example, alcohol detoxification, mental health treatment, and AIDS-related illnesses.
3. More employers are self-administering or self-funding their health plans, which means that highly personal medical information is, in some instances, routinely handled by fellow employees.
4. New HIPAA regulations require that all personnel involved in the health care process respect the patient's right to privacy and confidentiality.

HIPAA

In 1996, President William Clinton signed into law the Health Insurance Portability and Accountability Act. The portability issues will be addressed in another chapter. Here we will discuss the patient privacy and fraud and abuse issues.

The Act encompasses two main issues:

1. Portability, or the ability to transfer insurance companies and still be covered for pre-existing conditions (which will be discussed in more depth in a later chapter), and
2. Accountability, generally dealing with the patient's right to privacy from the medical provider, health insurer and any other parties required in the health care process (i.e., billers, clearinghouses, etc.).

Regarding the Privacy section of HIPAA, the Department of Health and Human Services states:

The privacy requirements limit the release of patient protected health information (PHI) without the patient's knowledge and consent beyond that required for patient care. Patient's personal information must be more securely guarded and more carefully handled when conducting the business of health care.

All health care entities were required to meet the standards set in the privacy issues section of HIPAA on April 14, 2003.

General Rules

Following are the general rules for ensuring that privacy guidelines are met:

1. Always obtain an authorization to release information before releasing any information. Most releases routinely signed in the medical practice only authorize the physician to release information necessary to process a patient's claim. Additional authorization should be obtained to release any information to other parties. These releases should state exactly what information is to be released, the dates of any services provided which fall within the release, the person to whom the information may be released, the signature of the patient, the date of the signature, and the date the release expires.
2. Make sure that a release was signed by the member prior to processing a claim. If possible, ask the provider for a copy of the patient's signature on the release form. This will ensure that you have the right to look at the information contained on the claim.
3. Gather only the information that is necessary and relevant to the billing or processing of the claim.
4. Use only legal and ethical means to collect the information required. Whenever permission is necessary, obtain written authorization from the

insured or claimant (guardian or parent if the claimant is a minor).

5. When requested, and subject to any applicable legal or ethical prohibition or privilege, the insured or claimant concerned should be advised of the nature and general uses to be made of the information.

6. Make every reasonable effort to ensure that the information upon which an action is based is accurate, relevant, timely, and complete.

7. Upon request, the claimant or insured should be given the opportunity to correct or clarify the information given by or about him or her, and the file should be amended to the extent that it is fair to both the insurer and the member or claimant. Requests for review or clarification of medical information will be accepted only from the health care provider from whom the information was obtained.

8. In general, disclosures of information to a third party (other than those described to the insured or claimant) should be made only with the written authorization of the member or claimant. This includes disclosure to employers, family members or former spouses.

9. All practical precautions should be taken to ensure that claim files are physically secure and that access to the use of such files is limited to authorized personnel. This includes not leaving files out, locking all files, and even turning your computer screen away from where it might be seen by other persons. Security passwords and other security measures may also be required, depending on your office situation.

10. All personnel involved in the processing of claims should be advised of the need to protect the Right of Privacy in obtaining required information and the need to treat all individually identifiable information as confidential. Willful abuse of the privacy of any insured or claimant by the employee may be cause for dismissal.

11. The disclosure of a diagnosis should never be made to a member or his or her family. If the member requests this information, refer the member to the physician. There may be a reason the patient does not know his or her diagnosis.

12. Never, release any information to an ex-spouse. This includes the member's address, phone number, when a claim was paid, to whom, and other information. The ex-spouse should be instructed to contact the member directly.

13. Do not leave files, member's records or appointment books open on your desk or in an area where they may be seen by others. This includes member files or information that may be displayed on a computer screen. The best way to handle this is to be sure that all files are closed or are turned over on your desk. Computer screens must be placed in such a way that they cannot be seen by anyone passing by. If necessary, use a screen saver or other unrestricted document that can be clicked on to replace the one you are working on instantaneously.

14. If a minor patient has the legal right to authorize treatment for services, disclosure to the parents, legal guardians of the minor or to other persons may be a violation of HIPAA and or the Confidentiality of Medical Information Act.

15. Be cautious about releasing information to a patient's employer, even if an authorization to release information has been obtained.

If in doubt as to whether specific information should be released, check with your supervisor before, not after, releasing it.

These guidelines cover some of the basic aspects of HIPAA privacy regulations. For detailed information regarding HIPAA guidelines, complete rules and regulations regarding HIPAA are printed in the Federal Register.

Faxing

When faxing items, be aware of sensitive information on a fax. All faxes should contain a cover sheet which announces who the fax is to, who it is from, and a notation that the enclosed information is personal and confidential. Information regarding diagnosis, treatments, sexually transmitted diseases, HIV, drug or alcohol abuse or financial information should never be faxed. Following is sample wording for the fax confidentiality statement:

The enclosed information is intended exclusively for the individual or entity to which it is addressed and contains information which is privileged, confidential or exempt from disclosure under federal or state laws. If the reader of this message is not the recipient or the agent or employee responsible for delivering this facsimile transmission to the intended recipient you are hereby notified that any dissemination, distribution or copying of the information contained in this facsimile is strictly prohibited. If you have received this facsimile in error, please notify our office immediately by telephone and return the original facsimile to us at the above address.

When faxing other information, consider asking the receiving party for a code number (i.e., the patient's ID number or birthdate), then black out all pertinent information on the patient and replace it with the code number.

Items should only be faxed in an emergency. Otherwise regular or certified mail should be used.

Fraud

Fraud is defined as deception to cause a person to give up property or something of lawful right. Fraud is synonymous with deceit, trickery, cheat, and imposter. Schemes for gain involve almost every conceivable form of deception, from a subtle omission of fact to the most flagrant lie.

Fraud can be perpetrated by anyone and involves every type of claim. Doctors, lawyers, hospitals, claimants, beneficiaries, and claims handlers working for an insurance company are capable of committing fraud. It is estimated that millions of dollars annually are paid out by the health benefits industry on fraudulent claims. Regardless of who or how the expenses are submitted for payment, the overall impact on claim payments, premiums, administrative costs, and other expenses is devastating.

Forms of Fraud

Fortunately, most claims are legitimate and forthright. Therefore, a claims examiner should not automatically assume fraud. However, awareness of the possibility is necessary to properly recognize and detect those instances of fraud. The two major areas of fraud concern are:

1. **Internal fraud**, which involves the employees of the company against which the fraud is perpetrated. The employee may act alone or with another or other employees.
2. **External fraud**, which involves people outside the company that it is directed against. Claims personnel are often the innocent parties that discover the existence of fraud during routine claim paying activities.

Fraud can assume many different shapes and forms and is as limitless as the creativity of the human mind. Some forms are more obvious than others. With training and experience, a competent examiner develops a sense about claims that do not appear just right. In such cases, the examiner needs to listen to that sense and take steps to explore such a possibility. The following scenarios may be of assistance in identifying fraudulent situations:

- A member is covered for group hospital benefits as both an employee and a dependent. This fact is concealed to avoid COB.
- A prospective insured has been receiving medical treatment for hypertension. This question is answered negatively on an application for life insurance in an effort to obtain coverage not otherwise available or at a more favorable premium rate.
- A member has a condition that requires prescription medication. Dates on the bills are altered and photocopies plus the originals are filed to receive multiple payments for the same charges.
- An employee photocopies another claimant's bills, replacing the actual claimant data with his or her own. The bills are marked paid and the fake claims are submitted as his or her own.
- The insured's attending physician signs a return to work release. Discarding this, the insured shops for another doctor who will extend disability.
- The insured stages an intentional injury to appear accidental.
- A worker strains his back lifting a TV set at home. The next day, co-workers find the insured lying at the bottom of a flight of stairs complaining of back pain. A Workers' Compensation claim for loss of wages and medical expenses is filed.
- The member's spouse sustains a stroke and requires constant custodial care at home. The member's stable, chronic condition suddenly becomes acute, thus, rendering the member unable to continue working and enabling the member to remain home and care for the spouse.

Although the list of potential fraud situations is endless, an attitude of alertness and thorough, conscious efforts can curb the success of the various scenarios.

The following four procedures can assist in establishing a case of fraud and subsequent successful prosecution.

1. If the file is out of the ordinary in any way or contains discrepancies, be inquisitive. Try to determine why file statements or circumstances conflict with expected conclusions. The claim should be filed in a timely manner. Information about other insurance, the how, when, and where of the accident, and the names and addresses of all attending physicians and witnesses should be freely available from the claimant. Appearance of undue anxiety or anger on the part of the claimant or beneficiary for a prompt payment could be a fraud indicator. Any alteration of a claim form or bill is to be questioned.

   Sometimes routine, in-depth reviews of original claim files disclose questionable elements or trends. Suspicious elements should not be ignored and should be pursued and developed.

   A questionable element in one area of a claim file often points to further discrepancies in other areas, until an entire series of payments may be found to have been made but not owed. Follow through on all leads and clues. Be sure claims are handled promptly. Use tact in pursuing possible fraud indicators.

   Attempts to recognize and deal with fraud are a basic part of an overall philosophy of good claim practices. There is not only a contractual obligation to properly handle possible fraudulent situations, but a social obligation as well. Like any other crime, insurance fraud is detrimental to society in many ways, including the influence it may have in increasing the overall price of benefit coverage.

2. Although investigation of fraudulent claims may be thorough and complete and the documentation may seem irrefutable, fraud is often difficult to prove in court. In some cases, depending on the nature of the fraud, the insurance company or administrator may be hesitant to prosecute because of the possibility of a counter suit on the charge of libel. This does not mean that efforts to resolve fraudulent claims should be restricted. Rather, this emphasizes the need for in-depth investigation and development of a complete, accurate claim file so that any fraud case that is prosecuted will be as solid as possible. Thorough investigation increases the chances that the case will be prosecuted in the courts, that prosecution will be successful, and that the occurrence of countercharges for libel will be reduced.

3. Although each examiner must recognize and investigate each case of potential fraud, actual and overall control should be retained by management. In the process of prosecuting fraud, many persons have certain definite responsibilities. Cooperation among and between several different departments is essential. Communication plays a critical role in the investigation process.

4. In identifying possible fraud, some indicators may help to isolate situations. No single indicator is necessarily suspicious, nor is it evidence that fraud has occurred. The claims examiner must assume an identity of an investigator and put all of the facts and indicators together to see whether fraud is actually present. Following are some indicators that have been put into categories for easier reference.

Fraud Indicators

Indicators associated with the claimant or insured (employee) are as follows:

- Claimant is overly pushy and demanding of a quick claim settlement.
- Claimant is unusually familiar with insurance terminology or claims procedures.
- Claimant handles business in person or by phone, apparently avoiding use of the mail. (Using the mail for such purposes is a federal offense.)
- Attorney or claimant is willing to accept less than the actual claim estimate just to help out and resolve the matter quickly.
- Insured/claimant contacts the insurance agent to verify coverage or extent of coverage just before loss.
- Attorney representation is coincident with or shortly after injury date and threatens a bad-faith lawsuit unless the carrier or administrator agrees to settle quickly.
- No police report was made or only an over-the-counter report occurred, when police would usually investigate the actual scene.
- Claimants or witnesses use post office box or a hotel address.
- Claimant has multiple policies covering the same loss.
- Un-witnessed, one-car or hit-and-run accidents.
- Medical treatment is declined at the time of the accident, but the injured party is later hospitalized for extensive injuries.
- History of previous loss with similar treatment exists, or the same doctor or attorney repeatedly handles medical or lost earnings claims following minor accidents.
- Claimant has a history of numerous past questionable claims.
- Trends can be observed on billing statements or treatments by providers that appear to show excessive charges. These may include same fees and treatment regardless of condition, differences between amounts billed to patient, and amounts on claim forms.

Claim Processing and Claim Inflation Indicators

During claim review, discrepancies seem to exist. Often, these are flags that should warn the claims examiner to go over the claim papers more thoroughly or to check past history at length. Rather than being obvious, these indicators are often seen only after a number of payments have occurred. Things to look for include:

- A minor accident produces major accident costs, lost wages, and so on.
- Medical bills indicate routine treatment being provided on Sundays, holidays, or on doctor's day off.
- Summary medical bills are submitted without itemization of office visits or treatments.
- Photocopies of medical, prescription, or dental bills; third or fourth generation bills are especially suspect. Photocopies of claim forms contain alterations or corrections.
- Receipts or bills are submitted without provider's letterhead.
- Several different typefaces, handwritings, or colors of ink are on claim forms or bills.

- Unusually high number of treatments are noted for relatively minor conditions. Such ailments persist for weeks or months.
- Insurance effective or employment commenced just a short time before the claim.
- Condition is diagnosed subjectively as nausea, fatigue, inability to sleep, headaches, low back pain, sprain, whiplash, and so on.
- Patient's statement that services were not received as shown on the billing.
- Provider accepts claim payment as payment in full for services rendered, regardless of the billed amount.
- Unassigned benefits are seen on large medical claim amounts with questionable evidence to support payment in full and with a claim form as the only information submitted. Supporting bills are seldom, if ever, included.
- Incorrect or incomplete forms are submitted. For example, there are questionable signatures from providers (i.e., doctor's name is signed Doctor J. Jones instead of J. Jones, MD).
- Unusual or unfamiliar medical terms, misspelled medical words, or a non-existent diagnosis are found.
- Claim file indicates no other coverage but claim consistently submits photocopies of unassigned medium to large dollar claims.
- Improbable, impossible treatment or unlikely surgery (i.e., second appendectomy, bilateral procedure questionable) is listed.
- Doctor's specialty is not related to the patient's diagnosis (i.e., male treated by an Ob-Gyn specialist, severe heart problem treated by a chiropractor).

Insurance Speculation Indicators

Insurance speculation means buying insurance or coverage for the purpose of making a profit. It may include staging a fake death or accident to file claims under more than one policy. Collusion with others may occur. Things to look for are as follows:

- An attorney demand or threat of lawsuit even before a claimant files a claim.
- Claims reported late.
- Instant pressure from the claimant or provider to pay fast.
- Multiple hospital indemnity coverage's held by claimant or combined hospital, medical, accident, and hospital indemnity policies.
- Denial or omission of information about other insurance coverage.

Other Indicators of Fraud

Indicators pointing to employee embezzlement usually apply to employees within or even outside the claim operation. Access to claim files is usually involved. Things to look for include:

- Payee name and address does not match claim form, bills, or other pertinent material.
- Change in lifestyle or lifestyle is inconsistent with expected income level.
- Undocumented claim file actions are found such as voids, reversals, reissued payments by employee.
- Provider bills and claim forms do not match explanation of benefits; unusual payee, questionable assignments/non-assignments are noted.
- Claim payments are split by examiner to allow payment to be within dollar authorized levels.
- No documentation is located for many payments on a claimant's file. System production records and manual counts of work do not match, with claim papers missing from daily correspondence files.
- Over utilization of certain benefits: claims are for hospitalization or extensive treatment indicating total disability, and the claimant was not observed to have been absent or ill from work.
- Pattern of accident claims by an individual or family is found.
- Alteration of bills is made for other family member's expense, to allow payment under another member's history to avoid deductible, etc.

HIPAA and Fraud and Abuse

The new HIPAA fraud statutes have greatly broadened the scope of the federal government for prosecuting fraud and abuse in the health care industry. HIPAA defines four new criminal healthcare fraud offenses: Health Care Fraud, Theft or Embezzlement in Connection with Health Care, False Statements Relating to Health Care Matters, and Obstruction of Criminal Investigations of Health Care Offenses.

HIPAA now defines a health care benefit program as: any public or private plan or contract, affecting commerce, under which any medical benefit, item, or service is provided to any individual, and includes any individual or entity who is providing a medical benefit, item, or service for which payment may be made under the plan or contract. By including private health benefit plans and any individual or entity, they have effectively given themselves the right to prosecute anyone involved in the health care industry for fraud or abuse.

The following four sections further define the HIPAA statutes:

Health Care Fraud (18 USC 1347): Whoever knowingly and willfully executes, or attempts to execute, a scheme or artifice to defraud any health care benefit program; or to obtain, by means of false or fraudulent pretenses, representations, or promises, any of the money or property owned by, or under the custody or control of, any health care benefit program, in connection with the delivery of or payment for health care benefits, items, or services, shall be fined under this title [up to $250,000 per offense] or imprisoned not more than 10 years, or both.

The health claims examiner needs to keep in mind that if he processes a health claim which he knows to be fraudulent he may be held liable under this portion of the statute.

Theft or Embezzlement in Connection with Health Care (18 USC 669): Whoever knowingly and willfully embezzles, steals, or otherwise without authority converts to the use of any person other than the rightful owner, or intentionally misapplies any of the moneys, funds, securities, premiums, credits, property, or other assets of a health care benefit program, shall be fined under this title or imprisoned not more than 10 years, or both; but if the value of such property does not exceed the sum of $100 the defendant shall be fined under this title or imprisoned not more than one year, or both.

Any health claims examiner that does any of the following: pays on claims which they know to be fraudulent; takes home office supplies, equipment or other items with the intent to keep; and drafts unauthorized checks to himself, may be held liable under this portion of the statute.

False Statements Relating to Health Care Matters (18 USC 1035): Whoever, in any matter involving a health care benefit program, knowingly and willfully falsifies, conceals, or covers up by any trick, scheme, or device a material fact; or makes any materially false, fictitious, or fraudulent statements or representations, or makes or uses any materially false writing or document knowing the same to contain any materially false, fictitious, or fraudulent statement or entry, in connection with the delivery of or payment for health care benefits, items, or services, shall be fined under this title or imprisoned not more than 5 years, or both.

A health claims examiner that creates false claims and/or claim documents, alters and/or falsifies claim information, lies about claims situations, and does not come forward to disclose fraudulent situations that they are aware of, may be held liable under this portion of the statute.

Obstruction of Criminal Investigations of Health Care Offenses (18 USC 1518): (a) Whoever willfully prevents, obstructs, misleads, delays or attempts to prevent, obstruct, mislead or delay the communication of information or records relating to a violation of a Federal health care offense to a criminal investigator shall be fined under this title or imprisoned not more than 5 years, or both. (b) As used in this section the term criminal investigator means any individual duly authorized by a department, agency, or armed force of the United States to conduct or engage in investigations for prosecutions for violations of health care offenses.

Destroying records, not turning over files or documents when asked, lying to investigators and generally being uncooperative during an investigation may cause a health claims examiner liability under this portion of the statute.

While it may seem that these statutes apply mostly to those who are billing health care claims, it is important for the health claims examiner to be aware of these issues. If you discover a possibly fraudulent claim, it is important to bring it to your supervisor's attention as soon as possible. Additionally, if an investigation is initiated, you should cooperate fully with the investigators. Not doing so could be construed as hindering their investigation, making you liable for fines and imprisonment up to five years. It is important to note that the statutes are written in such a way that you can be found guilty of hindering an investigation, even if that investigation later fails to turn up fraud.

Additionally, health claims examiners need to be cautious about the statements or comments they make regarding a claim, especially written comments which are placed in a file. If those comments turn out to be fraudulent, the health claims examiner may be held liable.

Investigation

Investigation means an organized effort to discover the facts or truth of the matter.

Legitimate claims should be paid promptly and in accordance with scheduled allowances. The handling of such claims should reflect a positive service attitude. The same amount of effort and determination should go into the denial of every illegitimate claim. The claims examiner cannot accomplish this purpose without exercising investigative efforts whenever claim discrepancies occur.

During review of every claim, the examiner must be alert to items that do not look right. Because most claims are payable without further questions, it is only necessary to investigate claims that raise questions.

Although investigation of facts takes time, it is absolutely necessary to properly document the claim file. Threats of contacting a State Department of Insurance or threat of lawsuit should not deter continued investigation as long as the examiner and his or her supervisor are relatively sure that the claim investigation is justified. The claimant or the provider should be kept well informed of the claim's status regarding what has been requested and what items are necessary or outstanding, in order to complete the processing of the claim. Be aware of legal time standards required in responding to claimants and in communicating regularly during investigation.

Be candid with persons inquiring about the claim to a point. Do not hesitate to let him or her know that the claim needs further research to determine the validity of the facts presented. Avoid words that can be damaging to a case, such as crook, and thief; and never make accusations (see **Table 2 – 1**).

Table 2-1: Investigation Terminology	
Words to avoid	**Words to use**
Investigation	Clarification of charges, services, etc.…
Fraud	Incomplete/ omitted information
Lied	Inconsistency in information reported
Any other derogatory remark/term	It appears that…

Prompt, cautious contact with information sources is essential in every investigation. When possible fraud indicators are present, a greater degree of caution must be exercised and the source of suspected fraud must be taken into account when various contacts are made.

Remember that all plans have the right to investigate and confirm the validity of the submitted information.

Inside Sources of Fraud

Whenever a company's employees within or outside the claim processing area appear to be involved in questionable activity, the claims examiner should contact his or her supervisor, personnel director, or others in management.

Under no circumstances should the matter be discussed with anyone other than management personnel in a secluded area. It is then up to management to decide how the matter will be handled.

Outside Sources of Fraud

Whenever insureds, members, claimants, or other persons (not including the provider of service) appear to be involved in fraud, careful contact with providers of services should be made. These contacts involve the verification of dates, type of service rendered, and amounts charged to the patient. Verification of disability and accident-related information should also be investigated. The use of an outside investigator may be required to expedite the

investigation. All contacts should be documented in writing. If possible, the information should be requested in writing, and the reply should also be given in writing with the name and the title of the person supplying the information.

When providers of services appear to be involved in fraud, careful contact with the member/claimant should be made. Limit verification to dates and types of treatment and to amounts of charges for those services. Avoid discussions regarding diagnoses. As previously indicated, all information requested and received should be documented in writing whenever possible.

Building the Claim File

The following five steps should be taken to build the evidence in a claim file.

1. Carefully document all discrepancies, conflicting facts and omissions. Do not write on any of the original submitted claim documents. Make notes on a note pad or separate pieces of paper.
2. Make a written record of pertinent points of phone conversations. Summarize conflicting facts that were obtained by phone and note any new information carefully. Include dates of conversations, names, and phone numbers of contacts.
3. Place all documents in the order in which they occurred or were received. Keep a log that clearly shows the dates of all communications and whom they were with.
4. Retain the envelopes for all documents mailed to the office. Attach it to the back of the documentation received.
5. Coordinate the investigation with the insurance company's or administrator's legal department or counsel.

Checkpoints for Spotting Provider Fraud and Insurance Abuse

Every claims examiner should be aware of the possibility of fraud and briefly check each claim for fraudulent indicators. The following checklist should alert you to the need for further investigation, although one or more of these factors does not prove that fraud exists. Look carefully for the following situations:

*   When the insured lists no insurance coverage on hospital admissions forms.
*   When the insured does not assign benefits on inpatient hospital bills.
*   When proof of accident or illness includes photocopies of documents, forms, or bills with altered dates or receipts with serialized numbers.
*   When prescription bills submitted for payment are consecutively numbered.

- When claimants say that the insurance company is being billed for services not received or treatment not provided.
- When claims are submitted for injuries not reported or not witnessed.
- When you notice the doctor's portion of the bill or claim form has erasures or strikeovers.

Embezzlement

Embezzlement is the act of an employee illegally taking funds from a company they work for. Embezzlement can be committed by anyone in a firm.

To protect against embezzlement:

1. Accurate records must be kept of all transactions. Be sure to follow all procedures when issuing claim payment checks.
2. Any amounts paid out should be clearly notated, including the payee, the amount, the date, the check number, and what the payment was for.
3. Any discrepancies should be reported immediately to a supervisor.
4. If embezzlement is suspected, the proper person should be notified. In the case of a coworker, this is usually their supervisor. If a worker knows of embezzlement by a coworker and says nothing, they are guilty of being an accomplice to the crime.
5. A bond (insurance against embezzlement) should be obtained for each member of the company who deals directly with the company's receipts or processes payments.
6. If you notice poor bookkeeping or inaccurate records which were kept by a previous employee or a current coworker, this should be brought to the attention of your supervisor or employer. You should then document the problems in writing and ask the supervisor or employer to initial a copy for you to keep. This may provide minimal protection in case the problems with the records were found to conceal embezzlement or mismanagement of funds.

Insurance carriers are responsible for the acts of their employees. If embezzlement is found, the insurance carrier may be considered guilty and may be responsible for monies embezzled by their employees.

Legal Damages

Legal damages are monetary awards that a plan member may attempt to recover, which are above and beyond the benefits provided by the group plan.

In the legal climate today, it is not uncommon for plan members to seek legal channels to obtain benefits or to obtain greater benefits than provided by a plan of benefits. Usually, such cases are based on what is known as bad faith.

An insurance policy or a health and welfare plan is considered a legal contract. Under contract law, the claimant can only recover benefits up to the policy or plan limits.

However, with the development of consumerism, the courts have become more liberal. In some states a body of law has developed that says there is an implied obligation of good faith and fair dealings in every contract. A breach of this obligation is termed bad faith. Generally, the law of bad faith allows an insured to attempt to recover various types of damages above and beyond the benefits provided by the plan. The courts will look at two concepts to determine whether a plan has met the obligation of good faith and fair dealing:

1. Did the plan give the claimant's interest equal consideration with that given the company's interest?
2. Was the claim handled or denied in accordance with the plan provisions and in a timely manner?

The following are examples of how courts often view policy interpretations.

1. The meaning of a plan of benefits is determined by the member's reasonable expectations of coverage,
2. Uncertain wording that could be subject to more than one interpretation will usually be resolved against the plan and in favor of the member, and
3. When two equally believable interpretations may be made, the one that gives the greatest amount of protection to the member will prevail.

There are two types of damages that a court may award: compensatory damages and punitive damages.

Compensatory damages are designed to compensate an insured for all of the actual losses or damages to make that person whole again. For example, if a person has not been able to pay his or her home mortgage or car payment because they did not receive a monthly disability check and, therefore, the person's home and car are repossessed, he or she may be able to recover equity in the home and car as well as attorney fees and also possible damages for emotional stress.

Punitive damages are often the larger of the two awards and are intended primarily to punish wrongdoing by the defendant and set them up as an example to help deter such actions in the future. Unlike compensatory damages, punitive damages are not automatically recoverable if bad faith is found. In addition to bad faith, a plan member in California, for example, must prove the plan to be guilty of fraud, oppression, or malice. **Malice** is defined as intentional conduct to cause injury or conduct that is carried on with the conscious disregard of the rights of others. **Oppression** is defined as putting a person through cruel and unjust hardships with conscious disregard of rights.

Bad Faith Awards

The dollar amount of a bad faith award is based on two concepts: (1) the degree of wrongfulness and (2) the wealth of the defendant.

All lawsuits are expensive not only in the dollar cost of the damages, but in other costs as well. These costs remain even if the case is settled out of court. If the case is settled out of court, the plaintiff's attorney costs, miscellaneous costs, the attorney costs for the plan, and the benefit not originally paid must be paid and, finally, substantial pain and suffering costs may be included. The value of the claim usually has no correlation to the amount of restitution (award) sought.

Part of the reason for the continuing escalation of premium costs is the necessity to be prepared for lawsuits, because whether the case is settled in court or out of court, the monetary damage to the plan is usually significant and often preventable.

In light of the foregoing information, it is important that every claim be handled quickly, correctly, and fairly. This responsibility falls on each and every claims examiner. To fulfill this responsibility, the following four guidelines should be incorporated into the routine handling and processing of claims.

1. Every customer and claimant is entitled to courteous, fair and just treatment. An acknowledgment of all communications with respect to a claim or bill should be received with reasonable promptness.
2. Customers and claimants should be treated equally and without outside considerations other than those dictated by the office policy or plan provisions.
3. Every claim is entitled to prompt investigation of all pertinent facts and objective evaluation in the fair and equitable settlement of the claim.
4. Recognize the obligation to pay all just claims promptly.

Maintenance of Records

Records should be accurate and contain details of the claims processing history. If information is to be changed on a record, a single line should be drawn through the information to be changed and the corrected information should be placed above or beside the changed information. The date of the change should be notated and should be initialed by the person responsible for the change.

All records should be kept as long as they are needed. Most insurance carriers put their medical records on microfiche and keep them indefinitely.

There are local and state laws governing how long claims records should be preserved. These usually range from seven to ten years.

Subpoenas

Occasionally the records of a member may be needed in a court action. In such a case a subpoena is issued requesting the records. A **subpoena** is a demand for a witness to appear. Sometimes a witness will need to turn the records over to the court personally, at other times they may be mailed.

One person in the office should be designated in charge of handling subpoenas. This person should be the only person to accept a subpoena of claims records. If you are designated that person, the subpoena must be served in person. It cannot be laid on a desk or sent through the mail. No one else should accept the subpoena in your absence.

A witness fee or mileage amount may be given to a witness. You should request any payable fees at the time the subpoena is served.

If the subpoena is only for the records, not for the records and for the record keeper as a witness, you should call the attorney who sent the subpoena and ask if the records can be sent. If so, send the records by certified mail, return receipt requested.

Usually you are given a specified amount of time to produce the records. Occasionally the records will need to be turned over at the time of the subpoena. In all cases, consult with your supervisor before turning over the records. If your supervisor is unavailable, let the server know that you are unable to turn over the records without proper authorization and let them know when they can come back and serve the subpoena directly on your supervisor. This will give you time to be sure that the record is complete, accurate and in good order. Also be sure all signatures are identifiable and make copies.

In most cases the original record must be sent. Always keep a copy of all records sent. This allows you to check for changes in the records and protects against loss of information if the records are lost. Number the pages before copying so you can determine if any pages are missing.

If you are unable to accept the subpoena and no one is present who is authorized to accept it, explain the situation to the person serving the subpoena. Suggest a time when they can come back or ask them to contact the insurance carrier's legal department. Then inform the legal department of the situation.

Once a subpoena has been served, check over the records to be sure they are accurate and complete, then number the pages and make the copy. The original file should then be sent out immediately (if delivery by certified mail is allowed), or placed under lock and key to avoid tampering. Find out the day of the trial and comply with all orders given by the court. Be sure not to allow anyone to see the records or tamper with them. The records should be turned over only to the judge and should only be left in the care of the judge or jury, never in the care of an attorney. Be sure to obtain a receipt for the records if leaving them.

Subpoena Notification

If a subpoena is served to request claims records, many insurance carriers will notify the member in writing that the records have been requested. This allows the member's attorney to file papers with the court to block the subpoena.

If there is very little time between the date the subpoena was served and the date the records have been requested, the letter may be faxed or the member may be contacted by phone. In either case, be sure to let the member know that they do not have the authority to stop you from releasing the records. They must have their attorney file a petition with the court in order to have the subpoena rescinded. A sample of a subpoena notification follows:

MEMBER NOTIFICATION OF SUBPOENA

Date: _____
To: _____
Address: _____

Dear Member and your Attorney of Record:

Please note that a subpoena for records pertaining to you are being sought by _____. from _____ as shown in the subpoena attached to this Notice.

If you object to us furnishing any part of the records described in this action, you must file papers with the court prior to our release of these records. This subpoena requires that we furnish the records on or by _____ (date).

You or your attorney of record may contact the attorney for the party seeking to examine such records and determine whether they are willing to agree to cancel or limit this subpoena. If no such agreement is reached and you are not already represented by an attorney in this action, **you should consult an attorney to advise you of your rights in this matter.**

If we do not have notification in writing regarding the cancellation or limitation of this subpoena, at least 24 hours prior to the above date, we will assume you have no objection to us releasing this information.

Signed: _____ Date: _____

Summary

Disclaimers should always be used when speaking to patients or providers. This can help prevent the insurance carrier from being held liable for a promise made by a claims examiner.

Submission of fraudulent claims has hit epidemic levels. Payments for fraudulent claims cost administrators millions of dollars annually.

One of the qualities of a good claims examiner is the ability to use good judgment in making claim decisions. Fraud is a very sensitive issue, and the guidelines we have just covered should be practiced along with your company guidelines to ensure accurate and fair claims decisions.

Records should be maintained properly and requests for subpoenas should be answered promptly and correctly.

Assignments

Complete the Questions for Review.
Complete Exercise 2 – 1.

Questions for Review

Directions: Answer the following questions without looking back into the material just covered. Write your answers in the space provided.

1. What are the two concepts that a court will usually look at to determine whether a plan has met the obligation of good faith and fair dealing?

    1. _____

    2. _____

2. When two equally believable interpretations may be made, the one which gives _____ _____ will prevail.

3. Name and explain the two types of damages that may be awarded in bad faith actions.

    1. _____

        _____

    2. _____

        _____

4. _____ is intentional misrepresentation of a fact with the intent to deprive a person of legal rights.

5. _____ is intentional conduct to cause injury, or conduct that is carried on with the conscious disregard of the rights of others.

6. _____ is to put a person through cruel and unjust hardships with the conscious disregard of rights.

7. The dollar amount of a bad faith award is based on two concepts:

    1. _____ and

    2. _____

8. What are the two main areas of fraud concern?

    1. _____

    2. _____

9. (True or False?) A claims examiner should avoid words that can be extremely damaging to a case. _____

10. (True or False?) Prompt, cautious contact with information sources is essential to every investigation. _____

If you were unable to answer any of the questions, refer back to the section and then complete the answers.

Exercise 2 – 1

Directions: Reword the statements below to include the use of a disclaimer in the sentence.

1. Yes, your plan does include that coverage. _____
_____

2. Yes, you are a member of that plan. _____
_____

3. Yes, that is a covered service and we will be paying for it. _____
_____

4. Your check will arrive in five days. _____
_____

5. Your deductible and stop loss have been met so you will not have to put out any more money on this bill. _____
_____
_____

6. You have worked for over 90 days so your company's insurance should cover the services. _____
_____

7. Do not worry; your insurance will cover the bill. _____
_____

8. All hospitalization expenses are covered under your plan. _____
_____

9. We pay 80% of the billed amount. _____

10. All preventive care is covered under your contract. _____
_____

11. Your insurance will cover the cost of these services. _____
_____

12. Your policy includes coverage for those services, so we will pay a portion of the cost. _____
_____

13. We process all claims upon receipt, so you should have your payment within 10 working days. _____
_____

14. Yes, your child is an eligible dependent. _____
_____

15. If your claim reaches us by the 15th, it should be paid by the end of the month. _____
_____

Honors Certification™

The Honors Certification™ for this chapter is two tests. The first test is a written test on the material covered in this chapter. You will also be presented with several scenarios and asked to respond to the situation using the guidelines in this chapter. Each incorrect answer will result in a deduction of 2% to 5% from your grade. You must achieve a score of 80% or higher to pass this test. If you fail the test on your first attempt you may retake the test one additional time. The items included in the second test may be different from those included in the first test.

3   Billing Forms

In this chapter you will learn:

- To understand and properly read the HCFA 1500 claim form.
- To gain speed and accuracy in understanding the HCFA 1500 claim form.
- To understand the UB-92 billing form and to properly read it.
- To identify hospital revenue codes.

Key words and concepts you will learn in this chapter:

HCFA-1500 – The claim form most commonly used to bill for provider's services.

UB-92 – The claim form most commonly used to bill for hospital services.

There are two types of forms most commonly used for billing claims, the HCFA-1500 and the UB-92.

HCFA-1500 Form

The **HCFA-1500** claim form is a standardized form, approved by the American Medical Association, for use as a "universal" form for billing professional services (see following pages for sample form). Many provider's offices use only the HCFA-1500 for billing, however, a few still use alternate forms unique to their office (entitled superbills).

As you use this form, you will become familiar with the various boxes and know where to obtain the information required for completing and processing claim forms. The following listing will assist in explaining the uses of the various fields. It contains the field number along with the name of the field and a brief description of the information needed. The word "same" refers to a description that is the same as the title of the box. Explanations which are too lengthy to be included here have been recorded after this brief listing.

Since it is easier to remember information in groups, we have broken the HCFA-1500 into sections. These sections include information about the patient, the insured, the secondary insurance, third party liability, authorization signature, the illness, the procedures performed, and the provider of services.

Field # Field Name/Description
Following are the numbers, titles and descriptions of the fields found on the HCFA-1500.

Information About the Patient
These boxes contain information about the patient.

1   *Medicare, Medicaid, Tri-Care (CHAMPUS), CHAMPVA, Feca Black Lung or Other.* Check the box of the organization to which you are submitting this claim for payment if you are submitting the form to one of those organizations listed.

2   *Patient's Name.* Same.

3   *Patient's Birth Date and Sex.* All dates should be recorded as Month/Day/Year. Check the box for the appropriate sex.

5   *Patient's Address and Phone Number.* Same.

6   *Patient's Relationship to Insured.* Same.

8   *Patient's Status.* Check applicable boxes.

Information About the Insured
These boxes contain information on the insured, their insurance and their employment.

1A   *Insured's ID Number.* Social Security number, ID number or policy number of insured.

4   *Insured's Name.* Subscriber's Name.

7   *Insured's Address and Phone Number.* Same.

11   *Insured's Policy Group or FECA Number.* Subscriber's Group Number. This number refers to primary insured listed in 1a above.

11A   *Insured's Date of Birth.* Same.

11B   *Employer's Name or School Name.* Employer or school name of insured party.

11C **Insurance Plan Name or Program Name.** Name of insurance company and/or group plan.

11D **Is There Another Health Benefit Plan.** Check appropriate box. If "YES" is checked, then items 9A-9D must be completed.

Information About the Secondary Insurance

These boxes contain information about a secondary insurance policy (if any), which may provide coverage on this patient.

9 **Other Insured's Name.** Other insured whose coverage may be responsible, in whole or in part, for the payment of this claim.

9A **Other Insured's Policy or Group Number.** Same.

9B **Other Insured's Date of Birth and Sex.** Same.

9C **Employer's Name or School Name.** Employer or School Name of other insured party.

9D **Insurance Plan Name or Program Name.** Name of insurance company and/or group plan for other insured.

Information About Third Party Liability

These boxes contain information on whether a third party may be liable for payment on this claim.

10A **Was Condition Related to: Employment?** If "YES" is marked, then there is Worker's Compensation Insurance involved. If "NO" is marked, then Worker's Compensation is not involved. Circle whether employment is current or previous.

10B **Was Condition Related to: Auto Accident?** If "YES" is marked, then check for an injury date (Block 14) and an injury diagnosis (Block 21). The state the accident occurred in should also be indicated. If "NO" is marked then the claim may not be for an injury.

10C **Was Condition Related to: Other Accident?** If "YES" is marked, then check for an injury date (Block 14) and an injury diagnosis (Block 21). If "NO" is marked then the claim may not be for an injury.

10D **Reserved for Local Use.** Same

Authorization Signatures

These boxes should be signed by the insured, or a permanent release of information and assignment of benefits should be kept on file. If there is a permanent release of information or assignment of benefits on file, the words SIGNATURE ON FILE should be placed in these boxes.

12 **Patient's or Authorized Person's Signature.** Patient's release of medical information.

13 **Assignment of Benefits.** This box should always be signed by the patient to allow the insurer to pay the physician directly instead of paying the patient and waiting for the patient to pay the provider.

Information About the Illness

These boxes contain information about the current illness.

14 **Date of Illness, Injury, Accident or Pregnancy.** All injury claims (i.e., injury diagnosis) must have an injury or accident date. If the patient's condition is a pregnancy, the date of the last menstrual period should be indicated.

15 **If Patient Has Had Same Or Similar Illness, Give First Date.** Same.

16 **Dates Patient Unable To Work In Current Occupation.** Same.

17 **Name Of Referring Physician Or Other Source.** If this patient was referred to the current physician by another physician, a hospital, or clinic, the referring party should be listed here.

17A **I.D. Number of Referring Physician.** Same

18 **Hospitalization Dates Relating to Current Services.** Same.

19 **Reserved for Local Use.**

20 **Outside Lab.** Was laboratory work performed outside your office? If so, check the yes box and indicate the total of the charges.

21 **Diagnosis or Nature of Illness or Injury.** The diagnosis states why the patient went to see the provider. Both an ICD-9 code and a description should be indicated.

22 **Medicaid Resubmission Code.** Leave blank.

Information About the Procedures Performed

These boxes contain information about the procedures which were performed.

23 **Prior Authorization Number.** Authorization number for services which were approved prior to being rendered.

24A **Date of Service.** The date service was rendered by the provider. A complete date must be given.

24B **Place of Service.** The location where the services were performed (see following section for further information).

24C **Type of Service.** Leave blank.

24D **Procedure Code.** The 5-digit procedure code as found in the CPT/RVS and HCPCS manuals. These are codes that have been assigned to each procedure the provider can perform. By selecting the proper code, billers can describe the type of service performed with a few numbers. This eliminates the confusion that used to arise from various abbreviations and descriptions of a procedure. It also allows for easy computer tabulation of the different procedures performed.

24D **Modifier Code.** The two-digit modifier from the CPT/RVS further describing the procedure code.

24E **Diagnosis Code.** This is used in conjunction with Field 21. The number placed in Field 24E (i.e., 1, 2, 3, 4) refers to diagnosis 1, 2, 3, or 4 in

PLEASE
DO NOT
STAPLE
IN THIS
AREA
☐☐☐ PICA

WINTER INSURANCE CO.
9763 WESTERN WAY
WHITTIER, CO 82963

APPROVED MOB-0938-0008

CLAIM: HCFA EX

HEALTH INSURANCE CLAIM FORM

PICA ☐☐☐

1. MEDICARE   MEDICAID   CHAMPUS   CHAMPVA   GROUP HEALTH PLAN   FECA BLK LUNG   OTHER

☐ (Medicare #) ☐ (Medicaid #) ☐ (Sponsor's SSN) ☐ (VA File #) ☒ (SSN or ID) ☐ (SSN) ☐ (ID)

1. INSURED'S I.D NUMBER   (FOR PROGRAM IN ITEM 1)

777-77-7777

2. PATIENT'S NAME (Last, First, Middle Initial)

NORMAL, NANCY N.

3. PATIENT'S BIRTH DATE MM | DD | YY   SEX

07 | 27 | 77   M☐ F☒

4. INSURED'S NAME (Last, First, Middle Initial)

NORMAL, NANCY N.

5. PATIENT'S ADDRESS (No., Street)

707 NATIONAL STREET

6. PATIENT'S RELATIONSHIP TO INSURED

Self ☒   Spouse ☐   Child ☐   Other ☐

7. INSURED'S ADDRESS (No., Street)

707 NATIONAL STREET

CITY

NANDO

STATE

NV

8. PATIENT STATUS

Single ☒   Married ☐   Other ☐

Employed ☒   Full-Time ☐   Part-Time ☐
Student   Student

CITY

NANDO

STATE

NV

ZIP CODE

89577

TELEPHONE (Include Area Code)

(775) 555-3377

ZIP CODE

89577

TELEPHONE (INCLUDE AREA CODE)

(775) 555-3377

9. OTHER INSURED'S NAME (Last, First, Middle Initial)

10. IS PATIENT'S CONDITION RELATED TO:

11. INSURED'S POLICY GROUP OR FECA NUMBER:

777-77-ABC

a. OTHER INSURED'S POLICY OR GROUP NUMBER

a. EMPLOYMENT? (CURRENT OR PREVIOUS)

☐ YES   ☒ NO

a. INSURED'S DATE OF BIRTH
MM | DD | YY   SEX

07 | 27 | 77   M☐ F☒

a. OTHER INSURED'S DATE OF BIRTH
MM | DD | YY   SEX
M☐ F☐

b. AUTO ACCIDENT?   PLACE (State)

☐ YES   ☒ NO |___|

b. EMPLOYER'S NAME OR SCHOOL NAME

ABC CORPORATION

c. EMPLOYER'S NAME OR SCHOOL NAME

c. OTHER ACCIDENT?

☐ YES   ☒ NO

c. INSURANCE PLAN NAME OR PROGRAM NAME

ABC PLAN

d. INSURANCE PLAN NAME OR PROGRAM NAME

10d. RESERVED FOR LOCAL USE

d. IS THERE ANOTHER HEALTH BENEFIT PLAN?

☐ YES   ☒ NO   *If yes, return to and complete item 9 a-d*

READ BACK OF FORM BEFORE COMPLETING & SIGNING THIS FORM
12. PATIENT'S OR AUTHORIZED PERSON'S SIGNATURE I authorize the release of any medical or other information necessary to process this claim. I also request payment of government benefits either to myself or to the party who accepts assignment below.

SIGNED **SIGNATURE ON FILE**   DATE **02/ 05/ 04**

13. INSURED'S OR AUTHORIZED PERSON'S SIGNATURE I authorize payment of medical benefits to the undersigned physician or supplier for services described below.

SIGNED   **SIGNATURE ON FILE**

14. DATE OF CURRENT: ◄ ILLNESS (1st symptom) INJURY (Accident) PREGNANCY (LMP)
MM | DD | YY

02 | 03 | 04

15. IF PATIENT HAS HAD SAME OR SIMILAR ILLNESS, GAVE FIRST DATE   MM | DD | YY

16. DATES PATIENT UNABLE TO WORK IN CURRENT OCCUPATION
FROM MM | DD | YY   TO MM | DD | YY

17. NAME OF REFERRING PHYSICIAN OR OTHER SOURCE

17a. I.D. NUMBER OF REFERRING PHYSICIAN

18. HOSPITALIZATION DATES RELATED TO CURRENT SERVICES
MM | DD | YY
FROM   TO MM | DD | YY

19. RESERVED FOR LOCAL USE

20. OUTSIDE LAB? $ CHARGES

☐ YES   ☐ NO

21. DIAGNOSIS OR NATURE OF ILLNESS OR INJURY, (RELATE ITEMS 1,2,3, OR 4 TO ITEM 24E BY LINE)

1. | 079 . 3
2. |
3. |
4. |

22. MEDICAID RESUBMISSION CODE   ORIGINAL REF. NO.

23. PRIOR AUTHORIZATION NUMBER

24.	A. DATE(S) OF SERVICE						B. Place of Service	C. Type of Service	D. PROCEDURES, SERVICES, OR SUPPLIES (Explain Unusual Circumstances) CPT/HCPS	MODIFIER	E. DIAGNOSIS CODE	F. $ CHARGES		G. DAYS OR UNITS	H. EPSDT Family Plan	I. EMG	J. COB	K. RESERVED FOR LOCAL USE
	From MM DD YY			To MM DD YY														
	02	05	04	02	05	04	11	1	99201		1	320	00	1				
	02	05	04	02	05	04	11	1	85025		1	130	00	1				
	02	05	04	02	05	04	11	1	87040		1	140	00	1				

25. FEDERAL TAX I.D. NUMBER   SSN EIN

70-7759777   ☐ ☒

26. PATIENT'S ACCOUNT NO.

NANNR001   737

27. ACCEPT ASSIGNMENT? (For govt. claims, see back)

☒ YES   ☐ NO

28. TOTAL CHARGE

$ 590 | 00

29. AMOUNT PAID

$

30. BALANCE DUE

$ 590 | 00

31. SIGNATURE OF PHYSICIAN OR SUPPLIER INCLUDING DEGREES OR CREDENTIALS (I certify that the statements on the reverse apply to this bill and are made a part thereof.)

SIGNED *Dee N. Aee*   DATE 02/18/04

32. NAME AND ADDRESS OF FACILITY WHERE SERVICES WERE RENDERED (If other than home or office)

33. PHYSICIAN'S, SUPPLIERS BILLING NAME, ADDRESS, ZIP CODE & PHONE #

DEE N. AEE M.D.
2577 NONE STREET, STE 575N
NOLTY, NV 89577 (775) 555-0077

PIN# DNA001 | GRP#

(APPROVED BY AMA COUNCIL ON MEDICAL SERVICE 8/88)
FORM OWCP-1500   FORM RRB-1500

PLEASE PRINT OR TYPE

FORM HCFA-1500   (12-90)

Figure 3 – 1: Front of HCFA-1500

BECAUSE THIS FORM IS USED BY VARIOUS GOVERNMENT AND PRIVATE HEALTH PROGRAMS, SEE SEPARATE INSTRUCTIONS ISSUED BY APPLICABLE PROGRAMS.

NOTICE: Any person who knowingly files a statement of claim containing any misrepresentation or any false, incomplete or misleading information may be guilty of a criminal act punishable under law and may be subject to civil penalties.

REFERS TO GOVERNMENT PROGRAMS ONLY

MEDICARE AND CHAMPUS PAYMENTS: A patient's signature requests that payment be made and authorizes release of any information necessary to process the claim and certifies that the information provided in Blocks 1 through 12 is true, accurate and complete. In the case of a Medicare claim, the patient's signature authorizes any entity to release to Medicare medical and nonmedical information, including employment status, and whether the person has employer group health insurance, liability, no-fault, worker's compensation or other insurance which is responsible to pay for the services for which the Medicare claim is made. See 42 CFR 411.24(a). If item 9 is completed, the patient's signature authorizes release of the information to the health plan or agency shown. In Medicare assigned or CHAMPUS participation cases, the physician agrees to accept the charge determination of the Medicare carrier or CHAMPUS fiscal intermediary as the full charge, and the patient is responsible only for the deductible, coinsurance and noncovered services. Coinsurance and the deductible are based upon the charge determination of the Medicare carrier or CHAMPUS fiscal intermediary if this is less than the charge submitted. CHAMPUS is not a health insurance program but makes payment for health benefits provided through certain affiliations with the Uniformed Services. Information on the patient's sponsor should be provided in those items captioned in "Insured"; i.e., items 1a, 4, 6, 7, 9, and 11.

BLACK LUNG AND FECA CLAIMS

The provider agrees to accept the amount paid by the Government as payment in full. See Black Lung and FECA instructions regarding required procedure and diagnosis coding systems.

SIGNATURE OF PHYSICIAN OR SUPPLIER (MEDICARE, CHAMPUS, FECA AND BLACK LUNG)

I certify that the services shown on this form were medically indicated and necessary for the health of the patient and were personally furnished by me or were furnished incident to my professional service by my employee under my immediate personal supervision, except as otherwise expressly permitted by Medicare or CHAMPUS regulations.

For services to be considered as "incident" to a physician's professional service, 1) they must be rendered under the physician's immediate personal supervision by his/her employee, 2) they must be an integral, although incidental part of a covered physician's service, 3) they must be of kinds commonly furnished in physician's offices, and 4) the services of nonphysicians must be included on the physician's bills.

For CHAMPUS claims, I further certify that I (or any employee) who rendered services am not an active duty member of the Uniformed Services or a civilian employee of the United States Government or a contract employee of the United States Government, either civilian or military (refer to 5 USC 5536). For Black-Lung claims, I further certify that the services performed were for a Black Lung-related disorder.

No Part B Medicare benefits may be paid unless this form is received as required by existing law and regulations (42 CFR 424.32).

NOTICE: Any one who misrepresents or falsifies essential information to receive payment from Federal funds requested by this form may upon conviction be subject to fine and imprisonment under applicable Federal laws.

NOTICE TO PATIENT ABOUT THE COLLECTION AND USE OF MEDICARE, CHAMPUS, FECA, AND BLACK LUNG INFORMATION
(PRIVACY ACT STATEMENT)

We are authorized by HCFA, CHAMPUS and OWCP to ask you for information needed in the administration of the Medicare, CHAMPUS, FECA, and Black Lung programs. Authority to collect information is in section 205(a), 1862, 1872 and 1874 of the Social Security Act as amended, 42 CFR 411.24(a) and 424.5(a) (6), and 44 USC 3101;41 CFR 101 et seq and 10 USC 1079 and 1086; 5 USC 8101 et seq; and 30 USC 901 et seq; 38 USC 613; E.O. 9397.

The information we obtain to complete claims under these programs is used to identify you and to determine your eligibility. It is also used to decide if the services and supplies you received are covered by these programs and to insure that proper payment is made.

The information may also be given to other providers of services, carriers, intermediaries, medical review boards, health plans, and other organizations or Federal agencies, for the effective administration of Federal provisions that require other third parties payers to pay primary to Federal program, and as otherwise necessary to administer these programs. For example, it may be necessary to disclose information about the benefits you have used to a hospital or doctor. Additional disclosures are made through routine uses for information contained in systems of records.

FOR MEDICARE CLAIMS: See the notice modifying system No. 09-70-0501, titled, 'Carrier Medicare Claims Record,' published in the Federal Register, Vol. 55 No. 177, page 37549, Wed. Sept. 12, 1990, or as updated and republished.

FOR OWCP CLAIMS: Department of Labor, Privacy Act of 1974, "Republication of Notice of Systems of Records," Federal Register Vol. 55 No. 40, Wed Feb. 28, 1990, See ESA-5, ESA-6, ESA-12, ESA-13, ESA-30, or as updated and republished.

FOR CHAMPUS CLAIMS: PRINCIPLE PURPOSE(S): To evaluate eligibility for medical care provided by civilian sources and to issue payment upon establishment of eligibility and determination that the services/supplies received are authorized by law.

ROUTINE USE(S): Information from claims and related documents may be given to the Dept. of Veterans Affairs, the Dept. of Health and Human Services and/or the Dept. of Transportation consistent with their statutory administrative responsibilities under CHAMPUS/CHAMPVA; to the Dept. of Justice for representation of the Secretary of Defense in civil actions; to the Internal Revenue Service, private collection agencies, and consumer reporting agencies in connection with recoupment claims; and to Congressional Offices in response to inquiries made at the request of the person to whom a record pertains. Appropriate disclosures may be made to other federal, state, local, foreign government agencies, private business entities, and individual providers of care, on matters relating to entitlement, claims adjudication, fraud, program abuse, utilization review, quality assurance, peer review, program integrity, third-party liability, coordination of benefits, and civil and criminal litigation related to the operation of CHAMPUS.

DISCLOSURES: Voluntary; however, failure to provide information will result in delay in payment or may result in denial of claim. With the one exception discussed below, there are no penalties under these programs for refusing to supply information. However, failure to furnish information regarding the medical services rendered or the amount charged would prevent payment of claims under these programs. Failure to furnish any other information, such as name or claim number, would delay payment of the claim. Failure to provide medical information under FECA could be deemed an obstruction.

It is mandatory that you tell us if you know that another party is responsible for paying for your treatment. Section 1128B of the Social Security Act and 31 USC 3801-3812 provide penalties for withholding this information.

You should be aware that P.L. 100-503, the "Computer Matching and Privacy Protection Act of 1988", permits the government to verify information by way of computer matches.

MEDICAID PAYMENTS (PROVIDER CERTIFICATION)

I hereby agree to keep such records as are necessary to disclose fully the extent of services provided to individuals under the State's Title XIX plan and to furnish information regarding any payments claimed for providing such services as the State Agency or Dept. of Health and Humans Services may request.

I further agree to accept, as payment in full, the amount paid by the Medicaid program for those claims submitted for payment under that program, with the exception of authorized deductible, coinsurance, co-payment or similar cost-sharing charge.

SIGNATURE OF PHYSICIAN (OR SUPPLIER): I certify that the services listed above were medically indicated and necessary to the health of this patient and were personally furnished by me or my employee under my personal direction.

NOTICE: This is to certify that the foregoing information is true, accurate and complete. I understand that payment and satisfaction of this claim will be from Federal and State funds, and that any false claims, statements, or documents, or concealment of a material fact, may be prosecuted under applicable Federal or State laws.

Public reporting burden for this collection of information is estimated to average 15 minutes per response, including time for reviewing instructions, searching existing date sources, gathering and maintaining data needed, and completing and reviewing the collection of information. Send comments regarding this burden estimate or any other aspect of this collection of information, including suggestions for reducing the burden, to HCFA, Office of Financial Management, P.O. Box 26684, Baltimore, MD 21207; and to the Office of Management and Budget, Paperwork Reduction Project (OMB-0938-0008), Washington, D.C. 20503.

Figure 3 – 2: Back of HCFA-1500

Block 21. In other words, the doctor can perform different services for different illnesses or injuries on different dates and submit them all on one claim form.

24F   *Charges.* The charge per line of service.

24G   *Days or Units.* The number of times a service was performed

24H   *EPSDT Family Plan.* Leave blank.

24I   *EMG.* If service was rendered in the hospital emergency room, this should match the service code in Item 24B.

24J   *COB.* Coordination of Benefits. Are there other insurance policies or plans which may be responsible for payment on this claim? Indicate a Y for yes, an N for no.

24K   *Reserved for Local Use.* Leave blank.

28   *Total Charge.* The total charge of the claim.

29   *Amount Paid.* The amount paid by the patient or subscriber.

30   *Balance Due.* The difference between the total charge and the amount paid by the patient or subscriber (if any).

Information About the Provider of Services
These boxes contain information about the provider of services.

25   *Federal Tax ID Number.* If the provider of service is a physician or an individual, his/her Social Security number should be used. If the provider of service is a facility, an Employer Identification Number should be used.

26   *Patient's Account Number.* Same

27   *Accept Assignment for Government Claims.* Refers only to Tri-Care or Medicare. Do not use to assign payment on this claim to the provider. Use Item 13 only for your assignment of payment.

31   *Signature of Physician or Supplier of Service.* Must be signed by the provider indicating that the said services have indeed been rendered. Degrees or credentials (ie, M.D., D.O., etc.) should follow the name.

32   *Name and Address of Facility Where Services Rendered.* If this information is the same as Item 33, it may be left blank.

33   *Physician's/Supplier's Billing Name, Address, Zip Code And Phone #.* The name, address and phone number of the physician or supplier of service. This is the address that payments will be addressed to if assignment of benefits has been signed for in Field 13.

Field 24B, Place of Service

This item needed further description for which space was not available in the above text. This is a numerical code to indicate the place where the service was rendered.

00-10   **Unassigned.**

11   **Office.** Location other than a hospital, Skilled Nursing Facility (SNF), Military Treatment Facility, Community Health Center, State or Local Public Health Clinic or Intermediate Care Facility (ICF), where the health professional routinely provides health examinations, diagnosis and treatment of illness or injury on an ambulatory basis.

12   **Home.** Location other than a hospital or other facility where the patient receives care in a private residence.

13-20   **Unassigned.**

21   **Inpatient Hospital.** A facility other than psychiatric, which primarily provides diagnostic, therapeutic (both surgical and nonsurgical) and rehabilitation services by, or under the supervision of, physicians to patient admitted for a variety of medical condition.

22   **Outpatient Hospital.** A portion of a hospital which provides diagnostic, therapeutic (both surgical and non surgical) and rehabilitation services to sick and injured persons who do not require hospitalization or institutionalization. A patient who is not admitted to a hospital (i.e., one who is under 24-hour supervision) is an outpatient.

23   **Emergency Room – Hospital.** A portion of a hospital where emergency diagnosis and treatment of illness or injury is provided. Patients in the emergency room are considered to be facility outpatients. Remember to also complete box 24I.

24   **Ambulatory Surgical Center.** A freestanding facility, other than a physician's office, where surgical and diagnostic services are provided on an ambulatory basis. When this code is used, the facility must be an HCFA-approved ASC.

25   **Birthing Center.** A facility, other than a hospital's maternity facilities or a physician's office, which provides a setting for labor, delivery and immediate post-partum care as well as immediate care of newborn infants.

26   **Military Treatment Facility (MTF).** A medical facility operated by one or more of the Uniformed Services. MTF also refers to certain former U.S. Public Health Service facilities now designated as Uniformed Service Treatment Facilities (USTF).

27-30   **Unassigned.**

31   **Skilled Nursing Facility.** A facility which primarily provides inpatient skilled nursing care and related services to patients who require medical, nursing, or rehabilitative services which does not provide the level of care or treatment available in a hospital.

32   **Nursing Facility.** A facility which provides skilled nursing care and related services for the rehabilitation of injured, disabled, or sick

persons or on a regular basis health-related care services above the level of custodial care to other than mentally retarded individuals.

33 **Custodial Care Facility.** A facility which provides room, board and personal assistance services, generally on a long-term basis, and which does not include a medical component.

34 **Hospice.** A facility, other than a patient's home, in which palliative and supportive care for terminally ill patients and their families are provided.

35-40 **Unassigned.**

41 **Ambulance – Land.** A land vehicle specifically designed, equipped and staffed for lifesaving and transporting the sick or injured.

42 **Ambulance – Air or Water.** An air or water vehicle specifically designed, equipped and staffed for lifesaving and transporting the sick or injured.

43-50 **Unassigned.**

51 **Inpatient Psychiatric Facility.** A facility that provides inpatient psychiatric services for the diagnosis and treatment of mental illness on a 24-hour basis, by or under the supervision of a physician.

52 **Psychiatric Facility – Partial Hospitalization.** A facility for the diagnosis and treatment of mental illness that provides a planned therapeutic program for patients who do not need full-time hospitalization, but who need broader programs than are possible from outpatient visits in a hospital-based or hospital-affiliated facility.

53 **Community Mental Health Center.** A facility that provides comprehensive mental health services on an ambulatory basis primarily to individuals residing or employed in a defined area. Includes a physician-directed mental health facility.

54 **Intermediate Care Facility/Mentally Retarded.** A facility which primarily provides health-related care and services above the level of custodial care of mentally retarded individuals but does not provide the level of care or treatment available in a hospital or SNF.

55 **Residential Substance Abuse Treatment Facility.** A facility which provides treatment for substance (alcohol and drug) abuse to live-in residents who do not require acute medical care. Services include individual and group therapy and counseling, family counseling, laboratory tests, drugs and supplies, psychological testing, and room and board.

56 **Psychiatric Residential Treatment Center.** A facility or distinct part of a facility for psychiatric care which provides a total 24-hour therapeutically planned and professionally staffed group living and learning environment.

57-60 **Unassigned.**

61 **Comprehensive Inpatient Rehabilitation Facility.** A facility that provides comprehensive rehabilitation services under the supervision of a physician to inpatients with physical disabilities. Services include rehabilitation nursing, physical therapy, occupational therapy, speech pathology, social or psychological services, and orthotics and prosthetics services. There are specific licensing requirements for these facilities.

62 **Comprehensive Outpatient Rehabilitation Facility.** A facility that provides comprehensive rehabilitation services under the supervision of a physician to inpatients with physical disabilities. Services include physical therapy, occupational therapy, and speech pathology services. There are specific licensing requirements for these facilities.

63-64 **Unassigned.**

65 **End Stage Renal Disease Treatment Facility.** A facility other than a hospital, which provides dialysis treatment, maintenance and/or training to patients or care givers on an ambulatory or home-care basis.

66-70 **Unassigned.**

71 **State or Local Public Health Clinic.** A facility maintained by either State or local health departments that provides ambulatory primary medical care under the general direction of a physician. Such facilities must be physician-directed.

72 **Rural Health Clinic.** A certified facility which is located in a rural medically undeserved area that provides ambulatory primary medical care under the general direction of a physician. Qualified facilities do not bill Part B of Medicare for items or services except for DME and orthotics and prosthetics.

73-80 **Unassigned.**

81 **Independent Laboratory.** A laboratory certified to perform diagnostic and/or clinical tests independent of an institution or a physician's office.

With the exception of hospital inpatients, the place of service for lab tests will be based on where "drawn" instead of where the test is actually performed. If the physician is billing for a lab service performed in his/her own office, then use the appropriate code for doctor's office. If an independent laboratory is billing, show the place where the sample is drawn. An independent laboratory drawing a sample in its laboratory should use the code for independent laboratory as the place of service. If an independent laboratory is billing for a test on a sample drawn on a hospital inpatient, then the appropriate code for hospital inpatient is entered as the place of service. If the independent laboratory is billing for a test on a sample drawn in a physician's office, then the appropriate code is for doctor's office.

82-98   **Unassigned.**

99   **Other Unlisted Facility.** Other service facilities not identified above.

Tips on Understanding the HCFA-1500

Properly using the HCFA-1500 is vital to paying the proper reimbursement on claims. The following tips will help to minimize errors and speed processing of a claim.

1. Be sure the patient information contained on the claim matches that in your records.
2. Be sure that all necessary boxes are filled in.
3. Be sure that all diagnoses have related procedures, and all procedures have a related diagnosis.
4. Do not write on the form, instead, attach a separate paper for comments.
5. Do not sign or write in red ink. Many scanners used by insurance carriers are programmed to pass over everything in red on the form and just pick up the data. Therefore, anything in red will not be picked up by the scanner.
6. Do not use a highlighter on the form. Some scanners will pick up the highlighter and turn it into a black mark, thus obliterating the information in that field.

UB-92

The **Uniform Bill-1992 (UB-92)** is intended to be used by hospitals or other hospital-type facilities for inpatient and outpatient billing (see **Figures 3 – 3** and **3 – 4**). The data elements and the design of the form were determined by the National Uniform Billing Committee. This form was designed to provide the basic data needed by most payors to adjudicate a large majority of their claims. The objective was to accommodate a wide range of needs while eliminating the need for attachments.

As you use this form, you will become familiar with the various boxes and know where to obtain the information required for completing and processing claim forms. The following list will assist in explaining the uses of the various fields. It contains the field number along with the name of the field and a brief description of the information needed. The word "same" refers to a description that is the same as the title of the box. Explanations that are too lengthy to be included here have been recorded after this brief listing.

Field #   Field Name/Description

1   *Provider Name, Address, and Telephone Number.* Name, address, and telephone number of hospital or clinic where services were rendered.

2   *Reserved (untitled).* All unlabeled fields are reserved for state or national use. Their use may be assigned by either the state or National Uniform Billing Committee.

3   *Patient Control Number.* Patient's account number.

4   *Type of Bill.* Three-digit code providing information regarding what type of bill is being submitted. (See following section for further information.)

5   *Federal Tax Number.* Provider's identification number or social security number.

6   *Statement Covers Period.* The dates of service that this billing statement represents. Dates should match those on the itemized billing statement. For services rendered on the same day, both dates should be the same.

7   *Covered Days.* Number of days services covered by the primary payor.

8   *Noncovered Days (inpatient only).* Number of days services not covered by the primary payor. For Medicare, the reason for noncoverage should be explained by occurrence codes, PSRO fields, or in remarks.

9   *Coinsurance Days.* Number of days for which the patient must pay a portion of the costs of services. For Medicare, the inpatient Medicare days occurring after the 60th and before the 91st day in a single spell of illness.

10   *Lifetime Reserve Days.* Under Medicare, each beneficiary has a lifetime reserve of 60 additional days of inpatient hospital services after using 90 days of inpatient hospital services during a spell of illness.

11   *Reserved for State Assignment.*

12   *Patient's Name.* Same.

13   *Patient's Address.* Same.

14   *Birth Date.* Patient's date of birth.

15   *Sex.* Patient's sex.

16   Marital Status. Patient's marital status (S = Single, M = Married, X = Legally Separated, D = Divorced, W = Widowed, U = Unknown)

17   *Date of Admission.* Date patient was admitted to hospital.

18   *Hour of Admission.* Hour patient admitted to hospital according to a 24-hour clock (ie, 10:10 p.m. would be written 22:10). 99 = unknown.

19   *Type of Admission.* Numerical code denoting the priority of this admission (see following section for further information).

20   *Source of Admission.* Numerical code denoting the source of this admission (see following section for further information).

21   *Discharge Hour.* Time patient was discharged from inpatient care. Time should be written according to a 24-hour clock. 99 = unknown. This element is not necessary for outpatient care.

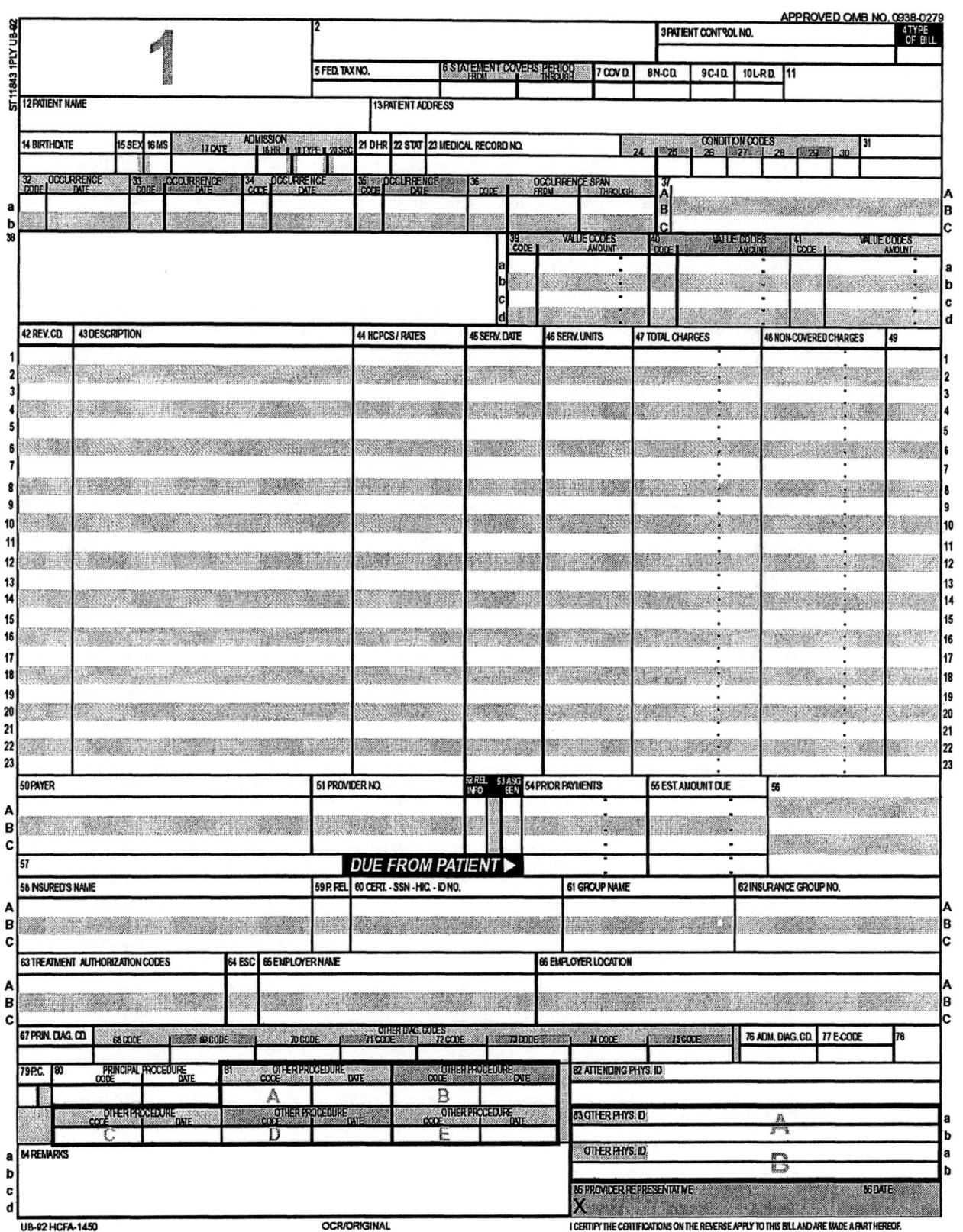

Figure 3 – 3: Front of UB-92

UNIFORM BILL: **NOTICE: ANYONE WHO MISREPRESENTS OR FALSIFIES ESSENTIAL INFORMATION REQUESTED BY THIS FORM MAY UPON CONVICTION BE SUBJECT TO FINE AND IMPRISONMENT UNDER FEDERAL AND/OR STATE LAW.**

Certifications relevant to the Bill and Information Shown on the Face Hereof: Signatures on the face hereof incorporate the following certifications or verifications where pertinent to this Bill:

1. If third party benefits are indicated as being assigned or in participation status, on the face thereof, appropriate assignments by the insured/beneficiary and signature of patient or parent or legal guardian covering authorization to release information are on file. Determinations as to the release of medical and financial information should be guided by the particular terms of the release forms that were executed by the patient or the patient's legal representative. The hospital agrees to save harmless, indemnify and defend any insurer who makes payment in reliance upon this certification, from and against any claim to the insurance proceeds when in fact no valid assignment of benefits to the hospital was made.

2. If patient occupied a private room or required private nursing for medical necessity, any required certifications are on file.

3. Physician's certifications and re-certifications, if required by contract or Federal regulations, are on file.

4. For Christian Science Sanitoriums, verifications and if necessary re-verifications of the patient's need for sanitorium services are on file.

5. Signature of patient or his/her representative on certifications, authorization to release information, and payment request, as required be Federal law and regulations (42 USC 1935f, 42 CFR 424.36, 10 USC 1071 thru 1086, 32 CFR 199) and, any other applicable contract regulations, is on file.

6. This claim, to the best of my knowledge, is correct and complete and is in conformance with the Civil Rights Act of 1964 as amended. Records adequately disclosing services will be maintained and necessary information will be furnished to such governmental agencies as required by applicable law.

7. For Medicare purposes:

   If the patient has indicated that other health insurance or a state medical assistance agency will pay part of his/her medical expenses and he/she wants information about his/her claim released to them upon their request, necessary authorization is on file. The patient's signature on the provider's request to bill Medicare authorizes any holder of medical and non-medical information, including employment status, and whether the person has employer group health insurance, liability, no-fault, workers' compensation, or other insurance which is responsible to pay for the services for which this Medicare claim is made.

8. For Medicaid purposes:

   This is to certify that the foregoing information is true, accurate, and complete.
   I understand that payment and satisfaction of this claim will be from Federal and State funds, and that any false claims, statements, or documents, or concealment of a material fact, may be prosecuted under applicable Federal or State Laws.

9. For CHAMPUS purposes:

   This is to certify that:

   (a) the information submitted as part of this claim is true, accurate and complete, and, the services shown on this form were medically indicated and necessary for the health of the patient;

   (b) the patient has represented that by a reported residential address outside a military treatment center catchment area he or she does not live within a catchment area of a U.S. military or U.S. Public Health Service medical facility, or if the patient resides within a catchment area of such a facility, a copy of a Non-Availability Statement (DD Form 1251) is on file, or the physician has certified to a medical emergency in any assistance where a copy of a Non-Availability Statement is not on file;

   (c) the patient or the patient's parent or guardian has responded directly to the provider's request to identify all health insurance coverages, and that all such coverages are identified on the face the claim except those that are exclusively supplemental payments to CHAMPUS-determined benefits;

   (d) the amount billed to CHAMPUS has been billed after all such coverages have been billed and paid, excluding Medicaid, and the amount billed to CHAMPUS is that remaining claimed against CHAMPUS benefits;

   (e) the beneficiary's cost share has not been waived by consent or failure to exercise generally accepted billing and collection efforts; and,

   (f) any hospital-based physician under contract, the cost of whose services are allocated in the charges included in this bill, is not an employee or member of the Uniformed Services. For purposes of this certification, an employee of the Uniformed Services is an employee, appointed in civil service (refer to 5 USC 2105), including part-time or intermittent but excluding contract surgeons or other personnel employed by the Uniformed Services through personal service contracts. Similarly, member of the Uniformed Services does not apply to reserve members of the Uniformed Services not on active duty.

   (g) based on the Consolidated Omnibus Budget Reconciliation Act of 1986, all providers participating in Medicare must also participate in CHAMPUS for inpatient hospital services provided pursuant to admissions to hospitals occurring on or after January 1, 1987.

   (h) if CHAMPUS benefits are to be paid in a participating status, I agree to submit this claim to the appropriate CHAMPUS claims processor as a participating provider. I agree to accept the CHAMPUS-determined reasonable charge as the total charge for the medical services or supplies listed on the claim form. I will accept the CHAMPUS-determined reasonable charge even if it is less than the billed amount, and also agree to accept the amount paid by CHAMPUS, combined with the cost-share amount and deductible amount, if any, paid by or on behalf of the patient as full payment for the listed medical services or supplies. I will make no attempt to collect from the patient (or his or her parent or guardian) amounts over the CHAMPUS-determined reasonable charge. CHAMPUS will make any benefits payable directly to me, if I submit this claim as a participating provider.

ESTIMATED CONTRACT BENEFITS

Figure 3 – 4: Back of UB-92

22   *Patient Status.* Numerical code denoting the status of the patient as of the statement-through date. This element is necessary only for inpatient care (see following section for further information).

23   *Medical Record Number.* Number assigned by the provider to the medical record.

24-30   *Condition Codes.* Codes used to identify conditions relating to the claim that may affect payor processing (see following section for further information). No specific date is associated with this code.

31   *Reserved for National Assignment.*

32-35   *Occurrence Codes.* The code and associated date defining a significant event relating to this bill that may effect payor processing (see following section for further information).

36   *Occurrence Span.* The code and the related dates that identify an event that relates to the payment of the claim. These codes identify occurrences that happened over a span of time (see following section for further information).

37   *Internal Control Number.* The control number assigned to the original bill by the payor or the payor's intermediary.

38   *Responsible Party Name and Address.* Name and address of person ultimately responsible for insuring payment of the bill. This is usually the patient, or the parent or legal guardian if the patient is a minor.

39-41   *Value Codes and Amounts.* Codes and the related dollar amount that identify data of a monetary nature that is necessary for the processing of this claim (see following section for further information).

42   *Revenue Code.* Revenue code referencing the type of services provided (see following section for further information).

43   *Revenue Description.* A description of the services provided. Abbreviations may be used. Accommodation (room) descriptions must be entered first on the bill and must be in chronologic order of appearance (ie, 03/01/89 ICU, 03/02/89 Semiprivate room).

44   *HCPCS/Rates.* The accommodation rate for inpatient bills, or the CPT or HCPCS code for ancillary or outpatient services. Outpatient Worker's Compensation and Medicaid require HCPCS coding in this space.

45   *Service Date.* The date the service was provided if this is a series bill where the date of service differs from the from/through date on the bill.

46   *Units of Service.* Quantitative measure of services, days, miles, pints of blood, units, or treatments (ie, if a patient was hospitalized for three days, a 3 would be placed here).

47   *Total Charges.* Total charges for that line of services.

48   *Noncovered Charges.* The amount per line of service that is not covered by the primary payor.

49   *Reserved for National Assignment.*

50   *Payor Identification.* Name of Insurer(s) covered by the patient who may be responsible for payment on this bill. Insurers should be listed in order of Primary Payor, Secondary Payor, Tertiary Payor(s). If required, numbers identifying each payor organization should be listed.

51   *Provider Number.* The number assigned to the provider by the listed payor.

52   *Release Information.* A Y (yes) or N (no) designation stating whether or not patient's signature is on file authorizing the release of information. An R may also be entered to show that a hospital has restricted authorization to release information. In such a case the authorization should be attached. If no Authorization to Release Information is on file, one must be obtained before sending in the claim.

53   *Assignment of Benefits.* A Y (yes) or N (no) designation stating whether or not patient's signature is on file authorizing the insurer to pay the provider of service directly instead of the patient. If a Y is placed in this box, you must have an assignment of benefits, signed by the insured, on file in your office (see following section for further information).

54   *Prior Payments.* The amount that has been paid toward this bill prior to the current billing date. These can include payments by the patient, other payors, and so on.

55   *Estimated Amount Due.* The amount estimated by the provider to be due from the indicated payor. This is usually the total amount due minus any previous payments.

56   *Reserved for State Assignment.*

57   *Reserved for National Assignment.*

58   *Insured's Name.* Name of the person listed on the insurance forms (subscriber's name). This may be a spouse or parent of the patient.

59   *Patient's Relationship to Insured.* Numerical code designation indicating the relationship between the patient and the insured (see following section for further information).

60   *Subscriber's Certificate Number.* The policy number under which the insured is covered if it is an individual policy. If the insured is covered under a group policy (such as one offered by his/her employer), often the insured's social security number is used as the subscriber number.

61   *Insured Group Name.* The name of the group or company that holds the insured's policy. Often this is the employer of the insured. This information is required by Medicare when Medicare is not the primary payor.

62   *Insurance Group Number.* The group number denoting the group policy or plan under which the insured is covered.

63   *Treatment Authorization Code.* A number indicating that the treatment described by this bill has been authorized by the payor.

64   *Employment Status Code.* A code denoting whether or not the employee is currently employed part- or full-time, is retired or is in active military service (see following section for further information).

65   *Employer Name.* Name of the employer of the insured person.

66   *Employer Location.* Address of the employer of the insured or responsible party.

67   *Principal Diagnosis Code.* ICD-9CM code for the diagnosis of the patient's condition. The diagnosis shown should reflect the information contained in the patient's medical record for the dates indicated in Item 6 even if the diagnosis is changed at a later date.

68-75 *Other Diagnosis Codes.* ICD-9CM, V, and E Codes for any additional diagnosis of the patient's condition.

76   *Admitting Diagnosis.* The ICD-9 code provided at the time of admission.

77   *External Cause of Injury Code (E Code).* The ICD-9 Code for an external cause of injury, poisoning or adverse effect.

78   *Reserved for State Assignment.*

79   *Procedure Coding Method Used.* An indicator code that identifies the coding method used for procedure coding on the claim.

      1-3   Reserved for State Assignment
      4   CPT-4
      5   HCPCS
      6-8   Reserved for National Assignment
      9   ICD-9CM

80   *Principal Procedure Codes and Date.* CPT code for principal procedure rendered and the date that procedure was rendered. For Medicare, ICD-9 codes must be entered here and on Item 81.

81   *Other Procedure Codes and Dates.* CPT code for additional procedures rendered and the dates of those procedures.

82   *Attending Physician ID.* Name and license number of the physician who is primarily responsible for the patient.

83   *Other Physician ID.* Name and license number of secondary physician, assistant surgeon, and so on.

84   *Remarks.* Pertinent data for which there is no other specific place on the form. Often this space is used to record the nature of an accident (ie, fell and hit head on concrete, 06/09/93). For Medicaid, required for abortion certification when the attending physician is an employee of

the hospital and does not submit a separate bill. Also, multiple visits to the ER on the same day should be recorded.

85   *Provider Representative Signature.* Signature of provider representative. In the case of a hospital billing, it is not necessary for the attending physician to sign, as long as a representative of the hospital signs the form certifying that the information entered is in conformance with the certifications specified on the reverse of the bill. Billers should make sure that the physician's certification is contained in the hospital records.

86   *Date Bill Submitted.* Date the bill was signed and submitted for payment.

The following items needed further description for which space was not available in the above text. Please study the following before processing the billing forms.

Field 4, Type of Bill
The following code structure is to be used to classify the type of bill. Each claim should have a 3-digit code entered in the space that corresponds with the following information.

First Digit--Type of Facility
1   **Hospital.**
2   **Skilled Nursing.**
3   **Home Health.**
4   **Christian Science.** Hospital.
5   **Christian Science.** Extended Care.
6   **Intermediate Care.**
7   **Clinic.***
8   **Special Facility.***
9   **Reserved For National Use.**
* If Type of Facility is a Clinic (Code 7), then the Bill Classifications for Clinics Only must be used. If Type of Facility is a Special Facility (Code 8), then the Bill Classifications for Special Facilities Only must be used.

Second Digit--Bill Classification
For All Except Clinics
1   **Inpatient.** Includes Medicare Part A
2   **Inpatient.** Medicare Part B only
3   **Outpatient.**
4   **Other.** For hospital referenced diagnostic procedures or home health not under plan of treatment. This is to be further defined at the state level.
5-7   **Reserved For National Use.**
8   **Swing Beds.**
9   **Reserved For National Use.**

Clinics Only
1   **Rural Health.**
2   **Hospital based or Independent Renal Dialysis Center.**
3   **Free Standing.**

4   **Outpatient Rehabilitation Facility (ORF).**
5   **Comprehensive Outpatient Rehabilitation Facility (CORF).**
6-8 **Reserved For National Use.**
9   **Other.**

Special Facilities Only
1   **Hospice.** Non-hospital-based.
2   **Hospice.** Hospital-based.
3   **Ambulatory Surgery Center.**
4   **Free Standing Birthing Center.**
5-8 **Reserved for National Use.**
9   **Other.**

Third Digit – Frequency of Billing
0   **Nonpayment/Zero Claim.** Claim being submitted for information only. Provider does not anticipate payment on the claim.
1   **Admit through Discharge Claim.** This claim is expected to be the only bill submitted for this course of treatment.
2   **Interim – First Claim.** This is the first claim in a series for the same course of treatment.
3   **Interim – Continuing Claim.** A prior claim has been submitted for this course of treatment or confinement, and a subsequent bill is also expected to be issued.
4   **Interim – Last Claim.** A prior claim has been submitted for this course of treatment or confinement and this is expected to be the last bill issued.
5   **Late Charge(s) Only Claim.** A prior claim or complete set of claims has been submitted to the provider and late charges are being added to the prior billing(s).
6   **Adjustment of Prior Claim.** This claim adjusts a prior claim. Adjustments should be made by altering the prior claim with the addition of an explanation and a credit or additional charge added to the claim.
7   **Replacement of Prior Claim.** This claim replaces a prior claim and the prior claim should be considered null and void.
8   **Void/Cancel Prior Claim.** This bill voids the prior bill that was submitted with the same information. In effect, submitting a bill with this code is the same as submitting a duplicate copy of the claim with the word VOID written across the front. This bill may be followed by a replacement claim.
9   **Reserved for National Assignment.**

For example, claims for the following types of bills would be coded the following way:

Hosp admit through discharge, inpatient   111
Hosp inpatient, replacement of prior claim   117
Hosp ER outpatient claim, only bill   131
Rural Clinic outpatient prior claim adjustment   716

Field 19, Type of Admission

This is a one-digit code indicating the priority of this admission according to the following structure:
1   **Emergency.** The patient requires immediate medical intervention as a result of severe, life-threatening, or potentially disabling conditions. Generally, the patient is admitted through the ER.
2   **Urgent.** The patient requires immediate attention for the care and treatment of a physical or mental disorder. Generally, the patient is admitted to the first available and suitable accommodation.
3   **Elective.** The patient's condition permits adequate time to schedule the availability of a suitable accommodation.
4   **Newborn.** A baby born within this facility. Use of this code necessitates the use of special Source of Admission Codes (Item 20).
5-8 **Reserved for National Assignment.**
9   **Information Not Available.**

Field 20, Source of Admission

This is a one-digit code indicating the source of this admission according to the following structure:

Emergency, Elective, or Other Admission Types
1   **Physician Referral.** The patient was admitted or referred to this facility upon the recommendation of his or her personal physician. If outpatient, the patient may request services (self-referral).
2   **Clinic Referral.** The patient was admitted or referred to this facility upon recommendation of this facility's clinic physician.
3   **HMO Referral.** The patient was admitted or referred to this facility upon the recommendation of a Health Maintenance Organization physician.
4   **Transfer from a Hospital.** The patient was admitted or referred to this facility as a transfer from an acute care facility where he/she was an inpatient.
5   **Transfer from a Skilled Nursing Facility.** The patient was admitted or referred to this facility as a transfer from a skilled nursing facility where he/she was an inpatient.
6   **Transfer from Another Health Care Facility.** The patient was admitted or referred to this facility as a transfer from a health care facility other than an acute care facility or a skilled nursing facility.
7   **Emergency Room.** The patient was admitted or referred to this facility upon the recommendation of this facility's ER physician.
8   **Court/Law Enforcement.** The patient was admitted or referred to this facility upon the direction of a court of law, or upon the request of a law enforcement agency representative.

9   **Information Not Available.** The means by which the patient was admitted or referred to this hospital, clinic, and so on, is not known.

A-Z   **Reserved for National Assignment.**

For Newborns

1   **Normal Delivery.** A baby delivered without complications.

2   **Premature Delivery.** A baby delivered with time and/or weight factors qualifying it for premature status.

3   **Sick Baby.** A baby delivered with medical complications, other than those relating to premature status.

4   **Extramural Birth.** A newborn baby born in a non-sterile environment.

5-8   **Reserved for National Assignment.**

9   **Information Not Available.**

Field 22, Patient Status

This is a two-digit code indicating the status of the patient at the last date covered by this billing statement.

01   **Discharged to home or self-care.** Routine discharge.

02   **Discharged/transferred to another short-term general hospital (inpatient).**

03   **Discharged/transferred to skilled nursing facility (SNF).**

04   **Discharged/transferred to an intermediate care facility (ICF).**

05   **Discharged/transferred to another type of institution (either inpatient or outpatient).**

06   **Discharged/transferred to home under care of home health service organization.**

07   **Left or discontinued care against medical advice.**

08   **Discharged/transferred to home under care of a Home IV provider.**

09   **Admitted as an inpatient to this hospital.** For use on outpatient Medicare claims.

10-19   **Discharge to be defined at state level, if necessary.**

20   **Expired.**

21-29   **Expired to be defined at state level, if necessary.**

30   **Still a patient or expected to return for outpatient services.**

31-39   **Still a patient to be defined at state level, if necessary.**

40*   **Expired at home.**

41*   **Expired in a medical facility. Hospital, free-standing clinic, hospice.**

42*   **Expired, place unknown.**

43-99   **Reserved for National Assignment.**
        *NOTE: Codes with an asterisk are for use only on Medicare claims for hospice care.

Fields, 24-30, Condition Codes

This is a two-digit code used to identify conditions relating to this bill that may affect payor processing. There is no specific date associated with this code as there is in Items 32-36. Condition codes should be entered in numeric sequence.

Insurance Codes

01   **Military Service-Related.** Medical condition incurred during military service.

02   **Condition is Employment-Related.** Patient alleges that medical condition is due to environment/events resulting from employment.

03   **Patient Covered By Insurance Not Reflected Here.** Indicates that patient/patient representative has stated that coverage may exist beyond that reflected on this bill.

04   **HMO Enrollee.** Indicates Medicare beneficiary is enrolled in an HMO and provider expects to receive payment from the HMO.

05   **Lien Has Been Filed.** Provider has filed legal claim for recovery of funds potentially due a patient as a result of legal action initiated by or on behalf of the patient.

06   **ESRD Patient in First 18 Months of Entitlement Covered by Employer Group Health Insurance.** Code indicates Medicare may be a secondary insurer if the patient is also covered by employer group health insurance during the first 18 months of end-stage renal disease entitlement.

07   **Treatment of Nonterminal Condition for Hospice Patient.** The patient is a hospice enrollee, but the provider is not treating his/her terminal condition and is requesting regular Medicare reimbursement.

08   **Beneficiary Would Not Provide Information About Other Insurance Coverage.** Same.

09   **Neither Patient Nor Spouse is Employed.** Same.

10   **Patient and/or Spouse is Employed But No Employer Group Health Plan Exists.** Same.

11   **Disabled Beneficiary But No Large Group Health Plan.** Patient is disabled (therefore no longer an employee) and is not covered by a large group health plan. A large group health plan is a health plan composed of a large group of individuals with a common bond (i.e., a national or state organization).

12-16   **Payor Codes.** These codes are reserved for payor processing.

Special Conditions

17   **Reserved for National Assignment.**

18   **Maiden Name Retained.** A dependent spouse entitled to benefits who does not use her husband's last name.

19 **Child Retains Mother's Name.** A patient who is a dependent child entitled to benefits that does not have his or her father's last name.

20 **Beneficiary Requested Billing.** Provider understands services are not covered or excluded, but beneficiary requests determination by payor.

21 **Billing for Denial Notice.** Provider understands services are not covered or excluded, but requests denial notice from payor.

22-25 **Reserved for National Assignment.**

26 **VA Eligible Patient Chooses to Receive Services in a Medicare Certified Facility.** Patient has chosen a Medicare certified facility rather than a VA certified facility.

27 **Patient Referred to a Sole Community Hospital for a Diagnostic Laboratory Test.** This code is for use by Sole Community hospitals only. It indicates patient was referred for a diagnostic laboratory test. Payment is generally made at 62%. This code should not be used when a specimen only is referred to a hospital.

28 **Patient and/or Spouse's Employee Health Plan is Secondary to Medicare.** Patient has indicated that there is employer group coverage through either the patient or the patient's spouse, however the employer health plan is under a single employer that has fewer than 20 full- and part-time employees or the employer health plan is a multi or multiple employer plan that has elected to pay secondary to Medicare for employees and their spouses aged 65 or older for those employers who have fewer than 20 employees.

29 **Disabled Beneficiary and/or Family Member's Large Group Health Plan is Secondary to Medicare.** Patient or family members have indicated that one or more is employed and covered by a large group health plan or other employer sponsored health plan, but the large group health plan is a single employer plan and the employer has less than 100 full- and part-time employees or the large group health plan is a multi- or multiple employer plan and that all employers participating in the plan have fewer than 100 full- and part-time employees.

30 **Reserved for National Assignment.**

Student Status

This information is required when the patient is a dependent child over age 18. Use only one of the following codes. The one with the lowest numerical value should take precedence.

31 **Patient is Student (full-time--day).** Patient declares that he or she is enrolled as a full time day student.

32 **Patient is Student (cooperative/work study program).** Same.

33 **Patient is Student (full-time night).** Patient declares that he or she is enrolled as a full-time night student.

34 **Patient is Student (part-time).** Patient declares that he or she is enrolled as a part-time student.

35 **Reserved for National Assignment.**

Accommodations

36 **General Care Patient in a Special Unit.** Patient temporarily placed in special care unit bed because no general care beds available.

37 **Ward Accommodation at Patient Request.** Patient assigned to ward accommodations at patient's request.

38 **Semiprivate Room Not Available.** Indicates that either private or ward accommodations were assigned because semiprivate accommodations were not available.

39 **Private Room Medically Necessary.** Patient needs a private room for medical reasons.

40 **Same Day Transfer.** Patient transferred to another facility before midnight on the day of admission.

41 **Partial Hospitalization.** Indicates claim is for partial hospitalization services. For outpatient Medicare this may include psychiatric services (i.e., drug and alcohol treatment).

42-45 **Reserved for National Assignment.**

Tri-Care (CHAMPUS) Information

46 **Nonavailability Certificate On File.** Any Tri-Care beneficiary who lives within forty miles of a military or public health service hospital has provided to the treating facility a certificate of nonavailability (DD1251) certifying the fact that medical care was not obtainable from a military or public health hospital.

47 **Reserved for Tri-Care.**

48 **Psychiatric Residential Treatment Centers for Children and Adolescents.** Indicates the claim is submitted by a Tri-Care authorized residential psychiatric treatment center for children and adolescents.

49-54 **Reserved for National Assignment.**

SNF Information

55 **SNF Bed not Available.** Patient's SNF admission was delayed more than 30 days after hospital discharge because a SNF bed was not available.

56 **Medical Appropriateness.** Patient's SNF admission was delayed more than 30 days after discharge from a hospital because his/her condition made it inappropriate to begin active care within that period.

57   **SNF Readmission.** Patient was previously receiving Medicare covered SNF care within 30 days of this readmission.

58-59   **Reserved for National Assignment.**

Prospective Payment

60   **Day Outlier.** A hospital being paid under a prospective payment system is reporting this stay as a day outlier. This entry may be made by either the provider or the payor.

61   **Cost Outlier.** A hospital being paid under a prospective payment system is requesting additional payment for this stay as a cost outlier.

62   **Payor Code.** This code indicates the claim was paid under a DRG. This code is for use by payors, not providers.

63-65   **Payor Codes.** These codes are set aside for payor use.

66   **Provider Does Not Wish Cost Outlier Payment.** A hospital being paid under a prospective payment system is not requesting additional payment for this stay as an outlier.

67-69   **Reserved for National Assignment.**

Renal Dialysis Setting

70   **Self-Administered Erythropoietin (EPO).** Home dialysis patient who self-administers EPO.

71   **Full Care in Unit.** Patient who received staff-assisted dialysis services in a hospital or renal dialysis facility.

72   **Self-Care in Unit.** Patient who managed his own dialysis services without staff assistance in a hospital or renal dialysis facility.

73   **Self-Care Training.** For special dialysis services where a patient and his helper (if necessary) were learning to perform dialysis.

74   **Home.** Patient who received dialysis services at home, but where condition code 75 does not apply.

75   **Home 100% Reimbursement.** Patient received dialysis services at home, using a dialysis machine that was purchased by Medicare under the 100% program.

76   **Back-up in Facility Dialysis.** Home dialysis patient who received back-up.

77   **Provider Accepts or is Obligated to Accept Payment by a Primary Payor as Payment in Full.** Provider has accepted or is obligated (by a contractual arrangement or by law) to accept payment as payment in full.

78   **New Coverage not Implemented by HMO.** A Medicare newly dialysis services in a facility covered service for which the HMO does not pay.

79   **CORF Services Provided Off-Site.** Physical therapy, occupational therapy, or speech pathology services were provided off-site.

80-99   **Reserved for State Assignment.**

Special Program Indicator Codes

This is a code indicating that the services on this claim are related to a special program.

A0   **Tri-Care External Partnership Program.** Identifies Tri-Care claims submitted under the External Partnership Program.

A1   **EPSDT – CHAP.** Early and Periodic Screening Diagnosis and Treatment.

A2   **Physically Handicapped Children's Program.** Services provided under this program receive special funding through Title 8 of the Social Security Act or the Tri-Care Program for the handicapped.

A3   **Special Federal Funding.** This code has been designed for uniform use by state uniform billing committees.

A4   **Family Planning.** This code has been designed for uniform use by state uniform billing committees.

A5   **Disability.** This code has been designed for uniform use by state uniform billing committees.

A6   **PPV/Medicare 100% Payment.** This code identifies that pneumococcal pneumonia vaccine (PPV) services given should be reimbursed under a special Medicare program provision.

A7   **Induced Abortion – Danger to Life.** Abortion was performed to avoid danger to the woman's life.

A8   **Induced Abortion Victim Rape/Incest.** Same.

A9   **Second Opinion – Surgery.** Services requested to support second opinion on surgery. Part B deductible and coinsurance do not apply.

B0-B9   **Reserved for National Assignment.**

PRO Approval Indicator Services

C0   **Reserved for National Assignment.**

C1   **Approved as Billed.** Approved by the PRO/UR as billed (only for cases that have actually been approved).

C2   **Automatic Approval as Billed Based on Focused Review.** Include categories of cases that the PRO/UR has determined it need not review under a focused review program.

C3   **Partial Approval.** PRO/UR approved of some services but disapproved others.

C4   **Admission/Services Denied.** All services denied by the PRO/UR.

C5   **Postponement Review Applicable.** PRO/UR review will take place after payment.

C6   **Admission Pre-authorization.** The PRO/UR authorized the admission but not the services.

C7   **Extended Authorization.** The PRO/UR has authorized these services for an extended period of time but has not reviewed the services provided.

C8-C9   **Reserved for National Assignment.**

Claim Change Reasons

Enter only one of the following claim change reasons. The codes have been prioritized. Use the first claim change reason that applies.

D0	**Changes to Service Dates.** Same.
D1	**Changes to Charges.** Same.
D2	**Changes in Revenue Codes/HCPCS.** Same.
D3	**Second or Subsequent Interim PPS Bill.** Same.
D4	**Change in GROUPER Input.** Same.
D5	**Cancel to Correct HICN or Provider#.** Same.
D6	**Cancel Only to Repay a Duplicate or OIG Overpayment.** Includes cancellation of an outpatient bill containing services required to be included on the inpatient bill.
D7	**Change to Make Medicare the Secondary Payor.** Same.
D8	**Change to Make Medicare the Primary Payor.** Same.
D9	**Any Other Change.** Same.
E0	**Change in Patient Status.** Same.
E1-W9	**Reserved for National Assignment.**
X1-Z9	**Reserved for State Assignment.**

Fields, 32-35, Occurrence Codes

The Occurrence Code is a code and associated date defining a significant event relating to this bill that may affect payor processing.

Due to the varied nature of occurrence and occurrence span codes, provisions have been made to allow the use of both types of codes within each. The occurrence span code can contain an occurrence code where the "through" date would not contain an entry. This allows as many as ten occurrence codes to be used.

When reporting occurrence span codes, Items 32a through 35a should be used before using Items 32b through 35b. If these spaces have been filled, you may use Items 36a and 36b to report additional occurrence span codes. In such a case, the beginning date is entered and the through date is left off.

Likewise, if there are more than two occurrence codes to report, additional codes may be entered in Items 32a through 36b.

Accident – Related

01	**Auto Accident.** Code indicating the date of an auto accident.
02	**No Fault insurance Involved.** Code indicating the date of an accident (either auto or other) where the state has applicable no fault liability laws (ie, legal basis for settlement without admission or proof of guilt).
03	**Accident/Tort Liability.** Code indicating the date of an accident resulting from a third party's action that may involve a civil court process in an attempt to require payment by the third party, other than no fault liability.
04	**Accident/Employment-Related.** Code indicating the date of an accident relating to the patient's employment.
05	**Other Accident.** Code indicating the date of an accident not described by the above codes.
06	**Crime Victim.** Code indicating the date on which a medical condition resulted from allegedly criminal action committed by one or more parties.
07-08	**Reserved for National Assignment.**

Medical Condition

09	**Start of Infertility Treatment Cycle.** The date of the start of infertility treatment cycle.
10	**Last Menstrual Period.** Code indicating the date of the last menstrual period; ONLY applies when patient is being treated for a maternity-related condition.
11	**Onset of Symptoms/Illness.** Code indicating the date the patient first became aware of symptoms/illness.
12	**Date of Onset for a Chronically Dependent Individual.** The date the patient/beneficiary became or becomes a Chronically Dependent Individual. This date begins the first month of the three month period prior to eligibility for respite care benefits.
13-16	**Reserved for National Assignment.**

Insurance-Related

17	**Date Outpatient Occupational Therapy Plan Established or Last Reviewed.** Same.
18	**Date of Retirement Patient/Beneficiary.** The beneficiary or patient's date of retirement.
19	**Date of Retirement Spouse.** The date of retirement of the spouse of the patient.
20	**Guarantee of Payment Began.** Code indicating the date on which the provider began claiming Medicare payment under the guarantee of payment provision (HIM 10, 402.1, Item 21).
21	**UR Notice Received.** Code indicating the date of receipt by the hospital of the UR Committee's (PSRO or other responsible group's) finding that an admission for further stay was not medically necessary.
22	**Date Active Care Ended.** Code indicating the date on which a covered level of care ended in a general hospital, or date on which active care ended in a psychiatric or tuberculosis hospital. (HIM 10, 402.1, Item 23). Code not required when PSRO/UR approval is completed.
23	**Reserved for National Assignment.**
24	**Date Insurance Denied.** Code indicating the date the denial of coverage was received by the hospital from any insurer.
25	**Date Benefits Terminated By Primary Payor.** Code indicating the date on which coverage (including Worker's Compensation benefits or

no-fault coverage) is no longer available to the patient.

26   **Date SNF Bed Available.** Code indicating the date on which a SNF bed became available to hospital inpatient who requires only SNF level care (HIM 10, 405C).

27   **Date Home Health Plan Established or Last Reviewed.** The date a home plan of treatment was established (this code is only to be used by Home Health providers), (HIM 11 402, Item 13).

28   **Date CORF Plan Established or Last Reviewed.** The date a comprehensive outpatient rehabilitation plan (CORF) was established or last reviewed.
NOTE: Codes 27 and 28 should only be used by hospitals with a Home Health (27) or CORF (28) program.

29   **Date Outpatient Physical Therapy Plan Established or Last Reviewed.** Same

30   **Date Outpatient Speech Pathology Plan Established or Last Reviewed.** Same.

31   **Date Beneficiary Notified of Intent to Bill Accommodations.** The date notice was provided to the beneficiary by the hospital to the patient that inpatient care is no longer required. Beyond this date the patient will be billed for accommodations.

32   **Date Beneficiary Notified of Intent to Bill Procedures or Treatments.** The date notice was given to the beneficiary that requested procedures or treatments are not reasonable or necessary under Medicare or Tri-Care. Beyond this date the patient will be billed for all procedures and services.

33   **First Day of the Medicare Coordination Period for ESRD Beneficiaries Covered by an Employee Group Health Plan.** The first day of the Medicare coordination period during which Medicare or Tri-Care benefits are secondary to benefits payable under an employee group health plan. This is required only for ESRD patients.

34   **Date of Election of Extended Care Facilities.** The date the patient elected to receive extended care services. This code is used by Christian Science Sanitoria only.

35   **Date Treatment Started for Physical Therapy.** Same.

36   **Date of Inpatient Hospital Discharge for Covered Transplant Patient.** The date of discharge for a hospital stay during which the patient received a covered transplant procedure and the hospital is billing for immunosuppressive drugs. If the patient received both a covered and a noncovered transplant, the covered transplant would take precedence.

37   **Date of Inpatient Hospital Discharge for Noncovered Transplant Patient.** The date of discharge for a hospital stay during which the patient received a noncovered transplant procedure and the hospital is billing for immunosuppressive drugs.

38-39   **Reserved for National Assignment.**

40   **Scheduled Date of Admission.** The date on which a patient will be admitted as an inpatient to the hospital. This code is for use on an outpatient claim.

41   **Date of First Test for Pre-Admission.** The date on which the first outpatient diagnostic test was performed as part of a pre-admission testing program. This code should be used only if a date of admission was scheduled prior to the administration of the test(s).

Service-Related Codes

42   **Date of Discharge.** Only to be used when "through" date in Item 6 is not the actual discharge date and the frequency code in Item 4 is that of a final bill.

43   **Scheduled Date of Canceled Surgery.** The date for which ambulatory surgery was scheduled.

44   **Date Occupational Therapy Treatment Started.** Same.

45   **Date Speech Therapy Treatment Started.** Same

46   **Date Cardiac Rehabilitative Treatment Started.** Same.

47-49   **Payor Codes.** These codes are reserved for use by the payor.

50-69   **Reserved for State Assignment.**

70-99   **Occurrence Span Codes and Dates.** See following section.

A0   **Reserved for National Assignment.**

A1   **Birth Date –Insured A.** The birth date of the insured individual covered by insurance considered as primary payor.

A2   **Effective Date – Insured A Policy.** The date insurance coverage under the primary payor began.

A3   **Benefits Exhausted – Payor A.** The last date for which benefits are available. No payments will be made after this date by the primary payor. This code is to be used by the payor, not the provider of services.

A4-A9   **Reserved for National Assignment.**

B0   **Reserved for National Assignment.**

B1   **Birth Date – Insured B.** The birth date of the insured individual covered by insurance considered as secondary payor.

B2   **Effective Date – Insured B Policy.** The date insurance coverage under the secondary payor began.

B3 **Benefits Exhausted – Payor B.** The last date for which benefits are available. No payments will be made after this date by the secondary payor. This code is to be used by the payor, not the provider of services.

B4-B9 **Reserved for National Assignment.**

C0 **Reserved for National Assignment.**

C1 **Birth Date – Insured C.** The birth date of the insured individual covered by insurance considered as tertiary payor.

C2 **Effective Date – Insured C Policy.** The date insurance coverage under the tertiary payor began.

C3 **Benefits Exhausted – Payor C.** The last date for which benefits are available. No payments will be made after this date by the tertiary payor. This code is to be used by the payor, not the provider of services.

C4-I9 **Reserved for National Assignment.**

J0-L9 **Reserved for State Assignment.**

M0-Z9 **Occurrence Span Codes and Dates.** See following section.

Field 33, Occurrence Span Codes and Dates

Occurrence span codes and dates refers to the code and the related dates that identify an event relating to the payment of the claim. These codes identify occurrences that happened over a span of time. Therefore, they have both a beginning and an ending date.

70 **Qualifying Stay Dates.** The beginning and ending dates of a hospital stay of at least 3 days that qualifies the patient for Medicare payment of SNF services billed. This code may only be used by skilled nursing facilities.

70 **Payor Code – Nonutilization Dates.** The beginning and ending dates during a PPS inlier stay for which the beneficiary has exhausted all full and/or coinsurance days, but which is covered on the cost report. This code is for payor use only.

71 **Prior Stay Dates.** The beginning and ending dates given by the patient of any hospital, SNF, or nursing home stay that ended within 60 days of this hospital or SNF admission (HIM 10, 310.1, Item 12).

72 **First/Last Visit.** The beginning and ending dates of outpatient services. This code is for use on outpatient bills only where the entire billing period is not represented by the billing statement dates reflected in Item 4.

73 **Benefit Eligibility Period (Primary Payor).** The inclusive dates during which Tri-Care medical benefits are available to a sponsor's beneficiary as shown on the beneficiary's ID card.

74 **Noncovered Level of Care.** The beginning and ending dates of noncovered care in an otherwise covered hospital stay. This should exclude any days reported with the use of occurrence span code 76, 77, or 79.

75 **SNF Level of Care.** The beginning and ending dates of a hospital stay for which SNF care was provided. This code should be used only when the payor has given approval for the patient to remain in the hospital due to a SNF bed not being available. This code should not be used for swing-bed cases. For hospitals under prospective payment, this code is needed in day outlier cases only.

76 **Patient Liability.** The beginning and ending dates of a Medicare patient's hospital stay for which the hospital is allowed to charge the Medicare beneficiary. This charge may be used only when prior approval for the stay has been received from the PRO or Medicare intermediary and the patient has been notified in writing at least 3 days prior to the beginning stay date.

77 **Provider Liability Period.** The beginning and ending dates of noncovered care for which the provider is liable. Utilization is charged.

78 **SNF Prior Stay Dates.** The beginning and ending dates given by the patient of a SNF or nursing home stay that ended within 60 days of this hospital or SNF admission.

79 **Payor Code.** The code is for payor use only.

80-99 **Reserved for State Assignment.**

M0 **PRO/UR Approved Stay Dates.** The beginning and ending dates of a hospital stay that were approved when the entire stay was not approved. Condition codes 3 should be used in Items 24-30.

M1-W9 **Reserved for National Assignment.**

X0-Z9 **Reserved for State Assignment.**

Fields 39-41, Value Codes and Amounts

These spaces are for codes and their related dollar amounts that identify data of a monetary nature that is necessary for processing the claim. The value code structure is intended to provide reporting capability for those data elements that are widely used but do not warrant dedicated fields. The codes should be written in numerical sequence. Negative numbers are not allowed except in Item 41.

01 **Most Common Semiprivate Rate.** To provide for the recording of the hospital's most common semiprivate rate.

02 **Hospital Has No Semiprivate Rooms.** Entering this code requires entering a 0.00 dollar amount.

03 **Reserved for National Assignment.**

04 **Inpatient Professional Component.** The amount shown is the total inpatient professional component charges combined together. For use on Medicare inpatient bills in which there is no Part A eligibility or Part A benefits have been

exhausted. Medicare uses the information for internal processing procedures and also for HCFA notice of utilization, which is sent to the patient to explain the Part B coinsurance portion that applies to the patient.

05   **Outpatient Professional Component included in Charges and also Billed Separately to Carrier.** For use on Medicare OP bills and all Medicaid bills if State specifies the need for this information.

06   **Medicare Blood Deductible.** Total cash blood deductible, if appropriate. Enter the Part A blood deductible amount.

07   **Reserved for National Assignment.**

08   **Medicare Life Time Reserve Amount.** Medicare life time reserve charged in the year of admission.

09   **Medicare Coinsurance Amount.** Medicare coinsurance amounts charged in the year of admission. This code is to be used only if 08 is used.

10   **Lifetime Reserve Amount in the Second Calendar Year.** The amount of the Medicare lifetime reserve in the year of discharge. This code is only used when the bill's beginning and ending dates fall into two different years.

11   **Coinsurance Amount in the Second Calendar Year.** The amount of the Medicare coinsurance in the year of discharge. This code is only used when the bill's beginning and ending dates fall into 2 different years.

12   **Working Aged Beneficiary/Spouse with Employer Group Health Plan.** The dollar amount shown is the amount that was paid by a employer group health plan whose payments were primary to Medicare. The provider signifies this amount is being applied toward Medicare covered services on this bill.

13   **ESRD Beneficiary in a Medicare Coordination Period With an Employer Group Health Plan.** The dollar amount shown is the amount that was paid on behalf of an ESRD beneficiary by a employer group health plan whose payments were primary to Medicare. The provider signifies this amount is being applied toward Medicare covered services on this bill.

14   **No Fault Auto/Other.** The dollar amount shown is the amount that was paid by no-fault insurance (including auto and other) whose payments were primary to Medicare. The provider signifies this amount is being applied toward Medicare covered services for a Medicare beneficiary on this bill.

15   **Worker's Compensation.** The dollar amount shown is the amount that was paid by Workers' Compensation insurance whose payments were primary to Medicare. The provider signifies this amount is being applied toward Medicare covered services for a Medicare beneficiary on this bill.

NOTE: If benefits were reduced due to the failure to file a proper claim, the provider should indicate the amount for codes 12-15 that would have been paid had the claim been properly completed.

16   **PHS or Other Federal Agency.** The dollar amount shown is the amount that was paid by a Public Health Service or the Federal Agency whose payments were primary to Medicare. The provider signifies this amount is being applied toward Medicare covered services for a Medicare beneficiary on this bill.

NOTE: If the provider is claiming conditional payment from Medicare on codes 12-16, six zeros should be entered in the amount field. Conditional payment signifies that no amount has been collected from the other insurance as yet and the provider will repay to Medicare any amounts that are subsequently paid by the other insurance.

17-20   **Payor Codes.** These codes are for payor use only.

Medicaid Specific Codes
21-24   **Reserved for State Assignment.**
25-29   **Reserved for National Medicaid Assignment.**

Code Structure
30   **Pre-admission Testing.** The amount indicated is the charge for outpatient pre-admission testing. Hospital Admission should have been previously scheduled.

31   **Patient Liability Amount.** The amount indicated is the amount approved for the provider to charge the beneficiary for noncovered diagnostic services, accommodations or procedures.

32-36   **Reserved for National Assignment.**

37   **Pints of Blood Furnished.** Total number of pints of whole blood or units of packed red cells furnished to the patient.

38   **Blood Deductible Pints.** The number of unreplaced blood units furnished for which the patient is responsible.

39   **Pints of Blood Replaced.** The number of blood pints or packed blood cells that have been replaced by and on behalf of the patient.

40   **New Coverage not Implemented by HMO.** The amount indicated is for inpatient charges covered by the HMO. This code is used when the bill includes inpatient charges for newly covered services that are not paid by the HMO. It should only be utilized for inpatient service. Condition codes 4 and 78 should also be reported.

41 **Black Lung.** The dollar amount shown is the amount that was paid on behalf of a Medicare beneficiary by a Black Lung payment, which payment was primary to Medicare. The provider signifies this amount is being applied toward Medicare covered services on this bill.

42 **VA.** The dollar amount shown is the amount that was paid on behalf of a Medicare beneficiary by a VA payment, which payment was primary to Medicare. The provider signifies this amount is being applied toward Medicare covered services on this bill.

43 **Disabled Beneficiary Under Age 65 With Large Group Health Plan.** The dollar amount shown is the amount that was paid on behalf of a Medicare beneficiary by a large group health plan whose payments were primary to Medicare. The provider signifies this amount is being applied toward Medicare covered services on this bill.
NOTE: If benefits were reduced due to the failure to file a proper claim, the provider should indicate the amount for codes 41 and 43 that would have been paid had the claim been properly completed.

44 **Amount Provider Agreed to Accept from Primary Payor Which Amount is Less Than Charges but Higher Than Payment Received and a Medicare Secondary Payment is Due.** The amount indicated is the amount the provider was required to accept from a primary payor. When this amount is less than the charges, a Medicare secondary payment is due.

45 **Accident Hour.** Medical treatment is the result of an accident. The time of the accident should be indicated in the amount column. Times should be written according to a 24-hour clock. 99 = unknown.

46 **Number of Grace Days.** The number of days necessary to arrange for post-discharge care for the patient. This number is determined by PRO/UR review.

47 **Any Liability Insurance.** The dollar amount shown is the amount that was paid by liability insurance whose payments were primary to Medicare. The provider signifies this amount is being applied toward Medicare covered services for a Medicare beneficiary on this bill. If the provider is claiming conditional payment from Medicare, 6 zeros should be entered in the amount field. Conditional payment signifies that no amount has been collected from the other insurance as yet and the provider will repay to Medicare any amounts that are subsequently paid by the other insurance (see TPL in the General Plan Provisions section).

48 **Hemoglobin Reading.** The latest hemoglobin reading taken during this billing cycle.

49 **Hematocrit Reading.** The hematocrit reading prior to the last administration of erythropoietin that was given during this billing cycle.

50 **Physical Therapy Visits.** The number of physical therapy visits given by this provider from the outset of the illness until the last date indicated in the billing period.

51 **Occupational Therapy Visits.** The number of occupational therapy visits given by this provider from the outset of the illness until the last date indicated in the billing period.

52 **Speech Therapy Visits.** The number of speech therapy visits given by this provider from the outset of the illness until the last date indicated in the billing period.

53 **Cardiac Rehabilitation Visits.** The number of cardiac rehabilitation visits given by this provider from the outset of the illness until the last date indicated in the billing period.
NOTE: Whole numbers for items 48-53 should be reported in the dollar portion of the item.

54-55 **Reserved for National Assignment.**

56 **Skilled Nurse – Home Visit Hours.** The number of skilled nursing hours provided during the billing period. This code should only be used by Home Health Aides. Only hours spent in the home are counted. This excludes travel time. Round out to the nearest whole hour.

57 **Home Health Aide – Home Visit Hours.** The number of home health aide services and home services hours provided during the billing period. This code should only be used by Home Health Aides. Only hours spent in the home are counted. This excludes travel time. Round out to the nearest whole hour.

58 **Arterial Blood Gas (PO2/PA2).** The arterial blood gas value at the beginning of each reporting period for oxygen therapy.

59 **Oxygen Saturation (O2 SAT/Oximetry).** The Oxygen saturation count at the beginning of each reporting period for oxygen therapy.
NOTE: Either code 58 or 59 is required on the initial bill and the fourth month bill for oxygen therapy. The value should be rounded to the nearest whole number and entered in the cents area to the right of the code.

60 **HHA Branch MSA.** Metropolitan Statistical Area in which the Home Health Agency is located. If the branch location is different than the HHA location, report the MSA in which the branch is located. The MSA number should be entered into the dollar column to the right of the code.

61-67 **Reserved for National Assignment.**

68 **EPO-Drug.** Number of units of erythropoietin administered or supplied during the billing period. Report amount in whole units.

69 **Reserved for National Assignment.**

70-72   **Payor Codes.** These codes are provided for payor use only.

73-74   **Reserved for National Assignment.**

75-79   **Payor Codes.** These codes are provided for payor use only.

80   **Most Common Ward Rate.** The amount indicated is the hospital's most common ward rate.

81-99   **Reserved for State Assignment.**

A0   **Reserved for National Assignment.**

A1   **Deductible Payor A.** The amount indicated is the amount assumed by the provider to be applied toward the deductible amount for the indicated payor.

A2   **Coinsurance Payor A.** The amount indicated is the amount assumed by the provider to be applied toward the coinsurance amount for the indicated payor.

A3   **Estimated Responsibility Payor A.** The amount indicated is the amount assumed by the provider to be the estimated responsibility for the indicated payor.

A4-A9   **Reserved for National Assignment.**

B0   **Reserved for National Assignment.**

B1   **Deductible Payor B.** The amount indicated is the amount assumed by the provider to be applied toward the deductible amount for the indicated payor.

B2   **Coinsurance Payor B.** The amount indicated is the amount assumed by the provider to be applied toward the coinsurance amount for the indicated payor.

B3   **Estimated Responsibility Payor B.** The amount indicated is the amount assumed by the provider to be the estimated responsibility for the indicated payor.

B4-B9   **Reserved for National Assignment.**

C0   **Reserved for National Assignment.**

C1   **Deductible Payor C.** The amount indicated is the amount assumed by the provider to be applied toward the deductible amount for the indicated payor.

C2   **Coinsurance Payor C.** The amount indicated is the amount assumed by the provider to be applied toward the coinsurance amount for the indicated payor.

C3   **Estimated Responsibility Payor C.** The amount indicated is the amount assumed by the provider to be the estimated responsibility for the indicated payor.

C4-C9   **Reserved for National Assignment.**

D0-D2   **Reserved for National Assignment.**

D3   **Estimated Responsibility Patient.** The amount indicated is the amount assumed by the provider to be the estimated responsibility for the patient.

D4-W9   **Reserved for National Assignment.**

X0-Z9   **Reserved for State Assignment.**

Field 42, Hospital Revenue Codes

Revenue codes identify a specific accommodation, ancillary service, or billing calculation. Subcategory classifications and standard abbreviations are listed below each major category. The correct subcategory classification should be added to the major category number to create a three-digit number. The use of a fourth digit has been approved by the NUBC for possible future needs. These four-digit numbers are thus far unassigned and therefore not in use.

Major Category
   Subcategory (Standard Abbreviation)

001   **Total Charges.** To reflect the total of all charges on this bill.

01X   **Reserved for internal payor use.**

02X-06X **Reserved for National Assignment.**

07X-09X **Reserved for State Assignment.**

10X   **All-Inclusive Rate.** Flat fee charge incurred on either a daily basis or total stay basis for services rendered. Charge may cover room and board plus ancillary services or room and board only.
   0   All-inclusive room and board plus ancillary (ALL-INCL R&B/ANC)
   1   All-inclusive room and board (ALL INCL R&B)

11X   **Room and Board – Private (Medical or General).** Routine service charges for single-bed rooms.
   0   General Classification (R&B/PVT)
   1   Medical/Surgical/Gyn (MED-SUR-GYN/PVT)
   2   OB (OB/PVT)
   3   Pediatric (PEDS/PVT)
   4   Psychiatric (PSYCH/PVT)
   5   Hospice (HOSPICE/PVT)
   6   Detoxification (DETOX/PVT)
   7   Oncology (ONCOLOGY/PVT)
   8   Rehabilitation (REHAB/PVT)
   9   Other (OTHER/PVT)

12X   **Room and Board – Semiprivate Two-Bed (Medical or General).** Routine service charges incurred for accommodations with two beds.
   0   General Classification (R&B/SEMI)
   1   Medical/Surgical/Gyn (MED-SUR-GYN/2 Bed)
   2   OB (OB/2 Bed)
   3   Pediatric (PEDS/2 Bed)
   4   Psychiatric (PSYCH/2 Bed)
   5   Hospice (HOSPICE/2 Bed)
   6   Detoxification (DETOX/2 Bed)
   7   Oncology (ONCOLOGY/2 Bed)
   8   Rehabilitation (REHAB/2 Bed)
   9   Other (OTHER/2 Bed)

13X   **Semiprivate – Three and Four Beds.** Routine service charges incurred for accommodations with three and four beds.

0   General Classification (R&B/3&4 Bed)
1   Medical/Surgical/Gyn (MED-SUR-GYN/3&4 Bed)
2   OB (OB/3&4 Bed)
3   Pediatric (PEDS/3&4 Bed)
4   Psychiatric (PSYCH/3&4 Bed)
5   Hospice (HOSPICE/3&4 Bed)
6   Detoxification (DETOX/3&4 Bed)
7   Oncology (ONCOLOGY/3&4 Bed)
8   Rehabilitation (REHAB/3&4 Bed)
9   Other (OTHER/3&4 Bed)

14X   Private (Deluxe). Deluxe rooms are accommodations with amenities substantially in excess of those provided to other patients.
0   General Classification (R&B/PVT/ DLX)
1   Medical/Surgical/Gyn (MED-SUR-GYN/DLX)
2   OB (OB/DLX)
3   Pediatric (PEDS/DLX)
4   Psychiatric (PSYCH/DLX)
5   Hospice (HOSPICE/DLX)
6   Detoxification (DETOX/DLX)
7   Oncology (ONCOLOGY/DLX)
8   Rehabilitation (REHAB/DLX)
9   Other (OTHER/DLX)

15X   Room and Board – Ward (Medical or General). Routine service charge for accommodations with five or more beds.
0   General Classification (R&B/ WARD)
1   Medical/Surgical/Gyn (MED-SUR-GYN/ WARD)
2   OB (OB/WARD)
3   Pediatric (PEDS/WARD)
4   Psychiatric (PSYCH/WARD)
5   Hospice (HOSPICE/WARD)
6   Detoxification (DETOX/WARD)
7   Oncology (ONCOLOGY/WARD)
8   Rehabilitation (REHAB/WARD)
9   Other (OTHER/WARD)

16X   Other Room and Board. Any routine service charges for accommodations that cannot be included in the more specific revenue center codes.
0   General Classification (R&B)
4   Sterile Environment (R&B/STRL)
7   Self-Care (R&B/SELF)
9   Other (R&B/Other)

17X   Nursery. Charges for nursing care to newborn and premature infants in nurseries.
0   General Classification (NURSERY)
1   Newborn (NURSERY/NEWBORN)
2   Premature (NURSERY/PREMIE)
5   Neonatal ICU (NURSERY/ICU)
9   Other (NURSERY/OTHER)

18X   Leave of Absence. Charges for holding a room while the patient is temporarily away from the provider.
0   General Classification (LOA)
1   Reserved (RESERVED)

2   Patient Convenience (LOA/PT CONV)
3   Therapeutic Leave (LOA THER)
4   ICF/MR – any reason (LOA/ICF/ MR)
5   Nursing Home (for hospitalization) (LOA/NURS HOME)
6   Other Leave of Absence (LOA/OTHER)

19X   Not Assigned.

20X   Intensive Care. Routine service charge for medical or surgical care provided to patients who require a more intensive level of care than is rendered with the general medical or surgical unit.
0   General Classification (ICU)
1   Surgical (ICU/SURGICAL)
2   Medical (ICU/MEDICAL)
3   Pediatric (ICU/PEDS)
4   Psychiatric (ICU/PSYCH)
6   Post-ICU (POST ICU)
7   Burn Care (ICU/BURN CARE)
8   Trauma (ICU/TRAUMA)
9   Other Intensive Care (ICU/OTHER)

21X   Coronary Care. Routine service charge for medical or surgical care provided to patients with coronary illness who require a more intensive level of care than is rendered in the general medical care unit.
0   General Classification (CCU)
1   Myocardial Infarction (CCU/MYO INFARC)
2   Pulmonary Care (CCU/PULMON)
3   Heart Transplant (CCU/TRANS-PLANT)
4   Post-CCU (POST CCU)
9   Other Coronary Care (CCU/OTHR)

22X   Special Charges. Charges incurred during an inpatient stay or on a daily basis for certain services.
0   General Classification (SPCL CHGS)
1   Admission Charge (ADMIT CHG)
2   Technical Support Charge (TECH SUPPT CHG)
3   UR Service Charge (UR CHG)
4   Late Discharge, Medically Necessary (LATE DISCH/MED NEC)
9   Other Special Charges (OTHER SPEC CHG)

23X   Incremental Nursing Charge Rate. Charge for nursing service assessed in addition to room and board.
0   General Classification (NURSING INCREM)
1   Nursery (NUR INCR/NURSERY)
2   OB (NUR INCR/OB)
3   ICU (NUR INCR/ICU)
4   CCU (NUR INCR/CCU)
5   Hospice (NUR INCR/ HOSPICE)
9   Other (NUR INCR/OTHER)

24X   All-Inclusive Ancillary. A flat rate incurred on either a daily basis or total stay basis for ancillary services only.

0   General Classification (ALL INCL ANCIL)

9   Other Inclusive Ancillary (ALL INCL ANCIL/ OTHER)

25X   Pharmacy. Charges for medication produced, manufactured, packaged, controlled, assayed, dispensed, and distributed under the direction of licensed pharmacist. This category includes blood plasma, other components of blood, and IV solutions.

0   General Classification (PHAR)

1   Generic Drugs (DRUGS/GENRC)

2   Nongeneric Drugs (DRUGS/ NONGENRC)

3   Take Home Drugs (DRUGS/ TAKEHOME)

4   Drugs Incident to Other Diagnostic Services (DRUGS/INCIDENT OTHER DX)

5   Drugs Incident to Radiology (DRUGS/INCIDENT RAD)

6   Experimental Drugs (DRUGS/ EXPERIMT)

7   Nonprescription (DRUGS/ NONPSCRPT)

8   IV Solutions (IV SOLUTIONS)

9   Other Pharmacy (DRUGS/OTHER)

26X   IV Therapy. Administration of intravenous solution by specially trained personnel to individuals requiring such treatment.

0   General Classification (IV THER)

2   Infusion Pump (IV THER/INFSN PUMP)

3   IV Therapy – Pharmacy Services (IV THER/PHARM/SVC)

4   IV Therapy/Drug/Supply Delivery (IV THER/DRUG/SUPPLY DELV)

9   Other IV Therapy (IV THERP/ OTHER)

NOTE: Providers billing for home IV therapy should use the HCPCS code that describes the pump in Item 44.

27X   Medical/Surgical Supplies and Devices. Charges for supply items required for patient care.

0   General Classification (MED-SUR SUPPLIES)

1   Nonsterile Supply (NON-STER SUPPLY)

2   Sterile Supply (STERILE SUPPLY)

3   Take Home Supplies (TAKE HOME SUPPLY)

4   Prosthetic/Orthotic Devices (PROSTH/ORTH DEV)

5   Pacemaker (PACE MAKER)

6   Intraocular Lens (INTRA OC LENS)

7   Oxygen-Take Home (O2/ TAKEHOME)

8   Other Implants (SUPPLY/ IMPLANTS)

9   Other Supplies/Devices (SUPPLY/ OTHER)

28X   Oncology. Charges for the treatment of tumors and related diseases.

0   General Classification ONCOLOGY

9   Other Oncology (ONCOLOGY/ OTHER)

29X   Durable Medical Equipment (Other Than Renal). Charge for medical equipment that can withstand repeated use (excluding renal equipment).

0   General Classification (DME)

1   Rental (MED EQUIP/RENT)

2   Purchase of new DME (MED EQUIP/NEW)

3   Purchase of used DME (MED EQUIP/USED)

4   Supplies/Drugs for DME Effectiveness (Home Health Agency Only) (MED EQUIP/SUPPLIES/ DRUGS)

9   Other Equipment (MED EQUIP/ OTHER)

30X   Laboratory. Charges for the performance of diagnostic and routine clinical laboratory tests.

0   General Classification (LAB)

1   Chemistry (LAB/CHEMISTRY)

2   Immunology (LAB/IMMUNLGY)

3   Renal Patient (Home) (LAB/RENAL HOME)

4   Nonroutine Dialysis (LAB/NR DIALYSIS)

5   Hematology (LAB/HEMAT)

6   Bacteriology & Microbiology (LAB/BACT-MICRO)

7   Urology (LAB/UROLOGY)

9   Other Laboratory (LAB/OTHER)

31X   Laboratory Pathological. Charges for diagnostic and routine laboratory tests on tissues and culture.

0   General Classification (PATHOLOGY LAB or PATH LAB)

1   Cytology (PATHOL/CYTOLOGY)

2   Histology (PATHOL/HYSTOL)

4   Biopsy (PATHOL/BIOPSY)

9   Other (PATHOL/OTHER)

32X   Radiology – Diagnostic. Charges for diagnostic radiology services provided for the examination and care of patients. Includes taking, processing, examining, and interpreting radiographs and fluorographs.

0   General Classification (DX X-RAY)

1   Angiocardiography (DX X-RAY/ ANGIO)

2   Arthrography (DX X-RAY/ARTH)

3   Arteriography (DX X-RAY/ ARTER)

4   Chest X-ray (DX X-RAY/CHEST)

9   Other (DX X-RAY/OTHER)

33X   Radiology – Therapeutic. Charges for therapeutic radiology services and chemotherapy that are required for care and treatment of patients. Included therapy by injection or ingestion of radioactive substances.

0   General Classification (RX X-RAY)

1   Chemotherapy – Injected (CHEMO-THER/INJ)

2   Chemotherapy – Oral (CHEMO-THER/ORAL)

3   Radiation Therapy (RADIATION RX)

    5   Chemotherapy – IV (CHEMOTHERP-IV)
    9   Other (RX X-RAY/OTHER)
34X **Nuclear Medicine.** Charges for procedures and tests performed by a radioisotope laboratory utilizing radioactive materials as required for diagnosis and treatment of patients.
    0   General Classification (NUCLEAR MEDICINE or NUC MED)
    1   Diagnostic (NUC MED/DX)
    2   Therapeutic (NUC MED/RX)
    9   Other (NUC MED/OTHER)
35X **CT Scan.** Charges for computed tomographic scans of the head and other parts of the body.
    0   General Classification (CT SCAN)
    1   Head Scan (CT SCAN/HEAD)
    2   Body Scan (CT SCAN/BODY)
    9   Other CT Scans (CT SCAN/OTHR)
36X **Operating Room Services.** Charges for services provided to patients in the performance of surgical and related procedures during and immediately following surgery.
    0   General Classification (OR SERVICES)
    1   Minor Surgery (OR/MINOR)
    2   Organ Transplant – Other than kidney (OR/ORGAN TRANS)
    7   Kidney Transplant (OR/KIDNEY TRANS)
    9   Other Operating Room Services (OR/OTHER)
37X **Anesthesia.** Charges for anesthesia services in the hospital.
    0   General Classification (ANESTHE)
    1   Anesthesia Incident to Radiology (ANESTHE/INCIDENT RAD)
    2   Anesthesia Incident to Other Diagnostic Services (ANESTHE/ INCDNT OTHER DX)
    4   Acupuncture (ANESTHE/ ACUPUNC)
    9   Other Anesthesia (ANESTHE/ OTHER)
38X **Blood.**
    0   General Classification (BLOOD)
    1   Packed Red Cells (BLOOD/PKD RED)
    2   Whole Blood (BLOOD/WHOLE)
    3   Plasma (BLOOD/PLASMA)
    4   Platelets (BLOOD PLATELETS)
    5   Leucocytes (BLOOD/ LEUCOCYTES)
    6   Other Components (BLOOD/ COMPONENTS)
    7   Other Derivatives (Cryoprecipitates) (BLOOD/DERIVATIVES)
    9   Other Blood (BLOOD/OTHER)
39X **Blood Storage and Processing.** Charges for storage and processing of whole blood.
    0   General Classification (BLOOD/ STOR-PROC)
    1   Blood Administration (BLOOD/ ADMIN)
    9   Other Blood Storage and Processing (BLOOD/OTHER STOR)
40X **Other Imaging Services.**
    0   General Classification (IMAGE SVS)

    1   Diagnostic Mammography (DIAG MAMMOGRAPHY)
    2   Ultrasound (ULTRASOUND)
    3   Screening Mammography (SCRN MAMMOGRAPHY)
    4   Positron Emission Tomography (PET SCAN)
    9   Other Imaging Services (OTHER IMAGE SVS)
NOTE: High-risk beneficiaries should be noted by the inclusion of one of the following ICD-9 diagnosis codes:
V10.3   Personal History – Malignant neoplasm breast cancer.
V16.3   Family History – Malignant neoplasm breast cancer (mother, sister or daughter with breast cancer).
V15.89   Other specified personal history representing hazards to health (not given birth prior to 30, history of biopsy proven breast disease). Must be coded to the appropriate 4th or 5th digit.
41X **Respiratory Services.** Charges for administration of oxygen and certain potent drugs through inhalation or positive pressure and other forms of rehabilitative therapy through measurement of inhaled and exhaled gases and analysis of blood and evaluation of the patient's ability to exchange oxygen and other gases.
    0   General Classification (RESPIR SVC)
    2   Inhalation Services (INHALATION SVC)
    3   Hyperbaric Oxygen Therapy (HYPERBARIC O2)
    9   Other Respiratory Services (OTHER RESPIR SVS)
42X **Physical Therapy.** Charges for therapeutic exercises, massage, and utilization of light, heat, cold, water, electricity, and assistive devices for diagnosis and rehabilitation of patients who have neuromuscular, orthopedic, and other disabilities.
    0   General Classification (PHYS THERP)
    1   Visit Charge (PHYS THERP/VISIT)
    2   Hourly Charge (PHYS THERP/ HOUR)
    3   Group Rate (PHYS THERP/ GROUP)
    4   Evaluation or Reevaluation (PHYS THER/EVAL)
    9   Other Physical Therapy (OTHER PHYS THERP)
43X **Occupational Therapy.** Charges for teaching manual skills and independent personal care to stimulate mental and emotional activity on the part of patients.
    0   General Classification (OCCUP THERP)
    1   Visit Charge (OCCUP THERP/ VISIT)
    2   Hourly Charge (OCCUP THERP/ HOUR)
    3   Group Rate (OCCUP THERP/ GROUP)
    4   Evaluation or Reevaluation (OCCUP THER/EVAL)

9   Other Occupational Therapy (OTHER OCCUP THERP)

44X   **Speech-Language Pathology.** Charges for services provided to persons with impaired functional communications skills.
0   General Classification (SPEECH PATHOL)
1   Visit Charge (SPEECH PATH/ VISIT)
2   Hourly Charge (SPEECH PATH/ HOUR)
3   Group Rate (SPEECH PATH/ GROUP)
4   Evaluation or Reevaluation (SPEECH PATH/EVAL)
9   Other Speech-Language Pathology (OTHER SPEECH PAT)

45X   **Emergency Room.** Charges for emergency treatment to those ill and injured persons who require immediate unscheduled medical or surgical care.
0   General Classification (EMERG ROOM)
9   Other Emergency Room (OTHER EMER ROOM)

46X   **Pulmonary Function.** Charges for tests that measure inhaled and exhaled gases and analysis of blood and for tests that evaluate the patient's ability to exchange oxygen and other gases.
0   General Classification (PULMON FUNC)
9   Other Pulmonary Function (OTHER PULMON FUNC)

47X   **Audiology.** Charges for the detection and management of communication handicaps centering in whole or in part on the hearing function.
0   General Classification (AUDIOL)
1   Diagnostic (AUDIOLOGY/DX)
2   Treatment (AUDIOLOGY/RX)
9   Other Audiology (OTHER AUDIOL)

48X   **Cardiology.** Charges for cardiac procedures rendered in a separate unit within the hospital. Such procedures include but are not limited to heart catheterization, coronary angiography, Swan-Ganz catheterization, and exercise stress test.
0   General Classification (CARDIOL)
1   Cardiac Cath Lab (CARDIAC CATH LAB)
2   Stress Test (STRESS TEST)
9   Other Cardiology (OTHER CARDIOL)

49X   **Ambulatory Surgical Care.**
0   General Classification (AMBUL SURG)
9   Other Ambulatory Surgical Care (OTHER AMBL SURG)

50X   **Outpatient Services.** Outpatient charges for services rendered to an outpatient who is admitted as an inpatient before midnight of the day following the date of service. These charges are incorporated on the inpatient bill of Medicare patients.
0   General Classification (OUTPATIENT SVS)
9   Other Outpatient Services (OUTPATIENT/OTHER)

51X   **Clinic.** Clinic (nonemergency/scheduled outpatient visit) charges for providing diagnostic, preventive, curative, rehabilitative, and education services on a scheduled basis to ambulatory patients.
0   General Classification (CLINIC)
1   Chronic Pain Center (CHRONIC PAIN CL)
2   Dental Clinic (DENTAL CLINIC)
3   Psychiatric Clinic (PSYCH CLINIC)
4   OB-GYN Clinic (OB-GYN CLINIC)
5   Pediatric Clinic (PEDS CLINIC)
9   Other Clinic (OTHER CLINIC)

52X   **Free-Standing Clinic.**
0   General Classification (FR/STD CLINIC)
1   Rural Health – Clinic (RURAL/ CLINIC)
2   Rural Health – Home (RURAL/ HOME)
3   Family Practice (FAMILY PRAC)
9   Other Freestanding Clinic (OTHER FR/STD CLINIC)

53X   **Osteopathic Services.** Charges for a structural evaluation of the cranium, entire cervical, dorsal, and lumbar spine by a doctor of osteopathy.
0   General Classification (OSTEOPATH SVS)
1   Osteopathic Therapy (OSTEOPATH RX)
9   Other Osteopathic Services (OTHER OSTEOPATH)

54X   **Ambulance.** Charges for ambulance service, usually unscheduled, to the ill/ injured who require immediate medical attention.
0   General Classification (AMBUL)
1   Supplies (AMBUL/SUPPLY)
2   Medical Transport (AMBUL/MED TRANS)
3   Heart Mobile (AMBUL/ HEARTMOBL)
4   Oxygen (AMBUL/OXY)
5   Air Ambulance (AIR AMBUL)
6   Neonatal Ambulance Services (AMBUL/NEONAT)
7   Pharmacy (AMBUL/PHARMACY)
8   Telephone Transmission EKG (AMBUL/TELEPHONIC EKG)
9   Other Ambulance (OTHER AMBULANCE)

NOTE: Units may be either miles or trips.
NOTE: On items 55-58, charges should be reported to the nearest hour.

55X   **Skilled Nursing.** Charges for nursing services that must be provided under the direct supervision of a licensed nurse to ensure the safety of the patient and to achieve the medically desired result. This code may be used for nursing home services or a service charge for home health billing.
0   General Classification (SKILLED NURS)
1   Visit Charge (SKILLED NURS/ VISIT)
2   Hourly Charge (SKILLED NURS/ HOUR)
9   Other Skilled Nursing (SKILLED NURS/OTHER)

56X **Medical Social Services.** Charges for services such as counseling patients, interviewing patients, and interpreting problems of social situation rendered to patients on any basis.
  0 General Classification (MED SOCIAL SVS)
  1 Visit Charge (MED SOC SERVS/ VISIT)
  2 Hourly Charge (MED SOC SERVS/HOUR)
  9 Other Medical Social Services (MED SOCIAL SERVS/OTHER)

57X **Home Health Aide (Home Health).** Charges made by a home health agency for personnel that are primarily responsible for the personal care of the patient.
  0 General Classification (AIDE/ HOME HEALTH)
  1 Visit Charge (AIDE/HOME HLTH/ VISIT)
  2 Hourly Charge (AIDE/HOME HLTH/ HOUR)
  9 Other Home Health Aide (AIDE/ HOME HLTH/ OTHER)

58X **Other Visits (Home Health).** Charges by a home health agency for visits other than physical therapy, occupational therapy or speech therapy, which must be specifically identified.
  0 General Classification (VISIT/ HOME HLTH)
  1 Visit Charge (VISIT/HOME HLTH/ VISIT)
  2 Hourly Charge (VISIT/HOME HLTH/ HOUR)
  9 Other Home Health (VISIT/HOME HLTH/ OTHER)

59X **Units of Service (Home Health).** Revenue code used by a home health agency that bills on the basis of units of service.
  0 General Classification (UNIT/ HOME HEALTH)
  9 Home Health Other Units (UNIT/ HOME HLTH/ OTHER)

60X **Oxygen Home Health.** Charges by a home health agency for oxygen equipment, supplies, or contents, excluding purchased items. If a beneficiary has purchased a stationary oxygen system, and oxygen concentrator or portable equipment, revenue codes 292 or 293 apply. DME other than oxygen systems is billed under codes 291, 292, or 293.
  0 General Classification (O2/HOME HEALTH)
  1 Oxygen – Stationary Equipment, Supplies or Contents (O2/STAT EQUIP/SUPPL/CONT)
  2 Oxygen – Stationary Equipment or Supplies Under 1 LPM (O2/STAT EQUIP/UNDER 1 LPM)

  3 Oxygen – Stationary Equipment or Supplies Over 4 LPM (O2/STAT EQUIP/OVER 4 LPM)
  4 Oxygen – Portable Add-on (O2/ PORTABLE ADD-ON)

61X **MRI.** Charges for Magnetic Resonance Imaging of the brain and other parts of the body.
  0 General Classification (MRI)
  1 Brain (including brain stem) (MRI-BRAIN)
  2 Spinal Cord (including spine) (MRI-SPINE)
  9 Other MRI (MRI-OTHER)

62X **Medical/Surgical Supplies.** Charges for supplies required for patient care. This code is an extension of code 27X and allows for the reporting of additional breakdown, if needed. Subcategory 1 is for providers who are not able to bill supplies used for radiology procedures under radiology. Subcategory 2 is for providers who are not able to bill supplies used for other diagnostic procedures under diagnostic procedures.
  1 Supplies Incident to Radiology (MED-SUR SUPP/INCDNT RAD)
  2 Supplies Incident to Other Diagnostic Services (MED-SUR UPP/INCDNT ODX)

63X **Drugs Requiring Specific Identification.** Charges for drugs and biologicals requiring specific identification required by the payor. If you are using HCPCS to identify the drug, the HCPCS code should be entered in Item 44.
  0 General Classification (DRUGS)
  1 Single Source Drug (DRUG/ SNGLE)
  2 Multiple Source Drug (DRUG/ MULT)
  3 Restrictive Prescription (DRUG/ RSTR)
  4 Erythropoietin (EPO) less than 10,000 units (DRUG/EPQ10,000 Units)
  5 Erythropoietin (EPO) more than 10,000 units (DRUG/EPQ10,000 Units)
  6 Drugs requiring Detailed Coding (DRUGS/DETAIL CODE)
  NOTE: Revenue Code 636 relates to a HCPCS code. Therefore, the appropriate HCPCS code should be entered in Item 44. The specific units of services to be reported should be in hundreds (100s) rounded to the nearest hundred.

64X **Home IV Therapy Services.** Charge for IV drug therapy services that are done in the patient's home. For home IV providers, the appropriate HCPCS code must be entered for all equipment and covered therapy.
  0 General Classification (IV THER SVC)
  1 Nonroutine Nursing, Central Line (NON RT NURSING/CENTRAL)
  2 IV Site Care, Central Line, HCPCS related(IV SITE CARE/CENTRAL)

3   IV Start/Change Peripheral Line (IV STRT/CHNG/PERIPHRL)

4   Nonroutine Nursing Peripheral Line (NON RT NURSING/PERIPHRL)

5   Training Patient/Caregiver, Central Line (TRNG PT/CAREGVR/ CENTRAL)

6   Training Disabled Patient, Central Line (TRNG DSBLPT/CENTRAL)

7   Training Patient/Caregiver, Peripheral Line (TRNG PT/ CAREGVR/PERIPHRL)

8   Training Disabled Patient, Peripheral Line (TRNG DSBLPT/ PERIPHRL)

9   Other IV Therapy Services (OTHER IV THERAPY SVC)

NOTE: Units need to be reported in 1-hour increments.

65X   **Hospice Service.** Charges for hospice care services for a terminally ill patient. The patient would need to elect these services in lieu of other services for a terminal condition.

0   General Classification (HOSPICE)

1   Routine Home Care (HOSPICE/RTN HOME)

2   Continuous Home Care (HOSPICE/ CTNS HOME)

3   RESERVED

4   RESERVED

5   Inpatient Respite Care (HOSPICE/ IP RESPITE)

6   General Inpatient Care (Nonrespite) (HOSPICE/IP NONRESPITE)

7   Physician Services (HOSPICE/ PHYSICIAN)

9   Other Hospice (HOSPICE/OTHER)

NOTE: There must be a minimum of 8 hours of care (not necessarily continuous) during a 24-hour period to receive the Continuous Home Care rate from Medicare under code 652. If less than 8 hours of care are provided, code 651 should be used. Any portion of an hour counts as an hour. When billing Medicare under code 657, a physician procedure code must be entered in Item 44. Code 657 is used by the hospice to bill for physician's services furnished to hospice patients when the physician is employed by the hospice or receives payment from the hospice for services rendered.

66X   **Respite Care.** Charges for hours of service under the Respite Care Benefit for homemaker or home health aide, personal care services, and nursing care provided by a licensed professional nurse.

0   General Classification (RESPITE CARE)

1   Hourly Charge/Skilled Nursing (RESPITE/SKILLED NURSE)

2   Hourly Charge/Home Health Aide/ Homemaker (RESPITE/HMEAID/ HMEMKR

67X   **Not Assigned.**

68X   **Not Assigned.**

69X   **Not Assigned.**

70X   **Cast Room.** Charges for services related to the application, maintenance, and removal of casts.

0   General Classification (CAST ROOM)

9   Other Cast Room (OTHER CAST ROOM)

71X   **Recovery Room.**

0   General Classification (RECOV RM)

9   Other Recovery Room (OTHER RECOV RM)

72X   **Labor Room/Delivery.** Charges for labor and delivery room services provided by specially trained nursing personnel to patients, including prenatal care during labor, assistance during delivery, postnatal care in the recovery room, and minor gynecological procedures if they are performed in the delivery suite.

0   General Classification (DELIVROOM/LABOR)

1   Labor (LABOR)

2   Delivery (DELIVERY ROOM)

3   Circumcision (CIRCUMCISION)

4   Birthing Center (BIRTHING CENTER)

9   Other Labor Room/Delivery (OTHER/DELIV-LABOR)

73X   **EKG/ECG (Electrocardiogram).** Charges for operation of specialized equipment to record electromotive variations in actions of the heart muscle on an electrocardiograph for diagnosis of heart ailments.

0   General Classification (EKG/ECG)

1   Holter Monitor (HOLTER MON)

2   Telemetry (TELEMETRY)

9   Other EKG/ECG (OTHER EKG/ECG)

74X   **EEG (Electroencephalogram).** Charges for operation of specialized equipment to measure impulse frequencies and differences in electrical potential in various areas of the brain to obtain data for use in diagnosing brain disorders.

0   General Classification (EEG)

9   Other EEG (OTHER EEG)

75X   **Gastrointestinal Services.**

0   General Classification (GASTR-INTS SVS)

9   Other Gastrointestinal (OTHER GASTROINTS)

NOTE: Use 759 with the procedure code for endoscopic procedure.

76X   **Treatment/Observation Room.** Charges for the use of a treatment room, or observation room charges for outpatient observation services.

0   General Classification (TREATMT/OBSERVATION RM)

1   Treatment Room (TREATMT RM)

2   Observation Room (OBSERV RM)

9   Other Treatment/Observation Room (OTHER TREAT/OBSERV RM)

77X **Not Assigned.**

78X **Not Assigned.**

79X **Lithotripsy.** Charges for using lithotripsy in the treatment of kidney stones.

    0   General Classification (LITHOTRIPSY)

    9   Other Lithotripsy (LITHOTRIPSY/ OTHER)

80X **Inpatient Renal Dialysis.** A waste removal process that uses an artificial kidney when the body's own kidneys have failed. The waste may be removed directly from the blood (hemodialysis) or indirectly from the blood by flushing a special solution between the abdominal covering and the tissue (peritoneal dialysis). In-unit lab nonroutine tests are medically necessary tests in addition to or at greater frequency than routine tests that are performed in the dialysis unit.

    0   General Classification (RENAL DIALY)

    1   Inpatient Hemodialysis (DIALY/ INPT)

    2   Inpatient Peritoneal (Non-CAPD) (DIALY/INPT/PER)

    3   Inpatient Continuous Ambulatory Peritoneal Dialysis (DIALY/ INPT/CAPD)

    4   Inpatient Continuous Cycling Peritoneal Dialysis (DIALY/ INPT/CCPD)

    9   Other Inpatient Dialysis (DIALY/ INPT/OTHER)

81X **Organ Acquisition.** The acquisition of a kidney, liver, or heart for use in transplantation. Organs other than these are included in category 89X. Living donor is a living person from whom kidney is obtained for transplantation. Cadaver is an individual who has been pronounced dead according to medical and legal criteria from whom organs have been obtained for transplantation.

    0   General Classification (ORGAN ACQUISIT)

    1   Living Donor – Kidney (KIDNEY/ LIVE)

    2   Cadaver Donor – Kidney (KIDNEY/ CADAVER)

    3   Unknown Donor – Kidney (KIDNEY/UNKNOWN)

    4   Other Kidney Acquisition (KIDNEY/OTHER)

    5   Cadaver Donor – Heart (HEART/ CADAVER)

    6   Other Heart Acquisition (HEART/ OTHER)

    7   Donor – Liver (LIVER ACQUISIT)

    9   Other Organ Acquisition (ORGAN/ OTHER)

82X **Hemodialysis – Outpatient or Home.** A program under which a patient performs hemodialysis away from the facility using his or her own equipment and supplies. Hemodialysis is the removal of waste directly from the blood.

    0   General Classification (HEMO/OP OR HOME)

    1   Hemodialysis/Composite or Other Rate (HEMO/COMPOSITE)

    2   Home Supplies (HEMO/HOME/ SUPPL)

    3   Home Equipment (HEMO/HOME/ EQUIP)

    4   Maintenance 100% (HEMO/HOME/ 100%)

    5   Support Services (HEMO/HOME/ SUPSERV)

    9   Other Outpatient Hemodialysis (HEMO/HOME/OTHER)

83X **Peritoneal Dialysis – Outpatient or Home.** A program under which a patient performs peritoneal dialysis away from the facility using his or her own equipment and supplies. Waste is removed by flushing a special solution between the tissue and the abdominal covering.

    0   General Classification (PERTNL/ OP OR HOME)

    1   Peritoneal/Composite or Other Rate (PERTNL/COMPOSITE)

    2   Home Supplies (PERTNL/HOME/ SUPPL)

    3   Home Equipment (PERTNL/ HOME/EQUIP)

    4   Maintenance 100% (PERTNL/ HOME/100%)

    5   Support Services (PERTNL/HOME/ SUPSERV)

    9   Other Outpatient Peritoneal (PERTNL/HOME/OTHER)

84X **Continuous Ambulatory Peritoneal Dialysis (CAPD) – Outpatient or Home.** A program under which a patient performs continual dialysis away from the facility using his or her own equipment and supplies. The patient's peritoneal membrane is used as a dialyzer.

    0   General Classification (CAPD/OP OR HOME)

    1   CAPD/Composite or Other Rate (CAPD/COMPOSITE)

    2   Home Supplies (CAPD/HOME/ SUPPL)

    3   Home Equipment (CAPD/HOME/ EQUIP)

    4   Maintenance 100% (CAPD/HOME/ 100%)

    5   Support Services (CAPD/HOME/ SUPSERV)

    9   Other Outpatient CAPD (CAPD/ HOME/OTHER)

85X **Continuous Cycling Peritoneal Dialysis (CCPD) – Outpatient or Home.** A program under which a patient performs continual dialysis away from the facility using his or her own equipment and supplies. A machine is used to make automatic exchanges at night.

    0   General Classification (CCPD/OP OR HOME)

1   CCPD/Composite or Other Rate (CCPD/COMPOSITE)
2   Home Supplies (CCPD/HOME/ SUPPL)
3   Home Equipment (CCPD/HOME/ EQUIP)
4   Maintenance 100% (CCPD/HOME/ 100%)
5   Support Services (CCPD/HOME/ SUPSERV)
9   Other Outpatient CCPD (CCPD/ HOME/OTHER)

86X   Reserved for Dialysis (National Assignment).
87X   Reserved for Dialysis (National Assignment).
88X   Miscellaneous Dialysis. Charges for dialysis services not identified elsewhere. Ultrafiltration is the process of removing excess fluid from the blood of dialysis patients by using a dialysis machine without the dialysis solution. The designation is only used when the procedure is not performed as a part of a normal dialysis session.
0   General Classification (DIALY/ MISC)
1   Ultrafiltration (DIALY/ ULTRAFILT)
2   Home Dialysis Aid Visit (HOME DIALY AID VISIT)
9   Miscellaneous Dialysis Other (DIALY/ MISC/OTHER)

89X   Other Donor Bank. Charges for the acquisition, storage, and preservation of all human organs (excluding kidneys).
0   General Classification (DONOR BANK)
1   Bone (DONOR BANK/BONE)
2   Organ (other than Kidney) (DONOR BANK/ORGN)
3   Skin (DONOR BANK/SKIN)
9   Other Donor Bank (OTHER DONOR BANK)

90X   Psychiatric/Psychological Treatments. Charges for treatment of emotionally disturbed patients, including those admitted for diagnosis and treatment.
0   General Classification (PSYCH TREATMENT)
1   Electroshock Treatment (ELECTRO SHOCK)
2   Milieu Therapy (MILIEU THER)
3   Play Therapy (PLAY THERAPY)
9   Other (OTHER PSYCH RX)

91X   Psychiatric/Psychological Services. Charges for providing nursing care and employee, professional services for emotionally disturbed patients, including patients admitted for diagnosis and those admitted for treatment.
0   General Classification (PSYCH SVS)
1   Rehabilitation (PSYCH/REHAB)
2   Day Care (PSYCH/DAYCARE)
3   Night Care (PSYCH/NIGHTCARE)
4   Individual Therapy (PSYCH/INDIV RX)
5   Group Therapy (PSYCH/GROUP RX)
6   Family Therapy (PSYCH/FAMILY RX)
7   Biofeedback (PSYCH/BIOFEED)
8   Testing (PSYCH/TESTING)

9   Other (PSYCH/OTHER)
92X   Other Diagnostic Services. Charges for other diagnostic services not otherwise categorized.
0   General Classification (OTHER DX SVS)
1   Peripheral Vascular Lab (PERI-VASCUL LAB)
2   Electromyogram (EMG)
3   Pap Smear (PAP SMEAR)
4   Allergy Test (ALLERGY TEST)
5   Pregnancy Test (PREG TEST)
9   Other Diagnostic Service (ADDL DX SVS)

93X   Not Assigned.
94X   Other Therapeutic Services. Charges for other therapeutic services not otherwise categorized.
0   General Classification (OTHER RX SVS)
1   Recreational Therapy (RECREATION RX)
2   Education/Training (EDUC/TRNG)
3   Cardiac Rehabilitation (CARDIAC REHAB)
4   Drug Rehabilitation (DRUG REHAB)
5   Alcohol Rehabilitation (ALCOHOL REHAB)
6   Complex Medical Equipment – Routine (CMPLX MED EQUIP-ROUT)
7   Complex Medical Equipment--Ancillary (CMPLX MED EQUIP-ANC)
9   Other Therapeutic Services (ADDITIONAL RX SVS)
NOTE: Use 930 with a procedure code for plasmapheresis. Use 932 for dietary therapy and diabetes-related services, education, and training.

95X   Not Assigned.
96X   Professional Fees. Charges for medical professionals that the hospitals or third party payors require to be separately identified.
0   General Classification (PRO FEE)
1   Psychiatric (PRO FEE/PSYCH)
2   Ophthalmology (PRO FEE/EYE)
3   Anesthesiologist (MD) (PRO FEE/ANES MD)
4   Anesthetist (CRNA) (PRO FEE/ANES CRNA)
9   Other Professional Fees (OTHER PRO FEE)

97X   Professional Fees (continued).
1   Laboratory (PRO FEE/LAB)
2   Radiology--Diagnostic (PRO FEE/RAD/ DX)
3   Radiology--Therapeutic (PRO FEE/RAD/ RX)
4   Radiology--Nuclear Medicine (PRO FEE/ NUC MED)
5   Operating Room (PRO FEE/OR)
6   Respiratory Therapy (PRO FEE/ RESPIR)
7   Physical Therapy (PRO FEE/ PHYSI)
8   Occupational Therapy (PRO FEE/ OCUPA)
9   Speech Pathology (PRO FEE/ SPEECH)

98X **Professional Fees (continued).**
   1 Emergency Room (PRO FEE/ER)
   2 Outpatient Services (PRO FEE/ OUTPT)
   3 Clinic (PRO FEE/CLINIC)
   4 Medical Social Services (PRO FEE/ SOC SVC)
   5 EKG (PRO FEE/EKG)
   6 EEG (PRO FEE/EEG)
   7 Hospital Visit (PRO FEE/HOS VIS)
   8 Consultation (PRO FEE/CONSULT)
   9 Private Duty Nurse (FEE/PVT NURSE)

99X **Patient Convenience Items.** Charges for items that are generally considered by payors to be strictly convenience items and not covered.
   0 General Classification (PT CONV)
   1 Cafeteria/Guest Tray (CAFETERIA)
   2 Private Linen Service (LINEN)
   3 Telephone/Telegraph (TELEPHN)
   4 TV/Radio (TV/RADIO)
   5 Nonpatient Room Rentals (NONPT ROOM RENT)
   6 Late Discharge Charge (LATE DISCH)
   7 Admission Kits (ADMIT KITS)
   8 Beauty Shop/Barber (BARBER/ BEAUTY)
   9 Other Patient Convenience Items (PT CONVENCE/OTH)

Field 53, Assignment of Benefits

This assignment of benefits will not allow you to release information regarding the patient. A written authorization to release information, signed by the patient or patient representative, is needed (see Item 53). Note the certification procedure on the back of the UB-92 before completing this item. The UB-92 eliminates the need to send an assignment of benefits to accident and health insurers.

Field 59, Relationship

Numerical code designation indicating that the patient is related to the insured in the following manner:
01 **Insured party.**
02 **Spouse of insured.**
03 **Child of insured.**
04 **Natural child/insured does not have financial responsibility for child.**
05 **Stepchild of insured.**
06 **Foster child of insured.**
07 **Ward of the Court.** Patient is a ward of the insured as a result of court order.
08 **Employee.** Patient is employed by the insured.
09 **Unknown.** Patient's relationship to the insured is unknown.
10 **Handicapped Dependent.** Dependent child whose coverage extends beyond normal termination age limits as a result of laws or agreement extending coverage.
11 **Organ Donor.** Used in cases where bill is submitted for care given to organ donor where such care is paid for by the receiving patient's insurance coverage.
12 **Cadaver Donor.** Used in cases where bill is submitted for procedures performed on a cadaver (deceased) donor where such procedures are paid for by the receiving patient's insurance coverage.
13 **Grandchild of insured.**
14 **Niece/nephew of insured.**
15 **Injured Plaintiff.** Used when patient claims insurance as a result of injury covered by insured.
16 **Sponsored Dependent.** Individual not normally covered by insurance, but coverage has been specially arranged to include relationships such as grandparent or former spouse that would require further investigation by the payor.
17 **Minor Dependent of a Minor Dependent.** This code is used when the patient is a dependent minor of a dependent minor (though not a child) of the insured.
18 **Parent of insured.**
19 **Grandparent.**
20-99 **Reserved.**

Field 64, Employment Status Code

Employment status Code is used to define the employment status of the individual in Item 63.
1 **Employed Full-Time.**
2 **Employed Part-Time.**
3 **Not Employed.**
4 **Self-Employed.**
5 **Retired.**
6 **On Active Military Duty.**
7-8 **Reserved for National Assignment.**
9 **Employment Status Unknown.**

Summary

The HCFA-1500 is the most accepted form for billing professional services. The information in each field allows the claim to be processed quickly and accurately. While understanding the form may seem simple, it takes practice to be able to accurately process this claim type.

The UB-92 is the claim form used when billing for hospital services. It was created by the National Uniform Billing Committee to allow for the necessary information needed by payors to be inserted on a single form, thus eliminating the need for attachments.

You should familiarize yourself with these forms and know where to find the necessary information for claims processing.

Assignments

Complete the Questions for Review.
Complete Exercise 3 – 1 and 3 – 2.

Questions for Review

Directions: Answer the following questions without looking back into the material just covered. Write your answers in the space provided.

1. What is the HCFA-1500 billing form used for? _____

2. If the provider of service is an individual, what should be placed in the box entitled Federal Tax ID Number? _____
    _____

3. Which HCFA-1500 box denotes that Worker's Compensation is involved in the claim?_____

4. What are the boxes at the top of the HCFA-1500 form, labeled "Medicare, Medicaid, Tri-Care, CHAMPVA, Feca,
    Black Lung, and Other" for? _____

5. What does the term "Assignment of Benefits" mean? _____
    _____

6. On the HCFA-1500, what does item 24J "COB" stand for and what does the term mean? _____
    _____

7. (True or False?) When a physician or provider of service signs a medical billing form, he/she is legally stating that
    the service(s) which they are seeking payment for have actually been performed. _____

8. What is a "Unit of Service?" _____

9. What is the UB-92 billing form used for? _____

10. What does item 17 on the UB-92 indicate? _____

11. What are occurrence codes and occurrence span codes and what is the difference between them? _____
    _____
    _____

12. What would the code 20 indicate in item 21 on the UB-92? _____

13. What would the code 03 indicate in item 22 on the UB-92? _____

14. On the UB-92, what is a value code used for? _____
    _____

15. How would you write the following times on a UB-92?

    a. 9:55 a.m.   _____   f. 2:48 p.m.   _____
    b. 10:25 p.m. _____   g. 5:56 p.m.   _____
    c. 1:18 a.m.   _____   h. Noon   _____
    d. 8:01 p.m.   _____   i. Midnight   _____
    e. 12:23 a.m. _____   j. 6:06 p.m.   _____

If you were unable to answer any of the questions, refer back to the section, and then fill in the answers.

Exercise 3 – 1

Directions: Look at the HCFA-1500 form in **Figure 3 – 1**, then answer the following questions.

1. What is the patient's name? _____ _____

2. What is the name of the insured person on this claim? _____

3. What is the procedure code for the procedure performed? _____

4. What is the diagnosis code given? _____

5. What is the patient's marital status? _____

6. What insurance plan is the patient covered under? _____

7. Has the authorization to release information been signed? _____

8. Is this patient covered under more than one insurance policy? _____

9. Have benefits been assigned on this claim? _____

10. What is the name of the provider on this claim? _____

Exercise 3 – 2

Directions: Look at the first claim in the Hospital Services chapter, then answer the following questions.

1. What is the patient's name? _____

2. What is the name of the insured person on this claim? _____

3. What is the procedure code for the procedure performed? _____

4. What is the diagnosis code given? _____

5. What is the patient's marital status? _____

6. What insurance plan is the patient covered under? _____

7. Has the authorization to release information been signed? _____

8. Is this patient covered under more than one insurance policy? _____

9. Have benefits been assigned on this claim? _____

10. What is the name of the provider on this claim? _____

Honors Certification™

The Honors Certification™ challenge for this chapter is a written test. You will be presented with several claim forms and asked to pull information from them, similar to that found in Exercise 3 – 1 and 3 – 2. Any errors will result in a deduction of between 3% and 5% from your grade. You must achieve a score of 85% or higher to pass this test. If you fail the test on your first attempt you may retake the test one additional time. The items included in the second test may be different from those in the first test.

4 Resource Manuals

In this chapter you will learn:

- To recognize the Merck Manual, PDR, Medical Dictionary, CPT, ICD9 and Red and Blue Books and explain their uses.

Key words and concepts you will learn in this chapter:

HCFA Common Procedure Coding System (HCPCS) – A coding book which came about because of the limitations in the CPT and RVS for billing injections, medication, supplies and durable medical equipment.

International Classification of Disease – 9th Revision Clinical Modification **(ICD-9CM)** – An indexing of conditions.

Medical Dictionary – A Book that lists medical terms and their definitions, synonyms, illustrations, and supplemental information.

Merck Manual – A manual that assists in identifying the symptomatology, prognosis, treatment protocols, etiology, and other miscellaneous information regarding diagnoses.

Physician's Current Procedure Terminology (CPT) – A systematic listing for coding the procedures or services performed by a physician.

*Physicians' Desk Reference (*PDR) – A manual that provided information on prescription drugs, including usage, dosage, appearance, prescription status, makeup and other factors.

Red Book and Blue Book – Are manuals which list drug product information, along with prevailing wholesale prices.

Relative Value Study (RVS) – Is another reference book used for coding physician services.

A resource manual or reference book is a source of information to which a reader is referred. In health claims billing, coding, and examining, there are a number of books that are utilized as reference books. These include the *International Classification of Diseases – 9th Revision (ICD-9), Physician's Current*

Procedure Terminology (CPT), Relative Value Study (RVS), HCFA Common Procedure Coding System (HCPCS), Physicians' Desk Reference (PDR), the medical dictionary, the Merck Manual,and the Red and Blue Books. We will discuss each of these books briefly in this chapter.

ICD-9

The *International Classification of Diseases – 9th Revision Clinical Modification (ICD-9CM)* is an indexing of conditions that serves a dual purpose for health benefits personnel. Mainly, it enables the medical biller and the claims examiner to convert English language descriptions of an illness, injury, or other condition into a numerical code and secondly, it allows for the classification of diseases for statistical purposes. Symptoms, diseases, injuries, and routine services are identified with either a three, four or five digit code, which may be entirely numerical or a combination of letters and numbers.

The ICD-9 consists of three volumes:

- Volume I – A tabular listing of diseases.
- Volume II – An alphabetical listing of diseases by English language description.
- Volume III – A numerical and alphabetical listing of surgical or nonsurgical procedures that may be performed by a physician.

The order of use and the degree of use of each of these volumes varies. However, Volume III is not widely used by health claims personnel.

Volume I

Volume I is structured numerically according to body system. It is used when:

1. An ICD-9 code is provided, but there is no language description of the diagnosis.

2. A language diagnosis is included, but an ICD-9 is not indicated and the terms used by the provider cannot be found in Volume II. If you can identify the body system, you may be able to locate an appropriate ICD-9 code.

Volume I is categorized as follows:

BODY SYSTEM/	
#	**CLASSIFICATION**
00-13	Infective and Parasitic Diseases
14-23	Neoplasms
24-27	Endocrine, Nutritional, Metabolic Diseases
28	Diseases of the Blood and Blood-Forming Organs
29-31	Mental/Nervous Disorders
32-38	Diseases of the Nervous System and Sense Organs
39-45	Diseases of the Circulatory System
46-51	Diseases of the Respiratory System
52-57	Diseases of the Digestive System
58-62	Diseases of the Genito-Urinary System
63-67	Complications of Pregnancy, Childbirth and the Puerperium
68-70	Diseases of the Skin and Subcutaneous Tissue
71-73	Diseases of the Musculoskeletal System and Connective Tissue
74-75	Congenital Anomalies
76-77	Certain Causes of Perinatal Morbidity and Mortality
78-79	Symptoms, Senility and Ill-Defined Conditions
80-86	Fractures, Dislocations, Sprains and Internal Injuries
87-90	Lacerations
91-99	Other Accidents, Poisoning and Violence (nature of the injury)
V0-Y24	Miscellaneous Informative Codings (a particular diagnosis is not indicated)

A number in parenthesis after a code is the page number in Volume II that can be checked to verify the code.

Volume II

Volume II is the alphabetical listing of diagnoses. This section is most commonly used first. It is divided into four sections:
1. An alphabetical index of diseases and injuries
2. A table of drugs and chemicals
3. An alphabetical index of external causes of injuries and poisonings (accidents) (E codes)
4. A listing of factors affecting the health status of an individual (V codes).

Volume III

Volume III of the ICD-9 is used for coding diagnoses and procedures performed in a hospital. Volume III contains both a tabular listing and index. The tabular listing has procedures arranged according to body sections. The body sections are arranged as follows:
1. Operations on the Nervous System
2. Operations on the Endocrine System
3. Operations on the Eye
4. Operations on the Ear
5. Operations on the Nose, Mouth and Pharynx
6. Operations on the Respiratory System
7. Operations on the Cardiovascular System
8. Operations on the Hemic and Lymphatic System
9. Operations on the Digestive System
10. Operations on the Urinary System
11. Operations on the Male Genital Organs
12. Operations on the Female Genital Organs
13. Obstetrical Procedures
14. Operations on the Musculoskeletal System
15. Operations on the Integumentary System
16. Miscellaneous Diagnostic and Therapeutic Procedures

The index has procedures listed in alphabetical order. Thus, it is the easiest way to look up a procedure. The medical biller should confirm their choice of code by looking in the tabular listing and checking all referrals, exclusions and notes included.

CPT/RVS

The *Physician's Current Procedure Terminology (CPT)* is a systematic listing for coding the procedures or services performed by a physician. Within this text the word "physician" is used generically to apply to any provider of services other than a hospital or other facility. Each procedure is identified with a five-digit numerical code. The purpose of the CPT is to provide a uniform method of accurately describing medical, surgical, and diagnostic services, which facilitates an effective means of communication among physicians, patients, and claim administrators.

The **Relative Value Study (RVS)** is another reference book used for coding physician services. The RVS preceded the CPT and was, in fact, the basis on which the CPT was designed. Consequently, the purpose of the RVS is the same as that of the CPT. These two manuals are referred to interchangeably even though the rules guiding their usage differ somewhat. Therefore, it is important for the medical biller and claims examiner to know which standard is specified by the plan being processed so that the appropriate rules can be used. The CPT and RVS each have six major sections:
1. Evaluation and Management 99201-99499
2. Medicine 90001-99199
3. Surgery 10000-69999

4. Anesthesia, CPT 00100-01999
    RVS 99100-99140 (same as surgery but add anesthesia modifier).
5. Radiology/Nuclear Medicine 70000-79999
6. Pathology & Laboratory Tests 80000-89999

To properly code using the CPT, choose the number code associated with the English-language description of the procedure performed. Sometimes the procedure will be phrased in different terminology (ie, testectomy is found under orchiectomy even though both are legitimate medical terms). Therefore it is important to check all related codes and alternate terminology for a procedure. It may also be necessary to consult a medical dictionary for alternate terminology for a specified procedure.

Each section of the CPT has specific instructions relating to that section prior to the first codes. It is important that you read each of these instructions in order to properly code the procedures contained in that section.

Some descriptions in the CPT are subprocedures of other descriptions. These subheading descriptions will be indented under the main procedure. To properly read an indented procedure, read the description of the main procedure (the one not indented) up to the semicolon. Then add the remaining description found in the indented wording.

For example, codes 21208 and 21209 read as follows:

21208   Osteoplasty, facial bones; augmentation
21209   reduction

Therefore the correct description for 21209 is Osteoplasty, facial bones; reduction. It is important to carefully read the full description of all related procedures before choosing the one which best describes the procedure performed. A slight change in the main description can significantly alter the meaning of the indented procedure.

Using the CPT Index

The CPT index lists all main procedures, often with a choice of several codes. Once again, some procedures are indented, indicating that the unindented procedure listed directly above them is part of the description.

Listings in the CPT are arranged by the procedure done, then by the site of the procedure. For example, the heading Amputation then lists numerous portions of the body which can be amputated, and their related codes. Some portions of the body also have a heading. Thus, the code for amputation of the lower arm can be located by looking under either Amputation, Arm, Lower or Arm, Lower, Amputation. In most cases it is best to check both descriptions since there may be additional codes located under one of the descriptions. By using the above example, we see that under Amputation, Arm, Lower we have codes of 25900, 25905, and 25915. However under Arm, Lower, Amputation the codes 24900-24920 are listed in addition to the above three codes.

HCPCS

The **HCFA Common Procedure Coding System (HCPCS)** came about because of the limitations in the CPT and RVS for billing injections, medication, supplies and durable medical equipment. These codes are most often used for billing Medicare claims, but may also be used for Medicaid claims and for some carriers. The HCPCS system actually includes three levels of coding:

- Level I utilized the current CPT codes for most procedures.
- Level II utilizes the HCPCS codes listed in the HCPCS manual.
- Level III utilizes codes which are specific to the local Medicare carrier.

To properly code using the HCPCS system, you should check Level III codes first. If no code exists for the service or item you are billing, check the Level II codes. Only if there is no Level III or Level II codes should you use the appropriate CPT code.

To use the HCPCS manual:

1. If you have a code number, but need the English language equivilent, look in the front section of the HCPCS. HCPCS codes have a letter, then several numbers. The codes are listed by the letter, then the numbers within that letter (i.e., J1111, J1112, J1113, etc.). Additionally, codes are assigned within groups. Therefore the items within a group will be found near each other (i.e., medications, orthopedic devices, etc.).
2. If you have an English language equivilent and need to look up a HCPCS code, look up the item in the index.

Physicians Desk Reference

Physicians' Desk Reference (PDR) – A manual that provided information on prescription drugs, including usage, dosage, appearance, prescription status, makeup and other factors. Among other things the PDR enables a person to determine whether a pharmaceutical product is a prescription or nonprescription drug. This is a very important distinction since most health plans do not cover nonprescription drugs.

The PDR is divided into six sections:

1. **Manufacturer's Index** (white) – arranged alphabetically by manufacturer, then by drug name. The name and address of the manufacturer are included. This section includes prescription and nonprescription drugs. The related information has been provided by the manufacturer.
2. **Product Name Index** (pink) – arranged alphabetically by brand name or generic name (if provided). Prescription and nonprescription

drugs are included. This section is usually used first to locate the manufacturers name and the page number for further information.

3. **Product Category Index** (blue) – arranged alphabetically by drug action category, that is, according to the most common use of the drug. If the drug is an antidepressant, it is listed under the antidepressant category; and if it is an antacid, it is listed under the antacid category.

4. **Product Identification Section** (gray) – jarranged alphabetically by manufacturer, then by brand name. This section contains the actual size and full-color reproductions. Only the reproductions submitted by the manufacturer are included.

5. **Product Information Section** (white) – arranged alphabetically by manufacturer, then by brand name. Most pharmaceuticals are described by indications and usage, dosage, administration, description, clinical pharmacology, supply warnings, contraindications, adverse reactions, overdosage precautions and other miscellaneous information.

6. **Diagnostic Product Information** (green) – oarranged alphabetically by manufacturer, then by product. This section provides a description of diagnostic products only.

Medical billers and claims examiners use the Product Information Section (white) the most. However, since generic drugs are cheaper than brand name medications, many plans encourage their members to purchase generically and offer increased payment incentives. Therefore, use of the Product Name Index (which includes both brand name and generic names) is increasing. For instance, instead of paying for generic drugs at the plan's regular coinsurance rate of 80%, 100% may be payable. As with all benefits, this varies widely by plan.

Medical Dictionary

Medical dictionaries list medical terms and their definitions, synonyms, illustrations, and supplemental information. Numerous medical dictionaries are on the market. These dictionaries can be very helpful in assisting the examiner to identify diagnoses, their symptoms, prognoses, and common treatment protocols. The use of a dictionary can assist the claims examiner in both coding the claim and determining whether or not the diagnosis or service is allowable under a plan.

As a rule, this manual should be used mainly for verifying a diagnosis or affected body area or checking definitions and the spelling of terms. For greater detail on symptomatology and treatment protocols, the *Merck Manual* is more definitive. As with most dictionaries, entries are arranged alphabetically.

When using the medical dictionary, it is important that you first read through the foreword and any instructions or general guidelines contained in the front of the book. Since each publisher uses different symbols and information, you must read these instructions to understand the symbols and terms and their meanings.

In addition to basic definitions, many medical dictionaries include other information regarding the word or term. These can include the following 14 pieces of information:

1. The etymology of the word (i.e., the original language and meaning).
2. The pronunciation of the word.
3. Biographical information on diseases, symptoms, conditions, procedures, or cures that have been given an eponym (named after a person, such as Addison's disease).
4. Synonyms. Often diseases or conditions are known by more than one name. In these instances they are listed as synonyms in the dictionary (i.e., Addison's disease: adrenocortical hypofunction).
5. Abbreviations. If a word or term has a standard abbreviation in the medical community, this abbreviation is often listed in the medical dictionary.
6. Etiology. The causes of the disease.
7. Treatment. Common medical treatments are stated for some diagnoses or conditions. It is understood that this may not be the only effective medical treatment and that specifics of the treatment are not given.
8. Cross-reference. Cross-references for treatments may be included, allowing the user to locate possible drugs or treatments that may prove to be effective.
9. Prognosis. A generalized prognosis for the disease is given. At times it will include a prognosis for patients who are not treated and for those that are.
10. Nursing implications. The implications of care of the patient are listed. This may include the need for monitoring of certain conditions or vital signs.
11. Nursing diagnosis cross-reference. Some dictionaries list an appendix of nursing diagnoses and implications. Certain diseases or conditions will be cross-referenced to this section.
12. Subentries. Subentries contain more specific information regarding a term or condition and list some of the different types of conditions that can occur. For example, the subentries under the term "acid" can include acetic a., boric a., citric a., fatty a., and sulfuric a., as well as many others. It is understood that a small letter followed by a period refers to a repetition

of the original term or condition. In the example above, the "a." would stand for the word "acid."

13. Illustration cross-reference. An illustration occurs in the dictionary – placed either near the word or under another heading – which illustrates either the term or a portion of the definition. The user is directed to the correct page or term under which the illustration can be found.

14. Cautions or warnings. Certain terms or conditions have a warning placed within the definition. This is most often used with drugs and treatments. This warning can include any side effects or adverse reactions or conditions that can occur from use of the drug or treatment. Often this caution or warning is in boldface or marked off within a section to help call attention to it.

When using the medical dictionary, it is imperative that the health claims examiner read through the entire entry. If terms are used in the definition that the health claims examiner does not understand, the unknown word should also be looked up, either in the medical dictionary (if it is a medical term) or in a standard dictionary (if it is not).

There are numerous diseases, conditions, or terms that are very similar to each other in spelling or pronunciation, but vastly different in meaning. It is important to use the proper term and its proper spelling when billing, coding, and examining a claim.

Merck Manual

Even the most experienced examiner occasionally has questions regarding the appropriateness of services for a reported diagnosis. The *Merck Manual* is relied on within the medical profession to assist in identifying the symptomatology, prognosis, treatment protocols, etiology, and other miscellaneous information regarding diagnoses.

When an examiner receives a claim with unusual services based on the diagnosis, using the *Merck Manual* may assist in identifying whether or not the treatment is appropriate for the reported diagnosis or symptoms.

The *Merck Manual* has two main sections: a listing of diseases and an index. The index is arranged alphabetically by disease. To look something up, simply turn to the index to find out what page the disease information is on.

The information provided includes the diagnosis, symptoms, prognosis, and treatment. If the treatment provided is not consistent with the diagnosis, it may be forwarded to a medical review board or a consultant, causing a delay in the processing of the claim.

Red Book and Blue Book

The *Red Book* and *Blue Book* are manuals which list drug product information, along with prevailing wholesale prices.

Some plans have a separate drug coverage. Drugs on these plans are often paid according to a set price schedule, regardless of the amount charged by the pharmacy or dispensing physician. These schedules are often based upon the Blue Book or the Red Book. These two books list wholesale prices of drugs.

Often the plan provisions will specify payment at 150% or 175% of the *Blue Book* or *Red Book* price.

Summary

The *ICD-9CM, CPT, RVS, HCPCS, PDR*, medical dictionary, and *Merck Manual* are the resource manual most commonly used by health claims examining personnel.

The *ICD-9CM* is used to code diagnoses and conditions. The *CPT* is used to code procedures and services rendered by providers. Use of the PDR assists in determining whether a drug is prescription or nonprescription, and lists some of the properties (i.e., manufacturer, chemical make-up, side effects, appearance) of a specific drug. Medical dictionaries list medical terms and their meanings, and the *Merck Manual* can assist in determining whether a service or Red and Blue Book procedure is appropriate for a given diagnosis or condition.

Health claims examiners should familiarize themselves with the use of each of the reference books just discussed. Without their proper utilization, delays and denials can result in claims submitted to payors.

Assignments

Complete the Questions for Review.
Complete Exercises 4 – 1 to 4 – 4.

Questions for Review

Directions: Answer the following questions without looking back into the material just covered. Write your answers in the space provided.

1. Which manual is used for coding diagnoses?_____

2. Name the two manuals that serve the same purpose and may be referred to interchangeably.

   1. _____

   2. _____

3. The full name of the PDR is_____

4. If you needed to verify a diagnosis, affected body area, or spelling of terms and definitions you would probably refer to the _____

5. _____is useful in determining the appropriateness of services for a reported diagnosis.

If you were unable to answer any of the questions, refer back to the section, then fill in the answers.

Exercise 4 – 1

Directions: Determine the correct resource manual needed to answer the question, then use that reference to find the answer. Do not be concerned if you do not understand all the words in the description or answer.

1. What is the English language description for diagnosis code 460 and 487.1? _____

   _____

2. Describe diagnosis 1 (code 460) from question 1? _____

   _____

3. Define catarrhal. _____

   _____

4. Is fever most commonly a symptom of diagnosis 1 or diagnosis 2? _____

5. What is a synonym for the common cold?   _____

6. How long is a person contagious with this disease?_____

   _____

7. Name two symptoms or signs of diagnosis 1. _____

   _____

8. What causes the condition from diagnosis code 1?_____

   _____

9. What is the incubation period for this disease?_____

10. What is the procedure code 87070 for and is it appropriate for diagnosis code 460? _____

    _____

Exercise 4 – 2

Directions: Determine the correct resource manual needed to answer the question, then use that reference to find the answer. Do not be concerned if you do not understand all the words in the description or answer.

1. What is the English Language description for the diagnosis code 696.1?_____

2. Describe the disease from question 1?_____

3. What are erythematous papules?_____

4. What is the cause of the disease in question 1?_____

5. Name two symptoms or signs of this disease._____

6. Name two possible treatments for this disease._____

7. What is the English language description for the procedure code 97028?_____

8. Is procedure code 97028 a valid treatment for diagnosis code 696.1? _____

9. Should a patient with this disease expose themselves to sunlight?_____

10. Does smoking affect this condition? If so, in what way?_____

Exercise 4 – 3

Directions: Determine the correct resource manual needed to answer the question, then use that reference to find the answer. Do not be concerned if you do not understand all the words in the description or answer.

1. What is the English Language description for the procedure code 26535?_____

2. What is the English Language description for the diagnosis code 345.90?_____

3. Is procedure code 26535 a valid treatment for diagnosis code 696.1?_____

4. Describe the disease from question 2?_____

5. Define paroxysmal disorder?_____

6. What is the cause of the disease in question 2?_____

7. Name two symptoms or signs of this disease._____

8. How effective are anticonvulsant drugs in treating this disease (give percentages of control or reduction of symptoms, if any)?_____

9. Can a patient with this disease lead a normal life?_____

10. What book would tell you if a specific drug was considered effective against the given condition?_____

_____

Exercise 4 – 4

Directions: Determine the correct resource manual needed to answer the question, then use that reference to find the answer. Do not be concerned if you do not understand all the words in the description or answer.

1. What do the initials AIDS and HIV stand for?_____

_____

2. Which of the following is the correct diagnosis code for AIDS? 079.53, V01.7, 042, or 795.71._____

_____

3. Describe the disease from question 1?_____

_____

4. How is the disease transmitted among adults?_____

_____

5. How is the disease transmitted to infants?_____

_____

6. What is the description of the code 43842 and is it an appropriate treatment for an AIDS patient?_____

_____

7. What are the descriptions of the codes 86701, 86702 and 86703 and is any of them an appropriate procedure for a suspected AIDS patient?_____

8. If the patient is a Medicare patient and receives and injection of Interferon, would you use the code J9213 or 90782 and why?_____

9. What precautions should medical personnel take when treating someone with AIDS?_____

_____

10. What book would tell you if a specific drug was considered effective against the given condition?_____

_____

Honors Certification™

The Honors Certification™ challenge for this chapter is a written test of the information contained within this chapter. Each incorrect answer will result in a deduction of between 1% and 5% from your grade. You must achieve a score of 85% or higher to pass this test. If you fail the test on your first attempt you may retake the test one additional time. The items included in the second test may be different from those in the first test.

5 Contracts

In this chapter you will learn:

- To differentiate between basic comprehensive and major medical benefits.
- To determine the order of benefits.
- The three usual roles for basic benefits.

Key words and concepts you will learn in this chapter:

Basic Benefits – Benefits which are paid before major medical benefits, and which are usually paid at 100%.

Coinsurance – An agreement to split insurance expenses (i.e., if the insurance carrier may pay 80% and the patient is responsible for 20%).

Contract – A legal and binding written document that exists between two or more parties.

Deductible – The amount the patient must pay before the insurance carrier pays anything on a claim.

Effective Date – The date a contract began to be in force.

Eligibility – The qualifications which make the person eligible for coverage.

Exclusions – Any condition or expense for which, under the terms of the policy, no coverage is provided.

Explanation of Benefits (EOB) – A form which shows which parts of a claim are being paid or denied, and the amount of any payments, exclusions or deductibles taken.

Group Policy Holder – An employer or entity (i.e., union) who purchases a group policy.

Lifetime Maximum – The total dollar payments the insurance carrier will make toward the care of this member.

Major Medical Benefits – Those benefits paid after basic benefits, and which are usually subject to a deductible and coinsurance.

Mental/Nervous Expenses – Expenses for psychiatric treatment, marriage and family counseling and drug and alcohol treatment.

Offer – To propose or undertake to do or give something in exchange for a return promise from the person to whom the act or gift is being offered.

Out-of-Pocket Limit – A member's costs which include the deductible, cost-sharing arising from the operation of the coinsurance clause, and medical expenditures that are deemed by the plan to be in excess of reasonable and customary charges.

Pre-Admission Testing – Testing done prior to admittance into a hospital for a scheduled surgery.

Preexisting Condition – A medical condition that existed before an insurance policy was purchased. Depending on the policy, a preexisting condition may be defined based on when it originated, when symptoms first appeared, or when treatment was first sought.

Preventive Care – Measures taken in advance of symptoms to prevent illness or injury.

Second Surgical Opinion – An opinion provided by a second physician, when one physician recommends surgery to an individual.

Termination of Coverage – Cessation of eligibility for benefits under the plan.

A contract is a legal and binding written document that exists between two or more parties. Written contracts are in every aspect of society. Essentially, any agreement between two or more persons that is enforceable by law is considered a contract. However, written contracts have several advantages over non-written (oral) contracts: the existence of a written contract cannot be denied, and the terms of a written contract can be enforced more easily in the event of death or incapacity (i.e., insanity, coma) of one of the parties of the contract.

In health insurance, the contract is used to determine eligibility requirements and covered services and to determine how those covered services are to be paid. The contract also indicates services that are excluded and services that have limitations. Therefore, the health claims examiner must learn to read and interpret the contract in order to pay the proper benefits.

Contract Validity

For a contract to be valid, the persons signing the contract must agree on the terms. For the parties to agree, there must be some form of offer and acceptance. To **offer** means to propose or undertake to do or give something in exchange for a return promise from the person to whom the act or gift is being offered. An offer must be communicated in one form or another before it can be accepted. However, acceptance need not always be communicated to create a contract.

For example, banks often send out a letter to their patrons informing them of a change in interest rates or other terms regarding their accounts. These letters often state that if the bank is not contacted within a specified period of time, it will be assumed that the patron has agreed to and accepted the new terms or rates.

For a contract to be valid and enforceable, the following principals must be met:

1. The contract must be based on a mutual agreement by the parties to do or not to do a specific thing or things.
2. The contract must be made by the parties who are able and competent to enter into the contract and to enforce the terms of the contract. In some states, this may mean that minors may not enter into certain types of contracts.
3. The contract must include consideration to pay money, deliver services, or promise to do or refrain from doing some lawful act that has not yet occurred (i.e., a contract cannot be made to enforce an event that has already occurred).
4. The purpose of the contract must be lawful. Contracts for unlawful acts are unenforceable.
5. If the contract falls into a class of contracts required by law to be in a special form, the format of the contract must meet those laws or requirements.

Group Contracts

Every health benefit plan, whether it is insured or not, is required by law to have a written document describing the plan benefits. This written legal document is used both by the plan members and by the administrator in determining how claims are to be paid. If any settlement disputes develop, the document is entered as evidence of what is and is not covered, what allowances are provided towards specific services, what books are used for reference in calculating benefits, and what the appeal procedures are.

Insured plans call this written document a **contract** or **policy**. Non-insured plans usually refer to it as a **summary plan description**. For our purposes, we will refer to the documents generically as contracts without implying whether or not a plan is insured.

The **group contract** is an instrument through which an insurance company can meet the financial security needs of a group of persons. In essence, it is an agreement between the insurance company and the policyholder to insure the lives and health of the members of a defined group of persons and to pay the insurance benefits to the insured person or their beneficiaries. The specific terms and conditions of the contract are determined by negotiation between the insurance company and the policyholder. With the exception of benefit provisions, they are largely determined by standard provisions, generally accepted throughout the industry.

The group contract must consist of the following three parts:

1. The group master policy,
2. The application of the group policyholder, and
3. The individual applications, if any, of the persons insured.

The parties to a group contract are the insurance company and the **group policy holder**. In most cases, this is an employer. However, the policyholder may be a union or the trustee of a fund established by employers, unions, or both. For a group contract to be valid, a written application must be made. For it to remain valid, premiums must continue to be paid.

A basic principal of the law of contracts is consideration. Consideration can be a very broad term. For our purposes, **consideration** will be defined as anything that is given, done, promised, forbidden, or suffered by one party as an inducement for the agreement. The most common form of consideration is the payment of money in exchange for a promise. For insurance, consideration is the premium paid by the group policyholder. The individual insured may contribute toward these premiums or provide the entire amount. In most cases, however, the premium is paid by the policyholder to the insurer, even though the individual insured may contribute part or all of the monies.

Interpreting and understanding contracts is one of the most important aspects of being a health claims examiner. The health care contract is the one document which is used to determine the benefits which the insurance carrier will pay for services rendered.

The wording and terminology of health insurance contracts can often be confusing to someone who is not well versed in the insurance field. For this reason, health claims examiners will often be called upon to interpret the provisions of a contract for billing purposes or to explain benefits to a patient.

Contract Provisions

In the following sections we will look at each of the items in a contract in brief. These items, and how to calculate them, will be discussed in more detail in subsequent chapters. For now just familiarize yourself with where to find items in a contract.

Eligibility

The first item which is considered on the contract is **eligibility,** or the qualifications which make the person eligible for coverage. Usually this includes items such as working full-time for a company, and the description of what is considered full time. For example, in the Winter contract, an employee must work a minimum of 30 hours per week to be eligible for coverage. The contract also discloses who is considered a dependent of the employee.

If a person has purchased individual coverage and is not covered by their place of work, there would be no minimum work requirements, however, there would still be qualifications to have coverage as a dependent under the plan.

Dependent eligibility is usually defined by the relationship to the employee and the age (if the dependent is a child). For example, in the Winter contract a child is covered until age 19 or to age 23 if they are a full-time student. If an eligible dependent becomes disabled before age 19, or if a student and the eligible dependent becomes disabled before age 23, dependent coverage would continue until age 23. Children includes unmarried natural children, legally adopted children, foster children and those for whom the employee is considered the legal guardian.

On some contracts there are provisions which state that if a husband and wife (or parent and child) work for the same employer and are covered under the same contract, the spouse or child cannot be covered as a dependent on the employees policy. Also, some contracts state that if both spouses are working at the same company and are covered under the same contract, the children may be covered by one parent or the other, but not both. This prevents the insurance carrier from having to pay twice for the same patient and services rendered.

Effective Date

The next item to be considered is whether or not the contract was in force at the time the services were rendered. This is often defined as a minimum length of time an employee has worked for a company.

There is also an **"actively-at-work"** stipulation that is included in many contracts. This clause states that a person must be at-work (or actively engaged in their normal activities if a dependent) on the date coverage becomes effective. If he or she is not at work or actively engaged in their normal activities, the contract does not become effective until the employee or dependent returns to work or their normal activities.

As a claims examiner, it is important that you ensure that a patient is eligible and is covered under an insurance policy in order to receive benefits. Many providers contact the insurance company prior to performing a procedure to be sure that the patient is covered. This is especially important when a patient is covered under an individual policy and pays a monthly premium for coverage.

Termination of Coverage

This section of a contract provides information regarding when coverage will terminate for both the employee and their dependents. It is important to note when coverage ceases as the insurance carrier should not pay benefits after this date. You should be aware that coverage will often continue until the end of the month in which an employee terminates.

Contract Benefits

The next section of the contract usually details the benefits which the contract covers. These can include basic benefits and major medical benefits. Premiums are based upon the number and amount of benefits which a contract covers. The greater the coverage, the higher the cost of the premiums. For example, a contract which covers charges at 90% of the allowed amount and has a $100 deductible will usually cost more than a comparative contract which covers charges at 70% of the allowed amount and has a $250 deductible.

Basic Benefits

Basic benefits are usually paid at 100% of covered expenses and are paid before major medical benefits are paid. Therefore, it is possible for the insurance plan to pay basic benefits even when the patient has not yet met their deductible. Not all contracts will have basic benefits. Most basic benefit plans have been replaced with managed care plans.

Some contracts have a basic benefit which is based upon the unit value (a number based upon the difficulty of a procedure and the overhead needed) being multiplied by a basic conversion factor (see Ball contract). This allows a small portion of most services to be paid at 100% with the remaining portion paid at the normal coinsurance percentage. Often these types of basic benefits do not cover all procedures.

Accident Benefits

One of the most common basic benefits is an accident benefit. An **accident** is defined as an unintentional injury which has a specific time, date and place. Under the Winter contract, the first $300 of services that are due to an accident are paid at 100%. After that, the remaining charges are paid at 90%. This benefit is for the first $300 of charges that are incurred within 120 days of the date of the accident.

On the HCFA-1500 form, box 10b & 10c indicate services due to an accident with the date of the accident indicated in box 14.

Pre-Admission Testing

In the past, a patient would enter the hospital the day before surgery for routine tests such as a chest x-ray and blood tests. The hospital would then admit the patient and watch over them to ensure that they had nothing to eat or drink in the 24 hours prior to surgery. Insurance carriers realized there would be a great cost savings if the patient were to visit the hospital for the tests, return home, and return the next day for the surgery. This eliminated the charges for an overnight hospital stay.

To encourage this practice, some insurance carriers offer an extra incentive for **pre-admission testing**, or testing done before the patient enters the hospital for surgery. Some insurance carriers now cover these charges at 100% rather than at their normal coinsurance percentage. Only tests done at the facility where the patient will be admitted, and done within 24 hours of admittance are usually allowed under this benefit.

Second Surgical Opinions
A **second surgical opinion** is an opinion provided by a second physician, when one physician recommends surgery to an individual. This provision is designed to insure that the diagnosis of diseases and recommendation of treatments are accurate; or to investigate alternative less invasive treatment.

Some insurance carriers pay 100% of allowable charges for a second surgical opinion. This originally started out as a cost containment measure. The hope was that only those surgeries that were necessary would be confirmed, with some patients receiving alternative (and less expensive) treatments or with treatment being considered completely unnecessary.

Second surgical opinions have become less popular among insurance carriers since the cost savings seems to be minimal, if any. Many doctors are reluctant to go against the word or prescribed treatments of another physician. They do not want to contradict their peers, and also do not want to open themselves up to a lawsuit by suggesting a less radical treatment which may eventually prove less effective. Therefore, they will often simply confirm the diagnosis and prescribed treatment of the original physician.

Outpatient Facility Charges
Some surgeries are simple or routine enough to be performed on an outpatient basis. This means that the patient enters the facility in the morning, has surgery, and, after a brief recovery period, returns home the same day. There are no overnight or room and board charges. To encourage outpatient surgery when and where possible, some insurance carriers will cover such charges at 100%.

Major Medical Benefits
Major Medical benefits are those benefits paid after Basic benefits, and which are usually subject to a deductible and coinsurance. Major medical plans usually cover a broad list of medical expenditures. This section lists the particular benefits and stipulations which a Major Medical contract generally provides.

Deductible
The first item usually listed is the amount of the **deductible**. This is the amount which the patient must pay prior to the insurance paying their benefits. Deductibles are usually accumulated according to a

calendar year. Thus, each January 1st, the amount the patient has paid toward their deductible returns to zero and the patient must start paying again.

The exception to this is in contracts which have a "carry-over provision." A **deductible carry-over provision** means that any amounts which the patient pays toward their deductible in the last three months of the year will carry-over and will be applied toward the next year's deductible. Remember, the member pays their deductible before the insurance is required to pay any benefits. Therefore, if the patient is still paying a deductible in the last three months of the year, the insurance carrier has not had to pay any major medical benefits on this patient up to that time.

Family Deductible
Family deductibles work the same way individual deductibles do in that once a certain limit is reached, no more deductible is taken. There are two ways to accumulate family deductible: aggregate and non-aggregate.

Aggregate means that any amounts paid toward the deductible by any member of the family will be added up to reach the deductible.

In **non-aggregate family deductible** limits, the added sum of what each family member has paid is not important. Rather, a specified number of individuals in the family must meet their individual deductible limit in order for the family limit to be met.

Out-of-Pocket Limit
A member's **"out-of-pocket"** costs include the deductible, cost-sharing arising from the operation of the coinsurance clause, and medical expenditures that are deemed by the plan to be in excess of reasonable and customary charges.

Co-payment
A **co-payment** provision is when the member is required to pay a set or fixed dollar amount (i.e., $5, $10, or $25) each time a particular medical service is used. Co-payment provisions are frequently found in PPO and HMO plans.

Coinsurance
Coinsurance is an agreement to share expenses between the member and the insurance carrier. This is usually expressed in percentages (i.e., the insurance covers 80% of the approved amount of a bill, and the member covers 20%).

Coinsurance Limit
Many insurance companies are aware that the financial effects of a catastrophic illness can ruin a family financially. Since insurance carriers want to keep people on the rolls, they must leave them with enough resources to consistently pay premiums. For this reason many insurance carriers have a **coinsurance limit**. This limit stipulates that if the coinsurance portion of a patient's bills reaches a certain amount, all subsequent claims will be paid at 100% of the allowed amount.

For example, the Ball Contract has a coinsurance limit of $400. Since the coinsurance amount is based upon 20% of the allowed amount (with the insurance covering 80% of the allowed amount), the patient must have bills with approved amounts totaling over $2,125 in a calendar year ($125 is applied toward deductible, $2,000 multiplied by 20% equals the $400 limit).

Mental/Nervous Expenses

Mental and nervous expenses include claims submitted for psychiatric services, marriage and family counseling services, and drug and alcohol treatment. A higher coinsurance percentage (i.e., 50%) and a lower lifetime benefit limit (i.e., $10,000 or $20,000) may apply. Also, the coverage may depend on whether treatment is provided on an in-patient or out-patient basis.

Many contracts have a calendar year maximum or a maximum number of visits for these types of services.

Lifetime Maximum

There is a lifetime maximum payment amount placed on most contracts. Once the patient reaches the **lifetime maximum** amount, the insurance carrier will not cover any additional expenses. Essentially this amount is the total dollar payments the insurance carrier will make toward the care of this member. However, this amount is so high that it is seldom reached, except in extreme cases.

Pre-existing Limitations

Many contracts will not cover conditions which existed prior to a patient becoming covered under a contract (called **pre-existing conditions**). This prevents a patient from not paying for insurance coverage, then suddenly discovering they have a serious illness and seeking insurance to cover that illness.

By law, pre-existing limitations must be included in the contract. The term pre-existing is different for each contract. Most often it is defined as a condition for which the patient has sought treatment within a given time period before insurance coverage has begun. If the patient has sought treatment for such a condition, within this time period benefits for treatment may not be covered, or may be limited to a certain dollar amount. Usually the restraints for benefits will cease once the patient has been covered under a contract for 6 months or longer.

Some contracts also have a "**treatment free**" period. With this provision, if the patient can go without treatment for a specified period of time (often 90 days), then the insurance carrier will no longer consider the condition to be pre-existing and will cover the illness or condition under the normal terms of the contract.

Remember that treatment includes any kind of contact in relationship with the illness, including the office visit or testing which were used to diagnose the illness. It also includes treatment of the condition, tests or office visits to monitor the condition and filling of prescriptions relating to the condition.

Exclusions

Every contract will have a list of exclusions, (conditions or expenses for which, under the terms of the policy, no coverage is provided). It is important to check the list of exclusions before verifying benefits for services. If the procedures or treatments are not covered, the member will be responsible for the entire amount of the bill.

Summary

The term "contract," in general, is an agreement among two or more persons that is enforceable by law. For a contract to be valid, the parties must agree on its terms. There must also be some form of offer and acceptance. As soon as an offer has been properly communicated and accepted, a binding contract is formed. A group contract is the instrument through which an insurance company can meet the financial security needs of a group of persons.

It is vital that health claims examiners understand how to interpret contracts. It will take practice to accurately understand the coverages provided under contracts and to pay benefits properly.

Basic and Major Medical plans are generally classified as indemnity contracts. These plans indemnify, or reimburse, the insured for medical expenses incurred and typically require the completion and filing of claims. These plans also often contain deductible and coinsurance provisions and may restrict coverage for certain types of medical care expenditures. Indemnity plans, in contrast to HMO and PPO plans, provide the member with substantial freedom regarding the choice of physicians or specialists seen. HMO and PPO plan coverage emphasizes comprehensive (including preventive) care and typically contain fewer exclusions, small or no deductibles, and nominal co-payments. However, there is much less freedom of choice of physician.

The three contracts found on the following pages will be used throughout the course to calculate benefits on sample claims and to add clarification to examples used to demonstrate the application of plan provisions.

These sample contracts are based on actual plans and should be used as examples of what is possible within the industry. There is no such thing as a definitive plan. As you will discover, there are a multitude of possible contract provisions. Therefore, use these samples as learning tools only.

Go through the following contracts and be sure that you understand what coverage's are provided. Additional practice with other contracts may also prove helpful.

Assignments

Study the contracts on the following pages.
Complete the Questions for Review.
Complete the Contracts Exercises 5 – 1 to 5 – 5.

Questions for Review

Directions: Answer the following questions without looking back into the material just covered. Write your answers in the space provided.

1. (True or False?) Every health benefit plan, whether it is insured or not, is required by law to have a written document describing the plan benefits. _____True_____

2. Define offer. _To propose or undertake to do or give something in exchange for a return promise from the person to whom the act/gift is being_

3. Define eligibility. _The first item which is considered on the contract is eligibility or the qualification which make the person eligible for coverage_

4. For a contract to be valid and enforceable, what five principals must be met?
    1. _The contract must be based on a mutual agreement by the parties to do or not to do a specific thing or things_
    2. _The contract must be made by the parties who are able and competent to enter into the contract and to enforce terms of contract._
    3. _The contract must include consideration to pay money deliver services or promise to do or refrain from doing some act that has not yet occurred_
    4. _The purpose of the contract must be lawful. Contracts for unlawful parts are unenforceable._
    5. _If the contract falls into a class of contracts required by law to be in a special form the format of the contract must meet those laws or requirements_

5. The group contract must consist of what three parts?
    1. _The Group master policy_
    2. _The application of group policyholder_
    3. _The individual application if any of the persons insured_

6. Basic benefits are usually paid at 100% and are _paid before any of medical benefits are paid_

7. Define accident. _An unintentional injury which have specific time, date & place_

8. What is pre-admission testing? _Testing done before the patient enters hosp. for surgery_

9. What is outpatient surgery? _patient enters facility in morning, after brief recovery sent home_

10. What is a deductible? _This is the amount which patient pays before insurance pays_

11. What is coinsurance? _is the agreement to share expenses between the member and the insurance carrier._

12. What are mental/nervous expenses? _Include claims submitted for psychiatric services, marriage and family counseling & drug & alcohol treatment._

13. What happens when a patient reaches their lifetime maximum? _the insurance will not cover additional exp._

14. What is a pre-existing condition? _a condition for which the patient has sought treatment within a given time period before ins coverage begun._

15. What is an exclusion? _condition or expenses for which under the term of the policy no coverage is provided._

If you were unable to answer any of the questions, refer back to the section and then complete the answers.

BALL INSURANCE CARRIERS   (800) 555-5432

3895 Bubble Blvd. Ste. 283, Boxwood, CO 85926   (970) 555-5432

RE: <u>XYZ Corporation</u>   **Basic/MajorMedical Plan**   Effective 09/1/93

ELIGIBILITY EMPLOYEE: Must work a minimum of 30 hours per week. Is eligible for coverage the first of the month following three consecutive months of continuous employment.

DEPENDENTS: Are eligible for coverage from birth to age 19, or to age 23 if a full-time student or handicapped prior to 19/23 (proof of disability must be furnished within 31 days after dependent reaches limiting age). Not eligible as a dependent if eligible as an employee. Unmarried natural children, legally adopted and foster children are included (includes legal guardianship). If both parents are covered by the plan, children may be covered by one employee only.

EFFECTIVE DATE EMPLOYEE: If written application is made prior to eligibility date, coverage becomes effective the first of the month following three months of continuous employment.

DEPENDENTS: The date acquired by the covered employee becomes the effective date if written application is made within 31 days of eligibility date. If confined in a hospital on date of eligibility, coverage will not start until the first of the month following the date the confinement ends. Newborns are automatically covered for the first 30 days following birth. Coverage will be terminated after 30 days unless written application for coverage is submitted by the employee within 31 days of birth.

TERMINATION OF COVERAGE EMPLOYEE: Coverage terminates the last day of the month following termination of employment, or when the employee ceases to qualify as an eligible employee, or following request for termination of coverage.

DEPENDENTS: Coverage terminates the date the employee's coverage terminates or the last day of the month during which the dependent no longer qualifies as an eligible dependent.

BASIC BENEFITS

PRE-ADMISSION TESTING - Out-patient diagnostic tests performed prior to inpatient admissions; paid at 100% of UCR. *Usual Customary Reasonable*

SUPPLEMENTAL ACCIDENT EXPENSE - 100% of the first $300.00 for services incurred within 90 days of accident.

INPATIENT HOSPITAL EXPENSE
   DEDUCTIBLE: $50.00.
   ROOM AND BOARD: Up to semi-private room charge. ICU up to $600.00 per day.
   MISCELLANEOUS FEES: Unlimited.
   MAXIMUM PERIOD: 10 days per period of disability.

SURGERY
   CONVERSION FACTOR: $8.50.
   CALENDAR YEAR MAXIMUM: $1,600.00 per person.
   REMARKS: Voluntary sterilizations covered.

ASSISTANT SURGERY
   CONVERSION FACTOR: $8.50.
   CALENDAR YEAR MAXIMUM ALLOWANCE: $320.00 per person. Maximum of 20% of surgeon's allowance or billed charge, whichever is less.
   REMARKS: Voluntary sterilizations covered for women only.

IN-HOSPITAL PHYSICIANS
   DAILY MAXIMUM: $21.00 for the first day; $8.00 per day thereafter.
   MAXIMUM PERIOD: Ten days per period of disability.
   REMARKS: Only one doctor can be paid per day.

ANESTHESIA
   CONVERSION FACTOR: $7.50.
   CALENDAR YEAR MAXIMUM: $300.00 per person.
   REMARKS: Voluntary sterilizations covered.

OUTPATIENT PHYSICIANS VISITS
   CONVERSION FACTOR: $7.50.
   CALENDAR YEAR MAXIMUM: $300.00 per person.
   REMARKS: Chiropractors, MDs, DOs and acupuncturists allowed. Mental and Nervous treatment not covered.

X-RAY AND LABORATORY
   CONVERSION FACTOR: $7.00.
   CALENDAR YEAR MAXIMUM: $200.00 per person.
   REMARKS: Professional component charges covered at 40% of UCR allowance for procedure. Routine procedures are not covered.

MAJOR MEDICAL EXPENSES

INDIVIDUAL CALENDAR YEAR DEDUCTIBLE: $125.00; three month carryover provision.

FAMILY MAXIMUM DEDUCTIBLE: Two family members must satisfy their individual calendar year deductible in order to satisfy the family deductible.

STANDARD COINSURANCE: 80%.

COINSURANCE LIMIT: $400.00 out-of-pocket per individual; $800.00 out-of-pocket per family (not to include deductible, mental and nervous expenses); aggregate.

APPLICATION OF COINSURANCE LIMIT: Coinsurance limit applies in the calendar year in which the limit is met and the following calendar year.

OUTPATIENT MENTAL/NERVOUS EXPENSE: 50% coinsurance while not a hospital inpatient. $500.00 calendar year maximum per person.

LIFETIME MAXIMUM: $1,000,000.00 per person.

ROOM LIMIT: Semi-private room rate.
HOSPITAL DEDUCTIBLE: Not covered.
HOME HEALTH CARE: 120 visits per calendar year. Prior hospital confinement required.
PRE-EXISTING LIMITATION: If treatment received within six months prior to effective date, $2,000.00 maximum payment until patient has been covered continuously under the plan for 12 months.
ANESTHESIA: Calculated using actual time.

MEDICARE

TYPE: Coordination of Benefits.
REMARKS: Assume all Medicare benefits whether or not individual actually enrolled. Subject to all other plan provisions.

EXCLUSIONS

1. Expenses resulting from self-inflicted injuries;
2. Work-related injuries or illnesses;
3. Services for which there is no charge in the absence of insurance;
4. Charges or services in excess of UCR or not medically necessary;
5. Charges for completion of claim forms and failure to keep appointments;
6. Routine or preventative or experimental services;
7. Eye refractions; contacts or glasses; orthotics (eye exercises); radial keratotomy or other procedures for surgical correction of refractive errors;
8. Custodial care;
9. Cosmetic surgery unless for repair of an injury or surgery incurred while covered or result of mastectomy;
10. Dental care of teeth, gums or alveolar process (TMJ) except: a) reduction of fractures of the jaw or facial bones; b) surgical correction of harelip, cleft palate or prognathism; c) removal of salivary duct stones; d) removal of bony cysts of jaw, torus palatinus, leukoplakia or malignant tissues;
11. Reversal of voluntary sterilization;
12. Diagnosis or treatment of infertility including artificial insemination, in vitro fertilization, etc.;
13. Contraceptive materials or devices;
14. Non-therapeutic abortions except where the life of the mother is endangered;
15. Expenses for obesity, weight reduction or diet control unless at least 100 lbs. overweight;
16. Vitamins, food supplements and/or protein supplements;
17. Sex-altering treatments or surgeries or related studies;
18. Orthopedic shoes or other devices for support or treatment of feet except as medically necessary following foot surgery;
19. Bio-feedback related services or treatment;
20. Experimental transplants; and
21. EDTA Chelation therapy.

COMPREHENSIVE DENTAL BENEFITS

DEDUCTIBLE: $50.00.
FAMILY DEDUCTIBLE LIMIT: $150.00; non-aggregate.
COINSURANCE: 80%.
MAXIMUM: No lifetime maximum. $1,000.00 per calendar year maximum.
SPACE MAINTAINER ELIGIBILITY: Employees and dependents.
FLUORIDE ELIGIBILITY: Dependents up to age 18 only.
ORTHODONTIA: No coverage.
CLAIM COST CONTROL: Predetermination of benefits and alternate course of treatment based on customarily employed methods.
PROSTHETIC REPLACEMENTS: Five-year replacement rule applies to replacements of any previously installed prosthetics.
ORDERED AND UNDELIVERED: Excludes expenses for any devices installed or delivered after 30 days following termination of insurance.
ORAL SURGERY: Covered at regular coinsurance rate, subject to calendar year maximum.
EXTENSION OF BENEFITS: 12 months.
MISSING AND UNREPLACED: Applies.

ROVER INSURERS INC
5931 ROLLING ROAD
RONSON, CO 81369
(970) 555-1369

POLICY: **NINJA ENTERPRISES, 1234 Nockout Road, Newton, NM 88012**   Effective 01/01/01

ELIGIBILITY EMPLOYEES must work a minimum of 30 hours per week. They are eligible for coverage the first of the month following one consecutive month of continuous employment. DEPENDENTS are eligible for coverage from birth to age 19, or to age 25 if a full-time student or handicapped prior to 19/25. Is not eligible as a dependent if eligible as an employee. Unmarried natural children, legally adopted children, foster children, and legal guardianship children are included. If both parents are covered by the plan, children may be covered by one parent only.

EFFECTIVE DATE - EMPLOYEE becomes effective, if written application is made prior to eligibility date, on the first of the month following 30 days of continuous employment. If employee is absent from work due to disability on the date of eligibility, coverage will not start until the first of the month following the date of return to active work.

DEPENDENTS become effective on the date the covered employee becomes effective, if written application is made within 31 days of eligibility date. If confined in a hospital on the date of eligibility, coverage will not start until the first of the month following the date the confinement ends. Newborns are automatically covered for the first 14 days following birth. Coverage terminates after 14 days unless written application for coverage is submitted by the employee within 31 days of birth.

TERMINATION OF COVERAGE - EMPLOYEE'S coverage terminates the last day of the month following termination of employment or when the employee ceases to qualify as an eligible employee, or following request for termination of coverage. DEPENDENTS' coverage terminates the date the employee's coverage terminates, or the last day of the month during which the dependent no longer qualifies as an eligible dependent.

EXTENSION OF BENEFITS - If covered under the plan when disabled, may continue coverage in accordance with COBRA. No other extension available.

COMPREHENSIVE MEDICAL BENEFITS

PRE-ADMISSION TESTING - Out patient diagnostic tests performed prior to inpatient admissions are paid at 100% whether through a network provider or not.

PRE-CERTIFICATION - Voluntary, non-emergency inpatient admissions must be approved at least five days prior to admission. Emergency admissions must be pre-certified within 48 hrs. of admission. Benefits are reduced to 50% if not performed as required.

SECOND SURGICAL OPINION - The SSO is paid at 100% of UCR. It is required for the following: bunionectomy, cataract extraction, chemonucleolysis, cholecystectomy, coronary bypass, hemorrhoidectomy, hysterectomy, inguinal herniorrhaphy, laparotomy, laminectomy, mastectomy, meniscectomy, oophorectomy, prostatectomy, salpingectomy, submucous resection, total joint replacement (hip or knee), tenotomy, varicose veins (all procedures). **IF SSO NOT PERFORMED, ALL RELATED EXPENSES PAYABLE AT 50%**

SUPPLEMENTAL ACCIDENT EXPENSE - 100% is paid on the first $500.00 for services incurred within 90 days of the date of accident. Subject to $20.00 co-payment. After $500.00, payments are subject to calendar year deductible. Provider does not have to be a network member to receive 100% benefit. Common accident provision applies.

OUT-PATIENT FACILITY CHARGES PAYABLE AT 100% - Network out-patient facility expenses for following procedures paid 100%. Does not include professional charges: arthroscopy, breast biopsy, cataract removal, bronchoscopy, deviated nasal septum, pilonidal cyst, myringotomy w/tubes, esophagoscopy, colonoscopy, herniorrhaphy (umbilical, to five years old), skin and subsequent lesions, benign and malignant (2cms+).

INDIVIDUAL CALENDAR YEAR DEDUCTIBLE - $150.00; three month carryover provision. All plan services subject to deductible unless otherwise indicated.

FAMILY MAXIMUM DEDUCTIBLE - $300.00, non-aggregate. Two family members must meet individual deductible limit.

STANDARD COINSURANCE - 80% Network; 60% Non-network.

COINSURANCE LIMIT - $1,250.00 out-of-pocket per individual; $2,500.00 out-of-pocket per family. Two individuals must meet their individual out of pocket limit to satisfy the family limit. Limits not to include deductible, mental/nervous expenses, or surgery expenses reduced because SSO not done. 100% of allowed amount paid thereafter for network providers; 80% for non-network providers.

LIFETIME MAXIMUM - $1,000,000.00 per person.

IN/OUTPATIENT MENTAL/NERVOUS - $15,000.00 per person (includes substance abuse and alcoholism).

PRE-EXISTING LIMITATION - If treatment is received within 90 days prior to effective date, no coverage on that condition for six months from the effective date (continuously covered for six consecutive months) unless treatment free for three consecutive months which ends after the effective date of coverage.

INPATIENT HOSPITAL EXPENSE   **IF NO PRE-CERTIFICATION, ADMISSION PAID AT 50%**
DEDUCTIBLE - $200.00, waived for network facilities, applies to non-network. Inpatient hospital expenses not subject to regular Major Medical deductible.
ROOM AND BOARD - Network: 80% of semi-private/ICU; Non-network: 60% of semi-private/ICU.
MISCELLANEOUS FEES - Network: 80%; Non-network: 60%.
EXCLUSIONS - Well baby care. Automatic coverage for first seven days if baby is ill. Otherwise, no coverage.
MENTAL/NERVOUS/PSYCHONEUROTIC - Includes substance abuse and alcoholism. Exclusions: psychological testing, hyperkinetic syndrome, learning disabilities, behavior problems or autistic disease of childhood.
   OUTPATIENT MENTAL AND NERVOUS TREATMENT
   PAYABLE - $60.00 per visit for first 5 visits; $30.00 per visit for next 21 visits.
   COINSURANCE - 80% for first five visits (maximum payable: $60.00 per visit) 50% per visit for next 21 visits (maximum payable: $30.00 per visit).
   CALENDAR YEAR MAXIMUM - 26 visits.
   INPATIENT MENTAL AND NERVOUS TREATMENT
   PHYSICIAN SERVICES - 70% applies to network and non-network providers.
   HOSPITAL SERVICES - 70% network and non-network providers.
   MAXIMUM - 30 days per lifetime or $15,000.00 combined inpatient and outpatient.
   DAY/PARTIAL PROGRAM - Each day in a partial/day program: equals half day in an acute setting.
   PROVIDERS - Psychiatrists and clinical psychologists only.
MAMMOGRAMS
COINSURANCE - 80% Network; 60% Non-network.
REQUIREMENTS - Baseline mammogram for women age 35-39; for ages 40-49, one allowed every two years; for ages 50+, one allowed every year.
X-RAY AND LABORATORY - PROFESSIONAL COMPONENTS - Professional charges paid at 25% of UCR.
DURABLE MEDICAL EQUIPMENT
COINSURANCE - 50%.
REQUIREMENTS - Prescribed by MD; must not be primarily necessary for exercise, environmental control, convenience, comfort or hygiene. Must be an article only useful for the prescribed patient. Covered up to purchase price only.
ANESTHESIA: Use actual time.
MEDICARE
TYPE - Maintenance of benefits.
REMARKS - Assume all Medicare benefits whether or not individual actually enrolled. Subject to all other plan provisions.

EXCLUSIONS
1. Expenses resulting from self-inflicted injuries;
2. Work-related injuries or illnesses;
3. Services for which there is no charge in the absence of insurance;
4. Charges or services in excess of UCR or not medically necessary;
5. Pre-existing conditions;
6. Charges for completion of claim forms and failure to keep appointments;
7. Routine or preventative or experimental services;
8. Eye refractions; contacts or glasses; orthotics (eye exercises); radial keratotomy or other procedures for surgical correction of refractive errors;
9. Custodial care;
10. Cosmetic surgery unless for repair of an injury or surgery incurred while covered or result of mastectomy;
11. Dental care of teeth, gums or alveolar process (TMJ) except: a) reduction of fractures of the jaw or facial bones; b) surgical correction of harelip, cleft palate or prognathism; c) removal of salivary duct stones; d) removal of bony cysts of jaw, torus palatinus, leukoplakia or malignant tissues.
12. Reversal of voluntary sterilization;
13. Diagnosis or treatment of infertility including artificial insemination, in vitro fertilization, etc.;
14. Contraceptive materials or devices;
15. Pregnancy; pregnancy-related expenses of dependent children for the delivery including Caesarian section. Related illnesses may be covered such as pre-eclampsia, vaginal bleeding, etc.;
16. Non-therapeutic abortions except where the life of the mother is endangered

WINTER INSURANCE CO, 9763 WESTERN WAY, WHITTIER, CO 82963, (970) 555-2963
COMPANY: ABC CORPORATION, POLICY NAME: ABC, EFFECTIVE DATE: 06/01/02

ELIGIBILITY

EMPLOYEE: Must work a minimum of 35 hours per week. Is eligible for coverage the first of the month following 60 consecutive days of continuous employment.
DEPENDENTS: Are eligible for coverage from birth to age 19, or to age 24 if a full-time student or handicapped prior to age 19/24 (proof of disability must be furnished within 31 days after dependent reaches limiting age). Dependent is not eligible as a dependent if eligible as an employee. Unmarried natural children, legally adopted and foster children are included (also includes legal guardianship). If both parents are covered by the plan, children may be covered by one employee only.

EFFECTIVE DATE

EMPLOYEE: If written application is made prior to the eligibility date, coverage becomes effective the first of the month following 60 days of employment.
DEPENDENTS: The date acquired by the covered employee becomes the effective date if written application is made within 31 days of the eligibility date. Newborns are automatically covered for the first seven days following birth. Coverage will terminate after seven days unless written application for coverage is submitted by the employee within 31 days of birth.

TERMINATION OF COVERAGE

EMPLOYEE: Coverage terminates the last day of the month following termination of employment or when the employee ceases to qualify as an eligible employee, or following request for termination of coverage.
DEPENDENTS: Coverage terminates the date the employee's coverage terminates, or the last day of the month during which the dependent no longer qualifies as an eligible dependent.

EXTENSION OF BENEFITS - If covered under the plan when disabled, employee may continue coverage for 12 months following the date of termination or until no longer disabled, whichever is less.

COMPREHENSIVE MEDICAL BENEFITS

SUPPLEMENTAL ACCIDENT EXPENSE - 100% of first $300.00 for services incurred within 120 days of date of accident. Not subject to deductible.

PLAN BENEFITS
INDIVIDUAL CALENDAR YEAR DEDUCTIBLE:$100.00; three month carry-over provision.
FAMILY MAXIMUM DEDUCTIBLE: $200.00, aggregate.
STANDARD COINSURANCE: 90% except 100% of hospital room and board expenses for 365 days per lifetime.

COINSURANCE LIMIT: $750.00 out-of-pocket per individual; $1,500.00 out-of-pocket per family. Two separate members must satisfy the individual limit, not to include deductible, mental or nervous expenses. Applies only in the calendar year in which the limit is met.
LIFETIME MAXIMUM: $300,000.00 per person.
OUTPATIENT MENTAL AND NERVOUS LIFETIME MAXIMUM: $10,000.00 per person (includes substance abuse and alcoholism). No inpatient maximum.
PRE-EXISTING LIMITATION: On 6/1/99 no restriction. After 6/1/99, if treatment received within 90 days prior to effective date, no coverage for that condition for 12 months from the effective date (continuously covered for 12 months) unless treatment free for three consecutive months ending after the effective date of coverage.

X-RAY AND LABORATORY
REMARKS: Professional component charges covered at 40% of UCR allowance for procedure.   Routine procedures are not covered.

INPATIENT HOSPITAL EXPENSE
Room and board payable at 100% of semi-private room rate. Miscellaneous expenses covered at 90%. Non-medically necessary, well baby care and cosmetic services excluded. Personal comfort items not covered.

MENTAL/NERVOUS/PSYCHONEUROTIC
INCLUDES SUBSTANCE ABUSE AND ALCOHOLISM. Exclusions: psychological testing.

OUTPATIENT MENTAL/NERVOUS TREATMENT
COINSURANCE: 50% while not hospital confined.
CALENDAR YEAR MAXIMUM: None.
LIFETIME MAXIMUM: $10,000.00 lifetime maximum, applies to outpatient expenses only.

INPATIENT MENTAL/NERVOUS TREATMENT
PHYSICIAN SERVICES: Covered at 90%.
HOSPITAL SERVICES: Covered at 90%.
ALLOWED PROVIDERS: Psychiatrists and clinical psychologists. Marriage and Family Child Counselor and Licensed Clinical Social Worker allowed with referral from MD.

EXTENDED CARE FACILITY
LIFETIME MAXIMUM: 60 days.
HOSPITAL SERVICES: 80% of billed room and board charge.
REQUIREMENTS: Stay must begin within 14 days of acute hospital stay of at least 3 days. Extended care must be due to same disability that caused hospitalization and continued hospital care would otherwise be required.

DURABLE MEDICAL EQUIPMENT
COINSURANCE: Covered at 90%.
REQUIREMENTS: Must be prescribed by MD. Must not be primarily necessary for exercise, environmental control,

convenience, comfort or hygiene. Must only useful for the prescribed patient. Covered up to purchase price only.

ANESTHESIA
Computed using block time.

REMARKS
Covered expenses include charges for the initial set of contact lenses which are necessary due to cataract surgery. Handicapped children are limited to a $15,000.00 lifetime maximum after attainment of age 19. Coordination of Benefits according to National Association of Insurance Carriers (NAIC) guidelines. Subject to Third Party Liability and subrogation.

MEDICARE INTEGRATION
TYPE: Non-duplication of benefits applies.
REMARKS: Assume all Medicare benefits whether or not individual actually enrolled.

EXCLUSIONS
1. Expenses resulting from self-inflicted injuries, work related injuries or illnesses;
2. Charges or services: in excess of UCR, not medically necessary, for completion of claim forms, for failure to keep appointments; for routine, preventative or experimental services;
3. Eye refractions; contacts or glasses; orthotics (eye exercises); radial keratotomy or other procedures for surgical correction of refractive errors;
4. Custodial care and/or convalescent facility coverage;
5. Cosmetic surgery unless for repair of an injury or surgery incurred while covered or result of mastectomy;
6. Diagnosis or treatment of infertility including artificial insemination, in vitro fertilization, etc., contraceptive materials or devices, non-therapeutic abortions except where the life of the mother is endangered, reversal of voluntary sterilization;
7. Pregnancy-related expenses for dependent children.
8. Expenses for obesity, weight reduction or diet control unless at least 100 lbs. overweight;
9. Vitamins, food supplements and/or protein supplements;
10. Sex altering treatments or surgeries or related studies;
11. Orthopedic shoes or other devices for support or treatment of feet except as medically necessary following foot surgery; and
12. Bio-feedback related services or treatment, EDTA chelation therapy.

COMPREHENSIVE DENTAL BENEFITS

INTEGRATED: Deductible provisions, lifetime maximum and coinsurance limit combined with comprehensive Major Medical.
CALENDAR YEAR DEDUCTIBLE: $100.00.
DEDUCTIBLE CARRYOVER: No carryover.
FAMILY DEDUCTIBLE LIMIT: $200.00, aggregate.
COINSURANCE: 90%.
COINSURANCE LIMIT: $500.00 (Patient responsibility, not to include disallowed amounts or the deductible.)
APPLICATION OF COINSURANCE LIMIT: Applies only in the calendar year in which the limit is met.
FAMILY COINSURANCE LIMIT: $1,000.00.
MAXIMUM: $300,000.00 lifetime.
MAXIMUM PER CALENDAR YEAR: $1,500.00.
ORTHODONTIA ELIGIBILITY: Dependents only.
SPACE MAINTAINER ELIGIBILITY: Dependents only.
FLUORIDE ELIGIBILITY: Employees and dependents.
ORTHODONTIA: 90% coinsurance.
ORTHODONTIC MAXIMUM: $800.00 lifetime; not subject to the 1,500.00 calendar year maximum.
CLAIM COST CONTROL OPTIONS: Predetermination of benefits required on claims over $500.00; alternate course of treatment based on customarily employed method.
PROSTHETIC REPLACEMENTS: Five-year rule applies to replacement of any previously installed prosthetics.
ORDERED AND UNDELIVERED: Excludes expenses for any devices installed or delivered after 30 days following termination date of insurance.
MISSING AND UNREPLACED EXCLUSION: Applies.
REMARKS: Orthodontic benefits are payable as incurred, rather than amortized over the period of time during which work is performed.

Exercise 5 – 1

Directions: Read through the ABC (Winter Insurance) contract and list the amounts for the following provisions in the space provided. Do not concern yourself with the definitions of terms or how to calculate the amounts, since these subjects will be covered in another chapter.

1. What is the individual deductible amount? _____ $100.00
2. What is the dependent eligibility age limit? _19 yrs — 24 or full time student._
3. What is the family calendar year deductible? _____ $200.
4. What is the individual coinsurance limit? _____
5. What is the coinsurance percentage? _____ 150%
6. What is the lifetime maximum amount? _____ $350
7. How many hours must the employee work to be eligible? _____ 35 hrs. week
8. Does the contract include dental coverage? _____ yes
9. What is the family coinsurance limit? _____ $1,500.00
10. Is the family coinsurance aggregate or non-aggregate? _____ aggregate
11. Is there a carryover provision on the individual deductible? _____ yes - 3 months
12. How many months must the employee work before coverage becomes effective? _2 months_
13. What is the amount of the basic accident benefit? _____ $350   100% of the $350
14. What basic benefits does it have? _____
15. What are the terms of the accident benefit? _100% of the first $300_

Exercise 5 – 2

Directions: Read through the XYZ (Ball Insurance Carriers) contract and list the amounts for the following provisions in the space provided.

1. What is the individual deductible amount? _____ $125 per year
2. What is the dependent eligibility age limit? _____ 19 or 23 if full-time
3. What is the family calendar year deductible? _____
4. What is the individual coinsurance limit? _____ $450.00
5. What is the coinsurance percentage? _____ 80%
6. What is the lifetime maximum amount? _____ 1 million dollar per person.
7. How many hours must the employee work to be eligible? _____ 30 hrs. per week
8. Does the contract include dental coverage? _____ yes
9. What is the family coinsurance limit? _____ $800.00
10. Is the family coinsurance aggregate or non-aggregate? _____ aggregate
11. Is there a carryover provision on the individual deductible? _____
12. How many months must the employee work before coverage becomes effective? _3 con. month_
13. What is the amount of the basic accident benefit? _100% of first $300._
14. What basic benefits does it have? _____
15. What are the terms of the accident benefit? _100% of the first $300 for services within 90 days of accident_

Exercise 5 – 3

Directions: Read through the Ninja (Rover Insurers) contract and list the amounts for the following provisions in the space provided.

1. What is the individual deductible amount? _$150.00_
2. What is the dependent eligibility age limit? _19 25 - Full time student_
3. What is the family calendar year deductible? _$300 - Two family must meet deductible_
4. What is the individual coinsurance limit? _$1250_
5. What is the coinsurance percentage? _80% in-network 60% out of network_
6. What is the lifetime maximum amount? _$1 million_
7. How many hours must the employee work to be eligible? _30 hrs_
8. Does the contract include dental coverage? _NO_
9. What is the family coinsurance limit? _$2500_
10. Is the family coinsurance aggregate or non-aggregate? _aggregate_
11. Is there a carryover provision on the individual deductible? _yes_
12. How many months must the employee work before coverage becomes effective? _1 month_
13. What is the amount of the basic accident benefit? _100% of first $500_
14. What basic benefits does the contract have? _____
15. What are the terms of the accident benefit? _100% on first $500 - $20 co-pay Regular policy will kick in._

Exercise 5 – 4

Directions: Read the dental contracts and list the amounts for the following dental provisions in the spaces provided.

	ABC	XYZ	Ninja
1. What is the individual deductible amount?	100	50	
2. What is the dependent eligibility age limit?	birth - 19	birth - 19 or 23	NA
3. What is the family calendar year deductible?		150	
4. What is the calendar year maximum?	1500	1000	NA
5. What is the coinsurance percentage?	90%	80%	NA
6. How many hours must the employee work to be eligible?	35	30	NA
7. Are orthodontics covered?	Dependent only	No	NA
8. Is oral surgery covered?	NO	yes	NA
9. Are fluoride treatments covered for a 20-year-old?	yes if full time	NO	N/A
10. Does the missing and unreplaced rule apply?	yes	yes	N/A

Exercise 5 – 5

Directions: Read the following list of exclusions and place an E in the space provided if the service is excluded under the contract. Place an N/E in the space provided if the service is not excluded under the contract.

	ABC	XYZ	Ninja
1. Sex-altering treatments or surgeries or related studies.			
2. Work-related injuries or illnesses.			
3. Changes or services in excess of UCR.			
4. Charge made for failure to keep an appointment.			
5. Routine or preventative or experimental services.			
6. Mental/Nervous expenses above $15,000			
7. Orthopedic shoes (medically necessary) following foot surgery.			
8. Radial keratotomy.			
9. Cosmetic surgery for breast following mastectomy.			
10. Services for which there is no charge in the absence of insurance.			
11. Surgical correction of cleft palate.			
12. Custodial care.			
13. Reversal of voluntary sterilization.			
14. Contraceptive materials or devices.			
15. Expenses resulting from self-inflicted injuries.			
16. Elective abortions.			
17. Expenses for weight reduction for someone 90 lbs. overweight.			
18. Charges for services not medically necessary.			
19. Vitamins, food supplements, and/or protein supplements.			
20. Experimental transplants.			

Honors Certification™

The Honors Certification™ challenge for this chapter is a written test. You will be given questions pertaining to the information covered in this chapter. In addition you will be given a number of questions dealing with the three contracts presented. Any incorrect answers will result in a deduction of between 3% and 5% from your grade. You must achieve a score of 80% to pass this test. If you fail the test on your first attempt you may retake the test one additional time. The information included in the second test may be different from that included in the first test.

6 Eligibility

In this chapter you will learn:

- To define eligibility and termination of coverage and explain their purposes.
- Basic eligibility guidelines.
- To determine the patient's eligibility status.
- To identify and explain COBRA.

Key words and concepts you will learn in this chapter:

Contributory Plan – The employees contribute to the cost of the coverage, usually through payroll deductions.

Dependent – The employee's legal spouse or domestic partner, and unmarried children within the age limitations specified by the plan who rely on the employee for daily maintenance and care.

Eligibility – Fit to be chosen or legally or morally qualified. The qualifications which make the person eligible for coverage

Evidence of Insurability – The employee will be required to submit proof of good health usually by filling out a health questionnaire.

Non-Contributory Plan – Insurance where the employer bears the complete cost of the coverage and the employee does not contribute.

Open Enrollment – A process that allows late applicants to enroll in a plan without having to complete evidence of insurability.

Eligibility is defined as the quality or qualities that make someone eligible. **Eligible** is defined as fit to be chosen or legally or morally qualified. Therefore, as far as insurance is concerned, eligibility means those qualities or requirements that a person must meet to be covered by the plan. Do not confuse "eligible" with "effective." In insurance, these are two very different concepts. A person can be eligible for coverage without the coverage ever becoming effective. (The concept of coverage becoming effective will be covered later in this chapter).

The definition of an eligible person varies from plan to plan. However, most plans have separate definitions for eligible employees or subscribers compared with eligible dependents. The requirements for the insured can include such things as the number of hours worked for the policyholder and a minimum of months that the employee has been employed by the policyholder. The requirements for the dependents of the insured can include such things as being a lawful spouse, domestic partner or dependent child of the insured, being under a certain age limit, or attending school full-time. The requirement for dependent coverage may also include a domestic partner. The eligibility of this relationship varies by plan as well as by insurance company. Before verifying eligibility and benefits, be sure to review the plan definition of an eligible dependent and the company policy for covering domestic partners.

It is important for the health claims examiner to understand the concept of eligibility and the eligibility requirements under each contract in order to process claims correctly.

Employee Eligibility

Most contracts define participants (also called employees, subscribers, members, or insureds) according to the minimum number of hours that the employee or subscriber must work per specified period of time, which is usually per week. Generally, part-time employees and full-time employees working fewer than 30 hours per week are not considered eligible for coverage.

Other contracts define the subscriber in terms of membership in an organization, such as the CPA Society or real estate societies. A minimum number of hours worked may also apply in these circumstances.

Partners and proprietors are also considered participants as long as they engage in the conduct of business on a full-time basis or a minimum number of hours per week.

For example, refer to the XYZ Contract. As indicated therein, the employee must:

- Routinely work a minimum of 30 hours per week.
- Be considered a full-time employee. (Even though the contract does not specifically indicate this, it is an industry standard). Therefore, unless the booklet or contract says otherwise, this is to be assumed.
- Work three consecutive months to be eligible. Coverage may become effective the first of the month following the completion of three months of work (application must still be made).

For example, suppose an employee is hired on 3/2 and works 40 hours per week. Since 6/2 is past the first of the month, coverage may become effective the first of the month following the completion of the three-month waiting period, or 7/1.

Under many union contracts, eligibility depends on the number of hours the member worked during the previous year or the previous month. With unions, a member may work for multiple employers during a month or week. As long as the employer is a member of the union and the employee is a member of the union, hours are accumulated toward the satisfaction of the hourly requirement.

For example, a common type of wording for union contracts is: If you are a bargaining unit employee, you will become eligible for benefits on the first day of the second month following any three consecutive months during which you worked for one or more contributing employers a minimum total of 300 hours. Once eligibility has been established, you and your dependents will be covered for a minimum of three consecutive months.

For example, if you worked:

January	110 hr	Your coverage
February	0 hr	will begin May 1.
March	190 hr	
Total	300 hr	

In this example, the requirements are:

- 300 hours in any consecutive three-month period.
- Eligibility begins on the first day of the second month following the three consecutive months.
- Coverage will be for a minimum of three consecutive months.

It is not unusual for a plan to have different eligibility provisions for different classifications of employees. For example, separate provisions may be given for employees classified as Active Officers, Board Members, Management Employees, or Retired Employees. Special provisions may also be applicable to employees who are laid off or on leave. Therefore, it is very important to check the plan provisions to determine whether there are a variety of classifications and, if so, to know how to verify the specific classifications of the claimants whose claims you are handling.

Dependent Eligibility

The first step in determining whether a dependent is eligible is to verify whether the dependent fits the definition of an eligible dependent. Defining a dependent is much more difficult than defining an employee because of the complex family and social dynamics in our society. A plan must try as much as possible to define all the dependents that can exist and to place those definitions into either covered or non-covered categories.

In general, "**dependent**" means:

1. The employee's legal spouse (either through marriage or through common-law status if recognized by the state in which they are residing. The employee and spouse cannot be divorced or legally separated, even if there is a court decree stating that the employee is responsible for providing medical coverage.)

2. Dependent, unmarried children within the age limitations specified by the plan. The term "dependent" means that the child must rely on the employee for daily maintenance and care. The term "children" always includes one's natural children and may include:

   a. Adopted children for whom the final court order has been issued or for whom it is specified by the adoption agreement during any state-mandated waiting period that the adoptive parents provide for all medical care.

   b. Stepchildren residing with the employee.

   c. Grandchildren residing with the employee, who depend on the employee for more than 50% of their support.

   d. Foster children whose foster child agreement specifies that the state is not responsible for their health care and that the foster parents are responsible. (Usually, the state maintains responsibility for the foster children's health care).

   e. Any other children related to the employee by blood or marriage, provided that they are living in a regular parent-child relationship and dependant on the employee for support and maintenance. In the case of grandchildren, a regular parent-child relationship does not exist if either of the child's parents also reside with the employee.

Plans will further specify that to be eligible, children must be under a certain age, usually 18 or 19 years. Unmarried children of a specified age limitation, usually 23 through 25 years of age, who attend a licensed or accredited school on a full-time basis, are generally also eligible. For coverage to continue during vacation periods, the child must be scheduled and registered to enter school on the next enrollment date.

In conjunction with this requirement, plans must define what is considered a "licensed" or "accredited" school. Many plans cover only colleges or universities. Other plans allow vocational schools and rehabilitation schools. The plan must specify what is considered to be full-time. Most schools define what constitutes a full-time student, and most plans accept the school specific definition. However, this must be verified by reading the contract provisions.

Many states have enacted legislation concerning coverage for dependent children from birth. Although specific wording and intent are determined by individual state legislation, the laws generally provide that newborn children can be afforded the same eligibility for accident and health coverage as any other dependent and are covered from birth for treatment of a disease or injury. Pre-existing limitations by definition cannot be applied to newborn children. This automatic coverage is generally for an initial 31-day period from date of birth. For such coverage to continue past the 31-day period, the employee must:

- Complete any required enrollment form.
- Make any required contributions, effective from the date of birth.

The law does not usually create an obligation for plans to pay for well-baby or custodial care, however, few states require insured plans to have well-child care provisions. Refer to the mandates listed in the **General Plan Provisions** chapter.

Many plans also specify that a person who is eligible as an employee cannot be enrolled as a dependent on the same plan. And, if both husband and wife are covered under the same plan as employees, one or the other, not both, may elect to cover their dependents. This prevents a particular child from being covered as a dependent under both parents. Some self-funded plans do permit dual coverage under the same plan, for husbands, wives, and dependent children. Unless specifically excluded from being covered as both employees and dependents or as a dependent under both parents, dual coverage is permitted. Be sure to review the contract for the definition of dependent coverage.

Employee Effective Date of Coverage

For an eligible employee's coverage or a dependent's coverage to become effective, the person is usually required to complete the necessary enrollment papers prior to the date of eligibility.

The rules defining the effective date of coverage vary, depending on whether the plan is considered a contributory or non-contributory plan.

In a **contributory plan**, the employees contribute to the cost of the coverage, usually through payroll deductions. In a **non-contributory plan**, the employer bears the complete cost of the coverage and the employee does not contribute.

In a contributory plan:

- The employee must complete the enrollment card listing himself or herself and the dependents he or she wants to be covered; usually, all eligible dependents must be listed.
- Such application must be received by the employer or by the plan administrator on or before the eligibility date of the coverage for coverage to become effective on that date.
- The employee must also authorize the applicable payroll deductions or make the necessary premium payments.

Example: Sammy Subscriber begins working for White Corp on 1/15. The winter contract states he will become eligible on the first of the month after 90 days of employment. Therefore, he became eligible on 4/1. If he has not completed the enrollment card, turned it in to the employer, and made arrangements for payment before 4/1, his insurance will not become effective. Thus, he will not be insured.

If the enrollment card is not received on or before the eligibility date of coverage, but is received within one month (or 30 or 31 days) after the date of eligibility, the employee is considered to be a "late applicant" and coverage will begin either on the date of application or the first or fifteenth of the month following the date of application (the plan provisions must specify which of the time limitations are to be applied).

Example: Sammy thought he had finished all the paperwork and would be enrolled on 4/1. However, on 4/2 the employer informed him that he never got the enrollment card. Sammy discovers it in his desk at work and turns it in on 4/2. Sammy is then considered a late applicant. Since his contract stipulates that late applicants' coverage becomes effective on the first of the month following application. Sammy will not be covered until 5/1.

If the enrollment application is not submitted within one month (or 30 or 31 days) after the date of eligibility, the employee may be required to submit proof of good health. Also known as **evidence of insurability** this is often a health questionnaire, required for the policy holder and all eligible dependents seeking coverage. The questionnaire will be submitted to the medical consultants of the insurer or plan administrator for review. If the participant appears to be a good "risk," that is, he or she does not appear to have any active illness or conditions, coverage may be approved. If the participant appears to be a poor risk because of active illnesses, coverage may not be approved and the employee and dependents may not be able to obtain coverage under the plan at that time (some plans provide for open enrollment periods, which will be discussed later.) Dependents cannot be covered unless the employee is covered. Therefore, if the dependents are healthy but the employee is not and the employee's eligibility is denied, even though the dependents may be a good risk, they will not be covered under the plan.

> *Example:* Patty Participant also began working for White Corporation on 1/15. However, she chose not to enroll in the insurance program at that time. On 6/1 she changed her mind, filled out the enrollment card, and made arrangements for the premiums to be deducted from her check. Since she is enrolling more than one month after becoming eligible, she must complete a health questionnaire. The insurer will review the questionnaire. If they decide she is a good risk, they will insure her. Her coverage will become effective on 6/1 or 7/1 depending on the terms of the contract.

In a non-contributory plan in which the employer pays the full cost, a request for coverage is not necessary except for record purposes and beneficiary designations. Coverage for employees and, in some instances, their dependents begins automatically on the employee's eligibility date, regardless of when the enrollment application is completed and submitted. If the insurer or administrator is not informed of an employee's eligibility on the appropriate date and a claim or an enrollment card is subsequently submitted, the insurer/administrator will automatically add the member and bill the employer for all back premiums due. After the back premiums are paid, the claim(s) will be paid. Evidence of insurability is not required in these cases and there are not considered to be any "late applicants" on the plan.

Be aware that a plan can be non-contributory for the employee and contributory for the dependents. Therefore, a combination of the above rules may apply. For example, a company provides free health insurance for their employees (non-contributory), but any employees who also want coverage for their spouse and children must pay for it (contributory).

Whether the group is contributory or non-contributory, the usual effective date of coverage is deferred if on the effective date the employee is absent from work because of illness or injury. Most plans stipulate that for coverage to become effective, the employee must have completed either a full day of active work on that date or a full day of active work on the last regularly scheduled work day and is able to work on the date of eligibility. If the employee does not meet these requirements, the coverage will become effective on the date he or she returns to active work.

> *Example:* Sammy Subscriber's insurance was to become effective on 5/1. However, on 4/30 he came down with a bad cold and was off for a week. He returned on 5/7. Therefore, his insurance coverage will not begin until 5/7.

Active work and **actively at work** usually means performing the regular duties for a full workday for the employer.

Dependent Effective Date of Coverage

The rules regarding the effective date of dependents are similar to the rules for employees, since the rules depend on whether the plan is contributory or non-contributory.

In the case of an employee, the plan usually makes a stipulation regarding being actively at work. A similar provision is also made for dependents. However, since a dependent often does not work, policies usually state that if a dependent is in the hospital, the coverage for that dependent becomes effective on the day after the date of discharge, or the date on which the dependent is able to perform all the duties he or she usually performs. In other words, if the dependent is of school age, coverage might begin when the child returns to school. An exception would be that of a newborn child, who is usually born in a hospital. In such a case, coverage begins immediately.

In a contributory plan, dependents are handled in the same way as with employees regarding late enrollment. However, many contributory plans require that for dependent coverage, all eligible dependents must be enrolled in the plan. This requirement prevents an employee from selectively putting sick dependents on one plan and healthy dependents on another plan.

Open Enrollment

Open enrollment is a process that allows late applicants to enroll in a plan without having to complete evidence of insurability. This enrollment process usually occurs on the anniversary date of the plan, and usually occurs when an employer has multiple plan options. For example, larger employers are required by law to offer their employees an HMO option. These employers often offer an HMO plan, a low-indemnity plan (i.e., higher deductibles, lower coinsurance payable by the plan), and perhaps a high-indemnity plan (lower deductible, higher coinsurance payable by the plan). By having an open enrollment period, employees may switch from one plan to another without penalties or a gap in coverage and without having to complete a health statement.

Termination of Coverage

The provisions for terminating an individual's coverage vary according to the type of group and how the employer wants the plan administered. In a union or association group, for example, coverage terminates when the employer terminates the group's membership in the union or association. The most common termination provisions are those based on conditions pertaining to employment. Coverage is usually terminated under one of these conditions:

- The group policy terminates (i.e., a company terminates the policy).
- The policy is amended to terminate the eligibility of the class of employees to which the individual belongs (i.e., the employer decides they will no longer cover commissioned sales people).
- The employee transfers out of a class covered by the policy (i.e., an employee goes from full time to part time).
- Active employment ceases (i.e., the employee quits).
- The employee ceases to pay the required contributions for the coverage.

When coverage ceases, regardless of the reason, some form of continuation of coverage may be available.

Continuation of Coverage

Many plans allow benefits to extend beyond the normal date or terms of eligibility. These extensions can be of several types, depending on the reason for the continuation (i.e., disability, COBRA). We will discuss the main situations in which benefits are extended beyond normal eligibility and the requirements for continuing such coverage.

An employee or dependent losing coverage may qualify for continuation of benefits under more than one provision. It should be noted that the order in which these provisions apply is important. Continuation is first considered under COBRA, because it is premium based and covers all conditions. The extension of benefits for disability is second because the only person eligible for coverage under this provision is the person and only the disabling condition is covered. The coverage is usually for 12 months and the premium contributions are waived. The conversion privilege is the last coverage option to be exercised.

Extension of Benefits

Because extension of benefits for disability and conversion are more easily explained, we will cover those first. Most plans contain an extended benefits provision for totally disabled members. This type of provision requires that:

- The person was eligible and covered under the plan when his or her coverage terminated.
- As of the termination date, the person was totally disabled due to an injury or illness.
- Only covered expenses (as defined by the plan provisions) incurred for the illness or injury causing the disability will be considered eligible for benefit consideration.
- Coverage will last only for the length of time as specified in the policy.

The latter requirements indicate that first there must be documented proof that the person was totally disabled with an injury or illness when he or she terminated. Second, only eligible expenses incurred for the injury or illness causing the disability are considered for benefits after the termination date.

Refer to the three contracts. As indicated, ABC and XYZ contracts both have a standard extension of benefits provision. Coverage will continue for 12 months from the date of termination under the plan or until the person is no longer totally disabled, whichever interval is less. Ninja Enterprises does not have an extension of benefits provision.

Therefore, in determining whether an extension of benefits provision is applicable, the following steps must be followed:

1. Was the member eligible and effective under the plan when coverage terminated? If no, the investigation would end, since the member could not continue coverage if he or she was not eligible and effective on the plan when the coverage terminated. If yes, then:
2. Was the member totally disabled at the time the coverage terminated? If no, extension of benefits would not apply. If yes, then:
3. A letter from the attending physician must be obtained stating the condition or conditions causing the disability, the date the member became totally disabled, and the anticipated end of the total disability.
4. Also, if the employee is claiming disability, try to find out if he or she is employed anywhere. Sometimes, members apply for this type of extension because premiums are not required (continuation is provided for the maximum 12 months free of charge to the employee but only for the person totally disabled) and the member wants coverage between jobs.

Conversion Policies

Most states have legislatively mandated that insurance policies contain a continuation of coverage provision known as conversion. **Conversion** permits employees and dependents to continue their insurance protection on an individual basis when their coverage under a group plan ceases because:

- The employee's employment in the class of employees insured under the group policy terminates.
- The policy is amended to terminate coverage for the class to which the employee belongs.
- The employee terminates employment with the employer.
- A dependent child reaches the plan limiting age.
- The employee and spouse are divorced or legally separated so that the spouse is no longer considered eligible under the provisions of the plan.

Evidence of insurability is not required, but the person must apply in writing and pay the required premiums within a specified time period of the date of termination of coverage under the group plan (usually 31 days). Those who voluntarily discontinue their insurance coverage while still employed are not eligible to convert, nor is the conversion privilege available when the employer's complete policy is terminated.

As a rule, conversion policies are extremely expensive. It is not uncommon for a quarterly conversion policy premium to be $5000 to $10,000. The reason for this high premium is that usually only those employees who are disabled and extremely ill convert their policy. Because of the high experience on the conversion policy, the resulting premiums are also very high.

Unfortunately, if an individual is so ill that he or she must cease working, it is extremely difficult to afford the high premiums. Nevertheless, it is an available option.

COBRA

On April 7, 1986, President Ronald Reagan signed into law HR3128, the Consolidated Omnibus Budget Reconciliation Act of 1985 (COBRA), also referred to hereafter as **continuation of coverage**. Within this act, there was a very significant provision, Title X, which has had profound effects on employee welfare benefits plans.

Previous to COBRA, employers were generally not required to provide continuation of group insurance coverage for individuals who ceased to be eligible for such coverage. The objective of Congress through Title X was to require employers to permit employees and their dependents to purchase transitional health care coverage at favorable group rates until replacement coverage could be obtained. The intended result was to reduce the number of people without health care coverage.

Title X is composed of the following amendments:

Section 10001	Amendments to the Internal Revenue Code (IRC).
Section 10002	Amendments to the Employee Retirement Income Security Act (ERISA).
Section 10003	Amendments to the Public Health Service Act (PHSA).

The effect of these amendments is to require virtually every type of group health plan, insured or self-funded, to provide the option of self-payment for continuation of coverage. And, since the penalties for nonconformance will be administered by the IRS, noncompliance will be costly.

Cobra Applicability

COBRA applies to all private employers who regularly employ 20 or more employees (including both full-time and part-time) on a typical working day. It applies to single employer health plans, multiple employer trust plans, collectively bargained plans, insured plans, and self-funded plans.

Under the amendment to the Public Health Service Act (PHSA) (Section 10003), certain state and local governmental employers of 20 or more employees are required to offer continuation of coverage even though these employers are exempt from both taxes and ERISA. The applicability of COBRA to state and local governmental employers is based on the receipt of funds under PHSA. If the state or local governmental employer received funds under PHSA, compliance is required.

In summation, all employee group health benefit plans are required to comply in offering continuation of coverage, with the exception of the following:

- Any group health plan for any calendar year if the employer normally maintained fewer than 20 employees on a typical business day during the preceding calendar year.
- Certain church plans.
- Group health plans maintained by state or local governmental employers who do not receive funds under PHSA.
- Group health plans maintained for employees by the government of the District of Columbia or any territory or possession of the United States.

Governmental and nongovernmental group health plans that are not collectively bargained were subject to the COBRA requirements as of the first of the plan year, beginning subsequent to June 30, 1986.

Qualified Beneficiaries

The option of self-payment continuation of coverage must be offered by the affected employers to certain individuals referred to as qualified beneficiaries. A **qualified beneficiary** is defined as anyone who, on the day before the Qualifying Event, is covered under the health coverage plan as an employee, a dependent spouse or a dependent child.

Qualifying Event

The term **qualifying event** refers to one of the following events, which results in the loss of eligibility under the employer sponsored health plan:

- Voluntary or involuntary termination of employment, with the exception of termination for gross misconduct.
- Reduction in work hours.
- Eligibility of the employee only for Medicare.
- Death of the employee.
- Divorce or legal separation.
- Disqualification of a dependent child as an eligible dependent.

Employers are required to offer the self-pay continuation of coverage option to the following:

- Terminated or laid-off employees (except those terminated for gross misconduct); employees for whom a reduction in work hours would result in the loss of coverage; retired employees who are not eligible for Medicare.
- The surviving spouse and dependent children of a deceased employee.
- Divorced spouses and their dependent children.
- Spouses and dependent children of employees who are eligible for Medicare.
- Dependent children who cease to meet the plan definition of a "dependent child."

There are no length of service requirements connected to COBRA. As long as the employee was covered under the employer-sponsored health plan prior to the qualifying event, he or she has the right to elect continuation. This right also applies to the employee's spouse and dependent children, provided they were covered under the plan the day before the event.

The covered employee or spouse (when spouse is the elector) may act as the agent for the entire family. It is not necessary for each family member to make an individual election.

Duration of Coverage

COBRA requires that affected employers permit employees and covered dependents, at the time their coverage would cease because of a qualifying event, to elect continuation of their insurance coverage for up to 18, 29, or 36 months, depending on the circumstances.

For employees and their dependents, a maximum of 18 months is allowed after one of the following events:

- Voluntary or involuntary termination of employment other than for gross misconduct.
- Reduction of work hours below the plan eligibility requirements.

For employees or dependents who are permanently disabled at the time of the event, coverage may be continued for up to 29 months rather than 18 months. The plan may use the Social Security standard of permanent disability as a qualifying condition of the extended coverage.

For covered dependents only, a maximum of 36 months of continued coverage is allowed after one of the following events:

- Death of the employee.
- Divorce or legal separation from the employee.
- The employee becomes eligible for Medicare.
- A child ceases to be an eligible dependent as defined by the plan provisions.

If a second qualifying event occurs during the time of the continuation of coverage for dependents, the maximum time allowed can be increased from 18 to 36 months if a qualifying event occurs as indicated above. For example, an employee terminates (18 months) during this 18 months; the child ceases to be an eligible dependent. That dependent may continue coverage but other family members may not. Also, it may be possible to extend coverage from 18 to 29 months if an employee becomes totally disabled while covered. However, coverage cannot be extended beyond 29 months for employees.

Notification of Eligibility

One of the most important aspects of the COBRA Act is the requirement that eligible members be informed of their eligibility for COBRA. Many employers have interpreted this to mean that when an employee terminates coverage, usually in the form of employment termination, he or she will be informed of the COBRA rights. However, this procedure addresses only a portion of those actually eligible for continuation of coverage.

Few personnel departments of large employers can maintain adequate monitoring of the mobility of all employees, much less of dependents. Yet, this segment of the eligible member base may represent a significant portion of continuation eligibility.

Figure 6 – 1 is an example of a document that may be used to enroll the applicant for continuation of coverage. In addition, the employer must provide notification of the availability of COBRA to all employees and their dependents. By early distribution of reference materials, liability for failure to notify affected employees/dependents can be avoided, and the responsibility for timely application would be shifted entirely to the affected employee if (1) dependents become overage, (2) if a divorce or separation occurs, or (3) if the employee abandons or terminates employment without advance notification. The applicant has 60 days from the date that such coverage is terminated due to a qualifying event in which to submit the application for continuation to the administrator or insurance company or 60 days from the date notice of the right to elect COBRA continuation is sent to the employee. Therefore, if the employer/plan fails to send out notification of the election right for two years after the actual event date, the employee would have to be given 60 days from the two year date in which to elect coverage. Mistakes like this can prove to be very costly to a plan.

Premium Payments
After COBRA has been elected, 45 days is allowed in which to pay the initial premium including all retroactive premiums due since the termination of coverage as a regular employee. If the initial premium and all back premiums are not paid within this time, coverage will remain terminated and COBRA coverage will not become effective.

ABC Company
333 Whata Way
Hollywood, CA 91731

CONTINUATION OF COVERAGE REQUEST

If you were eligible under your employer's group health insurance plan, you may be eligible to continue your coverage. In order to apply, this form must be completed and returned to the Administrator's office indicated above within 60 days of the date your eligibility under the group plan terminates. Within 14 days of our receipt of this request, you will be sent a copy of your Election Rights under the Consolidation Omnibus Reconciliation Act of 1985 (COBRA), Public Act 99-272, Title X.

EMPLOYEE NAME – LAST	FIRST	FACILITY	SOC. SEC.

COMPLETE HOME ADDRESS	CITY	STATE	ZIP

Qualifying Event: Check off the event and give the event date.
☐ Reduction in work hours. Effective: _____
☐ Employment Termination (Except due to "gross misconduct"). Last Work Day: _____
☐ Dependent Child Attained Maximum Age Defined by Plan. _____
☐ Legal Separation and/or Divorce. Date: _____
☐ Death of Covered Employee. Date: _____

CONTINUATION OF COVERAGE REQUESTED FOR: (Coverage(s) cannot be added. May be dropped only.)

☐ Employee Only	☐ Employee & Dependent(s)	☐ Dependent(s) Only
☐ Medical Only	☐ Medical Only	☐ Medical Only
☐ Dental + Vision Only	☐ Dental + Vision Only	☐ Dental + Vision Only
☐ Medical + Dental + Vision	☐ Medical + Dental + Vision	☐ Medical + Dental + Vision

ALL DEPENDENTS MUST BE LISTED BELOW. LIST THE SOCIAL SECURITY NUMBER OF THE EMPLOYEE'S SPOUSE AND OVERAGE DEPENDENT CHILDREN.

NAME	SO. SEC. #	BIRTHDATE	RELATIONSHIP

Signature of Applicant/ Date Signed

Figure 6 – 1: Continuation of Coverage Request

Normally, a monthly COBRA statement is provided to the employee, which reflects the premium due date for each month and the amount of the monthly premium based on the coverage elected by the applicant. However, the law permits a 30-day grace period from the premium due date. This allows the applicant 30 additional days in which to pay the required premium amount. If the premium is not mailed within the 30-day grace period, coverage will automatically lapse back to the last premium paid date. The amount of the premium can be up to 102% of the premium costs for employees. The 2% is to cover administrative costs. For employees who are eligible for the 29-month extension, the premium can be up to 150% of the employee premium cost for months 19 through 29.

Normally, claims are not paid until the member has paid the premium for the month in which the services were incurred or until the grace period has lapsed. Consequently, if the member consistently pays at the end of the grace period, claim payments may be consistently delayed (again, the incurred date of services will be compared with the paid through date. If the premium for the month in which services were incurred has not been paid, processing will be delayed until the end of the grace period).

Bounced checks or any type of non-paid check may result in lapse of coverage if the check is returned from the bank after the premium due date and a replacement check was not received prior to the end of the grace period. The mailing date of premiums should be strictly monitored with no exceptions. The date of receipt is not important. Judgment of whether or not a payment was received timely is based on the postmark on the envelope. By law, if the payment was mailed within the specified time, it must be accepted as being paid timely.

It is very important that all applicants/ members be treated equitably regarding the premium payment policy, since deviations may set precedents and extend plan liabilities above acceptable limits.

Termination of Coverage
An individual may terminate the continuation of coverage before the completion of the 18-, 29-, or 36-month period. However, if coverage is terminated before the completion of the maximum period, the employer is not required to offer a second election of extension. In other words, once continuation is discontinued, coverage will not be reinstated or restarted.

If any of the following events occurs before the end of the 18-, 29-, or 36-month continuation period, coverage will cease at the end of the month following the date of the occurrence:

- Termination of all of the employer's sponsored group health plans.
- Failure to pay required premium contributions within 30 days of premium due date.

- Becoming covered under another group sponsored health plan unless the replacement plan exempts coverage for a preexisting condition affecting the member. Under this circumstance, the member may continue COBRA with the COBRA plan covering only those expenses incurred as a result of the preexisting condition. The replacement plan would cover all other expenses.
- Becoming entitled to Medicare coverage.

HIPAA

In 1996 President William Clinton signed the Health Insurance Portability and Accountability Act (HIPAA). Among other provisions, HIPAA limits pre-existing condition exclusion periods. The employee must be issued a certificate of coverage by his employer; stating how long the employee was covered under the plan. The new carrier must apply the period of time covered under the prior coverage to the new pre-existing condition clause. Because the new carrier may have to waive or reduce the pre-existing condition clause, the need to carry COBRA for the pre-existing condition is also reduced.

Example: Mr. Jones has diabetes and has found a new job with the ABC Company. Mr. Jones obtained a certificate of coverage from his old employer showing 3 years coverage. ABC Company has a 12-month pre-existing condition clause, which because of the certificate of coverage is waived. Since Mr. Jones will be covered with no pre-existing condition restriction, there is no need to pay for COBRA to cover expenses for his diabetes.

Congress is constantly amending legislation regarding this provision, therefore, it is important to stay abreast of changes.

For more information on HIPAA and pre-existing conditions, see the chapter on General Plan Provisions.

Summary

Eligibility and effective dates of coverage are probably the greatest factors to be considered when processing a claim. Thus, eligibility and effective date is the first thing that should be checked when a claim is received for payment. If the patient is not eligible, no further action need be taken on the claim.

Assignments

Complete the Questions for Review.
Complete Exercises 6 – 1 to 6 – 3.

Questions for Review

Directions: Answer the following questions without looking back into the material just covered. Write your answers in the space provided.

1. <u>Eligibility</u> refers to the requirements that must be fulfilled for a person to be covered by the plan.

2. Most contracts define employees in terms of <u>the minimum number of hours that the employee must work per week.</u>

3. List the five conditions under which coverage is terminated.
    1. <u>The group policy terminates</u>
    2. <u>The policy is amended to terminate the eligibility of class to which the emp. belongs</u>
    3. <u>The employee transfer out of a class covered by the policy.</u>
    4. <u>Active employment ceases.</u>
    5. <u>The employee ceases to pay the required contribution for the coverage.</u>

4. <u>Conversion policy</u> permits employees and dependents to continue their insurance protection on an individual basis when their coverage under a group plan ceases.

5. To whom does the COBRA Act apply? <u>To employee who loses their job except for illegal reason.</u>

6. What is a qualified beneficiary? <u>The option of self payment continuation of coverage must be offered by an employer to certain individuals.</u>

7. What is a qualifying event? <u>refer to the reason why you were terminated. It can be for anything illegal</u>

8. What is the maximum time in which a dependent can continue COBRA? <u>18, 29, or 36 months depending on the circumstances</u>

9. What is the maximum time in which an employee can continue COBRA? <u>29 months</u>

10. How long does a member have to apply for COBRA after termination of coverage? <u>60 days</u>

If you were unable to answer any of the questions, refer back to the section and then complete the answers.

Exercise 6 – 1

Directions: Indicate whether the person listed would be considered an eligible dependent (ED) or a non-eligible dependent (NED) under the provisions of the plan. Assume that the first person is covered under the plan, and the second person is applying as his or her dependent.

1. Natalie's legally married spouse. _____ ED _____
2. Nathaniel's dependent child age four . _____ ED _____
3. Bryant's cousin Terrell. _____ NED _____
4. Tabari's divorced ex-spouse. _____ NED _____
5. Tiron's son, aged 45, fully functional. _____ NED _____
6. Kyra's dependent child, age 19, who is a full time student. _____ ED _____
7. Kayla's brother Kenneth. _____ NED _____
8. Ann's dog Pepper. _____ NED _____
9. Aaron's adopted daughter. _____ ED _____
10. Brittany's mother-in-law. _____ NED _____

Exercise 6 – 2

Directions: Place a "yes" or "no" next to each of the following to show whether coverage would be terminated under the circumstances given. Assume that each person listed is the member on the plan. Do not be concerned about whether the person is entitled to continuation of coverage.

1. Nancy goes from full-time to 20 hours per week. _____ yes _____
2. Alonzo is terminated by the company. _____ yes _____
3. Kerri's company terminates the policy. _____ yes _____
4. Sydney becomes self-employed but works on a contract basis for the same company. _____ yes _____
5. Sean stops paying the premium for his insurance. _____ yes _____
6. Thomas goes on vacation for two weeks. _____ No _____
7. Floree forgets to enroll during her company's open enrollment period. _____ yes _____
8. Mia is transferred out of a class covered by the policy. _____ yes _____
9. Mayra goes on maternity leave. _____ NO _____
10. Carol gets married. _____ NO _____

Exercise 6 – 3

Directions: Place a "yes" or "no" next to each of the following people to show which would be eligible for coverage under the Ninja contract.

1. Mother, Kanika, works 35 hours per week for Ninja. _____ yes _____

2. Father, Kenneth, is self-employed. He is Kanika's second husband. _____ yes _____

3. Ryan, 20-year-old son of Kanika and her first husband, is currently unemployed and is not a full-time student.
_____ NO _____

4. Ravyn, 20-year-old daughter (Ryan's twin) is going to the local university full-time. _____ yes _____

5. Jordan, 16-year-old daughter is a high school dropout. _____ yes _____

6. Sheila is a 13-year-old foster child who lives with the family. _____ yes _____

7. Sharon is a 10-year-old legally adopted child. _____ yes _____

8. Paris is the three-year-old daughter of Ravyn. _____ NO _____

9. Kytrena is Kanika's mother. She has Alzheimer's disease and is listed as a dependent on Kanika's income tax form. _____ NO, But if there were a court order. _____

10. Caitlind is Kanika's mentally retarded sister. Kanika is not her legal guardian. _____ NO _____

Honors Certification™

The Honors Certification™ challenge for this section is a written test. You will be asked questions regarding the material covered in this chapter. Additionally you will be presented with a number of scenarios and asked whether or not a person is eligible for coverage. Any incorrect answer will result in a deduction of between 3% and 5% from your grade. You must achieve a score of 80% or higher to pass this test. If you fail the test on your first attempt, you may retake the test one additional time. The items included in the first test may be different from those in the second test.

7 Usual, Customary, and Reasonable

In this chapter you will learn:

- To determine the correct unit value of the procedure code billed.
- To determine the appropriate conversion factor as indicated by geographic region and status of provider.
- To accurately calculate customary and reasonable allowances.

Key words and concepts you will learn in this chapter:

Allowed Amount — Same as UCR amount.

Conversion Factor — A dollar amount determined for a specific service type or a particular region. Each region may have a unique set of conversion factors, and each service type may be assigned a specific conversion factor.

Modifier Codes — Two-digit numerical codes attached to a CPT code to indicate special circumstances for that particular service. This may mean that the unit value or UCR amount should be increased or decreased because of those special circumstances.

Procedure Code — A five-digit numerical code used to designate medical services according to standardized, industry-accepted methods; usually reflected in a CPT manual.

Region — The geographic region of the country that is assigned a specific conversion factor. More expensive cost-of-living areas are assigned higher conversion factors than less expensive cost-of-living areas. Some states or cities are divided into multiple or different regions, whereas other states or cities may have only one area or may even be combined with other states or cities.

Type of Treatment — The type of service performed, which is usually classified by the following categories: surgery, medical, x-ray, laboratory, and anesthesia.

Unit Value — A numerical value assigned by a relative value study to a procedure code. The unit value is multiplied by the conversion factor to determine the UCR allowance or a basic allowance.

Usual, Customary and Reasonable — An amount usually charged by most providers within a geographic region for a specified service.

Benefit plans define covered expenses as charges for the following services and supplies:

- Those that are medically necessary for the treatment or diagnosis of an injury or illness,
- Those that are ordered or prescribed by a licensed provider, and
- Those that do not exceed the usual, customary, and reasonable (UCR) fee generally charged by like providers in the same geographic area for the same procedure.

At one time insurance companies covered a straight percentage of whatever the doctor charged. Over time, however, they found that some doctors were charging one amount for a procedure, and others were charging a much higher amount. This was because doctors were setting their fees based on their perceived needs. For example, if a doctor decided he needed a new car, he would raise his fees by several dollars to cover the costs of his new car. Because of this, fees were increasing at an alarming rate. Eventually, insurance carriers decided that they needed to put a lid on the charges, or at least on their payments. Therefore they created an "**allowed amount.**" This is the amount that they would allow for a procedure, based on what was **Usual, Customary and Reasonable (UCR)** for a given procedure. This is the amount insurance companies would base their payments on, regardless of what the doctor charged.

However, costs in one area of the country are often much less than those in another area of the country. Thus, insurance carriers began compiling data based on the usual amounts charged by doctors in different areas. The information on the average fees charged for a given service in a given area was developed, and fee schedules (or lists of amounts for each procedure) were developed. Eventually the RVS/Conversion Factor method was developed. This system bases amounts on the procedure performed, the geographic location (zip code area) of the provider of service's office, and the date the service was performed.

There are several sources that compile and publish UCR data. Using this data or compiling their own data, third-party administrators and insurance carriers determine the UCR allowances for their plans or clients. Amounts in excess of UCR are not considered to be an allowable expense under the plan and are therefore, excluded from all benefit calculations.

UCR is usually applicable only to professional services or to hospital billings that give CPT/RVS codes. Individually, some administrators are establishing daily UCR amounts for hospital services.

Not all procedures have UCR. For instance, new procedures, experimental procedures and very unusual, complex procedures may not have an established UCR amount. UCR can be established only when enough procedures of a particular type have been performed in a geographic area to allow for an "average" or "usual" amount to be determined. Usually, a minimum of 50 operations is required to provide even a rough estimate of the amount that should be considered as usual.

There are several reasons why a UCR amount will not be available, including:

- The CPT code is a BR (By Report) procedure. The value of this service is based on the operative report because the service is too unusual or variable to be assigned a unit value.
- The code entered is an RNE (Relatively Not Established) procedure. This indicates new or infrequently performed services for which sufficient data have not been collected to allow establishment of a relative value.
- The code entered is not listed in the most recent Current Procedural Terminology (CPT) book because it is a new procedure.

Resource-Based Relative Value Study

The studies that assign unit values to a particular procedure are called **Relative Value Studies (RVS)** (see **Figure 7 – 1**).

At one time providers were paid based on not only the procedure performed, but the title of the provider. Thus an M.D. and a chiropractor would receive different amounts for the same procedure.

With the passage of OBRA 90-Public Law 101-608, major changes for physician payment reform took place. One of these changes was the replacement of historic payment basis, with a fee schedule for physician payment. This fee schedule is to be based on relative value units that reflect the resources required to provide a service. OBRA 90 declared that after January 1, 1992, and each year thereafter, a fee schedule must be established for all physician services in all geographic areas. The fee schedule will be based on national uniform relative values for all physicians without respect to area of specialization. The relative value units (RVU's) represent the total RVS for components of the schedule.

Components for resource-based RVS include:

- **Physicians Work Component** — reflects the resources required to furnish the professional service including the time and the intensity of effort.
- **Overhead or Practice Expense Component** — reflects customary practice expenses (i.e., rent, salaries, staff, equipment cost and so on).
- **Malpractice or Professional Liability Component** — reflects the risk inherent in providing various procedures. This component does not reflect any specialties but reflects that some procedures are performed routinely by physicians with specialty training in the procedure.

The RVS are to be adjusted for various locales by a geographic adjustment factor. These factors are often referred to as conversion factors.

Calculating UCR

UCR calculation is the process of determining the fee usually charged by similar providers for the same procedure in the same geographic area during a specified period of time.

Conversion Factors

In determining UCR, the listed procedure unit value is multiplied by the plan's appropriate conversion factor or factors. Often there are separate conversion factors for medicine, surgery, diagnostic x-ray and laboratory (DXL), and anesthesia charges. (see **Figure 7 – 2**).

The CPT code for the procedure determines the appropriate conversion factor, not the description of the service. The ranges by conversion factor categories are:

Medicine	90701-99499
Anesthesia	00100-01999
Surgery	10040-69979
DXL	70010-89399

The conversion factor is a dollar amount based on the geographic area in which the provider practices. For example, Los Angeles may have a surgical conversion factor of $50.64, whereas Bismarck, North Dakota's surgical conversion factor may be $28.00.

Example: Tonsillectomy, 42842, RVS, Unit Value = 16.39. Geographic conversion factor for San Francisco (zip code 940XX) is $39.54. To determine UCR for this procedure, multiply the RVS 16.39 unit value by the conversion factor of $39.54 (for 940XX, San Francisco). The total UCR amount is $648.06. This amount would be placed in the Allowed Amount column on the Payment Worksheet (see Claims Administration chapter).

On a Basic-Major Medical plan, two limits must be calculated:

1. Basic allowed amount, and
2. Total plan or major medical allowed amount.

The Basic Benefit usually has a dollar conversion factor specified in the plan document. Consequently, all providers, regardless of their geographic location or when the service is performed, receive the same basic allowance for a specific procedure. Also, the basic allowance is usually paid at 100%. Conversely, the UCR allowance under Major Medical is not normally specified in the plan document because it is usually upgraded periodically due to inflation.

Basic Allowance

Refer to the contract for XYZ Corporation. As indicated, this is a Basic-Major Medical plan. For office visits, the conversion factor is $7.50 and for DXL it is $7.00. To calculate the Basic payment:

1. Look up the procedure code and determine the relative unit value that applies to the procedure for the specified schedule.
2. Multiply the RVS unit value by the plan basic conversion factor. (In the case of XYZ, it would be $7.00 for DXL or $7.50 for office visits.)

The resulting figure will be the amount payable at 100% under Basic Benefits.

Example: A claim is submitted with a charge for a definitive bacterial culture, blood (87070). This has a unit value of 1.3. Therefore, the basic conversion factor of $7.00 for DXL (XYZ contract) is multiplied by 1.3 for a basic unit value of $9.10.

Major Medical UCR

To calculate the Major Medical UCR limit:

1. Look up the procedure code and determine the relative unit value that applies to the procedure for the specified schedule.
2. Multiply the RVS unit value by the plan (or Major Medical) conversion factor based on:
   a. The specific time period during which the services were provided;
   b. The geographic location of the provider (using the first three digits of the zip code); and
   c. The type of service being performed, i.e., surgery, medical.
      This will give you the allowed amount for the procedure.
3. Subtract any amounts paid at the basic rate. This will give you the Major Medical amount.

Relative Value Study

CPT/HCPCS*	Description	Total RVUs	Follow-up Days
00144	ANESTHESIA FOR CORNEAL TRANSPLANT	6.0	--
00172	ANESTHESIA FOR REPAIR OF CLEFT PALATE	6.0	--
00215	ANESTHESIA FOR CRANIOPLASTY	9.0	--
00400	ANESTHESIA, INTEGUMENTARY SYSTEM, EXTREMITIES	3.0	--
00520	ANESTHESIA FOR CLOSED CHEST PROCEDURES	6.0	--
00534	ANESTHESIA FOR TRANSVENOUS INSERTION	7.0	--
00868	ANESTHESIA FOR RENAL TRANSPLANT	10.0	--
01230	ANESTHESIA FOR UPPER 2/3 OF FEMUR, OPEN	6.0	--
01480	ANESTHESIA, ON BONES OF LOWER LEG, OPEN	3.0	--
01990	PHYSIOLOGICAL SUPPORT, BRAIN-DEAD PATIENT	7.0	--
15570	FORMATION OF DIRECT OR TUBED PEDICLE	10.0	90
15952	EXCISION TROCHANTERIC PRESS ULCER	8.0	90
19125	EXCISION OF BREAST LESION	7.0	30
19126	EXCISION OF BREAST LESION, EACH ADDITIONAL	3.5	30
20205	BIOPSY, MUSCLE DEEP	2.4	15
21800	CLOSED TREATMENT OF RIB FRACTURE, EACH	18.0	90
24102	ARTHROTOMY, ELBOW WITH SYNOVECTOMY	14.5	90
25622	CLOSED TREAT OF CARPAL SCAPHOID FRACTURE	3.5	60
27350	PATELLECTOMY OR HEMIPATELLECTOMY	12.0	60
27372	REMOVAL OF FOREIGN BODY, DEEP, THIGH REGION	5.2	30
27758	OPEN TREATMENT OF TIBIAL SHAFT FRACTURE	12.7	30
27784	OPEN TREATMENT OF PROXIMAL FIBULA	12.7	90
28456	PERCUTANEOUS SKELETAL FIXATION OF TARSAL	3.9	90
30125	EXCISION DERMOID CYST UNDER BONE	8.5	30
31200	ETHMOIDECTOMY	7.0	90
31225	MAXILLECTOMY WITHOUT ORBITAL EXENTERATION	22.5	120
32800	REPAIR LUNG HERNIA THROUGH CHEST	12.0	30

Figure 7 – 1: RVS Schedule (continued on next page)

33217	INSERTION OF A TRANSVENOUS ELECTRODE	9.5	15
33225	INSERTION OF PACING ELECTRODE	BR	
33240	INSERTION OF SINGLE OR DUAL CHAMBER PACING	12.0	15
36430	TRANSFUSION, BLOOD	0.4	00
38100	SPLENECTOMY, TOTAL	16.0	45
39520	REPAIR, DIAPHRAGMATIC HERNIA	17.0	90
39545	IMBRICATION OF DIAPHRAGM FOR EVENTRATION	12.0	90
40808	BIOPSY, VESTIBULE OF MOUTH	0.7	00
43840	GASTRORRHAPHY, SUTURE PERFORATED ULCER	14.0	45
47630	BILIARY DUCT STONE EXTRACTION	7.0	45
49560	REPAIR INITIAL INCISIONAL OR VENTRAL HERNIA	11.5	45
52500	TRANSURETHRAL RESECTION OF BLADDER NECK	10.0	90
58700	SALPINGECTOMY, COMPLETE OR PARTIAL	11.4	90
59400	ROUTINE OBSTETRIC CARE	20.0	45
59820	TREATMENT OF MISSED ABORTION	4.5	30
61703	SURGERY OF INTRACRANIAL ANEURYSM	13.0	90
62000	ELEVATION OF DEPRESSED SKULL FRACTURE	8.3	90
65800	PARACENTESIS OF ANTERIOR CHAMBER OF EYE	3.0	00
69400	EUSTACHIAN TUBE INFLATION	0.3	00
70250	RADIOLOGIC EXAM, SKULL	3.1	--
70260	RADIOLOGIC EXAM, SKULL, COMPLETE	5.0	--
70450	CAT SCAN, SKULL	21.7	--
71020	RADIOLOGIC EXAM, CHEST	3.2	--
73100	RADIOLOGIC EXAM, RIGHT WRIST	2.5	--
73130	RADIOLOGIC EXAM, HAND, MINIMUM 3 VIEWS	2.8	--
73550	RADIOLOGIC EXAM, UPPER LEG	2.8	--
73590	RADIOLOGIC EXAM, LOWER LEG	2.5	--
73718	MRI LEG	55.0	--
74250	RADIOLOGIC EXAM, SMALL BOWEL	6.6	--
76090	MAMMOGRAPHY, UNILATERAL	4.5	--
76092	SCREENING MAMMOGRAPHY, BILATERAL	4.5	--
76870	ECHOGRAPHY, SCROTUM AND CONTENTS	8.0	--
76872	ECHOGRAPHY, TRANSRECTAL	13.8	--
78810	TUMOR IMAGING	100.0	--
80048	BASIC METABOLIC PANEL	1.3	--
80053	COMPREHENSIVE METABOLIC PANEL	1.6	--
81000	URINALYSIS	0.7	--
82310	CALCIUM, TOTAL	1.0	--
83540	IRON	1.6	--
83545	ANGIOGRAM	22.0	--
85025	BLOOD COUNT, COMPLETE, AUTOMATED	0.8	--
85610	PROTHROMBIN TIME	0.6	--
86901	BLOODTYPING, RH (D)	1.1	--
87040	CULTURE, BACTERIAL; BLOOD	1.2	--
87070	CULTURE, BACTERIAL DEFINITIVE BLOOD	1.3	--
88150	CYTOPATHOLOGY, SLIDES, CERVICAL OR VAGINAL	0.9	--
90782	THERAPEUTIC, INJECTION	2.5	--
93000	EKG	7.8	--
93585	INJECTION DURING ANGIOGRAPHY	22.0	--
94060	BRONCHOSPASM EVALUATION	20.0	--
97116	GAIT TRAINING	7.0	--
99025	INITIAL (NEW PATIENT) VISIT WHEN STARRED	4.0	--
99201	OFFICE OR OTHER OUTPATIENT VISIT, NEW	6.5	--
99213	ESTABLISHED PATIENT, EXPANDED	9.0	--
99284	EMERGENCY VISIT, DETAILED	25.0	--
99285	EMERGENCY VISIT, COMPREHENSIVE	37.0	--

Figure 7 – 1: RVS Schedule (continued)

UCR Conversion Factor Report

Zip	Area	Including Zip Codes	Surgery	Medicine	X-Ray & Lab	Anesthesia
006	Puerto Rico	006-009	35.58	31.13	26.68	22.14
039	Maine	039-049	31.01	27.13	23.26	31.34
100	New York City	100-102	66.02	57.77	49.51	30.30
125	Poughkeepsie, Monticello & N.E. NY	125, 127-129, 136	40.71	35.62	30.53	32.71
153	Southwestern PA	153-158	36.76	32.16	27.57	25.25
210	Baltimore Area	210, 211, 214	48.00	42.00	36.00	35.35
255	Huntington, Wheeling, Parkesburg, Morgantown	255, 257, 260, 261, 265	32.94	28.82	24.70	31.14
302	Atlanta	302, 303	38.86	34.00	29.14	47.43
354	Alabama-miscellaneous	354-357, 359-360, 363-365, 368, 324	30.90	27.04	23.18	32.06
441	Cleveland, Youngstown Area	441, 444	37.10	32.46	27.83	38.69
480	Detroit	480-482, 485	36.63	32.05	27.47	31.41
550	Minneapolis-St Paul Area	550, 551, 553	26.42	23.12	19.81	29.46
580	North Dakota	580-588	28.00	24.50	21.00	23.12
606	Chicago	606	45.64	39.94	34.23	49.57
640	Kansas City Area	640-641, 661-662	33.48	29.29	25.11	40.30
770	Houston	770, 772, 775	40.60	35.52	30.45	42.66
777	Austin & Beaumont	777, 779, 787, 788	33.10	28.96	24.82	50.31
801	Denver, Colorado Springs, Alamosa, Glenwood Springs Area	801-803, 806, 808 811, 816	32.32	28.28	24.24	41.69
890	Reno & Area	890, 895, 897	34.38	30.08	25.78	49.11
904	Santa Monica, Long Beach, Glendale	904, 908, 912	45.18	39.53	33.89	47.94
970	Portland & Western Oregon	970, 971, 974, 975	30.87	27.01	23.15	34.20

Figure 7 – 2: Conversion Factor Report

Example: A claim is submitted with a charge for a definitive bacterial culture, blood (87070). This has a unit value of 1.3. The provider lives in Atlanta, GA, in zip code 30325. The DXL conversion factor for zip codes starting with 303 is $29.14. Therefore, the conversion factor of $29.14 for DXL is multiplied by 1.3 for an allowed amount of $37.88. The basic amount (figured above) is $9.10. This amount is subtracted from the $37.88, leaving $28.78 (the Major Medical amount)

The figure arrived at will be the maximum amount allowed under the plan. "Allowed" does not necessarily mean the same as "paid."

Amounts over the Major Medical UCR allowance are not considered covered by the plan. The UCR amount or the lesser amount (if the amount is lower than the UCR amount) are applied toward all of the plan limitations, including the deductible and coinsurance. The amounts not covered by the plan are the patient's sole responsibility.

Normally, if the provider's charge exceeds the UCR allowance by more than 20% or 25%, a Peer Review (consultant) may be required.

Special Services
The services in the procedure code range of 99000-99199 are considered special services. Regardless of the type of service provided, the UCR calculation is based on the medicine conversion factor category.

UCR Modifications
Remember that the addition of modifiers will alter the percentage of the UCR that is allowed. There will also be adjustments based on whether or not there were multiple or asterisk procedures.

For standard adjustments on modifiers, consult the CPT book. For those modifications not listed, the adjustment will vary according to the insurance carrier's policy and the contract provisions.

Fee Schedules

Some plans have done their own calculations of the amount payable for particular services. These amounts are listed on what is commonly called a **fee schedule** (see **Figure 7-3**). Fees are assigned according to the particular CPT code, and this is considered the allowable amount for that particular procedure.

If a fee schedule is used, the claims examiner looks up the appropriate code to obtain the allowed amount. This eliminates the need for numerous calculations and can speed up the process of claims examining. However, the compensation with the schedules is the same in a large city as it is in outlying areas.

Summary

The concept of Usual, Customary, and Reasonable charges allows a payor to determine allowable charges based on what is considered to be a usual and reasonable charge for a given service performed in a given area. This prevents the paying of excessive benefits to doctors who may charge high fees on their bills. UCR allows for the payment of higher rates in areas in which there is a higher cost of doing business (i.e., building costs, personnel) and lower rates in areas in which there is a lower cost of doing business.

Assignments

Complete the Questions for Review.
Complete the UCR Exercises 7 – 1 to 7 – 4.

Fee Schedule

CPT/HCPCS*	Description	Allowed Amount	Follow-up Days
00144	ANESTHESIA FOR CORNEAL TRANSPLANT	196.26	--
00400	ANESTHESIA, INTEGUMENTARY SYSTEM, EXTREMITIES	98.13	--
19126	EXCISION OF BREAST LESION, EACH	142.49	30
24102	ARTHROTOMY, ELBOW WITH SYNOVECTOMY	590.30	90
28456	PERCUTANEOUS SKELETAL FIXATION OF TARSAL	158.77	90
36430	TRANSFUSION, BLOOD	16.28	00
49560	REPAIR INITIAL INCISIONAL OR VENTRAL HERNIA	468.17	45
59820	TREATMENT OF MISSED ABORTION	183.20	30
65800	PARACENTESIS OF ANTERIOR CHAMBER OF EYE	122.13	00
70250	RADIOLOGIC EXAM, SKULL	94.64	--
76090	MAMMOGRAPHY, UNILATERAL	137.39	--
80053	COMPREHENSIVE METABOLIC PANEL	48.85	--
99025	INITIAL (NEW PATIENT) VISIT WHEN STARRED	162.84	--
99201	OFFICE OR OTHER OUTPATIENT VISIT, NEW	264.61	--

*CPT codes, descriptions, and two digit numeric modifiers only are copyright 2003 American Medical Association. All Rights Reserved.

Figure 7 – 3: Fee Schedule (sample of various codes)

Questions for Review

Directions: Answer the following questions without looking back into the material just covered. Write your answers in the space provided.

1. What does UCR mean? _____

2. What is UCR based on? _____

3. Explain why a procedure may not have a UCR allowance. _____
   _____

4. Define the following words:

   1. Conversion factor _____
      _____

   2. Unit value _____
      _____

   3. Procedure code _____
      _____

   4. Region _____
      _____

   5. Modifier codes _____
      _____

5. How do you calculate Major Medical UCR? _____
   _____

6. How do you calculate the basic allowance? _____
   _____

7. (True or False?) The maximum amount allowed under the plan will always be the amount paid. _____

8. Are amounts in excess of the UCR allowance considered covered by the plan? _____

9. What is the procedure code range for special services? _____

10. What do BR and RNE stand for and what is the difference between them? _____
    _____

If you were unable to answer any of the questions, refer back to the section and then complete the answers.

Exercise 7 – 1

Directions: Using the Conversion Factor Report (**Figure 7 – 2**), list the Surgery, Medicine, DXL, and Anesthesia conversion factors for the following zip codes.

Zip Code	Surgery	Medicine	DXL	Anesthesia
1. 12345				
2. 75839				
3. 98023				
4. 78593				
5. 03464				
6. 89456				
7. 21438				
8. 63545				
9. 85679				
10. 00615				
11. 54632				
12. 76385				
13. 94612				
14. 27893				
15. 93480				
16. 36845				
17. 40267				
18. 52455				
19. 87754				
20. 14543				
21. 31778				
22. 94345				
23. 67845				
24. 02845				
25. 24176				
26. 54378				
27. 43127				
28. 68575				
29. 49956				
30. 78239				

Exercise 7 – 2

Directions: Using the ABC contract, calculate the plan UCR amounts. Use the conversion factor for zip code 90820.

Proc.Code	Description	Conversion Factor	Units	Amount
1. 15952	Excision Trochanteric Press Ulcer	45.18	8.0	$361.44
2. 93000	EKG	33.89	7.8	$264.34
3. 27372	Removal of Foreign Body, Deep, Thigh	45.18	5.2	$234.94
4. 78810	Tumor Imaging	33.89	160.0	$338.90
5. 70250	Radiologic Exam, Skull	33.89	3.1	$105.05
6. 19125	Excision of Breast Lesion	45.18	7.0	$316.26
7. 36430	Transfusion, Blood	45.18	0.4	$180.72
8. 87040	Culture, Bacterial; Blood	33.89	1.2	$40.66
9. 40808	Biopsy, Vestibule of Mouth	45.18	0.7	$316.26
10. 20205	Biopsy, Muscle Deep	45.18	2.4	$108.43
11. 47630	Bilary Duct Stone Extraction	45.18	7.0	$316.26
12. 59820	Treatment of Missed Abortion	45.18	4.5	$203.31
13. 86901	Blood Typing, RH (D)	$33.89	1.1	$37.28
14. 69400	Eustachain Tube Inflation	45.18	0.3	$135.54
15. 32800	Repair Hernia Through Chest	45.18	12.0	$542.16

Exercise 7 – 3

Directions: Using the Ninja contract, calculate the plan UCR amounts. Use the conversion factor for zip code 36810.

Proc.Code	Description	Conversion Factor	Units	Amount
1. 15952	Excision Trochanteric Press Ulcer	30.90	8.0	$247.20
2. 93000	EKG	23.18	7.8	$180.80
3. 27372	Removal of Foreign Body, Deep, Thigh	30.90	5.2	$160.68
4. 78810	Tumor Imaging	23.18	100.0	$231.18
5. 70250	Radiologic Exam, Skull	23.18	3.1	$71.85
6. 19125	Excision of Breast Lesion	30.90	7.0	$216.30
7. 36430	Transfusion, Blood	30.90	0.4	$123.60
8. 87040	Culture, Bacterial; Blood	23.18	1.2	$27.82
9. 40808	Biopsy, Vestibule of Mouth	30.90	0.7	$21.63
10. 20205	Biopsy, Muscle Deep	30.90	2.4	$74.16
11. 47630	Bilary Duct Stone Extraction	30.90	7.0	$216.30
12. 59820	Treatment of Missed Abortion	30.90	4.5	$139.05
13. 86901	Blood Typing, RH (D)	23.18	1.1	$25.50
14. 69400	Eustachain Tube Inflation	30.90	0.3	$9.27
15. 32800	Repair Hernia Through Chest	30.90	0.3	$370.80

Exercise 7 – 4

Directions: Using the XYZ contract, calculate both basic and plan UCR amounts. Use the conversion factor for zip code 04143.

Proc.Code	Description	Conversion Factor	Units	Basic Allowance	Major Medical Allowance
1. 15952	Excision Trochanteric Press Ulcer	$31.01	8.0	68.00	180.08
2. 93000	EKG	23.26			
3. 27372	Removal of Foreign Body, Deep, Thigh	31.01	5.2	44.20	117.05
4. 78810	Tumor Imaging	23.26	100.0	750.00	1626.00
5. 70250	Radiologic Exam, Skull	23.26	3.1	21.70	50.31
6. 19125	Excision of Breast Lesion	31.01	7.0	59.50	157.57
7. 36430	Transfusion, Blood	31.01	0.4	34.00	9.00
8. 87040	Culture, Bacterial; Blood	23.26	1.2	8.40	19.51
9. 40808	Biopsy, Vestibule of Mouth	31.01	0.7	5.95	15.75
10. 20205	Biopsy, Muscle Deep	31.01	2.4	20.40	54.02
11. 47630	Bilary Duct Stone Extraction	31.01	7.0	59.50	157.50
12. 59820	Treatment of Missed Abortion	31.01	4.5	38.25	101.29
13. 86901	Blood Typing, RH (D)	23.26	1.1	7.70	17.88
14. 69400	Eustachain Tube Inflation	31.01	0.3	25.50	6.75
15. 32800	Repair Hernia Through Chest	31.01	12.0	102.00	270.12

Page 70 is your get unit

Honors Certification™

The Honors Certification™ challenge for this section is a written test. You will be asked questions regarding the material covered in this chapter. Additionally, you will be presented with a number of procedure codes and zip codes, and asked to calculate the correct UCR amount. Any incorrect answer will result in a deduction of between 3% and 5% from your grade. You must achieve a score of 80% or higher to pass this test. If you fail the test on your first attempt, you may retake the test one additional time. The items included in the first test may be different from those in the second test.

8 Benefit Structures

In this chapter you will learn:

- To interpret contract provisions.
- To identify the type of treatment as indicated by service provided.

Key words and concepts you will learn in this chapter:

Accumulation Period – The period of time in which to satisfy the deductible, accumulate COB credit reserves, reach maximums, and so on.

Actively-at-Work Requirement – The provision that requires that an employee be actively at work on the day he or she is scheduled to become covered.

Aggregate Deductible – All Major Medical deductibles applied for all family members are added together in order to attain the family limit.

Automatic Annual Reinstatement (AAR) – A contractually specified amount of money that may be added to the balance of available lifetime benefits.

Coinsurance – The arrangement by which both the member and the plan share, in a specific ratio of the covered losses under the policy.

Common Accident Provision – A provision whereby only one deductible is taken for all members of a family involved in the same accident.

Extended Benefits – The continued entitlement of a member, under certain circumstances, to receive benefits after the coverage has terminated.

Individual Deductible – The amount of covered expense that must be paid by the individual family member before benefits become payable by the plan.

Loss Date – The date of an accident.

Maximum – The greatest amount payable by the plan.

Non-Aggregate Deductible – A specified number of individual deductibles must be satisfied before the family limit is met.

Out-of-Pocket Expense (OOP) – Expenses for which the insured is held responsible and must pay "out-of-pocket," such as the deductible and coinsurance.

Out-of-Pocket Maximum – A yearly limit on the OOP that the insured is responsible for paying.

Three Month Carryover Provision – Eligible charges incurred in the last quarter of the calendar year and applied toward the member's deductible will also count toward the following year's deductible.

Every health care plan is required by law to have a written description of the benefits available to the members of that plan. This plan document must indicate, in detail, and in layman's terms, the provisions of the coverage.

Three major types of indemnity coverage are currently available:
1. Basic only.
2. Basic-Major Medical.
3. Comprehensive Major Medical.

Within these types there may be numerous variations. Additionally, under managed care provisions there can be PPO and HMO contracts.

Since the benefit payments calculated under each type of coverage can be identical, do not let the names confuse you. It is the concept that is important. Be sure you understand the types of benefit payments before processing any claims, since accurate benefit payment calculation is essential to a good claims examiner. Inaccurate payments can cost an insurance carrier thousands of dollars.

Benefit Definitions

Following are some common terms that are used when dealing with benefits. These definitions may not have calculations associated with them, so they are covered here. Benefit definitions that require you to calculate items will be discussed in the Benefit Calculations section.

Accumulation Period – Period of time (normally January 1 through December 31) in which to satisfy the deductible, accumulate COB credit reserves, reach maximums, and so on.

Actively-at-Work Requirement – The provision of a group plan which requires that an otherwise eligible employee must be actively at work on the day he or she is scheduled to become covered. If the employee is not actively at work on the date that coverage should become effective, coverage will be delayed until the date of return to active work. It should be noted that the employee does not have to be actively at work, if the effective date of coverage falls on a date the employee would not normally be scheduled to work (i.e., someone who works Monday through Friday and is not scheduled to work on Saturday, but his effective date falls on Saturday.) In this instance the employee's coverage would become effective on Saturday. For an eligible dependent, if the dependent is hospital-confined on the date coverage was to become effective, the coverage will not become effective until after release from the hospital.

Covered Expense – Those expenses that are allowable under the plan. Services specifically excluded by the plan or in excess of UCR (usual customary and reasonable fees) are not considered to be covered expenses.

>   *Example:* Surgery is $500. The plan's UCR amount is $350. The covered expense would be $350. Therefore, any applicable deductible would be taken from the $350 allowance, and any remaining amount would be paid at the Major Medical coinsurance percentage. The difference between the submitted amount of $500 and the covered/allowable amount of $350 ($150) would be the member's responsibility.

Exclusions – Conditions or types of services that the policy does not cover.

Extended Benefits – The continued entitlement of a member, under certain circumstances, to receive benefits after the coverage has terminated. A doctor's certification of total disability is required before benefits can be extended. Usually, such coverage will continue only for expenses incurred from the condition that caused the disability and for a maximum of 12 months following the date of disability or the date that the member is no longer totally disabled, whichever is less.

Loss Date – The loss date is always the date of the accident. Regardless of the date of service, the loss date remains the same.

Maximum(s) – The maximum amount payable by the plan. The maximum may be a calendar year or lifetime maximum. In addition, it may apply only toward expenses paid under Basic or only toward expenses paid under Major Medical or a combination of all payments, Basic and Major Medical. The policy must specify the type.

Out-of-Pocket Expense (OOP) – Expenses for which the insured is held responsible and must pay "out-of-pocket," such as the deductible and coinsurance (see Stoploss in the following section.)

OOP Maximum – A yearly limit on the OOP that the insured is responsible for paying. When this limit or maximum is reached, the plan pays subsequent covered expenses at 100% (or other specified percentage) instead of the usual percentage for the remainder of the calendar year.

Per Period of Disability – Basic Benefit waiting periods and deductibles; may be based on a per illness basis or a waiting period basis. With a per illness waiting period, for each new illness or injury a new benefit amount may be applicable or a new waiting period may apply. If there is a time period basis for renewal of the benefit, the patient must go for a specified time period without treatment of the specific illness or any illnesses. This most often applies to medical treatment while hospitalized or office visit benefits.

Pre-Existing Exclusion – When specified by the plan, a condition that is treated within a specified time period before the effective date of coverage. All charges related to the condition would not be covered at all for a stated period of time, or payment for the condition would be limited to a stated dollar amount.

Benefit Calculations

The following items may need to be calculated in order to determine the proper benefit. This section will cover the calculation of each of these items. Since not all items are needed on every claim, we will look at each item separately. This way you can check back in this section when you are unsure of a calculation.

When you reach the Claims Administration chapter and the chapters which discuss the various types of claims, these calculations will be used to complete the Payment Worksheet. At this time, do not concern yourself too much with where these items go. Instead, concentrate on understanding how to calculate each item properly.

Automatic Annual Reinstatement (AAR) – A contractually specified amount of money (credit) that may be added to the balance of available lifetime benefits. Usually, this applies to Major Medical benefits and is important only when a member has a catastrophic illness or injury and is calculated only when lifetime benefits have been exhausted.

>   *Example:* $1000 yearly reinstatement (AAR). Plan in effect since 2002.

Monies Payable by Plan	Lifetime Maximum
2003	
$150,000 benefits	$300,000 Lifetime Max -$150,000 Payments Made $150,000

2004

$175,000 benefits $150,000 Remaining Lifetime Max
                     +1,000 2002 AAR
                     <u>+1,000 2003 AAR</u>
                     $152,000 Remaining and Payable
                     $152,000 Payments Made

                     $175,000 Benefits
                     <u>-152,000</u> Benefit Available
                     $23,000 Unpaid/Over Max.

$23,000 remains unpaid because it was over the lifetime maximum.

The maximum amount that can be reinstated in one year is either the amount specified in the plan or the amount paid out in that year, whichever is less. For example, if $800 had been paid out in 2000, only $800 could be reinstated. Usually, reinstatement is allowed for every year that the member is covered up to either the $1000 contract limit or the amount paid out, whichever is less. In essence, any amount not used will not be carried over to succeeding years.

Since it is very uncommon for a patient to reach their lifetime maximum, there is no specific box on the payment worksheet for this item. Instead, if an automatic annual reinstatement amount is included on a claim, the amount would be placed in the Adjustment field, and an explanation included under remarks.

Coinsurance – The arrangement by which both the member and the plan share, in a specific ratio of the covered losses under the policy. For example, the plan may reimburse the provider or member for 80% of covered expenses, and the member will be responsible for the remaining 20% of expenses.

To calculate this amount, simply multiply the amount subject to major medical (after all basic amounts, deductible and other benefits have been deducted) by the coinsurance amount the plan provides. For example, if the amount subject to major medical is $120 and the plan pays 80%, the plan's major medical payment would be $96.

Out-of-Pocket – The amount that the member/insured must pay "out-of-pocket" (OOP). This would normally include the deductible, cost-sharing arising from the operation of the coinsurance clause, and medical expenditures that are deemed by the plan to be in excess of reasonable and customary charges. The policy will state the specifics.

The calculation of this amount is the reverse of the coinsurance amount. Thus, if the insurance carrier pays 80% of the amount subject to Major Medical, then the out-of-pocket amount would be 20% of the amount subject to Major Medical.

Co-Payment - A provision where the member is required to pay a set fixed dollar amount (i.e., $10 or $15) each time a particular medical service is used. Co-payment provisions are frequently found in PPO and HMO plans.

Calculating Deductible

Deductible is the amount of covered expenses that must be paid by the insured/member before benefits become payable by the insurer/plan under the Major Medical portion of the contract. Usually, this is a calendar year deductible (taken once each calendar year), but not always. The deductible is always taken out of the first eligible expense(s) submitted each year.

- **Individual Deductible** – The amount of covered expense that must be paid by the individual family member before benefits become payable by the plan.
- **Aggregate Deductible** – All Major Medical deductibles applied for all family members are added together in order to attain the family limit.
  Example: if the Barton Family is covered under the Winter Contract. Their family deductible is $200, aggregate. Therefore:
  Billy has paid $25 toward his deductible.
  Barry has paid $45 toward his deductible.
  Bobby has paid $85 toward his deductible.
  Betty has paid $0 toward her deductible.
  Betty now submits a claim for $500 in services. She only needs only pay $45 toward her deductible, since, when all amounts are added up, the family will then have reached the $200 family deductible limit. Even though none of the family members have met their individual limit, the family limit has been satisfied. Therefore no more deductible will be taken on any member of this family.

- **Non-aggregate Deductible** – A specified number of individual deductibles must be satisfied before the family limit is met.
  Example: Non-aggregate family limits often require that the family pay more money toward the deductible. For example, if the Barton family were covered under the Ball contract, the family deductible limit would be two family members. Therefore if:
  Billy has paid $25 toward his deductible.
  Barry has paid $45 toward his deductible.
  Bobby has paid $85 toward his deductible.
  Betty has paid $0 toward her deductible.
  Betty now submits a claim for $500 in services. She must pay the full $125 toward her deductible. Even so, the family deductible has still not been satisfied.
  If the next claim is for Billy for $75, the full $75 amount would be considered part of the deductible, thus bringing the amount Billy has paid toward his deductible to $100. However the family deductible still has not been met since only one family member (Betty), not two have reached their individual family limit.

Only when either Billy, Barry or Bobby has paid $125 toward their deductible will the family deductible be considered to be met. At that time, no more deductible would be taken on any member of the family.

Three-Month Carryover Provision (C/O)

A **three month carryover provision** states that eligible charges incurred in the last quarter of the calendar year (October, November, December) and applied toward the member's deductible will also count toward satisfying the following year's deductible. However, if the plan year is different from the calendar year, the last three months of the plan year will constitute the carryover deductible period. These monies may or may not be applied toward the family limit (see the terms of the contract).

Example: The deductible for John is $100 per year. The first claim payment submitted was for services in June, 2003. Payment of $35 was applied toward the deductible. The second claim is for services dated November, 2003. The deductible paid on this claim is $65, thus, satisfying the deductible for 2003. However, since $65 was satisfied during the last three months of 2003, $65 of the 2004 deductible will also be considered satisfied.

Carryover deductibles reward a patient who has been treatment free for most of the year. If the patient is still paying their deductible during the last three months of the year, they have remained treatment free for most of the year. Since deductibles are paid before the insurance carrier pays out any benefits, this means that the insurance carrier has not had to pay out any benefits during the year.

Common Accident Provision

A **common accident provision** states that only one deductible, under Major Medical, will be taken for all members of a family involved in the same accident. After the one deductible, remaining deductibles will be waived on all other members for expenses incurred for that accident only.

As a claims examiner, try to be aware of where each member of a family stands in relation to their deductible payments. This can be done fairly simply by glancing at the patient ledger for each family member. The patient with the most charges during the year has probably gone the farthest toward meeting their deductible. Also, if the insurance carrier has previously made several payments, the deductible has usually (though not always) been satisfied.

If more than one member of a family is being treated, many insurance carrier will take the single deductible from the claim that comes in first. If several claims for the family come in at the same time, often the deductible is taken from the patient who owes the most on their deductible.

Example: The entire Barton family was involved in an accident and visited the doctor on the same day. All claims come in at the same time. You check their files and discover that they are covered by the Ball contract and:

Billy has paid $25 toward his deductible
Barry has paid $45 toward his deductible
Bobby has paid $85 toward his deductible
Betty has paid $0 toward her deductible

Most insurance carriers will take the full deductible from Betty, then will waive the deductible for the other family members.

Basic Benefits

A **Basic Benefit** provides a specified allowance for a certain type of service. Usually, the allowance is 100% of either UCR (as defined by the plan) or some other amount based on the relative value study (RVS) and conversion factors.

A Basic Benefit usually has a stated calendar year dollar maximum, or number of visits or treatments, or a combination of both.

For example, refer to the XYZ contract under "Surgical" benefits. As indicated, this Basic Benefit pays 100% of the allowable using an $8.50 conversion factor. A maximum of $1600 is payable under the Basic Benefits only per surgery or operative session. Any money charged in excess of either the $1600 or the allowable amount up to the UCR amount would be covered under Major Medical subject to any limitations specified by that provision. Basic Benefits are always paid first. It is possible for a single expense to be covered under multiple Basic Benefits. In this case, the first Basic Benefit would be computed, then any excess would be allowed under any other applicable Basic Benefit, and finally any remaining amount would be considered under Major Medical.

Following are some guidelines for calculating Basic Benefits:

- Basic Benefits are always paid first before applicable Major Medical benefits are calculated.
- Basic Benefits are usually paid at 100% of the stated amount. Any other applicable percentage must be specifically stated in the policy.
- Basic Benefits usually have a dollar or number limit.

Under a basic only plan, any amount not paid by the Basic Benefit would not be covered at all. The excess charges would be the patient's responsibility.

Common Basic Benefits

There are several different types of Basic Benefits. The most common are listed below.

Accident Benefits

An **accidental injury** is a sudden and unforeseen event, definite as to time and place. This includes trauma happening involuntarily or as a result of a voluntary act entailing unforeseen consequences. The following is terminology related to accidental injuries:

- **Aggravated physiologic weakness** – Injury caused when an individual has a physical weakness that is aggravated by some voluntary activity. Overexertion or unusual physical exertion is also considered an accident if there is a specific time and circumstance involved. Do not consider routine bodily movements to be an injury if there is a history of related illness, such as arthritis and chronic strain of the affected area. Strains or sprains resulting from an unknown cause would not be considered an accident.

- **Aggressor acts while intoxicated** – The aggressor may not be considered responsible for his or her actions. Therefore, resulting injuries may be covered under this provision. However, this role is changing due to tougher intoxication laws and the push toward encouraging responsible drinking.

- **Aggressor claims** – If someone is the victim of an aggressor, his or her injuries are usually considered accidental. When an investigation does not clearly show who the aggressor was, the determination is usually made in the claimant's favor. As a rule, a person who is the aggressor or who is injured in the commission of a crime is not usually covered under an accident benefit.

- **Family altercations** – If an employee unintentionally injures a member of his or her family without provocation, the injuries would be considered accidental. Cases of this sort need to be investigated to ascertain the facts.

- **Internal reaction with external trauma** – Injury incurred as the result of an internal condition (i.e., by falling after fainting) is considered accidental. There must be an external impact involved in the injury.

- **Reactions to external stimulus** – Unforeseen consequences of voluntary acts, such as insect bites, allergic reactions to poison ivy or other foliage, food poisoning, and animal bites.

Benefits under this provision usually pay the first charges submitted up to a specified limit at 100% for all expenses incurred within a specified time period of the date of the accident. Amounts over the dollar limit or after the time limit are covered under other plan provisions.

Note: Any complication involved in the treatment of what was originally deemed an "accident" would continue to be part of that accident. This includes reactions to drugs given as a result of the accident.

Example: Holly Hiker (covered under the XYZ contract) was hiking along a mountain trail when a snake jumped out and bit her. She ended up incurring allowable charges of $150 for the ambulance, $125 for the ER doctor, $225 for the second doctor, $1,100 in hospital fees, and $250 in lab fees. The total allowable amount is $1,850.

Under XYZ the first $300 is covered at 100%. Therefore, if the bills were submitted in the order shown above, the ambulance charge ($150), the ER doctor's charge ($125), and $25 of the second doctor's charge would be paid at 100%. Thus $200 for the second doctor, $1,100 for the hospital fees and $250 for the lab fees would be paid under Major Medical at the Major Medical rates.

It is important to note that accident benefits usually have a date provision attached. Benefits may be limited to charges incurred within the first 90 days. Therefore, any treatments that occurred after the 90 day limit would not be allowed under Basic Benefits. They would only be paid under Major Medical benefits.

Non-Accidental Injuries

Injuries received as a result of any of the following are usually not considered accidental. These include:

- Injuries resulting from willful or reckless actions, which are known to result in serious bodily injury, including extremes such as playing Russian roulette, parachute jumping, high-speed auto racing on city streets, and injuries sustained in the commission of a crime.

- Intentionally self-inflicted injuries, such as those sustained during an attempted suicide.

- Injury sustained as a result of a family quarrel, unless the injured party takes legal action and receives a favorable court decision and it is the injured party who is the insured.

- Sunburn for any person over the age of 16. However, severe sunburn resulting from being stranded (i.e., in a desert) is covered as an accident for a person of any age.

- Any trauma resulting from the normal risks a person takes when undergoing surgical or medical treatment for an illness. Included in this category would be circumstances similar to the following: the unintentional severing of a ureter during a hysterectomy, leaving a clamp or surgical instrument in the operative field, and allergic reactions to prescribed medications.

- Injuries sustained in a fight or brawl, if it is determined that the member was the aggressor.
- A "bad trip" as the result of voluntary injection, ingestion or inhalation of illegal drugs in anyone over 16 years of age. In a person under 16 years of age, the first such experience may be considered "accidental."
- Any injury, in which the patient cannot recall how it happened, with the exception of anything as obvious as a fracture, burn, or laceration, and except in a small child who cannot be expected to remember.

Attempted Suicide

Most plans will not cover attempted suicides as an accident. Some plans specifically exclude expenses incurred as a result of an attempted suicide or self-inflicted injury. Thus, the policy should be checked to determine whether such an exclusion is applicable.

Diagnostic X-ray and Laboratory (DXL)

Benefits for x-rays and labs can be handled in a variety of ways. In the past, it was not uncommon to have what was called a "scheduled benefit." This type of benefit specified that a set dollar amount was allowed for each test. Today, most basic plans provide an alternative type of benefit called an "unscheduled" Basic Benefit, which limits payment under the Basic Benefit to a specified dollar amount per calendar year based on UCR or based on a conversion factor and RVS units. Once the calendar year maximum has been paid, subsequent expenses would be paid under the Major Medical benefit. If a Basic DXL benefit is provided by the plan, inpatient charges are usually excluded. That is, inpatient expenses would be covered only under Major Medical. However, outpatient hospital claims would allow a Basic Benefit for DXL charges. Therefore, it is important to read the benefit plan before determining benefits.

Example: Gen Gym is covered under the ABC contract. He has lab tests performed by his doctor in which the allowed amount is $25. The unit value for the lab tests is .95. The contract pays a basic benefit of $7.00 as a conversion factor. Thus the .96 unit value would be multiplied by $7.00 to get $6.72. This $6.72 is paid at the basic benefit rate (100%) and the remaining $18.28 is paid at the Major Medical rate.

Hospital Benefits

With this Basic Benefit, there may be a per admission deductible that does not usually carry over to the Major Medical plan. This benefit usually applies not only to hospital expenses, but also to outpatient surgery expenses and charges incurred as a result of an accident within a specified time period (generally 24 hours).

Another fact of this type of benefit is that a dollar limit is allowed per day for room and board and a separate allowance limit for ancillary expenses. As with other Basic Benefits, the provisions of this type of benefit vary widely from plan to plan.

Example: The XYZ contract allows for an inpatient hospital Basic Benefit of room and board up to the semi-private room charge (ICU is limited to $600 per day). Miscellaneous fees (all other hospital fees) are unlimited, but the Basic Benefit only lasts for 10 days per period of disability. This amount is subject to a $50 deductible.

Therefore, if Emily Emerson was admitted to the hospital for 14 days, the Basic Benefit would pay the cost of the room and board up to the semi-private rate for 10 days. 4 days would be paid under Major Medical. Likewise, the miscellaneous fees would be covered for the first 10 days under Basic Benefits, and the remaining 4 days under Major Medical. Basic Benefits are paid at 100%, for this contract, the Major Medical portion is covered at 80%.

The $50 hospital deductible would apply to the hospital charges. However, the patient would also have to pay the full $125 Major Medical deductible on any Major Medical charges, since the hospital deductible is separate from the Major Medical deductible. Additionally, if Emily Emerson was hospitalized again at a later date, she would owe another $50 deductible for the hospital charges since the benefits (and deductible) in this case is per occurrence, not per year.

Medical While Hospitalized (MWH)

Inpatient hospital care is often known as medical while hospitalized. The patient is admitted into a facility, and the physician visits him or her in the hospital.

Cumulative Benefit

Many types of MWH benefits are available. One of the more common types is called a **cumulative benefit**. To calculate benefits under this provision, the number of days hospitalized is multiplied by the benefit amount.

Example: Bobby Brainerd was hospitalized from 3/1 through 3/14. His contract allows $21 for the first day and $7 per day thereafter.

Here, the day of admission and the day of discharge are counted to determine the maximum allowance. Then, $7 is multiplied by 13 days, which equals $91 plus $21 for the first day = $112.

This is the maximum amount of Basic Benefit that can be paid out for this admission, regardless how many doctors see the patient on a single day, or the actual number of visits during the 14-day period. Some provisions allow multiple doctors to receive the benefit, but most plans limit the benefit to one maximum, which may be split up and paid to multiple providers as long as it does not exceed the maximum as calculated above. For an example of this benefit type, see the XYZ Corporation contract.

Per Visit Benefit

A second type of benefit has multiple names, which may include the terms **non-disabling** or **per visit benefit**. In this type of benefit, there is a waiting period, a daily maximum, and a calendar year maximum. For instance, the provision may read: $10 per day payable after seven days and $200 per calendar year.

Using the same hospitalization as above, this benefit is substantially different from the prior example. The day of admission and the day of discharge are counted to determine the maximum allowance. The seven-day waiting period is subtracted from the 14 days, and the remaining number of days (seven) is multiplied by the daily benefit amount of $10 for a total of $70. Usually, this provision allows for the circumstance in which a patient is discharged and then readmitted within a specified period of time, and another seven-day waiting period is not required. The plan provisions must be checked for this and any other exceptions.

Surgery While Hospitalized

If surgery is performed during the hospitalization, there are many ways to apply an inpatient visit provision, depending on the wording of the benefit and how the services are provided. The following is a summary of some of the more common circumstances. These rules apply to visits performed by the operating surgeon.

- If surgery is performed, there should be no charge for a visit on the same day as a surgery, excluding diagnostic procedures such as proctosigmoidoscopy and other procedures with no follow-up days.
- If the surgery has follow-up days listed but the surgery is not performed on the day of admission:
  - Visits billed before the date of surgery are allowed. Calculate as indicated in the examples above, counting the date of admission and every day up to but not including the day of surgery.
  - Visits billed on the day of surgery are combined with the surgery charge. There should be no separate charge on the day of surgery. Allow up to the plan maximum for the surgery.
  - Visits billed on the days following surgery within the follow-up days listed are to be combined with the surgery charge. Visits billed after the follow-up days can be paid separately.
  - If surgery is performed on the first day of admission, all visits, billed separately from the surgery, occurring within the follow-up days should be combined with the surgery charge. An emergency consultation on the same day as surgery may be an exception to combining the visits with the surgery charge. The regular

surgery benefit will be calculated in accordance with the plan provisions.

Example: Araceli Alejandro enters the hospital for treatment of a bone cyst (code 20615) on 3/1. Surgery is performed on 3/2 and she is discharged on 3/12. The RVS lists 10 follow-up days for this procedure. Therefore, a physician visit benefit would be allowed on the first day, since surgery was not performed on that day. The visits for the next 10 days would be covered under the surgical charge. The visit for the last day would be paid since it occurred after the 10 follow-up days.

Office Visits

Like the MWH benefit, office visit benefits are usually based on a specified dollar limit per visit after a specified number of visits have been applied to the waiting period. The waiting period is often on a per illness basis. That is, a specified number of visits are not paid for under Basic Benefits for each illness. After the specified number of visits have been accumulated, Basic Benefits begin. The waiting period may be based on the illness, or it may be cumulative for all conditions based on a period of disability.

Example: Frank Fryeburger broke his arm while skateboarding. His XYZ contract allows $7.00 for each visit after three visits. He sees the doctor five times during the treatment of his broken arm. Therefore, the first three visits to the doctor for treatment of the broken arm would not be covered under Basic Benefits. However, the last two visits would be covered at $7.00 per visit under Basic Benefits. All remaining amounts on these charges would be paid under Major Medical.

Surgery, Assistant Surgery, and Anesthesia

For surgery, assistant surgery, and anesthesia, determination of the Basic Benefit is based on the RVS and plan designated conversion factors. The assistant surgeon's allowance is almost always 20% of the surgeon's basic allowance. Consequently, the conversion factors are the same for the surgeon and the assistant surgeon. The anesthesia benefit may have the same or a different conversion factor. To get the Basic Benefit for all of these provisions, the conversion factor is multiplied by the RVS unit factor. Usually, there is a maximum amount allowed per operative session and often also for a calendar year. After the maximums are reached, these services would be covered only under Major Medical unless excluded under that contract's provisions.

Example: Terry Tucker covered under the XYZ contract had a cholecystectomy (code 47610) on 3/5. The surgery used the services of an anesthesiologist, a surgeon and an assistant surgeon. The unit value for the surgery is 25.42 for the surgeons and 15.0 for the anesthesiologist.

The conversion factor for Surgery is $8.50. Therefore, $216.07 (25.42 X $8.5) is payable under the Basic Benefit for the surgeon. Assistant surgeons are paid at 20% of the surgeon's amount. Therefore, $43.21 ($216.07 X 20%) is payable to the assistant surgeon.

The anesthesia conversion factor is $7.50. Therefore, $112.50 (15 X $7.5) is payable as a Basic Benefit for the anesthesiologist.

Note: Each of the above providers should submit payment on a separate claim. Thus, only one Basic Benefit amount will be shown on each claim.

Order of Basic Benefit Payments

To best use the funds available for Basic Benefits, these benefits should be applied in the following order:

1. Hospital benefits.
2. Surgery, assistant surgery, and anesthesia benefits.
3. Physician's visits (in- or outpatient).
4. DXL benefits.
5. Supplemental accident benefits.

Basic Major Medical Benefits

On a Basic only plan, amounts not paid by the Basic Benefits would not be payable at all. With a Basic-Major Medical Plan, expenses not paid by the Basic portion of the contract may be payable under the Major Medical portion. Different limitations or restrictions may apply to Basic Benefits than to Major Medical benefits. Generally, the following guidelines apply:

- Pay all applicable Basic Benefits.
- Refer to the policy or plan document to see whether the excess amounts not paid under the Basic plan would be eligible under Major Medical.
- Apply all Major Medical limitations, deductibles, UCR maximums, and other limitations.
- Add the Basic allowance to the Major Medical allowance to determine the total claim payment.

Usually, the Major Medical portion has a specified dollar deductible amount that must be satisfied yearly before any payments are made. In addition, expenses under Major Medical are not usually paid at 100%, at least not initially. Normally, payments are calculated at 80%, 70%, and so on (this can be any percentage).

With a Basic-Major Medical plan, all Basic Benefits will have two limitations (assuming the services are covered under both the Basic provisions and the Major Medical provisions):

1. The Basic Benefit limitation.
2. The Major Medical UCR or plan limitation.

Example: Terry Tucker (from previous example above), lets assume that this is Terry Tucker's first visit this year and no deductible has been satisfied yet. If the surgeon billed $1,500 for the surgery, and the allowed amount was $1,100, here's how the claim would be processed:

Billed amount	$1,500.00
Allowed amount	$1,100.00
Excluded amount	$ 400.00
Basic Benefit	$ 216.07
Major Medical amount	$ 883.93
Applied to deductible	$ 125.00
Remaining	$ 758.93
Major medical (payment at 80%)	$ 607.14
Payment (MM + Basic)	$ 823.21

This will become easier and clearer as you gain practice processing claims.

Comprehensive Major Medical Benefits

The comprehensive Major Medical plan does not have Basic Benefits per se. However, there may be supplemental or built-in benefits that act the same as a Basic Benefit. In other words, some charges may be covered at 100%, the same as in a Basic plan. All of the definitions previously covered also apply to this type of plan.

All services would be subject to the Major Medical deductible (unless it is waived for certain types of services) and would then be paid at the designated coinsurance rate. Limitations are usually based on a lifetime maximum or calendar year maximum.

Computing Stop Loss

Many Major Medical contracts have a provision that provides for a greater reimbursement percentage (usually 100%) after payment of a certain dollar amount for a calendar year period. This provision limits the amount of money that the member/patient will be responsible for on allowable charges. Such a provision applies only toward "allowable" charges. Expenses not allowed under the plan such as UCR excess amounts, non-covered expenses and sometimes those expenses not paid at the regular plan benefit level such as 50% benefits would not be applied toward the stop loss. The patient would remain entirely responsible for payment of these items.

An example of such contract wording would be "80% of the first $5000, 100% thereafter."

To compute stoploss:

Example 1
The plan coinsurance rate is 90%.
Stop loss is $6,000.
Major Medical paid to date for the year is $5,200.
Claim: $2,225 eligible under Major Medical

Step 1: Subtract the amount in Major Medical paid to date for the year from the plan's stop loss limit.

$6000
- 5200
  $800

$800 is 90% of the amount that must be considered by the payor to max the stop loss for the year.

Step 2: Calculate the amount that $800 is 90% of to determine the amount of eligible charges subject to the coinsurance stop loss limit. This is done by dividing the remaining amount by the coinsurance percentage.

$800 divided by .90 = $888.89
$888.89 will be covered at 90% to meet the stop loss limitation.

Step 3: Subtract the amount covered at 90%, $888.89, from the allowable charges on the claim to determine the amount that will be paid at 100% because the stop loss limit has been met.

Description	Allowed Amount	Paid at 90%	Paid at 100%
Visit	$ 100	$ 100.00	0
Lab Tests	$ 125	$ 125.00	0
Surgery	$2,000	$ 663.89	$1,336.11
Total	$2,225	$ 888.89	$1,336.11

Step 4: Calculate all remaining items normally. However, since the plan's stop loss has now been met, all subsequent allowable charges will be payable at 100% (there are some exceptions on some plans). Some types of expenses, such as nervous and mental, remain at a specific coinsurance rate regardless of whether the coinsurance limit has been met.

Example 2
The plan's coinsurance rate is 80%.
Stop loss is $6,000.
Major Medical paid to date for the year is $5,700.
Claim: $2,000 eligible under Major Medical.

Step 1: Subtract the amount applied to the Major Medical stop loss limit to date.

$6,000.00
- 5,700.00
  $300.00

Step 2: Calculate the amount that $300 is 80% of to determine the amount of eligible charges subject to the coinsurance stop loss limit. This is done by dividing the remaining amount by the coinsurance percentage.

$300 divided by .80 = $375
$375 will be covered at 80% to meet the stop loss limitation.

Step 3: Subtract the amount covered at 80%, $375, from the allowable charges on the claim to determine the amount that will be paid at 100% because the stop loss limit has been met.

Description	Allowed Amount	Paid at 80%	Paid at 100%
Visit	$ 100	$ 100.00	0
Lab Tests	$ 75	$ 75.00	0
Surgery	$1,825	$ 200.00	$1,625.00
Total	$2,000	$ 375.00	$1,625.00

Step 4: Calculate all remaining items normally. However, since the plan's stop loss has now been met, all subsequent allowable charges will be payable at 100% (there are some exceptions on some plans). Some types of expenses, such as nervous and mental, remain at a specific coinsurance rate regardless of whether the coinsurance limit has been met.

Example 3
The plan's coinsurance rate is 70%.
Stop loss is $5,000.
Major Medical paid to date for the year is $4,000.
Claim: $4,500 eligible under Major Medical (Total submitted charges: $5,000).
This is a Basic/Major Medical contract.

Step 1: Subtract the amount applied to the Major Medical stop loss limit to date.

$5,000
- 4,000
$1,000

Step 2: Calculate the amount that $1,000 is 70% of to determine the amount of eligible charges subject to the coinsurance stop loss limit. This is done by dividing the remaining amount by the coinsurance percentage.

$1,000 divided by .70 = $1,428.57
$1,428.57 will be covered at 70% to meet the stop loss limitation.

Step 3: Subtract the amount covered at 70% ($1,428.57), from the allowable Major Medical charges on the claim to determine the amount that will be paid at 100%, since the stop loss limit has been met. Remember that Basic Benefits are paid first. Therefore, the amount of the Basic Benefits will be subtracted from the allowed amount to determine the Major Medical amount.

Desc	Allowed Amount	Basic Benefit	Paid at 70%	Paid at 100%
Visit	$ 100	$ 15.65	$ 84.35	0
Lab	$ 500	$110.78	$ 389.02	0
Surgery	$3,900	$232.16	$ 955.20	$2,712.64
Total	$4,500	$358.59	$1,428.57	$2,712.64

Even though the Basic Benefit and the stoploss benefit are paid at the same amount (100%), they are broken into separate columns on the claim form. This allows anyone reviewing the payment worksheet to see the amounts paid under each benefit.

Step 4: Calculate all remaining items normally. However, since the plan's stop loss has now been met, all subsequent allowable charges will be payable at 100% (there are some exceptions on some plans). Some types of expenses, such as nervous and mental, remain at a specific coinsurance rate regardless of whether the coinsurance limit has been met.

The amount(s) paid at the coinsurance percentage will be placed in the Maj Med (Major Medical) column and the amount(s) paid at 100% would be placed in the last column.

Summary

The three major types of indemnity coverage currently available are:
1. Basic only.
2. Basic-Major Medical.
3. Comprehensive Major Medical.

It is important to understand the terminology associated with contracts and how benefit payments are calculated under each type of coverage. Quick and accurate benefit payments are what makes a health claims examiner a valuable employee.

Assignments

Complete the Questions for Review.
Complete Exercises 8 – 1 through 8 – 3.

Questions for Review

Directions: Answer the following questions without looking back into the material just covered. Write your answers in the space provided.

1. Name the three major types of coverage which are currently available.

    1. _____

    2. _____

    3. _____

2. _____ is the arrangement by which both the member and the plan share in a specified ratio of the covered losses under a policy.

3. _____ are the amount of those expenses that are allowable under the plan.

4. What is an individual deductible? _____

    _____

5. A _____ provides a specified allowance for a certain type of service.

6. State the three usual rules for Basic Benefits.

    1. _____

    2. _____

    3. _____

7. (True or False?) Expenses not paid by the Basic portion of the contract may be payable under the Major Medical portion. _____

8. Define accumulation period. _____

_____

9. Define automatic annual reinstatement. _____

_____

10. Explain the three-month carryover provision. _____

_____

If you were unable to answer any of the questions, refer back to the section and then complete the answers.

Exercise 8 – 1   *Page 74*

Directions: Calculate the amount of deductible which will be taken and answer the following questions.

The Apple family is covered under the Winter Contract. Their previous deductible payments are as follows:

	Annie	Adam	April	August	Ashley
C/O paid	0.00	5.00	10.00	55.00	0.00
Deductible paid	10.00	0.00	5.00	5.00	0.00
	35.00				

1. What is the individual deductible limit on this contract? ___$100.00___
2. What is the family deductible limit on this contract? ___$200.00___
3. Is the family limit aggregate or non-aggregate? ___aggregate___
4. How much has been paid toward the family deductible? ___$20.00___
5. Annie incurs allowed charges of $35. How much will be applied to the deductible? ___$35___
6. How much has Annie now met on her deductible? ___$45.00___
7. How much has now been paid toward the family deductible? ___$55.00___
8. August incurs allowed charges of $55. How much will be applied to the deductible? ___$40.00___
9. How much has August now met on his deductible? ___$100.00___
10. How much has now been paid toward the family deductible? ___$95.00___
11. April incurs allowed charges of $55. How much will be applied to the deductible? ___$55.00___
12. How much has April now met on her deductible? ___$70.00___
13. How much has now been paid toward the family deductible? ___$150.00___
14. Adam incurs allowed charges of $60. How much will be applied to the deductible? ___$50.00___
15. How much has Adam now met on his deductible? ___$55.00___
16. How much has now been paid toward the family deductible? ___$200.00___
17. Annie incurs allowed charges of $35. How much will be applied to the deductible? ___∅___
18. How much has Annie now met on her deductible? ___$45___
19. How much has now been paid toward the family deductible? ___$200.00___

Exercise 8 – 2

Directions: Calculate the amount of deductible which will be taken and answer the following questions.

The Carpenter family is covered under the Ball Contract. Their previous deductible payments are as follows:

	Carrie	**Connie**	**Cathy**	**Chris**
C/O paid	0.00	5.00	10.00	55.00
Deductible paid	10.00	0.00	5.00	5.00

1. What is the individual deductible limit on this contract? _$125.00_
2. What is the family deductible limit on this contract? _$250.00_
3. Is the family limit aggregate or non-aggregate? _Non-aggregate_
4. How many people are needed to meet the family deductible? _2_
5. Connie incurs allowed charges of $35. How much will be applied to the deductible? _$35.00_
6. How much has Connie now met on her deductible? _$40.00_
7. How many people are now needed to meet the family deductible? _2_
8. Carrie incurs allowed charges of $55. How much will be applied to the deductible? _$55.00_
9. How much has Carrie now met on her deductible? _$65.00_
10. How many people are now needed to meet the family deductible? _2_
11. Chris incurs allowed charges of $60. How much will be applied to the deductible? _$60.00_
12. How much has Chris now met on his deductible? _$120.00_
13. How many people are now needed to meet the family deductible? _2_
14. Chris incurs allowed charges of $35. How much will be applied to the deductible? _$5.00_
15. How much has Chris now met on his deductible? _$125.00_
16. How many people are now needed to meet the family deductible? _2_
17. Connie incurs allowed charges of $95. How much will be applied to the deductible? _$85.00_
18. How much has Connie now met on her deductible? _$125.00_
19. How many people are now needed to meet the family deductible? _2_
20. Carrie incurs allowed charges of $45. How much will be applied to the deductible? _$45.00_
21. How much has Carrie now met on her deductible? _$110.00_
22. How many people are now needed to meet the family deductible? _2_
23. Cathy incurs allowed charges of $105. How much will be applied to the deductible? _$105.00_
24. How much has Cathy now met on her deductible? _$120.00_
25. How many people are now needed to meet the family deductible? _2_
26. Carrie incurs allowed charges of $85. How much will be applied to the deductible? _$15.00_
27. How much has Carrie now met on her deductible? _$125.00_
28. How many people are now needed to meet the family deductible? _1_
29. Chris incurs allowed charges of $85. How much will be applied to the deductible? _∅_
30. How much has Chris now met on his deductible? _$125.00_
31. How many people are now needed to meet the family deductible? _1_
32. Cathy incurs allowed charges of $90. How much will be applied to the deductible? _$5.00_
33. How much has Cathy now met on her deductible? _$125.00_
34. How many people are now needed to meet the family deductible? _1_

NB If 2 people must satisfy its NON-aggregate

Exercise 8 – 3

Directions: Calculate the amount of deductible which will be taken and answer the following questions.

The Bear family is covered under the Rover Contract. Their previous deductible payments are as follows:

	Brad	**Bonnie**	**Barbra**	**Brian**
C/O paid	0.00	5.00	10.00	55.00
Deductible paid	10.00	0.00	5.00	5.00

1. What is the individual deductible limit on this contract? _$150.00_
2. What is the family deductible limit on this contract? _$360.00_
3. Is the family limit aggregate or non-aggregate? _NON-aggregate_
4. How many people are needed to meet the family deductible for this year? _2_
5. Bonnie incurs allowed charges of $55. How much will be applied to the deductible? _$55.00_
6. How much has Bonnie now met on her deductible? _$60.00_
7. How many people are now needed to meet the family deductible? _2_
8. Brian incurs allowed charges of $85. How much will be applied to the deductible? _$85.00_
9. How much has Brian now met on his deductible? _$145.00_
10. How many people are now needed to meet the family deductible? _2_
11. Barbra incurs allowed charges of $105. How much will be applied to the deductible? _$105.00_
12. How much has Barbra now met on her deductible? _$120.00_
13. How many people are now needed to meet the family deductible? _2_
14. Brad incurs allowed charges of $60. How much will be applied to the deductible? _$60.00_
15. How much has Brad now met on his deductible? _$70.00_
16. How many people are now needed to meet the family deductible? _2_
17. Bonnie incurs allowed charges of $35. How much will be applied to the deductible? _$35.00_
18. How much has Bonnie now met on her deductible? _$95.00_
19. How many people are now needed to meet the family deductible? _2_
20. Brian incurs allowed charges of $35. How much will be applied to the deductible? _$5.00_
21. How much has Brian now met on his deductible? _$150.00_
22. How many people are now needed to meet the family deductible? _2_
23. Barbra incurs allowed charges of $55. How much will be applied to the deductible? _$30.00_
24. How much has Barbra now met on her deductible? _$150.00_
25. How many people are now needed to meet the family deductible? _2_
26. Brad incurs allowed charges of $60. How much will be applied to the deductible? _$60.00_
27. How much has Brad now met on his deductible? _$130.00_
28. How many people are now needed to meet the family deductible? _2_

Honors Certification™

The Honors Certification™ challenge for this chapter is a written test. You will be presented with general information and asked to make the calculations discussed in this chapter. Each incorrect response will result in a deduction of between 5% and 10% from your grade. You must score 80% or higher to pass this test. If you fail the test on your first attempt you may retake the test one additional time. The items included in the second test may be different from those in the first test.

9 Cost-Containment Programs

In this chapter you will learn:

- To identify cost-containment programs and describe their implementation.

Key words and concepts you will learn in this chapter:

Health Maintenance Organization (HMO) – A type of pre-payment policy in which providers agree to charge HMO members for their services in accordance with a fixed schedule of rates.

Management Service Organization (MSO) – A corporation set up to provide management services to a medical group for a fee.

Medical Case Management – The process of evaluating the effectiveness and frequency of medical treatments by reviewing to determine whether the care that is being rendered or that is going to be rendered is appropriate.

Preadmission Testing (PAT) – Routine laboratory and x-ray tests performed on an outpatient basis before a scheduled inpatient admission.

Pre-certification – To get pre-approval for admission on elective, non-emergency hospitalization.

Preferred Provider Organization (PPO) – A group of health care providers who agree to provide services to a specific pool of patients for an agreed fee.

Second Surgical Opinion (SSO) – A review of a proposed surgery by a second physician/surgeon to determine the necessity of the planned services.

Utilization Review (UR) – A review of a patient's hospitalization prior to, during or after confinement to determine the medical necessity of services.

Until the tremendous growth in health care costs triggered the need for new approaches, plan sponsors had been concerned primarily with improving employee's access to quality medical care. As a result of the increased health care costs of the last 40 years, many employers have been struggling to provide adequate care for their employees at an affordable cost. As a result, a variety of programs have been developed to slow down the rate of increase in both the premiums and the cost of health care.

Some of the more popular methods used in trying to slow down spiraling health care costs include the following:

- Preadmission Testing (PAT)
- Pre-certification of Inpatient Admissions
- Utilization Review (UR)
- Second Surgical Opinion (SSO) Consultation
- Preferred Provider Organizations (PPO)
- Health Maintenance Organizations (HMO)

Preadmission Testing

Preadmission testing (PAT) consists of routine laboratory and x-ray tests performed on an outpatient basis before a scheduled inpatient admission. PAT was designed to reduce the duration of elective hospital confinements. This benefit is appropriate for scheduled, non-emergency hospital admissions that require the standard prerequisite testing before surgery. As a rule, this type of testing is restricted to a period of three to seven days before admission. Additionally, some plans limit the place of testing to either the hospital where the surgery is performed or the patient's regular provider of services.

No payments under PAT is made for preadmission tests that are prepared during the hospitalization or whose results are rejected by the physician as unreliable. Since preadmission testing generally serves to reduce costs, most plans offer an incentive to the member to use PAT by paying these charges at a higher coinsurance rate than regular testing or hospital-related services.

Example: Outpatient diagnostic tests performed prior to inpatient admission paid at 100% whether through a network provider or not.

Pre-certification of Inpatient Admissions

To **pre-certify** means to get pre-approval for admission on elective, non-emergency hospitalization. Contact is made either to the plan administrator or to some other entity sanctioned to determine the necessity of the admission. Most often, these entities are composed of a specialized group of nurses working under the direction of a physician. The nurses deal directly with the physician's office and the facility to determine whether the admission is necessary and whether the number of days of care is medically necessary. If the patient stays longer than the approved number of days, the additional days of care may not be paid for or the usual payment may be reduced by a percentage specified in the plan document. The objective in this program is to prevent unnecessary admissions and to get the patient out of the hospital as soon as is medically appropriate.

Some programs provide for pre-certification only prior to or on the day of hospitalization. Other programs provide for a complete approach to managing the care, which entails a utilization review program.

As part of HIPAA the Federal Government has mandated that no pre-certification can be required on maternity confinements. The law stipulates a confinement for a normal delivery cannot be limited to less than 48 hours (two days) or in the case of a cesarean section 96 hours (four days). The law however, does not state that a concurrent review could not be done. Therefore, if the patient stays hospital confined beyond the two days for a normal delivery or a day for a C-section and the plan has concurrent review and extended stay provisions, applicable penalties can be imposed on those extra days.

Utilization Review

As previously indicated, pre-certification or a prospective review determines the need and appropriateness of the recommended care. A complete Utilization Review (UR) program contains the following three components:

1. Pre-certification (prior to) or prospective review.
2. Concurrent review (during the confinement).
3. Retrospective review (after termination of confinement).

Concurrent review determines whether the estimated length of time and scope of the inpatient stay is justified by the diagnosis and symptoms. This review is conducted periodically during the projected length of stay. If the length of stay exceeds the criteria or if there is a change in treatment, the matter is referred to the medical consultant for review. This consultant at no time dictates the method of treatment or the length of stay. These decisions are left entirely to the patient and the attending physician. However, the consultant is entitled to inform the patient, physician, and facility that the continued stay exceeds the approved number of days and may not be covered by the plan as medically necessary. It is then the patient's responsibility to decide what course to take.

Retrospective review is used to determine after discharge whether the hospitalization and treatment were medically necessary and covered by the terms of the benefit program. This type of review may be used as a substitute for admission and concurrent reviews when the failure to notify the UR program of an admission prevents the regular review procedures. However, the main drawback to the retrospective review is that the patient and providers are not notified about the services that will not be covered until after they have been provided. The best programs always work most effectively when the patient is notified beforehand that he or she will be primarily responsible for payment of services. This approach deters the member from incurring unnecessary expenses.

Second Surgical Opinion Consultations

Surgical claims represent the second highest categorical cost to benefit plans (hospitalization ranks first). The United States has the world's highest rate of surgical treatment because neither the physician nor the patient has any financial incentive to consider less expensive alternatives.

About **80%** of all surgeries can be considered "elective." That is, they are not required because of a life-threatening situation. The objective of a **Second Surgical Opinion (SSO)** is to eliminate elective surgical procedures that are classified as unnecessary.

Unnecessary surgery is that which is recommended as an elective procedure when an alternative method of treatment may be preferable for a number of reasons, including:

- The surgery itself may be premature, taking into consideration all pathologic indications.
- The risk to the patient may not justify the benefits of surgery.
- An alternative medical treatment may be superior for both medical and cost-effective reasons.
- A less severe surgical procedure may be preferable under the circumstances. Or, no medical or surgical procedure may be necessary at all.

In this program, the plan participant consults an independent specialist to determine whether the recommended elective surgical procedure is advisable.

This process is not intended to interfere with the patient-physician relationship nor to prevent the participant from receiving necessary elective operations.

This program may be administered in one of two ways:

1. A **mandatory program** requires the patient to obtain an SSO for special procedures, or there is an automatic reduction or denial of benefits. For an example of this type of program, see the Ninja Enterprises contract.

2. A **voluntary program** encourages participants to have an SSO, but there is no automatic reduction of benefits if the patient does not comply. In both approaches, the SSO and related tests are usually paid at 100% so that the patient will not have any out-of-pocket expenses for conforming to the program.

The SSO program has meet with much criticism because it has not effectively reduced the number of elective surgeries. One of the main reasons for this ineffectiveness is that physicians may be reluctant to tell a patient that a surgery is not necessary. This attitude stems from the growing number of malpractice lawsuits. For example, if a physician states that a patient does not need surgery and a sudden emergency situation arises that is related to the original need for surgery, the physician may be held liable under a malpractice suit. Consequently, many plans are abandoning the SSO plan provision.

Managed Care

Managed care is a strategy for reducing or controlling health care costs by tightly monitoring and restricting the use and cost of services. With this type of system, the insurer manages the delivery of health care and controls costs by emphasizing primary and preventive care services. Managed care plans use quality assurance and utilization review to ensure the appropriate delivery of care. Preferred provider organizations, HMO's, and point-of-service plans are examples of managed care plans.

Preferred Provider Organizations

A **Preferred Provider Organization** is a group of health care providers who agree to provide services to a specific pool of patients for an agreed fee (contractual). PPO's include doctors, dentists, hospitals, and any provider group that contracts with another entity to provide services at competitive fees.

PPO packages may involve contractual agreements for a limited number of health care services or for a full range of inpatient and outpatient medical services. Because the PPO group has agreed

to specific benefits, they usually have their own utilization review committees or guidelines to reduce the amount of testing performed, hospitalizations, and other services.

In some cases, a health plan may continue to offer a standard indemnity coverage but also offers special PPO arrangements in which the PPO provider is paid more quickly and at a higher rate than non-PPO providers. In such a case, the plan participant saves money because out-of-pocket expenses are also reduced.

Many PPO providers are available. Some are good and some are not. The benefits of a PPO provider compared with a non-PPO provider vary greatly from plan to plan. However, generally both the patient and the plan reduce costs by being members of a good PPO.

Some of the advantages for the patient associated with being in a PPO are:

- Reduced health care costs with no restriction (or with only a minimal restriction) of freedom of choice of providers. Reduced health care costs mean reduced out-of-pocket expenses.
- Less paperwork in filing claims because the PPO submits the claim directly to the payer and payment is made directly to the PPO.
- Generally, provision only of services that are medically necessary because there is usually a formal utilization review program.

Some of the advantages to the provider associated with being in a PPO are:

- Increased patient volume.
- Prompt claim payment.
- Reduced financial risk due to automatic assignment of benefits.
- Active participation in local cost-containment efforts.

Some of the advantages to the benefit plan associated with being in a PPO are:

- Reduced health care cost.
- Better utilization control.

The Ninja contract is an example of a PPO contract.

Health Maintenance Organizations

A **Health Maintenance Organization** is a type of pre-payment policy in which providers agree to charge HMO members for their services in accordance with a fixed schedule of rates. The HMO member (insured) may pay a certain portion of the charge at the time services are rendered, and the balance is either directly billed to the HMO or included in the monthly fee that the HMO pays the provider for participating.

If services are available through the HMO but the insured does not go through the HMO provider, either the benefit will be reduced or the member will be entirely responsible for the payment of care received. Any services provided outside the HMO network must be pre-approved by the HMO to be covered. If services are not approved, the HMO will not pay anything toward the charges.

The main difference between a PPO and an HMO is that an HMO provider receives a monthly fee based on capitation (number of covered plan members), whereas a PPO provider is paid only when a member is treated. A disadvantage of the HMO arrangement is the limitation of the patient's freedom of choice of physicians. In addition, the location of the HMO facilities may be limited or inconvenient for many plan members.

Exclusive Provider Organizations

In the **Exclusive Provider Organization**, the patient must select a primary care giver and can use only physicians who are part of the network or who are referred by the primary care physician. EPO physicians are paid as service is rendered, after which they get a capitation or utilization bonus from the carrier.

Gatekeeper PPO

In the **Gatekeeper PPO**, the member chooses a family provider or physician and must see him or her before being referred to a specialist. The specialist may or may not be within the network. In essence, the family physician is the "gatekeeper" to alternative services and can choose to refer the patient or not.

Physician Hospital Organizations

A **Physician Hospital Organization (PHO)** is an organization of physicians and hospitals that bands together for the purpose of obtaining contracts from payor organizations. The PHO bargains as an entity for preferred provider status with various payers. The organization also refers clients to each other.

Management Service Organizations

A **Management Service Organization (MSO)** is a separate corporation set up to provide management services to a medical group for a fee. Individual physicians and providers contract with the MSO for services. An MSO may be owned by a single hospital, several hospitals, or investors.

Medical Case Management

Medical Case Management (MCM) is the process of evaluating the effectiveness and frequency of medical treatments by reviewing to determine whether the care that is being rendered or that is going to be rendered is appropriate. When a situation arises in which the potential for high claims payment exists based on the diagnosis or the type of services needed by the claimant, the case is generally referred to the Medical Case Management Department. The MCM (in some instances, an outside company performs this function) reviews these cases and tries to minimize the company's loss by finding alternative solutions to provide patient care. This may necessitate providing the patient with equipment or care that is normally not covered under the plan, but based on the circumstances it is more cost-effective and beneficial to the patient to make these provisions. MCM often concentrates on high dollar claims involving inpatient hospital confinements. Less costly alternatives such as hospice, nursing home, and home health care with discounted nursing or equipment are explored.

An important goal of MCM is to save costs for the insured, the patient, the account, the health care providers, and the administrator. Even more important, this process can result in higher quality care.

Under most plans, MCM is a voluntary process. To be successful, the cooperation of the patient and family is important.

Situations that may indicate possible claims for MCM are included in **Appendix 9 – 1**; however, the health claims examiner should watch for certain factors. These include:

1. Pattern of repeated hospital admissions (or two within six months).
2. Outpatient therapies of more than six weeks (including nursing services).
3. Home care by an RN of more than four hours per day.
4. Skilled nursing care in an extended care facility of more than six weeks.
5. Any hospital interim bill (excessive length of stay).
6. Any terminal or progressive disease requiring long-term skilled care.

Use experience and common sense to identify claims that are unusual and may become "catastrophic" by virtue of chronicity or immediately high cost.

Summary

The cost of health care coverage in general is increasing faster than any other segment of service or commodity in our society. In general, although overall inflation has been very low in the last few years, the medical inflation rate, particularly as it relates to health insurance has increased by double digits. Because of these factors, it is essential to the survival of the health insurance industry that cost containment provisions be implemented to help reverse this trend.

Assignments

Complete the Questions for Review.

Questions for Review

Directions: Answer the following questions without looking back into the material just covered. Write your answers in the space provided.

1. List six of the more popular methods used in trying to slow down spiraling health care costs.

    1. _____

    2. _____

    3. _____

    4. _____

    5. _____

    6. _____

2. _____ is routine laboratory and x-ray tests performed on an outpatient basis before a scheduled inpatient admission.

3. To _____ means to get pre-approval for an admission on an elective, non-emergency hospitalization.

4. List the two ways that second surgical opinion programs may be administered.

    1. _____

    2. _____

5. A _____ is a type of prepayment policy in which providers agree to charge HMO members for their services in accordance with a fixed schedule of rates.

If you were unable to answer any of the questions, refer back to the section and then complete the answers.

Honors Certification™

The Honors Certification™ challenge for this chapter is a written test of the information contained within this chapter. You will be given 30 minutes to complete this test. Each incorrect answer will result in a deduction of between 1% and 5% from your grade. You must achieve a score of 85% or higher to pass this test. If you fail the test on your first attempt you may retake the test one additional time. The items included in the second test may be different from those in the first test.

Appendix 9 – 1

Potential Medical Case Management Claims

The following list consists of diagnoses that are potentially medical case management claims. This list is intended to be used for training and reference purposes only, since the particular company or plan guidelines may differ from those stated.

Section 1: Potential medical case management claims listing by condition are as follows:

Neonatal Patients
- Premature birth
- Hydrocephalus
- Respiratory distress and in ICU over one week
- Meningomyelocele
- Bronchopulmonary dysplasia
- Major or multiple congenital anomaly

Obstetric Patients
- Expected multiple birth of three or more infants
- Previous history of neonatal ICU-confined infant
- Bleeding during pregnancy
- Toxemia (hypertension) requiring hospitalization during pregnancy

Transplant/Dialysis Patients
- Heart, liver, or bone marrow transplant
- Organ rejection
- Cardiomyopathy
- Biliary atresia
- Renal failure

Neurologic Patients
- Brain tumors
- TIA (transient ischemic attack)
- Closed head injury
- Unconsciousness (any cause)
- Cerebral aneurysm or AV malformation
- Meningitis or encephalitis
- Reye's syndrome
- Anoxic encephalopathy
- Guillain-Barre
- Quadriplegia
- Paraplegia
- Chronic stroke
- Multiple sclerosis (MS)
- Amyotrophic lateral sclerosis (ALS)
- Alzheimer's disease

Psychiatric Conditions
- Anorexia nervosa
- Adolescent adjustment reaction
- Manic depression; bipolar disorder
- Schizophrenia
- Sexual abuse
- Chemical dependency
- Depression with or without suicide attempt

Cardiovascular Conditions
- Ruptured abdominal aortic aneurysm
- Myocardial Interaction (heart attack)
- Intractable angina
- Peripheral vascular disease, w/ pending amputation

Respiratory Conditions
- Respirator dependency (any cause)
- Emphysema
- Chronic bronchitis or asthma

Malignancy Patients
- Multiple surgeries
- Radiation treatments
- Cancer in children
- Chemotherapy
- Acute leukemia
- Aplastic anemia
- Kaposi's sarcoma

Other Diagnoses
- AIDS
- Lupus
- Any condition causing paralysis

Traumatically Injured Patients
- Thermal burns or frostbite
  - Child over 10% or adult over 20%
- Crash injuries
- Amputations
- Multiple trauma or fractures
- Spinal cord injury

Section II: Potential medical case management claims by ICD-9 codes are as follows:

Cases	ICD-9 Code	Description
High-risk mothers		
	640.x – 644.0	Complications of pregnancy
	646.x – 648.x	
	760 – 779	Perinatal conditions
Other		
	344.x	Other paralytic syndrome
	045.x	Poliomyelitis and other viral diseases of CNS
Highly suggestive of AIDS		
	031.0	Pulmonary infection by *Mycobacterium*
	112.0*	Candidiasis of mouth (thrush)
	112.4	Candidiasis pneumonia
	112.5	Systematic candidiasis
	112.81 – 112.89*	Candidiasis of other sites
	114	Coccidioidal meningitis
	114.0	Pulmonary coccidioidomycocis
	114.9	Coccidioidomycocis, unspecified
	115.0 – 115.9	Histoplasmosis
	130.0	Toxoplasmosis encephalitis
	130.3 – 130.9	Toxoplasmosis of other sites
	136.3	*Pneumocystis carinii* pneumonia
	173.9	Kaposi's sarcoma
	279.3	Deficiency of cell-mediated immunity
	279.3	Unspecified immunity deficiency
	279.9	Unspecified disorder of immune system
	279.10	Immunodeficiency with predominant T-cell defect, unspecified
	279.19	Other
	780.6*	Fever of unknown origin
	785.6*	Lymphadenopathy
	790.8*	Viremia, unspecified
Traumatic brain injury		
	850.x—854.x	Various types of head injury
	800.x—804.x	Skull fracture
	780.0	Coma and stupor

Cases	ICD-9 Code	Description
Nontraumatic brain injury		
	191.x	Brain tumors
	293.x	Transient organic condition
	294.x	Other organic psychotic conditions
	310.x	Mental disorders due to organic brain damage
	348.x	Brain conditions
	349.x	Other and unspecified diseases of CNS
Spinal cord injury		
	952.x	Spinal cord injury without evidence of spinal bone injury
	805.x – 806.x	Fracture of neck and trunk
	827.x – 828.x	Fracture of neck and trunk
	336.x	Diseases of spinal cord
Stroke		
	342.x	Hemiplegia
	430	Subarachnoid hemorrhage
	431	Intercerebral hemorrhage
	432	Other unspecified intracranial hemorrhage
	433.x	Occulsion and stenosis of cerebral arteries
Multiple fractures		
	733.81	Malunion (fx)
	733.82	Nonunion (fx)
Burns		
	940.x—949.x	Burns
High-risk infants		
	343.x	Infantile cerebral palsy
	741.x	Spina bifida
	742.x	Other congenital anomalies of the nervous system
	644.2	Early onset of delivery

*These codes appear frequently with AIDS-related complex (ARC) or AIDS. However, these codes also appear with a substantial number of non-AIDS related illnesses. "X" denotes the entire range of subset numbers describing variations on the particular diagnosis.

10 General Plan Provisions

In this chapter you will learn:

- The purpose and identification of possible third party liability and pre-existing claims.
- To thoroughly investigate possible third party liability and pre-existing claims.

Key words and concepts you will learn in this chapter:

Acts of Third Parties – A provision that allows the insurance carrier to recoup medical expenses paid if it is found that a third party is liable for damages.

Mandates – Laws enacted by state legislatures that require insurance carriers to cover certain services or dependents, or services provided by certain providers.

Pre-existing Condition – A condition that the patient was treated for within a specified time period before becoming effective under the plan.

Subrogation – The right for a portion of the recovery that the claimant may obtain from a third party.

Third Party Liability (TPL) – See Acts of Third parties.

Acts of Third Parties and Subrogation are provisions that are included in many benefit plans to allow for recovery of money paid on claims incurred as a result of a third party's act or acts for which that party is financially responsible.

> *Example:* A claimant is injured while on the premises of a grocery store. The losses are submitted to the benefit plan for payment. Subsequently, the claimant seeks recovery from the store. When recovery is successful, the claimant is required to reimburse the benefit plan for its losses.

Subrogation and Acts of Third Parties (ATP) (also known as Third Party Liability [TPL]) have some similarities but are actually different. Many older plans had Subrogation, whereas many new plans have TPL.

State laws affect general plan provisions. Although a plan may contain one of these provisions, it may not always be allowed to function if prohibited by a specific state statute or statutes.

A demand by the plan for reimbursement cannot be made until the insured has been compensated for the loss by the third party. Filing a lien against such compensation protects the plan by making it mandatory that the plan be reimbursed before the claimant receives such compensation. Although the loss claimed by the claimant may include medical expenses, property damage, loss of earnings, pain, suffering, and even future medical expenses, the plan is permitted to recover only the amount actually paid out as a result of the injury. A sample of a payment demand is shown in **Figure 10 – 1**. When any payments are received, they should be noted on a Right of Reimbursement Claims Ledger Sheet. A sample copy of such a ledger sheet is shown in **Figure 10 – 2**.

When a claim is received for expenses incurred as a result of an injury, determine how, when, and where the injury occurred. If this information is not indicated on the submitted forms, write to the member and request details. Samples of a letter and questionnaire are shown in **Figures 10 – 3 and 10 – 4**.

If the injury occurred as the result of another party's acts and the plan has a TPL or subrogation provision, a letter informing the claimant regarding the appropriate provision should be sent along with an agreement. A sample copy of such letter is shown in **Figure 10 – 5**. The claimant must sign the agreement indicating that if monies are received from another source to cover these expenses, he or she is legally obligated to reimburse the plan. A sample copy of the agreement is shown in **Figure 10 – 6**. This signed agreement is then kept on file with occasional follow-ups to track recovery; some payers file a lien against monies that the claimant might be entitled to. If the plan does not have either of these types of provisions, reimbursement from a third source cannot be sought.

As a rule, these provisions cannot be used to recover against the member's own auto liability carrier, or homeowner's insurance carrier.

Acts of Third Parties

Under **TPL**, the plan advances money to the injured person with the understanding that, if the claimant is successful in obtaining reimbursement monies from a third party, the plan will be reimbursed for its losses. The plan's interests lie with the claimant, not with the third party.

An example of a third party provision is:

A special provision applies when you or your dependent covered under the plan is injured through the act or omission of another person. When this happens, the plan will advance the benefits under the policy only under the condition that you or your dependents agree in writing to the following:

1. To repay the plan in full any sums advanced to cover such claims paid by the plan from the judgment or settlement you or a dependent receives.
2. To provide the plan with a lien to repay the plan to the extent of benefits advanced by the plan. The lien may be filed with the person whose act caused the injuries, his or her agent, the court, or the attorney of the person covered under the plan.

Thus, when such a claim is received, a repayment agreement must be sent to the claimant. This agreement requires the member to provide the information necessary to investigate the claim and subsequently, if appropriate, to file a lien with the member's attorney for reimbursement against any settlement procured by the member. Usually, payment of losses is not made until the claimant has signed the repayment agreement and returned it to the administrator.

Administration of this provision tends to be long-term and time-intensive. Therefore, many plans have retained special agencies responsible for tracking and recovering TPL monies .In exchange, the agency is paid from the proceeds that they recover.

ANY INSURANCE CARRIER, INC.
123 Any Drive, Anywhere, USA 12345 ● (800) 555-1234

Date: _____

Policyholder: _____
Control: _____
Employee: _____
Dependent: _____

Dear

This is to advise you that benefits totaling _____ have been paid to date to _____
_____ as a result of the accident on _____.

Under the terms of _____ group health coverage, the insurance carrier is entitled to claim reimbursement from any third party liability coverage applicable to the same accident. Therefore, subrogation rights are claimed. Please advise as soon as possible when we might expect payment.

Sincerely,

Any Insurance Carrier

Figure 10 – 1: Sample of a Payment Demand Letter

ANY INSURANCE CARRIER, INC.
123 Any Drive, Anywhere, USA 12345 ● (800) 555-1234

FOR RIGHT OF REIMBURSEMENT CLAIMS

Claimant: _____   Policyholder: _____

Date of Accident: _____   Control No.: _____

Amount of Payment	Payee	Date Paid	Total Amount Paid to Date

Figure: 10 – 2: Right of Reimbursement Claims Ledger Sheet

ANY INSURANCE CARRIER, INC.
123 Any Drive, Anywhere, USA 12345 ● (800) 555-1234

Social Security No.

Re:

Dear

The claim that you recently submitted for accidental bodily injuries expenses is under review. Circumstances of the accident indicate that a third party may be liable for the payment of your medical or dental bills.

Accordingly, the policy in force between _____ and _____ contains a Third Party Liability exclusion, which provides that no medical or dental benefits are payable for injuries or illness caused by a third party if payment for such expenses has been or will be received from the third party or insurer. A copy of the entire provision is attached.

To assist us in evaluating the claim, please complete the enclosed questionnaire detailing particulars regarding the accident and parties involved. Any additional information would be greatly appreciated.

Additionally, if a third party is liable for your expenses, we have enclosed a Third Party Liability Reimbursement Agreement, to be signed, witnessed, and returned to us before benefits can be released.

If you have any questions regarding this matter, please do not hesitate to contact me.

Sincerely,

Figure 10 – 3: Sample of a letter requesting further information on a possible TPL claim.

ANY INSURANCE CARRIER, INC.
0123 Any Drive, Anywhere, USA 12345 ● (800) 555-1234

TPL INVESTIGATION QUESTIONNAIRE

1. Name and address of responsible third party.

   _____

   City _____ State _____ Zip Code _____

2. Name and address of responsible third party insurance company and policy number.

   City _____ State _____ Zip Code _____

3. If an accident, what were the circumstances?

   _____
   _____

4. If Any Insurance Carrier, Inc. is to pay medical benefits under the terms of the contract, when is settlement expected or how often may we expect status reports?

   _____
   _____

5. Is legal counsel involved? If yes, please give name and address.

   _____
   _____

   City _____ State _____ Zip Code _____

Figure 10 – 4: Sample of TPL questionnaire.

ANY INSURANCE CARRIER, INC.
123 Any Drive, Anywhere, USA 12345 • (800) 555-1234

Third Party Liability Exclusion Rider Effective
Attached to and made part of Group Insurance Policy No. _____

Issued by _____

to _____

No benefits will be paid under this policy to or on behalf of an insured individual who has:

1. medical or dental charges or
2. loss of earnings

if the insured individual has received payment, in whole or in part, from a third party, or its insurer, for past or future medical or dental charges or loss of earnings as the result of negligence or intentional acts of a third party.

If an insured party makes a claim to Any Insurance Carrier for medical, dental, or loss of earnings benefits under this policy prior to receiving payment from a third party, or its insurer, the insured individual (or legal representative of a minor or incompetent) must agree in writing to repay Any Insurance Carrier from any amount of money received by the insured individual from the third party, or its insurer. The repayment will be to the extent of the benefits paid by Any Insurance Carrier. However, the reasonable pro rata expenses, such as lawyer's fees and court costs, incurred in affecting the third party payment may be deducted from the repayment to Any Insurance Carrier.

The repayment agreement will be binding upon the insured individual (or legal representative of a minor or incompetent) whether:

1. The payment received from the third party, or its insurer, is the result of:
   a. a legal judgment, or
   b. an arbitration award, or
   c. a compromise settlement, or
   d. any other arrangement, or
2. The third party, or its insurer, has admitted liability for the payment, or
3. The medical or dental charges or loss of earnings are itemized in the Third party payment.

Figure 10 – 5: Sample of a letter informing the claimant of TPL or subrogation provision

---

ANY INSURANCE CARRIER, INC.
123 Any Drive, Anywhere, USA 12345 • (800) 555-1234

Third Party Liability Reimbursement Agreement

I, _____, an insured individual (or his or her legal representative) under group insurance policy number _____ issued by Any Insurance Carrier, Inc. to _____, the policyholder, pursuant to the terms of the group insurance policy, do hereby agree to reimburse Any Insurance Carrier for any medical or dental expenses or loss of earnings benefits which are paid by Any Insurance Carrier or will be paid by it, which expenses or benefits arise out of the accident or sickness commencing _____, 20 _____, if payment is received from a third party, or its insurer.

I understand that this agreement to reimburse shall be binding on me regardless of whether:

1. the payment received from the third party, or its insurer, is the result of a legal judgment, arbitration award, compromise settlement or otherwise; or
2. such third party, or its insurer, has admitted liability in connection with such payment; or,
3. such medical or dental expenses actually incurred or loss of earnings realized are itemized in such third party payment.

I further understand that the reasonable pro rata costs, including attorney fees, actually incurred by me in effecting the third party payment for such medical or dental expenses or loss of earnings may be deducted from any such reimbursement.

_____
(Witness)

_____
(Insured Individual or his or her Legal Representative)

Figure 10 – 6: Third Party Liability Reimbursement Agreement

Subrogation

Under **subrogation**, the plan has an obligation to pay a benefit under the contract, but has a subrogated right for a portion of the recovery that the claimant may obtain from a third party. The plan has a direct interest with the third party.

An example of a subrogation provision is:

When benefits are paid to or for you or a dependent under the terms of the plan, the plan shall be subrogate, unless otherwise prohibited by law, to your right of recovery or the rights of recovery of a dependent against any person who might acknowledge to be liable or might be found legally liable by a court of competent jurisdiction for the injury that necessitated the hospitalization or the medical or surgical treatment for which the benefits were paid.

Such subrogation rights shall extend only to the recovery by the plan of the benefits it has paid for such treatment, and the plan shall pay fees and costs associated with such recovery.

When a claim is received for expenses incurred as a result of any injury involving another party, a subrogation letter along with a subrogation statement should be sent to the claimant.

The subrogation statement requires the member to provide information necessary to investigate the claim. The form also requires the member to agree to allow the plan to file a lien against any settlement made by another party.

Although, technically, these two provisions are not the same, from the health claims examiner's standpoint, the differences are moot. Do not be concerned with what the differences are at this point. Be concerned with the concepts behind them, what the objective is, and how to obtain that objective.

Pre-existing Conditions

A **pre-existing condition** is a condition that the patient was treated for within a specified time period before the member becoming effective under the plan. This provision must be read carefully because there are many variations. For example, it may apply to dependents only; time limits may be different for members versus dependents; or, the provision may be waived for all individuals who are covered on the effective date of the plan.

Whether the expense or expenses incurred are excluded completely or limited to a specific dollar benefit, most clauses provide that benefits will become payable after the member has been covered under the plan for a specific period of time and has not received any treatment for the pre-existing condition.

Handling Procedures

Improperly handled claims for pre-existing conditions are a frequent source of complaints and lawsuits. An examiner has an obligation to:

- Investigate thoroughly, at the earliest appropriate time, preferably on the very first claim receipt. If the expenses result from an injury incurred after the effective date of the plan or are not chronic, such as a cold or flu, an inquiry should not be made. Always consider the specific plan provisions.
- Notify the member and the provider, if appropriate, of the delay, in writing.
- Bring the investigation to a conclusion as rapidly as possible with either a decision to pay or a fully documented denial.

Treatment Free Provisions

To qualify for payment on the basis of having satisfied the treatment free provision and the total limitation (no payment of pre-existing conditions for 12 months), it must be determined that the patient did not receive any treatment for the pre-existing condition from a doctor, hospital, clinic, or other medical practitioner. Advice from a practitioner without treatment may be considered "treatment" in the case of a pre-existing condition. To determine whether a given condition is pre-existing, the following procedures should be followed:

1. Identify all potential pre-existing conditions by noting the diagnosis and the length of time between the effective date of the plan and the first treatment documented on the claim form or in the claim file. Special attention should be paid to claims for chronic conditions or for major surgery with little or no preliminary diagnostic work or medical treatment.

2. Initiate the investigation as soon as appropriate by writing to the attending physician and all other consulting or referring physicians whose names can be determined. Write the following sources as well:

    - All hospitals involved and request a copy of hospital records including the admitting history and physical, discharge summary, consultation, and operative reports.
    - Pharmacies to obtain drug names, dates filled, and names and phone numbers of prescribing physicians.
    - Attending physicians to request copies of treatment histories that should detail the onset of the condition, referring physicians, and so on.
    - Claimants to request the names, addresses, and phone numbers of all doctors seen and all medications taken during the appropriate time period stipulated in the plan.

    Many insurance carriers have a standard form letter for requesting information regarding a pre-existing condition.

3. Act immediately on leads or additional information supplied in response to the initial requests for information.
4. Bear in mind that the burden of proof lies with the plan to prove that a condition is pre-existing. No matter how certain you may be that a condition is pre-existing, a claim cannot be denied as such unless there is adequate documentation in the claim file.
5. If answers to the inquiries are not received, follow the administrator's guidelines for denying the claim. Do not deny the claim as pre-existing. Instead, deny pending receipt of previously requested information.
6. Determining whether a condition is a chronic illness or a new illness is essential in deciding whether the pre-existing exclusion would apply. For example, infectious conditions such as upper respiratory infection, otitis media, bronchitis, and urinary tract infection may occur repeatedly with resolution between episodes. If a period elapses between treatments, a new episode (and therefore, a new illness) may exist, in which the pre-existing exclusion would not apply.
7. Related conditions and complications of existing conditions may pose problems in determining whether an illness is pre-existing. Certain diseases are progressive, and a different diagnosis may be assigned to the successive stages of the disease. *The Merck Manual* may be helpful in researching such conditions, but any questionable case should be referred to the supervisor, medical review department, or a consultant for review.

Refer to the ABC contract. According to this plan, if the claimant was effective when the plan became effective 06/01/02, the pre-existing exclusion will not apply to that person. If the claimant was not effective on the plan effective date of 06/01/02, the exclusion would apply.

Example: Claimant effective 07/01/02 and a claim is received for a diagnosis of diabetes for the date of service 08/01/02. Diabetes is a chronic condition; therefore, it is possibly pre-existing. An investigation must be pursued in a manner previously indicated so that the claim file can be properly documented to substantiate the claims decision. Let's examine the claim form. Does it list the following: The date of the first treatment of the condition? Was the treatment before the effective date? If so, the condition is possibly pre-existing because persons with some diabetic conditions require insulin injections or pills on a daily basis.

If not, is there a name of a referring physician? If so, write to that physician and request treatment information. If the first treatment date is not indicated, write to the physician who submitted the claim and the claimant, requesting the following information:

- The names of all physicians seen between 03/01/02 and 07/01/02 (this covers the 90-day period prior to the effective date of coverage, up to and including the current treatment date).
- The names and dates of all prescriptions written during this same period of time.
- The names of all other medical providers referred to or from and the dates of treatments during this period of time.

The objective of this questioning is two-fold as follows:

1. To determine whether treatment commenced during the 90-day period of time before the effective date.
2. To determine whether a three-month period of time has intervened in which the claimant did not receive treatment (determine whether the three-month treatment free period provision applies).

Once the claimant has been covered under the plan for 12 consecutive months, the pre-existing exclusion no longer applies whether or not the condition was pre-existing.

On a plan that includes a specific money limit for pre-existing conditions, it is not necessary to pend the claims and request information. However, the allowable amounts that have been provided under the plan must be tracked so that once the specified limit has been reached for each condition, the pre-existing inquiry can be initiated.

Properly applying pre-existing limitations takes experience. Remember what is being investigated and what the plan provisions allow or do not allow. Also, request assistance at the beginning of the process until you are familiar with the application of the various provisions. In doing so you will not delay the claim unnecessarily.

HIPAA and Health Insurance Portability

On August 26, 1996, new laws regarding health insurance were signed into law by President William Clinton. This law was called the Health Insurance Portability and Accounting Act of 1996 (HIPAA). The most important changes include pre-existing limitations, prior coverage certification, and privacy issues. The privacy issues were covered in the **Legal Issues** chapter. Here we shall discuss pre-existing limitations and prior coverage certification.

This law has a direct impact on insurers unlike other health care legislation, which primarily impacts the employer.

HIPAA restricts the circumstances and the period for which a group health plan may exclude coverage for a pre-existing condition. The restriction has five parts:

1. A group health plan may not impose a pre-existing condition limit unless the plan provides prior notice to the member of the existence and terms of the pre-existing condition exclusion.
2. A group health plan may not impose a pre-existing condition exclusion unless the member received treatment or advice from a state-licensed medical practitioner regarding the condition within the six months preceding the date of enrollment under the group health plan.
3. The group health plan must credit an individual's prior health coverage toward satisfaction of the pre-existing condition limit unless that coverage was solely for excepted benefits (see below).
4. The maximum period allowed for a pre-existing condition exclusion is generally 12 months (18 months in the case of an individual who does not enroll when first eligible).
5. The group health plan may not impose any pre-existing condition exclusions for pregnancy or for a newborn or newly adopted child enrolled within 30 days.

Prior Notification

Unless the insurer gives the insured prior information regarding pre-existing limitations, they may not impose them. Most insurance carriers include pre-existing clauses in their contracts. Placing the information within the contract satisfies the requirement of prior notification.

Pre-Existing Requires Treatment

HIPAA limits the pre-existing period (also called the look back time) in determining whether a conditions is pre-existing to 6 months. A pre-existing condition is generally defined as medical advice, diagnosis, care or treatment that is either recommended or received. The look back period is taken from the enrollment date. Some states use the prudent person standard in determining a pre-existing condition. This means that a condition is pre-existing if a prudent person would have sought care or treatment. HIPPA rejects this standard. Therefore, a condition is only pre-existing if advise or care is actually sought.

Credit for Prior Coverage

HIPAA also states that an employee may be given credit for the period of time he was covered by his former employer provided the coverage is considered "credible". **Credible coverage** is defined as like coverage. For example if the former coverage was medical only, and the new coverage is medical, dental and vision only the medical portion would be considered credible. Therefore, the employee would be given credit for prior medical coverage, but pre-existing exclusions could be applied to dental and vision services.

Credible coverage does not take into consideration the benefits of the old and new plan only that the former plan was medical and the new plan is medical coverage. A new insurance carrier may choose to enact the pre-existing limitations on certain items that were not included in previous medical coverage. This allowance is limited to coverage for mental health, substance abuse treatment, prescriptions, dental care and vision care. For example, if a participant's old plan did not include coverage for mental health benefits, then the new plan may elect to enact a pre-existing limit on the mental health benefits that it normally offers in the plan.

Under the new law, pre-existing exclusions are limited to six months, and credit must be given for prior coverage. Therefore, if a person is covered by insurance, and transfers insurance coverage to a new company within 63 days of ceasing coverage at the old company, the new insurance carrier may not apply pre-existing limitations to treatment. If there was a break of more than 63 days between termination of the old coverage and the available date of new coverage, pre-existing exclusions are limited to six months.

If a person declines coverage under a new plan because they are covered under a previously existing plan, then they loose their benefits under the old plan, they can enroll under a new plan without pre-existing limitations. No pre-existing limitation may be applied to those who transfer from one plan to another during a company's open-enrollment period.

Employees are no longer allowed to continue COBRA coverage on a policy if they are covered under a new policy. In the past, many employees would continue coverage on an old policy until the existing limitation had been satisfied on the new insurance. Since the new insurance is no longer allowed to apply pre-existing limitations, the need for this coverage has been eliminated. Many people may still elect to continue coverage on the old policy until they have satisfied any length of employment (i.e., must be employed for 90 days) requirements. However, the waiting period is not considered a break in coverage for purposes of the 63-day break in coverage. Therefore, if an employee terminates at one company (and ceases coverage), and is hired at a second company within 63 days, they are considered continuously covered even if they must satisfy a 90-day waiting period before coverage begins with their new employer.

Employers are not allowed to discriminate against those with higher medical costs in their hiring practices. This is true even though the higher costs will eventually show an increase in the company's insurance premiums.

The employee leaving his employer, obtains a certificate of credible coverage which states the employee was covered and what type of plan (dental only, medical etc.) and for how long. This certificate of credible coverage is then applied to the new carriers pre-existing conditions clause.

Companies are also now required to provide written certification of all prior coverage. They must provide this information upon termination of coverage, and for up to 24 months after termination if the employee requests it.

Certificates must include the following:
- The date the certificate is issued,
- The name of the group health plan that provided the coverage described in the certificate,
- The name of the participant or dependent covered and identifying information on them (i.e., social security number, identification number, etc.),
- A telephone number to call for further information on the certificate;
- Either:
    a. A statement that the individual has had at least 18 months of creditable coverage, or
    b. The beginning date for any creditable coverage (and any waiting period), and
- The ending date of coverage, or (in cases of COBRA) a statement that the participant or dependent is continuing as of the date the certificate was issued.

If the information for a participant and their dependents is identical, one certificate may be issued, provided all persons are properly named and identified by the certificate. If information is different for each individual (i.e., beginning and ending dates of coverage), then a plan administrator may either issue a separate certificate for each person or the information for each person may be detailed on one certificate.

Example 1:   A new employee with ABC Company hired on 2/1/04 has a three-month waiting period. The employee signs up in a timely manner and is covered effective 5/1/04. He is taking medication for hypertension, which is considered pre-existing by the new carrier. The 12-month exclusion begins on 2/1/04. The employee was covered by his prior medical plan for a period of 6 months and has a certificate of credible coverage. Because the employee has credible coverage the new carrier must give the employee credit for the 6 month covered by the former plan. Therefore, the hypertension is only excluded for a period of 6 months.

Example 2:   A new employee with ABC Company hired on 2/1/04 has a three-month waiting period. The employee signs up in a timely manner and is covered effective 5/1/04.

He is taking medication for hypertension, which is considered preexisting by the new carrier. The 12-month exclusion clause begins on 2/1/04. The employee was covered by his prior medical plan for a period of 36 months and has a certificate of credible coverage. Because there is a certificate of credible coverage for 36 months the pre-existing exclusion period does not apply.

Maximum Periods
For those who do not satisfy the continuous coverage requirements, pre-existing exclusions are limited to conditions where treatment was received within six months prior to coverage. Exclusions are only allowed to remain in effect for 12 months. Therefore, after 12 months the carrier must cover the condition, whether it was pre-existing or not. If a person did not enroll when they first became eligible, then pre-existing exclusions are allowed to continue for up to 18 months. This is because some people will not apply for coverage until they have a condition that they know is going to require extensive treatment. They will then attempt to get coverage on that condition.

HIPAA also states that if a pre-existing condition exists, the 12-month period for imposing the pre-existing exclusion is measured from the employee's enrollment date. The enrollment date is defined as the earlier of the date of coverage in the plan or the first day of the waiting period before the coverage begins usually the employment date. The waiting period rule does not apply when the enrollee is a late entrant.

Example 1: A new employee with ABC Company, hired on 2/1/04, has a three-month waiting period before signing up for coverage. The employee sign up in a timely manner and is covered for benefits on 5/1/04. The employee takes medication for hypertension, which is considered a pre-existing condition. The plan's 12-month coverage exclusion for a pre-existing condition begins on 2/1/04 because that is the earliest date of enrollment under HIPAA.

Example 2: A new employee with ABC Company, hired on 2/1/04, has a three-month waiting period before signing up for coverage. The employee does not sign up right away and so does not become covered until 7/15/04. The employee takes medication for hypertension, which is considered a pre-existing condition. HIPAA states that the late enrollee does not get benefit of his waiting period, therefore, the 12-month pre-existing exclusion period begins on the actual effective date of coverage, in this case 7/15/04.

Note should be taken if an employer requires a physical examination as a condition of employment and that examination is done **after** the date of employment, any condition first identified during that examination cannot be applied to the pre-existing condition clause. If however, the physical examination takes place **prior** to the employment date and the condition is first identified at that time, the pre-existing condition clause can apply.

Pregnancies and Newborns Excluded
Pre-existing limitations are not allowed for pregnancy or newborns. Therefore, if a woman transfers coverage while she is pregnant, the new insurance carrier must cover the costs associated with the pregnancy.

HIPAA does much to reduce the burden placed on employees due to a pre-existing condition. It does not eliminate the right of a carrier to investigate and impose the pre-existing clause when applicable. This legislation is complex and all questions should be directed to your supervisor.

A good understanding of the pre-existing condition clause in a plan is essential for applying the rules under HIPAA.

Possible Pre-Existing Conditions

Following is a list of conditions by body system that are potentially pre-existing.

Cardiovascular System
Abnormal ECG
Aneurysm
Arteriosclerosis/ASHD
Coronary disease
Dyspnea
Edema
Enlarged heart
Fibrillation
Heart disease/ASHD
Heart failure
Heart murmurs
Hemophilia
High blood pressure
Irregular pulse
Leukemia
Pacemaker
Rapid pulse
Stroke/CVA

Endocrine System
Adrenal disorders
Diabetes
Elevated blood sugar
Hyperglycemia
Pituitary disorders
Thyroid disorders (except hypothyroidism)

Gastrointestinal System
Colostomy/ileostomy
Duodenal ulcer

Esophageal disorders
Gastric ulcers
GI hemorrhage
Liver disorders
Pancreas disorders
Peptic ulcer
Regional enteritis
Regional ileitis
Ulcerative colitis

Genitourinary System
Albuminuria
Congenital GU disorders
GU stone
Hematuria
Hydronephrosis
Hysterectomy
Kidney disorders
Nephrectomy
Nephritis
PID
Prostatic disorder
Pyelitis
Pyelonephrosis
Pyonephrosis
Sexually transmitted diseases
Toxemia/eclampsia
Unlisted or undiagnosed

Nervous System
Autism
Cerebral palsy
Headaches
Mental retardation
Down's syndrome
Multiple sclerosis
Parkinson's disease
Psychoses
Seizure disorders
Severe neuroses
Suicide (attempted)
Syncopy/vertigo
Tremors

Respiratory System
Asthma
Bronchiectasis
Chronic bronchitis
Constructive pulmonary disease
Emphysema
Obstructive pulmonary disease
TB/TBC

Miscellaneous Conditions
Arthritis
Back disorders, disc, sacro
Bone/joint disorders
Cancer
Cataracts

Eye disorder
Glaucoma
Gout
Hodgkin's lymphoma
Impaired vision
Lupus erythematosus
Lymph node disorders
Mastoiditis
Meniere's disease, labyrinthitis
Muscular dystrophy
Osteomyelitis
Otitis media
Regional disorders
Skin cancer
Spinal curvature
TB
Tumors, malignant
Tumors, benign

Non-Physical Conditions
Alcoholism
Drug addiction

Mandates

Mandates are laws enacted by state legislatures that require insurance carriers to cover certain services or dependents, or services provided by certain providers.

Mandates generally take one of two forms:
1. The insurance carrier is required to provide the coverage as part of all plans offered by the carrier, or
2. The insurance carrier within the state must offer the benefit, however, it is not required to be part of a standard policy.

The second requirement is satisfied if the insurance carrier offers a second policy (often with a higher premium) which includes the benefit. Since most insurance coverage is offered as a benefit of employment, most employers will opt for the lower priced coverage that does not include the benefit. For that reason, many people with health insurance coverage provided through their employer often are not covered by the benefit.

There are over 1,000 mandates on the books as of this writing, however special interest groups are constantly submitting bills to the state legislatures requesting additional coverage.

Each insurance carrier is required to obtain a copy of the mandates in any states they sell coverage in. Regardless of where the insurance carrier is located, if the policy is sold and coverage is offered in a state, then that states mandates apply to the coverage offered in that state.

Each state has the right to mandate insurance coverage of certain procedures, practitioners or persons covered. For more complete and current information for your state, contact your state's Department of Insurance.

Benefits
(1) Benefits that are required to be covered are shown below. These benefits must automatically be included in the contract.
(2) Benefits that are required to be offered are shown. These benefits must be made available as an optional addition to a policy. However, employers are not required to purchase them for employees. Individuals who buy an individual insurance plan may choose to have these options included or not. These additional options often require the payment of additional premiums.
(3) Some states require health plans to cover specific groups of people to ensure that they are not excluded from coverage.
(4) Some states limit how long a health plan can review your medical records to search for pre-existing conditions, often known as a "look-back period." In addition, some also limit how long a health plan can exclude coverage of your pre-existing conditions once your application is approved. HIPAA mandates that pre-existing conditions can be excluded for only 12 months, and that credit from any previous eligible group health plan must be applied to the 12-month waiting period; some state laws shorten that waiting period for group plans. If the listed state shortens the HIPAA requirement, the requirement is listed. If the word NO appears, it means the state does not shorten the HIPAA requirements.
(5) Do prompt-pay laws require health plans to pay health insurance claims within a specified time period, or face fines, added interest payments, and other penalties? Note that prompt-pay laws apply only to "clean claims" (meaning claims without defect and with full information provided).

Alabama – **(1)** Breast reconstruction, Drug abuse treatment, Mammography screening, Minimum maternity stays, Off-label drug use. **(2)** Alcoholism treatment **(3)** Newborns **(4)** No. **(5)** Health plans have 25 working days to pay claims to providers and 45 days to consumers.

Alaska – **(1)** Alcoholism treatment (only for group plans with more than five employees), Breast reconstruction, Cervical cancer screening (Pap smear), Diabetic supplies, education, Drug abuse treatment (only for group plans with more than five employees), Formula for PKU, Mammography screening, Minimum maternity stays, Prostate cancer screening. **(2)** Dental, vision, hearing benefits. **(3)** Adopted children, Newborns, Spouses. **(4)** No. **(5)** Health plans have 30 calendar days to pay claims.

Arizona – **(1)** Ambulatory surgery, Breast reconstruction, Contraceptives (all insurance plans that offer prescription drug coverage must cover contraceptives), Diabetic supplies, Education, Emergency services, Home health care, Mammography screening, Minimum maternity stays. (2) None. (3) Adopted children, Conversion to non-group, Handicapped dependents, Newborns. (4) No. (5) Yes. Insurers must pay clean claims within 30 days.

Arkansas – **(1)** Ambulatory surgery, Breast reconstruction, Diabetic supplies, education, Emergency services, Formula for PKU, Infertility services and/or in vitro fertilization, Mental health, parity, Minimum mastectomy stays, Minimum maternity stays, Off-label drug use. **(2)** Alcoholism treatment, Drug abuse treatment, Hospice care, Mammography screening, Mental health. **(3)** Adopted children, Continuation/dependents and employees and Conversion to non-group, Handicapped dependents, Newborns. **(4)** No. **(5)** No.

California – **(1)** Breast reconstruction, Cervical cancer screening, Clinical trials, for cancer patients only, Complications of pregnancy (only if maternity care is offered), Contraceptives, Dental anesthesia, Diabetic supplies, education, Emergency services, Formula for PKU, Mammography screening, Mental health, general, Mental health, parity, Minimum mastectomy stays, Minimum maternity stays, Off-label drug use, Osteoporosis, Prostate cancer screening, Second medical and surgical opinion, TMJ disorders, Well-child care. **(2)** Alcoholism treatment, Blood lead screening, Drug abuse treatment, Home health care, Infertility services and/or in vitro fertilization, Maternity care, Orthotics or prosthetics, Prescription drugs (medically necessary). **(3)** Continuation/dependents/spouses/employees, Conversion to non-group, Handicapped dependents, Newborns. **(4)** Health plans can review your medical records for the previous 12 months and can exclude coverage of pre-existing conditions for 12 months after you buy the policy. **(5)** Yes. Insurers have 30 working days to pay claims and HMOs have 45 working days to pay claims.

Colorado – **(1)** Breast reconstruction, Cleft palate, Complications of pregnancy, Dental anesthesia (children only), Diabetic supplies, education, Emergency services, Mammography screening, Maternity care (group plans only), Mental health, general (group plans only), Mental health, parity (group plans only), Minimum maternity stays (group plans only), Prostate cancer screening, Well-child care. **(2)** Alcoholism treatment, Home health care, Hospice care. **(3)** Adopted children, Continuation/dependents and employees, Conversion to non-group, Newborns. **(4)** Health plans can review your medical records for the previous 12 months and can exclude coverage of pre-existing conditions for 12 months after you buy the policy. **(5)** Yes. Health plans have 30 days to pay electronic claims, 45 days for nonelectronic claims, and 90 days for disputed claims.

Connecticut – **(1)** Alcoholism treatment, Ambulance transportation, Breast reconstruction, Cervical cancer screening (Pap smear), Clinical trials, Colorectal cancer screening, Contraceptives, Dental anesthesia, Diabetic supplies, education, Drug abuse treatment, Emergency services, Formula for PKU, Hearing aids, Home health care, Lyme disease, Mammography screening, Mental health, general, Mental health, parity, Minimum mastectomy stays, Minimum maternity stays, Off-label drug use, Orthotics or prosthetics, Prostate cancer screening, Well-child care. **(2)** Infertility services and/or in vitro fertilization, Rehabilitation services. **(3)** Adopted children, Continuation/dependents, Continuation/employees, Dependent students, Handicapped dependents, Newborns, Non-custodial children. **(4)** Health plans can review your medical records for the previous 12 months and can exclude coverage of pre-existing conditions for 12 months after you buy the policy. **(5)** Yes. Health plans have 45 days to pay claims before incurring interest charges.

Delaware – **(1)** Cervical cancer screening (Pap smear), Childhood immunizations (group plans only), Clinical trials, Colorectal cancer screening, Contraceptives (only if prescription drugs are covered, religious employers can opt out, group plans only), Diabetic supplies, education, Emergency services, Gynecological exams, Lead poisoning screening (only if outpatient services are covered), Mammography screening (group plans only), Mental health, parity (group plans only), Mental illness, serious (individual plans only), Midwife services, Minimum maternity stays, Newborn care, Ovarian cancer monitoring (individual plans only), Prescription drugs, Referrals. **(2)** None. **(3)** Newborns. **(4)** Small-employer and group plans can review your medical records for the previous 12 months and can exclude coverage of pre-existing conditions for 12 months after the effective date of the policy. Individual plans can review your medical records for the previous six months and can exclude coverage of pre-existing conditions for 12 months after the effective date of the policy. **(5)** Yes. Health plans have 45 calendar days to pay claims.

District of Columbia – **(1)** Alcoholism treatment, Breast reconstruction, Cervical cancer screening, Drug abuse treatment, Emergency services, Mammography screening, Mental health, general, Mental health, parity, Mental illness, serious, Minimum maternity stays, Newborn care, Well-child care. **(2)** None. **(3)** Newborns. **(4)** Health plans can review your medical records for the previous six months and can exclude coverage of pre-existing conditions for 12 months after you buy the policy. **(5)** No.

Florida – **(1)** Ambulance transportation, Ambulatory surgery, Bone marrow transplants, Cleft palate, Dental anesthesia, Diabetic supplies, education, Emergency services, Formula for PKU, Home health care, Mammography screening, Minimum mastectomy stays,

Minimum maternity stays, Off-label drug use, TMJ disorders, Well-child care. **(2)** Alcoholism treatment, Breast reconstruction, Drug abuse treatment, General mental health, Orthotics or prosthetics. **(3)** Adopted children, Continuation/dependents and employees Conversion to non-group, Dependent students, Handicapped dependents, Newborns. **(4)** Health plans can review your medical records for the previous 24 months and can exclude coverage of pre-existing conditions for 24 months after you buy the policy. **(5)** Yes. Insurers have 45 days to pay claims and HMOs have 35 days.

Georgia – **(1)** Breast reconstruction, Cervical cancer screening, Clinical trials, Contraceptives, Dental anesthesia, Emergency services, Mammography screening, Maternity care, Mental health, parity, Minimum mastectomy stays, Minimum maternity stays, Off-label drug use, Prostate cancer screening, TMJ disorders, Well-child care. **(2)** Alcoholism treatment, Bone marrow transplants, Bone mass measurement, Diabetic supplies/education, Drug abuse treatment, General mental health, Morbid obesity treatment. **(3)** Adopted children, Continuation/ dependents, Continuation/employees, Conversion to non-group, Dependent students, Handicapped dependents, Newborns. **(4)** There is no limit on how many years back health plans can review your medical records. Individual plans can exclude coverage of pre-existing conditions for 24 months. Group health plans cannot exclude pre-existing conditions for more than 12 months. **(5)** Yes. Health plans have 15 working days to pay claims.

Hawaii – **(1)** Alcoholism treatment, Ambulatory surgery, Breast reconstruction, Contraceptives, Diabetic supplies, education, Drug abuse treatment, Emergency services, Formula for PKU, Infertility services and/or in vitro fertilization, Mammography screening, Maternity care, Mental health, general, Mental health, parity, Minimum maternity stays, Well-child care. **(2)** None. **(3)** Adopted children, Continuation/employees, Handicapped dependents, Newborns. **(4)** Health plans can review your medical records for the previous six months and can exclude coverage of pre-existing conditions for 12 months after the effective date of the policy. **(5)** Yes. Health plans have 30 days to pay claims.

Idaho – **(1)** Breast reconstruction, Cleft palate, Emergency services, Mammography screening, Minimum maternity stays. **(2)** None. **(3)** Continuation/employees, Conversion to non-group, Handicapped dependents, Newborns. **(4)** Health plans can review your medical records for the previous six months and can exclude coverage of pre-existing conditions for 12 months after you buy the policy. **(5)** No.

Illinois – **(1)** Alcoholism treatment, Breast reconstruction, Cervical cancer screening (Pap smear; group plans only except for HMOs), Diabetic supplies, education (group plans only), Infertility services and/or in vitro fertilization (employer groups of more than 25 only), Mammography screening, Mental health, general (HMOs only), Minimum mastectomy stays, Minimum maternity stays, Off-label drug use (cancer patients only), Prostate cancer screening (group plans only). **(2)** Clinical trials (cancer patients only), TMJ disorders (group plans only). **(3)** Adopted children, Continuation/ dependents, Continuation/spousal (does not apply to HMOs), Conversion to non-group, Handicapped dependents, Newborns. **(4)** HMOs may not deny coverage for pre-existing conditions. However, they may apply a co-payment for the first 12 months of coverage of up to 50 percent for those conditions present in the 12 months prior to the effective date of coverage. Non-HMO insurance companies providing individual plans may review your medical records for the previous 24 months and can exclude coverage of pre-existing conditions for up to 24 months after the effective date of the policy. **(5)** Yes. Health plans have 30 days to pay claims.

Indiana – **(1)** Autism, Breast reconstruction, Cleft palate, Dental anesthesia, Diabetic supplies, education, Emergency services, Mental health, parity, Minimum maternity stays, Morbid obesity treatment (state employees only), Off-label drug use, Prostate cancer screening, Well-child care. **(2)** Mammography screening. **(3)** Adopted children, Conversion to non-group, Handicapped dependents, Newborns. **(4)** Health plans can review your medical records for the previous 12 months and can exclude coverage of pre-existing conditions for 12 months after you buy the policy. **(5)** Yes. Health plans have 45 days to pay claims; 30 if they are filed electronically.

Iowa – **(1)** Breast reconstruction, Contraceptives, Diabetic supplies, education, Emergency services, Mammography screening, Minimum maternity stays, Well-child care (group only). **(2)** None. **(3)** Adopted children, Continuation/dependents and employees Conversion to non-group, Newborns. **(4)** Health plans can review your medical records for the previous 12 months and individual health plans can exclude coverage of pre-existing conditions for up to 24 months after you buy the policy. **(5)** Yes. Health plans have 30 days to pay a claim (effective Jan 1, 2002).

Kansas – **(1)** Alcoholism treatment, Bone mass measurement, Breast reconstruction, Dental anesthesia, Diabetic supplies, education, Drug abuse treatment, Emergency services, Gynecological exams, Mammography screening, Mental health, general, Mental health, parity (45 day limit on in-patient and out-patient treatment, effective Jan. 1, 2002), Minimum maternity stays, Off-label drug use, Prostate cancer screening, Well-child care. **(2)** Maternity care. **(3)** Adopted children,

Continuation/dependents and employees Conversion to non-group, Newborns. **(4)** No restrictions on individual health plans. **(5)** Yes. Health plans have 30 days to pay a claim.

Kentucky – **(1)** Ambulatory surgery, Bone marrow transplants, Breast reconstruction, Diabetic supplies, education, Emergency services, Long term care, Mammography screening, Minimum mastectomy stays, Minimum maternity stays, Off-label drug use, TMJ disorders. **(2)** Alcoholism treatment, Bone mass measurement, General mental health, Home health care. **(3)** Continuation/dependents and employees Conversion to non-group, Newborns. **(4)** Health plans can review your medical records for the previous 12 months and can exclude coverage of pre-existing conditions for 12 months after you buy the policy. **(5)** Yes. Health plans have 30 days to pay claims, except in the case of organ transplants when health plans are allowed 60 days to pay claims.

Louisiana – **(1)** Ambulance transportation, Breast reconstruction, Cervical cancer screening, Cleft palate, Clinical trials, Dental anesthesia, Diabetic supplies, education, Emergency services, Mammography screening, Mental health, parity, Minimum maternity stays, Off-label drug use, Prostate cancer screening, Well-child care. **(2)** Alcoholism treatment, Drug abuse treatment, General mental health, Rehabilitation services. **(3)** Continuation/dependents and employees Conversion to non-group, Dependent students, Handicapped dependents, Newborns. **(4)** Health plans can review your medical records for the previous 12 months and can exclude coverage of pre-existing conditions for 12 months after you buy the policy. **(5)** Yes. Health plans have 25 days to pay electronic claims and 45 days for nonelectronic claims.

Maine – **(1)** Breast reconstruction, Cardiac rehabilitation, Cervical cancer screening, Chiropractic care, Contraceptives (only if carrier covers prescription drugs), Diabetic supplies, education, Drug abuse treatment, Formula for PKU, Mammography screening, Maternity care, Mental health, general, Mental health, parity, Metabolic formula, Minimum mastectomy stays, Minimum maternity stays, Newborn care, Off-label drug use, Prescription drugs (HMOs only). **(2)** Alcoholism treatment, Home health care, Prostate cancer screening. **(3)** Continuation/dependents and employees Newborns. **(4)** Health plans can review your medical records for the previous six months and can exclude coverage of pre-existing conditions for 12 months after you buy the policy. **(5)** Yes. Health plans have 30 days to pay claims.

Maryland – **(1)** Alcoholism treatment, Blood products, Bone mass measurement, Breast reconstruction, Chlamydia screening, Cleft palate, Clinical trials, Colorectal cancer screening, Contraceptives, Dental anesthesia (for children), Diabetic supplies, education, Drug abuse treatment, Emergency services, Formula for PKU, Hair prostheses (for cancer patients), Hearing aids (limited coverage, for children under 18 only), Home health care, Infertility services and/or in vitro fertilization, Mammography screening, Maternity care, Mental health, general, Mental health, parity, Minimum mastectomy stays, Minimum maternity stays, Minimum testicular cancer stays, Morbid obesity treatment, small group plans excluded, Off-label drug use, Orthotics or prosthetics (breast prostheses only), Prostate cancer screening, Rehabilitation services (for children), Second medical and surgical opinion, Well-child care. **(2)** Alzheimer's (only for large groups), Hospice care. **(3)** Adopted children, Continuation/dependents and employees Conversion to non-group, Handicapped dependents, Newborns. **(4)** Health plans can review your medical records for the previous six months and can exclude coverage of pre-existing conditions for 12 months after you buy the policy. Applies only to large groups. **(5)** Yes. Health plans have 30 days to pay claims.

Massachusetts – **(1)** Alcoholism treatment, Blood lead screening, Bone marrow transplants, Cardiac rehabilitation, Cervical cancer screening (Pap smear), Diabetic supplies, education, Formula for PKU, Hair prostheses (for cancer patients), Hearing screening for children, Home health care, Hospice care, Human leukocyte antigen testing, Infertility services and/or in vitro fertilization, Mammography screening, Maternity care, Mental health, parity (not for small group holders until January 2002), Minimum maternity stays, Non-prescription enteral formulas, Off-label drug use, Rehabilitation services, Speech, language, and hearing disorders, Well-child care. **(2)** None. **(3)** Adopted children, Children of dependents, Continuation/ employees, Handicapped dependents, Newborns. **(4)** Health plans can review your medical records and can exclude coverage of pre-existing conditions for six months after you buy the policy, but must give credit towards a six-month period of prior creditable coverage under the previous health plan. Currently, pre-existing condition exclusion limits cannot be applied to guaranteed issue products, but effective Nov. 1, 2001, there will be a six-month limitation for certain non-group enrollees. **(5)** Yes. Health plans have 45 days to pay claims before incurring interest charges.

Michigan – **(1)** Alcoholism treatment, Breast reconstruction, Diabetic supplies, education, Drug abuse treatment, Emergency services (only HMOs and Blue Cross & Blue Shield), Minimum maternity stays. **(2)** Hospice care, Mammography screening, Orthotics or prosthetics. **(3)** Conversion to non-group (some exceptions apply), Handicapped dependents (only HMOs and Blue Cross & Blue Shield), Newborns. **(4)** Commercial insurers can review your medical records for the previous six months and can exclude coverage of pre-existing conditions for 12 months after you buy the policy. Blue Cross plans and HMOs can review your medical records for the previous six months and can exclude coverage of pre-existing conditions for six months. **(5)** Yes. Health plans have 45 days to pay claims.

Minnesota – (1) Alcoholism treatment, Ambulatory surgery, Bone marrow transplants, Breast reconstruction, Cervical cancer screening, Cleft palate, Dental anesthesia, Diabetic supplies, education, Drug abuse treatment, Elimination of port-wine stains, Formula for PKU, Hair prostheses, Lyme disease, Mammography screening, Maternity care, Mental health, general, Mental health, parity, Minimum maternity stays, Off-label drug use, TMJ disorders, Well-child care. **(2)** None. **(3)** Adopted children, Continuation/dependents and employees Conversion to non-group, Dependent students, Handicapped dependents, Newborns, Non-custodial children. **(4)** Health plans can review your medical records for the previous six months and can exclude coverage of pre-existing conditions for 12 months after you buy the policy. **(5)** Yes. Health plans have 30 days to pay a claim.

Mississippi – (1) Alcoholism treatment, Ambulance transportation, Breast reconstruction, Mental health, general, Minimum maternity stays, Off-label drug use. **(2)** Dental anesthesia, Diabetic supplies/education, Mammography screening, TMJ disorders, Well-child care. **(3)** Continuation/dependents and employees Handicapped dependents, Newborns. **(4)** Health plans can review your medical records for the previous 12 months and can exclude coverage of pre-existing conditions for 12 months after you buy the policy. **(5)** Yes. Health plans have 45 days to pay claims.

Missouri – (1) Alcoholism treatment (30 days in an approved facility on the same basis as coverage for any illness), Breast reconstruction, Cervical cancer screening (Pap smear), Childhood immunizations, Colorectal cancer screening, Contraceptives, only for health plans that also cover prescription drugs. Religious organizations are exempt, Dental anesthesia (for severely disabled and children under age 5), Formula for PKU, Hearing screening for children (newborns only), Mammography screening, Mental health, general, Minimum maternity stays, Prostate cancer screening. **(2)** Chemotherapy (only for breast cancer, lifetime cap of $100,000), Diabetic supplies, education, Drug abuse treatment, Maternity care, Speech, language, and hearing disorders, Well-child care. **(3)** Continuation/ dependents, Continuation/employees, Conversion to non-group, Newborns. **(4)** No restrictions. **(5)** Yes. Health plans have 45 days to pay claims.

Montana – (1) Alcoholism treatment, Breast reconstruction, Drug abuse treatment, Formula for PKU, Infertility services and/or in vitro fertilization, Mammography screening, Mental health, general, Mental health, parity, Minimum mastectomy stays, Minimum maternity stays, Well-child care. **(2)** Home health care. **(3)** Adopted children, Continuation/ employees, Conversion to non-group, Handicapped dependents, Newborns, Non-custodial children. **(4)** Health plans can review your medical records for the previous three years and can exclude coverage of pre-existing conditions for 12 months after you buy the policy. **(5)** No.

Nebraska – (1) Alcoholism treatment (group plans only), Breast reconstruction (group plans only), Dental anesthesia (children under age 8 and developmentally disabled only), Diabetic supplies, education, Emergency services, Hearing screening for children (newborns only), Mammography screening, Mental health, parity (group plans only), Minimum maternity stays, Off-label drug use (cancer and AIDS patients only), Well-child care. **(2)** TMJ disorders (group plans only). **(3)** Adopted children, Continuation/dependents and employees Dependent students, Newborns. **(4)** No restrictions for individual plans. Group plans can review your medical records for the previous 12 months and can exclude coverage of pre-existing conditions for 12 months after you buy the policy. **(5)** No.

Nevada – (1) Alcoholism treatment, Breast reconstruction, Cervical cancer screening, Complications of pregnancy, Contraceptives, Diabetic supplies, education, Drug abuse treatment, Emergency services, Formula for PKU, Hospice care, Mammography screening, Mental illness, serious, Minimum maternity stays, Off-label drug use, TMJ disorders. **(2)** None. **(3)** Adopted children, Continuation/dependents and employees Conversion to non-group, Newborns. **(4)** No restrictions. **(5)** Yes. Health plans have 60 days to pay claims.

New Hampshire – (1) Bone marrow transplants, Breast reconstruction, Clinical trials (for cancer or other life threatening illnesses), Contraceptives, Dental anesthesia, Diabetic supplies, education, Emergency services, Formula for PKU, Hair prostheses, Mammography screening, Mental health, general, Mental health, parity, Minimum maternity stays, Off-label drug use. **(2)** None. **(3)** Continuation/dependents and employees Handicapped dependents, Newborns. **(4)** Health plans can review your medical records for the previous three months and can exclude coverage of pre-existing conditions for nine months after you buy the policy. **(5)** Yes. Health plans have 30 days to pay claims.

New Jersey – (1) Alcoholism treatment, Blood lead screening and treatment, Breast reconstruction, Cervical cancer screening (Pap smear), Childhood immunizations, Congenital bleeding disorders, Dental anesthesia,

Diabetic supplies, education (large group plans only), Emergency services, Formula for PKU, Hemophilia, Home health care, Infertility services and/or in vitro fertilization (only if pregnancy-related care is covered, large group plans only, other restrictions apply, Mammography screening, Mental health, parity, Minimum mastectomy stays, Minimum maternity stays, Off-label drug use, Prostate cancer screening, Wellness care (large group plans only), Wilm's tumor. **(2)** Bone marrow transplants, Second medical and surgical opinion. **(3)** Handicapped employees/dependents, Newborns. **(4)** For large group plans, insurers can review your medical records for the previous six months and can exclude coverage of pre-existing conditions for 12 months after you buy the policy. Late enrollees may be subject to an 18-month pre-exclusion period. For individual plans, the look-back period is six months and the exclusion period is 12 months. For small group plans, a six-month look-back rule and a six-month exclusion period apply. **(5)** Yes. Health plans have 30 days to pay electronic claims and 40 days for nonelectronic claims.

New Mexico – **(1)** Breast reconstruction, Cervical cancer screening (Pap smear), Contraceptives, only for health plans that also cover prescription drugs. Religious organizations are exempt, Diabetic supplies, education, Emergency services, Mammography screening, Minimum mastectomy stays, Minimum maternity stays, TMJ disorders, Well-child care. **(2)** Alcoholism treatment, Home health care. **(3)** Adopted children, Continuation/dependents, Conversion to non-group, Handicapped dependents, Newborns. **(4)** Health plans can review your medical records for the previous six months and can exclude coverage of pre-existing conditions for six months after you buy the policy. **(5)** Yes. Health plans have 45 days to pay claims.

New York – **(1)** Alcoholism treatment (outpatient care must be covered, inpatient care must be offered), Breast reconstruction, Cervical cancer screening (Pap smear), Chiropractic care, Diabetic supplies, education, Drug abuse treatment (outpatient care must be covered, inpatient care must be offered), Emergency services, Enteral formulas (includes modified solid food products), Home health care, Mammography screening, Maternity care, Minimum mastectomy stays, Minimum maternity stays, Off-label drug use (cancer patients), Prostate cancer screening, Second medical and surgical opinion, Well-child care (0-19 years). **(2)** Ambulatory care, Hospice care, Infertility services and/or in vitro fertilization (applies to people between ages of 21 and 44, but excludes in vitro fertilization and vasectomy reversal), Mental health, general, Nursing home care. **(3)** Adopted children, Continuation/dependents, Continuation/employees, Conversion to

non-group, Handicapped dependents, Newborns. **(4)** Health plans can review your medical records for the previous six months and can exclude coverage of pre-existing conditions for 12 months after the effective date of the policy. **(5)** Yes. Health plans have 45 days to pay undisputed claims.

North Carolina – **(1)** Bone mass measurement, Breast reconstruction, Cervical cancer screening (Pap smear), Cleft palate, Clinical trials, Colorectal cancer screening (effective Jan. 1, 2002), Complications of pregnancy, Contraceptives, Dental anesthesia, Diabetic supplies, education, Emergency services, Hearing screening for children (newborns only), Mammography screening, Minimum mastectomy stays, Minimum maternity stays, Off-label drug use (cancer patients only), Prescription drugs (medically necessary nonformulary), Prostate cancer screening, TMJ disorders. **(2)** Alcoholism treatment, Drug abuse treatment. **(3)** Adopted children, Continuation/ dependents, Conversion to non-group, Foster children, Handicapped dependents, Newborns. **(4)** There are no restrictions on the "look-back period" for determining pre-existing conditions, except in the case of direct insurance sales (i.e. no agent involved), which limits the insurer to asking about conditions treated within the last five years. Individual health plans may exclude coverage for pre-existing conditions for up to 12 months from the effective date of coverage, but must give credit for prior creditable coverage under the previous health plan. However, individual health plans may utilize exclusionary riders or endorsements to exclude certain conditions indefinitely. **(5)** Yes. Health plans have 30 days to pay a claim, deny a claim, or notify the claimant that additional information is required.

North Dakota – **(1)** Alcoholism treatment (group plans only), Breast reconstruction, Complications of pregnancy, Dental anesthesia, Drug abuse treatment (group plans only), Emergency services, Formula for PKU, Mammography screening, Mental health, general (group plans only), Minimum maternity stays, Prostate cancer screening, TMJ disorders. **(2)** Chiropractic care, Prescription drugs. **(3)** Adopted children, Continuation/dependents and employees Conversion to non-group, Dependent students, Handicapped dependents, Newborns, Non-custodial children. **(4)** Health plans can review your medical records for the previous six months and can exclude coverage of pre-existing conditions for 12 months after the effective date of the policy. **(5)** Yes. Health plans have 15 days to pay claims.

Ohio – **(1)** Alcoholism treatment, Breast reconstruction, Cervical cancer screening (Pap smear), Emergency services, Mammography screening, Minimum maternity stays, Off-label drug use. **(2)** Mental health, general, but only benefits of up to $550 annually if the plan offers mental health coverage. **(3)** Adopted children, Conversion to non-group, Handicapped dependents, Newborns. **(4)** Health plans can review your medical records for the previous six months and can exclude coverage of pre-existing conditions for 12 months after you buy the policy. **(5)** Yes. Health plans have 30 days to pay claims.

Oklahoma – **(1)** Ambulance transportation, Ambulatory surgery, Bone mass measurement, Breast reconstruction, Childhood immunizations, Colorectal cancer screening, Dental anesthesia (only for children), Diabetic supplies, education, Emergency services, Hair prostheses (only for cancer and only if policy covers cancer treatment), Hearing aids (only for children up to age 13), Mammography screening, Mental health, parity, Minimum mastectomy stays, Minimum maternity stays, Off-label drug use, Prostate cancer screening. **(2)** Well-child care. **(3)** Adopted children, Continuation/dependents and employees Newborns. **(4)** No restrictions. **(5)** Yes. Health plans have 60 days to pay claims.

Oregon – **(1)** Alcoholism treatment (groups plans only), Breast reconstruction, Cervical cancer screening, Diabetic supplies, education, Drug abuse treatment, Emergency services, Mammography screening, Maternity care, Mental health, general (groups plans only), Minimum maternity stays. **(2)** None. **(3)** Adopted children, Continuation/dependents and employees Conversion to non-group, Newborns, Non-custodial children. **(4)** Health plans can review your medical records for the previous six months and can exclude coverage of pre-existing conditions for six months after you buy the policy. Individual plans may also exclude coverage of certain conditions for up to two years. **(5)** Yes. Health plans have 30 days to pay claims.

Pennsylvania – **(1)** Alcoholism treatment, Breast reconstruction, Cancer hormone treatment, Cervical cancer screening (Pap smear), Chemotherapy, Childhood immunizations, Diabetic supplies, education, Drug abuse treatment, Emergency services, Formula for PKU, Gynecological exams, Hearing aids, Mammography screening, Maternity care, Mental health, parity (group plans only), Mentally retarded child care, Minimum mastectomy stays, Minimum maternity stays, Physically handicapped child care, Well-child care. **(2)** None. **(3)** Conversion to non-group, Handicapped dependents, Newborns. **(4)** Health plans can review your medical records for the previous five years and can exclude coverage of pre-existing conditions for three years after you buy the policy. Blue Cross & Blue Shield plans must "take all comers," regardless of pre-existing conditions. **(5)** Yes. Health plans have 45 days to pay all uncontested claims.

Rhode Island – **(1)** Alcoholism treatment, Blood lead screening, Breast reconstruction, Cervical cancer screening, Clinical trials, Diabetic supplies,

education, Drug abuse treatment, Infertility services and/or in vitro fertilization, Mammography screening, Mental health, parity, Minimum mastectomy stays, Minimum maternity stays, Newborn sickle cell testing, Off-label drug use, Well-child care. **(2)** Home health care, Second medical and surgical opinion, but does not apply to Blue Cross and Blue Shield plans. **(3)** Continuation/dependents, Conversion to non-group, Newborns. **(4)** No pre-existing condition exclusion periods are allowed. **(5)** Yes. Health plans have 40 days to pay written claims and 30 days to pay electronically filed claims.

South Carolina – **(1)** Breast reconstruction, Cervical cancer screening (Pap smear), Cleft palate/cleft lip, Dermatological care (referrals only), Diabetic supplies, education, Emergency services, Gynecological exams, Mammography screening, Mental health, parity (does not apply to small-employer group plans), Minimum mastectomy stays, Minimum maternity stays, Off-label drug use (cancer patients), Prostate cancer screening. **(2)** Alcoholism treatment, Chiropractic care, Drug abuse treatment, Home health care if nursing home care is offered, Mental illness. **(3)** Adopted children, Continuation/dependents and employees Conversion for former spouse, Handicapped dependents, Newborns. **(4)** There are no restrictions on the "look-back period" for determining pre-existing conditions. Individual health plans may exclude coverage for pre-existing conditions for up to 12 months from the effective date of coverage, but must give credit for prior creditable coverage under the previous health plan. **(5)** No.

South Dakota – **(1)** Breast reconstruction, Dental anesthesia, Diabetic supplies, education, Mammography screening, Mental health, parity, Minimum maternity stays, Prostate cancer screening. **(2)** Alcoholism treatment, Formula for PKU. **(3)** Adopted children, Continuation/dependents, Conversion to non-group, Handicapped dependents, Newborns. **(4)** Health plans can review your medical records for the previous 12 months and can exclude coverage of pre-existing conditions for 12 months after you buy the policy. **(5)** Yes, insurers have 45 days to pay claims.

Tennessee – **(1)** Bone mass measurement, Breast reconstruction, Chemotherapy, Diabetic supplies, education, Emergency services, Formula for PKU, Mammography screening, Mental health, parity, Minimum maternity stays, Off-label drug use, Prostate cancer screening. **(2)** Alcoholism treatment, Bone marrow transplants, Cervical cancer screening, Chlamydia screening, Drug abuse treatment, General mental health, Maternity care, but doesn't apply to employers with less than 15 workers. **(3)** Continuation/dependents and employees Conversion to non-group, Handicapped dependents, Newborns. **(4)** No restrictions on individual health plans. **(5)** Yes. Health plans have 30 days to pay claims.

Texas – **(1)** Alcoholism treatment (group only), Bone mass measurement, Breast reconstruction, Childhood immunizations, Contraceptives (oral only and only if prescription drugs are also covered), Diabetic supplies, education, Drug abuse treatment (group only), Emergency services, Formula for PKU (group only and only if prescription drugs are also covered), Hearing screening for children, Mammography screening, Mental health, parity (large-employer group only), Mental illness, serious (group only, mandated offer for small-employer groups), Minimum mastectomy stays, Minimum maternity stays, Off-label drug use, Prostate cancer screening, TMJ disorders (group only), Well-child care (HMO plans only). **(2)** Home health care, Infertility services and/or in vitro fertilization. **(3)** Adopted children, Continuation/dependents and employees Conversion to non-group, Dependent students, Handicapped dependents, Newborns, Non-custodial children. **(4)** No restrictions on the look-back period for making an underwriting decision. For claim purposes, a health insurer may look back five years for evidence of symptoms that would cause a prudent person to seek diagnosis, care, or treatment. Unless specifically excluded by contract provision or rider, the pre-existing condition exclusion period cannot exceed two years from the policy issue date. **(5)** Yes. Health plans have 45 days to pay undisputed claims.

Utah – **(1)** Breast reconstruction, Diabetic supplies, education, Emergency services, Formula for PKU, Mental illness, serious, Minimum maternity stays, Well-child care. **(2)** Alcoholism treatment, Drug abuse treatment. **(3)** Adopted children, Continuation/dependents and employees Conversion to non-group, Handicapped dependents, Newborns, Non-custodial children, Unmarried children up to age 26. **(4)** Health plans can review your medical records for the previous six months and can exclude coverage of pre-existing conditions for 12 months after you buy the policy. **(5)** Yes. Health plans have 30 days to pay claims.

Vermont – **(1)** Alcoholism treatment, Breast reconstruction, Cervical cancer screening (Pap smear), Chiropractic care, Clinical trials, Contraceptives, Diabetic supplies, education, Drug abuse treatment, Emergency services, Formula for PKU, Home health care, Mammography screening, Mental health, parity, Minimum maternity stays Prostate cancer screening, TMJ disorders. **(2)** General mental health. **(3)** Civil union same-sex partners, Continuation/dependents and employees Conversion to non-group, Handicapped dependents, Newborns. **(4)** Health plans can review your medical records for the previous 12 months and can exclude coverage of pre-existing conditions for 12 months after you buy the policy. **(5)** Yes. Health plans have 45 days to pay claims.

Virginia – **(1)** Breast reconstruction, Cancer pain drugs, Cervical cancer screening (Pap smear), Clinical trials, Congenital bleeding disorders, Contraceptives, Emergency services, Hearing screening for children, Hospice care, Mammography screening, Mental health, general, Mental health, parity, Minimum hysterectomy stays, Minimum mastectomy stays, Minimum maternity stays, Off-label drug use, Prostate cancer screening, TMJ disorders. **(2)** Alcoholism treatment, Bone marrow transplants, Drug abuse treatment, Morbid obesity treatment, Well-child care. **(3)** Adopted children, Continuation/dependents and employees Conversion to non-group, Handicapped dependents, Newborns. **(4)** Health plans can review your medical records for the previous 12 months and can exclude coverage of pre-existing conditions for 12 months after you buy the policy. **(5)** Yes. Health plans have 40 days to pay claims.

Washington – **(1)** Alcoholism treatment, Breast reconstruction, Contraceptives (effective Jan. 1, 2002; only if prescription drugs are covered), Drug abuse treatment, Emergency services, Formula for PKU, Mammography screening, Minimum maternity stays, Neurodevelopment therapy, Second medical and surgical opinion. **(2)** Home health care, Hospice care, Mental health, general, TMJ disorders. **(3)** Adopted children, Continuation/dependents and employees Conversion to non-group, Handicapped dependents, Newborns. **(4)** Health plans can review your medical records for the previous six months and can exclude coverage of pre-existing conditions for nine months after you buy the policy. **(5)** Yes. Health plans have 60 days to pay claims.

West Virginia – **(1)** Alcoholism treatment, Breast reconstruction, Diabetic supplies, education, Emergency services, Infertility services and/or in vitro fertilization, Long term care, Mental health, general, Minimum maternity stays, Rehabilitation services, Well-child care. **(2)** TMJ disorders. **(3)** Continuation/dependents and employees Newborns. **(4)** No restrictions. **(5)** Yes. Health plans have 30 days to pay electronic claims and 40 days to pay claims filed manually.

Wisconsin – **(1)** Alcoholism treatment, Breast reconstruction, Childhood immunizations, Dental anesthesia, Diabetic supplies, education, Drug abuse treatment, Emergency services, Home health care, Kidney disease, Mammography screening, Mental health, general, Newborn care, Second medical and surgical opinion, TMJ disorders, Well-child care. **(2)** None. **(3)** Continuation/dependents and employees Conversion to non-group, Grandchildren, Handicapped dependents, Newborns. **(4)** No restrictions on individual health plans. **(5)** Yes. Health plans have 30 days to pay claims.

Wyoming – **(1)** Breast reconstruction, Cervical cancer screening (Pap smear), Colorectal cancer screening, Diabetic supplies, education, Mammography screening, Minimum maternity stays, Prostate cancer screening. **(2)**

Alcoholism treatment. **(3)** Adopted children, Continuation/employees, Conversion to non-group, Handicapped dependents, Newborns, Non-custodial children. **(4)** Health plans can review your medical records for the previous six months and can exclude coverage of pre-existing conditions for 12 months after you buy the policy. **(5)** Yes. Health plans have 45 days to pay claims.

External or Independent Grievance Systems

External grievance systems allow you to take a dispute with your health plan to a doctor or review board unaffiliated with your health plan. Thus, both you and your health plan receive an impartial ruling on its decision to deny coverage of services or treatment. Additionally, you can file a complaint against your health insurer with your state's department of insurance.

The following information identifies whether a state requires an external or independent grievance system to appeal your health plan's unfavorable decisions.

Alabama – No.

Alaska – Yes on grounds of experimental, investigative, medical judgment, or medical necessity. Panel's decision is binding, unless appealed to state superior court within six months.

Arizona – Yes, for all health plans, on grounds of any denial. Panel's decision is binding

Arkansas – No.

California – Yes, for all health plans, on grounds of investigational treatment appeals and medical necessity. Panel's decision is binding.

Colorado – Yes, for all health plans, on grounds of medical necessity. Panel's decision is binding.

Connecticut –Yes, for all health plans, on grounds of investigational treatment appeals and medical necessity. Panel's decision is binding on both parties.

Delaware – Yes, for managed care plans only, on grounds of investigational treatment appeals and medical necessity. Panel's decision is advisory.

District of Columbia – Yes, for all health plans, on grounds of any denial. Panel's decision is advisory.

Florida – Yes, for HMOs, on grounds of any denial. Panel's decision is advisory.

Georgia – Yes, for HMO and PPO plans, on grounds of investigational treatment appeals and medical necessity. Panel's decision is binding.

Hawaii – Yes, for all health plans, on grounds of any except medical malpractice. Panel's decision is appealable to state court.

Idaho – No.

Illinois – Yes, but only for HMOs, on grounds of denial of medically necessary treatment, disputes over length of stay, disputes over referrals. Panel's decision is binding.

Indiana – Yes, for HMOs, on grounds of investigational treatment appeals, medical necessity, violation of prompt-pay laws. Panel's decision is binding.

Iowa – Yes, for all health plans, on grounds of medical necessity. Panel's decision is binding on both parties.

Kansas – Yes, for all health plans, on grounds of investigational treatment appeals and medical necessity. Panel's decision is advisory.

Kentucky – Yes, for all health plans, on grounds of any denial. Panel's decision is binding.

Louisiana – Yes, for all health plans, on grounds of medical necessity. Panel's decision is binding on both parties.

Maine – Yes, on grounds of investigational/experimental treatment, medical necessity, pre-existing conditions. Panel's decision is binding only on carrier.

Maryland – Yes, through the Maryland Insurance Administration, on grounds of medical necessity. Panel's decision is binding.

Massachusetts – Yes, once all internal plan appeals are exhausted. Panel's decision is binding.

Michigan – Yes, for all plans, on grounds of any denial. Panel's decision is advisory.

Minnesota – Yes, for all health plans, on grounds of any denial. Panel's decision is binding.

Mississippi – No.

Missouri – Yes, for all health plans, on grounds of investigational treatment appeal, medical necessity. Panel's decision is binding on both parties.

Montana – Yes, for all health plans, on grounds of medical necessity. Panel's decision is binding.

Nebraska – No.

Nevada – No.

New Hampshire – Yes, on grounds of investigational treatment appeals and medical necessity. Panel's decision is binding.

New Jersey – Yes, for all health plans, on grounds of investigational treatment appeal, medical necessity. Panel's decision is binding.

New Mexico – Yes, for all health plans, on grounds of any denial. Panel's decision is advisory.

New York – Yes, for all health plans, on grounds of medical necessity, investigational treatment, experimental treatment, clinical trials. Panel's decision is binding.

North Carolina – Yes, on grounds of medical necessity. Panel's decision is binding.

North Dakota – No.

Ohio – Yes, for all health plans, on grounds of investigational treatment appeal, medical necessity. Panel's decision is binding.

Oklahoma – Yes, for all health plans, on grounds of medical necessity. Panel's decision is advisory.

Oregon – Yes. Grounds unspecified. Panel's decision is binding for both sides.

Pennsylvania – Yes, on grounds of medical necessity, coverage disputes, and exclusions. Panel's decision is binding.

Rhode Island – Yes, for all health plans, on grounds of medical necessity and appropriateness of medical treatment. Panel's decision is binding.

South Carolina – Yes, (effective Jan. 1, 2002), on grounds of emergencies, experimental or investigational treatment, medical necessity, untimely internal appeal delay, waiver of internal appeal by carrier. Panel's decision is binding for both claimant and insurer.

South Dakota – No.

Tennessee – Yes, for HMOs only, on grounds of medical necessity. Panel's decision is binding.

Texas – Yes, for all health plans, on grounds of medical necessity. Panel's decision is binding.

Utah – Yes, on grounds of denial, modification, or reduction of claims payments or termination of coverage. Panel's decision is binding.

Vermont – Yes, for all health plans, on grounds of investigational treatment appeal, medical necessity. Panel's decision is binding.

Virginia – Yes, for all health plans, on grounds of medical necessity. Panel's decision is binding on both parties.

Washington – Yes, on grounds of denial, modification, or reduction of claims payments, or termination of coverage. Panel's decision is binding for the insurer.

West Virginia – Yes, on grounds of experimental treatment, medical necessity. Panel's decision is binding.

Wisconsin – Yes, on grounds of medical necessity. Panel's decision is binding.

Wyoming – No.

Summary

Acts of Third Parties and Subrogation can drastically alter the way a claim is paid and who is responsible for the claim payment. Pre-existing conditions account for one of the highest dollar amounts of claims paid incorrectly, costing insurance companies thousands of dollars. The health claims examiner must understand these concepts and when they come into play.

Assignments

Complete Questions for Review.
Complete Exercises 10 – 1 through 10 – 3.

Questions for Review

Directions: Answer the following questions without looking back into the material just covered. Write your answers in the space provided.

1. Why are Acts of Third Parties and Subrogation provisions included in many benefit plans? _____

   _____

2. Under _____, the plan advances money to the injured person with the understanding that if the claimant is successful in obtaining reimbursement monies from a third-party, the plan will be reimbursed.

3. Under _____, the plan has an obligation to pay a benefit under the contract, but a subrogated right for a portion of the recovery that the claimant may obtain from a third-party.

4. (True or False?) Improperly handled claims for pre-existing conditions are a common source of complaints and lawsuits. _____

5. (True or False?) An examiner should not notify the member and the provider of the delay of a claim. _____

If you were unable to answer any of the questions, refer back to the section and then complete the answers.

Exercise 10 – 1

Directions: Indicate whether or not the following situations would warrant a pre-existing investigation and why.

1. Thomas is covered under the ABC Corporation plan. His effective date of coverage is 1/1/04. He received treatment for chronic allergies on 12/15/03, and a claim was received for services rendered on 1/25/04. _____
    _____

2. Gerald is covered under the Ninja Enterprises plan. His effective date of coverage is 7/4/02. He received treatment for a finger laceration on 4/23/04. _____
    _____

3. Adam is covered under the XYZ Corporation plan. His effective date of coverage is 4/14/02. He received treatment for leukemia on 3/15/02, and a claim was received for this same diagnosis for services rendered on 5/15/04. _____
    _____

4. Alyse is covered under the Ninja Enterprises plan. Her effective date of coverage is 11/1/04. She received treatment for diabetes on 7/1/04, and a claim was submitted for services. _____
    _____

5. Sebastian is covered under the ABC Corporation plan. His effective date of coverage is 2/15/04. A claim with a diagnosis of hypertension is received with a date of service of 2/20/04. _____
    _____

Exercise 10 – 2

Directions: Read each scenario below and determine whether or not the certificate of prior insurance should be checked and why or why not.

1. Jennifer received treatment for a chronic ulcer on 7/1/2001 and again on 8/1/2001. On 10/01/2001 she quit her old job and began working for a new employer two weeks later, on 10/15/2001. She immediately signed up for insurance and her coverage became effective after a 30-day waiting period, on 11/15/2001. On 1/15/2002, she was seen by the doctor for additional ulcer treatment. Do you need a copy of her coverage certificate with the 1/15/2002 claim?_____
    _____

2. Mary received treatment for diabetes on 7/1/2000 and again on 8/1/2000. On 10/1/2000 she quit her old job and began working for a new employer two weeks later, on 10/15/2000. She immediately signed up for insurance and her coverage became effective after a 90-day waiting period, on 1/15/2001. On 10/15/2001, she was seen by the doctor for additional diabetes treatment. Do you need a copy of her coverage certificate with the 10/15/2001 claim?_____
    _____

3. Tom received treatment for kidney disease on 2/1/2001 and again on 3/1/2001. On 10/1/2001 he quit his old job and began working for a new employer two weeks later, on 10/15/2001. He immediately signed up for insurance and his coverage became effective after a 30-day waiting period, on 11/15/2001. On 12/15/2001, he was seen by the doctor for additional kidney disease treatment. Do you need a copy of his coverage certificate with the 11/15/2001 claim?_____

   _____

   _____

4. Betty received a routine visit for pregnancy on 7/1/2001 and again on 8/1/2001. On 10/1/2001 she began working for a new employer. She immediately signed up for insurance and her coverage became effective after a 30-day waiting period, on 12/15/2001. She did not have prior coverage. On 1/15/2002, she was seen by the doctor for an additional routine visit. Do you need a copy of her coverage certificate for the 1/15/2002 claim?

   _____

   _____

5. Jesse received treatment for anorexia on 7/1/2001 and again on 8/1/2001. On 10/16/2001 she quit her old job and chose not to continue coverage under COBRA rules. On 12/15/2001 she began working for a new employer. She immediately signed up for insurance and her coverage became effective after a 30-day waiting period, on 1/15/2002. On 1/25/2002, she was seen by the doctor for additional diabetes treatment. Do you need a copy of her coverage certificate with the 10/15/2001 claim?

   _____

   _____

   _____

   _____

Exercise 10 - 3

Directions: Obtain a copy of the mandated insurance coverage in your state. This information is usually available through your state's Department of Insurance. Then check the listing below. For each of the items listed, decide whether insurance carriers in your state:

1.   Are required to cover this service.
2.   Must offer the benefit, however it need not be covered under a standard policy.
3.   Are not required to provide coverage for the indicated service.

Place the corresponding number next to each item denote the requirements in your state.

Benefits:
Alcoholism Treatment   _____
Ambulance Transportation   _____
Ambulatory Surgery   _____
Antiabortion   _____
Breast reconstruction   _____
Cleft Palate   _____
Diabetic Education   _____
Drug Abuse Treatment   _____
Home Health Care   _____
Hospice Care   _____
In Vitro Fertilization   _____
Long Term Care   _____
Mammography Screening   _____
Maternity Services   _____
Mental Health Care   _____
Orthotic, Prosthetic Care   _____
Prescription Drugs   _____
Rehabilitation Services   _____
Second Surgical Opinion   _____
TMJ Disorder   _____
Well Child Care   _____

Providers
Acupuncturist   _____
Chiropractors   _____
Dentists   _____
Licensed Health Professions   _____

Naturopath   _____
Nurses (RNs)   _____
Nurse Midwives (CNMs)   _____
Nurse Anesthetist (CRNAs)   _____
Nurse Practitionsers   _____
Nurse Psychiatric   _____
Occupational Therapist   _____
Optometrists   _____
Oral Surgeons   _____
Osteopaths   _____
Physical Therapists   _____
Podiatrists   _____
Professional Counselors   _____
Psychologists   _____
Public and Other Facilities   _____
Social Workers   _____
Speech/Hearing Therapist   _____

Persons Covered
Adopted Children   _____
Continuation/Dependents   _____
Continuation/Employees   _____
Conversion to Non-group   _____
Dependent Students   _____
Handicapped Dependents   _____
Newborns   _____
Noncustodial Children   _____

Do the continuation items still apply since HIPAA?_____

_____

Honors Certification™

The Honors Certification™ challenge for this chapter is a written test of the information contained within this chapter. Each incorrect answer will result in a deduction of between 1% and 5% from your grade. You must achieve a score of 85% or higher to pass this test. If you fail the test on your first attempt you may retake the test one additional time. The items included in the second test may be different from those in the first test.

11 Claims Administration

In this chapter you will learn:

- To understand the job responsibilities of a health claims examiner.
- To understand the process of administering claims.
- To understand the guidelines for processing prescription claims.

Key words and concepts you will learn in this chapter:

Batch Files – Files which are kept in batches or groups based on the date they were processed and the person who processed them.

Claim Files – Files for holding claims and other processing information.

Claim Investigation – Making a detailed inquiry to verify facts pertaining to a claim submitted.

Claim Processing – To determine benefit amounts and pay a claim.

Family Files – Folders of claims that are kept for each family of claimants.

Patient Files – Files which hold information for only one patient.

Pended Claims – Claims that have not been completely adjudicated or closed.

Referral – To send a claim to be reviewed by a technical claims person.

The claims examiner's job entails a wide variety of administrative duties to ensure proper claims handling. In this chapter, we will address the importance of the following: verification of coverage and eligibility, accurate claim file documentation, investigation, referrals, and pending claims. Company guidelines vary from payor to payor, so please review your company guidelines upon employment.

Maintenance of Claim Files

When a claim is received by a payor, the department (the name of the department varies from company to company) documents the receipt of the claim usually via a microfilm medium that copies the claim and assigns it a claim number, which includes the date. The date is used to keep all the claims received in chronological order so that the oldest mail can be processed first. After the claim has been documented and received, it is routed to the claims processor for handling.

Some claims payors prefer to have a manual filing system, in which the physical claims are kept for ready access by examining personnel. Although manual filing systems may vary, they usually entail the maintenance of family files, patient files, or batch files.

Family Files

Family files are folders of claims that are kept for each family of claimants. The claimants/patients are usually identified by the same subscriber identification number. This identification number is used to group the members of a family together into a single file or folder. Most companies use the member's social security number as the identification number.

Within the family folder, each member's information and claims are grouped separately. This grouping is based on the calendar year in which the charges were incurred, the date the expenses were processed, and whether the claim is completed or pended for additional information.

Therefore, each member will have a separate inter-family sub-file for each calendar year. Within this sub-file, completed claims are usually arranged with the claims processed earliest in a calendar year placed at the bottom of the file and the claims processed later in the year placed at the top. In addition, there may be a separate correspondence sub-file and a separate pended claim file by year, or there may be only one of each of these sub files for each member with all years combined together. However, as with the completed claims, the correspondence or pending claims are usually arranged chronologically so that those received the earliest are placed at the bottom and those received later are placed at the top of the stack.

Patient Files

An alternative to having family files is to have member files. With this type of filing system, there is only one member per file. Claims for the member for all years are kept in the same file. Therefore, unlike the family files, in which the entire family is accessed when a claim or phone call is received for a family member, only a single member's file is accessed. Correspondence and pended claims are kept separate from completed claims, and all information is arranged chronologically according to the date of handling.

Unfortunately with the individual member file, it is difficult for the examiner to see trends, fraud, over-utilization, and other abuses being practiced by a family or provider, since the information is located in multiple files. However, member files tend to be neater and easier to handle than family files.

Batch Files

Batch files are batches of claims grouped together according to the date they were processed and the person who processed them. Every claim processed by an individual each day is placed in the same folder or secured together and filed. The claims are usually placed in order by claim number. Pended claims and correspondence are usually kept in separate files. When a pended claim is completed, it is placed in the batch file according to the date of completion.

With the batch system, when claims for one person need to be accessed, multiple batch files must be accessed as well. This process tends to be labor-intensive. In addition, as with patient files, trends and abuses cannot be easily recognized by examining personnel.

Claim File Documentation

Documentation is the orderly organization and communication of important facts that can be used to furnish decisive evidence of claim handling or processing. Documenting the claim file with pertinent information is an important job of the claims examiner. If the claim cannot be processed upon receipt, the claim file must be documented as to the disposition of the claim. The most common reason a claim cannot be processed is that additional information is needed from the provider or the member. The claims examiner's responsibility is to indicate in the claim file the information requested and the date of the request. The date that the follow-up letter should be sent (in the event that the information is not received within a certain amount of time,) should also be included in the claim file.

This documentation enables the examiner to refresh his or her memory at a future date. Since you may not be the person who follows up on the claim or

receives the information requested, be sure that the documentation is understandable and that it provides concise, informative and pertinent information. Refrain from marking claim documents unnecessarily, since this may be very confusing to others reviewing the claim at a later date. Proper documentation should have the following attributes:

- **Clean claim files.** Never include any derogatory references to the member. Never write down personal remarks. Likewise, there should never be any reference to ethnic origin unless the information is relevant to the case. Always keep your points objective. Do not highlight, or mark in any way sections, passages, or words of a narrative report, or claim form. As innocent as it may seem a judge, jury or plaintiff's attorney may see it as singling out, bad faith or discriminatory and arbitrary.

- **Document the files properly and show the basis for your decision.** Careless or poorly worded claim files can give an appearance of bad faith or a conscious disregard of the claimant's rights. The representative not only must be fair and reasonable but must also create a claim file that shows fairness, reasonableness, and factual accuracy when read by a jury. Always correctly record the basis for all claims decisions. Such a practice should also force you to carefully consider your action before taking that action and to discover and correct errors before any serious damage has occurred.

- **Be careful when using words of the trade.** Sometimes such words or phrases may be taken out of context and used to give a bad connotation. Be especially aware of words that may have a double meaning, especially if taken out of context.

- **Give initial, factual information to an attorney involved on behalf of the claimant, if there is one involved.** If the attorney requests further information, questions concerning the extent and nature of that information should be discussed with a member of your firm's legal department or a supervisor before responding to the attorney. All information or copies of documents should be clearly documented in the file.

Some firms retain specialists to handle attorney claims. In such instances, the case should be referred immediately to the specialist. Nothing should be said or sent to the attorney regarding the case unless you are directed to do so by the specialist. Since the handling of these claims differs significantly from office to office, always request clarification on the handling of such claims before taking any action.

- **All information regarding the claim should be put in writing.** This means that phone conversations should always be documented and summarized in writing. This is often done on a form called a Telephone Information Sheet. A sample copy of a Telephone Information Sheet is shown as **Figure 11 – 1**. Also, keep to the facts with what you have to say about a case or an individual and express no opinion either in oral or written communications.

- **Be careful when asked to furnish information.** Information furnished by a doctor or provider with regard to a claim may be privileged information. If medical information is requested by the claimant, normally the claimant should be advised to contact the provider directly. The fact that the claimant is a patient of the provider does not necessarily entitle him or her to the information that has been furnished.

Claim Investigation

Claim investigation is making a detailed inquiry to verify facts pertaining to a claim submitted. When a claim is received, the minimal information that should be obtained is a diagnosis, the age, marital status, and student status (if applicable) of the claimant. Reasons for investigation may include possible pre-existing conditions, fraud, work-related injuries, and coordination of benefits. When making your request for information, be as specific as possible regarding the type of information needed. Request information in a way to get narrative answers rather than yes or no answers. Avoid sending several requests for different information to the same provider or member. Request all information at once so that claims are not delayed unnecessarily. Always attach an Authorization to Release Information with your request.

Referrals

Upon receipt of the information requested, you may find that the claim decision is beyond your level of expertise or authorization. When this occurs, the claim must be referred and reviewed by a technical claims person. This person may be a lead examiner, supervisor, medical review person, or consultant. This referral process ensures that there is a consistent approach to unusual situations and maintains an avenue of communication to higher levels in the case of sensitive issues. Following is a list of claims that are usually referred to technical personnel:

- **Lawsuits, legal actions, or legislation issues.** An attorney letter may be received

demanding payment or making reference to insurance law, a summons or Notice of Complaint, or receipt of other lawsuit notification correspondence.

- **Providers who have been flagged.** Flagged providers are those who have been identified as being questionable; therefore, special handling is required. Some reasons why providers are flagged are questionable billing practices, overuse of certain benefits (i.e., chiropractic services, biofeedback), new providers pending state approval to perform qualified services (i.e., surgi-center).
- **Fraud.** Providers have submitted claims in which indications of fraud have been identified and the claims are pending for verification.

When claims are received for the above situations, a referral form should be completed and routed to the appropriate department. It is important that copies of all documents, letters, and forms be sent along with the referral claim. **Figure 11-2** shows an example of a claims referral form.

Pended Claims

Pended claims are claims that have not been completely adjudicated or closed. These claims may require follow-up investigation so that correct and prompt liability decisions can be made, which comply with legislative or regulatory requirements for fair claim handling.

When requesting information, make sure that you request all the information needed to complete processing of the claim to ensure that an additional delay does not occur. A letter notifying the insured and the provider that the claim payment will be delayed must be sent. Many companies use a standard form letter requesting further information. **Figures 11 – 3 and 11 – 4** show two standard request forms.

The first follow-up date should be scheduled three to four weeks after the original request. If the requested information is not received within the scheduled follow-up period, send a second notice letter with follow-up scheduled for three to four weeks. If the requested information is not received within 60 days, it may be necessary to close the claim. Send a final letter advising the insured and the provider that "because information requested has not been received, the claim is being closed. If the information is received within a reasonable length of time we will be happy to reopen the claim." If the company has a statute of limitations on filing a claim, this information should be indicated in the letter: "We are unable to process claims received more than six months after the date of service. If information is submitted prior to this time, we will be happy to reopen the claim."

ANY INSURANCE CARRIER, INC.
123 Any Drive
Anywhere, USA 12345
(800) 555-1234

TELEPHONE INFORMATION SHEET

Date: _____

Claim Identification: _____

Person making inquiry: _____

Person supplying information: _____

Telephone Number: _____

Briefly state information received or desired: _____

Indicate additional handling, if any: _____

This form, when completed should be placed in the claim file.

Figure 11 – 1: Sample Telephone Information Sheet

Claim Office Referral Sheet

To   From   Date

Policy #   Soc. Sec. #   Employee's Name   Dependent's Name

Eff. Date Term. Date   Patient's Age   Provider of Service

Reason for Referral: _____

Attachments:

( ) □ Denial/□ Attorney Letters   ( ) Preop Photos   ( ) □ Policy/□ Booklet Page
( ) □ Special Correspondence   ( ) Op/Anesthesia/Path Report   ( ) □ Billings
( ) □ Hospital/ □ Dr. Records   ( ) X-rays   ( ) □ Other:

Please make sure that all material referenced in any appeal letter (insured/provider/attorney) are enclosed with this file.

Reply: _____

Signature   Date

ANY INSURANCE CARRIER, INC.
123 Any Drive, Anywhere, USA 12345 (800) 555-1234

Figure 11 – 2: Sample Claim Referral Form

ANY INSURANCE CARRIER, INC.
0123 Any Drive
Anywhere, USA 12345
(800) 555-1234

Name _____

Control No. _____

Please refer to the paragraph checked below.

□ Careful attention is being given to this claim. We will write you further about it in a short time.

□ As you requested, we are returning the _____

□ Please let us know whether this claimant has returned to work and if so, when _____. If not, does total disability still exist? _____ Will proofs of claim be submitted? _____ Information as to the claimant's present condition will be appreciated.

□ Please have the _____ statement completed and return the attached form to us.

□ Consideration of further benefits can be given only after we receive the _____

□ The attached furnished our first knowledge of this claim. Will you please arrange for submission of the required proofs of claim if this is properly covered under our insurance.

Figure 11 – 3: Sample Request for Additional Information Letter

---

ANY INSURANCE CARRIER, INC.
0123 Any Drive
Anywhere, USA 12345
(800) 555-1234

Request Form
□ Medical □Dental

Please return requested information to: _____

□ **First Request** □ **Second Request**   □ **Third and Final Request**

Insured: _____   Date: _____

Patient: _____

BEFORE WE CAN PROCESS YOUR CLAIM, WE WILL NEED THE ADDITIONAL INFORMATION CHECKED BELOW:

□ Please complete in full the member portion of the claim form. Dental (employee section).

□ Itemized Statements from: _____

□ Copies of other Insurance Payments from: _____

□ Full-time Student Eligibility Form Request: Please have the Registrar of the College or University that _____ attends complete the attached Student Eligibility Form for the _____ Semester/Quarter.

□ Other: _____

□ THE FOLLOWING EXPENSES WILL BE HELD UNTIL THE ABOVE REQUESTED ITEMS ARE RECEIVED IN THIS OFFICE _____

□ We have attempted on _____ to obtain the above necessary information to properly process your claim. As of this date it has not been received. The file will **now** be considered **closed** until such time the information is received and proper evaluation can be given your claim.

Thank you,

Figure 11 – 4: Sample Request for Additional Information Letter

Claim Processing

In the following paragraphs, we will discuss coverage and guidelines for processing claims. These guidelines are generalized, and company guidelines will always supersede any of the guidelines discussed in this chapter. Use the guidelines when processing the claims in this course. To ensure success in the claims processing portion of this guide, review UCR before attempting to process claims if more than two months have elapsed since taking the UCR portion of the course

Claim Analysis

A good claims examiner must have a thorough and systematic process for analyzing claims. The same process is used on each claim no matter how simple or complex. This is how consistency and accuracy are developed. The following model may be used in the development of an individual systematic approach. Identify the issues involved in the claim. There may be many issues, including the following eight:

1. Eligibility:
    a. Has the policy lapsed for nonpayment of premiums?
    b. At the time of service, was the patient currently enrolled under the plan?
    c. If a dependent, is the patient within the proper age limit? If not, is the patient a full-time student or otherwise within the extended age limit?
    d. Have all eligibility requirements set forth in the policy been met?
    e. Was any material misrepresentation made in the original application for coverage?
2. Possible other coverage:
    a. Is an injury involved? If so, do you have the date, place, and circumstances of the injury on file?
    b. Is there evidence of other insurance? Could TPL be involved?
    c. Is the injury work-related? If so, has a Workers' Compensation claim been filed?
    d. Does the patient have other insurance that might cover these services?
3. Determine what the policy/plan language provides:
    a. What is the definition of total disability?
    b. What is the contract definition of accident and sickness?
    c. What plan provisions could apply to this claim? What plan limitations and maximums could apply to the claim?
    d. Is there a pre-existing limitation on the plan and, if so, how is it applied?

4. Is there any information missing from the claim which is necessary for determination of payment (diagnosis, patient, provider licensing, etc.)?
5. Obtain all relevant facts. Request all missing information or documentation at one time. Thoroughly investigate all available data. Do not pend a claim again and again and keep asking questions that should have been asked initially.
6. Make an honest evaluation of the facts and the plan benefits. Seek assistance from supervisors or lead examiners when necessary, before, not after, pending or denying a claim.
7. Keep the member informed. Each time a claim is pended or denied, a letter must be sent. In addition, usually every 30 days a follow-up letter should be sent on a claim remaining pended.
8. No decision is final. If the benefits are denied, there should always be an opportunity for reevaluation of the claim if new or different information is received.

Good Claim Practices

Consider the following five guidelines when processing claims:

1. **Fully analyze the claim initially.** Consider all possible basis for acceptance or denial. Look for a way to pay a claim, not deny it. Often, an initial review of a claim will reveal clear and obvious grounds for denial. Sometimes the obvious grounds disappear later when the denial is questioned. Always clearly document the grounds for denial. Resist the natural temptation to deny a claim without a complete investigation and without considering all other possible grounds for acceptance.
2. **Thoroughly investigate and document the facts within the claim file.** This may be one of the most important steps that each examiner needs to take before paying or denying a claim. The lack of a proper investigation or documentation has probably resulted in more bad faith charges than any other individual factor.
    a. Investigate and thoroughly document all aspects under investigation before taking a position on the status of the claim.
    b. After investigation, evaluate the facts in an impartial and objective manner. If the facts are technical or the decision appears close, seek assistance from a lead examiner or supervisor.
    c. Verify the authenticity of the date. Is the person providing the information a qualified provider or other qualified person?
    d. Never rely on incomplete or ambiguous claim forms or inspection reports.
    e. Consider all policy provisions.

3. **Handle claims promptly and keep claimants informed.**
   a. Give priority to delayed/pended claims.
   b. Resolve conflicting evidence or information promptly.
   c. Do not withhold or delay payments in hope of a compromise.
4. **Make proper use of medical evidence.**
   a. Always contact the doctor to clear up any medical questions concerning the claimant.
   b. When a second medical opinion is required, the proper selection of an independent medical examiner is very important. A specialist should be chosen for the specific disease or injury. The medical examiner must always be provided with all the claimant's relevant medical information and records, whether they are favorable or unfavorable. Also, the examiner cannot provide a correct conclusion unless the correct questions are asked. Sometimes asking the correct questions is the most difficult part of preparing a case for review.
5. **In keeping with good claim practices, vigilance for excessive charges must be maintained.** Some doctors will indicate a long list of diagnoses to match up the wide variety of tests given with a diagnosis, so that the patient is covered by the insurance carrier. Some situations to watch for are:
   a. High charges, a long list of diagnoses, and no subsequent visits.
   b. Multiple diagnoses involving multiple bodily functions.
   c. Services described in very technical and non-standard medical terminology, especially in connection with exotic extensive medical testing.
   d. Vague or ambiguous diagnoses.
   e. Diagnoses involving extensive testing, beginning with hyper- or hypo- (e.g., hypoglycemia, hypercholesterolemia, hypomineralism).
   f. Bills that appear to be preprinted or that include wordy descriptions of services either on the bill or enclosed with the bill.

These are only a few of the instances that should alert the attention of a good claims examiner. If necessary, medical records should be requested to investigate the patient's history and chief complaints, the tests performed, and their results.

In questionable cases, use common sense and seek advice early. Often a second opinion or different point of view can clarify the situation. Do not hesitate to seek the opinions of your supervisor or lead examiner. Two areas in which help is often needed is in questioning pre-existing conditions and usual and customary charges. Your responsibility is to make decisions, but prudent decisions come with time and experience. Until you have experience, consider asking questions as a part of your learning and training.

Payment Worksheet

Whenever claims are processed manually, a payment worksheet must be completed by the examiner, which explains to the member how the benefits on the claim were calculated. Although worksheets vary from company to company, the general format and requirements remain the same. Following as an explanation of the worksheet that you will be using to process the claims (see **Figure 11 – 5**).

Header Information
The header area is where the member and plan identification information are indicated. It is composed of the following fields:
1. *Eligible Employee.* The insured or employee's full name.
2. *Company.* The name of the employer or company.
3. *Social Security Number.* The insured or employee's social security number.
4. *Patient.* The patient/claimant's name.
5. *Relationship.* The relationship of the patient to the insured.

The following information should be filled in after completing the claim payment worksheet:
6. *Accident Benefit.* Amount of accident benefit year to date.
7. *Lifetime Max.* Amount of lifetime maximum to date.
8. *Deductible.* Amount of deductible, year to date.
9. *Carryover Deductible.* Amount of deductible carried over from the previous year.
10. *Coinsurance.* Amount of coinsurance paid year to date.

Claim Data Information
The body of the worksheet is where the billed services are itemized indicating the amount allowed for each service, the amount excluded, and at what percentage the amount allowed is payable. It includes the following 18 fields:
1. *Procedure/Type of Service.* The applicable CPT code or English language description of service.
2. *Dates of Service.* Date of service for the particular charge being coded out.
3. *Billed Amount.* The total amount of charges for the services indicated on this single line of coding.

Payment Worksheet

Eligible Employee: Nancy Normal
Company: XYZ Corporation
Social Security Number: 777-77-7777
Patient: Nancy Normal
Relationship: Self

Accident Benefit:	0.00	(20)
Lifetime Max:	$109.46	
Deductible:	$125.00	(2004)
Carryover Ded:	0.00	(2004)
Coinsurance:	$ 11.74	(2004)
Date of Injury:		/ /

Procedure Type of Service	Dates of Service	Billed Amount	Excluded Amounts*	Allowed	Basic 100%	Maj. Med. 80 %	%
1. 99021	02/05/04	$220.00	$ 24.48	$195.52	$48.75	$146.77	
2. 85025	02/05/04	$ 40.00	$ 19.38	$ 20.62	$ 5.60	$ 15.02	
3. 87040	02/05/04	$ 30.00	$ 0.00	$ 30.00	$ 8.40	$ 21.60	
4.							
5.							
6.							

Remarks:
*Individual deductible has now been met.

	Basic 100%	Maj. Med. 80 %
Totals: $ 43.86 $246.14	$62.75	$183.39
Deductible:	$ 0.00	$125.00*
Amount Subject to Coinsurance:	$62.75	$ 58.39
Coinsurance:	$ 0.00	$ 11.68
Amount Subject to Adjustment:	$62.75	$ 46.71
Adjustment (See Remarks):	$ 0.00	$ 0.00
Payment Amount: $109.46	$62.75	$ 46.71

*Denial Reasons
1. $24.48 not covered — charge exceeds amount covered by your plan
2. $19.38 not covered — charge exceeds amount covered by your plan
3.
4.
5.
6.

Payees
1. $90.00 – Dee N. Aee, M.D.
2. $19.46 – Nancy Normal
3.
4.
5.
6.

If you disagree with our decision on your claim, you have the right by law to request that your claim be reviewed by your plan administrator. This request must be made in writing within 60 days of receipt of this notice. If you wish, you may submit your written comments and views. Please consult your plan's claim review procedures. See your employer regarding any other ERISA questions.

Figure 11 – 5: Payment Worksheet

4. *Excluded Amounts.* * The amount of charges for this single line of coding that are not allowable under the plan. An explanation should be placed under Denial Reasons (asterisk reference).

5. *Allowed.* The amount remaining after the excluded expenses are subtracted from the total charge.

6. *Basic 100%.* The amount of the allowable expense that is payable at 100%. If there are multiple applicable plan percentages for a single charge, the allowable should be broken up based on the amount payable at each specific percentage.

7. *Maj. Med %.* The Major Medical amount allowed after any higher benefits such as Basic have been subtracted.

8. *%.* Any additional applicable percentage rate that may apply to an allowable amount. This can be due to OOP maximums, SSO not performed, etc.

9. *Totals.* The totals of all amounts within that column.

10. *Deductible.* The amount of the charges applied to the plan deductible.

11. *Amount Subject to Coinsurance.* Amount payable at the plan coinsurance rate after any deductible is taken.

12. *Coinsurance.* The coinsurance rate that is the patient's liability.

13. *Amount Subject to Adjustment.* The amount that would need to be adjusted because of COB, overpayment, or any other type of adjustment.

14. *Adjustment (see Remarks).* The actual adjustment being made.

15. *Payment Amount.* The final payment that would be paid by the plan.

16. *Remarks.* This space is used to explain the type and reason for any adjustments being made.

17. *Denial Reasons.* A reason for the denial, which must be explained to the member whenever a charge or portion of a charge is not covered under a plan. The reason should be entered in this area.

18. *Payees.* Up to six payees entered per claim. This normally includes a maximum of providers and the employee.

Processing the Claim

Now that you know the claims examiner's responsibilities and the basic guidelines used to process a claim, lets go step by step through the processing of a

medical claim using the payment worksheet just described and the guidelines just covered.

The claim information is taken from the sample HCFA-1500 found in the Billing Forms Chapter. This information is shown on the claim form, and on the description in parentheses. The information shown in brackets is either the calculation used to arrive at an amount, or the field on the HCFA-1500 that contains the information. We will be using the XYZ Corporation contract from the Contracts chapter and the RVS schedule and Conversion Factor Report from the Usual, Customary and Reasonable chapter.

After it has been determined that the claim is filled out properly, the patient is covered, the provider is appropriate, there is no other insurance, and the services are covered, it is time to begin processing the claim.

Completing the Claim Payment Worksheet

The claim payment worksheet is equivalent to an explanation of benefits. A copy of this form will be sent to the insured to explain the benefit payment for the claim. Therefore, each section should be filled out completely to decrease the possibility of confusion on the part of the claimant.

The claim payment worksheet used for this course is intended to be an example only. It contains the information in much the same format as other insurance carrier payment forms. This worksheet and the guidelines for completing it are to be used for training and reference purposes only, since the particular company or plan worksheets and guidelines may differ.

Each item below will explain how to complete a section of the payment worksheet.

1. Complete the information regarding the patient and insured first. This information is contained in the box in the upper left-hand corner of the payment worksheet.
   Eligible Employee. (Nancy Normal) [Field 4]
   Company. (ABC Corporation) [Field 11b]
   Social Security Number. (777-77-7777) [Field "Insured's I.D. Number"]
   Patient. (Nancy Normal) [Field 2]
   Relationship. (self) [Field 6]

2. Next, each CPT code should be listed in the first column on the claim payment worksheet. Only codes that are the same should be combined together, otherwise list one service per line, regardless of whether this means using more than one claim payment worksheet. (99201, 85025, 87040) [Field 24D]

3. List the date(s) of service in the second column. (020504 for each line/ service) [Field 24A]

4. Now enter the amount the provider billed in the third column. ($220, $40, $30) [Field 24F]

5. The next step is to determine the allowed amount for the service or procedure. Using the Relative Value Study shown in **Figure 6 – 1**, locate the unit value for the CPT code assigned to each service provided. The unit value for the procedure is located in the right-hand column titled Total RVU's.

Next, determine the conversion factor for the procedure from the UCR Conversion Factor Report (**Figure 6 – 2**). Using the first three numbers of the zip code of the provider, locate the type of service. Each of four categories is listed next to the zip code location. The categories are:

1. Surgery
2. Medicine
3. X-ray/Lab
4. Anesthesia

Multiply the appropriate conversion factor by the unit value for the procedure. Remember the appropriate category is determined by the CPT code, not the description of service. This gives you the allowable amount. However, if the billed amount is less than the allowable amount, the billed amount is considered to be the allowable amount.

Thus, you will have: (195.52, 20.62, 30.94) [6.5 (RVS) X 30.08 (Medicine Conversion factor for zip code starting 895) = 195.52, 0.8 (RVS) X 25.78 (x-ray/lab conversion factor) = 20.62, 1.2 (RVS) X 25.78 (x-ray/lab conversion factor) = 30.94. However, since the billed amount for line three is less that the UCR amount, the allowed amount will be the billed amount.]

Skip to the fifth column of the payment worksheet (Allowed) and enter the allowed amount as figured above.

6. Subtract the allowed amount from the billed amount. The resulting figure is the excluded amount that goes in the fourth column. Remember, if the allowed amount is greater than the billed amount, the billed amount will be the allowed amount. Therefore, the excluded amount will be $0.00. ($24.48, $19.38, 0.00) [$220.00 (billed amount) – $195.52 (allowed amount) = 24.48, $40.00 – $20.62 = 19.38, $30.00 – $30.00 = 0.00]

7. By law, each explanation of benefits must list any amounts that are denied and the reason for the denial. Therefore, skip to the Denial Reasons section and enter a denial reason on the corresponding line in the denial reasons section. Usually, a brief explanation such as "$21.83 not covered — charge exceeds amount covered by your plan" is sufficient. If the service is not covered, the corresponding code (or description) and an explanation should be listed in the same

manner (i.e., $300.00 not covered—cosmetic services are not covered by your plan).

8. If the plan has a basic allowance, the unit value should be multiplied by the basic allowance listed in the contract. For example, if the contract stipulates that the basic allowance for an office visit is $7.00 and the service has a unit value of 1.0, then the basic allowance is $7.00. The basic allowance amount should be placed in the sixth column (Basic 100%). ($48.75, $5.60, $8.40) [$7.50 (Outpatient Physicians Visits basic conversion factor from contract) X 6.5 (RVS units) = $48.75, $7.00 (x-ray and laboratory basic conversion factor from contract) X 0.8 (RVS units) = $5.60, $7.00 (x-ray and laboratory basic conversion factor from contract) X 1.2 (RVS units) = 8.40]

9. The basic allowance is now subtracted from the allowed amount and the remainder is placed in the seventh column. ($146.77, $15.02, $21.60) [$195.52 (allowed amount) - $48.75 (basic amount) = $146.77, $20.62 (allowed amount) - $5.60 (basic amount) = $15.02, $30.00 (allowed amount) - $8.40 (basic amount) = $21.60]

10. After all the charges have been figured individually, the total for each column is added up and placed at the bottom of the column. ($43.86, $246.14, $62.75, $183.39)

Check your totals for accuracy by adding the major medical amount to the basic amount. These two items should match the allowed amount. Then add the allowed amount to the excluded amount. The total of these two figures should match the billed amount on the claim.

If the contract allows different percentages depending on the type of service (i.e, basic services paid at 100%, major medical at 80%, accidents paid at 100%, and so on), then each different type of benefit (i.e., basic, major medical, accident) should be placed on a different line. If there are not enough lines on the payment worksheet, all services with a similar co-payment amount may be placed together in a single column. There is an additional, eighth column to allow for varying percentages.

11. Now you are ready to calculate the actual benefit payment. At the top of each payment column (columns six through eight), place the coinsurance percentage amount that applies to the figures in that column. (100%, 80%)

12. Check the contract for the deductible amount and the Beginning Financials for any previously paid deductible amounts.

- Is there a deductible amount for basic benefits?
- Has the deductible for this individual been satisfied?
- Does the deductible combine the medical plan with a dental plan (the plans are integrated)?
- If so, has the deductible been satisfied under the medical or dental portion of the contract?
- Has the family deductible been satisfied?
- Is there any carryover deductible from the previous year that needs to be calculated in?

Using the above questions and information, calculate both the basic and the major medical deductible amounts. Often the only deductible amount on a basic portion of a plan will be for hospital services.

13. Now do the basic column first. Enter the amount of the deductible on the deductible line in the basic benefits column. In this case there is no basic deductible on the services for Nancy Normal, since the only deductible specifically stated in the contract is a $50 inpatient hospital deductible and this claim is not for inpatient hospital services.

14. Subtract the deductible amount from the total of the column. Since the deductible amount is $0.00, the total of the basic column remains the same. ($62.75) [$62.75 - $0.00 = $62.75]

    This amount is placed in the amount subject to coinsurance.

15. Multiply the amount subject to coinsurance by the insured's portion of the coinsurance amount (the remaining amount needed to reach 100%). For example, if the plan's coinsurance amount is 80%, then the insured's responsibility is 20%. For this column the payment amount is 100%, so there is no coinsurance amount for the patient. ($62.75) [$62.75 X 0% = $0.00]

16. Now subtract the coinsurance amount from the amount subject to coinsurance. The remaining balance is the amount subject to adjustment and goes in the next column. ($62.75) [$62.75 - $0.00 = $62.75]

    Double check your answer by multiplying the amount subject to coinsurance by the insurance carriers portion. [$62.75 X 100% = $62.75]

17. Now move on to the next column and repeat these steps. First, calculate the major medical deductible that should be applied to this claim. The amount of the deductible is placed across from the word deductible in the first column in which benefits are payable at less than 100%. The major medical deductible is not taken from Basic Benefits. If the deductible remaining is more than the amount of the column, the amount of the column should be placed in the deductible box and any remaining amounts carried over to additional columns with less than a 100% coinsurance amount. ($125.00. Since treatment is for a new patient visit at the beginning of the year, we will designate that Nancy Normal has not yet paid any of her deductible)

    Note: If any individual or family deductible or coinsurance amounts have been met with this claim, an asterisk should be placed beside the deductible or coinsurance amount and a notation made in the remarks box (e.g., 2003 Family deductible has been met).

18. Subtract the deductible amount from the total of the column. The remaining amount is the portion that is subject to coinsurance. (58.39) [$183.39 - $125.00 = $58.39]

19. Multiply the amount subject to coinsurance by the insured's portion of the coinsurance amount (the remaining amount needed to reach 100%). For example, if the plan's coinsurance amount is 80%, then the insured's responsibility is 20%. ($11.68) [$58.39 X .2 = $11.68]

20. Next, ask the following questions:
    - What is the maximum coinsurance amount listed in the contract?
    - Has this coinsurance limit been met?
    - If the individual coinsurance limit has not been met, has the family coinsurance limit been met?

    If any coinsurance limits have been met, the coinsurance amount should be adjusted accordingly. For example, if the individual coinsurance limit is $1,500 and $1,495 has been paid by the individual, the coinsurance amount is $5.00. The correct coinsurance amount goes in the next space labeled coinsurance.

21. Now subtract the coinsurance amount from the amount subject to coinsurance. The remaining balance is the amount subject to adjustment and goes in the next column. ($46.71) [$58.39 - $11.74 = $46.71]

    Double check your answer by multiplying the amount subject to coinsurance by the insurance carriers portion. [$58.39 X 80% = $46.71]

22. Then ask:
    - If there is other insurance, what is the amount paid by the other insurance company?
    - Are there any other reasons why there would be an adjustment to this claim?
    - If so, what is the proper adjustment amount?

If there is an adjustment, the amount of the adjustment should be placed in the following box labeled "Adjustment (see remarks)," and an explanation should be placed in the remarks box to the left. Many claims will not have an adjustment amount. If there is an adjustment amount, place the amount in the adjustments row, up to the amount of the Amount Subject to Adjustment. For example, if there were an adjustment of $100 on Nancy's claim, $62.75 would be placed in the first column and $37.25 would be placed in the second column. Since there is no adjustment on this claim, we will leave these boxes blank.

23. The adjustment is then subtracted from the amount subject to adjustment, and results are written in the payment amount (following boxes).

24. Add up the payment amount from each column. The resulting payment amount should be placed in the box immediately to the right of the words "Payment Amount." This is the amount of the benefits being paid by the insurance carrier. ($109.46) ($62.75 + 46.71 = $109.46)

ERISA

Federal ERISA requirements affect all claim denials. The ERISA Right of Review statement must be included with every claim denial and on every EOB where all or part of a claim is denied. The following is wording that may be used on the EOB or statement:

> "If you disagree with our decision on your claim, you have the right by law to request that your claim be reviewed by your plan administrator. This request must be made in writing within 60 days of receipt of this notice. If you wish, you may submit your written comments and views. Please consult your plan's claim review procedures. See your employer regarding any other ERISA questions."

Payees

Now all that is left is to determine to whom to make out the check and to update the financial history. Look back on the claim form. Benefits may be assigned to the provider of services by the member. The assignment must bear the member's written signature on a form that authorizes benefits payable directly to the provider of service. An assignment or authorization to pay benefits is a statement usually included on the claim form, which permits the member to authorize the administrator to pay benefits directly to the person or institution that provided the service. The examiner is required to honor all valid assignments made by the member.

When reviewing a claim, note whether an assignment has been made. If payment is made because of failure to honor an assignment and benefits are released to the member, the provider of service can also request payment, and payment must be made to the provider as well. The incorrect payment made to the member must be recouped (this will be covered in the Chapter on Adjustments). Ensuring that all valid assignments are honored is a basic part of good claim handling.

When processing a claim, ask yourself, did the insured authorize payment directly to the provider of services or is there a mandatory assignment of benefits?

- If not, the payee would be the insured.
- If so, check the billed amount from the claim and the amount (if any) that the patient/insured has already paid. If the difference between the billed amount and the amount that the patient or insured paid (balance due) is less than the benefit payment amount, the payee would be the provider of services up to the balance due. Any remaining funds would then be paid to the insured.

25. In this case, Nancy has paid $290 on the claim, leaving a balance of $90.00 owed to the provider. Since the provider should not be paid more than he has charged, the payment must be split. $90.00 will be paid to the provider and the remaining $19.46 will be reimbursed to Nancy as an overpayment. This information is placed in the Payees section.

Updating History

Updating the payment history is vitally important to ensure that proper benefit payments are calculated. Each preceding question that related to previous payments of deductibles, coinsurance amounts, satisfaction of individual or family limits, accident benefits, and others will change with the processing of each claim. On our payment worksheet, the updated history appears in the upper left-hand corner of the sheet. If claims are processed by computer, the computer should handle the updating of the history for you.

If accident benefits were paid on this claim, add the payment amount of the accident benefits to any previous accident benefit amounts paid on this individual for this accident. The amount goes on the first line. The amount paid on all accidents in this calendar year should be placed to the right of this amount, along with the current year (in parentheses).

The amount of the benefits paid under Major Medical should be added to all previous major medical benefits paid. If the plan has a calendar year maximum rather than a lifetime maximum, the amount of the benefits paid should be added to all previous benefits paid during that calendar year. The result should be placed in the lifetime maximum space on the next line. Usually, Basic Benefits on Basic and Major Medical plans do not apply to lifetime paid amounts. Check the contract to see whether there are separate maximums for Basic and Major Medical payment amounts. If the plan calls for a calendar year maximum, the word lifetime should be replaced by the words "calendar year" and the current year should be included.

The amount of any deductibles calculated on this claim should be added to any previously paid deductible amounts and the result placed in the deductible space with the current year.

If any of the dates of service on this claim fall within the last three months of the calendar year and the contract includes a carryover provision, the amount of deductible paid on these services should be placed on the line labeled "carryover deductible," along with the year. If there is more than one date of service and if some are in the last three months and others are not, the deductible amount should be taken from the amount or amounts of the services in the order in which they are received.

Example: An exam and x-ray were performed on 9/18/03. Two moles were found and an appointment was made to remove them on 10/10/03. The billed amount for the exam and x-ray was $40, and all of it was allowed (the UCR amount was higher than the billed amount). The allowed amount for the mole removal was $120. The patient had previously satisfied $25 of the $100 deductible. The total paid deductible amount would be $75 on this claim. Forty dollars of the deductible would be for the first two services and $35 would be for the two moles removed. Therefore, $35 would be considered the carryover deductible amount.

Finally, add the amount listed on the coinsurance line with any previous coinsurance amounts for the calendar year. The total, along with the year, should be placed on the coinsurance line of the financial history box. You have now completed payment on this claim.

26. In this case, this is the first claim for Nancy. Thus, the following amounts are listed in her updated history:
    Accident Benefit: 0.00   (20___) [This was not an accident claim, so no accident benefits were paid.]
    Lifetime Max: $109.46   2004 [This is the total amount of all claims paid on Nancy during her lifetime. Since this is her first claim, it is just the amount from this claim.]
    Deductible: $125.00   (2004) [Nancy paid $125 in deductible on this claim. She has now met the calendar year deductible for 2004.]
    Carryover Ded: 0.00   (2004) [This claim was not paid in the last three months of the year so there is no caryyover deductible.]
    Coinsurance: $ 11.74   (2004) [This is the amount of Nancy's copayment on this claim.]
    Date of Injury [This would not apply since this claim is not an accident.]

You have now finished processing this claim!

Quick Reference Formulas

The following quick reference formulas will help you remember the calculation included on a payment worksheet.

Plan UCR
Unit value x plan conversion factor = plan UCR.

Anesthesia: Time units + procedure unit value x plan conversion factor.
(TU + UV) x CF = ANES. ALLOW.

Multiple Surgery: 100% of the basic or UCR allowance for the major procedure.

Non-covered Charges
Total charges minus allowable amounts (UCR).
TC – UCR = NC

Basic Allowance
Procedure unit value x basic conversion factor.
UV x BCF = BASIC

Major Medical Allowance
Plan UCR allowance minus basic allowance.
UCR – BASIC = MM ALLOWABLE

Major Medical Payment
Plan UCR minus basic allowance minus applicable deductibles multiplied by plan coinsurance rate.
(UCR – BASIC) – DEDS x % = MM PAYMT

Total Payment
Major Medical payment plus basic payment.
MM + Basic = TP

Processing Drug Claims

Many health plans cover expenses for prescription drugs. However, these drugs must often meet the following three criteria:
1. They must be prescribed by the member's physician. This physician must be duly licensed and able to prescribe medications in the state in which the prescription was issued.
2. They must be prescription medications (i.e., they must, by law, require a prescription from a licensed physician for their dispensation).
3. They must be prescribed to treat a disease, bodily injury, or a mental or nervous disorder.

Some plans may cover prescriptions that do not meet the above criteria. These can include antacids, eye and ear medications, compounded dermatalogic preparations, or other medications. If these drugs are listed, they will be specifically indicated in the policy.

Non-prescription drugs are generally not covered under the provisions of a contract. In addition, some prescription drugs may not be covered. These can include:

- Contraceptives prescribed for contraception.
- Dietary supplements, health foods, or vitamins (including prenatal vitamins).
- Appetite suppressants.

The *Physician's Desk Reference* should be consulted to determine whether a drug is a prescription or a non-prescription drug.

Handling Prescription Claims

Prescription drugs can be issued on an outpatient or inpatient basis. For the guidelines regarding payment for inpatient drugs (including those issued for take home), see the **Hospital Claims** chapter.

For outpatient drug claims, certain guidelines should be followed. These include the following:

1. A valid claim form must be on file showing the eligible diagnosis for which the drugs are being prescribed. This form shows that the patient was under the care of a physician for the covered diagnosis when the prescription was issued. After a valid claim form has been accepted, it is not necessary for a new claim form to accompany each drug claim as long as the patient is still under the doctor's care and the diagnosis is still valid. For example, if the diagnosis is of a chronic nature, drugs will often be refills of earlier prescriptions.

2. The pharmacy bill, receipt, or pharmacy statement for each prescription must accompany the request for payment.

3. All drug receipts or pharmacy bills must show the prescription number, the name of the physician, the name of the patient, the date of issuance, and the amount charged. If any of these items are omitted, the validity of the prescription should be checked prior to payment of the claim. Some receipts may also list the type of drug. This is helpful for determining whether the drug is a prescription drug or an over-the-counter drug.

4. The drugs must be appropriate for the condition being treated, the amount of time since the first diagnosis of the condition, and the amount of drug prescribed. For example, persons suffering from a serious heart disease or diabetes may require large amounts of drugs over an extended period of time, whereas a patient suffering from an ear infection would require a small amount of drugs over a much shorter period of time.

5. If prescriptions are questionable, further information should be obtained from the prescribing physician, not from the patient. Causes for review include:

   a. The amount of the prescription expense is not appropriate to the condition being treated.

   b. The drugs are generally used to treat conditions that are not covered under the policy (i.e., exogenous obesity, contraception).

   c. The claim is for contraceptive medications. If the woman is over the age of 45, many doctors prescribe contraceptive medications for hormone imbalance. Some plans may cover contraceptives issued for these reasons, but not for contraceptive reasons.

   d. A large number of prescription claims is submitted at one time. This may indicate claims being submitted for prescriptions that were issued to more than one person.

   e. The prescription or information on any claim appears to have been altered.

6. If a receipt or statement is received for more than one drug, care should be taken to determine which drugs are covered and which are not. Often several types appear on the same claim.

7. Plan provisions should be checked to determine which drugs are covered and which are not. Also, drugs issued for a non-covered diagnosis should be denied as not covered.

   Example: Morphine would be covered for heart surgery but not for cosmetic surgery.

8. Check the licensure of the prescribing doctor. In many states, physicians, dentists, podiatrists, and psychiatrists, are allowed to prescribe medications. However, chiropractors, naturopaths, optometrists and psychologists are not. These doctors may suggest or dispense non-prescription medications, food supplements, or vitamins. However, since these items are not generally covered under the plan, no benefits would be payable. If the drug appears to be a prescription drug, but the physician indicated is not a physician, dentist, podiatrist, or psychiatrist, further investigation is warranted.

9. Finally, check the appropriate coverages for drug claims. Most prescription drugs are covered under Major Medical benefits and would be processed according to the general guidelines provided in the Major Medical plan. However, there may be specific plan provisions on medications. Care should also be taken to check the exclusions listed in the policy because this is usually where the

exclusions to types of drugs and diagnoses will be listed.

Red Book and Blue Book

Some plans have a separate drug sub-coverage. Drugs on these plans are often paid according to a set price schedule, regardless of the amount charged by the pharmacy or dispensing physician. These schedules are often based upon the Blue Book or the Red Book. These two books list wholesale prices of drugs.

Often the plan provisions will specify payment at 150% or 175% of the Blue Book or Red Book price. Typical wording of the contract often reads as follows:

a. Eligible expenses are X% (150% or 175%) of the Red Book or Blue Book plus ($1.35, $1.50, or $1.65), or the charge, whichever is less.

b. Coverage is limited to a (31-day, 90-day, 100-day) supply, except for maintenance drugs, which are limited to a (100-day) supply.

c. Benefits are payable at (50%, 75%, or 100%).

To find the correct payment amount, first determine the manufacturer of the drug. If the drug manufacturer is not listed, the information should be looked up using the *Physician's Desk Reference*. The least expensive generic drug should be used to calculate benefits.

Determine the charge for the smallest quantity listed, and then determine the price per unit. The unit may be indicated in quantification by tables, by ounces, or by some other measurement. If the drugs are listed in metric units and the prescription is issued in non-metric units, the metric units must be converted to non-metric units (or vice versa). Metric conversion tables can be found in most medical dictionaries.

You then multiply the price per unit by the number of units dispensed. This is the wholesale price for the drug. This wholesale price should be multiplied by the X% (150% or 175%) indicated by the plan. Then, add any amount indicated as $A ($1.35, $1.50, or $1.65). If this amount is more than the amount charged, the amount charged should be used. If not, this amount is considered the allowable amount. This allowed amount is then paid at the (50%, 75%, or 100%) amount at which benefits are payable.

Summary

There are many important responsibilities of the claims examiner. By applying basic guidelines, the examiner will establish a practice that will enable him or her to routinely make clear and concise claim decisions.

Assignments

Complete the Questions for Review.

Questions for Review

Directions: Answer the following questions without looking back into the material just covered. Write your answers in the space provided.

1. Name the three types of manual claim files that may be used in a claim processing system.

    1. _____

    2. _____

    3. _____

2. If the claim cannot be processed upon receipt, the claim file must be _____

3. Referrals should be made for which three types of claims?

    1. _____

    2. _____

    3. _____

4. Briefly explain the pended claim follow-up procedure. _____

    _____

    _____

5. Why is it important to update payment history? _____

    _____

    _____

If you were unable to answer any of the questions, refer back to the section and then complete the answers.

Honors Certification™

The Honors Certification™ challenge for this chapter is a written test of the information contained within this chapter, including the formulas on how to calculate benefits. You will be given 30 minutes to complete this test. Each incorrect answer will result in a deduction of between 1% and 5% from your grade. You must achieve a score of 85% or higher to pass this test. If you fail the test on your first attempt you may retake the test one additional time. The items included in the second test may be different from those in the first test.

12 Effective Communication

In this chapter you will learn:

- To use effective verbal communication.
- To know how to use the ERISA Right of Review Statement.
- To properly communicate the need for reimbursement of paid benefits.

Key words and concepts you will learn in this chapter:

ERISA Right of Review Statement – A statement which must be included on all denied claims.
Postscript – (often abbreviated P.S.) A sentence tacked onto the bottom of a letter after the signature.

Most of our communication with claim contacts will be by letter or through telephone conversations. These contacts will include claimants, attorneys, physicians, hospital personnel and employers.

Regardless of whom you are communicating with, you must be versatile. You will deal with people of different educational and socio-economic backgrounds. Therefore, you must be able to adapt to any situation and make yourself understood by your contact.

All communication is persuasive. The significance of the message varies depending on the situation, as well as whether the message comes across positively or negatively.

You, the person processing health claims, will at times be communicating with someone who has lost a loved one or is experiencing stress due to severe illness of a family member. Although you need to be professional, be compassionate as well.

Many ideas can be transmitted through effective communication. Communication is relevant in the functioning of any organization. Communication can be used to influence, to show cooperation, but most frequently to give and obtain information. The more effective the communication skill is, the greater the chance of giving understandable answers or receiving the information you are seeking.

Verbal Communication

The most commonly used mode of communication is verbal (speech). We speak so others may listen. When you speak to someone it is a stimuli which produces a response. The manner in which you speak to someone usually has an influence on the response you receive.

The majority of your speaking with a claimant will be over the telephone. Rarely will a claimant come into the office. When dealing with an Employer Group Plan, your contact will usually be with the employer and you may never have any contact with the claimant.

Your telephone conversation will always be judged by the listener and be subject to interpretation. Therefore, you will always want to be tactful and professional in your speaking.

You should be very careful about giving out information, which may be contradicted at a later date. For example, unless a request is already in process for a check to be sent, you should not say a check will be sent, until you are sure a check will be sent. A situation may arise where you have approved the claim but your supervisor may not agree with your decision, or you may get correspondence that same day that sheds a different light on the claim. Therefore, be very careful about any commitment you make.

A part of verbal communication is listening. You must be as good a listener as you are a speaker, soaking in the conversation and transferring pertinent information to the claims file.

When speaking on the telephone speak slowly and distinctly. Keep in mind that you will usually be speaking to someone who has no knowledge of your procedures and in most cases little or no understanding of insurance terminology. Also, the claimant may have little knowledge of requirements necessary to claim benefits under the policy.

Be sure to thank people for complying with your requirements. Remember also to preface any requests for additional information with a "please."

The tone of one's voice is very important. Our words can sometimes be helpful but condescending. Avoid getting into arguments with contacts, even if the contact is irate. Try to understand the other's viewpoint.

When taking a message for a co-worker, always read the message back or ask for the spelling of names. Repeat telephone numbers and ask for area codes. It is very frustrating for a person to get a message they cannot return. Also never commit a co-worker to returning a call at or by a specific time or date. Your co-worker may not be able to comply with the commitment you made and it may put the company in a bad light. Instead of saying "I'll have her call you back at 11:15, "say" I'll have her call you at her earliest convenience."

Being an effective speaker is more important than being an effective writer. A letter can always be dictated again, however, once you speak you cannot take it back.

Letter Writing

Letters sent to clients have a primary purpose: to give and/or request information. Each letter also impacts your public image. Customers perceive a company's reliability and personality from its letters. Are they curt or friendly, threatening or helpful?

The key to a good letter is organization. Present the information in a manner which is understandable. A letter should be readable and project a professional image. This can be achieved through the use of basic letter structure and clear, concise language.

Many insurance carriers use form letters for most claim contracts. Be sure that when filling in information on these letters that you write clearly and carefully convey what you want the claimant to do.

Letter Structure

As you are probably aware, a letter consists of certain elements. While the body of the letter contains the significant information, the opening, "sets the scene" and the closing leaves the "lasting impression."

Openings

When writing letters to clients it is important to be personable but direct. The reader should be able to understand the reason for your letter by reading the first paragraph. Get your reader's attention by appealing to their interests. Think of the subject as the reader's point of view.

Do not give all the information in the first paragraph. Briefly explain your reason for writing (i.e., "a complete review has been made of your claim as you requested ..."). Then, explain the details of the situation.

Body

Details you want to relate go here. Often, a brief review of claim facts, an explanation of the policy provisions that apply and statements relating the facts and the policy are appropriate. The letter must come to grips with the "heart of the problem" without getting bogged down by words that do not matter.

Lead the reader step by step toward an objective. First clear their mind of any preconceived notions without "talking down" to them. Respect their opinions and views while proceeding to help them understand and accept the principles you advocate.

Closings

The closing paragraph of your letter should be friendly, but decisive. It serves any or all of the following purposes:

- Requests action on the part of the reader,
- Leaves the door open for future action, or
- Ends the correspondence.

If you are requesting action, be sure to tell the reader:

- What you want done ("send", "contact", etc.),
- When you want it done (be specific not "ASAP", but "within 14 days", etc.), and
- How to complete your request ("call me at (XXX) 555-1212, etc.).

Postscript

A **postscript** (often abbreviated P.S.) is a sentence tacked onto the bottom of a letter after the signature. Do not use a postscript to express an important thought you overlooked when writing the body of your letter. Instead rewrite the letter.

Language

When writing, consider the message you want to deliver. Choose words, which will convey your message, clearly and concisely.

Tone

Build goodwill by writing letters with a friendly tone. Cold, stiff letters often create the wrong impression. Keynote each letter with courtesy. If the occasion warrants, be sympathetic, but not overly apologetic. Always show respect to the reader.

Be positive. Some people would write: "We are sorry that we shall be unable to compile this information for you in less than one week." Good writers would say it this way: "We shall be glad to compile this information for you and we could have it ready in one week." Avoid using negative words such as "cannot," "unable" and "impossible."

Voice

Whenever possible, write in the active voice rather than the passive voice. Instead of "the enclosed form should be returned within 30 days," try using "please return the enclosed form in 30 days."

Terminology

The words chosen to express an idea can greatly impact a reader's interpretation. Generally, short words communicate better than long ones. For example, "begin" is better than "initiate," "try" is better than "endeavor." Also, break complex sentences down into several simple ones.

When writing to an insured, it is helpful to use everyday terminology rather than insurance jargon. Use words that everyone can understand. However, be extremely careful in paraphrasing the policy or certificate. Quote the policy verbatim and not in your own words, whenever possible.

There are other catch phrases that are overused and/or abused, such as the following:

- "N/A" – Try not to use this abbreviation, it may not be understood by the reader.
- "Above named insured," "Above captioned insured" – A better way is to state the insured's name, "Mr. Jones."
- "Enclosed is an envelope" – The insured can see the envelope and will usually realize from the rest of your letter its intended use.
- "Please be advised" – These are wasted words. Try writing your sentence then cross out these words; usually the sentence is complete without them.

When you Mean	Use
Addition	And, also, again, besides, plus, finally, then, too, furthermore.
Contrast	However, though, although, but, nevertheless, yet, rather, than, otherwise, instead.
Result	It, consequently, therefore, thus, since, so, hence, accordingly.
Concession	Naturally, of course, perhaps, admittedly, granted.

- "Thank you in advance for your anticipated cooperation" – Can easily be reworded into a much shorter phrase, as "Thank you for your cooperation."

The use of connectives can be a valuable tool. However, make sure that you use a connective that conveys your intended meaning.

Content

A letter is useful only when it clearly states the message that is being conveyed. While wordiness is not recommended, extreme shortness can create a poor impression. Use words sparingly, but not sparsely.

When writing, keep the reader in mind. Tailor your letters for effectiveness and readability. Get all of the facts, do your homework and do not guess.

Proofreading

Never send a letter you have not proofread. Check for errors as well as readability. Since many of the letters you write will deal with benefits, it is especially important to check any dollar amounts that are included.

Check the remainder of the letter as well because just one letter can make a difference between "unit" and "unite," "owning" and "owing."

When corrections are necessary, indicate changes to be made at the point in the text where they occur. Make corrections in red ink so that they stand out from the rest of the letter and can be located easily by the typist. Always have a corrected letter retyped – sloppy, handwritten corrections leave a poor impression.

The remainder of this section will discuss various guidelines to consider when writing to certain individuals.

Claimant

When writing to a claimant, remember that he is not usually an insurance company employee and may not understand certain terminology (i.e., pre-existing, proceeds, EOB, transfer, etc.).

It is important to use courtesy and tact when corresponding with claimants. When dealing with sensitive issues (i.e., medical status), choose your words carefully. Review the following paragraph:

"In reviewing the operative report for your surgery, we note that while cancer was removed from your lung, the entire lung did not have to be removed. So, we can only pay $1,200 as the customary and reasonable fee, rather than the $2,200 charged by the doctor."

This claimant may not have know about the cancer and it is not your responsibility to relay this information. A better way is as follows:

"The operative report for the surgery that Dr. Jones performed describes a procedure which suggests a benefit based on $1,200 as a reasonable fee, rather than the $2,200 charged by the doctor."

Physician

Correspondence with the claimant, physician or hospital can facilitate or prolong the claim evaluation process, depending upon the manner in which requests are presented.

In your opening paragraph, state your reason for writing (i.e., "evaluating Mrs. Smith's claim for medical benefits"). Include any policy requirements that the physician may need to take into consideration. Be careful not to use insurance jargon that may not be readily understood.

State your request as clearly and concisely as possible. Present your questions in either paragraph or list form, whichever is clearer. Try to keep in mind the intended use of the reply. Word your questions carefully so that the answers you obtain will be of use in the claim evaluation. Anticipate all the information needed then write for everything early and at one time. Doctors and hospitals do not easily cooperate when three or four letters are sent requesting additional information about the claimant.

Other Contacts

There are other parties with which you may communicate during the processing of claims (i.e., collection agencies, attorneys, and other insurance carriers.)

Remember that courtesy and professionalism go a long way towards gaining the cooperation of those involved in the claim process.

Communication of Details

All denials must meet the following standards:
- A prompt and complete investigation is needed before a claim can be denied. The file must maintain and document the basis for denial. This means that the facts substantiated by the claim material and investigations are appropriate to the policy provisions related to the denial. Denial letters, which are required for all claims denials, must state all defenses available.
- A reasonable, written explanation of denial quoting or providing reference to the proper

policy provisions is required. Investigations need to be complete and documented.
- Determining eligibility is considered the first line of defense. Any complete investigation starts with a proper determination of eligibility.

Unfair claim settlement practices require notification of:
- All reasons for denial,
- The policy provisions on which the denial is based, and
- An explanation of how those provisions apply to the facts of the claim.

Where specific policy exclusions are involved a letter is necessary. If no payment is due, a reasonable explanation is required relating the denial to a specific policy provision. It should be standard practice to write a letter when a comparatively low payment is made compared to the total expense submitted, or compared to total benefits claimed.

Sensitive denial categories requiring letters include, but are not limited to, the following:
- Pre-existing conditions,
- Extension of benefits requirements not met,
- Questionable medical necessity,
- Questionable eligibility, and
- Distinction between accident vs. illness.

For medical claims, not every little disallowed charge has to have a denial letter. Explanation of Benefits form (EOB) messages are often used appropriately to expedite denials but they may not always adequately meet denial requirements outlined by some regulatory authorities. When small, non-covered charges are included on a bill where essentially everything is payable, use of an EOB message is adequate. Also, when numerous services are submitted with a few expenses incurred before insurance became effective, or which occurred after termination, an EOB message is usually sufficient. Although telephone calls do not meet the policy definition of "Notice Claim," when a claimant does notify you of a claim or loss and if the claimant is advised the claim is not covered, a follow-up, written confirmation of the denial must be given. This requirement does not apply to hypothetical, "what if" questions or to general questions about coverages.

Getting Your Point Across
If you are writing to the claimant or any claimant contacts such as the attorney or employer, denying benefits, the notification to them should contain elements such as:
- What was required (i.e., bodily "injury caused by and accident....")

- What happened (i.e., "death was caused by conditions more properly classified as a sickness"),
- What is the result (i.e., "no benefits are payable"), and
- What alternatives are available (i.e., "we will be glad to review any additional information you may wish to submit").

Each aspect of the denial should contain certain key information. The requirements should be quoted or carefully paraphrased from the certificate. All reasons for denials should be included and clearly stated, referencing medical terms when appropriate. However, terms should be simplified when possible. For example, use broken arm instead of fractured arm, or refer to heart condition instead of myocardial infarction.

Be very careful about giving the claimant information that the physician has submitted. You do not want to start a conflict between the doctor and the patient, nor violate the confidentiality of sensitive medical information. Instead of saying "your doctor said," consider using wording such as "medical information received." If additional details are requested, you may then be in a position to be more specific or refer the person to her doctor to clarify medical information.

Tying Up Loose Ends

The final paragraph(s) of the denial letter should inform the insured of any alternatives that are available (i.e., submit additional information, ERISA, etc.). If a reservation of rights is appropriate, it should be stated here also.

Notice Of Availability

Where all or a part of a claim is denied and the claimant is a resident of a state requiring a Notice of Availability by the State Insurance Department, all denial letters and EOB must contain the appropriately worded notice, as required by the state of residence.

Right Of Review/ERISA

Federal **ERISA** requirements affect all claim denials. The ERISA Right of Review Statement must be included with every claim denial letter and on every EOB when all or part of a claim is denied: The wording to be used is as follows:

If you disagree with the decision on your claim, you have the right by law to request that your claim be reviewed by your Plan Administrator (or your plan's claim reviewer). This request must be made in writing within sixty (60) days of receipt of this notice. If you wish, you may submit your written comments and views. Please consult your Plan's claim review procedures. See your employer on any other ERISA questions.

Adjustments

Overpayments
Overpayments usually fall into the three categories listed below:
1. A simple calculating error when all the necessary information is available in the claim file,
2. Professional or claimant errors which, because of misunderstanding, are unavoidable, and
3. Deliberate misstatement or fraudulent acts by the insured or others upon whom we rely for claim information.

Overpayments will usually be discovered while processing a claim for possible payment.

Overpayment Reimbursement Requests
When forwarding a request for reimbursement of an overpayment to an insured or other party, the following should be included:
- A statement of the facts as to why an overpayment of insurance benefits has been made, including a reference to an EOB and the relevant policy provisions,
- The amount of the overpayment,
- A request for reimbursement of the overpayment,
- A statement to the effect that if a lump sum repayment is not feasible, the willingness to discuss an alternative method of repayment, (i.e., monthly installment payments), and
- A statement informing the insured or other party that you will be happy to answer any questions or consider any comments or additional facts which the insured may have with regard to the matter, but that in any event you wish to hear from him within a reasonable amount of time regarding reimbursement (usually two weeks).

The examiner should retain a copy of all outgoing correspondence in case the need arises to clarify any misunderstandings resulting from the correspondence.

When contacting an insured regarding reimbursement for an overpayment of benefits, you should not:
- State or threaten that if reimbursement is not made, you will garnish the insured's wages. (**Garnishment** is a method of collecting an

unpaid debt, which may only be utilized after a lawsuit has been filed, and a judgment is obtained),

- Threaten independent legal action, or
- Threaten that if reimbursement is not made, that you will turn the matter over to a collection agency.

A follow-up to an overpayment letter should be sent to the insured, with a copy to the provider if an assigned claim, every two weeks, and these attempts should continue for a reasonable period of time.

If no acknowledgement of the overpayment is received from the claimant or provider after a six-week period, the letter should be referred to the legal department or to supervisory personnel.

wording when speaking, since the listeners will often judge their experience with the company by their conversations with a claims examiner.

When creating letters or completing form letters, it is important to be sure that you convey the correct intent of the letter. Be sure it is clear what you want the reader to do, or how you want them to respond.

When communicating with others, it is important to remember that they may not be familiar with all the terminology used in insurance communications. Abbreviations should be avoided, and terminology which can be misunderstood should be fully explained.

ERISA requirements state that any claim that is denied must contain the ERISA Right of Review Statement. This statement must appear on each letter or EOB associated with the denied claim.

Summary

Most communication with claim contacts will be through letters (often form letters) and telephone conversations. It is important to use tact and careful

Assignments

Complete the Questions for Review.
Complete Exercise 12 – 1.

Questions for Review

Directions: Answer the following questions without looking back into the material just covered. Write your answers in the space provided.

1. What is the most commonly used mode of communication?_____

_____

2. What is a postscript?_____

3. What does the body of a letter contain?_____

_____

4. Instead of the wording "Above named insured" what should you use in a letter?_____

_____

5. Unfair claim settlement practices require notification of what three items?

   1.   _____

   2.   _____

   3.   _____

6. There are several sensitive denial categories which require letters. List them._____

_____

7. What is the Right of Review Statement?_____

_____

8. Overpayments usually fall into what three categories?

    1. _____

    2. _____

    3. _____

9. What five items should be included when requesting reimbursement of an overpayment?

    1. _____

    2. _____

    3. _____

    4. _____

    5. _____

10. What three things should you not do when contacting an insured regarding reimbursement for an overpayment of benefits?

    1. _____

    2. _____

    3. _____

If you were unable to answer any of the questions, refer back to the section and then complete the answers.

Exercise 12 – 1

Directions: Write a letter to handle the following situations.

1. To the insured: A surgery claim is denied because the patient was not covered under the insurance plan when the surgery was performed.

2. To a physician: You need the operative report on a surgery before you can process the claim.

3. To a claimant: The claim was overpaid due to a clerical error at the insurance company (the wrong code was entered). You need the insured to reimburse the company $135.78.

Honors Certification™

The Honors Certification™ for this section will be a written test on the information covered in this chapter. Additionally, students will be asked to write two letters. These letters should be completely correct. Any errors or omissions will result in a deduction of between 2% and 10% of your grade. You must achieve a score of 80% or higher to pass this test. If you fail the test on your first attempt, you may retake the test one additional time. The items included in the second test may be different from those in the first test.

13 Physician's Services

In this chapter you will learn:

- To identify services that fall within the medical/physician's services 90000 code range of the CPT.
- To understand how the physician's services section is broken down, when codes should be used, and which providers may bill using these codes.
- To properly code and process physician's services claims.

Key words and concepts you will learn in this chapter:

Biofeedback – Training an individual to consciously control automatic, internal bodily functions.

Consultation – An opinion provided by a specialist.

Custodial Care – Care that is primarily for the purpose of meeting the personal daily needs of the patient and can be provided by personnel without medical care skills or training.

Dialysis – A maintenance procedure used for End-Stage Renal Disease when the kidneys cease functioning. This procedure helps to clean impurities out of the blood.

Maintenance Therapy – A repetitive service rendered to maintain a level of function with no other neurological function or other function gained.

Office Visit – Office visits or other encounters between a physician and patient that occur outside a hospital setting.

Ophthalmology Care – Eye care provided either by an optometrist or an ophthalmologist (MD).

Physical Medicine – The manipulation and physical therapy associated with the non-surgical care and treatment of the patient.

Second Surgical Opinion Consultation (SSO) – An opinion provided by a specialist regarding a proposed surgical treatment plan.

Speech Therapy – Therapy for the correcting of speech impairments.

The most common services billed by a physician are office and hospital visits. We will review and discuss some specific physician's services and basic guidelines

and coverage for these services. When referring to medical services, there are three basic categories:

1. Professional services,
   a. Surgical
   b. Non-surgical
2. Facility services, and
3. Miscellaneous services.

Professional services are those performed by a licensed individual such as a medical doctor, physician's assistant, nurse, or chiropractor. **Facility services** are those provided by a "place," for example, a hospital or clinic. Equipment usage and room fees (i.e., x-ray equipment, operating room) are considered facility expenses. **Miscellaneous services** are all other types of expenses not included in the previous categories. For example, prescriptions, medical equipment (i.e., wheelchairs, crutches), and ambulance expenses all are considered miscellaneous types of expenses.

In the remainder of this chapter we will discuss each of the sections of the CPT and any guidelines for that section. Follow along in the CPT and read any guidelines included there.

The first section of the CPT includes the 992XX series of numbers, for evaluation and management of a patient.

Office or Other Outpatient Services (99201 – 99215)

This section is used to report **office visits** or other encounters between a physician and patient that occur outside a hospital setting.

There are different codes for new and established patients. In general, codes for new patients (99201 –

99205) carry a higher unit value since the physician is expected to spend additional time completing introductory paperwork on the patient and performing a more in-depth history and exam. Because of this, claims examiners should be sure to double check if a patient has previously seen the physician before processing a claim for a new patient.

Hospital Observation Services (99217 – 99220)

These codes are used to denote that the patient was kept in the hospital "for observation." This generally happens when there is a chance that the patient's condition may worsen and the doctor wants to be sure that immediate medical help is available if that should happen.

Skilled Nursing Facility (99301 – 99316)

A skilled nursing facility is a specially qualified facility that has the staff and equipment to provide skilled nursing care or rehabilitation services and other related health services.

A patient may be transferred from an inpatient hospital to a nursing facility for supervised care when the patient no longer requires the skill levels of the inpatient hospital. They may also come directly from home or any other environment.

Custodial Care (99321-99333)

Custodial care is primarily for the purpose of meeting the personal daily needs of the patient and can be provided by personnel without medical care skills or training. For example, custodial care includes assistance with walking, bathing, dressing, eating and other activities. Skilled nursing personnel are not required for this non-medical type of care, which is commonly referred to as "meeting the daily living needs" of the patient. Most plans do not provide coverage for these types of services and for those that do, payment is very limited. If there is a question as to whether care is custodial, copies of the provider's nursing notes or the Admit and /or Discharge Summary reports should be requested.

Emergency Department Services (99281-99288)

When a patient goes to the outpatient or emergency department of a hospital, a physician is usually in attendance who has a contract to provide professional care at the facility. The contracting physician's charges may appear on the hospital bill or may be billed separately. Many hospitals have two types of outpatient departments: the emergency room (ER) and outpatient medical clinics.

When a billing is received from a hospital for clinic charges, there is often a room charge for the use of the facility and a separate physician charge. The coding of these types of claims varies greatly from payor to payor, so the handling procedures need to be clarified. However, there are two main handling procedures:
1. CPT services are coded separately and subjected to usual, customary, and reasonable (UCR).
2. Generic or UB-92 codes are used and not subjected to UCR.

The following rules provide some common handling suggestions:
- If a hospital is billing for professional component charges separately from the actual lab or x-ray charges, combine the two together because they represent one total service.
- Physician treatment charges (professional fees) may be coded separately from other fees. This will depend on whether or not the payor is cost-conscious. If coded separately, the charge is usually subject to UCR, whereas if not coded separately, it will not be subject to UCR.
- State fees should also be combined with the actual laboratory or x-ray charges.

These guidelines vary from company to company, so verification must be requested.

If the patient wants to have his regular physician in attendance and the physician is called in from outside the hospital to provide services, code 99056 should be used. If the patient visits the outpatient clinic of a facility, regular office visit coding should be used, since a clinic is conceptually the same as an office. That is, the same doctors see the same patients, visits are scheduled the same as in the office, the treatment provided is the same as what would be provided in an office, and so on. In essence, the physician is using the facility as his office.

Consultations (99241-99263)

Usually, a **consultation** is provided by a specialist who has been requested to provide an opinion only. The specialist examines the patient at the request of another physician. He or she may request diagnostic services and may take therapeutic recommendations to the referring physician. However, the specialist does not usually take over the day-to-day treatment or management of the patient. In fact, to qualify as a consultation, the consulting physician cannot be responsible for the regular management of the patient.

If the physician subsequently assumes responsibility for the routine care of the patient, the services should be coded as visits and not consultations even if billed as consultations. (The initial consultation would be allowed as such.) If the consultant is seeing the patient, in addition to the regular attending physician, 99231-99233 should be used.

Second Surgical Opinion Consultations (99271-99275)

A **second opinion** is designed as a benefit to the patient by confirming the need for surgeries that have a reputation for being done needlessly. Many plans provide a special benefit called an SSO Benefit, which provides 100% payment on services provided by a second, independent specialist whom the patient consults before the scheduling of an elective, non-emergency surgery. Normally, for an SSO benefit to be payable, the following requirements must be satisfied:

- The second or third opinion physician must be totally uninvolved with the original recommending physician. Therefore, he or she cannot be part of the same medical group and will often be picked by the administrator, medical management firm, or payor.
- The consultation must be completed before the scheduling of surgery.
- The second opinion physician cannot perform the recommended surgery.

Depending on the plan, failure to obtain an SSO may result in:

- Complete denial of all charges for the surgery and related services.
- Application of a special, reduced coinsurance. For instance, instead of paying 80% of the expenses, 50% would be paid. Non-compliance penalties vary substantially.
- No change of benefits. In this case, the SSO is considered to be a benefit for the member and is not used to penalize for non-compliance.

Immunizations (90700-90749)

Immunizations are considered to be preventive treatment. Therefore, usually an active illness or disease is not present. Consequently, many plans do not cover such routine services except under five special circumstances:

1. 90724 – Influenza virus – may be covered for senior citizens who have a history of respiratory illness.
2. 90726 – Rabies – may be covered as active treatment of an animal bite.
3. 90732 – Pneumococcal – may be covered for young or older patients with a history of respiratory illness.
4. 90703 – Tetanus toxoid – may be covered when provided due to an injury such as stepping on a nail. Some firms code this injection as 90782 rather than 90703.
5. The state in which the plan operates may have mandated laws that specify that all plans must provide specific levels of routine care for children. In such a case, the plan may be obligated to provide such benefits.

Nervous/Mental Care and Treatment (90801-90899)

Nervous/mental care and treatment includes:
- Psychotic and neurotic disorders,
- Organic brain dysfunction,
- Alcoholism, and
- Chemical dependency.

The language description on the claim form generally indicates "psychotherapy," "individual therapy," or "group therapy." The ICD-9 coding is usually in the range of 290.00 – 319.00. The providers of service are usually medical doctors (typically psychiatrists) or clinical psychologists.

If one of the following providers is indicated, most benefit plans require a referral by an MD:
- Marriage, Family and Child Counselor (MFCC),
- Licensed Clinical Social Worker (LCSW), and
- Master of Social Work (MSW).

These CPT codes are used only when psychiatric counseling or therapy is provided. If such therapy is not provided, even if the service is performed by one of the above licensed providers, a different code range should be used.

Most plans pay a reduced benefit for this type of treatment. There may be a limit on the number of visits per year or per lifetime, along with a dollar limit per visit, per calendar year, or per lifetime. Also, many plans only cover certain provider licensing. Therefore, read the plan document carefully before processing any psychiatric care claims.

Biofeedback (90900-90915)

Biofeedback is training an individual to consciously control automatic, internal bodily functions. For instance, through conscious control, some body rhythms that control the constriction of blood vessels or the beating of the heart can be increased or decreased. This type of treatment can be used for a variety of illnesses or symptoms. A common use is for the control of intractable pain.

Biofeedback is controversial in that its effectiveness is very hard to prove or disprove. In addition, it does not cure anything. Instead, it is used as a tool in dealing with the symptoms of a condition, not in its treatment. Most plans do not cover biofeedback treatment, or if it is covered, it is very limited and only for certain diagnoses.

Dialysis (90918-90999)

Dialysis is a maintenance procedure used for End-Stage Renal Disease when the kidneys cease functioning. Notice that this is not really a treatment because it is only handling the functions normally performed by the body (however, it is still referred to generically as "treatment"). For a patient with this disease to survive, the blood cleansing function must be performed artificially by one of three processes currently available:

1. Hemodialysis,
2. CAPD – continuous ambulatory peritoneal dialysis, or
3. Transplantation of a new kidney.

Most hemodialysis is performed at private dialysis centers. A small percentage of the patients have a machine in their own home. The fees for dialysis are usually billed on a monthly basis. When coding, either the actual dates of service should be indicated or a monthly from/through date is used. Normally, the only time you see these bills is for the first 30 months of treatment. After that, Medicare becomes the primary payor (refer to the Medicare section for additional information). If the dialysis is performed in an acute facility, you may be billed separately for the facility fees and the physician fees. Remember, the CPT codes are to be used only on physicians services. Dialysis treatment costs approximately $7,000 per month.

CAPD is performed by the patient at home. The peritoneum of the stomach is used to cleanse the blood. Surgery is required for the implantation of catheters and the construction of the internal bag (made of the peritoneum) to hold the dialysate fluids. Monthly supplies must be purchased, and there will be monthly examination charges by the attending physician. This type of treatment costs about $3,000 per month.

Transplants are coded in accordance with the surgery section of the CPT.

Ophthalmology (92002-92499)

Ophthalmology care is eye care provided either by an optometrist or an ophthalmologist (MD). Most health plans do not cover routine vision care services related to the refraction and subsequent prescription of glasses or contact lenses. If they are covered, the benefits are usually very limited in both the dollar allowance and the time restraints and are often provided under a separate vision care plan or benefit. Therefore, always be sure to verify plan benefits before processing a vision claim. Also be aware that not all vision care is routine. Some vision care is essential for the proper care and treatment of eye disease. Most payors have a listing of payable diagnoses, but even then the important point will be in what type of services are being provided. Prescriptive services for glasses or contact lenses are still considered routine (except possibly if the lens of the eye has been removed, as in cataract surgery).

Orthoptics is a retaining of the muscles that control vision. Some plans allow for this therapy for certain conditions such as strabismus and binocular vision. If the plan does allow therapy, it is usually very limited and may require a second opinion from an ophthalmologist.

Speech Therapy (92507-92508)

Speech therapy is usually for the correcting of speech that has been impaired because of sickness or injury and occurred while the individual was insured under the plan. The services must also be performed by a qualified practitioner. Conditions such as restoration of speech ability after a stroke or throat surgery would be covered. However, speech therapy for conditions such as stuttering or congenital deafness is usually not be covered.

If you are unsure of the underlying need for the speech therapy services, the claim should be referred to a specialist for further review.

Cardiovascular (92950-93981)

This is a very large section, and it is heavily used by the examiner. The following codes are some of the more commonly billed services:

93000   EKG
93010   EKG Interpretation Only
93015   Cardiovascular Stress Test
93224   24-hr EKG Monitoring

As a rule, the codes from 93000 through 93350 and 93600 through 93981 are considered to be DXL (Diagnostic x-ray and laboratory) expenses. Codes 93501 through 93545 are considered surgical procedures.

Physical Medicine (97010-98929)

Physical medicine is the manipulation and physical therapy associated with the non-surgical care and treatment of the patient. The most common form of physical medicine is chiropractic manipulation of the spine (theoretically, any joint can be involved). The chiropractor's scope of practice is limited in most states. For instance, in California, chiropractors are not allowed to draw blood or prescribe prescription medicines. The limitations vary by state.

Chiropractic care and billing used to be limited to manipulation of the spine and x-rays. Now, chiropractors use many different physical therapy modalities. Consequently, there has evolved an intense monitoring and restricting of payment for chiropractic services. Such restrictions may limit the number of visits per year, per month, or per condition, along with specifying daily money maximums or limiting the number of modalities that may be performed in a single visit. A wide variety of techniques have emerged to handle the overutilization of chiropractic care. As a result, it is important to check the coverage, as the administrative policies vary from payor to payor.

Many chiropractors use accident diagnosis, 84x.xx series, for billing purposes. Unless an accident or injury has actually occurred with a date, place, and circumstances indicated, the coding should be changed to reflect a non-injury skeletal condition, (72x.xx). (This varies by administrator.) Situations that should warrant further review include:

- Possible over utilization.
- Over three physical medicine visits in a week.
- Over 12 visits in a month.
- Over three months and at least 34 visits of physical medicine visits.
- Second provider of physical medicine on the same day.
- Over four physical medicine codes per day.
- More than one initial office visit by the same physician.
- Claims when the only physical medicine charges are for modalities or massage (97010-97039 procedure codes). Modalities are a method therapy, usually physical (i.e., a massage).
- Claims for use of an orthion table or orthion therapy.

If a particular claim appears to be excessive, the attending physician should be contacted and the following information obtained:

- An outline of the therapy program recommended.
- A list of goals to be achieved through the program.
- A narrative description of how the physician sees each procedure being performed as working toward one or more of the goals listed.

If the physician's reply justifies the use of therapy, frequency, and duration, then process the claim. It takes time and skill to be able to interpret or determine necessity of services rendered. Therefore, if you are not sure what action should be taken after compiling the information necessary to make a claims determination, refer the information to a claims specialist. Any of these limitations would depend on the individual contract and the administrator's policy. Please check with your administrator before processing this type of claim.

Maintenance Therapy

Maintenance therapy is a repetitive service rendered to maintain a level of function with no other neurological function or other function gained. Maintenance services must be considered under standard practice of medicine and must be skilled. Most payor's do not cover services for maintenance therapy or for therapy in which there is no improvement in the patient's condition.

Summary

Physician's services includes a wide array of services from treating a patient in the office to providing services in an emergency room setting, or at a skilled nursing facility. Physician's services charges may be billed by a variety of practitioners. Learn to identify the covered providers, and use these guidelines to determine whether the charges billed are covered services.

Assignments

Complete the Questions for Review.
Complete Exercises 13 – 1 to 13 – 3. Remember, company guidelines always supersede the guidelines provided here.

Questions for Review

Directions: Answer the following questions without looking back into the material just covered. Write your answers in the space provided.

1. (True or False?) If the diagnosis is for psychiatric care, regardless of the service provided, codes 90801 to 90899 are used. _____

2. What are dialysis services?_____

_____

3. (True or False?) Custodial care is usually a covered service. _____

4. The three types of end stage renal disease treatment are:

    1. _____

    2. _____

    3. _____

5. What is biofeedback? _____

6. Consultations are usually provided by a _____

7. (True or False?) A clinical psychologist requires a referral from an MD. _____

8. A Skilled Nursing Care Facility provides this type of care. _____

9. (True or False?) A second opinion physician can be in the same medical group as the surgeon. _____

10. What type of care is usually provided by an MFCC? _____

_____

If you were unable to answer any of the questions, refer back to the section and then complete the answers.

Exercises 13 – 1 to 13 – 3

Directions: Process each of the physicians services claims found on the following pages.

Honors Certification™

The Honors Certification™ challenge for this chapter is a written test of the information contained within this chapter. Additionally you will be given three claims to process, using the contracts contained in this book. You will be given 60 minutes to complete this test. Each incorrect answer will result in a deduction of between 1% and 5% from your grade. You must achieve a score of 80% or higher to pass this test. If you fail the test on your first attempt you may retake the test one additional time. The items included in the second test may be different from those in the first test.

APPROVED MOB-0938-0008

ROVER INSURERS INC.
5931 ROLLING ROAD
RONSON, CO 81369

CLAIM PHYS1

HEALTH INSURANCE CLAIM FORM

PICA ☐☐☐

1. MEDICARE	MEDICAID	CHAMPUS	CHAMPVA	GROUP HEALTH PLAN	FECA BLK LUNG	OTHER	1a. INSURED'S I.D. NUMBER	(FOR PROGRAM IN ITEM 1)
☐ (Medicare #)	☐ (Medicaid #)	☐ (Sponsor's SSN)	☐ (VA File #)	☒ (SSN or ID)	☐ (SSN)	☐ (ID)	999-99-9999	

2. PATIENT'S NAME (Last, First, Middle Initial)	3. PATIENT'S BIRTH DATE	SEX	4. INSURED'S NAME (Last, First, Middle Initial)
BOSSY, BETTY B.	09 / 19 / 39	M☐ F☒	BOSSY, BETTY B.

5. PATIENT'S ADDRESS (No., Street)	6. PATIENT'S RELATIONSHIP TO INSURED	7. INSURED'S ADDRESS (No., Street)
7991 BAGEL BLVD.	Self ☒ Spouse ☐ Child ☐ Other ☐	7991 BAGEL BLVD.

CITY	STATE	8. PATIENT STATUS	CITY	STATE
BARSTOW	NY	Single ☐ Married ☒ Other ☐	BARSTOW	NY

ZIP CODE	TELEPHONE (Include Area Code)		ZIP CODE	TELEPHONE (INCLUDE AREA CODE)
12899	(914) 555-3399	Employed ☒ Full-Time ☐ Part-Time ☐ Student Student	12899	(914) 555-3399

9. OTHER INSURED'S NAME (Last, First, Middle Initial)	10. IS PATIENT'S CONDITION RELATED TO:	11. INSURED'S POLICY GROUP OR FECA NUMBER:
		999-99-NIN

a. OTHER INSURED'S POLICY OR GROUP NUMBER	a. EMPLOYMENT? (CURRENT OR PREVIOUS) ☐ YES ☒ NO	a. INSURED'S DATE OF BIRTH 09 / 19 / 39 SEX M☐ F☒

b. OTHER INSURED'S DATE OF BIRTH MM / DD / YY SEX M☐ F☐	b. AUTO ACCIDENT? PLACE (State) ☐ YES ☒ NO	b. EMPLOYER'S NAME OR SCHOOL NAME NINJA CORPORATION

c. EMPLOYER'S NAME OR SCHOOL NAME	c. OTHER ACCIDENT? ☐ YES ☒ NO	c. INSURANCE PLAN NAME OR PROGRAM NAME NINJA PLAN

d. INSURANCE PLAN NAME OR PROGRAM NAME	10d. RESERVED FOR LOCAL USE	d. IS THERE ANOTHER HEALTH BENEFIT PLAN? ☐ YES ☒ NO If yes, return to and complete item 9 a-d

READ BACK OF FORM BEFORE COMPLETING & SIGNING THIS FORM

12. PATIENT'S OR AUTHORIZED PERSON'S SIGNATURE I authorize the release of any medical or other information necessary to process this claim. I also request payment of government benefits either to myself or to the party who accepts assignment below.

SIGNED **SIGNATURE ON FILE** DATE 02/06/04

13. INSURED'S OR AUTHORIZED PERSON'S SIGNATURE I authorize payment of medical benefits to the undersigned physician or supplier for services described below.

SIGNED **SIGNATURE ON FILE**

14. DATE OF CURRENT: ◄ ILLNESS (1st symptom) INJURY (Accident) ◄ PREGNANCY (LMP) 02 06 04	15. IF PATIENT HAS HAD SAME OR SIMILAR ILLNESS, GAVE FIRST DATE MM / DD / YY	16. DATES PATIENT UNABLE TO WORK IN CURRENT OCCUPATION FROM MM/DD/YY TO MM/DD/YY

17. NAME OF REFERRING PHYSICIAN OR OTHER SOURCE	17a. I.D. NUMBER OF REFERRING PHYSICIAN	18. HOSPITALIZATION DATES RELATED TO CURRENT SERVICES FROM 02 06 04 TO 02 14 04

19. RESERVED FOR LOCAL USE	20. OUTSIDE LAB? ☐ YES ☐ NO	$ CHARGES

21. DIAGNOSIS OR NATURE OF ILLNESS OR INJURY, (RELATE ITEMS 1,2,3, OR 4 TO ITEM 24E BY LINE)

1. 410 . 91   3. __ . __
2. __ . __   4. __ . __

22. MEDICAID RESUBMISSION CODE ___ ORIGINAL REF. NO.

23. PRIOR AUTHORIZATION NUMBER

24. A. DATE(S) OF SERVICE From MM DD YY To MM DD YY	B. Place of Service	C. Type of Service	D. PROCEDURES, SERVICES, OR SUPPLIES (Explain Unusual Circumstances) CPT/HCPS MODIFIER	E. DIAGNOSIS CODE	F. $ CHARGES	G. DAYS OR UNITS	H. EPSDT Family Plan	I. EMG	J. COB	K. RESERVED FOR LOCAL USE
02 06 04 02 06 04	23		99285	1	1,600 00	1		Y		
02 06 04 02 06 04	23		93000	1	420 00	1		Y		

25. FEDERAL TAX I.D. NUMBER SSN EIN	26. PATIENT'S ACCOUNT NO.	27. ACCEPT ASSIGNMENT? (For govt. claims, see back)	28. TOTAL CHARGE	29. AMOUNT PAID	30. BALANCE DUE
90-9999779 ☐ ☒	BETBS001 939	☐ YES ☒ NO	$ 2,020 00	$ 0 00	$ 2,020 00

31. SIGNATURE OF PHYSICIAN OR SUPPLIER INCLUDING DEGREES OR CREDENTIALS (I certify that the statements on the reverse apply to this bill and are made a part thereof.) SIGNED *Gal Bladder* DATE 02/19/04	32. NAME AND ADDRESS OF FACILITY WHERE SERVICES WERE RENDERED (If other than home or office) HEADACHE HOSPITAL 2000 HAZARD STREET HELP, NY 12899 (914) 555-9989	33. PHYSICIAN'S, SUPPLIERS BILLING NAME, ADDRESS, ZIP CODE & PHONE # GAL BLADDER, M.D. **NETWORK PROVIDER** 1990 GATEWAY DRIVE. STE 919G GOVERN, NY 12899 (914) 555-8899 PIN# GAL001 GRP#

PLEASE
DO NOT
STAPLE
IN THIS
AREA
□□□ PICA

WINTER INSURANCE CO.
9763 WESTERN WAY
WHITTIER, CO 82963

AREAAPPROVED MOB-0938-0008

CLAIM PHYS2

HEALTH INSURANCE CLAIM FORM

PICA □□□

1. MEDICARE MEDICAID CHAMPUS CHAMPVA GROUP HEALTH PLAN FECA BLK LUNG OTHER	INSURED'S I.D NUMBER (FOR PROGRAM IN ITEM 1)
□ (Medicare #) □ (Medicaid #) □ (Sponsor's SSN) □ (VA File #) ☒ (SSN or ID) □ (SSN) □ (ID)	444-44-4444

2. PATIENT'S NAME (Last, First, Middle Initial)	3. PATIENT'S BIRTH DATE MM DD YY SEX	4. INSURED'S NAME (Last, First, Middle Initial)
DINGBAT, DANNY D.	04 24 90 M☒ F□	DINGBAT, DANA D.

5. PATIENT'S ADDRESS (No., Street)	6. PATIENT'S RELATIONSHIP TO INSURED	7. INSURED'S ADDRESS (No., Street)
404 DOORWAY DRIVE	Self □ Spouse □ Child ☒ Other □	404 DOORWAY DRIVE
CITY STATE	8. PATIENT STATUS	CITY STATE
DENVER ND	Single ☒ Married □ Other □	DENVER ND
ZIP CODE TELEPHONE (Include Area Code)	Employed□ Full-Time ☒ Part-Time □ Student Student	ZIP CODE TELEPHONE (INCLUDE AREA CODE)
58444 (701) 555-3344		58444 (701) 555-3344

9. OTHER INSURED'S NAME (Last, First, Middle Initial)	10. IS PATIENT'S CONDITION RELATED TO:	11. INSURED'S POLICY GROUP OR FECA NUMBER:
		444-44-ABC
a. OTHER INSURED'S POLICY OR GROUP NUMBER	a. EMPLOYMENT? (CURRENT OR PREVIOUS) □ YES ☒ NO	a. INSURED'S DATE OF BIRTH MM DD YY SEX 04 04 64 M□ F☒
a. OTHER INSURED'S DATE OF BIRTH MM DD YY SEX M□ F□	b. AUTO ACCIDENT? PLACE (State) □ YES ☒ NO	b. EMPLOYER'S NAME OR SCHOOL NAME ABC CORPORATION
c. EMPLOYER'S NAME OR SCHOOL NAME	c. OTHER ACCIDENT? ☒ YES □ NO	c. INSURANCE PLAN NAME OR PROGRAM NAME ABC PLAN
d. INSURANCE PLAN NAME OR PROGRAM NAME	10d. RESERVED FOR LOCAL USE	d. IS THERE ANOTHER HEALTH BENEFIT PLAN? □ YES ☒ NO If yes, return to and complete item 9 a-d

READ BACK OF FORM BEFORE COMPLETING & SIGNING THIS FORM
12. PATIENT'S OR AUTHORIZED PERSON'S SIGNATURE I authorize the release of any medical or other information necessary to process this claim. I also request payment of government benefits either to myself or to the party who accepts assignment below.

SIGNED **SIGNATURE ON FILE**   DATE **01/ 26/ 04**

13. INSURED'S OR AUTHORIZED PERSON'S SIGNATURE I authorize payment of medical benefits to the undersigned physician or supplier for services described below.

SIGNED **SIGNATURE ON FILE**

14. DATE OF CURRENT: MM DD YY ◄ ILLNESS (1st symptom) ◄ INJURY (Accident) ◄ PREGNANCY (LMP) 01 26 04	15. IF PATIENT HAS HAD SAME OR SIMILAR ILLNESS, GAVE FIRST DATE MM DD YY	16. DATES PATIENT UNABLE TO WORK IN CURRENT OCCUPATION MM DD YY MM DD YY FROM TO
17. NAME OF REFERRING PHYSICIAN OR OTHER SOURCE	17a. I.D. NUMBER OF REFERRING PHYSICIAN	18. HOSPITALIZATION DATES RELATED TO CURRENT SERVICES MM DD YY MM DD YY FROM 01 26 04 TO 02 10 04
19. RESERVED FOR LOCAL USE		20. OUTSIDE LAB? $ CHARGES □ YES □ NO

21. DIAGNOSIS OR NATURE OF ILLNESS OR INJURY. (RELATE ITEMS 1,2,3, OR 4 TO ITEM 24E BY LINE)

1. 807 . 01   3. 800 . 40
2. 823 . 32   4. E884 . 9

22. MEDICAID RESUBMISSION CODE   ORIGINAL REF. NO.

23. PRIOR AUTHORIZATION NUMBER

24.	A. DATE(S) OF SERVICE From / To MM DD YY MM DD YY	B. Place of Service	C. Type of Service	D. PROCEDURES, SERVICES, OR SUPPLIES (Explain Unusual Circumstances) CPT/HCPS MODIFIER	E. DIAGNOSIS CODE	F. $ CHARGES	G. DAYS OR UNITS	H. EPSDT Family Plan	I. EMG	J. COB	K. RESERVED FOR LOCAL USE
	01 26 04 01 26 04	23	1	99285	1 2 3 4	882 00	1		Y		

25. FEDERAL TAX I.D. NUMBER SSN EIN	26. PATIENT'S ACCOUNT NO.	27. ACCEPT ASSIGNMENT? (For govt. claims, see back)	28. TOTAL CHARGE	29. AMOUNT PAID	30. BALANCE DUE
40-9999774 □ ☒	DANDI001 434	☒ YES □ NO	$ 882 00	$ 0 00	$ 882 00

31. SIGNATURE OF PHYSICIAN OR SUPPLIER INCLUDING DEGREES OR CREDENTIALS (I certify that the statements on the reverse apply to this bill and are made a part thereof.) SIGNED *Art Terry* DATE *2/10/04*	32. NAME AND ADDRESS OF FACILITY WHERE SERVICES WERE RENDERED (If other than home or office) HACKIM HOSPITAL 1000 HIDE STREET HUSHTOWN, ND 58444 (701) 555-4004	33. PHYSICIAN'S, SUPPLIERS BILLING NAME, ADDRESS, ZIP CODE & PHONE # ART TERRY, M.D. 4567 DOVER DRIVE, STE 404D DOLTER, ND 58444 (701) 555-0044 PIN# ART001 GRP#

(APPROVED BY AMA COUNCIL ON MEDICAL SERVICE 8/88)   PLEASE PRINT OR TYPE   FORM HCFA-1500 (12-90) FORM OWCP-1500   FORM RRB-1500

APPROVED MOB-0938-0008

BALL INSURANCE CARRIERS
3895 BUBBLE BLVD., STE.283
BOXWOOD, CO 85926

CLAIM PHYS3

HEALTH INSURANCE CLAIM FORM

PICA ☐☐☐   PICA ☐☐☐

1. MEDICARE	MEDICAID	CHAMPUS	CHAMPVA	GROUP HEALTH PLAN	FECA BLK LUNG	OTHER	INSURED'S I.D NUMBER (FOR PROGRAM IN ITEM 1)
☐ (Medicare #)	☐ (Medicaid #)	☐ (Sponsor's SSN)	☐ (VA File #)	☒ (SSN or ID)	☐ (SSN)	☐ (ID)	555-55-5555

2. PATIENT'S NAME (Last, First, Middle Initial)
PATIENT, PATTY P.

3. PATIENT'S BIRTH DATE MM DD YY   SEX
05 15 75   M☐ F☒

4. INSURED'S NAME (Last, First, Middle Initial)
PATIENT, PATTY P.

5. PATIENT'S ADDRESS (No., Street)
655 PAIN LANE

CITY: PEN   STATE: PA
ZIP CODE: 15522   TELEPHONE (Include Area Code) (878) 555-3355

6. PATIENT'S RELATIONSHIP TO INSURED
Self ☒ Spouse☐ Child☐ Other☐

8. PATIENT STATUS
Single ☒ Married ☐ Other ☐
Employed ☒ Full-Time ☐ Student Part-Time ☐ Student

7. INSURED'S ADDRESS (No., Street)
655 PAIN LANE

CITY: PEN   STATE: PA
ZIP CODE: 15522   TELEPHONE (INCLUDE AREA CODE) (878) 555-3355

9. OTHER INSURED'S NAME (Last, First, Middle Initial)

10. IS PATIENT'S CONDITION RELATED TO:

11. INSURED'S POLICY GROUP OR FECA NUMBER:
555-55-XYZ

a. OTHER INSURED'S POLICY OR GROUP NUMBER

a. EMPLOYMENT? (CURRENT OR PREVIOUS)
☐ YES ☒ NO

a. INSURED'S DATE OF BIRTH MM DD YY   SEX
05 15 75   M☐ F☒

a. OTHER INSURED'S DATE OF BIRTH MM DD YY   SEX
M☐ F☐

b. AUTO ACCIDENT?   PLACE (State)
☐ YES ☒ NO

b. EMPLOYER'S NAME OR SCHOOL NAME
XYZ CORPORATION

c. EMPLOYER'S NAME OR SCHOOL NAME

c. OTHER ACCIDENT?
☐ YES ☒ NO

c. INSURANCE PLAN NAME OR PROGRAM NAME
XYZ PLAN

d. INSURANCE PLAN NAME OR PROGRAM NAME

10d. RESERVED FOR LOCAL USE

d. IS THERE ANOTHER HEALTH BENEFIT PLAN?
☐ YES ☒ NO   If yes, return to and complete item 9 a-d

READ BACK OF FORM BEFORE COMPLETING & SIGNING THIS FORM

12. PATIENT'S OR AUTHORIZED PERSON'S SIGNATURE I authorize the release of any medical or other information necessary to process this claim. I also request payment of government benefits either to myself or to the party who accepts assignment below.

SIGNED   SIGNATURE ON FILE   DATE   02/02/04

13. INSURED'S OR AUTHORIZED PERSON'S SIGNATURE I authorize payment of medical benefits to the undersigned physician or supplier for services described below.

SIGNED   SIGNATURE ON FILE

14. DATE OF CURRENT: MM DD YY ◄ ILLNESS (1st symptom) ◄ INJURY (Accident) ◄ PREGNANCY (LMP)
02 02 04

15. IF PATIENT HAS HAD SAME OR SIMILAR ILLNESS, GAVE FIRST DATE MM DD YY

16. DATES PATIENT UNABLE TO WORK IN CURRENT OCCUPATION
FROM MM DD YY   TO MM DD YY

17. NAME OF REFERRING PHYSICIAN OR OTHER SOURCE

17a. I.D. NUMBER OF REFERRING PHYSICIAN

18. HOSPITALIZATION DATES RELATED TO CURRENT SERVICES
FROM MM DD YY   TO MM DD YY

19. RESERVED FOR LOCAL USE

20. OUTSIDE LAB? $ CHARGES
☐ YES ☐ NO

21. DIAGNOSIS OR NATURE OF ILLNESS OR INJURY, (RELATE ITEMS 1,2,3, OR 4 TO ITEM 24E BY LINE)
1. |___233__.__0__   3. |___.___
2. |___.___   4. |___.___

22. MEDICAID RESUBMISSION CODE   ORIGINAL REF. NO.

23. PRIOR AUTHORIZATION NUMBER

24. A. DATE(S) OF SERVICE From MM DD YY — To MM DD YY	B. Place of Service	C. Type of Service	D. PROCEDURES, SERVICES, OR SUPPLIES (Explain Unusual Circumstances) CPT/HCPS — MODIFIER	E. DIAGNOSIS CODE	F. $ CHARGES	G. DAYS OR UNITS	H. EPSDT Family Plan	I. EMG	J. COB	K. RESERVED FOR LOCAL USE
02 02 04 02 02 04	11	1	99213	1	330 00	1				

25. FEDERAL TAX I.D. NUMBER SSN EIN
50-9999775   ☐ ☒

26. PATIENT'S ACCOUNT NO.
PPP-0425501   535

27. ACCEPT ASSIGNMENT? (For govt. claims, see back)
☐ YES ☒ NO

28. TOTAL CHARGE
$ 330 00

29. AMOUNT PAID
$ 150 00

30. BALANCE DUE
$ 180 00

31. SIGNATURE OF PHYSICIAN OR SUPPLIER INCLUDING DEGREES OR CREDENTIALS (I certify that the statements on the reverse apply to this bill and are made a part thereof.)

SIGNED *Amber U. Lance* DATE 02/10/04

32. NAME AND ADDRESS OF FACILITY WHERE SERVICES WERE RENDERED (If other than home or office)

33. PHYSICIAN'S, SUPPLIERS BILLING NAME, ADDRESS, ZIP CODE & PHONE #
AMBER U. LANCE, M.D.
5005 ANSWER STREET, STE. 5123A
AGE, PA 15522 (878) 555-3155

PIN# AUL001   GRP#

(APPROVED BY AMA COUNCIL ON MEDICAL SERVICE 8/88)

PLEASE PRINT OR TYPE

FORM HCFA-1500 (12-90)
FORM OWCP-1500
FORM RRB-1500

PLEASE DO NOT STAPLE IN THIS AREA
☐☐☐ PICA

14 X-ray and Laboratory Services

In this chapter you will learn:

- To identify services that fall within the DXL 70000 - 80000 CPT codes.
- To identify common diagnostic tests performed in a physician's office.
- The normal range of specific DXL test values.
- How this section is broken down, when codes are used, and which providers may bill using these codes.

Key words and concepts you will learn in this chapter:

CT (Computed Tomography) Scans – 360-degree pictures of specific body areas.
Laboratory Examinations – The analyzing of body substances to determine their chemical or tissue make-up.
Nuclear Medicine – The use of radioactive elements and x-rays to image an organ or body part.
Panel Tests – Multiple tests that are combined and run from one specimen.
Papanicolaou or "Pap Smear" – A diagnostic laboratory test for detecting the absence or presence of infection, viruses, trauma, or cancer.
Professional Component – The reading or interpreting of the lab results or the x-ray.
Radiation Oncology – The use of radiation to treat a condition.
Technical Component – Taking the specimen or x-ray.
Ultrasonography – A picture made by bouncing sound waves off a desired area.
Unbundling – When a provider bills separately for each test performed even though all the tests came from the same specimen and were done simultaneously.
X-rays – Flat or two-dimensional pictures of a particular body part or organ.

Radiology and laboratory charges are charges that may be billed by a physician, an independent laboratory, or a freestanding radiology facility. Here we will discuss some of the basic guidelines used in determining whether billed diagnostic x-ray and laboratory (DXL) services are covered. We will also cover the guidelines for processing laboratory and radiology charges.

Laboratory examinations consist of the analyzing of body substances to determine their chemical or tissue make-up. Body fluids or tissues are collected and are either run through analyzing machines or looked at under a microscope to identify any abnormal substances or tissues.

There are basically two types of x-ray and laboratory charges: diagnostic x-ray/lab and medical management x-ray/lab. **Diagnostic charges** are for initial testing to confirm a diagnosis or to rule out other diagnoses. The physician orders the appropriate lab tests to confirm or rule out a diagnosis. **Medical management** x-ray/lab charges are incurred to control or manage a diagnosis (i.e., monitoring blood glucose levels on a patient with diabetes).

Laboratory tests are considered covered charges and may be payable under an x-ray and laboratory benefit. This benefit pays for the x-ray and laboratory test up to the policy maximum necessary to diagnose or manage a condition, as long as the expense is not payable under another Basic Benefit (i.e., inpatient hospital, preadmission testing, accident). The laboratory benefit is usually not payable for charges incurred in connection with any examination or test that is not necessary or incident to the establishment of a diagnosis for an injury or illness.

The XYZ plan has a Basic Benefit that covers a maximum of $200 per calendar year for x-ray/lab charges.

The CPT and DXL

CPT codes are used to list services on a billing form. These five-digit codes allow providers to designate which services were performed quickly and easily.

Radiology

Radiology services range from code 70010 to 79999. The radiology section of the CPT is arranged according to the anatomic position, that is, by body part, starting at the head and moving downward toward the feet. Knowledge of anatomy will make it much easier to locate which area of this section to refer to. This section is divided into several subsections. The four main subsections are:

- Diagnostic radiology   70010 – 76499
- Diagnostic ultrasound   76506 – 76999
- Radiation oncology   77261 – 77799
- Nuclear medicine   78000 – 78299

Diagnostic x-rays are flat or two-dimensional pictures of a particular body part or organ. X-rays are created by sending low-level radiation through the body onto a sheet of film. The image on the exposed piece of film looks like a negative from a roll of camera film. X-rays are most useful for looking at bones and dense tissue since softer tissue is not clearly defined.

Ultrasonography provides a more definitive type of picture than x-rays. Instead of using radiation, sound waves are bounced off the desired structure. The pattern and amount of sound returned constitute what forms a picture of the organ. This type of viewing is less potentially damaging than x-rays. This is why ultrasound scanning can be used during pregnancy, whereas x-rays are not.

Radiation oncology services is the use of radiation to treat a condition. This treatment is used in conjunction with chemotherapy to treat malignant cancers. Normally, radiation therapy is composed of multiple treatments and does not include a "picture" of the body part. It is done for treatment purposes only, not for diagnostic reasons.

Nuclear medicine combines the use of radioactive elements and x-rays to image an organ or body part. Certain radioactive elements collect in different organs. Therefore, to see whether an organ is working effectively or to see whether it is enlarged, for example, a radioactive element is injected into the patient, then pictures are taken of the organ at specified intervals to see how, where, and how much of the element collects in a specific organ.

CT scans (computed tomography) are 365-degree pictures of specific body areas. This scan provides a three-dimensional picture of the area and is used to help identify tumors and cancers located in an organ. CT scans are much more definitive than x-rays.

Pathology (Lab)

Laboratory examinations are the analyzing of body substances to determine their chemical or tissue type make-up. Body fluids or tissues are collected and then either run through analyzing machines or looked at under a microscope to identify any abnormal substances or tissues. Pathology services range from code 80000 to 89399 in the CPT.

For laboratory coverage, it is important to establish whether the tests are being done as part of a routine check-up or because the patient has symptoms that are being diagnosed. Also, the testing must be appropriate

for the reported symptoms. Thus, some tests would be routine for some diagnoses but not for others. This type of discrimination is learned through experience and time.

Automated Laboratory Charge
Automated laboratories offer their services primarily to doctor's offices. Usually, the doctor's office is furnished with all the necessary supplies for securing samples of blood and urine with lab sheets indicating which tests are to be performed on which specimens. Lab reports are usually received from the laboratory within approximately three days. The doctor is billed, usually monthly, for this service.

Panel Tests
Panel tests are composed of multiple tests that are combined and run from one specimen. These tests can be requested from one or two specimens and cost substantially less than several tests ordered separately from several separate specimens. These services are very sophisticated, highly computerized, and usually very reliable. CPT codes 80049-80092 refer to various types of panel tests. The number of tests performed determines which code to use. Doctors are allowed to bill for the collection of the specimen, a venipuncture if the specimen is blood, and the handling charge for packaging the specimen.

Unbundling
It is not uncommon for providers to do what is known as "unbundling" when billing. **Unbundling** is when a provider bills separately for each test performed even though all the tests came from the same specimen and were done simultaneously. In this circumstance, the provider gets significantly more money for doing nothing additional. When a bill is received "unbundled," the examiner needs to re-bundle it. An example of unbundling is shown in **Table 14 – 1**.

Table 14 – 1: Unbundling			
Bill from Doctor	CPT/RVS Code	Charges	Coding by Examiner/Charge
CO2	82347	$15.00	80048
Calcium	82310	20.00	
Chlorides	82435	25.00	
Creatinine	82565	15.00	
Glucose	82947	10.00	
Potassium	84132	15.00	
Sodium	84295	15.00	
BUN	84520	30.00	
		$195.00	$195.00

In **Table 14-1**, all the billed charges should be combined and coded under one panel code. Benefits would then be determined based on the one code.

Papanicolaou (PAP) Smear

A **Papanicolaou** or **"Pap smear"** is a diagnostic laboratory test for detecting the absence or presence of infection, viruses, trauma, or cancer. The expense for a Pap smear is eligible when one of the following six conditions exists:

1. The result of the Pap smear is abnormal.
2. A previous cancer of the cervix, uterus, or vagina has been present or is presently being treated.
3. The patient complains of symptoms referable to the female reproductive system.
4. The results of a Pap smear taken in the last 12 months were abnormal.
5. Signs or symptoms are present which, in the physician's opinion, are reasonably related to a gynecologic disorder.
6. The physical examination indicates any abnormal findings of the vagina, cervix, uterus, ovaries, or adnexa.

Usually, routine Pap smears performed in conjunction with a routine physical examination are not covered unless the contract specifically indicates coverage or the state mandates coverage.

Component Charges

Whenever a lab or an x-ray test is performed, two distinct services are actually performed:

1. The first service is the taking of the specimen or x-ray. This charge should include the expense for the personnel performing the test and the cost of the necessary equipment. This is called the **technical component** and is denoted by adding modifier – 27 to the CPT code.
2. The second service is the interpretation or the reading of the results of the test. This is called the **professional component** and is denoted by adding modifier – 26 to the CPT code.

An independent pathologist or radiologist often bills separately for the interpretation of the report. This interpretation-only charge is a professional component (PC) charge. To figure the cost of an x-ray or lab test, the PC charge (if billed separately) needs to be added to the base or technical charge (TC - the charge for performing the test). Sometimes, both the TC charge and the PC charge are billed by the same provider but are broken down into separate charges (not uncommon on hospital bills). When coding the claim, the two charges should be combined and coded as one charge. If the professional component and the technical component are performed by different providers, they are not to be combined and coded as a single expense. In such a case, these separate charges should be coded and paid separately.

A professional component charge ranges from 25% to 40% of the cost of the actual test. And the technical component ranges from about 60% of the cost of the test. (For training purposes, contracts that do not state a professional component percentage have had their claims computed at 40% of UCR).

Summary

X-ray and laboratory services are essential in determining the patient's problems, ruling out illnesses, and managing illnesses or injuries. It is now possible to perform certain tests in the privacy of one's home (i.e., pregnancy and glucose level tests).

We have discussed only some of the rules and guidelines used to process charges received for laboratory and radiology services. These guidelines should enable you to identify covered services and determine the correct processing procedures for services that are covered.

Assignments

Complete the Questions for Review.
Complete Exercise 14 – 1 to 14 – 3.

Questions for Review

Directions: Answer the following questions without looking back into the material just covered. Write your answers in the space provided.

1.   What is the numeric range of the CPT laboratory panel codes? _____

2.   What are panel tests? _____
      _____

3.   What is unbundling? _____
      _____
      _____

4.   What are professional and technical components? _____
      _____
      _____
      _____

5.   What does modifier –26 denote? _____
      _____

If you were unable to answer any of the questions, refer back to the section and then complete the answers.

Exercises 14 – 1 to 14 – 3

Directions: Process each of the DXL services claims found on the following pages.

Honors Certification™

The Honors Certification™ challenge for this chapter is a written test of the information contained within this chapter. Additionally you will be given three DXL claims to process, using the contracts contained in this book. Each incorrect answer will result in a deduction of between 1% and 5% from your grade. You must achieve a score of 80% or higher to pass this test. If you fail the test on your first attempt you may retake the test one additional time. The items included in the second test may be different from those in the first test.

PLEASE
DO NOT
STAPLE
IN THIS
AREA
□□□ PICA

ROVER INSURERS INC.
5931 ROLLING ROAD
RONSON, CO 81369

APPROVED MOB-0938-0008

CLAIM DXLI

HEALTH INSURANCE CLAIM FORM

PICA □□□

1. MEDICARE	MEDICAID	CHAMPUS	CHAMPVA	GROUP HEALTH PLAN	FECA BLK LUNG	OTHER	1a. INSURED'S I.D NUMBER	(FOR PROGRAM IN ITEM 1)
□ (Medicare #)	□ (Medicaid #)	□ (Sponsor's SSN)	□ (VA File #)	☒ (SSN or ID)	□ (SSN)	□ (ID)	999-99-9999	

2. PATIENT'S NAME (Last, First, Middle Initial)	3. PATIENT'S BIRTH DATE	4. INSURED'S NAME (Last, First, Middle Initial)
BOSSY, BETTY B.	MM 09 DD 19 YY 39 SEX M□ F☒	BOSSY, BETTY B.

5. PATIENT'S ADDRESS (No., Street)	6. PATIENT'S RELATIONSHIP TO INSURED	7. INSURED'S ADDRESS (No., Street)
7991 BAGEL BLVD.	Self ☒ Spouse □ Child □ Other □	7991 BAGEL BLVD.

CITY	STATE	8. PATIENT STATUS	CITY	STATE
BARSTOW	NY	Single □ Married ☒ Other □	BARSTOW	NY

ZIP CODE	TELEPHONE (Include Area Code)		ZIP CODE	TELEPHONE (INCLUDE AREA CODE)
12899	(914) 555-3399	Employed ☒ Full-Time □ Part-Time □ Student Student	12899	(914) 555-3399

9. OTHER INSURED'S NAME (Last, First, Middle Initial)	10. IS PATIENT'S CONDITION RELATED TO:	11. INSURED'S POLICY GROUP OR FECA NUMBER:
		999-99-NIN

a. OTHER INSURED'S POLICY OR GROUP NUMBER	a. EMPLOYMENT? (CURRENT OR PREVIOUS) □ YES ☒ NO	a. INSURED'S DATE OF BIRTH MM 09 DD 19 YY 39 SEX M□ F☒

b. OTHER INSURED'S DATE OF BIRTH MM DD YY SEX M□ F□	b. AUTO ACCIDENT? PLACE (State) □ YES ☒ NO	b. EMPLOYER'S NAME OR SCHOOL NAME NINJA CORPORATION

c. EMPLOYER'S NAME OR SCHOOL NAME	c. OTHER ACCIDENT? □ YES ☒ NO	c. INSURANCE PLAN NAME OR PROGRAM NAME NINJA PLAN

d. INSURANCE PLAN NAME OR PROGRAM NAME	10d. RESERVED FOR LOCAL USE	d. IS THERE ANOTHER HEALTH BENEFIT PLAN? □ YES ☒ NO If yes, return to and complete item 9 a-d

READ BACK OF FORM BEFORE COMPLETING & SIGNING THIS FORM

12. PATIENT'S OR AUTHORIZED PERSON'S SIGNATURE I authorize the release of any medical or other information necessary to process this claim. I also request payment of government benefits either to myself or to the party who accepts assignment below.

SIGNED **SIGNATURE ON FILE** DATE **02/06/04**

13. INSURED'S OR AUTHORIZED PERSON'S SIGNATURE I authorize payment of medical benefits to the undersigned physician or supplier for services described below.

SIGNED **SIGNATURE ON FILE**

14. DATE OF CURRENT: ◄ ILLNESS (1st symptom) INJURY (Accident) ◄ PREGNANCY (LMP) MM 02 DD 06 YY 04	15. IF PATIENT HAS HAD SAME OR SIMILAR ILLNESS, GAVE FIRST DATE MM DD YY	16. DATES PATIENT UNABLE TO WORK IN CURRENT OCCUPATION FROM MM DD YY TO MM DD YY

17. NAME OF REFERRING PHYSICIAN OR OTHER SOURCE	17a. I.D. NUMBER OF REFERRING PHYSICIAN	18. HOSPITALIZATION DATES RELATED TO CURRENT SERVICES FROM MM 02 DD 06 YY 04 TO MM 02 DD 14 YY 04

19. RESERVED FOR LOCAL USE	20. OUTSIDE LAB? □ YES □ NO $ CHARGES

21. DIAGNOSIS OR NATURE OF ILLNESS OR INJURY, (RELATE ITEMS 1,2,3, OR 4 TO ITEM 24E BY LINE)

1. | 410.91
2. | __.__
3. | __.__
4. | __.__

22. MEDICAID RESUBMISSION CODE ____ ORIGINAL REF. NO. ____

23. PRIOR AUTHORIZATION NUMBER

24. A. DATE(S) OF SERVICE From To MM DD YY MM DD YY	B. Place of Service	C. Type of Service	D. PROCEDURES, SERVICES, OR SUPPLIES (Explain Unusual Circumstances) CPT/HCPS MODIFIER	E. DIAGNOSIS CODE	F. $ CHARGES	G. DAYS OR UNITS	H. EPSDT Family Plan	I. EMG	J. COB	K. RESERVED FOR LOCAL USE
02 06 04 02 06 04	21		93000	1	340 00	1		Y		
02 06 04 02 06 04	21		93545	1	770 00	1		Y		
02 06 04 02 06 04	21		85025	1	40 00	1		Y		
02 06 04 02 06 04	21		86901	1	45 00	1		Y		
02 06 04 02 06 04	21		85610	1	30 00	1		Y		

25. FEDERAL TAX I.D. NUMBER SSN EIN	26. PATIENT'S ACCOUNT NO.	27. ACCEPT ASSIGNMENT? (For govt. claims, see back)	28. TOTAL CHARGE	29. AMOUNT PAID	30. BALANCE DUE
92-8989779 □ ☒	BETBS001 939	☒ YES □ NO	$ 1,225 00	$ 0 00	$ 1,225 00

31. SIGNATURE OF PHYSICIAN OR SUPPLIER INCLUDING DEGREES OR CREDENTIALS (I certify that the statements on the reverse apply to this bill and are made a part thereof.)

SIGNED *Daniel Drawblood* DATE 02/12/04

32. NAME AND ADDRESS OF FACILITY WHERE SERVICES WERE RENDERED (If other than home or office)

HEADACHE HOSPITAL
2000 HAZARD STREET
HELP, NY 12899 (914) 555-9989

33. PHYSICIAN'S, SUPPLIERS BILLING NAME, ADDRESS, ZIP CODE & PHONE #

DANIEL DRAWBLOOD, M.D.   **NETWORK PROVIDER**
HEADACHE HOSPITAL
2000 HAZARD STREET
HELP, NY 12899 (914) 555-9989

PIN# DAD106 | GRP#

(APPROVED BY AMA COUNCIL ON MEDICAL SERVICE 8/88)

PLEASE PRINT OR TYPE

FORM HCFA-1500 (12-90)
FORM OWCP-1500   FORM RRB-1500

AREAAPPROVED MOB-0938-0008

WINTER INSURANCE CO.
9763 WESTERN WAY
WHITTIER, CO 82963

CLAIM DXL2

PLEASE
DO NOT
STAPLE
IN THIS
AREA
□□□ PICA

HEALTH INSURANCE CLAIM FORM

PICA □□□

1. MEDICARE	MEDICAID	CHAMPUS	CHAMPVA	GROUP HEALTH PLAN	FECA BLK LUNG	OTHER	1a. INSURED'S I.D NUMBER (FOR PROGRAM IN ITEM 1)
☐ (Medicare #)	☐ (Medicaid #)	☐ (Sponsor's SSN)	☐ (VA File #)	☒ (SSN or ID)	☐ (SSN)	☐ (ID)	444-44-4444

2. PATIENT'S NAME (Last, First, Middle Initial)	3. PATIENT'S BIRTH DATE MM DD YY SEX	4. INSURED'S NAME (Last, First, Middle Initial)
DINGBAT, DANNY D.	04 24 90 M ☒ F ☐	DINGBAT, DANA D.

5. PATIENT'S ADDRESS (No., Street)	6. PATIENT'S RELATIONSHIP TO INSURED	7. INSURED'S ADDRESS (No., Street)
404 DOORWAY DRIVE	Self ☐ Spouse ☐ Child ☒ Other ☐	404 DOORWAY DRIVE

CITY: DENVER	STATE: ND	8. PATIENT STATUS Single ☒ Married ☐ Other ☐	CITY: DENVER	STATE: ND

ZIP CODE: 58444	TELEPHONE (Include Area Code) (701) 555-3344	Employed ☐ Full-Time Student ☒ Part-Time Student ☐	ZIP CODE: 58444	TELEPHONE (INCLUDE AREA CODE) (701) 555-3344

9. OTHER INSURED'S NAME (Last, First, Middle Initial)	10. IS PATIENT'S CONDITION RELATED TO:	11. INSURED'S POLICY GROUP OR FECA NUMBER: 444-44-ABC

a. OTHER INSURED'S POLICY OR GROUP NUMBER	a. EMPLOYMENT? (CURRENT OR PREVIOUS) ☐ YES ☒ NO	a. INSURED'S DATE OF BIRTH MM DD YY SEX 04 04 64 M ☐ F ☒

a. OTHER INSURED'S DATE OF BIRTH MM DD YY SEX M ☐ F ☐	b. AUTO ACCIDENT? ☐ YES ☒ NO PLACE (State)	b. EMPLOYER'S NAME OR SCHOOL NAME ABC CORPORATION

c. EMPLOYER'S NAME OR SCHOOL NAME	c. OTHER ACCIDENT? ☒ YES ☐ NO	c. INSURANCE PLAN NAME OR PROGRAM NAME ABC PLAN

d. INSURANCE PLAN NAME OR PROGRAM NAME	10d. RESERVED FOR LOCAL USE	d. IS THERE ANOTHER HEALTH BENEFIT PLAN? ☐ YES ☒ NO If yes, return to and complete items 9 a-d

READ BACK OF FORM BEFORE COMPLETING & SIGNING THIS FORM
12. PATIENT'S OR AUTHORIZED PERSON'S SIGNATURE I authorize the release of any medical or other information necessary to process this claim. I also request payment of government benefits either to myself or to the party who accepts assignment below.

SIGNED SIGNATURE ON FILE   DATE 01/26/04

13. INSURED'S OR AUTHORIZED PERSON'S SIGNATURE I authorize payment of medical benefits to the undersigned physician or supplier for services described below.

SIGNED SIGNATURE ON FILE

14. DATE OF CURRENT: ILLNESS (1st symptom) / INJURY (Accident) / PREGNANCY (LMP) MM DD YY 01 26 04	15. IF PATIENT HAS HAD SAME OR SIMILAR ILLNESS. GIVE FIRST DATE MM DD YY	16. DATES PATIENT UNABLE TO WORK IN CURRENT OCCUPATION FROM MM DD YY TO MM DD YY

17. NAME OF REFERRING PHYSICIAN OR OTHER SOURCE	17a. I.D. NUMBER OF REFERRING PHYSICIAN	18. HOSPITALIZATION DATES RELATED TO CURRENT SERVICES FROM MM DD YY 01 26 04 TO MM DD YY 02 08 04

19. RESERVED FOR LOCAL USE	20. OUTSIDE LAB? ☐ YES ☐ NO $ CHARGES

21. DIAGNOSIS OR NATURE OF ILLNESS OR INJURY. (RELATE ITEMS 1,2,3, OR 4 TO ITEM 24E BY LINE)

1. 807.01   3. 800.40
2. 823.32   4. E884.9

22. MEDICAID RESUBMISSION CODE   ORIGINAL REF. NO.

23. PRIOR AUTHORIZATION NUMBER

24. A. DATE(S) OF SERVICE From / To MM DD YY / MM DD YY	B. Place of Service	C. Type of Service	D. PROCEDURES, SERVICES, OR SUPPLIES (Explain Unusual Circumstances) CPT/HCPCS MODIFIER	E. DIAGNOSIS CODE	F. $ CHARGES	G. DAYS OR UNITS	H. EPSDT Family Plan	I. EMG	J. COB	K. RESERVED FOR LOCAL USE
01 26 04 01 26 04	21	1	70260 -27	3 4	70 00	1		Y		
01 26 04 01 26 04	21	1	71020 -27	1 4	55 00	1		Y		
01 26 04 01 26 04	21	1	73550 -27	2 4	80 00	2		Y		
01 26 04 01 26 04	21	1	73590 -27	2 4	100 00	2		Y		
01 26 04 01 26 04	21	1	70450 -27	3 4	325 00	1		Y		
01 26 04 01 26 04	21	1	73718 -27	2 4	770 00	1		Y		

25. FEDERAL TAX I.D. NUMBER SSN EIN 49-8989774 ☐ ☒	26. PATIENT'S ACCOUNT NO. DANDI001 434	27. ACCEPT ASSIGNMENT? (For govt. claims, see back) ☒ YES ☐ NO	28. TOTAL CHARGE $ 1,400 00	29. AMOUNT PAID $ 0 00	30. BALANCE DUE $ 1,400 00

31. SIGNATURE OF PHYSICIAN OR SUPPLIER INCLUDING DEGREES OR CREDENTIALS (I certify that the statements on the reverse apply to this bill and are made a part thereof.) SIGNED *Rita X. Ray* DATE 2/8/04	32. NAME AND ADDRESS OF FACILITY WHERE SERVICES WERE RENDERED (If other than home or office) HACKIM HOSPITAL 1000 HIDE STREET HUSHTOWN, ND 58444 (701) 555-4004	33. PHYSICIAN'S, SUPPLIERS BILLING NAME, ADDRESS, ZIP CODE & PHONE # RITA X. RAY, M.D. HACKIM HOSPITAL 1000 HIDE STREET HUSHTOWN, ND 58444 (701) 555-4004 PIN# RXR106 GRP#

(APPROVED BY AMA COUNCIL ON MEDICAL SERVICE 8/88)   PLEASE PRINT OR TYPE   FORM HCFA-1500 (12-90)

PLEASE
DO NOT
STAPLE
IN THIS
AREA
□□□ PICA

BALL INSURANCE CARRIERS
3895 BUBBLE BLVD., STE.283
BOXWOOD, CO 85926

APPROVED MOB-0938-0008

CLAIM DXL3

HEALTH INSURANCE CLAIM FORM

PICA □□□

1. MEDICARE MEDICAID CHAMPUS CHAMPVA GROUP HEALTH PLAN FECA BLK LUNG OTHER	INSURED'S I.D NUMBER (FOR PROGRAM IN ITEM 1)
□ (Medicare #) □ (Medicaid #) □ (Sponsor's SSN) □ (VA File #) ☒ (SSN or ID) □ (SSN) □ (ID)	555-55-5555

2. PATIENT'S NAME (Last, First, Middle Initial)	3. PATIENT'S BIRTH DATE MM DD YY SEX	4. INSURED'S NAME (Last, First, Middle Initial)
PATIENT, PATTY P.	05 15 75 M□ F☒	PATIENT, PATTY P.

5. PATIENT'S ADDRESS (No., Street)	6. PATIENT'S RELATIONSHIP TO INSURED	7. INSURED'S ADDRESS (No., Street)
655 PAIN LANE	Self☒ Spouse□ Child□ Other□	655 PAIN LANE

CITY	STATE	8. PATIENT STATUS	CITY	STATE
PEN	PA	Single☒ Married□ Other□	PEN	PA

ZIP CODE	TELEPHONE (Include Area Code)		ZIP CODE	TELEPHONE (INCLUDE AREA CODE)
15522	(878) 555-3355	Employed☒ Full-Time□ Part-Time□ Student Student	15522	(878) 555-3355

9. OTHER INSURED'S NAME (Last, First, Middle Initial)	10. IS PATIENT'S CONDITION RELATED TO:	11. INSURED'S POLICY GROUP OR FECA NUMBER:
		555-55-XYZ
a. OTHER INSURED'S POLICY OR GROUP NUMBER	a. EMPLOYMENT? (CURRENT OR PREVIOUS) □ YES ☒ NO	a. INSURED'S DATE OF BIRTH MM DD YY SEX 05 15 75 M□ F☒
a. OTHER INSURED'S DATE OF BIRTH MM DD YY SEX M□ F□	b. AUTO ACCIDENT? PLACE (State) □ YES ☒ NO	b. EMPLOYER'S NAME OR SCHOOL NAME XYZ CORPORATION
c. EMPLOYER'S NAME OR SCHOOL NAME	c. OTHER ACCIDENT? □ YES ☒ NO	c. INSURANCE PLAN NAME OR PROGRAM NAME XYZ PLAN
d. INSURANCE PLAN NAME OR PROGRAM NAME	10d. RESERVED FOR LOCAL USE	d. IS THERE ANOTHER HEALTH BENEFIT PLAN? □ YES ☒ NO If yes, return to and complete item 9 a-d

READ BACK OF FORM BEFORE COMPLETING & SIGNING THIS FORM
12. PATIENT'S OR AUTHORIZED PERSON'S SIGNATURE I authorize the release of any medical or other information necessary to process this claim. I also request payment of government benefits either to myself or to the party who accepts assignment below.

SIGNED SIGNATURE ON FILE   DATE 02/16/04

13. INSURED'S OR AUTHORIZED PERSON'S SIGNATURE I authorize payment of medical benefits to the undersigned physician or supplier for services described below.

SIGNED _____

14. DATE OF CURRENT: ◄ ILLNESS (1st symptom) ◄ INJURY (Accident) ◄ PREGNANCY (LMP) MM DD YY 02 16 04	15. IF PATIENT HAS HAD SAME OR SIMILAR ILLNESS, GAVE FIRST DATE MM DD YY	16. DATES PATIENT UNABLE TO WORK IN CURRENT OCCUPATION MM DD YY FROM TO MM DD YY

17. NAME OF REFERRING PHYSICIAN OR OTHER SOURCE	17a. I.D. NUMBER OF REFERRING PHYSICIAN	18. HOSPITALIZATION DATES RELATED TO CURRENT SERVICES MM DD YY FROM 02 16 04 TO 02 16 04

19. RESERVED FOR LOCAL USE	20. OUTSIDE LAB? □ YES □ NO $ CHARGES

21. DIAGNOSIS OR NATURE OF ILLNESS OR INJURY, (RELATE ITEMS 1,2,3, OR 4 TO ITEM 24E BY LINE)

1. 233.0   3. ____ . ____
2. ____ . ____ 4. ____ . ____

22. MEDICAID RESUBMISSION CODE   ORIGINAL REF. NO.

23. PRIOR AUTHORIZATION NUMBER

24. A. DATE(S) OF SERVICE From MM DD YY To MM DD YY	B. Place of Service	C. Type of Service	D. PROCEDURES, SERVICES, OR SUPPLIES (Explain Unusual Circumstances) CPT/HCPCS MODIFIER	E. DIAGNOSIS CODE	F. $ CHARGES	G. DAYS OR UNITS	H. EPSDT Family Plan	I. EMG	J. COB	K. RESERVED FOR LOCAL USE
02 16 04 02 16 04	11	1	76092	1	165 00	1				

25. FEDERAL TAX I.D. NUMBER SSN EIN	26. PATIENT'S ACCOUNT NO.	27. ACCEPT ASSIGNMENT? (For govt. claims, see back)	28. TOTAL CHARGE	29. AMOUNT PAID	30. BALANCE DUE
52-8989775 □ ☒	PATPA001 535	☒ YES □ NO	$ 165 00	$ 0 00	$ 165 00

31. SIGNATURE OF PHYSICIAN OR SUPPLIER INCLUDING DEGREES OR CREDENTIALS (I certify that the statements on the reverse apply to this bill and are made a part thereof.) SIGNED *Irene N. Jection* DATE 02/11/04	32. NAME AND ADDRESS OF FACILITY WHERE SERVICES WERE RENDERED (If other than home or office) HELPER HOSPITAL 25450 HAMMER AVE. HUMMER TOWN, PA 15522 (878) 555-6455	33. PHYSICIAN'S, SUPPLIERS BILLING NAME, ADDRESS, ZIP CODE & PHONE # IRENE N. JECTION, M.D. HELPER HOSPITAL 25450 HAMMER AVE. HUMMER TOWN, PA 15522 (878) 555-6455 PIN# INJ106 GRP#

(APPROVED BY AMA COUNCIL ON MEDICAL SERVICE 8/88)

PLEASE PRINT OR TYPE

FORM HCFA-1500 (12-90)
FORM OWCP-1500   FORM RRB-1500

15 Surgery

In this chapter you will learn:

- The definition of surgery.
- To list the four general classifications of surgical procedures.
- To process surgery claims.
- To identify possible cosmetic procedures.
- To define pre- and postoperative care and to determine when it is included in surgery.
- To apply surgical guidelines as they relate to maternity and cosmetic procedures.

Key words and concepts you will learn in this chapter:

Assistant Surgeon – A surgeon who assist a primary surgeon. An assistant surgeon may do the closing of the operative wound, hemostasis of the wound edges, and suturing of vessels.

Asterisk Procedures – Surgical procedures denoted by an asterisk to the left of the CPT code. These procedures require special handling.

Block Procedures – Multiple surgical procedures performed during the same operative session, in the same operative area.

By Report (BR) – Procedures that are so unusual or variable that it is impossible to determine a standard UCR or unit value allowance.

Co-Surgeons – Under some circumstances, two surgeons, usually with similar skills, may operate simultaneously as primary surgeons performing distinct, separate parts of a total surgical service.

Cosmetic Surgery – A surgical procedure performed solely to improve appearance.

Diagnostic Procedures – Procedures performed to determine the presence of disease or the cause of the patient's symptoms.

Follow-up Days – Days immediately following a surgical procedure in which a doctor must monitor a patient's condition in regard to that particular procedure.

Multiple Procedures – More than one surgical procedure performed during one operative session.

Reconstruction – Procedures performed to rebuild or restore aesthetically a part of the body that was damaged or defective as a result of an illness or injury.

Therapeutic Procedures – Procedures performed to remove or correct the functioning of a body part that is diseased or injured.

Surgery is defined as the branch of medicine that treats diseases, injuries, and deformities by operative or invasive methods. Although surgery usually involves cutting, cutting does not have to be involved for a procedure to be considered surgery. The surgery concept is anything that involves removing, altering, repairing, entering, or the carrying out of any other invasion of the body. Therefore, insertion of a tube into a person's throat does not involve cutting but is considered surgical in nature because it invades the body. There are also many laser procedures that are considered surgical.

Most benefit plans cover only surgeries that are necessitated by disease or injury. In other words, the procedure must be considered medically necessary to repair or improve function or diagnose an illness. In addition, because a procedure is listed in the surgery section of the CPT does not mean that the procedure is allowable under a benefit plan nor does it mean that it will necessarily be coded as a surgical procedure. The coding of procedures varies from company to company.

Surgical Procedures

In general, surgical procedures can be classified as one of the following types:
- Diagnostic
- Therapeutic
- Reconstructive
- Cosmetic

Diagnostic procedures are procedures performed to determine the presence of disease or the cause of the patient's symptoms. One of the most commonly used forms of diagnostic surgery is the endoscopic procedure. This type of procedure involves making a small incision on the exterior part of the patient's body in the area near the organ or space being examined. Then, a very small instrument, called a scope, is inserted through the incision into the body cavity. The surgeon can then look through the scope and see the interior condition of the examination area. If desired, pictures or a video may be taken of the area. Examples of diagnostic procedures include bronchoscopy (31622), gastroscopy (43234), and sigmoidoscopy (45330).

Therapeutic procedures are performed to remove or correct the functioning of a body part that is diseased or injured. As a rule, failure to perform the therapeutic procedure may result in either the patient's loss of life or a progressive functional decline.

A removal, repair, or manipulation may be involved in the correction of the abnormally functioning organ. Some cutting is usually required. However, with continual medical advances, more and more procedures are being performed without cutting or with minimal incisions. Examples of therapeutic procedures are liver transplant (47135), craniectomy (removal of tumor of the brain) (61510), and appendectomy (44950).

Reconstruction is performed to rebuild or restore aesthetically a part of the body that was damaged or defective as a result of an illness or injury. Reconstruction is necessary to return the body to its normal or near-normal appearance and may or may not affect the functioning of the organ/area. Even though reconstruction may be necessary for purely cosmetic reasons, it is considered eligible under most plans as long as it is necessitated as a result of a disease or injury occurring while the patient was covered under the plan. If the injury or illness occurred prior to the date that the patient was covered under the plan, the repair may be considered cosmetic, not reconstructive. Examples of reconstructive procedures are rhinoplasty (surgical correction of the external appearance of the nose; 30400—30450) and breast augmentation/reconstruction (after mastectomy resulting from breast cancer; 19324—19499).

Cosmetic procedures are those procedures performed solely to improve the appearance of a body part and are not usually covered by benefit plans. If the procedure is functional in nature, cosmetic exclusions do not apply. For example, a scar revision is performed as a result of a contracture of a scar received in an accident. The release of the contracture is considered functional in nature, although the appearance of the scar might also be significantly improved.

Situations may arise in which it is difficult to ascertain whether a procedure should be considered cosmetic or reconstructive. In these instances, a professional opinion is required. For examples, refer to the section entitled Possible Cosmetic Procedures (later in this chapter).

General Guidelines

The following guidelines will assist you in the processing of surgery claims.

Surgery in a Physician's Office

Billings for surgery performed in a physician's office are often itemized for each charge incurred such as the surgery, local anesthesia, medication, surgical trays, and dressings.

Generally, the charge made by the physician for surgery should include performing the surgical procedure, administering local anesthetic (if required), and all routine follow-up care. The charge for surgery always includes:
- The immediate preoperative visit.
- The surgical procedure.
- Local anesthesia (i.e., topical, digital block)
- Routine follow-up care (visits) provided within the follow-up days listed in the RVS.

Non-routine follow-up visits due to complications or other reasons may be billed and considered separately from the original surgical charge. Medical supplies, medications, x-rays, facility fees, and other services are usually considered and covered (or not covered) separately.

Preoperative Care

The immediate preoperative visit in the hospital or elsewhere is generally necessary to examine the patient, complete the hospital records, and initiate the treatment program. Charges for these procedures are included in the surgical allowance. However, a separate allowance may be warranted for preoperative services in the following circumstances:
- When the preoperative visit is the initial visit (i.e., in an emergency room), and prolonged detention or evaluation is required to prepare the patient or to establish the need for the surgery.
- When the preoperative visit is a consultation. Be sure the physician has not "up coded" a

pre-operative visit to increase benefits. An example is a surgeon billing for a consultation prior to surgery when in fact the visit was a simple pre-operative visit.

- When procedures that are not usually part of the basic surgical procedure (i.e., bronchoscopy prior to chest surgery) are provided during the immediate preoperative period.
- When a procedure could normally be performed in the office, but under certain circumstances requires hospitalization (i.e., patient's age, condition. See modifier code – 22 in the CPT).

Follow-Up Days

Follow-up days are days immediately following a surgical procedure in which a doctor must monitor a patient's condition in regard to that particular procedure. The RVS lists unit values for surgical procedures that include the surgery, local anesthesia, and the normal, uncomplicated follow-up care associated with the procedure for the time period indicated in the section titled Follow-up Days.

Complications or other circumstances requiring additional or unusual services concurrent with the procedure or procedures, or during the listed period of normal follow-up care, may warrant additional charges on a fee-for-service basis. However, unless the physician specifically indicates unusual circumstances, it should be assumed that the follow-up care is routine. Regardless of how the physician bills, all visits occurring within the listed follow-up days should be combined with the surgical charge. The following are categories of follow-up care:

- Follow-up care for diagnostic procedures (i.e., endoscopy, injection procedures for radiology) includes only care that is related to recovery from the diagnostic procedure itself. Care of the underlying condition for which the diagnostic procedure was performed or other accompanying conditions is not included and may be charged separately in accordance with the services rendered.
- Follow-up care for therapeutic procedures generally includes all normal postoperative care. Complications, exacerbations, recurrence, or the presence of other diseases or injuries requiring additional services concurrent with the surgical procedure(s) or during the indicated period of normal follow-up care may warrant additional charges coded and allowable separately.
- When additional surgical procedure(s) are carried out within the listed period of follow-up care for a previous surgery, the follow-up periods will run concurrently through their normal termination.

Separate charges for routine follow-up care should be added to the surgical charge and the total compared with the UCR fee for the procedure performed. Some plans follow this approach while others deny the visit as being within the follow-up period, if they are billed separately

For example:
Procedure: 40808, 10f/u days

Description	Date	CPT Code	Charge
Office visit	4/1	99213	$25
Surgery	4/3	40808	350
F/up hsp visit	4/4	99221	25
F/up hsp visit	4/5	99231	25
F/up office visit	4/10	99213	30
			$455

Based on administrative practices, the preoperative visit may or may not be considered part of the surgery charge. In the latter example, and unless you are told otherwise, assume that the preoperative visit is part of the surgery charge. Therefore, $455 would be compared against the plan's UCR limitation for the surgery.

Asterisk Procedures

Asterisk procedures are surgical procedures denoted by an asterisk to the left of the CPT code. These procedures require special handling. If an asterisk (*) follows a CPT code, the following six rules apply:

1. The listed value is for the surgical procedure only.
2. Pre- and postoperative care is to be added on a fee-for-service basis.
3. When the (*) procedure is carried out at the time of an initial interview (new patient) visit and this surgery constitutes the major services at that visit, procedure code 99025 is listed in lieu of the usual initial visit as an additional service (under CPT guidelines).
4. When the (*) procedure is carried out at the time of an initial or other visit involving significant identifiable services (i.e., removal of a small skin lesion at the time of a comprehensive history and physical examination), the appropriate visit is coded in addition to the (*) procedure and its follow-up care (under CPT and RVS guidelines).
5. When the (*) procedure is carried out at the time of a follow-up (established patient) visit and this procedure constitutes the major service at the visit, the service visit usually is not coded separately (under CPT and RVS guidelines).
6. When the (*) procedure requires hospitalization, the appropriate hospital visit is coded in addition to the (*) procedure and its follow-up care (under CPT guidelines).

By Report Procedures

Some procedures are so unusual or variable that it is impossible to determine a standard UCR or unit value allowance. These procedures are called **By Report (BR)** procedures. The RVS may refer to these procedures as **Relative Value Not Established (RNE)**. BR and RNE procedures need to be referred to a professional review unit, a supervisor, or a consultant for review to determine the allowance. For proper review, a copy of the operative report is required. The anesthesia record may also be needed. If the operative report is not submitted with the claim, the claim should be pended and a copy requested before referral.

Multiple or Bilateral Procedures

Multiple procedures are more than one surgical procedure performed during one operative session. **Bilateral procedures** are surgeries that involve a pair of similar body parts (i.e., breasts, eyes). There are two main types of multiple or bilateral procedures: same time, different operative field and same time, same operative field.

Same Time, Different Operative Field

Same time, different operative field, incision, or orifice: When more than one surgery is performed during the same operative session but through a different orifice (opening) or incision or in a different operative field, 100% of the actual charge or UCR (or scheduled amount) is allowable for the major procedure, and 50% of the UCR (or actual charge, whichever is less) is allowable for the second procedure. 25% of UCR (or actual charge, whichever is less) is allowed for each additional procedure. Podiatry surgery and most PPO's handle surgery in this manner. Some insurance carriers however, do not apply the 25% rule allowing 100% for the primary procedure and 50% thereafter. Bilateral procedures follow the same rules as multiple procedures performed through different incisions. Multiply the UCR allowance for the single procedure by 150% or 1.5. If there is an established bilateral procedure code, that code would be allowable at 100% only because the units have already been assigned at 1.5 times the units of the single procedure. There are two ways to identify a bilateral procedure. The provider will list the CPT and use modifier 50 to denote a bilateral procedure. Sometimes the provider will identify LT (Left) or RT (right) next to each procedure. When in doubt obtain an operative report.

Same Time, Same Operative Field

Same time, same operative field, incision or orifice: Usually, when multiple procedures are performed during the same operative session through the same incision, orifice, or operative field, the additional procedures are sometimes considered to be incidental.

An **incidental procedure** is one that does not add significant time or complexity to the operative session.

In such a case, the allowable amount will be that of the major procedure only. No additional amount will be allowable for the extra procedures.

However, if the additional procedures are not incidental, the rules for handling multiple procedures previously explained would apply. That is, the major procedure would be considered at 100% of UCR and the lesser at 50%.

Example: The following bill is received from the provider:

	Billed Amt	UCR
Tonsillectomy (42821)	$600	$600
Eustachian tube inflation (69400)	300	200

Following the rules previously indicated, 100% of the major procedure plus 50% of the lesser procedure would be allowed. Therefore, the allowable amount in this example would be:

100% of $600	$600
+ 50% of $200	$100
Total allowance	$700

Total billed amount	$900
Less allowed amount	-$700
Member's responsibility	$200

It is important to look at the total billing so as not to penalize the patient for the way the physician bills.

Example: The same procedures as above were billed in the following way:

	Billed Amt	UCR
Tonsillectomy (42821)	$300	$600
Eustachian tube inflation (69400)	+600	+100
	$900	$700

By referring to the RVS, you can determine that the major procedure is the tonsillectomy, which allows 16.39 units, whereas eustachian tube inflation allows only 1.39 units. Therefore, using the multiple surgery rules but following the doctor's billing, you can determine the allowable to be:

100% of $600 up to the actual charge of	$300
50% of $200 or the actual charge, whichever is less	+100
Total allowance would be	$400

As shown, this calculation would be financially detrimental to the patient solely because the doctor's office did not properly allocate the expenses. Therefore, when expenses are improperly allocated, a **"global approach"** should be used. The total billed amount should be compared with the total UCR amount. In our example, the total UCR amount is $700 versus the total billed amount of $900. The objective is to deny amounts in excess of the global UCR.

Therefore, even though the doctor billed incorrectly, when you use the global approach, $700 would be allowable toward the total billed amount of $900, and the patient would not be penalized by being allowed only $400.

Some insurance companies use HCFA guidelines. When multiple surgeries are performed and the additional procedures are not incidental, HCFA guidelines are to allow:

Major procedure: 100% of UCR or the billed amount, whichever is less.

2nd procedure: 50% of UCR or billed amount, whichever is less.

3rd through 5th procedures: 25% of UCR or billed amount, whichever is less.

Multiple procedures (more than two) are often referred to Consultants or Professional Review Departments, which consist of medical doctors and nurses, for analysis before payment. The Consultants or Review Department may give alternative instructions based on the actual operative report. Check with the administrator for guidelines for multiple surgeries before processing the claim.

Block Procedures

Block procedures are multiple surgical procedures performed during the same operative session, in the same operative area. The objective of these codes is to handle multiple repetitions of the same service. A block procedure consists of a primary code and subsequent modifying codes.

Example:

11100 is for biopsy of skin, subcutaneous tissue or mucous membrane, single lesion.

11101 is for each separate/additional lesion.

Therefore, if a bill was received for the removal of five lesions, the total allowance would be based on the following unit factors:

1.24	Units for the lesion
2.6	Units total for lesions 2, 3, 4, and 5 (4x .65)
3.84	Total units allowed

For another example of a block procedure, or add-ons refer to Moh's surgery in the CPT. The CPT is now a great source for identifying add-ons and procedures exempt from the multiple surgery rule. Usually you will see either a "+" or O next to the procedure code indicating the procedure is not subject to multiple surgery reduction.

Unbundling

As briefly discussed in the DXL chapter, some physicians practice what is known as "unbundling." The surgeon is considered to have "unbundled" when he bills for separate procedures that are a part of the primary procedure. For example a hysterectomy can be performed with or without the removal of the ovaries and/or the fallopian tubes. Therefore, a physician billing for a hysterectomy and removal of the ovaries has unbundled the surgery. The maximum allowance is the UCR for the hysterectomy. An extreme example is a surgeon billing for the removal of a gallbladder and also billing for the repair of an open wound. Of course the repair is not covered, as it is inherently part of the gallbladder surgery. Care in processing multiple surgeries should be taken to ensure that there is no unbundling and the secondary procedures are reduced accordingly.

Maternity Expenses

Most plans provide coverage for maternity-related expenses on the same basis as any other illness. Some plans, however, limit or exclude maternity related expenses for either spouse or the dependent children or occasionally for the subscriber/member. The services normally provided in maternity cases include all routine, ante-partum care (prior to delivery), delivery, and all routine, postpartum care (after delivery). The maternity procedure codes are based on this premise unless the specific code indicates otherwise. Therefore, if a doctor breaks up his or her bill into different segments, the charges should be combined and lumped together under the single appropriate code. This would apply unless the patient sees different doctors for ante-partum care and for delivery or for any other combination. In such a case the benefits would be broken up in a way to compensate the doctors appropriately for their services.

Ante-partum care (pre-natal) includes:

- Initial and subsequent history.
- Physician's exams, usually one per month for the first eight months, then weekly during the 9th month.
- Weight, blood pressure, urinalysis (monthly or weekly).
- Fetal heart tones.
- Maternity counseling on food requirements, vitamins and related items.

Delivery includes:

- Vaginal delivery (with or without episiotomy, forceps or breech delivery).
- Cesarean delivery.

Post-partum care (after delivery) includes:

- Post-delivery hospital visits.
- Post-delivery office visits (usually one or two routine check-ups) during the first six weeks following delivery.

Maternity Billing Procedures

Maternity cases are usually billed in a unique manner. Most Ob-Gyn physicians require full payment from the patient before the delivery date. Conversely, most benefit plans will not process the claim for any benefits until after the delivery. Therefore, the patient often has a substantial, initial out-of-pocket amount. The following are some of the more common maternity billing procedures:

- **Lump sum billings:** When a lump sum charge (a single, all-encompassing charge) is made for total obstetric care, the charge should be coded and processed under the appropriate CPT/RVS code for total obstetric care.
- **Itemized billings after delivery:** When charges for ante-partum care, delivery, and post-partum care are itemized by the physician, the charges should be combined into one charge and processed under the CPT/RVS code for total obstetric care. Charges for routine ultrasonography may or may not be covered by the plan. Usually, these charges are considered and coded separately from obstetric care. Charges for lab studies, especially urinalysis, are usually considered part of the complete care unless the physician indicates medical necessity for services beyond routine care. (Routine lab expenses may be coded and allowed separately. This varies by payor.)
- **Pre-delivery billings:** When a physician bills for the total obstetric care prior to delivery (based on monthly installments, for example, 80% of the charge by the 7th month), the plan may deny the claim and ask the doctor to re-bill after delivery. Other plans may consider payment on the part of the services that have been provided as of the date of the billing. Clarification needs to be requested.
- **Two or more physicians (unrelated, not in the same medical group):** If two or more physicians are involved in the total obstetric care of a patient (usually one performs the delivery and the other provides the ante-partum or post-partum care), each physician's charge should be processed separately for the services rendered. CPT code 59410 is for a vaginal delivery only (including in-hospital post-partum care. For ante-partum care only (up to three office visits), use the appropriate office visit code range of 99201 – 99205 for the initial visit and 99211 – 99215 for subsequent visits. Ante-partum care beyond three visits should use CPT code 59425 or 59426. 59430 is for post-partum care only.

Other Maternity-Related Procedures
The following are other types of maternity billings that you may encounter:

- **Artificial insemination** is the introduction of semen into the vagina or cervix by artificial means. Some plans consider this a covered expense, and some do not since it is not for the treatment of a disease or injury.
- **Amniocentesis/chromosomal analysis** is the trans-abdominal perforation of the uterus for the purpose of withdrawing amniotic fluid surrounding the fetus. The **chromosomal analysis** is the diagnostic study performed on the fluid to study the number and structure of the chromosomes to see whether any abnormalities are present.

An amniocentesis/chromosomal analysis is performed:
- To identify genetic defects of the fetus.
- To determine whether the fetus has attained an adequate state of gestation.
- To determine the sex of the fetus.

Charges for amniocentesis and chromosomal analysis are usually covered if the attending physician can demonstrate the medical necessity of the testing for the patient, such as a family history of specific genetic defects, or maternal age of greater than 35 years. The use of these tests to determine fetal sex alone is not covered by most plans.

In-utero fetal surgery has made it possible to perform surgery on a fetus while it is in the mother's womb; and also to remove the fetus from the womb, perform surgery, and return it back to the womb, with the pregnancy continuing to term. If the surgery is covered, it is often covered as the mother's expense as a complication of pregnancy.

In vitro fertilization is the fertilization of the ovum within a test tube. Charges for in vitro fertilization may be covered. Refer to the plan for verification.

Abortion is a pre-mature expulsion of an embryo or non-viable fetus. There are three different types of abortions:
1. A spontaneous abortion occurring naturally.
2. A therapeutic abortion intentionally induced because the life of the mother would be endangered if the pregnancy were allowed to continue to term.
3. An elective abortion intentionally induced to terminate an unwanted pregnancy.

Coverage for abortions varies greatly from plan to plan. Spontaneous and therapeutic abortions are covered by most plans. Whereas, elective abortions are often excluded. In addition, some plans may pay for certain services for spouses and then exclude these services for dependent children. Therefore, read the plan document carefully before processing these types of expenses.

Delivery with Tubal Ligation
Not all plans cover sterilization. For those plans that do not cover sterilization, the expense for a tubal ligation, regardless of when it is performed, would be denied as not a covered expense.

When the plan provides coverage for sterilization procedures and a tubal ligation is performed during the same operative session as that for a vaginal delivery, the UCR fee (or the surgeon's fee, whichever is less) for the delivery would be allowable at 100% and the sterilization fee would be allowable at 50% of UCR.

When a sterilization procedure is performed during the same hospitalization as that for a vaginal delivery but not in the same operative session, 100% of the fee or UCR would be allowable for each procedure.

When a tubal ligation is performed during the same operative session as that for a cesarean section or intra-abdominal surgery, the C-section should be processed under the appropriate CPT/RVS code and the tubal under CPT code 58611. The UCR for both the C-section and the tubal ligation should be allowed at 100%, since the relative value for 58611 has already been reduced.

Vaginal delivery with:
Tubal ligation   59400—100%
During same operative session   58605—50%

Vaginal delivery with:
Tubal ligation   59400—100%
Not during same operative session   58605—100%

C-section delivery with:
Tubal ligation   59510—100%
During same operative session   58611—50%

C-section delivery with:
Tubal ligation   59510—100%
Not during same operative session   58605—100%

Cosmetic Surgery

Cosmetic surgery is a surgical procedure performed solely to improve appearance and is usually not covered by benefit plans.

To properly handle possible cosmetic claims, you must become familiar with the terminology. The following are some of the more common cosmetic procedures and are therefore, not usually covered. However, each claim should be investigated and evaluated on an individual basis. The primary intent of each procedure must be established to determine whether the procedure is cosmetic or reconstructive.

Although some procedures are cosmetic in nature, they may also be performed for functional reasons. For instance, a blepharoplasty is the removal of excessive skin and fat from the eyelids. Certainly, removal of excessive skin and fat improves the person's appearance. However, most plans cover blepharoplasty when the skin overhang is so extensive that it interferes with the patient's peripheral vision. Therefore, the fact that a cosmetic procedure is performed does not necessarily mean that it is considered solely cosmetic.

When the restorative or cosmetic nature of the procedure is not obvious, claim investigation must be initiated with a careful review of the following documentation:

- Hospital admission history and physical.
- Operative report.
- Pathology report.
- Pre- and post-operative photographs.
- A narrative report from a referring physician, if available.

Pre-Operative and Post-Operative Photographs

Providers routinely take pre-operative and post-operative photographs. These photos are sometimes needed to determine whether a surgery was cosmetic in nature.

To request photographs, use a standard request for additional information form letter. The operative report for the procedure should be requested at the same time.

When the operative report and photographs are received, they should be compared with the claim to determine the reason for the surgery. If the surgery appears to be cosmetic in nature, the claim, along with the photographs and any reports, should be forwarded to a consultant for review.

Cosmetic Procedure Guidelines

Following are three general guidelines regarding cosmetic surgeries:

1. Cosmetic surgery preformed purely for cosmetic reasons is not covered. However, cosmetic surgery after an accident, injury, or surgical procedure may be covered (i.e., breast reconstruction after a mastectomy).
2. When there is an underlying condition, the surgery is not considered cosmetic, regardless of the nature of the surgery (i.e., removal of a scar if there is an underlying disease).
3. When processing a surgical claim, determine the primary reason for the surgical procedure. If the treatment is due to injury or disease, the surgery is not considered cosmetic.

Possible Cosmetic Procedures

Following is a list of procedures that can be considered cosmetic in nature. These are some of the more common surgeries that might be questioned as to their being cosmetic or not. Keep in mind that numerous other procedures and services would fall under a cosmetic heading. This sample list is for training purposes only, and the individual plan guidelines should be consulted prior to processing a surgery claim.

Blepharoplasty – Surgical repair of the eyelids. This surgery is done to correct blepharoptosis, which is a drooping of the upper eyelid. This condition may cause impairment of peripheral vision. The surgery may be of the upper lid only, the lower lid only, or both upper and lower lids. Surgery of both lids requires the use of modifier-50.

When blepharoplasty is done on the upper lid, the removal of the fat decreases the bulging lid, relieving the patient of a perpetual "tired look" about the eyes and thus imparting a more youthful appearance. The diagnosis most often listed on the claim is blepharochalasis, which means "acquired atrophy of the skin of the upper eyelid as in aging."

Blepharoplasty may also be preformed for ptosis, which is an abnormal downward displacement of the eyelid due to muscle weakness, eyelid trauma, facial nerve paralysis, or loss of innervation. As this condition worsens, vision is progressively impaired by the tissue obstructing the pupil. The operative report for treatment of functional blepharoptosis will describe structural rearrangement such as palpebral muscle shortening, resection of the part of the upper lid including the tarsal plate, nerve and muscle transplantation, and facial sling.

Vision impairment is the only condition for which an upper lid blepharoplasty would be considered non-cosmetic. The documentation required to assess visual impairment includes at least one of the following:

- Results of a tangent screen examination.
- Results of a confrontation test.
- Results of perimeter testing.

The latter tests measure the patient's peripheral vision and support the medical record and preoperative photos in establishing the functional need for surgery.

Claims received for lower lid blepharoplasty are usually purely cosmetic. The surgery consists of removing the herniated fat pads in the lower lid and excising the redundant skin. Three conditions in which a blepharoplasty of the lower lid may be indicated and not considered cosmetic are:

1. **Ectropion** – A condition in which the margin of the upper or lower eyelid turns outward. When the lower lid is involved, involuntary tearing often constitutes the most annoying symptom. Surgery consists of removing a portion of the inside of the lid to cause the eyelid to turn inward. This is a functional correction.
2. **Entropion** – A condition in which the margin of the upper or lower eyelid turns in, causing the eyelashes to rub against and irritate the eyeball. If a secondary infection occurs, scarring of the cornea may ensue with subsequent loss of vision. Therefore, correcting the condition in the early stages of development is important. Surgery consists of cutting away a portion of the inside of the eyelid in a way that causes the eyelid to turn outward. This is a functional correction.

3. **Lid lesions** – Most often a chalazion that is a cyst like mass resulting in chronic inflammation of the meibomian gland in the eyelid. This may also be called a meibomian or tarsal cyst. Another lesion is a hordeolum or sty, which is an infection of the eyelash and is associated with whitish pus under the skin. When medical treatment fails to alleviate the condition, surgery may be preformed to remove the affected area. Tumors constitute the third type of lesion that might require surgical care.

In a blepharoplasty, the pockets of fat in the upper and lower lids beneath the skin are removed. The ellipse of skin has to be cut off to elevate the drooping eyebrow. The margins are sewn together, with the final suture line lying with the eyebrow's upper hairline. The redundant skin of the lower lid is undermined, and the excess fat is removed along with the redundant skin. The wound is then sutured with fine silk.

The structure line in the upper eyelid partially coincides with the old; the one in the lower lid is disguised by the eyelashes. The rest of the two sutures coincide with the natural creases about the eye.

Breast augmentation – Surgical enlargement of the breast by use of implants. Implants come in various types but are most often gel- or fluid-filled sacs.

Breast prosthesis – An artificial sac implanted in the chest muscles to replace or enlarge the breast. Many types of prostheses are available.

Breast reconstruction – A procedure in which an implant is placed under the skin or muscle of the chest wall to restore the contour of a missing breast. This procedure is usually covered when it is used to restore the appearance of patients who have had a mastectomy due to cancer, fibroadenoma, or fibrocystic breast disease. Claims submitted for breast reconstruction should include the diagnosis of the underlying disease and the date of the previously performed mastectomy. In cases of breast cancer, only those charges submitted for reconstruction for the removed breast are considered covered expenses. Charges submitted for reduction mammoplasty on the unaffected side (to make the unaffected breast appear similar in size and shape to the reconstructed breast) are considered cosmetic and are usually not covered.

Asymmetry is a condition in which the breasts are grossly dissimilar in size, shape, or arrangement on the chest wall. Since a slight discrepancy in the breasts is normal, the condition must be severe to be considered functional.

Breast reduction – Surgical procedure to reduce the size of the breast. This may be covered in extreme cases (usually when over one pound of fat is removed on each side).

Chemical peel or chemical abrasion – This has the same affect as dermabrasion except that caustic chemicals such as phenol or trichloracetic acid (TCA) are used. The technique creates a superficial chemical burn which, when healed, has flattened fine wrinkles and tightened the skin. This is considered purely cosmetic.

Cheiloplasty – Surgery for the lips. The lips, like the skin and mucous membranes of other parts of the body, are subject to pre-cancerous and cancerous lesions. These lesions most often occur in fair-skinned persons with a long history of exposure to sunlight.

A common pre-cancerous condition is known as *hyperkeratosis*, a condition in which the mucosa of the lip becomes paler, thinner, and more fragile with numerous cracks and fissures. Gradually, ulcerations appear, which continue to break down and heal. Treatment consists of removing all of the involved lip surface and advancing the inner lining of the lip to cover the defect. This procedure is called *lip stripping and resurfacing* and is considered medically necessary.

A cheiloplasty can also be done to make the lips narrower, to enlarge thin lips, and to create a "cupid's bow" (the dip in the edge line of the upper lip). When done for these reasons, cheiloplasty would be considered cosmetic.

Cleft lip and palate – A birth defect in which the two sides of the face fail to unite properly in the early stage of prenatal development, resulting in a fissure or split in the lip and/or palate (roof) of the mouth. A cleft lip may occur unilaterally or bilaterally. An incomplete cleft lip occurs when a bridge of skin connects the cleft and non-cleft sides. If a skin bridge does not exist, the cleft is complete. Deformity of the nose usually accompanies a cleft lip in the form of distortion and displacement of the lower lateral nasal cartilage.

Surgery to correct a cleft lip and/or palate is scheduled when a child is old enough to tolerate the procedure safely, usually at about 10 weeks of age with a weight of about 10 pounds and a hemoglobin of 10g. By that time, the tissues are large enough to allow accurate repair. Further correction of the nasal deformity, often with simultaneous revision of minor lip irregularities, may be done when the child is older and final surgery may be delayed until adolescence to allow for full maturity of the facial features. Services to correct this congenital defect are considered functional.

However, claims for services related to cleft lip (and possibly palate) repair in persons older than adolescent age should be reviewed for possibly purely cosmetic repair and not functional repair of the defect.

Collagen or zyderm injections – Zyderm is a medical grade of collagen (taken from cows), which is injected into fine lines or small defects in the skin. It is a temporary measure, which plumps up the indented areas making them appear less pronounced. Usually, supplemental injections must be performed about every six to nine months. Collagen injections are strictly cosmetic.

Congenital anomaly – A birth defect. Depending on the defect, a congenital abnormality may or may not be covered by a plan.

Dermabrasion – A procedure using abrasive materials (sandpaper, emery paper, or wire brushes) to remove acne scars, birthmarks, fine wrinkles, or other skin defects. When the skin grows back, the surface irregularities have been smoothed away. Although this is considered a cosmetic procedure, check the plan guidelines because it may be covered to restore the skin to the appearance of a pre-sickness state. Some plans may cover dermabrasion for cases of severe acne.

Deviated nasal septum – A condition in which the dividing wall between the two nasal cavities is deflected (turned) away from the center of the nose.

Electrolysis epilation – Removal of hair by destruction of the hair follicle (root) with an electric current. For women, the usual diagnosis submitted is hirsutism, which is a condition of adult male hair growth in a female. Electrolysis does not treat the underlying condition, which is a hormonal imbalance and is therefore, considered purely cosmetic.

Gynecomastia – A swelling of the breast tissue in the male. If an underlying hormonal disease has been ruled out, the condition is treated by removing a small section of the breast tissue. This may be considered eligible under some plans.

Hair transplantation – Moving healthy hair follicles from one location on the body to another location – usually the head. Alopecia areata is a condition in which patchy areas of baldness occur. Alopecia means the absence of hair from areas where it normally occurs. Male pattern baldness (androgenic alopecia) is loss of hair from the crown of the head. This occurs in about 30% of adult males. A few medications have been shown to assist in re-growing hair in some instances. Transplantation does not treat the condition, only the symptoms and is therefore, usually considered purely cosmetic.

Hypertrophied/macromastia breasts – An abnormal enlargement of the female breasts caused by hormonal factors or obesity. The condition may require a mastectomy when the weight of the breast tissue causes physical complaints. Among the symptoms present are shoulder, neck, and back pain; numbness of the hand and arm caused by the bra straps compressing the brachial plexus (the group of nerves in the area between the neck and the shoulder that innervate the arm); and chronic inflammation of the skin of the opposed surfaces (intertrigo). Documentation to substantiate the functional nature of this procedure includes pre- and post-operative photos, admission history and physical examination information including the patient's height and weight, discharge summary, operative report, and pathology report.

Each administrator has their own guidelines. Therefore, all claims involving hypertrophied breasts should be researched before payment after verification of the applicable guidelines.

Keloid – A thick scar resulting from excessive growth of fibroid tissue. Any open wound can develop keloid scarring. Therefore, this scarring may occur following surgery. Keloid scar surgery is not usually considered cosmetic.

Lipectomy – The surgical removal of fatty tissue. Common in women over 50 or persons who have lost a large amount of weight. Redundant skin and tissue hanging from the upper arms is known as the "bat wing" deformity. Bat wings do not present any impairment to the function of the arms, and such surgical removal of the redundant fatty tissue and hanging skin is purely aesthetic.

In some persons, excess fat accumulates predominantly on the hips, buttocks, and thighs. This condition is referred to as "riding breeches syndrome." Like bat wing deformity, no functional impairment is involved. The removal of this fatty tissue may be accomplished by standard surgical techniques (incisional approach) or by liposuction, which consists of "sucking" out the fatty tissue through a vacuum tube inserted through small incisions. Regardless of the method used, the surgical reduction of hips, thighs, and buttocks is considered cosmetic.

Mammoplasty – Surgery to reduce (reduction mammoplasty) or enlarge (augmentation mammoplasty) the size of the breast.

Amastia or *amazia* is defined as the congenital absence of mammary tissue. These terms refer to masculine breast characteristics in an adult female. Amastia can be unilateral (one-sided) or bilateral (two-sided).

Hypomastia or *hypomazia* is defined as abnormal smallness of the mammary gland and, like amastia, it can affect one or both breasts. In cases in which one breast is normal and the other is markedly small or absent, asymmetery results. Augmentation mammoplasty is performed for both of these conditions.

Mastectomy – Excision or amputation of the breast, usually required as a result of a malignant disease. This is not the same as a reduction mammoplasty. The three types of mastectomies are:

1. *Radical mastectomy* is the removal of the breast tissue (mammary gland), pectoral muscles, axillary lymph nodes, and associated skin and subcutaneous tissue. This procedure is used for the treatment of cancer but may result in the partial loss of arm movement. Usually, radical mastectomy is followed by reconstructive surgery to restore the appearance of the remaining tissue.

2. *Modified radical mastectomy* is the same as the radical procedure except that the pectoral muscles are left in tact. This procedure can usually be performed during the earlier stages of cancer (stage I or II). Modified radical mastectomy is usually also followed by reconstructive procedures.

3. *Subcutaneous mastectomy* is a technique in which most of the breast tissue is removed but the skin and areola are preserved. Unlike the other two methods, immediate reconstruction can usually be done by inserting a Silastic prothesis into the subcutaneous pocket left by the excision of the breast tissue or under the pectorals major muscle. Subcutaneous mastectomy and reconstruction for multipathology breasts (i.e., fibrocystic disease, fibroadenoma) consists of removing the mammary tissue and inserting a prosthesis (implant) under the remaining skin to maintain the breast contour. The surgery is used to treat chronic mastitis in patients who experience incapacitating breast pain or those who have repeated breast biopsies of the cystic nodules to rule out cancer.

To determine the medical necessity of a mastectomy, the documentation requested from the physician should include a history of removal of the lumps or repeated aspirations of the cysts as well as the laboratory results of the previous biopsies.

Mentoplasty/genioplasty – Surgery to change the size and shape of the chin with an implant. This procedure is done for a small (microgenic) or moderately receding chin in persons in whom there is no underlying effect with the jaw itself. A small incision is made under the chin and a silicone implant is inserted, giving increased prominence to the chin.

Otoplasty – Plastic surgery to change the position or configuration of the ear or ears. The most common deformities that require an otoplasty are:

- **Protruding or lop ears** – Ears normally set at about a 25-degree angle from the skull. They may protrude due to cartilage deformities to such an extent that they form a right angle on the side of the head. In lop ears, the ear is bent upon itself. Prominent ears are usually caused by lack of definition of the anti-helical fold. This defect is referred to in the diagnosis and operative report.

  The best age to perform corrective surgery for these conditions is about 13 to 14 years, when the ear has attained almost maximum growth. However, because of the emotional and psychological problems associated with these conditions, surgery may be done before the child reaches school age. This surgery is usually considered cosmetic.

- **Microtia** – A congenital defect characterized by a small, malformed, malpositioned ear remnant. A hearing deficit is almost always present in affected children. Repair begins at age five or six years and is performed in a series of surgeries. The surgery is considered reconstructive.

Palatoplasty – Plastic surgery of the palate, usually to correct a cleft palate.

Panniculectomy – Removal of a sheet or layer of fatty tissue. This procedure is most often done to remove excess fatty tissue from the abdomen.

"-Plasty" – The surgical suffix that means to mold or shape.

Ptosis – Drooping or sagging of an organ part.

Removal of tattoos – This procedure is always considered cosmetic.

Rhinoplasty – Cosmetic repair of the external part of the nose to change its size or shape. This procedure does not involve the internal functioning of the nose, although it is performed entirely within the nose to prevent scarring.

A rhinoplasty consists of five major steps:

1. Elevating the skin from the bony and cartilaginous dorsum.
2. Removing the hump or lowering a prominent dorsum.
3. Narrowing the nasal pyramid to compensate for the flatness caused by the hump removal.
4. Shortening the nose if necessary.
5. Modeling the tip or lower cartilaginous complex to proportions consistent with the previous steps.

Key words to look for in determining whether surgery on the nose is cosmetic are "modifications of alar cartilages" and "lowering the dorsum." It is never necessary to modify the alar cartilages or lower the dorsum other than for cosmetic reasons. It is also never necessary to do alar base excisions for functional reasons. In fact, this constricts the airway and is against the principal of improving air flow.

Rhinoplasties are often combined with a septoplasty or submucous resection. Therefore, proper claim investigation is essential to determine whether and what part of the nasal procedure is necessary to correct a functional defect versus what part is for purely cosmetic purposes.

The test used to document airway obstruction is called *rhinomanometry*. It is the measurement of the airflow and pressure within the nose during respiration, and the resistance or obstruction is calculated. Unfortunately, this test is not often performed.

The structures of the nose responsible for airway obstruction are the septum and the nasal turbinates. The septum is made up of the downward projection of the ethmoid bone at the back, the vomer bone at the bottom, and the triangular shaped septal cartilage. It divides the nasal cavity (internal nose) into two wedge shaped cavities.

An accident can displace the septal cartilage where it meets the vomer or ethmoid bones, causing one side of the nasal cavity to become narrower and to obstruct the airway.

Rhytidectomy – Surgical removal of wrinkles. This procedure is usually cosmetic unless it interferes with the normal function of a body part.

Rhytidoplasty (facelift) – Removal of facial wrinkles. Wrinkles are related to the absorption of subcutaneous fat, a decrease in the thickness and elasticity of the skin, and a failure in adherence of the skin to the deeper tissues—all processes that are part of the normal physiology of aging. This is possibly one of the most graphic examples of a purely cosmetic procedure.

Senile ptosis of the eyelids – A condition in which the skin of the eyelids sags or droops. This may cause vision impairment.

Septoplasty – Surgical correction of a deviated nasal septum, the dividing wall between the two nasal cavities. This involves only the internal functioning of the nose and is usually covered. Septoplasty or submucous resection of the septum involves undermining the mucous membrane that covers the septum. This procedure is also referred to as "raising the mucoperichondrial and mucoperiosteal flaps." The cartilage is then cut into at its base so as to allow it to be moved over and straightened.

Submental lipectomy – Removal of fat deposits under the chin. The region under the chin (sub-mental region) and the neck often requires special attention. A submental lipectomy through a separate incision may be required to remove the fat deposits beneath the chin, thus correcting double chins. Suturing and repositioning of the neck muscle (platysma) is done to obliterate jowls. This is usually considered cosmetic.

Submucous resection – Removal of a portion of the nasal septum.

TMJ surgery – Osteoplastic surgery of the jaw for prognathism (projection of the jaw(s) beyond the projection of the forehead), micrognathism (abnormal smallness of jaws), and other variations may be cosmetic or functional, depending on the degree of malocclusion.

Turbinates – Bony projections from the sidewalls of the internal nose. The purpose of the turbinates is to warm and moisten air. Each nasal cavity is divided into three passageways by the turbinates. A submucous resection of the turbinates consists of undermining the mucous membrane that covers them and removing a portion of the bone, thereby enlarging the nasal passageway. A submucous resection is a functional correction and is therefore, an eligible expense.

Wart and mole removal – Moles and warts are discolorations of the skin which protrude above the normal skin elevation. Often warts and moles are associated with other diseases and conditions, especially cancer. Therefore, many plans will cover the removal of warts and moles.

Obesity Surgery

Exogenous obesity is obesity caused by overeating. Treatment for this condition is not considered treatment of a disease and is usually not covered by most plans until the level of obesity reaches a point at which it is life threatening. Most administrators have defined this level as being 100 pounds or 30% over the weight considered optimal for a person of a particular height and bone frame.

Endogenous obesity is obesity caused by an internal malfunction usually hormonal (i.e., thyroid disorder). Treatment for this type of obesity or for the underlying cause is considered treatment of a disease and is eligible under most plans. This is a comparatively rare condition.

Most administrators require the following documentation to be submitted before the scheduled treatment for review:

- Current weight and height.
- Frame type (small, medium, large).
- History of weight loss in the past (i.e., what diets have been tried, what level of success).
- Concurrent medical complications such as high blood pressure, diabetes.
- Family history of obesity or other health problems.

The following three procedures are the most common procedures used to combat exogenous obesity:

1. **Gastric balloon/garren gastric bubble** – A procedure in which a balloon is inserted into the stomach, thus giving the impression of being "full." Since many overweight people do not eat because they are hungry but because of habit or compulsion, this has not been an effective method. In addition, many complications, including death, have resulted from this procedure. Therefore, it is no longer considered an accepted medical practice.

2. **Gastric bypass** – A procedure in which the stomach is bypassed, allowing food to empty directly into the large intestine. The theory behind this procedure is that the food, nutrients, and fats are not thoroughly broken down and digested, resulting in fewer calories being accessible to the body for storing. Therefore, weight is lost. This is usually considered to be a permanent procedure, although it can be reversed. See CPT codes 43844, 43846.

3. **Gastric stapling** – A procedure in which a portion of the stomach is stapled off so as to reduce the size of the stomach. This procedure decreases the amount of food that may be eaten at a single meal. See CPT code 43843.

All procedures for obesity involving surgery have side effects. Some of the side effects for some people may be so severe that the procedure will need to be reversed. Therefore, only the severely obese should consider any of these methods of treatment.

The alternatives to surgery include the following services that are usually not covered under benefit plans:

Special diets and dietary supplements.
HCG (human chorionic gonadotropin) and vitamin injections.
Acupuncture.
Appetite suppressants.
Biofeedback.
Hypnosis.
Hospital confinements for weight reduction.
Exercise programs.
Health centers, weight loss centers, or other similar programs.
Diet books and instructions.

Co-Surgeons

Under some circumstances, two surgeons, usually with similar skills, may operate simultaneously as primary surgeons performing distinct, separate parts of a total surgical service. For example, two surgeons may simultaneously apply skin grafts to different parts of the body or two surgeons may repair different fractures of the same patient.

Different plans and different administrators handle co-surgeons differently. There are no set rules. Therefore, when a claim is received for co-surgeons, plan guidelines or administrative guidelines have to be referred to before processing. Usually co-surgeon procedures are referred to a consultant, supervisor, or Medical Review Department before processing.

Assistant Surgeons

Extensive surgeries require a primary surgeon and an assistant surgeon. The assistant surgeon may do the closing of the operative wound, hemostasis of the wound edges, and suturing of vessels. The job of the assistant surgeon is to assist the primary surgeon as required. Since the assistant surgeon is not the physician primarily responsible for the patient, the UCR allowance is considerably less than that for the surgeon.

The first consideration is that the complexity of the surgical procedure must medically require an assistant (**see Appendix 15-1** Assistant Surgeon Procedures). Obviously, an assistant surgeon would not be covered for minor surgery such as acne surgery (CPT code 10040).

As a rule, the following guidelines may be used in determining whether an assistant is required:

- The place of service is either an inpatient or outpatient hospital, or a surgicenter. Seldom are major surgeries performed in an office.
- Usually, follow-up days are listed in the RVS for the procedure. Services without follow-up days are usually not complex enough to require an assistant.

The allowance for an assistant surgeon is 20% of the surgery allowance (UCR). Modifier –80 is used to designate the assistant surgeon's fee.

Example: Procedure 20205 has a unit value of 10.0. The conversion factor is $38.50. Therefore, 10 units x $38.50 = $385.00. 20% of $385.00 = $77.00.

Based on the previously stated guidelines, $77.00 would be considered UCR for an assistant surgeon.

Some procedures do not require the expertise of an M.D. assistant, but do require technical help. For these procedures physician assistants (PA's) are often used. When these professionals are used in lieu of an M.D. assistant, Modifier 81 is used. The allowable amount is calculated at 10%-15% of the surgeon's allowance depending on the insurance company's practice and plan definition. The most common percentage used is 10%.

Example: Procedure 20205 has a unit value of 10 units. The conversion factor for surgery is $38.50. Therefore, 10 units x $138.50 = $385.00. $385.00 x 10% = $38.50, therefore, the allowable amount for the PA is $38.50.

It should be noted that although an assistant surgeon is eligible when a C-section is performed, the physician's coding should be reviewed. The assistant is entitled to 20% (or 10% if a PA) of the delivery only and not the global code that includes the antepartum and postpartum care.

If there is more than one procedure performed, the multiple/bilateral guidelines apply. The reasoning is that the assistant surgeon allowable is 20% of the surgeon's allowable. Thus, the first procedure would be calculated at 20% of the allowed amount and the subsequent procedures would be calculated at the allowed amount x 50% x 20%.

New Technology

The medical field is always developing new methods and technologies to improve care. One of the most significant improvements in surgery is the development of the laparoscopic procedure. A laparoscopic procedure is performed through two or three small incisions in which magnifying scopes and instruments are passed. Many procedures can be performed in this manner, among them are cholecystectomy (gall bladder removal), hysterectomy, and hernia repair. These procedures were normally performed through a large abdominal incision requiring several days hospital confinement, lengthy recovery and loss of time from work, and potential high risk for complications. Performing these procedures laparoscopically has reduced anesthesia time, hospital stays, risk of complications, recovery time and loss of wages, and the cosmetic benefit of reduced scarring.

New procedures and new ways to perform the old procedures improves care, but it is also important to investigate new procedures or those not specifically listed in the CPT for their efficacy and experimental nature which may not be covered under the plan.

Summary

Surgery charges may be the most complicated charges you will encounter. That is why there are so many guidelines covering surgery, multiple surgery, assistant surgery and cosmetic surgery. If for any reason you are unsure, request the medical opinion of a senior examiner or technical person.

The use of an assistant surgeon always depends on the medical necessity of the procedure performed. Using these guidelines and the Assistant Surgeon Procedures list will enable you to determine whether the assistant surgeon is necessary and what portion of the charges are covered.

Assignments

Complete the Questions for Review.
Complete Exercises 15 – 1 to 15 – 6.

Questions for Review

Directions: Answer the following questions without looking back into the material just covered. Write your answers in the space provided.

1. Define surgery. _____

   _____

   _____

2. Are cosmetic surgical procedures usually covered by benefit plans? _____

3. What are the four types of surgical procedures? (List and define.)

   1. _____

      _____

   2. _____

      _____

   3. _____

      _____

   4. _____

      _____

4. What does the physician's charge for surgery performed in the office generally include? _____

   _____

   _____

5. Identify two situations that would warrant separate payment for preoperative care.

   _____

   _____

   _____

   _____

6. What does the surgical unit value include? _____

   _____

7. When is the follow-up care allowed separately? _____

   _____

   _____

8. What are asterisk procedures? _____

   _____

9. What are By Report procedures and what other term may be used to indicate these procedures? _____

   _____

   _____

10. What services are normally provided in maternity cases? _____

    _____

11. What are therapeutic procedures? _____

    _____

12. What is the difference between a cosmetic procedure and a reconstructive procedure? _____ _____

13. What is a blepharoplasty? _____ _____

14. Define lump sum billing in relation to maternity charges. _____ _____

15. When would charges for amniocentesis or chromosomal analysis usually be covered? _____ _____

16. What is cheiloplasty? _____ _____

17. Are collagen injections a cosmetic procedure? _____

18. What is the name of the surgical procedure for reduction or enlargement of the breasts? _____

19. What is the name of the surgical procedure for excision or amputation of the breast? _____

20. What is a deviated nasal septum? _____ _____

21. (True or False?) An extensive surgery requires an assistant surgeon without a primary surgeon. _____

22. (True or False?) Major surgeries are normally preformed in the doctor's office. _____

23. Modifier _____ is used to designate the assistant surgeon's fee.

24. The allowance for an assistant surgeon is _____ of the surgery allowance?

25. Would an assistant surgeon be required for acne surgery? _____

If you were unable to answer any of the questions, refer back to the section and then complete the answers.

Exercise 15 – 1 to 15 – 6

Directions: Process each of the surgery and assistant surgery claims found on the following pages.

Honors Certification™

The Honors Certification™ challenge for this chapter is a written test of the information contained within this chapter. Additionally you will be given three claims to process, using the contracts contained in this book. You will be given 60 minutes to complete this test. Each incorrect answer will result in a deduction of between 1% and 5% from your grade. You must achieve a score of 80% or higher to pass this test. If you fail the test on your first attempt you may retake the test one additional time. The items included in the second test may be different from those in the first test.

PLEASE DO NOT STAPLE IN THIS AREA

ROVER INSURERS INC.
5931 ROLLING ROAD
RONSON, CO 81369

APPROVED MOB-0938-0008

CLAIM SUR1

PICA

HEALTH INSURANCE CLAIM FORM

PICA

1. MEDICARE (Medicare #) ☐ MEDICAID (Medicaid #) ☐ CHAMPUS (Sponsor's SSN) ☐ CHAMPVA (VA File #) ☐ GROUP HEALTH PLAN (SSN or ID) ☒ FECA BLK LUNG (SSN) ☐ OTHER (ID) ☐

1a. INSURED'S I.D. NUMBER (FOR PROGRAM IN ITEM 1): 999-99-9999

2. PATIENT'S NAME (Last, First, Middle Initial): BOSSY, BETTY B.

3. PATIENT'S BIRTH DATE MM DD YY: 09 | 19 | 39 SEX M ☐ F ☒

4. INSURED'S NAME (Last, First, Middle Initial): BOSSY, BETTY B.

5. PATIENT'S ADDRESS (No., Street): 7991 BAGEL BLVD.
CITY: BARSTOW STATE: NY
ZIP CODE: 12899 TELEPHONE (Include Area Code): (914) 555-3399

6. PATIENT'S RELATIONSHIP TO INSURED: Self ☒ Spouse ☐ Child ☐ Other ☐

7. INSURED'S ADDRESS (No., Street): 7991 BAGEL BLVD.
CITY: BARSTOW STATE: NY
ZIP CODE: 12899 TELEPHONE (INCLUDE AREA CODE): (914) 555-3399

8. PATIENT STATUS: Single ☐ Married ☒ Other ☐ Employed ☒ Full-Time Student ☐ Part-Time Student ☐

9. OTHER INSURED'S NAME (Last, First, Middle Initial):
a. OTHER INSURED'S POLICY OR GROUP NUMBER:
b. OTHER INSURED'S DATE OF BIRTH MM DD YY | | SEX M ☐ F ☐
c. EMPLOYER'S NAME OR SCHOOL NAME:
d. INSURANCE PLAN NAME OR PROGRAM NAME:

10. IS PATIENT'S CONDITION RELATED TO:
a. EMPLOYMENT? (CURRENT OR PREVIOUS) ☐ YES ☒ NO
b. AUTO ACCIDENT? ☐ YES ☒ NO PLACE (State) ____
c. OTHER ACCIDENT? ☐ YES ☒ NO
10d. RESERVED FOR LOCAL USE

11. INSURED'S POLICY GROUP OR FECA NUMBER: 999-99-NIN
a. INSURED'S DATE OF BIRTH MM DD YY: 09 | 19 | 39 SEX M ☐ F ☒
b. EMPLOYER'S NAME OR SCHOOL NAME: NINJA CORPORATION
c. INSURANCE PLAN NAME OR PROGRAM NAME: NINJA PLAN
d. IS THERE ANOTHER HEALTH BENEFIT PLAN? ☐ YES ☒ NO *If yes, return to and complete item 9 a-d*

READ BACK OF FORM BEFORE COMPLETING & SIGNING THIS FORM

12. PATIENT'S OR AUTHORIZED PERSON'S SIGNATURE I authorize the release of any medical or other information necessary to process this claim. I also request payment of government benefits either to myself or to the party who accepts assignment below.
SIGNED SIGNATURE ON FILE DATE 02/ 06/ 04

13. INSURED'S OR AUTHORIZED PERSON'S SIGNATURE I authorize payment of medical benefits to the undersigned physician or supplier for services described below.
SIGNED SIGNATURE ON FILE

14. DATE OF CURRENT: ILLNESS (1st symptom) INJURY (Accident) PREGNANCY (LMP) MM DD YY: 02 | 06 | 04

15. IF PATIENT HAS HAD SAME OR SIMILAR ILLNESS, GIVE FIRST DATE MM DD YY

16. DATES PATIENT UNABLE TO WORK IN CURRENT OCCUPATION FROM MM DD YY TO MM DD YY

17. NAME OF REFERRING PHYSICIAN OR OTHER SOURCE

17a. I.D. NUMBER OF REFERRING PHYSICIAN

18. HOSPITALIZATION DATES RELATED TO CURRENT SERVICES FROM 02 | 06 | 04 TO 02 | 14 | 04

19. RESERVED FOR LOCAL USE

20. OUTSIDE LAB? ☐ YES ☐ NO $ CHARGES

21. DIAGNOSIS OR NATURE OF ILLNESS OR INJURY, (RELATE ITEMS 1,2,3, OR 4 TO ITEM 24E BY LINE)
1. 410 . 91
2. ___ . ___
3. ___ . ___
4. ___ . ___

22. MEDICAID RESUBMISSION CODE ORIGINAL REF. NO.

23. PRIOR AUTHORIZATION NUMBER

24.

A. DATE(S) OF SERVICE From MM	DD	YY	To MM	DD	YY	B. Place of Service	C. Type of Service	D. PROCEDURES, SERVICES, OR SUPPLIES (Explain Unusual Circumstances) CPT/HCPCS	MODIFIER	E. DIAGNOSIS CODE	F. $ CHARGES		G. DAYS OR UNITS	H. EPSDT Family Plan	I. EMG	J. COB	K. RESERVED FOR LOCAL USE
02	06	04	02	06	04	21	1	33217		1	245	00	1		Y		
02	06	04	02	06	04	21	1	33225		1	500	00	1		Y		
02	06	04	02	06	04	21	1	33240		1	295	00	1		Y		

(Global Billing)

25. FEDERAL TAX I.D. NUMBER: 07-0089773 SSN ☐ EIN ☒

26. PATIENT'S ACCOUNT NO.: BETBS001 939

27. ACCEPT ASSIGNMENT? (For govt. claims, see back) ☒ YES ☐ NO

28. TOTAL CHARGE: $ 1,040 | 00

29. AMOUNT PAID: $ 0 | 00

30. BALANCE DUE: $ 1,040 | 00

31. SIGNATURE OF PHYSICIAN OR SUPPLIER INCLUDING DEGREES OR CREDENTIALS (I certify that the statements on the reverse apply to this bill and are made a part thereof.)
SIGNED *Abe Domin* DATE 02/21/04

32. NAME AND ADDRESS OF FACILITY WHERE SERVICES WERE RENDERED (If other than home or office)
HEADACHE HOSPITAL
2000 HAZARD STREET
HELP, NY 12899 (914) 555-9989

33. PHYSICIAN'S, SUPPLIER'S BILLING NAME, ADDRESS, ZIP CODE & PHONE #
ABE DOMIN, M.D. NETWORK PROVIDER
9909 DATEWAY DRIVE, STE 9A
DOVE, NY 12899 (914) 555-5199
PIN# ABD002 GRP#

(APPROVED BY AMA COUNCIL ON MEDICAL SERVICE 8/88) *PLEASE PRINT OR TYPE* FORM HCFA-1500 (12-90) FORM OWCP-1500 FORM RRB-1500

PLEASE
DO NOT
STAPLE
IN THIS
AREA

WINTER INSURANCE CO.
9763 WESTERN WAY
WHITTIER, CO 82963

AREAAPPROVED MOB-0938-0008

CLAIM SUR2

□□□ PICA

HEALTH INSURANCE CLAIM FORM

PICA □□□

1. MEDICARE MEDICAID CHAMPUS CHAMPVA GROUP HEALTH PLAN FECA BLK LUNG OTHER	INSURED'S I.D NUMBER	(FOR PROGRAM IN ITEM 1)
□ (Medicare #) □ (Medicaid #) □ (Sponsor's SSN) □ (VA File #) ☒ (SSN or ID) □ (SSN) □ (ID)	444-44-4444	

2. PATIENT'S NAME (Last, First, Middle Initial)	3. PATIENT'S BIRTH DATE MM DD YY SEX	4. INSURED'S NAME (Last, First, Middle Initial)
DINGBAT, DANNY D.	04 24 90 M ☒ F □	DINGBAT, DANA D.

5. PATIENT'S ADDRESS (No., Street)	6. PATIENT'S RELATIONSHIP TO INSURED	7. INSURED'S ADDRESS (No., Street)
404 DOORWAY DRIVE	Self □ Spouse □ Child ☒ Other □	404 DOORWAY DRIVE

CITY	STATE	8. PATIENT STATUS	CITY	STATE
DENVER	ND	Single ☒ Married □ Other □	DENVER	ND

ZIP CODE	TELEPHONE (Include Area Code)	Employed □ Full-Time ☒ Part-Time □ Student Student	ZIP CODE	TELEPHONE (INCLUDE AREA CODE)
58444	(701) 555-3344		58444	(701) 555-3344

9. OTHER INSURED'S NAME (Last, First, Middle Initial)	10. IS PATIENT'S CONDITION RELATED TO:	11. INSURED'S POLICY GROUP OR FECA NUMBER:
		444-44-ABC

a. OTHER INSURED'S POLICY OR GROUP NUMBER	a. EMPLOYMENT? (CURRENT OR PREVIOUS) □ YES ☒ NO	a. INSURED'S DATE OF BIRTH MM DD YY SEX 04 04 64 M □ F ☒

a. OTHER INSURED'S DATE OF BIRTH MM DD YY SEX M □ F □	b. AUTO ACCIDENT? PLACE (State) □ YES ☒ NO	b. EMPLOYER'S NAME OR SCHOOL NAME ABC CORPORATION

c. EMPLOYER'S NAME OR SCHOOL NAME	c. OTHER ACCIDENT? ☒ YES □ NO	c. INSURANCE PLAN NAME OR PROGRAM NAME ABC PLAN

d. INSURANCE PLAN NAME OR PROGRAM NAME	10d. RESERVED FOR LOCAL USE	d. IS THERE ANOTHER HEALTH BENEFIT PLAN? □ YES ☒ NO If yes, return to and complete item 9 a-d

READ BACK OF FORM BEFORE COMPLETING & SIGNING THIS FORM

12. PATIENT'S OR AUTHORIZED PERSON'S SIGNATURE I authorize the release of any medical or other information necessary to process this claim. I also request payment of government benefits either to myself or to the party who accepts assignment below.

SIGNED   SIGNATURE ON FILE   DATE   01/26/04

13. INSURED'S OR AUTHORIZED PERSON'S SIGNATURE I authorize payment of medical benefits to the undersigned physician or supplier for services described below.

SIGNED   SIGNATURE ON FILE

14. DATE OF CURRENT: ◄ ILLNESS (1st symptom) ◄ INJURY (Accident) ◄ PREGNANCY (LMP) MM DD YY 01 26 04	15. IF PATIENT HAS HAD SAME OR SIMILAR ILLNESS. GAVE FIRST DATE MM DD YY	16. DATES PATIENT UNABLE TO WORK IN CURRENT OCCUPATION FROM MM DD YY TO MM DD YY

17. NAME OF REFERRING PHYSICIAN OR OTHER SOURCE	17a. I.D. NUMBER OF REFERRING PHYSICIAN	18. HOSPITALIZATION DATES RELATED TO CURRENT SERVICES FROM MM DD YY 01 26 04 TO MM DD YY 02 08 04

19. RESERVED FOR LOCAL USE	20. OUTSIDE LAB? □ YES □ NO $ CHARGES

21. DIAGNOSIS OR NATURE OF ILLNESS OR INJURY. (RELATE ITEMS 1,2,3, OR 4 TO ITEM 24E BY LINE)

1. 807.01   3. 800.40
2. 823.32   4. E884.9

22. MEDICAID RESUBMISSION CODE   ORIGINAL REF. NO.

23. PRIOR AUTHORIZATION NUMBER

24. A DATE(S) OF SERVICE From / To MM DD YY MM DD YY	B Place of Service	C Type of Service	D PROCEDURES, SERVICES, OR SUPPLIES (Explain Unusual Circumstances) CPT/HCPS MODIFIER	E DIAGNOSIS CODE	F $ CHARGES	G DAYS OR UNITS	H EPSDT Family Plan	I EMG	J COB	K RESERVED FOR LOCAL USE
01 26 04 01 26 04	21	1	21800	1 4	560 00	1		Y		
01 26 04 01 26 04	21	1	27758	2 4	215 00	1		Y		
01 26 04 01 26 04	21	1	27784	2 4	200 00	1		Y		
01 26 04 01 26 04	21	1	62000	3 4	150 00	1		Y		

25. FEDERAL TAX I.D. NUMBER SSN EIN 41-0089772 □ ☒	26. PATIENT'S ACCOUNT NO. DANDI001 434	27. ACCEPT ASSIGNMENT? (For govt. claims, see back) ☒ YES □ NO	28. TOTAL CHARGE $ 1,125 00	29. AMOUNT PAID $ 0 00	30. BALANCE DUE $ 1,125 00

31. SIGNATURE OF PHYSICIAN OR SUPPLIER INCLUDING DEGREES OR CREDENTIALS (I certify that the statements on the reverse apply to this bill and are made a part thereof.) SIGNED *Ray Machine* DATE 02/08/04	32. NAME AND ADDRESS OF FACILITY WHERE SERVICES WERE RENDERED (If other than home or office) HACKIM HOSPITAL 1000 HIDE STREET HUSHTOWN, ND 58444 (701) 555-4004	33. PHYSICIAN'S, SUPPLIERS BILLING NAME, ADDRESS, ZIP CODE & PHONE # RAY MACHINE, M.D. 4044 ROOMER ROAD, STE 4R ROLLER, ND 58444 (701) 555-1144 PIN# RAM002 GRP#

(APPROVED BY AMA COUNCIL ON MEDICAL SERVICE 8/88)

PLEASE PRINT OR TYPE

FORM HCFA-1500 (12-90)
FORM OWCP-1500   FORM RRB-1500

PLEASE
DO NOT
STAPLE
IN THIS
AREA
□□□ PICA

BALL INSURANCE CARRIERS
3895 BUBBLE BLVD., STE.283
BOXWOOD, CO 85926

APPROVED MOB-0938-0008

CLAIM SUR3

HEALTH INSURANCE CLAIM FORM

PICA □□□

1. MEDICARE MEDICAID CHAMPUS CHAMPVA GROUP HEALTH PLAN FECA BLK LUNG OTHER	INSURED'S I.D NUMBER (FOR PROGRAM IN ITEM 1)
□ *(Medicare #)* □ *(Medicaid #)* □ *(Sponsor's SSN)* □ *(VA File #)* ☒ *(SSN or ID)* □ *(SSN)* □ *(ID)*	555-55-5555

2. PATIENT'S NAME (Last, First, Middle Initial)	3. PATIENT'S BIRTH DATE MM DD YY SEX	4. INSURED'S NAME (Last, First, Middle Initial)
PATIENT, PATTY P.	05 15 75 M□ F☒	PATIENT, PATTY P.

5. PATIENT'S ADDRESS (No., Street)	6. PATIENT'S RELATIONSHIP TO INSURED	7. INSURED'S ADDRESS (No., Street)
655 PAIN LANE	Self ☒ Spouse □ Child □ Other □	655 PAIN LANE

CITY	STATE	8. PATIENT STATUS	CITY	STATE
PEN	PA	Single ☒ Married □ Other □	PEN	PA

ZIP CODE	TELEPHONE (Include Area Code)		ZIP CODE	TELEPHONE (INCLUDE AREA CODE)
15522	(878) 555-3355	Employed ☒ Full-Time □ Part-Time □ Student Student	15522	(878) 555-3355

9. OTHER INSURED'S NAME (Last, First, Middle Initial)	10. IS PATIENT'S CONDITION RELATED TO:	11. INSURED'S POLICY GROUP OR FECA NUMBER:
		555-55-XYZ

a. OTHER INSURED'S POLICY OR GROUP NUMBER	a. EMPLOYMENT? (CURRENT OR PREVIOUS) □ YES ☒ NO	a. INSURED'S DATE OF BIRTH MM DD YY SEX 05 15 75 M□ F☒

a. OTHER INSURED'S DATE OF BIRTH MM DD YY SEX M□ F□	b. AUTO ACCIDENT? PLACE (State) □ YES ☒ NO	b. EMPLOYER'S NAME OR SCHOOL NAME XYZ CORPORATION

c. EMPLOYER'S NAME OR SCHOOL NAME	c. OTHER ACCIDENT? □ YES ☒ NO	c. INSURANCE PLAN NAME OR PROGRAM NAME XYZ PLAN

d. INSURANCE PLAN NAME OR PROGRAM NAME	10d. RESERVED FOR LOCAL USE	d. IS THERE ANOTHER HEALTH BENEFIT PLAN? □ YES ☒ NO If yes, return to and complete item 9 a-d

READ BACK OF FORM BEFORE COMPLETING & SIGNING THIS FORM
12. PATIENT'S OR AUTHORIZED PERSON'S SIGNATURE I authorize the release of any medical or other information necessary to process this claim. I also request payment of government benefits either to myself or to the party who accepts assignment below.

SIGNED   SIGNATURE ON FILE   DATE 02/ 02/ 04

13. INSURED'S OR AUTHORIZED PERSON'S SIGNATURE I authorize payment of medical benefits to the undersigned physician or supplier for services described below.

SIGNED   SIGNATURE ON FILE

14. DATE OF CURRENT: ILLNESS (1st symptom) INJURY (Accident) PREGNANCY (LMP) MM DD YY 02 02 04	15. IF PATIENT HAS HAD SAME OR SIMILAR ILLNESS, GAVE FIRST DATE MM DD YY	16. DATES PATIENT UNABLE TO WORK IN CURRENT OCCUPATION MM DD YY FROM TO MM DD YY

17. NAME OF REFERRING PHYSICIAN OR OTHER SOURCE	17a. I.D. NUMBER OF REFERRING PHYSICIAN	18. HOSPITALIZATION DATES RELATED TO CURRENT SERVICES MM DD YY FROM 02 16 04 TO 02 16 04

19. RESERVED FOR LOCAL USE	20. OUTSIDE LAB? □ YES □ NO $ CHARGES

21. DIAGNOSIS OR NATURE OF ILLNESS OR INJURY, (RELATE ITEMS 1,2,3, OR 4 TO ITEM 24E BY LINE) 1. 233 . 0 2. 3. 4.	22. MEDICAID RESUBMISSION CODE ORIGINAL REF. NO. 23. PRIOR AUTHORIZATION NUMBER

24. A. DATE(S) OF SERVICE From — To MM DD YY MM DD YY	B. Place of Service	C. Type of Service	D. PROCEDURES, SERVICES, OR SUPPLIES (Explain Unusual Circumstances) CPT/HCPCS MODIFIER	E. DIAGNOSIS CODE	F. $ CHARGES	G. DAYS OR UNITS	H. EPSDT Family Plan	I. EMG	J. COB	K. RESERVED FOR LOCAL USE
02 16 04 02 16 04	22	1	19125	1	360 00	1				
02 16 04 02 16 04	22	1	19126	1	740 00	4				

25. FEDERAL TAX I.D. NUMBER SSN EIN 35-0089771 □ ☒	26. PATIENT'S ACCOUNT NO. PATPA001 :535	27. ACCEPT ASSIGNMENT? (For govt. claims, see back) □ YES ☒ NO	28. TOTAL CHARGE $ 1,100 00	29. AMOUNT PAID $ 0 00	30. BALANCE DUE $ 1,100 00

31. SIGNATURE OF PHYSICIAN OR SUPPLIER INCLUDING DEGREES OR CREDENTIALS (I certify that the statements on the reverse apply to this bill and are made a part thereof.) SIGNED *Sam A. Piller* DATE 3/1/04	32. NAME AND ADDRESS OF FACILITY WHERE SERVICES WERE RENDERED (If other than home or office) HELPER HOSPITAL 25450 HAMMER AVE. HUMMER TOWN, PA 15522 (878) 555-6455	33. PHYSICIAN'S, SUPPLIERS BILLING NAME, ADDRESS, ZIP CODE & PHONE # SAM A. PILLER, M.D. 155 SOFT AVENUE, STE. 505P SUMMERVILLE, PA 15522 (878) 555-0055 PIN# SAP002 GRP#

(APPROVED BY AMA COUNCIL ON MEDICAL SERVICE 8/88)

PLEASE PRINT OR TYPE

FORM HCFA-1500 (12-90)
FORM OWCP-1500   FORM RRB-1500

PLEASE
DO NOT
STAPLE
IN THIS
AREA

ROVER INSURERS INC.
5931 ROLLING ROAD
RONSON, CO 81369

CLAIM ASUR1

☐☐☐ PICA

HEALTH INSURANCE CLAIM FORM

PICA ☐☐☐

1. MEDICARE MEDICAID CHAMPUS CHAMPVA GROUP HEALTH PLAN FECA BLK LUNG OTHER	INSURED'S I.D NUMBER (FOR PROGRAM IN ITEM 1)
☐ (Medicare #) ☐ (Medicaid #) ☐ (Sponsor's SSN) ☐ (VA File #) ☒ (SSN or ID) ☐ (SSN) ☐ (ID)	999-99-9999

2. PATIENT'S NAME (Last, First, Middle Initial)	3. PATIENT'S BIRTH DATE MM DD YY SEX	4. INSURED'S NAME (Last, First, Middle Initial)
BOSSY, BETTY B.	09 19 39 M ☐ F ☒	BOSSY, BETTY B.

5. PATIENT'S ADDRESS (No., Street)	6. PATIENT'S RELATIONSHIP TO INSURED	7. INSURED'S ADDRESS (No., Street)
7991 BAGEL BLVD.	Self ☒ Spouse ☐ Child ☐ Other ☐	7991 BAGEL BLVD.

CITY	STATE	8. PATIENT STATUS	CITY	STATE
BARSTOW	NY	Single ☐ Married ☒ Other ☐	BARSTOW	NY

ZIP CODE	TELEPHONE (Include Area Code)		ZIP CODE	TELEPHONE (INCLUDE AREA CODE)
12899	(914) 555-3399	Employed ☒ Full-Time Student ☐ Part-Time Student ☐	12899	(914) 555-3399

9. OTHER INSURED'S NAME (Last, First, Middle Initial)	10. IS PATIENT'S CONDITION RELATED TO:	11. INSURED'S POLICY GROUP OR FECA NUMBER:
		999-99-NIN

a. OTHER INSURED'S POLICY OR GROUP NUMBER	a. EMPLOYMENT? (CURRENT OR PREVIOUS) ☐ YES ☒ NO	a. INSURED'S DATE OF BIRTH MM DD YY SEX 09 19 39 M ☐ F ☒

a. OTHER INSURED'S DATE OF BIRTH MM DD YY SEX M ☐ F ☐	b. AUTO ACCIDENT? PLACE (State) ☐ YES ☒ NO	b. EMPLOYER'S NAME OR SCHOOL NAME NINJA CORPORATION

c. EMPLOYER'S NAME OR SCHOOL NAME	c. OTHER ACCIDENT? ☐ YES ☒ NO	c. INSURANCE PLAN NAME OR PROGRAM NAME NINJA PLAN

d. INSURANCE PLAN NAME OR PROGRAM NAME	10d. RESERVED FOR LOCAL USE	d. IS THERE ANOTHER HEALTH BENEFIT PLAN? ☐ YES ☒ NO If yes, return to and complete item 9 a-d

READ BACK OF FORM BEFORE COMPLETING & SIGNING THIS FORM

12. PATIENT'S OR AUTHORIZED PERSON'S SIGNATURE I authorize the release of any medical or other information necessary to process this claim. I also request payment of government benefits either to myself or to the party who accepts assignment below.

SIGNED   SIGNATURE ON FILE   DATE 02/06 04

13. INSURED'S OR AUTHORIZED PERSON'S SIGNATURE I authorize payment of medical benefits to the undersigned physician or supplier for services described below.

SIGNED   SIGNATURE ON FILE

14. DATE OF CURRENT: ILLNESS (1st symptom) / INJURY (Accident) / PREGNANCY (LMP) MM DD YY 02 06 04	15. IF PATIENT HAS HAD SAME OR SIMILAR ILLNESS, GAVE FIRST DATE MM DD YY	16. DATES PATIENT UNABLE TO WORK IN CURRENT OCCUPATION FROM MM DD YY TO MM DD YY

17. NAME OF REFERRING PHYSICIAN OR OTHER SOURCE	17a. I.D. NUMBER OF REFERRING PHYSICIAN	18. HOSPITALIZATION DATES RELATED TO CURRENT SERVICES FROM MM DD YY 02 06 04 TO MM DD YY 02 14 04

19. RESERVED FOR LOCAL USE	20. OUTSIDE LAB? ☐ YES ☐ NO $ CHARGES

21. DIAGNOSIS OR NATURE OF ILLNESS OR INJURY, (RELATE ITEMS 1,2,3, OR 4 TO ITEM 24E BY LINE) 1. 410 . 91 2. 3. 4.	22. MEDICAID RESUBMISSION CODE ORIGINAL REF. NO. 23. PRIOR AUTHORIZATION NUMBER

24. A. DATE(S) OF SERVICE From / To MM DD YY MM DD YY	B. Place of Service	C. Type of Service	D. PROCEDURES, SERVICES, OR SUPPLIES (Explain Unusual Circumstances) CPT/HCPS	MODIFIER	E. DIAGNOSIS CODE	F. $ CHARGES	G. DAYS OR UNITS	H. EPSDT Family Plan	I. EMG	J. COB	K. RESERVED FOR LOCAL USE
02 06 04 02 06 04	21	1	33217	-80	1	49 00	1		Y		
02 06 04 02 06 04	21	1	33225	-80	1	100 00	1		Y		
02 06 04 02 06 04	21	1	33240	-80	1	59 00	1		Y		

25. FEDERAL TAX I.D. NUMBER SSN EIN 90-0089779 ☐ ☒	26. PATIENT'S ACCOUNT NO. BETBS001 939	27. ACCEPT ASSIGNMENT? (For govt. claims, see back) ☒ YES ☐ NO	28. TOTAL CHARGE $ 208 00	29. AMOUNT PAID $ 0 00	30. BALANCE DUE $ 208 00

31. SIGNATURE OF PHYSICIAN OR SUPPLIER INCLUDING DEGREES OR CREDENTIALS (I certify that the statements on the reverse apply to this bill and are made a part thereof.) SIGNED Tim Percher DATE 02/19/04	32. NAME AND ADDRESS OF FACILITY WHERE SERVICES WERE RENDERED (If other than home or office) HEADACHE HOSPITAL 2000 HAZARD STREET HELP, NY 12899 (914) 555-9989	33. PHYSICIAN'S, SUPPLIERS BILLING NAME, ADDRESS, ZIP CODE & PHONE # TIM PERCHER, M.D. NETWORK PROVIDER 99 TANK STREET, STE 9T TREE, NY 12899 (914) 555-2599 PIN# TIM003 GRP#

(APPROVED BY AMA COUNCIL ON MEDICAL SERVICE 8/88)   PLEASE PRINT OR TYPE

FORM HCFA-1500 (12-90)
FORM OWCP-1500   FORM RRB-1500

PLEASE
DO NOT
STAPLE
IN THIS
AREA
☐☐☐ PICA

WINTER INSURANCE CO.
9763 WESTERN WAY
WHITTIER, CO 82963

CLAIM ASUR2

HEALTH INSURANCE CLAIM FORM

PICA ☐☐☐

1. MEDICARE MEDICAID CHAMPUS CHAMPVA	GROUP HEALTH PLAN FECA BLK LUNG OTHER	INSURED'S I.D NUMBER (FOR PROGRAM IN ITEM 1)
☐ (Medicare #) ☐ (Medicaid #) ☐ (Sponsor's SSN) ☐ (VA File #)	☒ (SSN or ID) ☐ (SSN) ☐ (ID)	444-44-4444

2. PATIENT'S NAME (Last, First, Middle Initial)	3. PATIENT'S BIRTH DATE	4. INSURED'S NAME (Last, First, Middle Initial)
DINGBAT, DANNY D.	MM 04 DD 24 YY 90 SEX M ☒ F ☐	DINGBAT, DANA D.

5. PATIENT'S ADDRESS (No., Street)	6. PATIENT'S RELATIONSHIP TO INSURED	7. INSURED'S ADDRESS (No., Street)
404 DOORWAY DRIVE	Self ☐ Spouse ☐ Child ☒ Other ☐	404 DOORWAY DRIVE
CITY STATE DENVER ND	8. PATIENT STATUS Single ☒ Married ☐ Other ☐	CITY STATE DENVER ND
ZIP CODE TELEPHONE (Include Area Code) 58444 (701) 555-3344	Employed ☐ Full-Time ☒ Part-Time ☐ Student Student	ZIP CODE TELEPHONE (INCLUDE AREA CODE) 58444 (701) 555-3344

9. OTHER INSURED'S NAME (Last, First, Middle Initial)	10. IS PATIENT'S CONDITION RELATED TO:	11. INSURED'S POLICY GROUP OR FECA NUMBER: 444-44-ABC
a. OTHER INSURED'S POLICY OR GROUP NUMBER	a. EMPLOYMENT? (CURRENT OR PREVIOUS) ☐ YES ☒ NO	a. INSURED'S DATE OF BIRTH MM 04 DD 04 YY 64 SEX M ☐ F ☒
a. OTHER INSURED'S DATE OF BIRTH MM DD YY SEX M ☐ F ☐	b. AUTO ACCIDENT? PLACE (State) ☐ YES ☒ NO ☐	b. EMPLOYER'S NAME OR SCHOOL NAME ABC CORPORATION
c. EMPLOYER'S NAME OR SCHOOL NAME	c. OTHER ACCIDENT? ☒ YES ☐ NO	c. INSURANCE PLAN NAME OR PROGRAM NAME ABC PLAN
d. INSURANCE PLAN NAME OR PROGRAM NAME	10d. RESERVED FOR LOCAL USE	d. IS THERE ANOTHER HEALTH BENEFIT PLAN? ☐ YES ☒ NO If yes, return to and complete item 9 a-d

READ BACK OF FORM BEFORE COMPLETING & SIGNING THIS FORM

12. PATIENT'S OR AUTHORIZED PERSON'S SIGNATURE I authorize the release of any medical or other information necessary to process this claim. I also request payment of government benefits either to myself or to the party who accepts assignment below.

SIGNED   SIGNATURE ON FILE   DATE   01/26/04

13. INSURED'S OR AUTHORIZED PERSON'S SIGNATURE I authorize payment of medical benefits to the undersigned physician or supplier for services described below.

SIGNED ____

14. DATE OF CURRENT: ◄ ILLNESS (1st symptom) MM 01 DD 26 YY 04 ◄ INJURY (Accident) ◄ PREGNANCY (LMP)	15. IF PATIENT HAS HAD SAME OR SIMILAR ILLNESS. GAVE FIRST DATE MM DD YY	16. DATES PATIENT UNABLE TO WORK IN CURRENT OCCUPATION MM DD YY TO MM DD YY FROM
17. NAME OF REFERRING PHYSICIAN OR OTHER SOURCE	17a. I.D. NUMBER OF REFERRING PHYSICIAN	18. HOSPITALIZATION DATES RELATED TO CURRENT SERVICES MM DD YY TO MM DD YY FROM 01 26 04 02 07 04
19. RESERVED FOR LOCAL USE		20. OUTSIDE LAB? $ CHARGES ☐ YES ☐ NO

21. DIAGNOSIS OR NATURE OF ILLNESS OR INJURY. (RELATE ITEMS 1,2,3, OR 4 TO ITEM 24E BY LINE)

1. 807.01
2. 823.32
3. 800.40
4. E884.9

22. MEDICAID RESUBMISSION CODE   ORIGINAL REF. NO.

23. PRIOR AUTHORIZATION NUMBER

24. A. DATE(S) OF SERVICE		B. Place of Service	C. Type of Service	D. PROCEDURES, SERVICES, OR SUPPLIES (Explain Unusual Circumstances) CPT/HCPCS MODIFIER	E. DIAGNOSIS CODE	F. $ CHARGES	G. DAYS OR UNITS	H. EPSDT Family Plan	I. EMG	J. COB	K. RESERVED FOR LOCAL USE
From MM DD YY	To MM DD YY										
01 26 04	01 26 04	21	1	21800 -80	1	132 00	1	Y			
01 26 04	01 26 04	21	1	27758 -80	2	35 00	1	Y			
01 26 04	01 26 04	21	1	27784 -80	2	50 00	1	Y			
01 26 04	01 26 04	21	1	62000 -80	3	40 00	1	Y			

25. FEDERAL TAX I.D. NUMBER SSN EIN	26. PATIENT'S ACCOUNT NO.	27. ACCEPT ASSIGNMENT? (For govt. claims, see back)	28. TOTAL CHARGE	29. AMOUNT PAID	30. BALANCE DUE
47-0089775 ☐ ☒	DANDI001 434	☐ YES ☒ NO	$ 257 00	$ 0 00	$ 257 00

31. SIGNATURE OF PHYSICIAN OR SUPPLIER INCLUDING DEGREES OR CREDENTIALS
(I certify that the statements on the reverse apply to this bill and are made a part thereof.)

SIGNED *Rod Diology*   DATE 2/7/04

32. NAME AND ADDRESS OF FACILITY WHERE SERVICES WERE RENDERED (If other than home or office)

HACKIM HOSPITAL
1000 HIDE STREET
HUSHTOWN, ND 58444 (701) 555-4004

33. PHYSICIAN'S, SUPPLIERS BILLING NAME, ADDRESS, ZIP CODE & PHONE #

ROD DIOLOGY, M.D.
4557 DREAMER DRIVE, STE 41D
DAYS, ND 58444 (701) 555-6044

PIN# ROD003   GRP#

(APPROVED BY AMA COUNCIL ON MEDICAL SERVICE 8/88)

PLEASE PRINT OR TYPE

FORM HCFA-1500   (12-90)
FORM OWCP-1500   FORM RRB-1500

APPROVED MOB-0938-0008

PLEASE
DO NOT
STAPLE
IN THIS
AREA
☐☐☐ PICA

APPROVED MOB-0938-0008

BALL INSURANCE CARRIERS
3895 BUBBLE BLVD., STE.283
BOXWOOD, CO 85926

CLAIM ASUR3

HEALTH INSURANCE CLAIM FORM

PICA ☐☐☐

1. MEDICARE MEDICAID CHAMPUS CHAMPVA GROUP HEALTH PLAN FECA BLK LUNG OTHER	INSURED'S I.D. NUMBER	(FOR PROGRAM IN ITEM 1)

☐ (Medicare #) ☐ (Medicaid #) ☐ (Sponsor's SSN) ☐ (VA File #) ☒ (SSN or ID) ☐ (SSN) ☐ (ID)

INSURED'S I.D. NUMBER: 555-55-5555

2. PATIENT'S NAME (Last, First, Middle Initial)
PATIENT, PATTY P.

3. PATIENT'S BIRTH DATE MM | DD | YY SEX
05 | 15 | 75 M☐ F☒

4. INSURED'S NAME (Last, First, Middle Initial)
PATIENT, PATTY P.

5. PATIENT'S ADDRESS (No., Street)
655 PAIN LANE

6. PATIENT'S RELATIONSHIP TO INSURED
Self ☒ Spouse ☐ Child ☐ Other ☐

7. INSURED'S ADDRESS (No., Street)
655 PAIN LANE

CITY: PEN STATE: PA

8. PATIENT STATUS
Single ☒ Married ☐ Other ☐
Employed ☒ Full-Time Student ☐ Part-Time Student ☐

CITY: PEN STATE: PA

ZIP CODE: 15522 TELEPHONE (Include Area Code): (878) 555-3355

9. OTHER INSURED'S NAME (Last, First, Middle Initial)

ZIP CODE: 15522 TELEPHONE (INCLUDE AREA CODE): (878) 555-3355

10. IS PATIENT'S CONDITION RELATED TO:

11. INSURED'S POLICY GROUP OR FECA NUMBER:
555-55-XYZ

a. OTHER INSURED'S POLICY OR GROUP NUMBER

a. EMPLOYMENT? (CURRENT OR PREVIOUS)
☐ YES ☒ NO

a. INSURED'S DATE OF BIRTH MM | DD | YY SEX
05 | 15 | 75 M☐ F☒

a. OTHER INSURED'S DATE OF BIRTH MM | DD | YY SEX M☐ F☐

b. AUTO ACCIDENT? PLACE (State)
☐ YES ☒ NO

b. EMPLOYER'S NAME OR SCHOOL NAME
XYZ CORPORATION

c. EMPLOYER'S NAME OR SCHOOL NAME

c. OTHER ACCIDENT?
☐ YES ☒ NO

c. INSURANCE PLAN NAME OR PROGRAM NAME
XYZ PLAN

d. INSURANCE PLAN NAME OR PROGRAM NAME

10d. RESERVED FOR LOCAL USE

d. IS THERE ANOTHER HEALTH BENEFIT PLAN?
☐ YES ☒ NO If yes, return to and complete item 9 a-d

READ BACK OF FORM BEFORE COMPLETING & SIGNING THIS FORM
12. PATIENT'S OR AUTHORIZED PERSON'S SIGNATURE I authorize the release of any medical or other information necessary to process this claim. I also request payment of government benefits either to myself or to the party who accepts assignment below.

SIGNED   SIGNATURE ON FILE   DATE 02/16/04

13. INSURED'S OR AUTHORIZED PERSON'S SIGNATURE I authorize payment of medical benefits to the undersigned physician or supplier for services described below.

SIGNED SIGNATURE ON FILE

14. DATE OF CURRENT: ◄ ILLNESS (1st symptom) ◄ INJURY (Accident) ◄ PREGNANCY (LMP)
MM | DD | YY 02 | 02 | 04

15. IF PATIENT HAS HAD SAME OR SIMILAR ILLNESS, GAVE FIRST DATE MM | DD | YY

16. DATES PATIENT UNABLE TO WORK IN CURRENT OCCUPATION
FROM MM | DD | YY TO MM | DD | YY

17. NAME OF REFERRING PHYSICIAN OR OTHER SOURCE

17a. I.D. NUMBER OF REFERRING PHYSICIAN

18. HOSPITALIZATION DATES RELATED TO CURRENT SERVICES
FROM MM | DD | YY 02 | 16 | 04 TO MM | DD | YY 02 | 16 | 04

19. RESERVED FOR LOCAL USE

20. OUTSIDE LAB? ☐ YES ☐ NO $ CHARGES

21. DIAGNOSIS OR NATURE OF ILLNESS OR INJURY. (RELATE ITEMS 1,2,3, OR 4 TO ITEM 24E BY LINE)
1. 233.0
2.
3.
4.

22. MEDICAID RESUBMISSION CODE ORIGINAL REF. NO.

23. PRIOR AUTHORIZATION NUMBER

24. A. DATE(S) OF SERVICE From MM DD YY To MM DD YY	B. Place of Service	C. Type of Service	D. PROCEDURES, SERVICES, OR SUPPLIES (Explain Unusual Circumstances) CPT/HCPCS	MODIFIER	E. DIAGNOSIS CODE	F. $ CHARGES	G. DAYS OR UNITS	H. EPSDT Family Plan	I. EMG	J. COB	K. RESERVED FOR LOCAL USE
02 16 04 02 16 04	22	1	19125	-80	1	72 00	1				
02 16 04 02 16 04	22	1	19126	-80	1	160 00	4				

25. FEDERAL TAX I.D. NUMBER SSN EIN
58-0089774 ☐ ☒

26. PATIENT'S ACCOUNT NO.
PATPA001 535

27. ACCEPT ASSIGNMENT? (For govt. claims, see back)
☒ YES ☐ NO

28. TOTAL CHARGE $ 232 00

29. AMOUNT PAID $ 0 00

30. BALANCE DUE $ 232 00

31. SIGNATURE OF PHYSICIAN OR SUPPLIER INCLUDING DEGREES OR CREDENTIALS (I certify that the statements on the reverse apply to this bill and are made a part thereof.)
SIGNED *Ann Tiseptic* DATE 03/2/04

32. NAME AND ADDRESS OF FACILITY WHERE SERVICES WERE RENDERED (If other than home or office)
HELPER HOSPITAL
25450 HAMMER AVE.
HUMMER TOWN, PA 15522 (878) 555-6455

33. PHYSICIAN'S, SUPPLIERS BILLING NAME, ADDRESS, ZIP CODE & PHONE #
ANN TISEPTIC, M.D.
232 AMSTER AVE., STE. 228A
AFTERALL, PA 15522 (878) 555-1055
PIN# ANN003 GRP#

(APPROVED BY AMA COUNCIL ON MEDICAL SERVICE 8/88)

PLEASE PRINT OR TYPE

FORM HCFA-1500 (12-90)
FORM OWCP-1500 FORM RRB-1500

APPROVED MOB-0938-0008

Appendix 15 – 1

Assistant Surgeon Procedures
The following is a list of surgical procedures by CPT code for which an assistant surgeon is considered NOT necessary. These procedures use an assistant surgeon in fewer than 5% of these surgeries performed in the United States. This is a partial list and is intended to be used for training and reference purposes only, as the particular company or plan guidelines may differ from those guidelines stated. Each company or plan will generally provide its own similar list. However, the list may run several hundred codes in length.

11921	25295	30140	54430	65155
17108	25909	31502	55040	66605
19125	26037	33470	55680	67101
19126	26358	36469	59821	67311
19328	26516	37700	61556	67875
21616	27358	42220	62142	68505
23020	27619	46700	63308	69631
24101	27831	52510	63746	69670
24351	28290	54110	64862	

16 Podiatric Surgery

In this chapter you will learn:

- Common foot conditions and surgical procedures.
- To process podiatric surgery claims.

Key words and concepts you will learn in this chapter:

Bone Spur – A bony overgrowth on the bone.
Bunion – An enlargement of a bone in a joint at the base of the big toe.
Ganglion – A fluid-filled sac that may grow on a joint capsule or tendon.
Hammertoes – Inherited muscle imbalances or abnormal bone lengths that can make the toes buckle under, causing the joints to contract.
Ingrown Toenail – A nail where one or both corners or sides of the nail grow into the skin of the toe.
Joint – The place where two bones meet.
Ligaments – Flexible bands of fiber joining bone to bone.
Matrixectomy – Removal of a nail margin.
Neuroma – A tumor arising from the connective tissue of the nerves.
Plantar Callus – A callus which develops when a bone is longer or lower than the others so that it hits the ground first at every step, with more force than it is equipped to handle.
Podiatry – An area of medicine that provides services for the feet.
Positional Bunion – A bony growth on the side of the metatarsal bone that enlarges the joint, forcing the joint capsule to stretch over it.
Structural Bunion – Occurs when the angle between the first and second metatarsal bones increases to a point at which it is greater than normal.
Wart – A growth caused by a virus.

Podiatry is an area of medicine that provides services for the feet. The services are usually provided by a podiatrist with the professional designation, DPM, (Doctor of Podiatric Medicine).

The joints of the feet are very complex. When surgery is performed, the claims that are received by the claims examiner will also be complex. In this chapter we will discuss some of the procedures performed on the foot and some guidelines that have been established regarding payment of podiatry claims.

General Guidelines

Because of the complexity of podiatry claims, most administrators have special handling guidelines for podiatric care and for podiatry surgery. Many plans have provisions that place a UCR limitation and a daily maximum on podiatric claims. In addition, most of these claims may also be referred to a consultant for review, prior to payment.

The UCR fee allowance for podiatric surgery is determined the same way as any other surgical procedure. The most common problem in determining the correct UCR allowance is the excessive detail in which the surgery is sometimes described. At times, the podiatrist describes and bills each procedure independently, even though some procedures are incidental to the major operation performed. Refer to the **Surgery** chapter for further information on multiple, bilateral, and incidental surgeries. The following four handling procedures may be helpful in identifying the correct breakdown of the surgeries performed:

1. Separate the procedures performed on each foot. The foot that has the most or major surgery is identified as the primary foot.
2. List the independent procedures and identify the metatarsal or phalange by digit (i.e., great toe #1, second toe #2).
3. Determine whether more than one procedure has been performed on one joint, one toe, or adjacent parts of the foot. If this has been identified, no additional allowance is made for

secondary procedures, because all such procedures are to be considered incidental (part of the major procedure).

4. After all the independent procedures for both the primary and secondary foot have been identified, the correct CPT surgical procedure code can be located.

Surgical Coding

To select the correct procedure code, identify the diagnosis and the required procedures necessary to correct the medical problem. For example, a bill with a diagnosis of "hammertoe" may list service for an arthroplasty, a capsulotomy, and a tenotomy with a separate charge for each procedure. The benefit for correction of the diagnosis (hammertoe), repair of hammertoe (CPT code 28285), should be allowed. No additional allowance is available for each separate procedure because they are included in the hammertoe repair procedure code. The following eight rules are important to consider when trying to determine the correct surgical codes:

1. Only one bunion surgery is allowable per foot.
2. Only one bone operation is allowable per toe.
3. Only one capsulotomy/tenotomy is allowable per metatarsal.
4. No increase is allowable for K wires (stabilizing wires placed in the foot). These are considered a necessary part of the procedure and do not warrant an extra benefit.
5. Generally one operation is allowable per incision.
6. Taylor's bunion is not a bunion.
7. Unna's boot (gauze soaked in zinc oxide) is considered part of the surgery itself and does not warrant an additional allowance. When the boot is used for treatment of leg ulcers, additional benefits may be allowed.
8. Flexible casts are nothing more than a tape or bandage and do not warrant a casting benefit.

Remember that these are general guidelines only. The actual administration of podiatry claims varies greatly among companies. Therefore, you should refer to the benefit plan summary prior to claim payment.

Conditions of the Foot and Treatment Procedures

The following are explanations of common foot conditions and some of the procedures performed to treat or correct problems.

Foot surgeries usually involve some incision of the skin and, in some cases, of the bone. Skin heals in phases. In the first phase, skin grows together, which allows stitches to be removed. The scar may look slightly inflamed. Some redness and swelling are normal. After about six months, the scar blends with the surrounding skin. However, scarring varies according to the individual.

Bone also heals in phases. A bone-like "cement" forms first, which bridges the affected bone and enables it to bear some weight. Later, this extra bone dissolves. The healing process varies from person to person and also depends on the health and age of the person.

Ligaments are flexible bands of fiber joining bone to bone. **Joints** are where two bones meet. Thirty-three complex joints in each foot permit flexibility.

Bunions

A **bunion** is an enlargement of a bone in a joint at the base of the big toe. Bunions are most often inherited. Contrary to what many people believe, bunions are not caused by tight shoes, although tight-fitting shoes can aggravate them. The simplest bunion procedure is the Silver procedure. The Silver procedure does not involve any surgery in the first metatarsal interspace; all other bunion procedures do.

The McBride procedure is performed to remove the bump on the outside of the first metatarsal, remove the sesamoid, and sever the abductor and short tendon. If tenotomies are not performed, the procedure is a Silver.

Reverdin or Reverdin and Green bunionectomy involves the removal of the bunion on the outside of the first metatarsal and a wedge osteotomy of the first metatarsal to bring the toe into proper alignment.

The Austin, Reverdin, Peabody, Mitchell, Wilson, and Rue bunionectomies all involve some kind of osteotomy in the head of the metatarsal and all have the same procedure code of 28296. A metatarsal base osteotomy is a valid second procedure (28306).

The Akin osteotomy involves the removal of a cylindrical wedge of the proximal phalanx of the great toe and is closed with a screw, wire or pin. This cylindrical wedge can be taken from either the distal or proximal end of the phalanx. If done with the Akin bunionectomy, the procedure code is 28298. When the Akin osteotomy and bunionectomy are performed at the same time, there should be one surgery per foot.

The Keller bunionectomy with Silastic implant involves the removal of a bunion from the first metatarsal and excision of the head of the proximal phalanx with insertion of the Silastic head into the end of the phalanx so that it forms a new gliding joint.

Positional Bunions

A **positional bunion** develops when a bony growth on the side of the metatarsal bone enlarges the joint, forcing the joint capsule to stretch over it. As this growth pushes the big toe toward the others, the tendons on the inside tighten. This then forces the big toe further out of alignment. The bunion presses against the shoe, irritating the skin and causing increased pain.

In treatment of a positional bunion (positional bunionectomy), the bump is removed (**Figure 16 – 1**). A wedge of the joint capsule may also be removed to reposition it. Tight tendons may also have to be released. A special wooden shoe or splint may be required for about three weeks postoperatively.

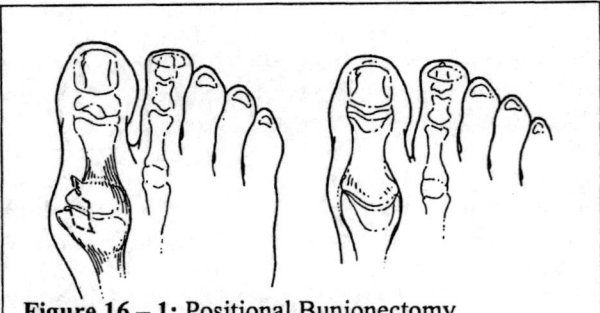

Figure 16 – 1: Positional Bunionectomy

Structural Bunions

A mild **structural bunion** occurs when the angle between the first and second metatarsal bones increases to a point at which it is greater than normal. The increased angle of the metatarsal makes the big toe bow toward the other toes. This is usually an inherited tendency. Treatment of a structural bunion (structural bunionectomy) involves repositioning the bone (**Figure 16 – 2**). A splint or a special shoe may be required for about six weeks postoperatively.

A structural bunion becomes severe when the angle between the metatarsal bones of the first and second toes grows greater than the angle of a mild structural bunion. The big toe bows toward the others, sometimes causing the second and third toes to buckle.

For a severe structural bunion, a base osteotomy may be performed to remove a wedge of bone so that the metatarsal can be repositioned. Tiny K wires or screws may be used to stabilize the bone.

The foot and ankle may be immobilized with a cast; no weight should be placed on the foot for several weeks.

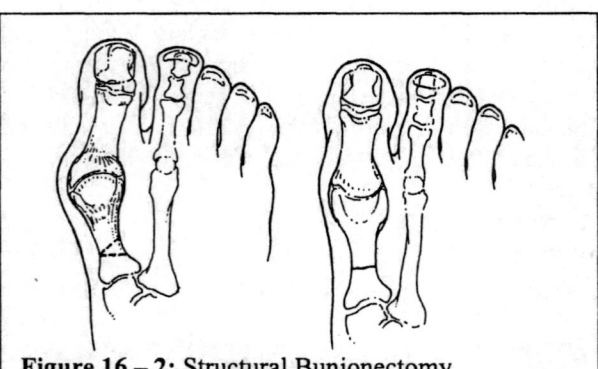

Figure 16 – 2: Structural Bunionectomy

Degenerative Disease

Degenerative disease is not a bunion, but it is often associated with bunions. This is because an untreated bunion can increase wear and tear on the joint of the big toe, break down the cartilage, and pave the way for degenerative disease such as arthritis, osteoarthritis, and rheumatoid arthritis.

Treatment of degenerative conditions involves removal of all bunions; the degenerated joint is then removed and replaced with a Silastic (plastic) implant. A splint or a special shoe may be worn for several weeks. However, the ability to walk may return within one or two days after surgery.

Taylor's Bunionectomy

Taylor's procedure is not a bunion operation, but the removal of a small bone portion of the fifth metatarsal. It is often done with an osteotomy. When the portion of the fifth metatarsal is removed, it may accompany an incidental removal of the outside of the first phalanx.

Hammertoes

Hammertoes are inherited muscle imbalances or abnormal bone lengths that can make the toes buckle under, causing their joints to contract. Subsequently, the tendons shorten. A flexible hammertoe is one in which the buckled joint can be straightened manually with the hand. These may progress and become rigid over time. Rigid hammertoes are fixed and cannot be manually straightened. Corns, irritation, pain, and loss of function are common symptoms and may be more severe in rigid than in flexible hammertoes.

Surgical Repair

There are two different types of hammertoe repair: simple and radical. Regardless of the procedure, only one hammertoe operation is allowable per toe. Some of the more common hammertoe repair procedures are tenotomy, capsulotomy, osteotomy, arthroplasty, and arthrodesis.

A **tenotomy** and **capsulotomy** are performed to release the buckling and the top and bottom tendons. The joint capsules may also have to be cut (see **Figure 16 – 3**). When a tenotomy and capsulotomy are performed on the same joint, only one operation is allowable per joint.

When an osteotomy is performed in conjunction with a tenotomy and capsulotomy, the additional procedure is incidental.

Arthroplasties and osteotomies on the same digit are generally the same procedure. In other words, one surgery is necessary to perform the other, with the latter fee covering the arthroplasty.

When an arthrodesis is being performed, only one operation is allowable per toe. The fusion may be accomplished by either screw or pin. CPT coding is determined by the procedure and the appropriate toe on which the procedure was performed. The joint most commonly fused is the second joint; occasionally, the distal joint is fused (there is no additional complexity for fusion of the distal joint).

Triple arthrodesis is an operation to fuse the three bones of the ankle joint. Multiple osteotomies are performed, and then the area is packed with bone chips and fixed in a stationary position with either pins or staples and placed in a cast for three to six months.

An **arthroplasty** is a procedure in which a portion of the joint is surgically removed and the toe is straightened. The resulting gap will fill in with fibrous tissue. Removal of the joint and fusion of the bones constitute an alternative treatment.

The fifth (little) toe may curl inward beneath the fourth toe, so that the nail faces outward. This inherited problem results in corns and pain. A derotation anthroplasty is performed to remove a wedge of skin and bone to uncurl (derotate) the toe. A bandage, splint, and sometimes a surgical shoe are required for several weeks following surgery.

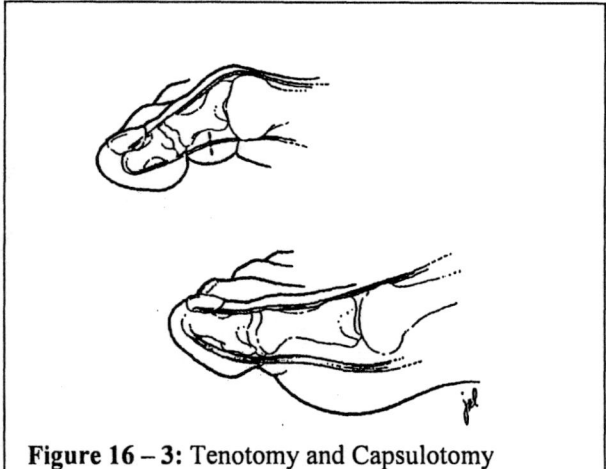

Figure 16 – 3: Tenotomy and Capsulotomy

Plantar Calluses

A **metatarsal plantar callus** occurs when the metatarsal bone is longer or lower than the others so that it hits the ground first at every step, with more force than it is equipped to handle. As a result, the skin under this bone thickens and becomes hardened into callus. The callus causes irritation and pain. The treatment is a V osteotomy in which the metatarsal bone is cut in a V shape. The end of the bone is then lifted and aligned with the other bones. The V shape holds the bone in its new position, preventing it from rocking to the left or the right.

A fifth metatarsal plantar callus is caused by walking improperly on the outside of the foot. The extra pressure may cause the skin under the bone to thicken causing irritation and pain.

Dwyer Osteotomy Surgical Procedure
The **Dwyer procedure** is the treatment for a deformity of the calcaneus or large heel bone. It consists of a wedge resection of a portion of the calcaneus bone and is closed with a staple, pin, or screw fixation.

A **dorsal osteotomy** is performed by removing a small wedge of bone from the top (dorsal) side of the base of the fifth metatarsal bone. This elevates the bone and relieves pressure on the callus. The bone is then fixated with tiny wires or screws.

Bone Spurs

A **spur** is a bony overgrowth on the bone. Bone spurs have a variety of causes and usually result in pain, interfere with the use of the foot, and detract from its appearance.

A **heel spur** is an overgrowth on the heel bone. It may be stimulated by muscles that pull from the heel bone along the bottom of the foot. High-arched feet are especially apt to have excessively tight muscles in this area.

Treatment of bone spurs involves releasing the band of tight muscles to relieve the stress. The bone spur is then surgically removed (see **Figure 16 – 4**). Crutches may be required for up to two weeks after surgery to avoid weight bearing on the foot.

A bone spur may occur alone or with a hammertoe, usually resulting in pain and interfering with the use of the foot. An overgrowth under the toe nail can press up into the tissue underneath the growth plate, deforming the nail above. This is especially painful when shoes are worn.

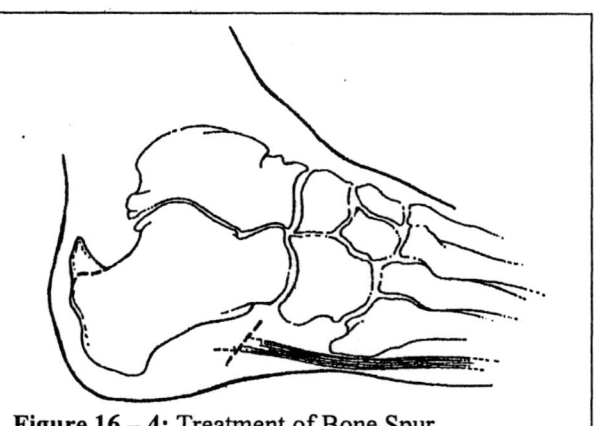

Figure 16 – 4: Treatment of Bone Spur.

Common Surgical Procedures
The most common exostosis (bony growth) on the foot is the heel spur. In most cases, surgery is the most effective way to treat a heel spur. A plantar fasciotomy performed at the same time as a surgery for heel spurs is an incidental procedure, since a fasciotomy must be done to cut through the area before the heel spur is located. In many cases, the use of **orthosis** (an orthopedic appliance) is as effective as the surgery.

Treatment for subungual exostosis is performed to smooth down the spur with a tiny rasp. The rasp resembles a dental burr and is inserted through a small incision.

Ingrown Toenails

A **nail** is **ingrown** when one or both corners or sides of the nail grow into the skin of the toe. Irritation, redness, an uncomfortable sensation of warmth, swelling, pain, and infection can result.

Surgical Procedures

Removal of a nail margin can be done with or without the excision of the root or matrix. To allow surgical benefits for the total excision of the nail and matrix, it must be indicated that the root and matrix are being permanently removed. Excision of subungual exostosis is sometimes used to describe the removal of one or two margins. This is not a separate procedure.

On a partial ingrown toenail, only one or two sides grow into the skin. The treatment is a partial matrixectomy in which a wedge of the nail and the underlying nail bed are removed. The nail portion can be surgically removed with a scalpel or by chemical means. This is a simple and brief procedure.

In severe cases of ingrown toenails, the entire nail grows into the skin on both sides. This is called a completely ingrown toenail. Usually, significant pain is present. Treatment is a total **matrixectomy** in which the nail and growth plate are removed either surgically or chemically (see **Figure 16 – 5**). The body then produces a "**false nail**," that is, tough skin that mimics a real nail. This false nail usually grows in within a few months after the surgery.

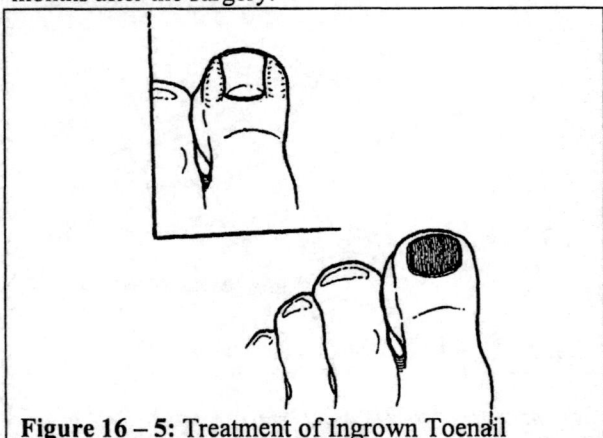

Figure 16 – 5: Treatment of Ingrown Toenail

Warts

Warts are caused by a virus and are contagious. They often grow in groups and spread to the fingers and other areas of the body. Warts occurring on the soles of the feet are called plantar warts, which are painful and may affect walking. Usually, these warts grow on the soles, but may occur on the toes or on the top of the foot. Treatment entails scooping out the wart with a curette, a

spoon-shaped surgical instrument. The base is then cauterized (burned either electrically or chemically) to discourage regrowth.

Neuromas

A **neuroma** is a tumor arising from the connective tissue of the nerves. Although there are four interspaces, neuromas most often occur in the second interspace. Neuromas are commonly bilateral, but rarely does more than one occur on the same foot or in the first interspace.

If any other surgical procedure is preformed on the first toe or on the M-P joint of the second, third, fourth, or fifth toes, no additional allowance is available for removal of neuromas from the adjacent interspace. This procedure should not call for any increased allowance for microsurgery.

When a nerve is pinched between two metatarsal bones (usually the third and fourth metatarsal), enlargement of the nerve may occur. Abnormal bone structure contributes to the cause, but too-tight shoes can aggravate the condition. The treatment is to remove a small portion of the nerve. As a result, this area is permanently numbed.

Ganglions

Ganglions are fluid-filled sacs that may grow on a joint capsule or tendon (**see Figure 16 – 6**). The location and size vary. The cause is unknown. Ganglions cause irritation, swelling, and pain when they press against nerves.

Treatment involves excision of the ganglion by separating it from the surrounding tissues. If not removed completely, a ganglion may grow back.

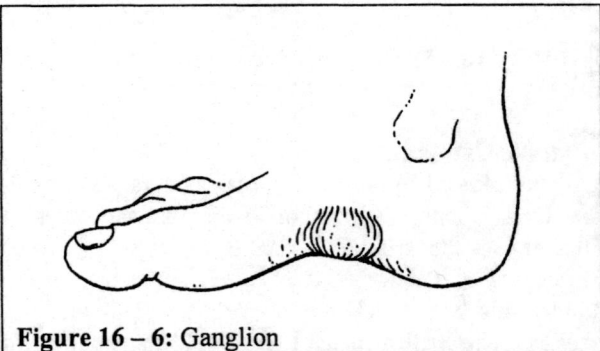

Figure 16 – 6: Ganglion

Miscellaneous

High-arched feet (pes cavus) are caused by an imbalance of muscles and nerves and is often inherited. High arches can cause various problems such as foot, heel, ankle, or tendon pain and calluses. Treatment depends on specific problems. Usually, surgery or orthosis is prescribed.

Flat feet (pes planus) are also hereditary and are caused by a muscle imbalance. Feet with low, relaxed arches may create problems such as hammertoes and bunions; arch, foot, and leg fatigue; calf pain; and an overly tight heel cord (which makes the foot even flatter). Loose joints move too freely causing pain and instability. Surgery and orthoses may also be used to treat this condition. **Orthotic devices** are prescribed custom-made arch supports that fit inside most shoes and "bring the floor up to your feet." To make this support, a plaster impression of the feet is made. The orthotic device is made of leather, plastic, or other material, depending on the particular foot problem based on the impression.

Assistant Surgeon

Because of the complexity of the bones, joints, and tendons in the foot, many podiatric surgeries that are performed on an inpatient basis require an assistant surgeon. However, some of these surgeries when performed in a doctor's office may also require an assistant surgeon.

It is generally accepted medical practice to allow an assistant surgeon when doing soft tissue work. The exception to this is for ingrown toenails. Multiple or bilateral procedures may also require an assistant surgeon.

Single-toe procedures for excision of dome and simple hammertoe procedures usually do not warrant the use of an assistant surgeon.

When allowed, the assistant surgeon's benefits are paid according to the standard policy provisions for assistant surgeons.

Referrals

Because of the difficulty in determining allowable expense and the correct surgical allowance, questionable claim situations should be referred to a supervisor, review department or consultant. Following are some guidelines or situations that may warrant a consultant's review:
- Charges for the insertion or removal of K wire.
- Microsurgical repair of nerves.
- **Serial surgery.** (Serial surgery is surgery on several individual toes or joints with one surgical procedure being performed in a single operative visit, i.e., surgery on one toe followed by surgery on another toe one week later, followed by still other surgeries after that. Or, it is surgery on one joint, followed by surgery on a different joint of the same toe at a later date.) It can last days, weeks, or even months.
- Fragmented fees billed at 100% for each procedure. This situation may also include misrepresented procedure codes.
- Vascular studies (i.e., temperature gradient studies, Doppler studies, or plethysmography).

These tests can be considered medically necessary in certain situations or for certain conditions (i.e., diabetes, peripheral vascular disease). Test results and the patient's history are needed for review.
- Possible unnecessary services or procedures. These can include:
  - Use of nitrous oxide anesthesia.
  - Operating room charge for office surgery.
  - Preoperative sedatives.
  - Use of steroid injections, arthrocentesis or power equipment on the day of surgery.
  - Rental of TENS unit.
  - More than two post-operative x-rays. The exception is in the case of major bone surgery and delayed bunion surgery.

When referring a claim for review, the claims examiner should request all necessary documentation before referring the claim. Necessary documentation includes the operating report and the patient diagnosis and history as well as the claim. In addition, diagnostic tests, before and after photos, x-rays, and the physician's daily office notes may also be necessary for review on some claims.

If a claim is sent for referral, the claims examiner should first make a determination and payment on any and all services that are not being questioned. Written notification should accompany the payment regarding which services are being held, pending a consultant's review.

When the consultant's review is received, some services may be allowed and others denied. The claims examiner should verify the plan guidelines and benefits, and make a payment determination on the claim.

The consultant's report and the name, address, and phone number of the consultant are the property of the company and should never be given to the claimant.

This information should be retained as part of the claim file.

Summary

The charges for podiatry services vary from simple to complex. These guidelines will assist you in identifying podiatry services. They will also enable you to determine which podiatry services are covered and which services have limitations.

Because podiatry surgery guidelines vary from company to company, check with the administrator before processing these types of claims.

Assignments

Complete the Questions for Review.

Questions for Review

Directions: Answer the following questions without looking back into the material just covered. Write your answers in the space provided.

1. What is podiatric surgery? _____

   _____

2. Define ligaments. _____

   _____

3. How many complex joints are in the foot? _____

4. How many bunion surgeries are normally allowed per foot? _____

5. What is an orthotic device? _____

   _____

   _____

If you were unable to answer any of the questions, refer back to the section and then complete the answers.

Honors Certification™

The Honors Certification™ challenge for this chapter is a written test of the information contained within this chapter. Each incorrect answer will result in a deduction of between 1% and 5% from your grade. You must achieve a score of 85% or higher to pass this test. If you fail the test on your first attempt you may retake the test one additional time. The items included in the second test may be different from those in the first test.

17 Anesthesia

In this chapter you will learn:

- To define the four methods of anesthesia administration.
- The anesthesia CPT code ranges (00100 - 01999).
- The anesthesia RVS code ranges (10000 - 69999).
- To identify anesthesia modifiers.
- To calculate anesthesia benefits (both base and time units).

Key words and concepts you will learn in this chapter:

Acupuncture – An ancient Chinese procedure in which fine needles are inserted into various points in the body to relieve pain and to regulate and improve body functions.

Epidural Anesthesia – Anesthesia which blocks the nerves in the epidural space.

General Anesthesia – Anesthesia that produces a state of unconsciousness.

Hypnosis – A state where the subconscious mind is allowed to take over, and the conscious mind is more or less inactive.

Intravenous (IV) Sedation – A medication composed of a sedative and a painkiller administered intravenously. A semiconscious state is produced.

Local Anesthesia – Anesthesia that affects only a localized area.

Monitored Anesthesia Care (MAC) – The monitoring of a patient's vital signs during an operation, in anticipation of the need for a general anesthesia.

Regional Anesthesia – Anesthesia that produces the loss of sensation of a part of the body due to the interruption of nerve conduction.

Topical Anesthesia – An anesthetic that is applied directly to the surface of the area to be anesthetized.

Nerve Block Anesthesia – Anesthesia produced by injecting a drug close to the nerve so that the nerve impulses are interrupted, thereby producing a loss of sensation.

Spinal Anesthesia – A specialized type of nerve block where the spinal nerves are blocked in either the subarachnoid or the epidural space.

Anesthesia is the artificially induced loss of feeling and sensation with or without loss of consciousness. The four kinds of anesthesia administration are:
1. General anesthesia
2. Regional anesthesia
3. Intravenous (IV) sedation
4. Acupuncture

General Anesthesia

General anesthesia produces a state of unconsciousness. It may be brought about by inhalation of drugs such as ether, nitrous oxide, and ethylene or by drugs administered intravenously such as sodium pentothal. General anesthesia produces preliminary excitement, replaced by a loss of voluntary control. Loss of consciousness occurs when the anesthetic reaches the brain, with hearing being the last sense to be lost. Most major operations, particularly on the upper abdomen, chest, head, and neck, are performed under general anesthesia. A number of side effects may accompany general anesthesia, many of which cannot be controlled or predicted. General anesthesia is considered more dangerous than other forms of anesthesia. Therefore, anesthesiologists have one of the highest malpractice insurance rates.

Prior to surgery requiring general anesthesia, the anesthesiologist usually meets with the patient to assess his or her general health, and record age, weight, concurrent medical problems, family history, and other pertinent data. Anesthesiologists are reluctant to administer general anesthesia to patients who are extremely obese or who have blood pressure or respiratory problems because they have the highest risk factors.

General anesthesia can be used in outpatient surgery. However, it requires a prolonged post-operative recovery period (usually 2 to 4 hours) and therefore, is commonly reserved for use in a facility setting (outpatient hospital, surgicenter). The administration of general anesthesia in a doctor's or dentist's office is considered very dangerous, although some specialists do so routinely.

Regional Anesthesia

Regional anesthesia is the loss of sensation of a part of the body due to the interruption of nerve conduction. While regional anesthesia is in effect, the patient remains conscious. This method is adequate for many operations and is considerably less dangerous than general anesthesia. Regional anesthesia can be safely performed on an outpatient basis. The three types of regional anesthesia are topical, local, and nerve block.

Topical anesthesia is applied directly to the surface of the area to be anesthetized. The conjunctiva and mucous membranes of the mouth, throat, urethra, and bladder are examples of areas that are most effectively anesthetized by a topical application.

Local anesthesia affects only a localized area. The drug is directly introduced by injection into the skin and subcutaneous tissues. The anesthesia injection wears off very quickly; therefore, only short procedures can be performed painlessly. Superficial biopsies, mole excisions, and suturing of lacerations are the most common procedures performed with local anesthesia.

For a **nerve block anesthesia**, a drug is injected close to the nerve so that the nerve impulses are interrupted, thereby producing a loss of sensation.

Spinal anesthesia is a specialized type of nerve block. The spinal nerves are blocked in either the subarachnoid or the epidural space. The term **spinal anesthesia** generally refers to nerves blocked in the subarachnoid space. **Epidural anesthesia** refers to the nerves blocked in the epidural space. Epidural anesthesia is frequently used for maternity claims.

According to the American Society of Anesthesiologists (ASA) guidelines, the anesthesia value for maternity claims is base units + time units. Since the epidural is administered throughout labor and the physician is not in constant attendance, many insurance carriers and PPO organizations have developed special guidelines for maternity anesthesia. To process these claims accurately, be sure to develop a full understanding of the office procedures.

Another type of spinal anesthetic is a **saddle block**. This is so named because the injection produces a loss of feeling in the region of the body that corresponds to the area that makes contact with a riding saddle (buttocks, perineum, and thighs). Spinal anesthesia was formerly used frequently for normal deliveries. Now, it is mainly used on operations within the peritoneal cavity and on the lower extremities.

Intravenous Sedation

Intravenous (IV) sedation is a medication composed of a sedative and a painkiller administered intravenously. A semiconscious state is produced. A common mixture is meperidine (Demerol) and diazepam (Valium). This type of anesthesia is often used in dental surgical procedures and in many diagnostic procedures such as bronchoscopy and esophagogastroduodenoscopy in which the surgical invasion is obtained through an existing orifice. This type of anesthesia is commonly referred to as "**twilight sleep**."

Acupuncture

Acupuncture is an ancient Chinese procedure in which fine needles are inserted into various points in the body to relieve pain and to regulate and improve body functions. There are more than 1000 acupuncture locations on the body. A different physiological effect is produced in each location or combination of locations. Sometimes, only one needle is necessary to achieve the desired result; and sometimes many needles are required. The patient remains awake and can talk during the procedure. Acupuncture works similarly to the way nerve block anesthesia works. Although this type of anesthesia is popular in China, it is also used in the United States.

Hypnosis

Hypnosis is a state where the subconscious mind is allowed to take over, and the conscious mind is more or less inactive. Some patients will choose hypnosis rather than conventional forms of anesthesia.

Most plans do not cover hypnosis services, though a few may allow coverage for hypnosis used in lieu of covered anesthesia.

Handling Procedures

An anesthesiologist may be classified as either a **hospital staff anesthesiologist** (employed by the hospital) or an **independent anesthesiologist** (self-employed or not employed by the hospital). Charges made by a hospital for the services of a staff anesthesiologist are usually covered as a hospital ancillary expense.

Charges by an outside anesthesiologist vary according to plan provision, but are usually covered under either a separate Basic anesthesia benefit or under a Major Medical benefit. When processing claims, do not confuse the professional anesthesia expense with the charges that may appear on a hospital bill. The anesthesia charges on a hospital bill are for the actual anesthesia drug, the anesthesia machine, and other associated supplies.

Anesthesia may be administered by any of the following individuals:

Medical doctor (M.D.)
Anesthesiologist (Anes.)
Certified registered nurse anesthetist (CRNA)
Anesthesia assistant (AA)

RVS Ground Rules

The American Society of Anesthesiologists developed a coding system which has been adopted by the CPT. The CPT code range for anesthesia is 00100 – 01999. The RVS uses 00100 – 01999 or 10000 – 69999 (same as surgery) for coding anesthesia services. Anesthesia unit values are listed in the RVS for procedures that require that anesthesia be administered by an anesthesiologist. Remember that local anesthesia is never allowable separately. Therefore, anesthesia benefits are those that are allowed on procedures that require more than a local anesthesia.

These units (for all schedules) are used when:

- The anesthesia is personally administered by a licensed physician.
- The physician remains in constant attendance during the procedure for the sole purpose of administering and monitoring the anesthesia service.

Basic/Base Units

The basic or base anesthesia units are designed to allow for the usual pre- and post-operative care, the administration of anesthesia, and the administration of fluids or blood incident to the anesthesia or surgery. Usually monitoring services such as ecg, blood pressure oximetry, capnography, mass spectrometry, and monitoring of blood gases are also included in the basic value and should not be billed separately.

Remember that the surgical unit values include surgery, local infiltration, and digital block or topical anesthesia.

Time Units

The length of time that a person is under anesthesia determines the amount of money that will be considered allowable for the procedure. Anesthesia time begins when the anesthesiologist starts to physically prepare the patient for the induction of anesthesia in the operating room area (or its equivalent). The time ends when the anesthesiologist is no longer in constant attendance, usually when the patient is ready for post-operative supervision.

There are two ways of calculating the anesthesia time, depending on individual payor guidelines:

1. Actual time, and
2. Block time.

Actual Time

Some carriers allow one time unit for each fifteen minutes, regardless of the amount of time a patient is under anesthesia. Any fractional portions of a fifteen minute block (i.e., five minutes) are calculated to the nearest tenth of a unit. Thus, each 1.5 minutes is worth 0.1 units.

Block Time

For the first four hours, time units are computed by allowing 1.0 time unit for each 15 minutes, or if less than 15 minutes, 1.0 unit is allowed for spans between five and 15 minutes. After four hours, 1.0 unit is allowed for each 10 minutes, or if less than 10 minutes, 1.0 unit is allowed for spans between five and 10 minutes. The reason for this is that the risks of injury or adverse effects significantly increase with time. Therefore, extra compensation is provided for extended anesthesia time.

For example, if the anesthesia time were 50 minutes, a total of 4.0 time units would be allowed: 1.0 unit for every 15 minutes = 3.0 units, plus 1.0 unit for the additional five minutes. Therefore, the same number of units would be allowed for a 50-minute procedure, a 55-minute procedure, or a one-hour procedure.

Anesthesia Time	Units of Occurrence
5 min – 19 min	1 unit
20 – 34 min	2 units
35 min – 49 min	3 units
50 min – 1 hr 49 min	4 units
1 hr 5 min – 1 hr 19 min	5 units
1 hr 20 min – 1 hr 34 min	6 units
1 hr 35 min – 1 hr 49 min	7 units
1 hr 50 min – 2 hr 4 min	8 units
2 hr 5 min – 2 hr 19 min	9 units
2 hr 20 min – 2 hr 34 min	10 units
2 hr 35 min – 2 hr 49 min	11 units
2 hr 50 min – 3 hr 4 min	12 units
3 hr 5 min – 3 hr 19 min	13 units
3 hr 20 min – 3 hr 34 min	14 units
3 hr 35 min – 3 hr 49 min	15 units
3 hr 50 min – 4 hr 4 min	16 units
4 hr 5 min – 4 hr 14 min	17 units
4 hr 15 min – 4 hr 24 min	18 units
4 hr 25 min – 4 hr 34 min	19 units
4 hr 35 min – 4 hr 44 min	20 units
4 hr 45 min – 4 hr 54 min	21 units
4 hr 55 min – 5 hr 4 min	22 units

Many anesthesiologists bill time according to a military clock, that is, by a 24-hour standard. When using military time, do not worry about converting the time to a regular clock. The regular time is unimportant.

Instead, concentrate only on determining the time units involved. For instance:

1. Total time: 13:15 to 14:25
   13:15 to 14:15 = 1 hour = 4.0 units
   14:15 to 14:25 = <u>10 min = 1.0 unit</u>
   1 hr 10 min = 5.0 units

2. Total time: 15:20 to 18:25
   15:20 to 18:20 = 3 hours = 12.0 units
   18:20 to 18:25 = <u>5 min = 1.0 unit</u>
   3 hr 5 min = 13.0 units

Exceptions

Time units are not allowed for the following procedures/situations:

- Regional anesthesia upper or lower extremity (01995).
- Daily management of epidural of subarachnoid drug administration (01996).
- Administration of epidural anesthesia for maternal delivery (62282).
- 01997
- 02020
- 99100
- 99116
- 99135
- 99140

These codes are normally paid at the base units multiplied by the conversion factor. No allowance is made for time units.

Calculating Anesthesia

The anesthesia allowance is calculated by adding the basic units to the time units and multiplying that amount by the conversion factor. This procedure applies to all schedules.

Basic Unit Value for the procedure
+ Time Unit Value
+ <u>Modifier Unit Value (if applicable)</u>
Total Anesthesia Value

Total Anesthesia Value X plan/Basic Conversion Factor = Anesthesia basic allowance or plan UCR.

Multiple Procedures

For anesthesia claims with multiple procedures, the basic units for the major procedure (the procedure with the greatest number of basic units) are the only basic units allowed. The basic units for the secondary procedure are not taken into account. The additional expense is accommodated by allowing the extra time units necessitated for completion of the multiple procedures.

Network Anesthesia

Carriers which pay different percentages for network and non-network providers will often base anesthesia payments on the network schedule, regardless of whether the anesthesiologist is a part of their network or not. This is because the surgeon usually chooses the anesthesiologist. Thus, the patient is not penalized for a choice they were not allowed to make.

Modifiers

In addition to the modifiers listed above which denote who performed the services, some carriers use additional modifiers for anesthesia services.

Physical status modifiers are represented by the initial P, followed by a single digit from 1 to 6.

P1: A normal healthy patient

P2: A patient with mild systemic disease

P3: A patient with severe systemic disease

P4: A patient with severe systemic disease that is a constant threat to life

P5: A moribund patient who is not expected to survive without the operation

P6: A declared brain-dead patient whose organs are being removed for donor purposes

Optional modifiers denote special conditions. The following are the valid anesthesia two-digit modifier codes (for additional information, consult your CPT):

-22: Unusual services

-23: Unusual anesthesia

-32: Mandated services

-47: Anesthesia by surgeon

-51: Multiple procedures, but not bilateral

-75: Concurrent care, services rendered by more than one physician

Some carriers require that a modifier be used to identify who performed the anesthesia service and the type of service. These modifiers are HCPCS Level II modifiers. The following modifier codes are used for this purpose:

AA: Anesthesia services performed by anesthesiologist.

AD: Anesthesia was medically supervised by a physician for more than four concurrent procedures.

QK: Medically directed by a physician: two through four concurrent procedures.

QX: Anesthesia administered by a CRNA with medical direction by a physician.

QY: Medical direction on one CRNA by an anesthesiologist.

QZ: Anesthesia administered by CRNA without medical direction by a physician.

Many providers will allow additional units for some modifiers.

Example:

P1 – No additional value
P2 – No additional value
P3 – 1 additional unit
P4 – 2 additional units
P5 – 3 additional units
P6 – No additional units

Unusual Circumstances

Occasionally the use of modifier –22 or –23 will indicate that unusual procedures were performed. This modifier is often used to explain why the amount of time shown on an anesthesia claim is greater than usual. **Unusual services** are services that are rarely provided, unusual, or variable and may warrant an additional anesthesia fee. These situations can include:

- Severe or multiple injuries,
- Procedures in the head, neck or shoulder region which can disrupt the administration of anesthesia,
- Unusual or lengthy monitoring,
- Procedures where care must be taken to avoid certain areas of the body, and
- Procedures or situations where the patient must be placed in an unusual position (i.e., sitting).

When processing these claims, the examiner should request a copy of the operative report, the hospital medical records, detailed records from the anesthesiologist regarding the services performed and the length of time under anesthesia. These reports will provide information to determine if the correct code was billed by the anesthesiologist, or if additional complications were involved which could increase the amount of time the anesthesiologist was in attendance with the patient.

Some insurance carriers will allow an additional percentage for unusual services claims (i.e., an additional 25% benefit), and some will allow a specific amount of units (i.e., an additional 3 units is not uncommon). Additionally, there are a number of other carriers who do not allow any additional benefit. The rationale for not allowing more is that the additional time involved in the procedure is enough to compensate the anesthesiologist for the unusual services. Be sure to consult plan guidelines prior to processing claims with unusual services modifiers. Many of these claims may need to be referred for medical review.

Qualifying Circumstances

Many anesthesia services are provided under particularly difficult circumstances, depending on factors such as extraordinary conditions of the patient, notable operative conditions, and unusual risk factors. This section includes a list of important qualifying circumstances that make a significant impact on the character of the anesthesia service provided. These procedures would not be reported alone, but as additional procedures qualifying an anesthesia procedure or service. More than one may be selected.

99100   Anesthesia for patient of extreme age, under one year or over 70 years.

99116   Anesthesia complicated by use of total body hypothermia.

99135   Anesthesia complicated by use of controlled hypotension.

99140   Anesthesia complicated by emergency conditions. Most plans require emergency conditions to be specified. Treatment is considered emergency treatment when its delay would lead to a significant increase in the threat to life or body part.

Many providers will allow additional units for qualifying circumstances.

Example:

99100 – 1 additional unit
99116 – 5 additional units
99135 – 5 additional units
99140 – 2 additional units

Monitored Anesthesia Care

Monitored anesthesia care (MAC) is the monitoring of a patient's vital signs during an operation, in anticipation of the need for general anesthesia. This can be due to:

- The anticipation of an adverse physiological reaction by the patient to the procedure.
- Patients with low pain thresholds or who may experience intense pain.
- Expected expansion of the operative field (i.e., a mass is biopsied under a local anesthetic, however, if the surgeon locates additional tumors, more radical surgery would be done during the same operative session).
- Combative patients.
- Neonatal or pediatric patients who may become frightened and/or combative.
- Mentally impaired patients who may become uncooperative due to their impairment.
- The administration of drugs which are required to be administered by an anesthesiologist, even though they may not produce unconsciousness in a patient.

In order for an anesthesiologist to be reimbursed for MAC, the following services are required:

- Pre-operative visit and evaluation, including medical history, anesthesia history, taking of medication information, and physical exam,
- Pre-operative evaluation of all available pertinent reports (lab, x-ray, etc.),
- Patient discussion and informed consent,
- Monitoring of vital signs during the operative procedure, including oxygenation, ventilation, circulation, temperature, and maintenance of the patient's airway,
- Diagnosis and treatment of any clinical problems which occur during the procedure,
- Administration of medications or other agents to ensure patient safety and comfort during the procedure,
- Post-operative patient management, including evaluation of the patient, time based record of vital signs and level of consciousness, reporting of any complications, adverse reactions or unusual events,
- Post-anesthesia visits (as needed), and
- A complete record of all drugs used and amounts.

In order for MAC to be reimbursed, the anesthesiologist must be present during the entire operative procedure. If all above requirements are met, a MAC anesthesiologist is reimbursed at the same amount as routine anesthesiology, since the same level of attention and care is required.

The modifier –QS on the claim will denote that the claim is for MAC services.

Medical Direction of Anesthesiology

At times the actual monitoring of the patient will be performed by an anesthesia assistant or a CRNA under the direction of a physician. In such cases, the physician is responsible for:

- The pre-operative evaluation of the patient,
- Ordering the drugs,
- Determining the anesthesia treatment plan,
- Handling or participating in the most demanding anesthesia procedures, including induction and emergence,
- Monitors the course of anesthesia and the patient's situation at frequent intervals,
- Handles any emergency situations, and
- Provides all post-anesthesia care.

The assistant anesthesiologist or CRNA is responsible for:

- Understanding the anesthesia plan,

- The continuous administration of the anesthesia ,
- Monitoring the patient's vitals, and
- Remaining in contact with the physician and summoning him or her if needed.

This allows a directing physician to handle anesthesia for several patients at the same time. However, most payors limit the number of patient's a physician may direct at one time to four or less.

In such cases most carriers will split the anesthesiologist allowance 50% to the directing physician and 50% to the assistant anesthesiologist or CRNA, provided the directing physician is not directing the care of more than four patients concurrently. If the physician is directing the care of more than four patients at a time, some payor will reduce reimbursement to 25% for the directing physician and 75% for the assistant anesthesiologist or CRNA. Others will consider the anesthesiologists services to be supervisory. In other words, they are simply overseeing the work of the assistant anesthesiologist or CRNA, not directing their work. Reimbursement for supervisory anesthesiologists is often calculated at three base units per procedure. No time units are allowed, unless an anesthesiologist can document that they were present and attending during the induction of the anesthesia. If this can be documented, one time unit is allowed.

Anesthesiologists are required to certify the number of patients for whom concurrent care was handled at any given time during the operative session.

Pain Control

Occasionally an anesthesiologist may be called upon to perform services to ease intractable or chronic pain. **Intractable pain** is pain which is hard to manage, and is often severe enough to limit a patient's movement or abilities.

In such cases, relief may be obtained through an injection or intravenous infusion of pain medication.

Many insurance carriers will allow payment for these services if certain conditions are met, as follows:

- The pain cannot be managed through other means (i.e., oral or traditional pain medications),
- The pain is severe enough that it interferes with daily living,
- A complete medical evaluation has been performed to asses the source of the pain,
- All other reasonable medical treatments (including psychological approaches) were considered or tried and found to be unsuccessful or potentially harmful,
- Electrical stimulation (TENS) was found to be unsuccessful, and

- Pharmacological or physical therapy programs were found to be unsuccessful or potentially harmful.

Often block treatments for intractable pain are limited to three per year. Medical records should be requested to evaluate the success of the treatment. These cases will often need to be referred for review.

Patient Controlled Anesthesia

Some conditions allow the patient to administer their own pain medication (or anesthetic). This is often done through an **infusion pump**. This is a machine which contains medication and administers a small dose when a button is depressed. The machine is attached to the outside of the body, with a line running into a vein (for intravenous medications) or under the skin (for subcutaneous medications). Safeguards on the machine prevent an overdose, and prevent a second dose from being administered before a first dose has had a chance to take effect.

Infusion pumps have been shown to provide equal or better pain relief with a lower overall dosage level.

Many carriers will allow benefits for the placement and use of an infusion pump if all of the following criteria are met:

- The unit and pain medication are prescribed by a licensed physician,
- The medical condition being treated is a covered expense,
- The medical condition being treated requires long-term pain control,
- The pain is manageable by pharmacological means and no other pain control (or very limited additional pain control) is necessary, and
- The unit is used in a hospital setting, or, if used in a home setting, the use is monitored by an RN on a regular basis.

As with many other new forms of anesthesia, plan guidelines vary widely. Be sure to check contract provisions before processing infusion pump claims. If the plan does allow for payment, there will often be separate charges for the infusion pump, professional charges for the placement of the infusion pump, and charges for the medications to be placed in the infusion pump.

Miscellaneous

Epidural anesthesia is often provided during labor for normal deliveries. Time of administration tends to run 4 or more hours. Some administrators provide their own rules, and some plans do not cover anesthesia during labor at all. Therefore, verify the guidelines that apply to the plan you are processing.

General anesthesia is usually administered when shock therapy is provided. Many plans do not cover it for this purpose or may have special handling guidelines. Verify before processing.

A standby anesthetist may be asked to be available while diagnostic procedures are performed on a patient who may require emergency surgery. If the anesthesiologist is not rendering treatment, administering anesthesia, monitoring vital signs, etc., but is merely making a charge for being available, the charge is usually not a covered expense. However, verify first before processing.

If surgery is cancelled for medical reasons, prior to the surgery, the anesthesiologist may be allowed reimbursement for evaluation and management. In such cases an E&M code should be used. Full documentation of the reason for the cancellation of surgery should be included with the claim.

Summary

Anesthesia plays an important role in patient care. Anesthesia in certain situations has been shown to help the patient recover more rapidly than if anesthesia were not used.

The guidelines we have just covered will enable you to process anesthesia charges, no matter what method or type of anesthesia is administered. There is almost always an anesthesia charge when major surgery is performed and you as the claims examiner are responsible for processing these charges. Use the preceding guidelines to calculate anesthesia time and to identify the provider of services (anesthesiologist, nurse anesthetist, or surgeon).

Assignments

Complete the Questions for Review.
Complete Exercises 17 – 1 to 17 – 3.

Questions for Review

Directions: Answer the following questions without looking back into the material just covered. Write your answers in the space provided.

1. What are the four methods of anesthesia administration?

    1. _____

    2. _____

    3. _____

    4. _____

2. What is the ASA code range for anesthesia? _____

3. What is the RVS code range for anesthesia? _____

4. The total anesthesia unit values consist of _____ and _____ units.

5. (True or False?) Most plans cover anesthesia for shock therapy. _____

If you were unable to answer any of the questions, refer back to the section and complete the answers.

Exercises 17 – 1 to 17 – 3

Directions: Process each of the anesthesia service claims found on the following pages.

Honors Certification™

The Honors Certification™ challenge for this chapter is a written test of the information contained within this chapter. Additionally you will be asked to process three anesthesia claims. Each incorrect answer will result in a deduction of between 1% and 5% from your grade. You must achieve a score of 85% or higher to pass this test. If you fail the test on your first attempt you may retake the test one additional time. The items included in the second test may be different from those in the first test.

PLEASE
DO NOT
STAPLE
IN THIS
AREA
☐☐☐ PICA

ROVER INSURERS INC.
5931 ROLLING ROAD
RONSON, CO 81369

APPROVED MOB-0938-0008

CLAIM ANESI

HEALTH INSURANCE CLAIM FORM

PICA ☐☐☐

1. MEDICARE MEDICAID CHAMPUS CHAMPVA GROUP HEALTH PLAN FECA BLK LUNG OTHER	INSURED'S I.D NUMBER (FOR PROGRAM IN ITEM 1)
☐ (Medicare #) ☐ (Medicaid #) ☐ (Sponsor's SSN) ☐ (VA File #) ☒ (SSN or ID) ☐ (SSN) ☐ (ID)	999-99-9999

2. PATIENT'S NAME (Last, First, Middle Initial)
BOSSY, BETTY B.

3. PATIENT'S BIRTH DATE MM DD YY SEX
09 19 39 M☐ F☒

4. INSURED'S NAME (Last, First, Middle Initial)
BOSSY, BETTY B.

5. PATIENT'S ADDRESS (No., Street)
7991 BAGEL BLVD.
CITY BARSTOW STATE NY
ZIP CODE 12899
TELEPHONE (914) 555-3399

6. PATIENT'S RELATIONSHIP TO INSURED
Self ☒ Spouse ☐ Child ☐ Other ☐

8. PATIENT STATUS
Single ☐ Married ☒ Other ☐
Employed ☒ Full-Time ☐ Part-Time ☐ Student Student

7. INSURED'S ADDRESS (No., Street)
7991 BAGEL BLVD.
CITY BARSTOW STATE NY
ZIP CODE 12899
TELEPHONE (914) 555-3399

9. OTHER INSURED'S NAME (Last, First, Middle Initial)

a. OTHER INSURED'S POLICY OR GROUP NUMBER

a. OTHER INSURED'S DATE OF BIRTH MM DD YY SEX M☐ F☐

c. EMPLOYER'S NAME OR SCHOOL NAME

d. INSURANCE PLAN NAME OR PROGRAM NAME

10. IS PATIENT'S CONDITION RELATED TO:
a. EMPLOYMENT? (CURRENT OR PREVIOUS) ☐ YES ☒ NO
b. AUTO ACCIDENT? ☐ YES ☒ NO PLACE (State)
c. OTHER ACCIDENT? ☐ YES ☒ NO
10d. RESERVED FOR LOCAL USE

11. INSURED'S POLICY GROUP OR FECA NUMBER:
999-99-NIN
a. INSURED'S DATE OF BIRTH MM DD YY SEX
09 19 39 M☐ F☒
b. EMPLOYER'S NAME OR SCHOOL NAME
NINJA CORPORATION
c. INSURANCE PLAN NAME OR PROGRAM NAME
NINJA PLAN
d. IS THERE ANOTHER HEALTH BENEFIT PLAN? ☐ YES ☒ NO

12. PATIENT'S OR AUTHORIZED PERSON'S SIGNATURE
SIGNED SIGNATURE ON FILE DATE 02/06/04

13. INSURED'S OR AUTHORIZED PERSON'S SIGNATURE
SIGNED SIGNATURE ON FILE

14. DATE OF CURRENT: ILLNESS/INJURY/PREGNANCY
02 06 04

15. IF PATIENT HAS HAD SAME OR SIMILAR ILLNESS

16. DATES PATIENT UNABLE TO WORK
FROM TO

17. NAME OF REFERRING PHYSICIAN

17a. I.D. NUMBER OF REFERRING PHYSICIAN

18. HOSPITALIZATION DATES
FROM 02 06 04 TO 02 14 04

19. RESERVED FOR LOCAL USE

20. OUTSIDE LAB? ☐ YES ☐ NO $ CHARGES

21. DIAGNOSIS OR NATURE OF ILLNESS OR INJURY
1. 410.91
2.
3.
4.

22. MEDICAID RESUBMISSION CODE ORIGINAL REF. NO.
23. PRIOR AUTHORIZATION NUMBER

24. A DATE(S) OF SERVICE From To MM DD YY MM DD YY	B Place	C Type	D PROCEDURES CPT/HCPS MODIFIER	E DIAGNOSIS CODE	F $ CHARGES	G DAYS/UNITS	H EPSDT	I EMG	J COB	K RESERVED
02 06 04 02 06 04	21	1	00534 17:08-18:48 (Actual Time)	1	430 00	1		Y		

25. FEDERAL TAX I.D. NUMBER 98-3539779 ☐SSN ☒EIN
26. PATIENT'S ACCOUNT NO. BETBS001 939
27. ACCEPT ASSIGNMENT? ☒YES ☐NO
28. TOTAL CHARGE 430 00
29. AMOUNT PAID 0 00
30. BALANCE DUE 430 00

31. SIGNATURE OF PHYSICIAN OR SUPPLIER
SIGNED Tom Sillitis DATE 02/20/04

32. NAME AND ADDRESS OF FACILITY
HEADACHE HOSPITAL
2000 HAZARD STREET
HELP, NY 12899 (914) 555-9989

33. PHYSICIAN'S BILLING NAME
TOM SILLITIS, M.D. NETWORK PROVIDER
9909 TRIMMER STREET, STE 1T
TRAVEL, NY 12899 (914) 555-6789
PIN# TOS004 GRP#

(APPROVED BY AMA COUNCIL ON MEDICAL SERVICE 8/88)   PLEASE PRINT OR TYPE   FORM HCFA-1500 (12-90) FORM OWCP-1500 FORM RRB-1500

PLEASE
DO NOT
STAPLE
IN THIS
AREA
□□□ PICA

WINTER INSURANCE CO.
9763 WESTERN WAY
WHITTIER, CO 82963

AREAAPPROVED MOB-0938-0008

CLAIM ANES2

HEALTH INSURANCE CLAIM FORM

PICA □□□

1. MEDICARE MEDICAID CHAMPUS CHAMPVA GROUP HEALTH PLAN FECA BLK LUNG OTHER	INSURED'S I.D NUMBER	(FOR PROGRAM IN ITEM 1)
□ (Medicare #) □ (Medicaid #) □ (Sponsor's SSN) □ (VA File #) ☒ (SSN or ID) □ (SSN) □ (ID)	444-44-4444	

2. PATIENT'S NAME (Last, First, Middle Initial)	3. PATIENT'S BIRTH DATE	4. INSURED'S NAME (Last, First, Middle Initial)
DINGBAT, DANNY D.	MM 04	DD 24	YY 90 SEX M☒ F☐	DINGBAT, DANA D.

5. PATIENT'S ADDRESS (No., Street)	6. PATIENT'S RELATIONSHIP TO INSURED	7. INSURED'S ADDRESS (No., Street)
404 DOORWAY DRIVE	Self ☐ Spouse ☐ Child ☒ Other ☐	404 DOORWAY DRIVE

CITY DENVER	STATE ND	8. PATIENT STATUS Single ☒ Married ☐ Other ☐	CITY DENVER	STATE ND

ZIP CODE 58444	TELEPHONE (Include Area Code) (701) 555-3344	Employed ☐ Full-Time Student ☒ Part-Time Student ☐	ZIP CODE 58444	TELEPHONE (INCLUDE AREA CODE) (701) 555-3344

9. OTHER INSURED'S NAME (Last, First, Middle Initial)	10. IS PATIENT'S CONDITION RELATED TO:	11. INSURED'S POLICY GROUP OR FECA NUMBER: 444-44-ABC
a. OTHER INSURED'S POLICY OR GROUP NUMBER	a. EMPLOYMENT? (CURRENT OR PREVIOUS) ☐ YES ☒ NO	a. INSURED'S DATE OF BIRTH MM 04	DD 04	YY 64 SEX M☐ F☒
a. OTHER INSURED'S DATE OF BIRTH MM	DD	YY SEX M☐ F☐	b. AUTO ACCIDENT? PLACE (State) ☐ YES ☒ NO	b. EMPLOYER'S NAME OR SCHOOL NAME ABC CORPORATION
c. EMPLOYER'S NAME OR SCHOOL NAME	c. OTHER ACCIDENT? ☒ YES ☐ NO	c. INSURANCE PLAN NAME OR PROGRAM NAME ABC PLAN
d. INSURANCE PLAN NAME OR PROGRAM NAME	10d. RESERVED FOR LOCAL USE	d. IS THERE ANOTHER HEALTH BENEFIT PLAN? ☐ YES ☒ NO If yes, return to and complete item 9 a-d

READ BACK OF FORM BEFORE COMPLETING & SIGNING THIS FORM
12. PATIENT'S OR AUTHORIZED PERSON'S SIGNATURE I authorize the release of any medical or other information necessary to process this claim. I also request payment of government benefits either to myself or to the party who accepts assignment below.

SIGNED   **SIGNATURE ON FILE**   DATE 01/26/04

13. INSURED'S OR AUTHORIZED PERSON'S SIGNATURE I authorize payment of medical benefits to the undersigned physician or supplier for services described below.

SIGNED   **SIGNATURE ON FILE**

14. DATE OF CURRENT: ◄ ILLNESS (1st symptom) ◄ INJURY (Accident) ◄ PREGNANCY (LMP) MM 01	DD 26	YY 04	15. IF PATIENT HAS HAD SAME OR SIMILAR ILLNESS, GAVE FIRST DATE MM	DD	YY	16. DATES PATIENT UNABLE TO WORK IN CURRENT OCCUPATION FROM MM	DD	YY TO MM	DD	YY
17. NAME OF REFERRING PHYSICIAN OR OTHER SOURCE	17a. I.D. NUMBER OF REFERRING PHYSICIAN	18. HOSPITALIZATION DATES RELATED TO CURRENT SERVICES FROM MM 01	DD 26	YY 04 TO MM 02	DD 08	YY 04
19. RESERVED FOR LOCAL USE		20. OUTSIDE LAB? ☐ YES ☐ NO $ CHARGES

21. DIAGNOSIS OR NATURE OF ILLNESS OR INJURY, (RELATE ITEMS 1,2,3, OR 4 TO ITEM 24E BY LINE)

1. 807 . 01
2. 823 . 32
3. 800 . 40
4. E884 . 9

22. MEDICAID RESUBMISSION CODE   ORIGINAL REF. NO.

23. PRIOR AUTHORIZATION NUMBER

24. A. DATE(S) OF SERVICE		B. Place of Service	C. Type of Service	D. PROCEDURES, SERVICES, OR SUPPLIES (Explain Unusual Circumstances) CPT/HCPS	MODIFIER	E. DIAGNOSIS CODE	F. $ CHARGES	G. DAYS OR UNITS	H. EPSDT Family Plan	I. EMG	J. COB	K. RESERVED FOR LOCAL USE
From MM 01	DD 26	YY 04	To MM 01	DD 26	YY 04	21	1	01480		1 4	170 00	1		Y		
01	26	04	01	26	04	21	1	00520		2 4	240 00	1		Y		
01	26	04	01	26	04	21	1	00215		3 4	300 00	1		Y		
								18:20—21:40								
								(Block Time)								

25. FEDERAL TAX I.D. NUMBER SSN EIN 60-3539774 ☐ ☒	26. PATIENT'S ACCOUNT NO. DANDI001 434	27. ACCEPT ASSIGNMENT? (For govt. claims, see back) ☐ YES ☒ NO	28. TOTAL CHARGE $ 710 00	29. AMOUNT PAID $ 0 00	30. BALANCE DUE $ 710 00

31. SIGNATURE OF PHYSICIAN OR SUPPLIER INCLUDING DEGREES OR CREDENTIALS (I certify that the statements on the reverse apply to this bill and are made a part thereof.)

SIGNED *Perry Cardiectomy* DATE 2/11/04

32. NAME AND ADDRESS OF FACILITY WHERE SERVICES WERE RENDERED (If other than home or office)

HACKIM HOSPITAL
1000 HIDE STREET
HUSHTOWN, ND 58444 (701) 555-4004

33. PHYSICIAN'S, SUPPLIERS BILLING NAME, ADDRESS, ZIP CODE & PHONE #

PERRY CARDIECTOMY, M.D.
4404 CLOVER COURT, STE 4C
COOL, ND 58444 (701) 555-1234

PIN# PEC004 | GRP#

(APPROVED BY AMA COUNCIL ON MEDICAL SERVICE 8/88)

PLEASE PRINT OR TYPE

FORM HCFA-1500 (12-90)
FORM OWCP-1500   FORM RRB-1500

APPROVED MOB-0938-0008

BALL INSURANCE CARRIERS
3895 BUBBLE BLVD., STE.283   **CLAIM ANES3**
BOXWOOD, CO 85926

PLEASE
DO NOT
STAPLE
IN THIS
AREA
□□□ PICA

HEALTH INSURANCE CLAIM FORM

PICA □□□

1. MEDICARE MEDICAID CHAMPUS CHAMPVA GROUP HEALTH PLAN FECA BLK LUNG OTHER	INSURED'S I.D NUMBER (FOR PROGRAM IN ITEM 1)
□ (Medicare #) □ (Medicaid #) □ (Sponsor's SSN) □ (VA File #) ☒ (SSN or ID) □ (SSN) □ (ID)	555-55-5555

2. PATIENT'S NAME (Last, First, Middle Initial)	3. PATIENT'S BIRTH DATE MM DD YY SEX	4. INSURED'S NAME (Last, First, Middle Initial)
PATIENT, PATTY P.	05 15 75 M□ F☒	PATIENT, PATTY P.

5. PATIENT'S ADDRESS (No., Street)	6. PATIENT'S RELATIONSHIP TO INSURED	7. INSURED'S ADDRESS (No., Street)
655 PAIN LANE	Self☒ Spouse□ Child□ Other□	655 PAIN LANE

CITY	STATE	8. PATIENT STATUS	CITY	STATE
PEN	PA	Single☒ Married□ Other□	PEN	PA

ZIP CODE	TELEPHONE (Include Area Code)		ZIP CODE	TELEPHONE (INCLUDE AREA CODE)
15522	(878) 555-3355	Employed☒ Full-Time□ Part-Time□ Student Student	15522	(878) 555-3355

9. OTHER INSURED'S NAME (Last, First, Middle Initial)	10. IS PATIENT'S CONDITION RELATED TO:	11. INSURED'S POLICY GROUP OR FECA NUMBER:
		555-55-XYZ

a. OTHER INSURED'S POLICY OR GROUP NUMBER	a. EMPLOYMENT? (CURRENT OR PREVIOUS) □ YES ☒ NO	a. INSURED'S DATE OF BIRTH MM DD YY SEX 05 15 75 M□ F☒
b. OTHER INSURED'S DATE OF BIRTH MM DD YY SEX M□ F□	b. AUTO ACCIDENT? PLACE (State) □ YES ☒ NO	b. EMPLOYER'S NAME OR SCHOOL NAME XYZ CORPORATION
c. EMPLOYER'S NAME OR SCHOOL NAME	c. OTHER ACCIDENT? □ YES ☒ NO	c. INSURANCE PLAN NAME OR PROGRAM NAME XYZ PLAN
d. INSURANCE PLAN NAME OR PROGRAM NAME	10d. RESERVED FOR LOCAL USE	d. IS THERE ANOTHER HEALTH BENEFIT PLAN? □ YES ☒ NO If yes, return to and complete item 9 a-d

READ BACK OF FORM BEFORE COMPLETING & SIGNING THIS FORM
12. PATIENT'S OR AUTHORIZED PERSON'S SIGNATURE I authorize the release of any medical or other information necessary to process this claim. I also request payment of government benefits either to myself or to the party who accepts assignment below.

SIGNED   SIGNATURE ON FILE   DATE   02/16/04

13. INSURED'S OR AUTHORIZED PERSON'S SIGNATURE I authorize payment of medical benefits to the undersigned physician or supplier for services described below.

SIGNED   SIGNATURE ON FILE

14. DATE OF CURRENT: ◄ ILLNESS (1st symptom) ◄ INJURY (Accident) ◄ PREGNANCY (LMP) MM DD YY 02 16 04	15. IF PATIENT HAS HAD SAME OR SIMILAR ILLNESS, GAVE FIRST DATE MM DD YY	16. DATES PATIENT UNABLE TO WORK IN CURRENT OCCUPATION MM DD YY MM DD YY FROM TO
17. NAME OF REFERRING PHYSICIAN OR OTHER SOURCE	17a. I.D. NUMBER OF REFERRING PHYSICIAN	18. HOSPITALIZATION DATES RELATED TO CURRENT SERVICES MM DD YY MM DD YY FROM 02 16 04 TO 02 16 04
19. RESERVED FOR LOCAL USE		20. OUTSIDE LAB? $ CHARGES □ YES □ NO

21. DIAGNOSIS OR NATURE OF ILLNESS OR INJURY, (RELATE ITEMS 1,2,3, OR 4 TO ITEM 24E BY LINE)

1. | 233 . 0   3. | .
2. | .   4. | .

22. MEDICAID RESUBMISSION CODE   ORIGINAL REF. NO.

23. PRIOR AUTHORIZATION NUMBER

24. A. DATE(S) OF SERVICE From To MM DD YY MM DD YY	B. Place of Service	C. Type of Service	D. PROCEDURES, SERVICES, OR SUPPLIES (Explain Unusual Circumstances) CPT/HCPCS MODIFIER	E. DIAGNOSIS CODE	F. $ CHARGES	G. DAYS OR UNITS	H. EPSDT Family Plan	I. EMG	J. COB	K. RESERVED FOR LOCAL USE
02 16 04 02 16 04	22	1	00400	1	175 00	1				
			1:45 - 2:35							
			(Actual Time)							

25. FEDERAL TAX I.D. NUMBER SSN EIN	26. PATIENT'S ACCOUNT NO.	27. ACCEPT ASSIGNMENT? (For govt. claims, see back)	28. TOTAL CHARGE	29. AMOUNT PAID	30. BALANCE DUE
51-3539775 □ ☒	PATPA001 535	☒ YES □ NO	$ 175 00	$ 0 00	$ 175 00

31. SIGNATURE OF PHYSICIAN OR SUPPLIER INCLUDING DEGREES OR CREDENTIALS (I certify that the statements on the reverse apply to this bill and are made a part thereof.) SIGNED *Diane Ignosis* DATE 02/18/04	32. NAME AND ADDRESS OF FACILITY WHERE SERVICES WERE RENDERED (If other than home or office) HELPER HOSPITAL 25450 HAMMER AVE. HUMMER TOWN, PA 15522 (878) 555-6455	33. PHYSICIAN'S, SUPPLIERS BILLING NAME, ADDRESS, ZIP CODE & PHONE # DIANE IGNOSIS, M.D. 656 DAIRY DRIVE, STE. 101D DEER, PA 15522 (878) 555-2455 PIN# DIA004 GRP#

(APPROVED BY AMA COUNCIL ON MEDICAL SERVICE 8/88)   PLEASE PRINT OR TYPE

FORM HCFA-1500 (12-90)
FORM OWCP-1500   FORM RRB-1500

18 Hospital Services

In this chapter you will learn:

- To identify hospital room and board charges and hospital ancillary charges.
- To break out hospital room and board charges from hospital ancillary charges.
- The different levels of care and different types of rooms within a hospital.
- The advantages of preferred provider organization (PPO) networks.

Key words and concepts you will learn in this chapter:

Ancillary Expenses – Miscellaneous services or supplies that are provided by the hospital on an inpatient or outpatient basis, which are necessary for the medical care or treatment of an individual.

Alternative Birthing Centers (ABC) – Are outpatient care centers that provide special rooms for routine deliveries.

Day Care Centers – Provide treatment during the daylight hours with the patient being released at night.

Hospice Care – A health care program providing coordinated services in a home setting.

Inpatient – The patient must be admitted into a hospital or a similar facility and stay for a period of time, usually a minimum of 24 hours. There must be a room and board charge.

Nursing Homes – Specialize in custodial care, that is, care that is primarily for the purpose of meeting the personal needs of the patient and that could be provided by personnel without professional skills or training.

Outpatient – "Come-and-go" or outpatient surgery is when the patient is not admitted to the hospital after surgery because it is not medically necessary. There are no room and board charges.

Personal items – Those items that are primarily for the comfort of the patient and are not medically necessary.

Rehabilitation Facilities – Specialize in long-term, post sickness, or post-injury care.

Surgicenters (Ambulatory Surgical Centers) – Facility that allows for the performance of surgery on an outpatient basis.

Take-Home Prescriptions – Medications to be taken after the patient is released from the hospital.

Urgent Care Centers – A facility that provides urgent or emergency treatment.

Hospital services are those services performed in a hospital setting. The term is used generically to refer to charges billed by a hospital, urgent care center, surgicenter, alternative birthing center, or similar institution. This chapter deals with the various types of facilities available, their billing formats, and general handling guidelines.

The term **"hospital"** means an institution that meets most of the following:

- It mainly provides medical treatment to inpatients.
- It provides treatment only by or under a staff of physicians.
- It provides care by registered nurses 24 hours per day.
- It maintains facilities for diagnosis.
- It maintains a daily medical record for each patient.
- It complies with all licensing and other legal requirements.
- It maintains permanent facilities for surgery

Most carriers have a file of established hospitals, surgicenters, skilled nursing facilities or birthing facilities that are licensed to treat patients in the state where they practice business. Occasionally, a new facility opens and, when claims are received, the information must be requested and verified to determine whether the facility is eligible for payment.

Hospital services are covered under the hospital benefits portion of the contract. Whether the contract is a Basic/Major Medical plan or a Comprehensive Major

Medical plan, hospital charges are usually a covered benefit. The following are typical hospital expenses:
- The daily room and board charge of a hospital.
- The charges for outpatient emergency treatment of illness and injuries.
- The charge for outpatient surgery.
- The charges for medical services and supplies during confinement, excluding private duty nursing.
- The charge for administration of anesthesia.
- The ambulance care if billed through the hospital.
- The charges for lab tests and other services performed by an outside facility at the hospital's request.

UB-92 Billing Form

The **Uniform Bill-92 (UB-92)** is intended to be used by hospitals or other hospital-type facilities for inpatient and outpatient billing. The data elements and the design of the form were determined by the National Uniform Billing Committee. This form was designed to provide the basic data needed by most payors to adjudicate most of their claims. The objective was to accommodate a wide range of needs while eliminating the need for attachments.

A review of the UB-92 is necessary before processing to determine whether inpatient or outpatient benefits apply. An inpatient billing will usually have a room and board charge. The statement from and to dates will correspond with the number of room and board days billed. Outpatient bills have an outpatient indicator such as 131 in item 4. The statement from and to dates are usually the same. The admit and discharge dates are usually the same. There is no charge for room and board. Some hospitals do not put the discharge time on the outpatient bill, however, you may want to request this information if the billing appears excessive or that the patient might have stayed overnight in an extended stay or observation room.

Inpatient Hospital Claims

On inpatient hospital claims, the provider of service is a facility that provides inpatient care. This may be a hospital, an acute care facility, a skilled nursing facility, a custodial care facility, or a similar facility.

For **inpatient care**, the patient must be admitted into the hospital and stay for a period of time, usually a minimum of 24 hours. There must be a room and board charge. A hospital room and board charge is similar to that for staying in a hotel. The day entered is paid but not the day discharged as long as the discharge time is before the required checkout time. The UB-92 form should always indicate admission and discharge dates.

When coding inpatient hospital claims, the CPT or RVS books are not used unless the billing has itemized some charges according to valid CPT/RVS codes. Each payor has its own coding guidelines. Therefore, before a claim can be coded for processing, the payor-specific codes must be obtained. Most payors break-up the bills according to:
- Room and board charges.
- Ancillary charges.
- Take-home prescriptions.
- Professional fees for exams, surgery, etc.

Providers of service use revenue codes in box 42 of the UB-92 form to indicate or identify the specific accommodation, ancillary service, or billing calculation. (See the **Billing Forms** chapter for further information.)

Room and Board
Hospitals have a variety of rooms available, which include but are not limited to:
- **Private** – a single-occupancy room. The extra cost for a private room is not covered by most plans unless the room was necessary due to the patient's illness (i.e., highly contagious disorder).
- **Semi-private** – a double-occupancy room. Most plans cover the cost of a semi-private room. The cost may vary based on the type of floor on which the room is located. That is, a semi-private room in a burn ward may cost more than a semi-private room in a maternity ward because of the increased level of care required.
- **Ward** – a room with three or more beds. A ward is also covered by most plans. Aside from county hospitals, most facilities no longer offer this type of room.
- **Nursery** – a large room for newborn babies. Twenty or 30 babies may be in a nursery.
- **Specialized units** – areas in which special monitoring equipment and a higher ratio of nurses to patients are required. These units are established for extremely ill or terminal patients with different illnesses or injuries that require more acute, intensive care. Specialized units tend to be considerably more expensive than other units. This type of room may cost $1,000 or more per day. Examples are the Intensive Care Unit (ICU), Coronary Care Unit (CCU), and Definitive Observation Units (DOU).

Telemetry charges (specialized observation equipment) may be billed separately from the base room and board amount. In addition, nursing charges may also be billed separately. If so, the telemetry charges and nursing charges should be combined with the base room and board amount to obtain the actual room and board charge.

To code the room and board amount, the number of days in the hospital is determined by counting the day of admission but not the day of discharge. If there is a charge for the day of discharge, the facility will need to be contacted to see why the last day is being charged. Usually, the charge will be for a late discharge. In this case, the late discharge is covered if it was caused or ordered by the attending physician. A late discharge for the patient's convenience however is not usually a covered expense.

Each type of room accommodation is coded on a separate line, and the quantity (number of days) applies to that type of room only. In addition, if either the type of room (semi-private, private, or other) or the per-day charges are different, even if the room type is the same, separate lines of coding are required. For instance, the following claim is received:

5/1, 5/2 Semi-private $650.00 per day
5/3, 5/4 Semi-private $675.00 per day

In this case, the two different semi-private room rates must be coded on two different lines, with the number of services shown on each line as two (unless 5/4 is the discharge date). If the charge per day was the same for all of the semi-private rooms, only one line of coding would be required with the number of services as four.

Check the following revenue code ranges on the UB-92 for room and board expenses: 110-179 and 200-219.

Ancillary Expenses

Ancillary expenses are miscellaneous services or supplies that are provided by the hospital on an inpatient or outpatient basis, which are necessary for the medical care or treatment of an individual. The most common charges include x-rays, lab fees, pharmacy, med-surgical supplies, operating room expenses, surgery room supplies, recovery room time, anesthesia supplies, occupational therapy, and inhalation therapy. All these expenses can be combined under a single line of coding for ancillary expenses. The only items that may be separated and coded on separate lines are charges for personal items, non-covered items, doctor's emergency room examination charges, other professional exam charges, or other expenses that may be limited by the plan. This does not include professional component charges (unless specified by the plan).

Take-Home Prescriptions

Often doctors in a hospital setting prescribe medications, called **take-home prescriptions**, to be taken after the patient is released from the hospital.

These medications may be dispensed by the hospital pharmacy and the charges included on the hospital bill. The medications are often covered under Major Medical benefits rather than standard hospital benefits. For this reason, these items are usually billed and coded separately, since they are not considered to be hospital expenses and may be subject to other plan provisions. Sometimes the plan has a separate payer for prescriptions, in which case the take home drugs should be denied.

Professional Fees

Bills for doctors, anesthesiologists, technicians, and other hospital professionals are often included on the hospital bill rather than billed separately on a HCFA-1500. These bills are broken out from the regular hospital bill and paid under the normal plan provisions as if they had been billed on a HCFA-1500. Therefore, it is important to go through the itemized billing and determine whether the charges were for materials, equipment, and overhead (rendered by the hospital), or for professional services (rendered by a provider).

Personal Items

Personal items are those items that are primarily for the comfort of the patient and are not medically necessary. The following items are considered to be personal items and are not usually covered by a benefit plan. These charges may have to be coded separately or they may be combined with other ancillary charges and then denied with an appropriate explanation indicating that they are not covered under the plan. Handling procedures varies from payor to payor. Personal items can include:

Barber expenses	Personal hygiene kit
Videotaping of birth	Birth certificate, photos
Cot rental	Room transfer requested
Lotion	Television
Telephone	Toothbrush, toothpaste,
Guest trays	Mouthwash
Gift shop expenses	Slippers

Most hospitals automatically issue an admission kit to incoming patients. An admission kit usually includes an emesis basin, carafe, cup, lotion, tissue, and mouthwash. Some plans administratively allow for one kit. Additional kits are not covered. This type of kit may also be called a maternity kit, Ob-Gyn kit, hygiene kit, patient comfort kit, and other names. Therefore, if items such as mouthwash and toothpaste are billed separately in addition to a kit, they are not usually considered covered charges. (Even if a kit is not billed, these types of charges are not usually allowable.) It is important to consider if there is a medical necessity for an item prior to denying it. For example, the hospital bill may list a razor. If the patient was scheduled for surgery and the nurse shaved the operative area, the razor would be considered medically necessary.

Outpatient Hospital Claims

The **outpatient** provider of service is a hospital facility (the title may be Hospital or Medical Center, Surgicenter, Birthing Center) in which there are no room and board charges. Commonly, "come-and-go" or outpatient surgery is performed in the outpatient department because an inpatient admission is not medically necessary. An outpatient hospital facility may have two departments:
1. The Emergency Room, and
2. Outpatient Clinics.

There may be facility charges such as emergency room usage fees, examination room usage charges, operating room expenses, and recovery room expenses. In an outpatient setting, ancillary expenses include everything except professional fees for examinations, surgery, and other professional services. Clinic charges should be treated as an office visit as far as coding for the physician. The actual facility usage fee is not coded with or considered a professional fee. It is coded separately.

Other commonly submitted outpatient charges may be for lab or x-ray services, pharmacy or durable medical equipment.

Miscellaneous Facilities

Many other types of treatment centers may be classified as facilities. Usually, they are designed to handle specialized treatment programs such as psychiatric care, alcoholism, and emergency care. The following is a sampling of other types of facilities in existence.

Day Care Centers
As the name implies, **day care centers** provide treatment during the daylight hours with the patient being released at night. The converse of this are centers that allow the patient to pursue a normal routine during the day such as working, and be treated at the center and maintained there overnight. Generally, these type of centers are for treatment of mental or nervous disorders.

A great disparity is seen in the handling of these claims from payor to payor. Usually, the following is required by the examiner to determine whether the treatment or the facility is eligible for benefits:
- A complete review of the facility must be made including:
  - Staffing—the type of licensing required for the staff.
  - Type of billing—how the bills are broken down, whether they are inclusive, itemized, and so on.
  - Type of state or federal licensing the facility has.

  - The facility's primary purpose (custodial care, active treatment, or other).
  - A detailed description of the type of treatment including length of each treatment, licensing of person actually performing the treatment, ancillary services, and other pertinent data.

Often, senior examiners may handle day care claims to ensure that the proper correspondence is prepared and mailed. They also review the documentation when a reply is received. Before any benefits are denied, all plan provisions and limitations must be verified.

Urgent Care Centers
An **urgent care center** is a facility that follows professionally recognized standards to provide urgent or emergency treatment. Many plans have specialized benefits to handle this type of center. An urgent care center generally meets the following eight requirements:
1. Mainly provides urgent or emergency medical treatment for acute conditions.
2. Does not provide services or accommodations for overnight stays.
3. Is open to receive patients every day of the calendar year.
4. Has a physician trained in emergency medicine, nurses, and other supporting personnel specially trained in emergency care on duty at all times.
5. Has x-ray and laboratory diagnostic facilities, emergency equipment, trays, and supplies available, for use in life-threatening events.
6. Has a written agreement with a local acute care inpatient facility for the immediate transfer of patients who require more intensive care than can be furnished at an outpatient facility, has written guidelines for stabilizing and transporting such patients, and has immediate and reliable direct communication channels with the acute care facility.
7. Complies with all state and federal licensing and other legal requirements.
8. Is not the office or clinic of any physician.

Generally, a medical emergency exists when:
- Severe symptoms occur. The symptoms must be severe enough to cause a person to seek immediate medical aid regardless of the hour of the day or night.
- The severe symptoms must occur suddenly and unexpectedly. A chronic condition with sub-acute symptoms that have existed over a period of time usually does not qualify as a medical emergency. However, symptoms that

become severe enough to require immediate medical aid may qualify.

- Immediate care was secured. Usually, a medical emergency would not be considered to exist if medical care is not received immediately after the appearance of acute symptoms. A telephone call to a doctor does not fulfill this requirement if the actual examination and treatment are deferred until the next day.

The administration of the urgent care benefit varies greatly. Therefore, refer to the plan provisions prior to taking any action on such claims.

Some patients will seek urgent care treatment for non-emergency reasons (i.e., the patient is suffering from flu symptoms and doesn't want to take time off to see a doctor). Some payors will deny or reduce payment on these claims based on the reasoning that the level of care obtained was not consistent with the situation.

Surgicenters

Ambulatory surgical centers (surgicenters) are equipped to allow for the performance of surgery on an outpatient basis. These centers may be freestanding or attached to a major acute care facility. Surgicenters provide financial savings by eliminating the need for admission into an inpatient facility. An ambulatory surgical facility is a specialized facility that meets all eight of the professionally recognized standards indicated below:

1. Provides a setting for outpatient surgeries.
2. Does not provide services or accommodations for overnight stays.
3. Has at least two operating rooms and one recovery room; all the medical equipment needed to support the surgery being performed; x-ray and laboratory diagnostic facilities; and emergency equipment, trays, and supplies for use in life-threatening events.
4. Has a medical staff that is supervised full time by a physician including a registered nurse when patients are in the facility.
5. Maintains a medical record for each patient.
6. Has a written agreement with a local acute care facility for the immediate transfer of patients who require greater care than can be provided on an outpatient basis.
7. Complies with all state and federal licensing and other legal requirements.
8. Is not an office or clinic for any physician.

Usually, plans provide benefits on a global basis, covering the facility room usage charge, supplies (i.e., anesthesia gases, medications, trays) on the same basis as inpatient hospital services. However, as with other benefits, coverage provisions vary greatly.

Alternative Birthing Centers

Alternative birthing centers (ABC) are outpatient care centers that provide special rooms for routine deliveries. As a rule, these centers provide quiet, non-traditional types of home-style rooms, which are designed to allow the parents to be together and participate in the birthing experience.

Often, a nurse practitioner rather than a physician is in attendance. The mother normally goes home within five to 12 hours after the delivery. As with other types of outpatient facilities, the following six or similar requirements are necessary for a facility to qualify as a birthing center:

1. Does not provide services or accommodations for overnight stays.
2. Has a medical staff that is supervised full-time by a physician. A registered nurse is also in attendance when patients are in the facility.
3. Maintains a medical record for each patient.
4. Has a written agreement with a local acute care facility for the immediate transfer of patients who require greater care than can be provided on an outpatient basis.
5. Complies with all state and federal licensing and other legal requirements.
6. Is not an office or clinic for any physician.

Most confinements at an ABC should not exceed a 24-hour period without the transfer to an acute care facility. If the stay exceeds 24 hours, charges should be referred for investigation as to the medical necessity of the continued stay.

Rehabilitation Facilities

Rehabilitation facilities specialize in long-term, post-sickness, or post-injury care. Rehabilitative treatment rather than active medical care is provided. This treatment is designed to return a patient to a normal or more normal state. Rehabilitative care is designed for those who are left paralyzed, deformed, handicapped, or otherwise not totally functional as a result of an accident, injury, or illness such as a stroke or spinal cord injury.

This type of care is very similar to convalescent care, although generally, care at a rehabilitation facility is more aggressive than that provided in a convalescent facility.

Many plans provide for some type of rehabilitative care. The limitations are usually based on a point at which progress ceases and the condition or status of the patient is stabilized. However, some plans do not provide any benefits for rehabilitative treatment.

Convalescent Hospitals

Convalescent facilities are usually considered to be midrange facilities, which provide non-acute care for persons recovering from an acute illness or injury. Usually, admission into a convalescent facility must commence within a specified number of days following a discharge from an acute care facility. The care provided must be active treatment, not custodial care.

The institution generally must meet all seven of the following requirements to be considered an eligible convalescent facility:

1. Is primarily engaged in providing skilled nursing care to sick or injured persons as inpatients under 24-hours supervision of a physician or registered nurse.
2. Has on duty at all times a registered nurse, licensed vocational nurse, or skilled practical nurse. A registered nurse must be on duty at least eight hours a day.
3. Is not, other than incidentally, a place for drug addicts, alcoholics, mentally ill persons, or senile or mentally deficient persons.
4. Maintains a medical record for each patient.
5. Has a written agreement with a local acute care facility for the immediate transfer of patients who require greater care than can be provided in a non-acute care facility.
6. Complies with all state and federal licensing and other legal requirements.
7. Is not an office or clinic for any physician.

Many plans provide very limited convalescent care benefits. However, always verify that the care being provided is not custodial. Some rehabilitative services may be provided and may be billed separately or included on a global basis (no breakdown).

Nursing Homes

Nursing homes specialize in custodial care, that is, care that is primarily for the purpose of meeting the personal needs of the patient and that could be provided by personnel without professional skills or training. **Custodial care** may include assistance with walking, bathing, dressing, eating, and other activities. Most plans do not provide custodial care coverage or, if they do, payment is limited. If there is a question whether or not care is custodial, copies of the provider's nursing notes and admission or discharge summary should be requested.

Hospice Care

A **hospice** is a health care program providing coordinated services in a home setting. Sometimes care is provided in the patients home by visiting specialists and sometimes patients are admitted to a hospice facility. Usually, such care is provided only for persons suffering from a terminal condition, generally with a life expectancy of six months or less. The hospice concept is based on the following principals:

- The beneficiaries of the program are both the terminally ill person and his or her family.
- An interdisciplinary team is required to serve the patient, which includes nurses, social workers, psychologists, clergy, volunteers, and other professionals.
- The alleviation of pain and suffering is emphasized rather than the treatment of the illness.
- Support is provided for all family members to help offset emotional pain.

Hospice care is billed in a variety of methods. If the patient is in a hospice facility the facility will submit a single bill for all charges. If the patient is receiving treatment in their own home the billing may be provided by a hospice agency, which is then responsible for paying other providers. Another method may be that of separate bills from the various providers. Usually, such services include the rental of beds, commodes, and other equipment, along with various medications and supplies required to care for a terminally ill person. For hospice care to be covered, the contract usually specifies such benefits.

Summary

Hospitals provide a sterile environment to have medically necessary services and treatments, surgical or otherwise. They also provide a controlled environment in which to recover.

The foregoing is by no means a complete list of all available facilities but provides a guide for the most common types of facilities that you will encounter when processing claims. Most plans and payors have specific handling guidelines that should be checked before processing.

Assignments

Complete the Questions for Review.
Complete Exercises 18 - 1 to 18 - 3.

Questions for Review

Directions: Answer the following questions without looking back into the material just covered. Write your answers in the space provided.

1. Define hospital services: _____

2. What type of claim form is used to bill for hospital services? _____

3. Name the four categories of hospital charges that most payors use:

     1. _____
     2. _____
     3. _____
     4. _____

4. Name the five varieties of hospital rooms.

     1. _____
     2. _____
     3. _____
     4. _____
     5. _____

5. What are ancillary services? _____
   _____

6. List at least three items that may be considered personal items. _____
   _____

7. What are the two departments of an outpatient hospital facility?

     1. _____
     2. _____

8. What are urgent care centers? _____
   _____

9. What are surgicenters? _____
   _____

10. What does the abbreviation ABC stand for and what is it? _____
    _____

If you were unable to answer any of the questions, refer back to the section and then complete the answers.

Exercises 18 - 1 to 18 - 3

Directions: Process each of the hospital claims found on the following pages.

Honors Certification™

The Honors Certification™ challenge for this chapter is a written test of the information contained within this chapter. Each incorrect answer will result in a deduction of between 1% and 5% from your grade. You must achieve a score of 85% or higher to pass this test. If you fail the test on your first attempt you may retake the test one additional time. The items included in the second test may be different from those in the first test.

CLAIM HOSP1

APPROVED OMB NO. 0938-0279

HEADACHE HOSPITAL		2					3 PATIENT CONTROL NO.				4 TYPE OF BILL
2000 HAZARD STREET							7654321				111
HELP, NY 12899	5 FED. TAX NO.	6 STATEMENT COVERS PERIOD FROM THROUGH		7 COV D	8 N-C D	9 C-I D	10 L-R D	11			
	BB-1234567	2/6/04	2/14/04	08	0						

12 PATIENT NAME	13 PATIENT ADDRESS								
BOSSY, BETTY B.	7991 BAGEL BLVD., BARSTOW, NY 12899								

14 BIRTHDATE	15 SEX	16 MS	17 DATE	ADMISSION 18 HR	19 TYPE	20 SRC	21 D HR	22 STAT	23 MEDICAL RECORD NO.	24	CONDITION CODES 25 26 27 28 29 30	31
09/19/39	F	M	2/6/04	10	1	7	13	01				

32 OCCURRENCE CODE DATE	33 OCCURRENCE CODE DATE	34 OCCURRENCE CODE DATE	35 OCCURRENCE CODE DATE	36 OCCURRENCE SPAN CODE FROM THROUGH	37
a				A	A
b				B	B
38				C	C

	39 VALUE CODES CODE AMOUNT	40 VALUE CODES CODE AMOUNT	41 VALUE CODES CODE AMOUNT
BETTY B. BOSSY	a 01 360 00	a	a
7991 BAGEL BLVD.	b	b	b
BARSTOW, NY 12899	c	c	c
	d	d	d

42 REV. CD.	43 DESCRIPTION	44 HCPCS / RATES	45 SERV. DATE	46 SERV. UNITS	47 TOTAL CHARGES	48 NON-COVERED CHARGES	49	
1	130	ROOM-BOARD/3 & 4 BED	395.00		8	3,160 00		1
2	250	PHARMACY			108	3,416 00		2
3	260	IV THERAPY			40	1,400 00		3
4	270	MED-SUR SUPPLIES			48	1,125 00		4
5	300	LABORATORY			13	772 00		5
6	410	RESPIRATORY SVC			9	294 00		6
7	730	EKG/ECG			1	79 00		7
8								8
9								9
10								10
11								11
12								12
13								13
14								14
15								15
16								16
17								17
18								18
19								19
20								20
21								21
22								22
23	001	TOTAL CHARGES				10,246 00		23

50 PAYER	51 PROVIDER NO.	52 REL INFO	53 ASG BEN	54 PRIOR PAYMENTS	55 EST. AMOUNT DUE	56	
A NINJA PLAN		X	X	0 00	10,246 00		A
B							B
C							C

57	DUE FROM PATIENT ▶	

58 INSURED'S NAME	59 P. REL	60 CERT. - SSN - HIC - ID NO.	61 GROUP NAME	62 INSURANCE GROUP NO.	
A BETTY B. BOSSY	01	999-99-9999	NINJA PLAN		A
B					B
C					C

63 TREATMENT AUTHORIZATION CODES	64 ESC	65 EMPLOYER NAME	66 EMPLOYER LOCATION	
A	1	NINJA CORPORATION		A
B				B
C				C

67 PRIN. DIAG. CD.	68 CODE	69 CODE	70 CODE	71 CODE	OTHER DIAG. CODES 72 CODE	73 CODE	74 CODE	75 CODE	76 ADM. DIAG. CD.	77 E-CODE	78
410.91											

79 PC	80	PRINCIPAL PROCEDURE CODE DATE	81	OTHER PROCEDURE CODE DATE	OTHER PROCEDURE CODE DATE	82 ATTENDING PHYS. ID	ABD002	
		A		B		ABE DOMIN, M.D.		
	OTHER PROCEDURE CODE DATE		OTHER PROCEDURE CODE DATE	OTHER PROCEDURE CODE DATE		83 OTHER PHYS. ID		a
	C		D	E				b

84 REMARKS		OTHER PHYS. ID		a
NETWORK PROVIDER				b
Pre-certification received	85 PROVIDER REPRESENTATIVE X			86 DATE

UB-92 HCFA-1450   OCR/ORIGINAL   I CERTIFY THE CERTIFICATIONS ON THE REVERSE APPLY TO THIS BILL AND ARE MADE A PART HEREOF.

CLAIM HOSP2

APPROVED OMB NO. 0938-0279

HACKIM HOSPITAL 1000 HIDE STREET HUSHTOWN, ND 58444	2			3 PATIENT CONTROL NO. 3221100	4 TYPE OF BILL 111

5 FED. TAX NO. DD-0011223	6 STATEMENT COVERS PERIOD FROM 1/26/04　THROUGH 2/08/04	7 COV D. 24	8 N-CO. 0	9 C-I D.	10 L-R D.	11

12 PATIENT NAME DINGBAT, DANNY D.	13 PATIENT ADDRESS 404 DOORWAY DRIVE, DENVER, ND 58444

14 BIRTHDATE	15 SEX	16 MS	17 DATE	18 HR	19 TYPE A	20 SRC	21 DHR	22 STAT	23 MEDICAL RECORD NO.	24	CONDITION CODES 25 26 27 28 29 30	31
04/24/90	M	S	1/26/04	18	1	7	11	03				

32 OCCURRENCE CODE DATE	33 OCCURRENCE CODE DATE	34 OCCURRENCE CODE DATE	35 OCCURRENCE CODE DATE	36 OCCURRENCE SPAN CODE FROM THROUGH	37

38	39 VALUE CODES CODE AMOUNT	40 VALUE CODES CODE AMOUNT	41 VALUE CODES CODE AMOUNT
DANA D. DINGBAT 404 DOORWAY DRIVE DENVER, ND 58444	a 01　395 00		

42 REV. CD.	43 DESCRIPTION	44 HCPCS / RATES	45 SERV. DATE	46 SERV. UNITS	47 TOTAL CHARGES	48 NON-COVERED CHARGES	49
130	ROOM-BOARD/3 & 4 BED	395.00		24	9,480 00		1
250	PHARMACY			396	10,671 00		2
260	IV THERAPY			96	3,252 00		3
270	MED-SUR SUPPLIES			336	12,853 50		4
300	LABORATORY			114	5,250 00		5
310	PATH LAB			12	630 00		6
320	DX X-RAY			5	901 00		7
351	CT SCAN-HEAD			1	3,182 97		8
360	OR SERVICES			2	956 00		9
370	ANESTHESIA			5	879 00		10
410	RESPIRATORY SVC			2	73 00		11
710	RECOVERY ROOM			1	79 00		12
001	TOTAL CHARGES				48,207 47		23

50 PAYER	51 PROVIDER NO.	52 REL INFO	53 ASG BEN	54 PRIOR PAYMENTS	55 EST. AMOUNT DUE	56
A DANA DINGBAT		Y	Y	2,500 00	0 00	
B ABC PLAN				0 00	45,707 47	
C						

57	DUE FROM PATIENT ▶	

58 INSURED'S NAME	59 P. REL	60 CERT.-SSN-HIC.-ID NO.	61 GROUP NAME	62 INSURANCE GROUP NO.
A DANA D. DINGBAT	03	444-44-4444	ABC PLAN	
B				
C				

63 TREATMENT AUTHORIZATION CODES	64 ESC	65 EMPLOYER NAME	66 EMPLOYER LOCATION
A	3	ABC CORPORATION	
B			
C			

67 PRIN. DIAG. CD.	68 CODE	69 CODE	70 CODE	71 OTHER DIAG. CODES 72 CODE	73 CODE	74 DIAG. CD.	75	76 ADM. DIAG. CD.	77 E-CODE	78
807 01	823 32	800 40	E884 9							

79 P.C.	80 PRINCIPAL PROCEDURE CODE DATE	81 OTHER PROCEDURE CODE DATE	OTHER PROCEDURE CODE DATE	82 ATTENDING PHYS. ID RAM002
		A	B	RAY MACHINE, M.D.
	OTHER PROCEDURE CODE DATE	OTHER PROCEDURE CODE DATE	OTHER PROCEDURE CODE DATE	83 OTHER PHYS. ID
	C	D	E	a
				OTHER PHYS. ID
				b

84 REMARKS	85 PROVIDER REPRESENTATIVE X	86 DATE
a		
b		
c		
d		

UB-92 HCFA-1450　　　OCR/ORIGINAL　　　I CERTIFY THE CERTIFICATIONS ON THE REVERSE APPLY TO THIS BILL AND ARE MADE A PART HEREOF.

CLAIM HOSP3

APPROVED OMB NO. 0938-0279

HELPER HOSPITAL 25450 HAMMER AVE. HUMMER TOWN, PA 15522	2			3 PATIENT CONTROL NO. 9876543	4 TYPE OF BILL 131

5 FED. TAX NO. PP-3456789	6 STATEMENT COVERS PERIOD FROM 2/16/04 THROUGH 2/16/04	7 COV D. 0	8 N-C D. 0	9 C-I D.	10 L-R D.	11

12 PATIENT NAME PATIENT, PATTY P.	13 PATIENT ADDRESS 655 PAIN LANE, PEN, PA 15522

14 BIRTHDATE	15 SEX	16 MS	17 DATE	ADMISSION 18 HR	19 TYPE	20 SRC	21 D HR	22 STAT	23 MEDICAL RECORD NO.		24	CONDITION CODES 25 26 27 28 29 30	31
05/15/75	F	S	2/16/04	07	3	1		17	01				

32 OCCURRENCE CODE DATE	33 OCCURRENCE CODE DATE	34 OCCURRENCE CODE DATE	35 OCCURRENCE CODE DATE	36 OCCURRENCE SPAN CODE FROM THROUGH	37
a					A
b					B

38		39 VALUE CODES CODE AMOUNT	40 VALUE CODES CODE AMOUNT	41 VALUE CODES CODE AMOUNT
PATTY P. PATIENT 655 PAIN LANE PEN, PA 15522		a b c d	a b c d	a b c d

42 REV. CD.	43 DESCRIPTION	44 HCPCS / RATES	45 SERV. DATE	46 SERV. UNITS	47 TOTAL CHARGES	48 NON-COVERED CHARGES	49	
1	250	PHARMACY			8	360 90		1
2	270	MED-SUR SUPPLIES			23	628 50		2
3	300	LABORATORY			3	146 90		3
4	360	OR SERVICES			6	1,407 60		4
5	370	ANESTHESIA			1	299 75		5
6	410	RESPIRATORY SVC			1	12 35		6
7								7
8								8
9								9
10								10
11								11
12								12
13								13
14								14
15								15
16								16
17								17
18								18
19								19
20								20
21								21
22								22
23	001	TOTAL CHARGES				2,856 00		23

50 PAYER	51 PROVIDER NO.	52 REL INFO	53 ASG BEN	54 PRIOR PAYMENTS	55 EST. AMOUNT DUE	56
A XYZ PLAN		Y	Y	500 00	2,356 00	
B						
C						

57	DUE FROM PATIENT ▶	

58 INSURED'S NAME	59 P. REL	60 CERT - SSN - HIC - ID NO.	61 GROUP NAME	62 INSURANCE GROUP NO.	
A PATTY P. PATIENT	01	555-55-5555	XYZ PLAN		A
B					B
C					C

63 TREATMENT AUTHORIZATION CODES	64 ESC	65 EMPLOYER NAME	66 EMPLOYER LOCATION	
A	1	XYZ CORPORATION		A
B				B
C				C

67 PRIN. DIAG. CD. 233.0	68 CODE	69 CODE	70 CODE	OTHER DIAG. CODES 71 CODE	72 CODE	73 CODE	74 CODE	75 CODE	76 ADM. DIAG. CD.	77 E-CODE	78

79 P.C.	80	PRINCIPAL PROCEDURE CODE DATE	81	OTHER PROCEDURE CODE DATE	OTHER PROCEDURE CODE DATE	82 ATTENDING PHYS. ID SAP002	
		A		B		SAM A. PILLER, M.D.	
		OTHER PROCEDURE CODE DATE		OTHER PROCEDURE CODE DATE	OTHER PROCEDURE CODE DATE	83 OTHER PHYS. ID	a
a		C		D	E	OTHER PHYS. ID	b
b	84 REMARKS						a
c						85 PROVIDER REPRESENTATIVE	86 DATE
d						X	

UB-92 HCFA-1450   OCR/ORIGINAL   I CERTIFY THE CERTIFICATIONS ON THE REVERSE APPLY TO THIS BILL AND ARE MADE A PART HEREOF.

19 Ambulance Expenses

In this chapter you will learn:

- To identify ambulance services billings and determine benefits payable.
- To process ambulance claims.

Key words and concepts you will learn in this chapter:

Air Ambulance – A helicopter or other flight vehicle used to transport a severely injured or ill person to a hospital.

Ambulance Expenses – Charges billed for transporting an injured or ill person to a medical facility.

Emergency Medical Technician (EMT) – A person trained in basic life support.

Mobile Intensive Care Unit – A life support vehicle equipped to provided care to critically ill patients during transportation to a hospital.

Paramedics – Specially trained emergency medical personnel who render emergency treatment at the scene of the injury or illness.

Van Transportation Units – Vehicles specially equipped to handle wheelchairs and patients who are unable to get in and out of a regular vehicle.

Ambulance expenses are charges billed for transporting an injured or ill person to a medical facility. Ambulance services are not considered professional or hospital services.

When ambulance services occur and charges are received, an investigation to determine whether the charges are eligible for coverage under the insured plan must be under taken. Under most plans, charges must be from a professional ambulance service; private automobiles, taxicabs, or similar vehicles are usually not covered.

Guidelines for Coverage

Benefits are usually payable for transfer to another hospital when medically necessary. For example, if one hospital does not have the facilities to treat the patient's medical condition, the patient may be transferred to the closest hospital with appropriate facilities.

An ambulance expense is covered under Major Medical, basic ambulance, and basic hospital benefits under the following conditions:

- The ambulance must be medically necessary and not for the patient's convenience.
- Transportation is provided by a professional ambulance/paramedic service.
- Transportation is to the nearest facility capable of treating the patient.
- Transportation is provided from one facility to another when the necessary treatment cannot be obtained from the first hospital.
- Transportation home from a facility is provided if the patient is unable to travel in an upright position. Exceptions such as this vary by plan, so refer to the plan provisions before processing.
- Charges for ambulance services are covered when either emergency room or inpatient hospital charges are also billed. An exception would be in the case of an insured who is dead on arrival at the hospital.
- Transportation to a facility if the claimant is dead on arrival, even though no treatment or charges are incurred at the facility.

Basic benefits usually designate a maximum allowable/payable amount for:
- Each trip to and from a facility.
- All trips made during a period of disability.
- All expenses incurred during a calendar year.

The plan provisions will indicate which limitations apply. Major Medical plans usually designate a maximum allowable/payable amount for each trip based on usual and customary guidelines. Expenses commonly billed by an ambulance service include:
- **Base call charge.** This is the amount automatically charged for the ambulance to

respond to a call even if the patient is not subsequently transported.

- Oxygen and oxygen supplies.
- Mileage.
- Linens.
- Emergency response charge. This is an extra expense, in addition to the base charge, which may be added if the patient's condition is severe enough that resuscitation efforts or other types of stabilization measures are required.
- Paramedic response charge. If paramedics rather than emergency medical technicians (EMTs) are used, an extra expense may be added.

Air Ambulance

An **air ambulance** is a helicopter or other flight vehicle used to transport severely injured or ill person to a hospital. Air medical transport may be covered if:

1. The facility in the area where the patient is injured cannot manage the patient's condition and it is medically necessary to transfer the patient by air to another facility more equipped to treat the patient, or
2. Ground transport time would be prolonged and thus, compromise the patient's medical status.

Coverage limited to the regular air ambulance charge for transportation to the nearest facility in the area that can handle the case.

Under a Basic plan, all trip or per disability limitations apply. A few Basic plans may have a special allowance designated to cover air medical transport. However, many plans do not cover this type of service, regardless of the reason required. The cost of air ambulance ranges upward from a base charge of about $1,200 and is usually based on an hourly rate.

When a person becomes ill while traveling, he or she may want to be transferred to a hospital near home or be treated by a specific specialist in another city, even though the city where he or she is located has qualified specialists in the field. In these instances, ambulance expenses are not covered, regardless of whether an air ambulance or a conventional ambulance is used. This is because the transportation is not considered "medically necessary."

Charges for commercial or private airplane transportation, regardless of the reason required, are usually not covered.

Paramedics

Paramedics are specially trained emergency medical personnel who render emergency treatment at the scene of the injury or illness. They are trained in advanced life support, whereas **Emergency Medical Technicians (EMTs)** are trained in basic life support. There are significant differences in educational requirements and certification of a paramedic compared with those of an EMT. Consequently, when a paramedic is required, an additional fee is usually charged.

Paramedic fees may be covered under a Basic ambulance benefit or may be strictly allowable under Major Medical. The plan provisions should stipulate the handling of this expense.

Mobile Intensive Care Unit

A **mobile intensive care unit** is a life support vehicle equipped to provided care to critically ill patients who require transportation to a hospital or from one hospital to another. It is designed to serve as an extension of an intensive care unit at a hospital.

The staffing of this unit usually involves a registered nurse and several other allied health professionals. The fees are in the same range as that for an air ambulance. Such charges may be covered if they are determined to be medically necessary in lieu of regular ambulance services.

Van Transportation Unit

Many companies provide non-emergency transportation of the disabled to doctors' offices or hospital facilities. **Van transportation units** are specially equipped to handle wheelchairs, and patients who are unable to get in and out of a regular vehicle. As a rule, it is required that the patient be able to sit in an upright position. The driver may have very basic medical training, such as cardiopulmonary resuscitation (CPR), but is generally not able or equipped to handle acute patients. This type of transportation is not covered by most plans because it is not considered medically necessary.

Summary

Ambulance expenses are expenses that are incurred to transfer an injured or sick person to a medical facility. These expenses are not considered professional or hospital services. Charges for an ambulance, air ambulance, paramedics and/or a mobile intensive care unit are often payable under Basic or Major Medical if services are considered medically necessary.

Assignments

Complete the Questions for Review.
Complete Exercises 19 – 1 to 19 – 2.

Questions for Review

Directions: Answer the following questions without looking back into the material just covered. Write your answers in the space provided.

1. Name the three different types of benefits that may cover ambulance expenses.

    1. _____

    2. _____

    3. _____

2. The base call charge is _____

    _____

3. (True or False?) If a person is injured while on vacation, most plans will pay to have the patient transported to

    the nearest facility to his or her home, even if there is no other reason for the transfer. _____

4. (True or False?) In an emergency, taxicab fees would be covered since the transportation was medically

    necessary. _____

5. Name the two circumstances in which air ambulance charges may be covered under a plan.

    1. _____

    2. _____

If you were unable to answer any of the questions, refer back to the section and then complete the answers.

Exercises 19 – 1 to 19 – 2

Directions: Process each of the ambulance services claims found on the following pages.

Honors Certification™

The Honors Certification™ challenge for this chapter is a written test of the information contained within this chapter. Additionally, you will be given three ambulance claims to process, using the contracts contained in this book. You will be given 45 minutes to complete this test. Each incorrect answer will result in a deduction of between 1% and 5% from your grade. You must achieve a score of 80% or higher to pass this test. If you fail the test on your first attempt you may retake the test one additional time. The items included in the second test may be different from those in the first test.

PLEASE
DO NOT
STAPLE
IN THIS
AREA
□□□ PICA

ROVER INSURERS INC.
5931 ROLLING ROAD
RONSON, CO 81369

APPROVED MOB-0938-0008

CLAIM AMB1

HEALTH INSURANCE CLAIM FORM

PICA □□□

1. MEDICARE MEDICAID CHAMPUS CHAMPVA GROUP HEALTH PLAN FECA BLK LUNG OTHER	INSURED'S I.D NUMBER (FOR PROGRAM IN ITEM 1)
□ (Medicare #) □ (Medicaid #) □ (Sponsor's SSN) □ (VA File #) ☒ (SSN or ID) □ (SSN) □ (ID)	999-99-9999

2. PATIENT'S NAME (Last, First, Middle Initial)	3. PATIENT'S BIRTH DATE MM DD YY SEX	4. INSURED'S NAME (Last, First, Middle Initial)
BOSSY, BETTY B.	09 19 39 M□ F☒	BOSSY, BETTY B.

5. PATIENT'S ADDRESS (No., Street)	6. PATIENT'S RELATIONSHIP TO INSURED	7. INSURED'S ADDRESS (No., Street)
7991 BAGEL BLVD.	Self ☒ Spouse □ Child □ Other □	7991 BAGEL BLVD.

CITY	STATE	8. PATIENT STATUS	CITY	STATE
BARSTOW	NY	Single □ Married ☒ Other □	BARSTOW	NY

ZIP CODE	TELEPHONE (Include Area Code)		ZIP CODE	TELEPHONE (INCLUDE AREA CODE)
12899	(914) 555-3399	Employed ☒ Full-Time □ Student Part-Time □ Student	12899	(914) 555-3399

9. OTHER INSURED'S NAME (Last, First, Middle Initial)	10. IS PATIENT'S CONDITION RELATED TO:	11. INSURED'S POLICY GROUP OR FECA NUMBER:
		999-99-NIN

a. OTHER INSURED'S POLICY OR GROUP NUMBER	a. EMPLOYMENT? (CURRENT OR PREVIOUS) □ YES ☒ NO	a. INSURED'S DATE OF BIRTH MM DD YY SEX 09 19 39 M□ F☒

a. OTHER INSURED'S DATE OF BIRTH MM DD YY SEX M□ F□	b. AUTO ACCIDENT? □ YES ☒ NO PLACE (State)	b. EMPLOYER'S NAME OR SCHOOL NAME NINJA CORPORATION

c. EMPLOYER'S NAME OR SCHOOL NAME	c. OTHER ACCIDENT? □ YES ☒ NO	c. INSURANCE PLAN NAME OR PROGRAM NAME NINJA PLAN

d. INSURANCE PLAN NAME OR PROGRAM NAME	10d. RESERVED FOR LOCAL USE	d. IS THERE ANOTHER HEALTH BENEFIT PLAN? □ YES ☒ NO If yes, return to and complete item 9 a-d

READ BACK OF FORM BEFORE COMPLETING & SIGNING THIS FORM
12. PATIENT'S OR AUTHORIZED PERSON'S SIGNATURE I authorize the release of any medical or other information necessary to process this claim. I also request payment of government benefits either to myself or to the party who accepts assignment below.

SIGNED   SIGNATURE ON FILE   DATE   02/ 06/ 04

13. INSURED'S OR AUTHORIZED PERSON'S SIGNATURE I authorize payment of medical benefits to the undersigned physician or supplier for services described below.

SIGNED   SIGNATURE ON FILE

14. DATE OF CURRENT: MM DD YY ◄ ILLNESS (1st symptom) INJURY (Accident) PREGNANCY (LMP) 02 06 04	15. IF PATIENT HAS HAD SAME OR SIMILAR ILLNESS, GAVE FIRST DATE MM DD YY	16. DATES PATIENT UNABLE TO WORK IN CURRENT OCCUPATION MM DD YY MM DD YY FROM TO

17. NAME OF REFERRING PHYSICIAN OR OTHER SOURCE	17a. I.D. NUMBER OF REFERRING PHYSICIAN	18. HOSPITALIZATION DATES RELATED TO CURRENT SERVICES MM DD YY MM DD YY FROM TO

19. RESERVED FOR LOCAL USE	20. OUTSIDE LAB? □ YES □ NO $ CHARGES

21. DIAGNOSIS OR NATURE OF ILLNESS OR INJURY, (RELATE ITEMS 1,2,3, OR 4 TO ITEM 24E BY LINE) ·

1. |___·__   3. |___·__
2. |___·__   4. |___·__

22. MEDICAID RESUBMISSION CODE   ORIGINAL REF. NO.

23. PRIOR AUTHORIZATION NUMBER

24.	A. DATE(S) OF SERVICE						B. Place of Service	C. Type of Service	D. PROCEDURES, SERVICES, OR SUPPLIES (Explain Unusual Circumstances) CPT/HCPCS MODIFIER	E. DIAGNOSIS CODE	F. $ CHARGES	G. DAYS OR UNITS	H. EPSDT Family Plan	I. EMG	J. COB	K. RESERVED FOR LOCAL USE
	From MM	DD	YY	To MM	DD	YY										
	02	06	04	02	06	04	41	1	A0433	1	610 00	1		Y		

25. FEDERAL TAX I.D. NUMBER SSN EIN	26. PATIENT'S ACCOUNT NO.	27. ACCEPT ASSIGNMENT? (For govt. claims, see back)	28. TOTAL CHARGE	29. AMOUNT PAID	30. BALANCE DUE
10-8888779 □ ☒	BETBS001 939	☒ YES □ NO	$ 610 00	$ 0 00	$ 610 00

31. SIGNATURE OF PHYSICIAN OR SUPPLIER INCLUDING DEGREES OR CREDENTIALS (I certify that the statements on the reverse apply to this bill and are made a part thereof.)

SIGNED Nico Ring   DATE 2/21/04

32. NAME AND ADDRESS OF FACILITY WHERE SERVICES WERE RENDERED (If other than home or office)

HEADACHE HOSPITAL
2000 HAZARD STREET
HELP, NY 12899 (914) 555-9989

33. PHYSICIAN'S, SUPPLIERS BILLING NAME, ADDRESS, ZIP CODE & PHONE #

AWESOME AMBULANCE SERVICE NETWORK PROVIDER
909 ANDY AVENUE
ANNSTOWN, NY 12899 (914) 555-9876

PIN# AAS911   GRP#

(APPROVED BY AMA COUNCIL ON MEDICAL SERVICE 8/88)

PLEASE PRINT OR TYPE

FORM HCFA-1500 (12-90)
FORM OWCP-1500   FORM RRB-1500

PLEASE
DO NOT
STAPLE
IN THIS
AREA
□□□ PICA

WINTER INSURANCE CO.
9763 WESTERN WAY
WHITTIER, CO 82963

AREAAPPROVED MOB-0938-0008

CLAIM AMB2

HEALTH INSURANCE CLAIM FORM

PICA □□□

1. MEDICARE MEDICAID CHAMPUS CHAMPVA GROUP HEALTH PLAN FECA BLK LUNG OTHER	INSURED'S I.D NUMBER (FOR PROGRAM IN ITEM 1)
□ (Medicare #) □ (Medicaid #) □ (Sponsor's SSN) □ (VA File #) ☒ (SSN or ID) □ (SSN) □ (ID)	444-44-4444

2. PATIENT'S NAME (Last, First, Middle Initial): **DINGBAT, DANNY D.**
3. PATIENT'S BIRTH DATE: 04 | 24 | 90 SEX M☒ F□
4. INSURED'S NAME (Last, First, Middle Initial): **DINGBAT, DANA D.**

5. PATIENT'S ADDRESS (No., Street): **404 DOORWAY DRIVE**
CITY: **DENVER** STATE: **ND**
6. PATIENT'S RELATIONSHIP TO INSURED: Self □ Spouse □ Child ☒ Other □
7. INSURED'S ADDRESS (No., Street): **404 DOORWAY DRIVE**
CITY: **DENVER** STATE: **ND**

ZIP CODE: **58444** TELEPHONE: **(701) 555-3344**
8. PATIENT STATUS: Single ☒ Married □ Other □ Employed □ Full-Time ☒ Part-Time □ Student
ZIP CODE: **58444** TELEPHONE: **(701) 555-3344**

9. OTHER INSURED'S NAME:
10. IS PATIENT'S CONDITION RELATED TO:
11. INSURED'S POLICY GROUP OR FECA NUMBER: **444-44-ABC**

a. OTHER INSURED'S POLICY OR GROUP NUMBER:
a. EMPLOYMENT? (CURRENT OR PREVIOUS) □ YES ☒ NO
a. INSURED'S DATE OF BIRTH: 04 | 04 | 64 SEX M□ F☒

b. OTHER INSURED'S DATE OF BIRTH: SEX M□ F□
b. AUTO ACCIDENT? PLACE (State) □ YES ☒ NO
b. EMPLOYER'S NAME OR SCHOOL NAME: **ABC CORPORATION**

c. EMPLOYER'S NAME OR SCHOOL NAME:
c. OTHER ACCIDENT? ☒ YES □ NO
c. INSURANCE PLAN NAME OR PROGRAM NAME: **ABC PLAN**

d. INSURANCE PLAN NAME OR PROGRAM NAME:
10d. RESERVED FOR LOCAL USE:
d. IS THERE ANOTHER HEALTH BENEFIT PLAN? □ YES ☒ NO

12. PATIENT'S OR AUTHORIZED PERSON'S SIGNATURE: SIGNED **SIGNATURE ON FILE** DATE **01/26/04**
13. INSURED'S OR AUTHORIZED PERSON'S SIGNATURE: SIGNED **SIGNATURE ON FILE**

14. DATE OF CURRENT: ILLNESS/INJURY/PREGNANCY: 01 26 04
15. IF PATIENT HAS HAD SAME OR SIMILAR ILLNESS:
16. DATES PATIENT UNABLE TO WORK: FROM — TO —

17. NAME OF REFERRING PHYSICIAN:
17a. I.D. NUMBER:
18. HOSPITALIZATION DATES: FROM 01 | 26 | 04 TO —

19. RESERVED FOR LOCAL USE:
20. OUTSIDE LAB? □ YES □ NO $ CHARGES

21. DIAGNOSIS OR NATURE OF ILLNESS OR INJURY:
1. **959 . 01**   3. **E884 . 9**
2. **823 . 32**   4. **E885 . 2**

22. MEDICAID RESUBMISSION CODE ORIGINAL REF. NO.
23. PRIOR AUTHORIZATION NUMBER

24. A DATE(S) OF SERVICE From — To	B Place	C Type	D PROCEDURES/CPT/HCPCS MODIFIER	E DIAGNOSIS CODE	F $ CHARGES	G DAYS/UNITS	H EPSDT	I EMG	J COB	K RESERVED
01 26 04 01 26 04	41	1	A0427	1 2 3 4	535 00	I		Y		

25. FEDERAL TAX I.D. NUMBER: **41-8889774** SSN □ EIN ☒
26. PATIENT'S ACCOUNT NO.: **DDD52801** 434
27. ACCEPT ASSIGNMENT? ☒ YES □ NO
28. TOTAL CHARGE: $ **535 00**
29. AMOUNT PAID: $ **0 00**
30. BALANCE DUE: $ **535 00**

31. SIGNATURE OF PHYSICIAN OR SUPPLIER: SIGNED **Cy Run** DATE **2/11/04**
32. NAME AND ADDRESS OF FACILITY:
33. PHYSICIAN'S BILLING NAME, ADDRESS: **ANSWER AMBULANCE SERVICE 1140 ANY WAY AMBLER, ND 58444 (701) 555-4532** PIN# **AAM422** GRP#

(APPROVED BY AMA COUNCIL ON MEDICAL SERVICE 8/88)   PLEASE PRINT OR TYPE   FORM HCFA-1500 (12-90) FORM OWCP-1500 FORM RRB-1500

20 Durable Medical Equipment

In this chapter you will learn:

- To define and explain what qualifies as durable medical equipment.
- To identify DME services billings and to determine benefits payable.
- The common criteria for equipment covered under the DME provision.

Key words and concepts you will learn in this chapter:

Durable Medical Equipment (DME) – Items that can be used for an extended period of time without significant deterioration.

Medically Oriented Equipment – Items primarily and customarily used for medical purposes.

Necessity – Equipment is necessary when it is expected to make a meaningful contribution to the treatment of the patient's illness or injury or to the improvement of the functioning of a malformed body part.

Prosthetic Devices – Devices designed to replace a missing body part or to restore some function to a paralyzed body part.

Reasonableness – This evaluates the soundness and practicality of the DME approach

Durable medical equipment (DME) is an item that can be used for an extended period of time without significant deterioration; that is, it can stand repeated use. Therefore, an item that can be rented and returned for re-use would meet the requirement for durability. Medical supplies of a disposable nature, such as incontinent pads and surgical stockings, would not qualify as durable. (However, these items may be covered under the plan as medical supplies.)

Medically oriented equipment is primarily and customarily used for medical purposes; that is, it is designed to fulfill a medical need. Therefore, it is generally not useful in the absence of an illness or injury. For example, an air conditioner may be used in the case of a heart patient to lower room temperature and reduce fluid loss. However, since the primary and customary use is non-medical in nature, an air conditioner cannot be considered medical equipment. If the item could be used in a regular manner in the absence of a diagnosis, it is probably non-medical in nature.

DME Billing Procedures

Most plans allow for the purchase or temporary rental of equipment and supplies when prescribed by a physician. However, certain requirements must be satisfied before authorizing payment.

Basically, three tests must be applied to items billed as DME in determining whether or not the items may be covered under a plan:

1. Does the item satisfy the definition of DME?
2. Is the item reasonable and necessary for the treatment of an illness or injury or for improvement of the functioning of a malformed body part?
3. Is the item prescribed for use in the patient's home?

Only when all three conditions are met will the item be covered by the plan.

Reasonable and Necessary

An item may meet the definition of DME and yet not be covered by the plan. Two things to be considered are:

1. **Reasonableness.** This evaluates the soundness and practicality of the DME approach to therapy, including such factors as:
   a. Is the need for the unit based on failures of other less costly approaches?
   b. Have more conservative means been attempted?
   c. What benefits will be derived from the unit?

d.   Do the benefits justify the expense?

2.   **Necessity.** Equipment is necessary when it is expected to make a meaningful contribution to the treatment of the patient's illness or injury or to the improvement of the functioning of a malformed body part. Physicians tend to prescribe equipment based on a variety of reasons including:

a.   Familiarity. The physician is familiar with a particular piece of equipment. Other less expensive, more effective means of treatment or equipment may be available.

b.   Current popularity. As with clothes fashions, treatment and equipment popularity runs in cycles. Patients may even request the use of some pieces of equipment because it is hyped by the news media or some other medium. The particular equipment may not be the best or least expensive treatment available.

c.   Monetarily beneficial. Some equipment suppliers provide monetary inducements to physicians who use their equipment. Therefore, some physicians may routinely prescribe certain equipment based on this factor.

Even with a physician's prescription, it may be necessary to refer the claim to a consultant for review prior to payment or approval for purchase.

Patient's Home

For DME to be purchased or temporarily rented, the equipment must be prescribed for use in the home. Therefore, any facility that meets at least the minimum requirements of the definition of a hospital or skilled nursing facility is usually excluded from consideration.

A patient's home can be considered, but not limited to:

- His or her own home, apartment, or dwelling.
- A relative's home.
- A home for the elderly.
- A nursing home.

Oxygen

Many plans cover the use of oxygen under DME benefits. Even though the oxygen itself is not durable, the canister in which the oxygen is contained and transported is durable, and it therefore, falls under the category of DME.

Remember that these are general guidelines only. The specific guidelines may vary from payor to payor.

Billing Requirements

All claims for DME should be documented with the following information:

- A description of the equipment prescribed by the physician. If the item is a commonly used item, a detailed description may not be necessary. However, with new equipment, it is important to try to obtain a marketing or manufacturer's brochure, which indicates how the item is constructed and how it functions.
- A statement of the medical necessity of the equipment. This should be in the form of a prescription showing the imprinted name, address, and telephone number of the prescribing physician. The related diagnosis should also be indicated.
- An indication as to whether the item is to be rented or purchased and the rental or purchase price.
- The estimated length of time that the equipment will be needed. This information will aid in the analysis of whether a rental or a purchase is more economical.
- An indication as to where the equipment will be used and for how long.

Rental Versus Purchasing Determinations

The following four steps will assist in determining the most cost-efficient means of reimbursement.

1.   Determine the period of time in months in which the item will be medically required from the information provided by the attending physician.

2.   Multiply the number of months by the monthly rental fee. (This must be obtained from the supplier. Do not include the costs of perishable supplies, batteries, electrodes and other items).

>   Estimated length of use in months
>   X monthly rental fee
>   = total estimated equipment rental fee

3.   Request the supplier's purchase price for the equipment. Compare the purchase price to the calculated total estimated rental fee obtained in step #2.

4.   If the total estimated rental fee is less than or equal to the purchase price, allow for the rental. If the rental fee is greater than the purchase price, rental is allowed up to but not exceeding the purchase price. Purchase of the item is not required. However, both the member and the supplier need to be notified that an expense that is higher than the purchase price will not be allowed under the plan.

Repairs, Replacement, and Delivery

Repairs are covered when necessary to make the equipment functional. If the expense for repairs exceeds the estimated cost of purchasing or renting new equipment for the remaining period of medical need, payment is limited to the lower amount. Verify manufacturer's warranties before payment of repair fees.

Replacements are usually covered in cases of irreparable damage or wear or when the patient's physical condition has changed. Replacements due to wear or changes in the patient's physical condition must be supported by a current physician's order. Replacements due to loss may or may not be covered, depending on the circumstances. Usually, replacement is not covered when disrepair or loss results from a patient's carelessness. Other reasons for repair or replacement may be covered based on the plan provisions.

Charges for delivery of the DME and oxygen are usually covered.

Prosthetic Devices

Prosthetic devices are designed to replace a missing body part or to restore some function to a paralyzed body part.

Prosthetic devices include the making and application of an artificial part medically necessary to replace a lost or impaired body part or function, such as an artificial arm or leg, obturator, urinary collection and retention systems, or other loss.

Covered expenses associated with prosthetics include:
- Shipping and handling as part of the purchase price.
- Temporary post-operative prostheses.
- Replacement charges when replacement is due to a change in the patient's physical condition. (Children often need replacement prostheses every 6 to 12 months depending on their growth rate and other factors.) Replacement is not covered for wear and tear.

Medical/Surgical Supplies

Perishable medical/surgical supplies may be covered under the plan if the items can be used only by the patient and are medically necessary in the treatment of the illness or injury. Medical and surgical supplies include:
- Disposable, non-durable supplies and accessories required to operate medical equipment or prosthetic devices.
- Necessary drugs and biological items put directly into equipment (such as non-prescription nutrients).
- Initial and replacement accessories essential for operating medical equipment.
- Supplies furnished and charged by a hospital, surgical center, or physician as part of active therapy, such as ace bandage, cast, cervical collar.

Do not include items or supplies that could be used by the patient or a member of the patient's family for purposes other than medical care.

Questionable items should be referred to your supervisor or other designated person with the following information:
- Patient's diagnosis.
- Prescription from attending physician.
- Product description, literature, and prices.

See **Appendix 20-1** for a list of DME and coverage guidelines. This list is provided as a guide only. Actual administration may vary from company to company.

Summary

Durable medical equipment includes medical-surgical equipment that can stand repeated use, is not useful in the absence of illness or injury, and is prescribed by a physician. In addition, the item must be necessary and reasonable for the treatment of the illness or injury or to replace an injured or lost bodily part or function and must be appropriate for home use.

In addition to the cost of the item, charges are also covered for shipping, handling, and postage, which is considered part of the purchase price. Necessary repairs to purchased equipment (if the equipment is not covered under warranty) are also covered. However, the cost of repairs is usually not covered for rented equipment. Broken rental equipment should be returned to the supplier for repair or replacement.

Charges are not usually covered for modification of the structure of the patient's home (including wiring, plumbing, or structural modifications), the installation of the equipment, or modifications to transportation vehicles.

Assignments

Complete the Questions for Review.
Complete Exercises 20 – 1 to 20 – 2.

Questions for Review

Directions: Answer the following questions without looking back into the material just covered. Write your answers in the space provided.

1. What three tests must be applied in determining whether items billed as DME may be covered under a plan?

   1. _____

   2. _____

   3. _____

2. All DME claims should be documented with the following information:

   1. _____
      _____

   2. _____
      _____

   3. _____
      _____

   4. _____
      _____

   5. _____
      _____

3. Repairs are covered when necessary to make the equipment _____
   _____

4. Replacements are usually covered in cases of irreparable damages or because of _____
   _____

5. _____ are designed to replace a missing body part or to restore function to a paralyzed part.

If you were unable to answer any of the questions, refer back to the section and then complete the answers.

Exercises 20 – 1 to 20 – 2

Directions: Process each of the DME services claims found on the following pages.

Honors Certification™

The Honors Certification™ challenge for this chapter is a written test of the information contained within this chapter. Additionally you will be given three claims to process, using the contracts contained in this book. Each incorrect answer will result in a deduction of between 1% and 5% from your grade. You must achieve a score of 80% or higher to pass this test. If you fail the test on your first attempt you may retake the test one additional time. The items included in the second test may be different from those in the first test.

PLEASE
DO NOT
STAPLE
IN THIS
AREA
□□□ PICA

ROVER INSURERS INC.
5931 ROLLING ROAD
RONSON, CO 81369

APPROVED MOB-0938-0008

CLAIM DME1

HEALTH INSURANCE CLAIM FORM

PICA □□□

1. MEDICARE	MEDICAID	CHAMPUS	CHAMPVA	GROUP HEALTH PLAN	FECA BLK LUNG	OTHER	INSURED'S I.D NUMBER	(FOR PROGRAM IN ITEM 1)
□ (Medicare #)	□ (Medicaid #)	□ (Sponsor's SSN)	□ (VA File #)	☒ (SSN or ID)	□ (SSN)	□ (ID)	999-99-9999	

2. PATIENT'S NAME (Last, First, Middle Initial)	3. PATIENT'S BIRTH DATE		SEX	4. INSURED'S NAME (Last, First, Middle Initial)
BOSSY, BETTY B.	MM 09	DD 19	YY 39	M □ F ☒	BOSSY, BETTY B.

5. PATIENT'S ADDRESS (No., Street)	6. PATIENT'S RELATIONSHIP TO INSURED	7. INSURED'S ADDRESS (No., Street)
7991 BAGEL BLVD.	Self ☒ Spouse □ Child □ Other □	7991 BAGEL BLVD.

CITY	STATE	8. PATIENT STATUS	CITY	STATE
BARSTOW	NY	Single □ Married ☒ Other □	BARSTOW	NY

ZIP CODE	TELEPHONE (Include Area Code)		ZIP CODE	TELEPHONE (INCLUDE AREA CODE)
12899	(914) 555-3399	Employed ☒ Full-Time □ Student Part-Time □ Student	12899	(914) 555-3399

9. OTHER INSURED'S NAME (Last, First, Middle Initial)	10. IS PATIENT'S CONDITION RELATED TO:	11. INSURED'S POLICY GROUP OR FECA NUMBER:
		999-99-NIN

a. OTHER INSURED'S POLICY OR GROUP NUMBER	a. EMPLOYMENT? (CURRENT OR PREVIOUS) □ YES ☒ NO	a. INSURED'S DATE OF BIRTH MM 09 DD 19 YY 39 SEX M □ F ☒

b. OTHER INSURED'S DATE OF BIRTH MM DD YY SEX M □ F □	b. AUTO ACCIDENT? PLACE (State) □ YES ☒ NO	b. EMPLOYER'S NAME OR SCHOOL NAME NINJA CORPORATION

c. EMPLOYER'S NAME OR SCHOOL NAME	c. OTHER ACCIDENT? □ YES ☒ NO	c. INSURANCE PLAN NAME OR PROGRAM NAME NINJA PLAN

d. INSURANCE PLAN NAME OR PROGRAM NAME	10d. RESERVED FOR LOCAL USE	d. IS THERE ANOTHER HEALTH BENEFIT PLAN? □ YES ☒ NO If yes, return to and complete item 9 a-d

READ BACK OF FORM BEFORE COMPLETING & SIGNING THIS FORM

12. PATIENT'S OR AUTHORIZED PERSON'S SIGNATURE I authorize the release of any medical or other information necessary to process this claim. I also request payment of government benefits either to myself or to the party who accepts assignment below.

SIGNED __SIGNATURE ON FILE__   DATE __02/06/04__

13. INSURED'S OR AUTHORIZED PERSON'S SIGNATURE I authorize payment of medical benefits to the undersigned physician or supplier for services described below.

SIGNED __SIGNATURE ON FILE__

14. DATE OF CURRENT: ILLNESS (1st symptom) INJURY (Accident) PREGNANCY (LMP) MM 02 DD 06 YY 04	15. IF PATIENT HAS HAD SAME OR SIMILAR ILLNESS, GAVE FIRST DATE MM DD YY	16. DATES PATIENT UNABLE TO WORK IN CURRENT OCCUPATION MM DD YY FROM TO MM DD YY

17. NAME OF REFERRING PHYSICIAN OR OTHER SOURCE	17a. I.D. NUMBER OF REFERRING PHYSICIAN	18. HOSPITALIZATION DATES RELATED TO CURRENT SERVICES FROM MM 02 DD 06 YY 04 TO MM 02 DD 14 YY 04

19. RESERVED FOR LOCAL USE	20. OUTSIDE LAB? □ YES □ NO	$ CHARGES

21. DIAGNOSIS OR NATURE OF ILLNESS OR INJURY, (RELATE ITEMS 1,2,3, OR 4 TO ITEM 24E BY LINE) 1. 410 . 91 2. 3. 4.	22. MEDICAID RESUBMISSION CODE ORIGINAL REF. NO.
	23. PRIOR AUTHORIZATION NUMBER

24. A. DATE(S) OF SERVICE From MM DD YY To MM DD YY	B. Place of Service	C. Type of Service	D. PROCEDURES, SERVICES, OR SUPPLIES (Explain Unusual Circumstances) CPT/HCPS | MODIFIER	E. DIAGNOSIS CODE	F. $ CHARGES	G. DAYS OR UNITS	H. EPSDT Family Plan	I. EMG	J. COB	K. RESERVED FOR LOCAL USE
02 06 04 02 06 04	99	1	E0617	1	2,275 00	1		Y		
			Prescription on File							

25. FEDERAL TAX I.D. NUMBER SSN EIN 90-0013779 □ ☒	26. PATIENT'S ACCOUNT NO. BETBS001 939	27. ACCEPT ASSIGNMENT? (For govt. claims, see back) □ YES ☒ NO	28. TOTAL CHARGE $ 2,275 00	29. AMOUNT PAID $ 0 00	30. BALANCE DUE $ 2,275 00

31. SIGNATURE OF PHYSICIAN OR SUPPLIER INCLUDING DEGREES OR CREDENTIALS (I certify that the statements on the reverse apply to this bill and are made a part thereof.) SIGNED Trina Ment DATE 02/19/04	32. NAME AND ADDRESS OF FACILITY WHERE SERVICES WERE RENDERED (If other than home or office) HEADACHE HOSPITAL 2000 HAZARD STREET HELP, NY 12899 (914) 555-9989	33. PHYSICIAN'S, SUPPLIERS BILLING NAME, ADDRESS, ZIP CODE & PHONE # MISSING MEDICAL EQUIPMENT 88 MAD ROAD MILES, NY 12899 (914) 555-0509 PIN# MME103 | GRP#

(APPROVED BY AMA COUNCIL ON MEDICAL SERVICE 8/88)   *PLEASE PRINT OR TYPE*   FORM HCFA-1500 (12-90) FORM OWCP-1500   FORM RRB-1500

PLEASE
DO NOT
STAPLE
IN THIS
AREA

AREAAPPROVED MOB-0938-0008

WINTER INSURANCE CO.
9763 WESTERN WAY
WHITTIER, CO 82963

CLAIM DME2

□□□ PICA

HEALTH INSURANCE CLAIM FORM

PICA □□□

1. MEDICARE	MEDICAID	CHAMPUS	CHAMPVA	GROUP HEALTH PLAN	FECA BLK LUNG	OTHER	INSURED'S I.D NUMBER	(FOR PROGRAM IN ITEM 1)
□ (Medicare #)	□ (Medicaid #)	□ (Sponsor's SSN)	□ (VA File #)	☒ (SSN or ID)	□ (SSN)	□ (ID)	444-44-4444	

2. PATIENT'S NAME (Last, First, Middle Initial)	3. PATIENT'S BIRTH DATE MM DD YY SEX	4. INSURED'S NAME (Last, First, Middle Initial)
DINGBAT, DANNY D.	04 24 90 M☒ F☐	DINGBAT, DANA D.

5. PATIENT'S ADDRESS (No., Street)	6. PATIENT'S RELATIONSHIP TO INSURED	7. INSURED'S ADDRESS (No., Street)
404 DOORWAY DRIVE	Self ☐ Spouse ☐ Child ☒ Other ☐	404 DOORWAY DRIVE

CITY	STATE	8. PATIENT STATUS	CITY	STATE
DENVER	ND	Single ☒ Married ☐ Other ☐	DENVER	ND

ZIP CODE	TELEPHONE (Include Area Code)		ZIP CODE	TELEPHONE (INCLUDE AREA CODE)
58444	(701) 555-3344	Employed☐ Full-Time☒ Part-Time☐ Student Student	58444	(701) 555-3344

9. OTHER INSURED'S NAME (Last, First, Middle Initial)	10. IS PATIENT'S CONDITION RELATED TO:	11. INSURED'S POLICY GROUP OR FECA NUMBER:
		444-44-ABC

a. OTHER INSURED'S POLICY OR GROUP NUMBER	a. EMPLOYMENT? (CURRENT OR PREVIOUS) ☐ YES ☒ NO	a. INSURED'S DATE OF BIRTH MM DD YY SEX 04 04 64 M☐ F☒

b. OTHER INSURED'S DATE OF BIRTH MM DD YY SEX M☐ F☐	b. AUTO ACCIDENT? PLACE (State) ☐ YES ☒ NO	b. EMPLOYER'S NAME OR SCHOOL NAME ABC CORPORATION

c. EMPLOYER'S NAME OR SCHOOL NAME	c. OTHER ACCIDENT? ☒ YES ☐ NO	c. INSURANCE PLAN NAME OR PROGRAM NAME ABC PLAN

d. INSURANCE PLAN NAME OR PROGRAM NAME	10d. RESERVED FOR LOCAL USE	d. IS THERE ANOTHER HEALTH BENEFIT PLAN? ☐ YES ☒ NO If yes, return to and complete item 9 a-d

READ BACK OF FORM BEFORE COMPLETING & SIGNING THIS FORM

12. PATIENT'S OR AUTHORIZED PERSON'S SIGNATURE I authorize the release of any medical or other information necessary to process this claim. I also request payment of government benefits either to myself or to the party who accepts assignment below.

SIGNED   SIGNATURE ON FILE   DATE   01/26/04

13. INSURED'S OR AUTHORIZED PERSON'S SIGNATURE I authorize payment of medical benefits to the undersigned physician or supplier for services described below.

SIGNED   SIGNATURE ON FILE

14. DATE OF CURRENT: ◄ ILLNESS (1st symptom) ◄ INJURY (Accident) ◄ PREGNANCY (LMP) MM DD YY 01 26 04	15. IF PATIENT HAS HAD SAME OR SIMILAR ILLNESS, GAVE FIRST DATE MM DD YY	16. DATES PATIENT UNABLE TO WORK IN CURRENT OCCUPATION FROM MM DD YY TO MM DD YY

17. NAME OF REFERRING PHYSICIAN OR OTHER SOURCE	17a. I.D. NUMBER OF REFERRING PHYSICIAN	18. HOSPITALIZATION DATES RELATED TO CURRENT SERVICES FROM MM DD YY TO MM DD YY

19. RESERVED FOR LOCAL USE	20. OUTSIDE LAB? $ CHARGES ☐ YES ☐ NO

21. DIAGNOSIS OR NATURE OF ILLNESS OR INJURY. (RELATE ITEMS 1,2,3, OR 4 TO ITEM 24E BY LINE)

1. 823.32
2.
3.
4.

22. MEDICAID RESUBMISSION CODE   ORIGINAL REF. NO.

23. PRIOR AUTHORIZATION NUMBER

24.	A. DATE(S) OF SERVICE From MM DD YY To MM DD YY	B. Place of Service	C. Type of Service	D. PROCEDURES, SERVICES, OR SUPPLIES (Explain Unusual Circumstances) CPT/HCPS MODIFIER	E. DIAGNOSIS CODE	F. $ CHARGES	G. DAYS OR UNITS	H. EPSDT Family Plan	I. EMG	J. COB	K. RESERVED FOR LOCAL USE
	02 08 04 02 08 04	99	1	E0114	1	121 00	1				
	02 08 04 02 08 04	99	1	L2122	1	200 00	1				
	02 20 04 02 20 04	99	1	E0145	1	160 00	1				
				Prescription on File							

25. FEDERAL TAX I.D. NUMBER SSN EIN	26. PATIENT'S ACCOUNT NO.	27. ACCEPT ASSIGNMENT? (For govt. claims, see back)	28. TOTAL CHARGE	29. AMOUNT PAID	30. BALANCE DUE
40-0012774 ☐ ☒	DANDI001 434	☐ YES ☒ NO	$ 481 00	$ 0 00	$ 481 00

31. SIGNATURE OF PHYSICIAN OR SUPPLIER INCLUDING DEGREES OR CREDENTIALS (I certify that the statements on the reverse apply to this bill and are made a part thereof.) SIGNED *Missy Maker* DATE 2/20/04	32. NAME AND ADDRESS OF FACILITY WHERE SERVICES WERE RENDERED (If other than home or office)	33. PHYSICIAN'S, SUPPLIERS BILLING NAME, ADDRESS, ZIP CODE & PHONE # MIRACLE MEDICAL EQUIPMENT 44 MALL BLVD. MANNER, ND 58441 (701) 555-1341 PIN# MME012 GRP#

(APPROVED BY AMA COUNCIL ON MEDICAL SERVICE 8/88)   PLEASE PRINT OR TYPE   FORM HCFA-1500   (12-90)   FORM OWCP-1500   FORM RRB-1500

Appendix 20 - 1

Durable Medical Equipment Coverage Guidelines

The following is a list of commonly billed DME items and coverage guidelines. This list is intended to be used for training and reference purposes only, since the particular company or plan guidelines may differ from the guidelines stated.

Item, (Description,) and Coverage Guidelines

Action bath hydro massage – (See Whirlpool.) Rx required. Refer for medical review.

Adjust-a-bed – (Lounger.) Not covered. Comfort item.

Aero-massage – (See Whirlpool.) See Whirlpool.

Aero-pulse surgical leggings – (Non-reusable support leggings.) Rx required following surgery.

Air conditioner – (Re-circulates and cools the air in a home.) Not covered. Environmental control equipment.

Air-fluidized bed – (Institutional equipment.) Not covered. Not for home use.

Air purifier – (Electronically cleans house environment.) Not covered. Environmental control equipment.

Allergy-free items – (Not primarily medical.) Not covered. Preventive in nature, non-durable

Alternating pressure pads – (Prevents pressure sores in bed or wheelchair confined person.) Rx required when ordered for treatment of decubitus ulcers or when a person is susceptible to ulcers.

Ankle weights – (As exercise equipment for post-operative care.) Not a covered medical expense. Covered only when prescribed in a post-op situation to return function (i.e., knee surgery).

Apnea monitor – (Monitors apnea, cessation of breathing, episodes in infants.) Medical documentation of condition necessary. Rx required.

Aqua-matic K-pad – (Heating pad.) Not covered. Comfort item, non- durable medical equipment.

Aqua-matic K-thermia – (Warm water system.) Used only in institutions or acute care facility. Not covered.

Aqua massage pump – (See Whirlpool.) See Whirlpool.

Aqua-whirl – (See Whirlpool.) See Whirlpool.

Arch supports – (Removable in-shoe support. See Orthotics.) Not covered. Non-durable medical equipment.

Arterio Sonde – (Automatic blood pressure monitor.) Covered as home blood pressure monitoring device.

Artificial kidney – (Home hemodialysis unit.) Covered for chronic renal disease; ancillary supplies essential to medical use may also be covered. Refer to medical review.

Astromatic bed, Astropedic bed, Comfort-a-bed – (Comfort bed. Not medical equipment.) Not covered. Comfort tem.

Autolift, bathtub – (Bathtub lift.) Possible convenience item. Rx required, patient's weight and statement of medical necessity; refer for medical review.

Backtrak, Cotrell – (Home back traction unit.) Not covered.

Barbells – (As exercise equipment. For post-op rehabilitation.) Not a covered medical expense. Covered only if prescribed in a post-op situation to return function.

Bathtub rail and seat – (Attached to bathtub for patient assistance.) Rx required or statement of medical necessity. Covered for paraplegics, quads, or stroke patients.

Beautyrest adjustable bed – (Not a hospital bed, not primary medical.) Not covered. Convenience item. See Hospital bed (standard).

Bed bath – (Hygienic equipment.) Convenience item. Not for treating disease or injury.

Bedboard – (Provides firm support under mattress.) Not covered. Not for treatment of disease or injury.

Bed lift – (Sling, either manual or electronic; lifts person to and from bed.) See Bathtub rail and seat. Rx required, patient's weight and statement of medical necessity.

Bed lounge, power or manual – (Not a hospital bed.) Convenience item (power or manual). Not covered. See Hospital beds (standard).

Bed mattress – (Standard mattress for adjustable hospital bed.)Covered when hospital bed is allowed.

Bedpan – (Hospital type.) Covered for bed-confined or immobilized patients.

Bed siderail – (Attached to hospital bed, protective device, often standard bed equipment.) Covered if person is bed confined, or if condition of vertigo, seizure, or neurologic disorder is present; also covered for small children.

Bed, oscillating type – (Swings back and forth.) Not covered for home use. Institutional equipment.

Bell & Howell Master – (Speech teaching machine, training aid.) Not covered.

Bendix-type oxygen concentrator – (Concentrates room air oxygen to a therapeutic level.) Rx required. Covered for person with severe breathing impairment.

Bennett IPPB machine – (Intermittent positive-pressure breathing.) Rx required. Covered for person with severe breathing impairment.

Bicycle, standard – Not covered.

Bicycle, stationary – (For cardiac medical exercise program only.) Refer for medical review.

Bidet – (Hygienic toilet item.) Not primarily for treatment of disease or medical condition. Not covered.

Bimler appliance – (Orthodontic dental appliance, corrects tongue thrust.) Not covered.

Bi-osteogenic electromagnetic treatment system – (Electrical currents used to treat non-union fracture.) Covered to treat fractures. Medical documentation required.

Bird respirator – (IPPB Machine for respiratory therapy .) Rx required. Covered for person with severe breathing problem.

Blood pressure cuff – (Measures blood pressure; necessary for home management.) Covered with documented diagnosis of hypertension; also use with home hemodialysis units.

Body braces, back, foot, leg, arm – (Supportive devices.) Rx required. Covered if durable and necessary.

Bra, Jobst Surgical – (Support item following surgery.) Initial bra only following post-surgical reconstruction and mastectomy.

Braille teaching aid – (Training and vocational equipment.) Not covered.

Breast pump – (Assists mother in breastfeeding; may be either manual or electric.) Not covered. Elective device for patient comfort.

Canes – (Straight, quad, ambulatory aids.) Covered for ambulatory impairments.

Cardiac phone monitor – (Telephone-relayed EKG reporting devices.) Charges covered within physician's office fee.

Cast guards – (A waterproof (usually plastic) coverlet for casts.) Covered for all covered casting procedures.

Cast shoes (fracture boot) – (A wood or rubber-based shoe with canvas sides to support casts in ambulation.) Covered with documentation by diagnosis.

Catheter – (Medical supply item, not reusable.) For bed-confined or similarly disabled persons; for urinary retention problems.

Centrifuge Readocrit – (Blood testing equipment.) Rx required. Covered for person on home dialysis.

Cervical collar – (Neck support item.) Covered for appropriate diagnosis, such as cervical sprain.

Cervical pillow – (Neck support item.) Covered for appropriate diagnosis, such as cervical sprain.

Colostomy supplies, bags and accessories – (Used after ostomy procedures.) Covered for colostomy patients, post-rectal surgery.

Commode – (Bedside toilet chair.) Covered for bed or wheelchair-confined person.

Computerized equipment for mobility and speech – (For paraplegics.) Not covered.

Contact lens, bandage – (Protects cornea following surgery or injury.)   Rx required.

Contact lens, orthokeratology – (Myopia or refractive.) Refer for medical review.

Corset – (Supportive item.) Covered with appropriate diagnosis such as thoracic sprain.

Crutches – (Ambulatory aids.) Covered for ambulatory impairments.

Cushion-lift power seat – (Assist person in/out of seat.) Covered for person with hip, knee arthritis, or other neuromuscular conditions.

Dehumidifier – (Room or central system type.) Not covered. Environmental control equipment.

Deluxe padding – (Comfort item, special order for wheelchairs, other seating.) Not covered.

Denis Browne splint or bar – (Metal support to maintain and correct adduction.) Covered for child with clubfoot or metatarsus deformity, (includes 1 pair of shoes).

Dextrometer/glucometer/diabetic supplies – (Measures blood sugar levels.) Rx required. For diabetic treatment.

Dialysis equipment and supplies – (Artificial kidney.) Covered for chronic renal disease. See hemodialysis.

Diapulse machine – (Diathermy machine.) Not covered for home use.

Diathermy equipment – (Heat treatment.) Not covered for home use.

Disposable sheets and bags – (Supplies.) Not covered. Non-durable medical equipment.

Ear molds – (Prevents water from entering inner ear canal.) Refer for medical review.

Ease-o-matic Bed Spring – (Comfort item, not adaptable to hospital bed.) Not covered. See Hospital bed (standard).

Eaton E-Z Bath – (Bathtub seat.) See Bathtub rail and seat.

Egg-crate pad, mattress – (Portable pad for preventing bedsores.) Rx required. For treatment of decubitus ulcers.

Elastic stocking, Jobst type – (Supportive, medical item following surgery.) Rx required. Covered post-surgical expense or for diagnosis of circulatory problems.

Electra-Rest Bed – (Not a hospital bed) Not covered.

Electrocardiocorder – (Diagnostic equipment.) Covered only as part of a physician's diagnostic charge.

Electrostatic air purifier machines – (Air cleanser, environment control apparatus.) Not covered. Environmental control equipment.

Elevators – (Convenience item.) Not covered.

Emesis basin – (Basin for vomitus fluids.) Covered expense for home bed-confined patients.

Enema supplies – (For stimulating lower colon activity.) Rx required.

Enuresis equipment – (Monitoring and training devices for involuntary urination.) Not covered.

Enurtone – (Training device for enuresis) Not covered.

Ergometer – (Tension measuring device for stationary bicycle.) See bicycle (stationary).

Esophageal dilator – (To open esophagus.) Used only by physician. Not covered for home use.

Exercise equipment – (Not primarily medical.) Not covered.

Exercise pad – (Flat soft surface.) Not covered.

Exercycle – (Stationary bicycle.) Rx required. For cardiac patients in active program. See Bicycle (stationary).

Face mask, oxygen – (Necessity for oxygen therapy.) Covered when oxygen therapy is required.

Face mask, surgical – (For contagious diseases, isolation care.) Rx required.

Flowmeter, oxygen – (Oxygen regulator.) Covered when oxygen therapy is required.

Fluidic breathing assistor – (Positive-pressure machine.) Covered when IPPB care is necessary.

Foundation garment – (Padding, bras, etc.) Not covered. Check under specific items such as Corsets.

Freika pillow splint – (Maintains adduction.) Covered for small child with hip disorder.

Gatchboard – (Bedboard.) Not covered.

Gel flotation pad and mattress – (Treats and prevents pressure sores.) Covered for treatment of decubitus ulcers.

Glideabout chair – (Chair with small wheels.) Rx required. Covered in lieu of wheelchair.

Glucometers – (Measures blood sugar levels.) Rx required. For medical management of covered conditions.

Gravitronics gravity device – (Anti-gravity treatment for back condition.) Not generally accepted medical practice.

Hand-E-Jet – (Portable whirlpool machine.) See Whirlpool.

Hand-D-Vent – (Similar to IPPB machine; manual respiratory therapy.) Rx required. Covered for severe respiratory impairment.

Hearing aid – (To assist hearing.) No coverage when specifically excluded by policy.

Heating lamp – (External thermal applicator.) Not covered outside hospital setting.

Heating pad – (Applies external heat.) Not covered. Non-durable medical equipment.

Hemodialysis equipment – (Artificial kidney device for blood filtering.) Rx required. For chronic renal disease.

Holter monitor – (24-hour cardiac measurement.) Used only in physician's office. Charges payable within office fee as billed by physician.

Hospital bed, electric – (Power multipurpose bed.) Rx required. May be necessary when person is required to self-change bed position. Refer for medical review.

Hospital bed, standard – (Multilevel positioning bed.) Rx required. For bed-confined person who requires frequent position changes.

Hot tub – (Thermal home spa system.) Not covered.

Hoyer lift, hydraulic – (Hydraulic patient lift.) Rx required. Generally a convenience for lifting person from bed to wheelchair, etc. Patient's weight and statement of medical condition necessary. Refer for medical review.

Humidifier, component of oxygen equipment – (Adds moisture to oxygen.) Covered when oxygen therapy unit is covered.

Humidifier, room or central – (Environmental control.) Not covered. Environmental control equipment.

Hydrocollator heating unit – (Applies local external heat.) Rx required. Expense should be incurred through physician's office.

Hydro-jet whirlpool bath – (Comfort whirlpool.) See Whirlpool.

Hypodermic needles and supplies, hypospray – (Administration of intra-muscular, intra-dermal injections.) Rx required. For medical management of covered condition.

Incontinence pads – (Non-durable, disposable supply.) Covered only for post-surgical urinary conditions for 1month.

Infusion pump – (Stimulates constant infusions of medication subcutaneously or intra arterially.) Rx required. Refer for medical review.

Insulin pump – (Artificial pancreas function surgically implanted.) Procedures still investigational. Submit records for medical review.

Inhalator – (Respiratory assistance.) Rx required.

IPPB machines – (For respiratory therapy.) Rx required.

Irrigation kit – (For hygienic use.) Covered for respiratory paralysis, wound drainage, etc... 60 days rental.

Jacuzzi portable pump – (For use in bathtubs.) Rx required. Refer for whirlpool medical review.

Jobst Hydro Float – (Special floatation cushion.) Covered for prevention or treatment of decubitus ulcers.

Jobst pneumatic appliance and compressor, pump – (Pneumatic full-limb appliance that maintains surface pressure.) Rx required. Covered for intractable edema, post-radical mastectomy, etc. Refer for medical review.

Jobst Fabric Support, Houses, sleeves, stockings – (Non-reusable items, anti-embolism hose.) Rx required. For circulatory conditions, pre- and post-op situations.

Lambs wool pad – (Soft padding, deluxe item, non-durable.) Covered for bed sores, etc.

Laser equipment, any kind – (High-intensity light source.) Covered service only in physician's office.

Lattoflex spring base – (Not a hospital-type bed.) Not covered. Comfort item.

Lenox Hill knee brace – (Supportive orthopedic device.) Rx required. Charges based on individual custom-ordered appliance.

Leotards – (Tight body apparel.) Not covered.

Life-O-Gen tank – (Portable oxygen.) Rx required. Covered for persons with respiratory impairment.

Limb-O-Cycle – (Exercise equipment.) Not covered.

Linde Oxygen Walker – (Portable oxygen system.) Rx required. Covered for persons with respiratory impairment.

Lumex chair table – (Like a rollabout chair.) Covered in lieu of regular wheelchair.

Lymphedema pump – (Appliance that maintains surface pressure.) Rx required. Covered for intractable edema of extremity.

Mask devices – (To mask out ringing in ears.) Refer for medical review.

Mask, oxygen – (Used to deliver oxygen.) Covered for persons who require oxygen.

Massage devices – (Comfort item.)   Not covered.

Massage pillow – (Comfort item.) Not covered.

Mattress, medical – (For use with hospital bed.) Covered when hospital bed is allowed.

Maxi-Mist Machine – (Delivers medicines as mist to be inhaled.) Rx required.

Medasphere portable oxygen unit – (Portable oxygen system.)   Covered when oxygen is necessary with exercise or walking.

Medcolator – (Physical therapy equipment.) Not covered.

Medi-Cool refrigerator – (For cooling medication.) Not covered.

Medi-Jector, injection gun – (Delivers insulin without use of needles, Convenience item.) Not covered.

Micronaire environmental control – (Equipment to control environment; air purifier.) Not covered. Environmental control equipment.

Milwaukee back brace – (Supportive orthopedic brace.) Rx required.

Mobile geriatric chair – (Wheelchair with smaller than normal wheels.) Covered in lieu of regular wheelchair.

Nebulizer – (Delivers medicine in mist form for inhalation.) Covered for respiratory impairment.

Neck halter – (Supportive device.) Rx not required.

Nolan bath chair – (For assistance in bathtub.) Rx required. Possible convenience item. Statement of medical necessity. See Bathtub rail and seat.

Non-vocal communication system – (Daily living assistance system, electronic.) Not covered.

Obturator – (Oral prosthesis.) Rx required. Cleft palate prosthesis.

Orthopedic shoes – (Custom shoes.) Not covered.

Orthosis – (Adjustable back brace.) Rx required.

Orthotics, foot stabilizers – (Acrylic arch supports.) Covered only when dispensed by physician and when not excluded for policy provisions.

Osci Lite – (Heat lamp.) Not covered.

Oscillating bed – (Alternating motion bed.) Not covered for home use.

Ostomy bags – (Used after ostomy procedures.) Covered post-surgically.

Ottobock cosmetic stockings – (Covers existing prosthesis.) Not covered. Non-durable medical equipment.

Overbed tables – (For use with hospital bed, comfort item.) Not covered.

Oxygen – (Compressed gas or liquid in tank.) Rx required.

Oxygen concentrator – (Condenses oxygen from room air.) Rx required. Covered for persons with severe respiratory impairment.

Oxygen humidifier – (Adds moisture to oxygen before inhalation.) Rx required. Used in conjunction with oxygen tank system.

Oxygen regulator – (Measures oxygen flow.) Covered when oxygen unit is allowable.

Oxygen tent – (Plastic overbed cover.) Rx required.

Oxygen tank, spare – (Precautionary supply.) Not covered.

Pace Trac – (Pacemaker monitor.) Rx required. Refer for medical review.

Poli-Axial knee cage brace system – (Lightweight supportive athletic knee cage and brace; very costly.) Not covered. Athletic support device.

Paraffin bath unit, portable and standard – (Wax immersion of affected joints.) Covered for home use for arthritis patients.

Parallel bars – (Exercise equipment.) Not covered.

Penile implant – (Inflatable penile prosthesis.) Covered for those with diabetes, spinal cord injury, vascular disease, hypertension, post-surgical impotence.

Penile monitor – (Electronic measuring device.) Covered only in hospital under medical supervision.

Percusser – (Striking instrument used to perform percussion.) **Refer for medical review.**

Phonic mirror, Handi-Voice – (Electronic device that produces words by pressing buttons.) Not covered.

Pogon buggy, stroller type – (Adaptive wheelchair for child.) Covered for non-ambulatory child who requires more support than standard wheelchair provides.

Pollen extractor – (For home environment use air purifier.) Not covered. Environmental control equipment.

Portable oxygen system – (Transportable.) Rx required.
- Regulated, adj. flw. Rate – Rx required.
- Preset, one flow rate – (For general use.) Not covered.

Portable room heater – (Environmental control.) Not covered.

Posture support chairs – (Comfort item.) Not covered.

Posturpedic mattress – (Special mattress.) Covered only when a hospital bed is allowable.

Pressure-Eze pad – (Alternating pressure pad.) Covered for treatment of decubitus ulcer.

Pressure leotard – (Form-fitting apparel.) Not covered.

Pulmo-Aide – (Medicated nebulizer system.) Covered for upper respiratory disease.

Pulse tachometer – (Electronic pulse reader.) Not covered.

Reading lamp – (For home use.) Not covered.

Rib belt – (Supportive elastic item.) Rx not required. Covered for appropriate diagnosis such as rib injury.

Sacro-Ease car seat – (For auto use.) Not covered.

Sanitation equipment – (For environmental use.) Not covered.

Sauna bath – (Comfort item.) Not covered.

Scolitron stimulator – (For curvature of the back, similar to TENS unit.) Refer for medical review.

Seat lift – (Seat that raises and lowers person in and out of chair.) Rx required. For arthritis or other degenerative type diseases when the person is ambulatory.

Selectron air purifier – (Air cleaner for environmental control.) Not covered. Environmental control equipment.

Shoe wedging – (Sole modification.) Rx required.

Shoes – (Wearing apparel item.) Not covered. See Orthopedic shoes.

Sitz bath – (Moist heat application.) Not covered for home use.

Sleek seat. – (Supportive chair for atonic child.) Rx required. For children with atonic muscle condition.

Spectrowave machine – (Diathermy machine.) Not covered for home use.

Speech teaching aids – (Education devices.) Not covered.

Sphygmomanometer – (Blood pressure equipment.) Covered with documented diagnosis of hypertension; also used with home hemodialysis units

Spircare incentive breathing device – (Usually shows pulmonary function.) Not covered.

Stairglide – (Home elevator system.) Not covered.

Stand alone – (Device that allows a paraplegic to stand without assistance. Comfort item.) Not covered.

Standing table – (Special table for use in standing position.) Not covered.

Stethoscope – (Blood pressure monitoring equipment.) Covered only with home blood pressure monitoring system.

Stimulators, TENS – (Electronic pulse.) Rx required. Refer for medical review.

Stryker flotation pad and mattress – (Gel flotation pad treats and prevents pressure sores.) Rx required.

Suction machine – (Removes secretions from airway, etc.) Rx required. Must have qualified person in home to handle machine.

Sun lamp – (Thermal application to skin.) Not covered.

Superpulse machine – (Diathermy machine.) Not covered for home use.

Surgical stockings and leggings – (Support apparel, anti-embolism hose.) Rx required. See Jobst fabric.

Telemedic II – (Telephone cardiac monitor.) Covered only when done in physician's office.

Telephone arm – (Attaches to receiver, comfort item.) Not covered.

Thermo-Jet – (Whirlpool pump.) See Whirlpool.

Thermometer, clinical – (Measures temperature.) Not covered.

Thermophore fomentation device – (Heat applicator, external heat source moist heating pad.) Not covered. Non-durable medical equipment.

Tilt table – (Adjustable exercise table.) Not covered.

Toilet seat, raised – Rx required. Hip replacement surgeries. See seat lift for other conditions.

Traction device – (Weighted device for physical therapy.) Rx required.

Trapeze bar – (Supportive device used for lifting self in hospital bed.) Rx required. For use with a standard hospital bed only.

Treadmill devices – (Home walking exercise unit.) Rental covered with Rx and appropriate cardiac diagnosis.

Truss – (Hernia support.) Rx not required. Covered with appropriate diagnosis.

Tub chair – (Bathtub use. Comfort item.) Not covered.

Twister cable medical device – (Pediatric orthopedic.) Rx required. Refer for medical review.

Ultrasound machine – (Sound waves applied to muscles, tendons, etc.) Covered only in physician's office. Not for home use.

Ultraviolet equipment – (Directs ultraviolet light to body areas.) Covered for persons with psoriasis when medical necessity is documented and home use approved by physician.

Urinal, autoclaveable hosp. Type – (Not a comfort item) Rx not required. Covered for bed-confined able person.

Vaporizer – (Delivers water mist to limited area in home.) Not covered. Does not dispense medication as a nebulizer does.

Vasculating bed – (Special hospital bed providing movement.) Not covered for home use.

Vision therapy training aids – (For adjunctive home use with vision therapy program.) Not covered.

Walker – (Ambulatory aid.) Rx not required.

Water bed – (Comfort item.) Not covered. See standard adjustable hospital bed.

Water pressure pad and mattress – (Treats and prevents pressure sores, hospital bed type.) Rx required.

Weighted quad boot – (Physical fitness equipment.) Not covered. See ankle weights.

Wheel-O-Vater – (Home elevator.)   Not covered.

Wheelchair
- Regular manual standard model – Rx not required if documented by diagnosis.
- Electric type – Rx required. Person must require independent mobility.
- Accessories and repair to function – (Rubber wheel linings, ball appropriate and bearings, batteries, seat pad.) Rx required. Covered only when policy provisions do not exclude. Convenience items or modifications not functional in nature such as color coordination, deluxe padding, and trays are not covered expense.
- Travel type – Covered in lieu of regular wheelchair.

Wheelchair insert – (For small child, when chair seat does not fit.) Rx not required.

Whirlpool pumps – (Portable units for home use in baths.) Rx required. Refer for medical review.

Wigs and toupees – (Cosmetic appliance for conditions of alopecia, hair loss.) Refer for medical review.

21 Managed Care

In this chapter you will learn:

- To understand what managed care is and why it was created.
- How to process managed care claims.
- How to maintain reports and member files in a managed care setting.

Key words and concepts you will learn in this chapter:

Capitation – A monthly fee paid to a provider in exchange for handling the health care needs of a patient.

Copayment – The amount the member pays for each visit, usually a nominal fee of $10 to $30.

Eligibility Roster – A listing which shows the ffective dates of the patient's coverage, what contract they are covered under, and their Primary Care provider.

Group Model – An HMO that contracts with providers or provider groups to provide services. These practitioners agree to see only HMO members, but they do so at their own facilities.

Health Maintenance Organization (HMO) – A policy where members pay a set amount every month and the HMO agrees to provide all their care, or to pay for the covered care they cannot provide.

Independent Practice Associations – Several medical organizations or providers who band together to form their own HMO.

Managed Care – An attempt by insurers to control health care costs.

Network Model – An HMO that contracts with several providers in a given area, allowing some overlap of geographic area.

Preventive Coverage – Items such as an annual physical, cancer screening (pap smears, mammograms, etc.), flu shots, immunizations, and well-baby care.

Primary Care Provider (PCP) – The provider a member has chosen who is responsible for all their health care needs.

Staff Model – An HMO that hires physicians or providers to work at the HMOs own facility.

Stoploss – An attempt to limit payments by an insured person, or a Group/IPA in the case of a catastrophic illness or injury to a member.

Treatment Authorization Request (TAR) – A form used to request authorization for services which are the financial responsibility of the HMO.

Utilization Review is a process whereby insurance carriers review the treatment of a patient and determine whether or not the costs will be covered.

Health care costs in the American economy have escalated out of control. Higher prices for services and insurance have American consumers screaming for some type of reform. Managed care contracts were created in an attempt to bring health care costs under control by having doctors share some of the financial risks of health care with the patient and the insurance carrier.

Decreasing Costs

Numerous ideas have been batted about regarding health care reform. Everything from health maintenance organizations to a national, federally run health insurance program, have been proposed or tried. Many with varying degrees of success.

More often than not the issue is not whether to cut costs, but how. The ideas most often proposed include limiting unnecessary services and restricting access to providers who have not agreed to cut costs.

Each idea seems to have its good and bad points, and often the idea itself is not at issue, but rather where the line is to be drawn.

Cutting Unnecessary Costs

Cutting unnecessary costs is often the first idea proposed when considering how to trim the health care budget. But what is unnecessary to one person may be considered vital to another. For example, if costs are trimmed among administrative personnel, causing delays in service and/or delays in payments for services, many patients may complain. In America we have grown accustomed to the idea of having health care on demand. When we are injured or do not feel well, we want attention and a remedy immediately. Patients who have to wait a week or more for services often express dissatisfaction regarding their health care. Additionally, some patients will refuse to wait, instead seeking care in a hospital emergency room, thus creating higher costs.

But what about cutting out procedures which are unnecessary. Currently the health care system is run on a fee for service basis; that is, doctors are paid according to the number of services they provide. This type of system encourages doctors to order tests or procedures that may be of limited value in diagnosing or treating the patient. However, the more tests the doctor requests, the higher he is paid. Additionally, many patients are uncomfortable with doctors who do not prescribe a battery of tests or procedures. They want to be sure the health care provided to them is the best they can get. In the patient's mind, this often means that the more testing provided, the better their overall care must be.

When these factors are added to the threat of malpractice, doctors are often reluctant to consider a test or procedure unnecessary if there is any chance that it may benefit the patient.

But at what point does a test become unnecessary? Currently doctors may prescribe an MRI (magnetic resonance imaging) scan of the head for patients who are showing signs of stupor or confusion which indicate a blood clot or other life threatening condition. But they may also often prescribe an MRI for a patient complaining of headaches and dizziness. In only one of every 2,000 cases does this MRI reveal a blood clot or life threatening condition, at a cost of two million dollars per life saved. Whether the cost is justified often depends on whether or not that one life that was or was not saved is someone you know.

At what point do you draw the line? If a test or procedure results in a life saved for every $100 of testing done, it is easy to make a determination. But what if the cost were $2,000 or $10,000 for every life saved? At what point does that one life become not worth the cost of testing patients with similar symptoms?

Restricting Access to Providers

Many plans are experimenting with limiting patients to those doctors who have agreed to limit or curb their costs. Some plans pay nothing for a patient who sees a doctor outside the limits set by the plan. Others pay a smaller portion of costs than they normally would (i.e., 60% rather than the 80% they would pay to a provider on their list for the same services).

These types of arrangements (most common in HMOs and PPOs) force a patient to see a specified doctor, perhaps giving up the trusted physician they have

seen for years. This has become less of an issue since so many patients have less allegiance to their family physician (due perhaps to frequent moves to a new area or more frequent job changes than in past history). Additionally, many physicians understand that managed care is here to stay and are signing up with HMO and PPO organizations. This creates a situation where patients may not need to change providers even though they change insurance carriers.

Managed Care

Managed care is the wave of the future. It is touted by experts as one of the ways of gaining control over spiraling health care costs. But what is managed care and how does it work?

Managed care is simply an attempt by insurers to control health care costs.

Due to the dilemmas listed above, there are many different types of managed care organizations, including Health Maintenance Organizations, Preferred Provider Organizations, Gatekeeper PPOs, Exclusive Provider Organizations, Physician Hospital Organizations, and Management Service Organizations, just to mention a few. Several of these types of care were previously discussed in the Introduction chapter under Types of Insurance. In this chapter we will focus on processing claims in a Health Maintenance Organization setting.

Health Maintenance Organizations

Health Maintenance Organizations (HMOs) are one of the most common managed care trends. Many other managed care models may start with an HMO base and modify it based upon the needs of the members. HMOs are organizations or companies that provide both the coverage for care, and the care itself.

Under an HMO policy, members pay a set amount every month and the HMO agrees to provide all their care, or to pay for the covered care they cannot provide. The HMO hires physicians and sets up hospitals (or contracts with existing physicians and hospitals). The member chooses a specific provider for their care (called a **primary care provider** or **primary care physician (PCP)**). This provider is paid a set amount every month to take care of the enrolled members, called a **capitation** amount).

HMOs (and independent providers) are based on the principal that in any given month most of its members will not need treatment. The payments these members make will be offset by the treatment which the other portion of the membership incurs. Often capitation amounts paid to a physician for a single member are far less than the cost for a single office visit. However if a physician has 500 members who have chosen him as a PCP, the payments for the 500 people will offset the costs of treating the 50 or so people who seek treatment during any given month.

Members can sign up for HMO coverage through their employer or with an individual policy.

Many HMOs require a **copayment** amount from the member for each visit, usually a nominal fee of $10 to $30. This is the entire amount the patient must pay. Additionally, members often receive benefits that are not usually covered under regular indemnity service such as annual physicals, mammograms and pap smears. Another benefit is the lack of paperwork for the patient since the provider completes any paperwork for reimbursement for treatment.

In return, the member is locked into visiting one physician or provider. If the member wishes to see a provider other than their PCP, they must seek pre-approval from the HMO or must cover the costs themselves. One complaint that many members often have of HMOs is the lack of freedom of choice in choosing providers. Many also find the location of HMO facilities inconvenient. Some members also feel their provider is reluctant to give referrals as often as the member feels they should. This is an attempt by the HMO to cut costs by eliminating visits to specialists which they feel are medically unnecessary.

Health Maintenance Organizations are so named because of their initial belief that health care costs could be cut by providing services that maintained and encouraged the health of its members. By adding benefits such as low cost physician visits and annual check-ups, they felt members would be encouraged to seek medical attention for minor medical problems before they became serious medical emergencies.

Since the doctor is paid a set amount according to the number of participants enrolled in his office, it forces the doctor to live within a budget. This is far different from the traditional plan whereby doctors were paid for each service performed, encouraging them to perform as many tests or procedures as the patient's condition could justify. Traditional insurance has placed limits on how much will be reimbursed (or allowed) for each service performed, however the doctor who wished to increase his income simply performed more procedures rather than charged more for the ones he did. Thus, health care costs kept increasing year after year.

With the HMO philosophy, the doctor is rewarded for keeping testing and procedures to a minimum while ensuring the health of the patient.

There are several different types of HMO organizations. The most common include:

Staff model. This is the original concept of HMO services. A physician or provider is hired to work at the HMOs own facility. They are usually paid a salary and may receive additional bonuses. The provider works only for the HMO and sees no outside patients.

Group model. The HMO contracts with providers or provider groups to provide services. These practitioners agree to see only HMO members, but they do so at their own facilities.

Staff Model HMOs

In a staff HMO, the HMO owns the facility and hires the staff. When a patient comes for a visit, the copayment amount is collected from the patient by the HMO. This money is kept by the HMO and added to premiums to cover their costs of doing business.

The practitioners on staff, whether physicians, nurses, or specialists (i.e., x-ray technicians, cardiac specialists, etc.) are paid a standard salary based on the work they do and the hours they are at work. In essence they receive an hourly wage. The amount stays the same regardless of the number of patients they see or the procedures they perform.

The HMO covers all costs, including the costs of the facilities, equipment and supplies, and personnel (including doctors, nurses, specialists, accountants and any other personnel needed to keep the company running).

In this arrangement, appointments are often made through the HMO, rather than through the provider. This allows the HMO to monitor the number of patients the provider sees and the services performed. If the patient needs additional services (i.e., a referral to a specialist, lab tests, x-rays, etc.) the staff provider will input information into a system, letting the HMO know that these services are needed.

Since providers are not reimbursed per procedure, there is little benefit to performing or ordering services the patient does not need. Additionally, if an HMO feels a provider is referring too many patients for additional services, they will limit the number of referrals he may make, or may insist on additional documentation to justify the services, thus increasing the provider's paperwork.

In this model there are no claims to process since all costs are handled by the HMO.

Group Model HMOs

In a Group model HMO, a facility or Group bands together to provide services for HMO patients at their own facilities. This is much like the staff model HMO in that the providers receive a salary based on their qualifications and working hours. However, rather than receiving payment directly from the HMO, they receive their salary from the Group. The Group itself receives a capitation amount from the HMO to cover a wide range of services.

Example: The HMO signs up 10,000 members, who each pay an average premium of $150 per month. The HMO contracts with a Group to provide all provider visits, outpatient x-ray and DXL charges, and outpatient/minor surgery charges for 1,000 of these patients (other Groups will handle the remaining patients). In exchange for these services, the HMO will pay a capitated payment of $50 per member for these 1,000 members. Thus, the Group receives $50,000 per month to cover these services. The Group then hires or contracts with providers to work for them for a salary. Thus, the providers are paid from this pool of money a set amount each month.

If there are any services which the Group is contracted to provide, which they cannot supply themselves, they must cover the cost of these services.

Example: The Group contract requires the Group to provide chiropractic services for those patients who need it. However, there is not enough need for the Group to keep a chiropractor on staff on a regular basis. Thus, the Group will make an arrangement with a chiropractor to provide these services at a reduced fee (say $50 per visit). Then, when patient's need chiropractic services, they are referred to this contracted chiropractor. The chiropractor collects the copayment amount from the patient (i.e., $20), and the remaining $30 for the visit is paid to the chiropractor by the Group.

If the patient needs services which are not covered by the provider group (i.e., hospital services), they are referred back to the HMO. The HMO will then provide these services at one of their facilities. These facilities may be either wholly owned by the HMO and thus paid as a staff model, or they may be another Group who has contracted with the HMO to provide all inpatient hospital treatment. If the hospital is a staff arrangement, the HMO covers all costs. If it is a grou arrangement, they receive a capitated amount (i.e., $75 per person per month). Any amount remaining from the premiums after all Groups have been paid their capitated amounts are used to cover the costs of services which they are contractually obligated to cover, but for which there is no provider under contract (i.e., prescriptions).

In a Group set-up, patients may see different doctors in the Group each time they visit the Group offices. The copayment amount for each visit is collected by the Group and is used to cover their costs (including staff, facilities and supplies).

Some HMOs are contracting with hospitals to take over a specified number of beds, or a wing of an existing hospital rather than build their own facilities. This has come about due to the increased costs associated with building a new hospital facility, and the lowered utilization of hospitals. With HMO doctors are encouraged to shorten the length of stays at hospitals, some hospitals have only 40% to 50% of their beds filled at any given time. Sharing a facility can be a good way to provide an HMO the resources and treatment options needed while at the same time increasing the revenues of the hospital. HMO personnel are usually used to care for patients at these facilities.

Independent Practice Associations (IPAs)

Independent Practice Associations (sometimes called **Individual Practice Organizations** or IPOs) came about in the 1950s in Central California. Concerned by the amount of business the Kaiser-Permanente plan was gaining, several county medical organizations banded together to form their own HMO.

There are two arms to this type of organization. The HMO arm acts as an insurer, oversees the program, enrolls members, collects premiums and handles the claims. The medical Group arm organize physicians and contract with the HMO for discounted rates on services. The medical Group as a whole is paid a capitation amount for each member, and the Group oversees the care of the members and attempts to control costs.

The individual physicians (who are members of the medical Groups) agree to see patients in their own offices along with their regular fee-for-service clients. The doctors were able to easily gather a large number of patients by joining the HMO, and at the same time they retained their autonomy and freedom, unlike the traditional HMO doctors who were hired by the HMO and placed on salary.

This type of arrangement allows the HMO to add numerous doctors which allows patients a wider freedom of choice. Since doctors are paid a capitation amount according to the number of members they see, there is no additional cost to the HMO for adding numerous additional doctors.

The doctors agree to provide discounted fees to the medical group for their services, and the medical group covers the fees from the capitation amount. In addition to the discounted fees, the individual physicians will usually have a small amount deducted from each claim which is placed into a general fund. This is placed in an escrow account to cover any unexpected fees the medical group or HMO might encounter. Any excess money in the escrow fund at the end of the year would be reimbursed to the physicians as a bonus.

The medical groups create their own cost-control measures and some are more successful than others. For those who pay their physicians a capitation amount, the physicians seem to do very well at managing their own costs. However, some still pay the physicians on a discounted fee-for service basis. These doctors still gain higher rewards by performing more services and there is less chance to limit costs.

The fee-for-service type physician HMO reacts by performing utilization reviews, which attempt to limit unnecessary treatment. Pre-authorization, or prior approval, for hospital stays may also be required. However these measures alone do not limit costs since doctors still received a fee for each treatment or test performed. Doctors are now making sure to substantiate the reasons for each test or treatment, but are continuing to utilize more services than in group HMO practices. Because of these increased costs, some IPA type HMOs often have higher premiums than group practice HMOs.

Network model. In this instance the HMO contracts with several providers in a given area, allowing some overlap of geographic area. This allows more of a choice for subscribers and allows an HMO to increase its subscriber base without worrying about unduly overloading a single provider. In the network model, providers see not only the HMO members, but continue to see their regular fee-paying patients as well.

There are two payment types within HMOs, those that utilize capitation, and those that pay according to services provided. Capitation pays a provider a set amount per month for the treatment of a patient. The provider is paid each month, regardless of whether or not the patient visits the provider. The savings of being paid for those that do not visit is usually offset by those people who require more treatment than the average member.

Most HMOs require the Group or IPA to have a certain number of physicians in varying specialties. For example, they must often have a general practitioner or internist, a pediatrician, an OB-GYN, a cardiologist, etc. This allows the Group to treat all aspects of the patient's care and to provide appropriate services to all members who choose that Group/IPA as their PCP.

HMO Coverage

Most HMOs offer a higher level of coverage than traditional indemnity plans. For example, not only do HMOs cover physician visits and necessary testing, but treatment by a specialist (when the patient is referred by their PCP) is also often covered. HMOs also tend to cover prenatal care, emergency care, home health care, skilled nursing care, drug and alcohol abuse treatment, physical therapy, allergy treatment and inhalation therapy, often to a higher degree than coverage provided by indemnity plans. Most physician visits require a small copayment from the member, usually between $10 and $30.

Hospitalization is covered in full by some plans, however some plans require a copayment. A $100 per day copayment for the first five days is not uncommon. If a patient is seen in the emergency room there is often a $25 to $50 copayment.

Additionally, HMOs often cover preventive services. **Preventive coverage** includes items such as an annual physical, cancer screening (pap smears, mammograms, etc.), flu shots, immunizations, and well-baby care. Many also cover health education, cessation of smoking classes and nutrition counseling, (especially for diabetics and those needing weight control) or exercise classes. Traditional indemnity plans either limit or restrict coverage of such services.

Eye exams for both children and adults are covered by most HMOs, however, additional vision services (glasses, contacts, etc) may not be covered.

For those plans that cover prescription drugs, there is often a small copayment required from the member ($3 to $25) for each prescription. Prescriptions are often limited to a 30 day supply, but many HMOs have no limit to the number of prescriptions which may be filled in a month.

Mental health treatment often requires a higher copayment than physician visits ($15-$35) and are often limited to short term care. There are also limits on the number of visits (often 20 a year).

Physical therapy is often covered only for a brief period of time (6 to 10 weeks) and only if significant improvement is expected for the patient.

Controversial or experimental procedures (i.e., temporomandibular joint (TMJ) surgery, radial keratotomy, and gastric stapling) are often not covered. Cosmetic procedures are virtually never covered.

Likewise, coverage is generally not provided for nontraditional treatments. These can include those provided by chiropractor, homeopaths, naturopaths and reflexologists. Some states mandate coverage for certain providers (i.e., California law mandates that chiropractic care be covered). In such instances such care will usually be covered (if deemed medically necessary) however, the HMO may not have such practitioners on staff and the patient may need to be referred to an outside provider.

Treatment provided by non-licensed or certified practitioners are usually not covered.

Those HMOs which are federally qualified must provide the following minimum benefits:

1. Preventive care.
2. All hospital inpatient services with no limits on costs or days.
3. Hospital outpatient diagnosis and treatment services, including rehabilitative services, with some limitations.
4. Skilled nursing home and home health care services.
5. Short-term detoxification treatment for drug and alcohol abuse.
6. Medical treatment and referral for substance abuse.

Groups/IPAs

In many HMO situations, the risk for patient services is shared between the Group/IPA and the HMO. The contract between the HMO and the Group/IPA will outline who is responsible for what services and any conditions or limitations that apply to those services.

Risk determinations are usually considered to be:

*   **No risk** – The HMO collects and keeps the monthly capitation amount, and merely pays providers on a fee for service basis for the treatment rendered to members. This is similar to a regular insurance carrier set-up, except that the member pays only the copay amount, no deductibles or copayment percentage. This arrangement is almost never seen.

- **Partial risk** – The HMO is responsible for most services, however the capitation covers basic services.
- **Shared risk** – The HMO and the Group/IPA share the responsibility for services. A contract will designate which services or treatments are covered by the HMO and which are covered by the provider.
- **Full risk** – The Group/IPA is responsible for most, if not all of the services, the HMO is just in the business of selling policies and writing contracts with groups/IPAs.

Most HMO contracts with providers are on a shared risk basis. The HMO will provide a list to the Group/IPA of all possible services (often indicated by CPT code and description), and an indication of who is responsible for those services (see **Figure 21 – 1**). A letter code will often designate who is responsible for payment for that service (i.e., G = Group/IPA responsibility, H = HMO responsibility, etc.).

If an HMO offers numerous different types of policies (i.e., group coverage, individual coverage, Medicare HMO coverage, etc.), then each of these plans may be listed on the same sheet. It is important for the biller to be sure they are looking at the correct procedure code, and the correct plan to determine who is financially responsible for a service.

This document will also list any services which are denied, and the appropriate copayment amount for many of these services. It is important to note that if the plan is a Medicare HMO, any services which are normally covered by Medicare should be covered services under the HMO contract (regardless of whether the group or the HMO has financial responsibility). Therefore, if Medicare determines that they will begin covering a specific type of treatment, then the HMO Medicare contract must also begin covering that type of treatment.

Group/IPA to Physician Risk
In addition to the HMO transferring all or part of the risk to the Group/IPA, the Group/IPA may turn around and transfer some or all of their risk to an individual capitated provider. The levels of risk transferred to the capitated provider include:

- **No risk** – The Group/IPA keeps the entire capitation payment and providers are paid on a fee-for-service basis. There are usually no withholds or bonuses as part of the provider's contract. However, there will often be a fee schedule incorporated as part of the contract agreement, so the amount the provider receives for services will be determine by the fee schedule.
- **No referral risk transferred** – This means that all or part of the payment to the provider involves risk, but that the risk is not tied to referrals. Only the capitation amount, bonuses and withholds are at risk (ie, the provider may perform more services than the capitation, withholds and bonuses cover). Under this arrangement, referral means any service not provided for by the provider. Essentially, it is expected that the capitation, withholds and bonuses are the only payments for any and all care which the provider renders to the member. The provider is not responsible for paying for referrals, and the amount of money paid to the provider is not affected by the decision of the provider to make referrals to other providers.
- **Referral risk is transferred, but is not substantial** – This means that part of the payment to the provider is dependent on the decisions the provider makes to refer patients to other providers. However, that part of the payment is not substantial (ie, is under 25%). Therefore, if this type of provider makes too many patient referrals to other providers, up to 25% of his or her capitation amount may be withheld.
- **Substantial risk for referrals is transferred, but stop-loss protection is in place** – If more than 25% of total payments to the provider are at risk for referrals, the Group/IPA must have aggregate or per-patient stoploss protection in place. Stoploss protection means that if the costs to the provider exceed a specified amount, the provider will be reimbursed by the group/ IPA for at least 90% of expenditures over that amount.

In general, the higher the risk that is transferred to the provider, the higher the capitation amount. If less risk is transferred to the provider, the Group/IPA keeps a higher percentage of the capitation amount to cover it's expenses.

Capitation Payments

Capitation refers to a monthly payment made to a provider. When a contract is signed between an HMO and a provider, an agreement is made regarding a capitated fee. This fee is often dependent upon the type of plan the patient is covered under. Varying factors such as the gender and age of the patient and their overall health may also be considered. The provider and HMO will also agree which services are covered by the capitation amount.

Often capitation amounts pay for all the basic treatment the patient needs during the month. If the patient does not see the physician that month, the physician keeps the fee. If the patient becomes ill requires treatment, the physician is expected to provide the necessary services without additional compensation by the HMO. Usually the amount saved and the extra amount spent balances out.

Covered Services	MEDICARE Standard	MEDICARE Medi-Medi	COMMERCIAL AMG	Rocky	CAT	MIPC	CAIT	SBA	RICE
Abortion - Elective (CPT 59840 - 59841)	G/P[1]	G/P[2]	G/P[2]	G/P[1]	G/P[2]	G/P[2,3]	G/P[4]	G/P[4]	G/P[4]
Note: Refer to Super Panel contracts for financial responsibility for specific procedures									
Abortion - Therapeutic (CPT 59812 - 59857)	-	G	G	G	G	G	G	G	G
If the life of the mother could be endangered if the fetus is carried to term, or in cases of fetal genetic defect.									
Acupuncture	-	-	-	-	-	-	-	-	G
Acute Care									
• Facility Component	P	P	P	P	P	P	P	P	P
• Hospital Based Physicians, including clinical and anatomical pathologist (CPT 80002 - 83999), radiologist (CPT 70010 - 76499), anesthesiologist (CPT 00100 - 01999, 99100 - 99140)	P	P	P	P	P	P	P	P	P
• Professional Component, including consultations and follow up care visits (CPT 99217 - 99239, 99251 - 99275)	G	G	G	G	G	G	G	G	G
• Closed panel physicians under contract with a hospital for test reading (e.g. EKG)[5]	P	P	P	P	P	P	P	P	P
• Special services and reports, miscellaneous (CPT 99000 - 99090, 99175 - 99199)	G	G	G	G	G	G	G	G	G

[1]Not covered except in cases of rape or incest, or when the life of the mother would be endangered if the fetus were brought to term.
[2]Covered for the first thirteen (13) weeks of pregnancy only.
[3]Copay for HIPC is the same as for in-patient hospitalization.
[4]Covered through the second trimester (24 weeks) of pregnancy only.
[5]Plan to confirm closed panel status.

Legend: G = Medical Group Responsibility; P = Plan/HMO Responsibility; G/P = Shared Responsibility; -- = Not Covered

This chart shows a sampling of CPT codes and the party that bears responsibility for covering costs for each procedure under numerous different plans. It is important to check the correct column for the plan being processed to determine if services are covered or not.

Figure 21-1: Distribution of Responsibility

The capitation amount for each provider is determined by those who are included on either the active or new member roster. The PCP usually receives capitation payments for the prior month. The amount of the capitation payment will vary according to the coverages or plans which have been selected

Additional amounts may be provided for patients who have entered a hospice or skilled nursing care facility, as well as those who have been diagnosed with specific diseases (i.e., HIV or ESRD).

The HMO may withhold a portion of the monthly capitation amount to protect the HMO from inadequate patient care or financial management by the PCP. They may also withhold a portion to insure the quality of care given to patients and promptness of payments to outside providers. This amount is outlined in the contract signed by the group and the HMO.

For example: The 123 HMO withholds 3% of the capitation amount to cover financial insolvency and unpaid claims by the Group/IPA. If all obligations have been met, this amount will be returned when the group terminates its contract with the HMO.

Additionally the 123 HMO will withhold 5% of the capitation for its Medical Management Incentive Program. This program stipulates that the 5% will be reimbursed to the Group/IPA if the following guidelines are met:

- 25% of the withheld amount will be reimbursed if the Group/IPA has submitted less than their budgeted amount of hospital expenses which are covered by the HMO.
- 15% of the amount will be reimbursed for customer satisfaction. The HMO will randomly survey patients to determine their satisfaction with the provider and the services rendered. If the provider is above the average in customer satisfaction, he or she will receive this amount.
- 20% of the withheld amount will be reimbursed for low disenrollment. If the provider/group maintains less than 2% disenrollment (those terminating HMO coverage or transferring to another provider), then they will receive this amount.
- 40% of the withheld amount will be reimbursed for quality of care. This will be determined by a review of medical records by the HMO. If the Medical Review Panel agrees with the treatment given at least 80% of the time, the provider will receive this amount.

Billing for Services

While the monthly capitation amount covers most services, some services will be reimbursed on a fee for service basis. This means that the provider will bill the HMO for these services when they are performed. Most agreements between a provider and an HMO will have a list of those services which are covered by the capitation amount, and/or those which are considered to be on a fee for service basis. Fee for service procedures are billed on an HCFA-1500 or superbill the same as non-HMO services.

Authorizations, Referrals and Second Opinions

In an effort to contain their costs, HMOs will often require pre-authorizations for treatment that is their financial responsibility. They may also require a Second Surgical Opinion regarding the proposed treatment.

Pre-Authorization

Most HMOs require that the provider or member obtain pre-authorization for services which are the financial responsibility of the HMO. This is often done on a **Treatment Authorization Request (TAR)** form. The provider lists the diagnosis and proposed treatment plan, along with any needed follow-up care.

The TAR is submitted to the HMO for approval, and the HMO evaluates the proposed treatment and informs the provider and member whether or not they will cover the services. If the HMO decides that the services are not necessary, they will deny payment. The provider and member must then decide whether they will abandon the treatment, seek authorization for an alternate treatment, or if they will go ahead with the treatment with the understanding that the patient is completely responsible for the charges.

The HMO may decide that a Second Surgical Opinion (SSO) is needed before they make a determination. In such a a case, the member must have the SSO performed prior to the services, and with enough time for the HMO to evaluate the second surgeon's response to determine whether or not they will cover the services.

Often a TAR approval will be valid for a limited time, usually 30 days. If services are not performed within that time the provider will need to complete an additional TAR and obtain another pre-authorization. In the case of ongoing treatments (i.e., chemotherapy, dialysis), the provider may need to obtain monthly authorization of services covered by the HMO.

All routine follow-up care and/or hospital stays should be included in the one authorization.

If a specific date of surgery is listed on the TAR, and the surgery is approved, the surgery should have been performed on the date indicated on the TAR. If there is no date listed, TARs are often good for 30 days from the date of approval. Services must have been performed within that time period for the TAR approval to be valid. If a TAR was approved, but services were not performed within the required time period, and no additional TAR was submitted, the Group/IPA may be responsible for payment of services, not the HMO.

The TAR approval will also indicate the number of days allowed for the patient to remain in the hospital (if it is an inpatient admit). Any days beyond this are not covered by the HMO unless an additional TAR was submitted and approved, verifying the need for additional services.

Example: John Johnson received approval for treatment in the HMO hospital facility for surgery to remove gallstones. During the surgery there were complications, which necessitated the need for an additional three days in the hospital. A TAR was not submitted for the additional three days. Therefore, the services are covered for the main surgery, but the additional three days are the financial responsibility of the member or the Group.

Different rules may apply for inpatient admission for psychiatric care or chemical dependency.

Emergency TARs

Many HMOs have an emergency request procedure which allows faxing of the TAR and overnight approval.

If the member is unable to wait the 24 hours for treatment, they should seek assistance in the emergency room of the nearest hospital. The hospital will then contact the HMO for an emergency treatment request. Many HMOs have a clause that the member must seek emergency treatment at an HMO facility, if possible. Only if the emergency is threatening to life or limb, should the member go to a non-HMO facility.

In such cases the hospital is required to provide life-saving measures. Any measures not required to sustain life must be approved by the HMO before they are rendered. Many hospitals are aware of this situation, and will immediately call the HMO before treating an HMO member who has sought treatment at their facility.

The HMO will do an immediate review of the patient's situation and authorize individual services. However, each service will need to be authorized prior to being rendered, unless it is necessary to sustain the life of the patient.

If the patient is stable, the HMO will often have the patient transferred to their own facility for treatment.

Example: June Jenkins was involved in a diving accident. When she was pulled from the water, she was not breathing and it appeared her neck was broken. At the emergency room the doctors were able to perform life-saving measures (i.e., CPR, insertion of a respirator tube). However, before being able to do a spinal x-ray or MRI, authorization was needed from the HMO. Only when the HMO authorized these procedures would the hospital be assured of payment on the services done to determine the extent of her injury. If the hospital had performed these services prior to receiving authorization, June would have been responsible for full payment on the unauthorized procedures.

If the Group/IPA is considered financially responsible for emergency room services, then they are responsible for managing the member's utilization of ER services and for paying for the cost of these services. The group must provide written information to its members on how to access these services. The Group/IPA must have procedures for the authorization of these services. Payment may not be denied based on lack of notification or lack of authorization for these services.

If the member seeks ER services from a non-contracted provider, the Group/IPA usually has 30 minutes to respond from the time of the non-contracted providers first call. Lack of response means that the ER may provide whatever services it deems necessary to treat the emergency situation and the Group/IPA is often obligated to pay for all charges.

Utilization Review

Utilization review is a process whereby insurance carriers review the treatment of a patient and determine whether or not the costs will be covered. Many nsurance carriers began creating utilization review departments in an effort to control costs and avoid unnecessary procedures. While this process was started with traditional insurance carriers, managed care carriers have taken the concept a step further, creating complete UR departments and reviewing every outside procedure which may require additional costs and every referral to a specialist.

Many doctors dislike the utilization review process. They feel the UR committee cannot always make an effective decision based on the data provided in the medical report. They dislike being second guessed by a committee that is not familiar with the patient and their problems.

Additionally, UR committees are becoming more selective in the items and providers they choose to review. Those procedures which are nearly always allowed, such as a cystourethroscopy, are being automatically allowed while more questionable procedures such as MRIs on the knees are being reviewed. Additionally, some insurers are tracking the records of providers. Those that are known for ordering tests or procedures that are nearly always necessary are less closely watched than those who have a history of ordering questionable procedures.

Specialist Referrals

If a member requests to see a specialist, the PCP must discuss the request with the member. If the request is denied, the procedures for denial of services must be followed, including the sending of a denial letter to the member.

If the PCP agrees with the members request, or recommends the member to see a specialist, an appropriate referral form should be completed and approved by the Group/IPA. The decision to refer or not to refer a member is a medical judgment which should be made by the PCP and the Group/IPA, especially since the financial responsibility for these visits often falls with the PCP or Group/IPA. Of course if the member wishes a referral to a specialist for a service that is the financial responsibility of the HMO, pre-authorization must be obtained.

If the referral authorization is approved, a written notice must advise the member of the name, address and phone number of the specialist and either state an appointment time, or inform the member how to schedule an appointment.

The Group/IPA is required to have contracts with its specialists. They must maintain contracts with a sufficient number of specialists so that members are not inconvenienced by excessive appointment waiting times.

Second Opinions

If a member requests a specific treatment and the HMO determines that this treatment or service is not medically necessary, would be detrimental to the patient, or would provide no medical benefit to the member, they may deny the service (i.e., refuse to cover the treatment). The denial letter should contain a statement regarding why services are denied.

Many HMOs have a second opinion policy designed to resolve differences of opinion regarding proposed treatment among PCP, members, specialists, and/or the HMO. Second opinions are often provided in the following instances:

- At the request of the member before a surgical or other invasive procedure,
- If the PCP's opinion is contrary to the member's expressed expectations, even after the physician has counseled the member,
- If the opinion of the PCP differs substantially from the recommended treatment plan of the specialist on the case, or
- At the request of the HMO.

There are several steps to the second opinion process:

1. A request is made by the PCP, member, consultant or HMO for a second opinion. This request may be either verbal or in writing.
2. The patient's chart is documented with the request.
3. An internal review is done. This is a second opinion performed by another physician affiliated with the same Group/IPA as the PCP.
4. If the member is still dissatisfied, or if the two opinions differ substantially, an external review may be performed. This is an opinion provided by a physician who is not a member of the Group/IPA to which the member belongs. If the member is still dissatisfied, they may contact the HMO to request the external review. The HMO reviews the records and, if they deem it necessary to have an external review, they will inform the PCP and the member. The HMO

may send the member to a physician of their choosing.
5. All records are forwarded to the HMO's Chief Medical Officer who makes a determination of the proper course of treatment. The PCP will then be informed of the decision and it is their responsibility to carry out the proposed treatment plan. This may mean treating the patient themselves, or referring the member to a specialist for treatment.

Financial responsibility for second opinions is usually split among the Group/IPA and the HMO as follows:

1. The Group/IPA is responsible for the internal review.
2. The HMO is responsible for the external review unless the Group/IPA failed to document the internal review, did not properly complete a TAR and obtain authorization before sending the member for an external review and/or if the opinion of the external review physician differs substantially from the Group/IPA decision.

All activities regarding the second opinion process must be thoroughly documented in the patient's record. Any time the HMO must bear financial responsibility for any services, including the external review, a TAR must be completed and the treatment pre-authorized.

Because of substantial delays in receiving authorizations and/or referrals, and member complaints, some HMOs are now allowing members to refer themselves for a second opinion. However, they are limited to obtaining a second opinion from another provider who is affiliated with the same HMO, and the number of times they may refer themselves for a second opinion is limited (i.e., once every six months).

Denials of Service after a Second Opinion

Once the member has exhausted the second opinion process, or chooses not to proceed with the process (i.e., accepts the decision of the internal review), the Group/IPA must send a denial letter to the member. A copy of this letter must also be sent to the HMO with any supporting documentation.

This letter must state the patient's name, the date services were requested, the services that were requested, and the reason for the denial of services.

The HMO will often keep a log of these denials. If they feel a Group/IPA is denying too many treatments, they may ask for a review of the record to monitor the quality of care given to the patients.

Miscellaneous Services

Certain rules can apply to select types of service under an HMO agreement. These services can include outpatient surgery, emergency room services, durable medical equipment, and prescriptions.

Outpatient Surgery

Some HMOs will provide a list of surgeries that must be performed in an outpatient setting. This is most often done in a shared risk contract when the Group/IPA is financially responsible for outpatient services and the HMO is responsible for inpatient services.

It is important to know which surgeries must be performed on an outpatient basis. If these guidelines are not followed, the Group/IPA may be financially responsible for all inpatient costs in relation to the surgery.

The examiner should be aware of this list and keep it handy. If a claim is received for inpatient surgery that should have been performed on an outpatient basis, the claim should be denied and returned to the provider/PCP.

If the provider feels the surgery should be done inpatient due to complications or other circumstances, a TAR should have been submitted and approval received prior to surgery.

Prescription Coverage

When an HMO offers prescription coverage to a member, there are often limitations as follows:
1. The member must purchase the drugs from an HMO contracted facility. If they obtain prescriptions from a non-contracted pharmacy, the member will bear the cost of the pharmacy services. There may be exceptions to this rule for emergency situations, or situations where the patient is outside the service area, or the prescription is not available from a contracted pharmacy.
2. They may limit drugs and medications to a 30 day supply.
3. They will usually only cover prescription drugs. Over the counter medications are usually not covered.
4. They may only include oral and topical drugs. Injectable drugs are often not covered under the pharmacy benefit. They may, however be covered under the medical benefit. This is especially true for injectable medications which the patient needs for survival (i.e., insulin for a diabetic).
5. They may also insist that the generic equivalent of a drug be prescribed if it is available. If there is no generic equivalent, the HMO will often cover the brand name at the standard copayment amount. However, if there is a generic equivalent, the HMO may only cover the cost of the generic equivalent. Thus, the member will be charged the standard copay, plus the difference between the generic and the brand name medication.

Some generic drugs are not the same as their brand name counterparts. They may have a similar, but different active ingredient, or they may be in a different dosage amount from the brand name drug. In such a case they are not considered to be therapeutically equivalent. For these drugs, the HMO may require the physician to prescribe the generic drug, or they may allow the full benefit for the brand name drug.

Claim Payments

Now that you understand some of the basic rules regarding eligibility, pre-authorizations, referrals and second opinions, we will discuss processing a claim from the HMO point of view. Below is a brief overview of the process. Each item will then be discussed in more detail.

1. Check the members eligibility, which contract they are covered under, and who is their PCP.
2. Check the member's contract to determine if the services are covered and any copayment or other amounts.
3. Determine who is financially responsible for payment on the claim by using the Distribution of Responsibility chart.
4. Check if the proper referrals, pre-authorizations or second opinions where done.
5. If the referrals, pre-authorizations or second opinions were done, process the claims.
6. If the referrals were not done, deny or reduce benefits accordingly and process the claim.

To process the claim:
1. Determine the allowed amount for the procedure.
2. Determine if there should be a reduction of benefits due to improper referrals, incompleted authorizations or other limitations.
3. Subtract the amount of any copayment given by the member.
4. Pay the remaining amount.

Check Member Eligibility

When processing HMO claims, as with other types of claims, eligibility is the first item to consider. Check the **eligibility roster** to determine the effective dates of the patient's coverage, what contract they are covered under, and their PCP (the Group/IPA responsible for their primary care).

The HMOs providers will often have three eligibility rosters to consider:
1. The **active member roster** lists those whose coverage has continued into the next month. This usually means the insured or their employer has paid the monthly premium to continue coverage for another month.

2. The **new member roster** shows those patients who have signed up for HMO coverage and have chosen the provider as their PCP. The new member roster also shows those patients who have recently chosen this provider as their PCP.

3. The **terminated member roster** shows those members whose coverage has been terminated.

The claims examiner will often have a computerized eligibility roster which shows not only the dates the member was eligible, but also what plan they are covered under and who their primary care physician is. The plan the patient is covered under will not only determine the covered services, but will also determine who is responsible for payment of each individual service.

Check the Member Contract

Once you have determined the plan, go through the member's contract. As with other contracts, this will list the items covered, the amount of copayments, and any excluded items. Any amounts that are excluded would be automatically denied.

Determine Financial Responsibility

For items that are covered, you will need to determine who is responsible for payment of the item. When a Group or a provider signs up with an HMO, they agree to cover certain services in exchange for a capitation amount. When each provider signs up, they will sign up for certain plans. They may be providers on some plans, but not on others.

Refer to the Distribution of Responsibility chart (see **Figure 21 – 1**). This is a chart (often many pages long) that will show who is responsible for the payment on each plan. This will be either the provider (regardless of whether it is a group of individual provider), or the HMO. On some items, the responsibility may be shared. In these cases you will need to refer to the specific contracts written for that plan and with the providers. This will explain in greater detail who has financial responsibility for the services.

Items are often listed on the Distribution of Responsibility chart by CPT number. If a chart lists items alphabetically, it may be necessary to look up the procedure code in the CPT to determine what the service is. Additionally, many Distribution of Responsibility charts that are listed alphabetically may have an indexed listing by CPT code in the back.

Once you have located the proper procedure code, follow the line across until you are under the plan name for the plan the member is covered under. Determine whether the responsibility is with the provider or the HMO. Be sure to check if there are any provisions regarding coverage. These will often be referenced by a small number, with a more detailed explanation at the bottom of the page (i.e., see Abortion on **Figure 21 – 1**).

If the provider is responsible for payment of the services, then these items are considered covered by the capitation amount and no further payment is due on those services. Check who the provider was on the claim. If the provider submitting the claim was the members PCP, then charges should be denied as being covered by the capitation amount. If the provider on the claim is not the PCP, the claim should be forwarded to the PCP for payment.

If there are services that the PCP is responsible for and services that the HMO is responsible for on the same claim, process the claim and pay those items the HMO is responsible for. Items the PCP is responsible for should be denied and the claim should be forwarded to the PCP for further processing, if needed.

Check Referrals, Pre-authorizations or Second Opinions

Those items that are the financial responsibility of the HMO should have had referral or pre-authorizations performed. In some cases a second opinion may also have been required. Check to be sure that all the proper paperwork was done.

If the paperwork was not done, check the contract to determine what the impact will be on the coverage of those services.

The pre-authorization will often be accessible by computer, so the claims examiner should be able to check it quickly and easily. Often a pre-authorization number will be included on the claim (see box 23 on the HCFA-1500). If a pre-authorization number is not included you must check the system for the pre-authorization. Not having a pre-authorization number on the claim is often not considered a valid reason for denying payment on a service since the claims examiner has access to that information.

If the referrals, pre-authorizations or second opinions were done, process the claims.

If the referrals were not done, deny or reduce benefits accordingly and process the claim.

Patient Encounter Forms

The group/IPA must report all patient encounters (i.e., visits) to the HMO. This is true regardless of whether the visit occurs at the group/IPA, or at one of its contracted providers. This reporting is often done using an encounter form. If the Group/IPA does not have data regarding an encounter (which may happen if they are not contractually obligated to cover the services), but they receive information regarding the encounter, they should report what they know of the encounter to the HMO.

The HMO may specify the use of a designated form for reporting encounters, or they may use the HCFA-1500.

Encounters for consultation, second opinions and other outside visits should be reported prior to adjudication and/or payment of the claim.

Some HMOs have their providers or group/IPAs report patient encounters on an HCFA-1500. When this is done, the only difference between this and a normal HCFA-1500 is in item 24F, the charges. If the charges are covered by a capitation amount, then there is no charge for these services. Therefore the indicated charges will be $0. The total charges and the balance due will, likewise, be $0.

If there are services which a provider renders which are not covered by the normal capitation amount, the amount for these charges should be placed in item 24F. Some HMOs may have providers or group/IPAs submit charges that are the HMOs responsibility on a separate claim form from those that are covered under capitation. Thus, two claim forms for the same provider, patient and dates of service may be necessary.

Processing the Claim

You are now ready to begin the actual calculations to process the claim. When claims are submitted, they will often be submitted with a Claim Transmittal Form (see **Figure 21 – 2**). This form will indicate the type of claim being submitted and the authorization number for these claims.

Determine the Allowed Amount
Start by determining the allowed amount for the procedure. Most HMOs will have a fee schedule which will list each CPT code and the allowed amount for that code. Some HMOs which cover a wide area may have an RVS and Conversion Factor Report. In these cases, calculate the allowed amount using these factors in the same way you would calculate indemnity claims (see the **Usual, Customary and Reasonable** chapter for more information).

If there is a contracted amount for services, the terms in the contract should be adhered to. Usually a fee schedule will accompany contracted terms. This fee schedule may be different for each provider which the Group/IPA contracts with. The proper contract should be pulled and the correct allowed amount determined.

Calculate Any Reduced Benefits
If the member or PCP did not obtain the proper referrals, pre-authorizations, or second opinions, determine the impact on the payment. This will often be stated in either the contract with the member (if it was the member's responsibility to obtain the proper paperwork) or the HMO's contract with the Group/IPA.

If the benefits are reduced calculate the impact of the reduction, (i.e., if benefits are reduced to 50% if pre-authorization is not obtained, multiply the allowed amount by 50%).

Be sure that you look at all paperwork carefully. If the pre-authorization allowed three days of inpatient care and the member spent four days in the hospital, services for the last day may not be covered, or may be reduced. In such a case you may need to request an itemized billing to determine the dates that services were provided so you can determine which services should be denied.

Subtract the Copayment
Check the member's contract. Each item should list a copayment amount if a copayment is required from the member. Be sure you are checking the proper category. Often there will be different copayment amounts for different types of services.

The amount of the members copayment is always subtracted from the allowed amount. If the provider neglected to collect this amount at the time services were rendered they are responsbile for contacting the patient and collecting it. Thus, even if the claim states that no money was collected from the member, the copayment amount should always be subtracted.

Pay the Remaining Amount
Pay any amount remaining after you have reduced the allowed amount and subtracted the copayment amount. Since the member is always responsible for the copayment, and usually only the copayment, any resulting benefits are generally due to the provider. The member should not have paid more than the copayment amount. If the member did pay more than the copayment amount, the provider is responsible for reimbursing the member for any amounts they overpaid.

An EOB should accompany all claim payments showing the calculation of the benefits and providing an explanation for why any services were denied or reduced. A notice should also accompany the EOB stating that this is the contracted amount for this service and no amounts other than the copayment may be collected from the member.

Of course if you are working for a staff model HMO, there is no payment due for those services rendered by the HMO owned facility. This is because the providers in this type of facility are paid a salary, regardless of the members they see or the services they perform.

Denial of a Claim or Service

If a claim or service is denied, a denial letter must be included with the EOB indicating the reason for the denial. The denial notice must also include a statement that the provider has the right to appeal the denial within 60 days, and the address of where to file an appeal. If it is believed that services were not medically necessary, or were not true emergency services, then the claim must be sent through a medical review process. The medical review should use the presenting diagnosis, rather than the

Provider Network Services
CLAIMS TRANSMITTAL FORM

Date:

To: Claims Services

From: _____, Administrator for _____

The attached claims are the responsibility of [the HMO].

Authorization Number

____   Inpatient Hospital (IP) Charges

____   Outpatient Surgery (OPS) Facility Charges

____   Anesthesia for approved IP or OPS

____   Radiology for approved IP, OPS or SNF

____   Pathology for approved IP, OPS or SNF

____   Emergency services which resulted in admission to Inpatient status

____   Ambulance

____   Durable Medical Equipment

____   Dialysis Facility Charges

____   Radiation Therapy

____   Member not on roster for date of service. Include relevant roster page(s).

NOTE: Use a separate form for each type of Plan expense. Multiple providers may be grouped if the authorization number is the same.

[The HMO] will not send denial notices for services which are the responsibility of the Group/IPA.

Refer to the Medical Services Agreement for questions of coverage and financial responsibility.

Figure 21 – 2: Transmittal Form

Excess Risk Limit Cost Summary

I.

Group Name: _____

Address: _____

_____

Contact Person: _____

Phone Number: _____

Date Submitted: _____

II.

Enrollee Name: _____

Enrollee PF#: _____

Date of Eligibility: _____

Contract Year: _____

For HIV/AIDS cases, list qualifying hospital stays:

_____

_____

_____

Type of Submission
___ Original   ___ Medicare
___ Supplemental   ___ Commercial
___ Resubmittal   ___ OO Care
___ AIDS/HIV   ___ CCC

III.

Provider of Service / Provider #	Date of Service	CPT4, RVS, or SMA code	Units	Billed Amount	Amount Paid	For HMO use only
		TOTAL THIS PAGE:				

Figure 21 – 3: Excess Risk (Stoploss) Form

discharge diagnosis as the basis for their decision making, and must consider the member's understanding of the medical circumstances which led to the emergency service

All denial notices must contain an explicit reason, in laymans terms, of why the service(s) are being denied. If the HMO provides a list of denial reasons, then the appropriate denial reason should be written on the denial letter. You may not use a code unless you indicate the meaning of that code on the denial letter. Additionally, all denial letters must meet the following criteria:

1. The decision to deny must be correct and based upon approved medical practices.
2. The denial reason must be clear to the member and must use HCFA-approved denial reasons.
3. The denial letter must include mandated appeals language and the correct health plan address.
4. The denial letter must be sent to the appropriate parties (either the provider, the member, or both).
5. The denial notice must be issued within required time frames.

Appeals

Any member or provider has the right to appeal a denied claim. All denial letters, by law, must include a statement saying that the receiver has the right to appeal the decision and whom to contact to begin the appeal process.

If a member or provider appeals a denied claim, the HMO will review the claim and make a determination of whether to uphold or reverse the denial. If the HMO determines that the services should have been covered, and the services were the financial responsibility of the Group/IPA, it will inform the Group/IPA of its decision and will instruct the Group/IPA to pay the claim.

Reinsurance/Stoploss

Stoploss is an attempt to limit payments by an insured person, or a Group/IPA in the case of a catastrophic illness or injury to a member.

Many HMO contracts have a stoploss or reinsurance clause included in them. This clause may state that the

Group/IPA will be financially responsible for the first set amount (i.e., $7,000) in expenses for each member in a contract year. After those expenses have been paid, the HMO will reimburse the Group/IPA for verified expenses which exceed the set amount.

If the provider's contract has a stoploss clause, it is important that the claims examiner be aware of the amount. Any services which exceed that set amount should be covered by the HMO.

Often the HMO will require that a claim for reimbursement be submitted on specific forms. An example of this form is shown in **Figure 21 – 3**.

Summary

Health care costs in the American economy have escalated out of control. Higher prices for services and insurance have American consumers screaming for some type of reform. Managed care contracts were created in an attempt to bring health care costs under control by having doctors share some of the financial risks of health care with the patient and the insurance carrier.

HMOs are one of the most common managed care trends. HMOs pay providers a set capitation amount each month for the patients on their eligibility roster, and in return the provider is expected to cover many of the services that member needs. A written contract will dictate those services which the provider will cover and those which the HMO will cover.

For those services that are the financial responsibility of the HMO, the provider will submit a claim. The claim must be processed and paid or denied in a timely manner.

The rules governing payment of HMO claims will vary from those of indemnity claims. In an HMO the financial responsibility must be determined, along with determinations of whether or not pre-authorizations, referrals or second opinions were handled properly.

Assignments

Complete the Questions for Review.
Complete Exercise 21 – 1.

Questions for Review

Directions: Answer the following questions without looking back into the material just covered. Write your answers in the space provided.

1. What is an HMO?_____

    _____

    _____

2. In a _____ the insurance carrier will contract with a group of facilities and/or providers to

    provide services at a set fee per month.

3. What is a capitation payment?_____

    _____

4. What is a TAR and what is its purpose?_____

    _____

5. What is stoploss? _____

    _____

If you were unable to answer any of the questions, refer back to the section, and then fill in the answers.

Exercise 21 – 1 to 21 – 5

Directions: Process the following HMO claims based on information provided in the member contract (Appendix 21 – 1), the Distribution of Responsibility schedule in Appendix 21 – 2, and the Fee Schedule in Appendix 21 – 3.

Honors Certification™

The Honors Certification™ challenge for this chapter is a written test of the information contained within this chapter. Additionally you will be given three claims to process, using the contracts contained in this book. You will be given 60 minutes to complete this test. Each incorrect answer will result in a deduction of between 1% and 5% from your grade. You must achieve a score of 80% or higher to pass this test. If you fail the test on your first attempt you may retake the test one additional time. The items included in the second test may be different from those in the first test.

SUMMER INSURANCE CO.
70065 SUNNY STREET
SANDY CITY, CO 82963

APPROVED MOB-0938-0008

CLAIM HM01

HEALTH INSURANCE CLAIM FORM

PICA □□□

1. MEDICARE MEDICAID CHAMPUS CHAMPVA GROUP HEALTH PLAN FECA BLK LUNG OTHER	INSURED'S I.D NUMBER (FOR PROGRAM IN ITEM 1)
□ (Medicare #) □ (Medicaid #) □ (Sponsor's SSN) □ (VA File #) ☒ (SSN or ID) □ (SSN) □ (ID)	222-22-2222

2. PATIENT'S NAME (Last, First, Middle Initial): **MORPHINE, MIKE M.**

3. PATIENT'S BIRTH DATE: 02 | 12 | 65 SEX: M ☒ F □

4. INSURED'S NAME (Last, First, Middle Initial): **MORPHINE, MINDY M.**

5. PATIENT'S ADDRESS (No., Street): 522 MUSHROOM STREET

6. PATIENT'S RELATIONSHIP TO INSURED: Self □ Spouse ☒ Child □ Other □

7. INSURED'S ADDRESS (No., Street): 522 MUSHROOM STREET

CITY: MIGRAINE STATE: ME

8. PATIENT STATUS: Single □ Married ☒ Other □ Employed ☒ Full-Time □ Part-Time □

CITY: MIGRAINE STATE: ME

ZIP CODE: 04022 TELEPHONE: (207) 555-3322

ZIP CODE: 04022 TELEPHONE: (207) 555-3322

9. OTHER INSURED'S NAME:

10. IS PATIENT'S CONDITION RELATED TO:

11. INSURED'S POLICY GROUP OR FECA NUMBER: 222-22-ROC

a. OTHER INSURED'S POLICY OR GROUP NUMBER:

a. EMPLOYMENT? □ YES ☒ NO

a. INSURED'S DATE OF BIRTH: 12 | 22 | 65 SEX: M □ F ☒

a. OTHER INSURED'S DATE OF BIRTH: M □ F □

b. AUTO ACCIDENT? □ YES ☒ NO PLACE (State)

b. EMPLOYER'S NAME OR SCHOOL NAME: ROCKY CORPORATION

c. EMPLOYER'S NAME OR SCHOOL NAME:

c. OTHER ACCIDENT? ☒ YES □ NO

c. INSURANCE PLAN NAME OR PROGRAM NAME: ROCKY PLAN

d. INSURANCE PLAN NAME OR PROGRAM NAME:

10d. RESERVED FOR LOCAL USE

d. IS THERE ANOTHER HEALTH BENEFIT PLAN? □ YES ☒ NO

12. PATIENT'S OR AUTHORIZED PERSON'S SIGNATURE: SIGNED **SIGNATURE ON FILE** DATE 01/30/04

13. INSURED'S OR AUTHORIZED PERSON'S SIGNATURE: SIGNED **SIGNATURE ON FILE**

14. DATE OF CURRENT ILLNESS/INJURY/PREGNANCY: 01 | 30 | 04

16. DATES PATIENT UNABLE TO WORK: FROM TO

17. NAME OF REFERRING PHYSICIAN:

18. HOSPITALIZATION DATES: FROM TO

19. RESERVED FOR LOCAL USE Transported To: Hurry Hospital, 8000 Halls Way, Huntersville, Me 04022

20. OUTSIDE LAB? □ YES □ NO $ CHARGES

21. DIAGNOSIS OR NATURE OF ILLNESS OR INJURY:
1. 729.5
2.
3.
4.

22. MEDICAID RESUBMISSION CODE ORIGINAL REF. NO.

23. PRIOR AUTHORIZATION NUMBER

24. A. DATE(S) OF SERVICE From / To	B. Place	C. Type	D. PROCEDURES CPT/HCPCS MODIFIER	E. DIAGNOSIS CODE	F. $ CHARGES	G. DAYS/UNITS	H. EPSDT	I. EMG	J. COB	K. RESERVED
01 30 04 01 30 04	41	1	A0429	1	355 00	1				

25. FEDERAL TAX I.D. NUMBER: 20-6659776 ☒ EIN

26. PATIENT'S ACCOUNT NO.: A001125 232

27. ACCEPT ASSIGNMENT? ☒ YES □ NO

28. TOTAL CHARGE: $ 355 00

29. AMOUNT PAID: $ 0 00

30. BALANCE DUE: $ 355 00

31. SIGNATURE OF PHYSICIAN OR SUPPLIER: SIGNED *Anna Bell* DATE 2/14/04

32. NAME AND ADDRESS OF FACILITY:

33. PHYSICIAN'S, SUPPLIER'S BILLING NAME, ADDRESS: AMAZING AMBULANCE SERVICE, 21 ARCH WAY, APPLEVILLE, ME 04022 (207) 555-8882
PIN# AAS122 GRP#

CLAIM HMO2

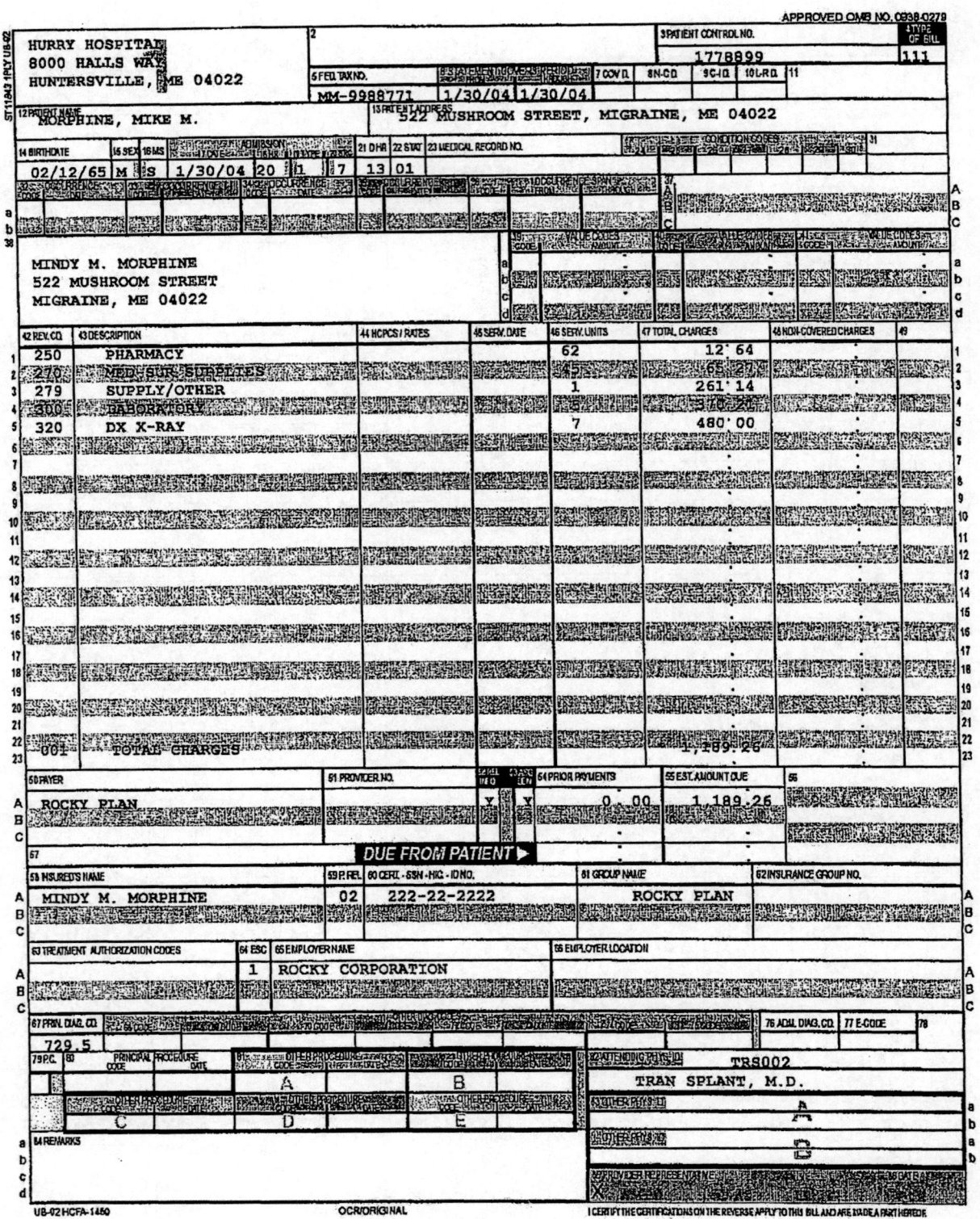

PLEASE
DO NOT
STAPLE
IN THIS
□□□ PICA

SUMMER INSURANCE CO.
70065 SUNNY STREET
SANDY CITY, CO 82963

APPROVED MOB-0938-0008

CLAIM HMO3

HEALTH INSURANCE CLAIM FORM

PICA □□□

1. MEDICARE　MEDICAID　CHAMPUS　CHAMPVA　GROUP HEALTH PLAN　FECA BLK LUNG　OTHER	INSURED'S I.D NUMBER　(FOR PROGRAM IN ITEM 1)

□ (Medicare #)　□ (Medicaid #)　□ (Sponsor's SSN)　□ (VA File #)　☒ (SSN or ID)　□ (SSN)　□ (ID)

INSURED'S I.D NUMBER: 222-22-2222

2. PATIENT'S NAME (Last, First, Middle Initial)
MORPHINE, MIKE M.

3. PATIENT'S BIRTH DATE MM | DD | YY　SEX
02 | 12 | 65　M ☒　F □

4. INSURED'S NAME (Last, First, Middle Initial)
MORPHINE, MINDY M.

5. PATIENT'S ADDRESS (No., Street)
522 MUSHROOM STREET

6. PATIENT'S RELATIONSHIP TO INSURED
Self □　Spouse ☒　Child □　Other □

7. INSURED'S ADDRESS (No., Street)
522 MUSHROOM STREET

CITY: MIGRAINE　STATE: ME

8. PATIENT STATUS
Single □　Married ☒　Other □
Employed ☒　Full-Time □ Student　Part-Time □ Student

CITY: MIGRAINE　STATE: ME

ZIP CODE: 04022　TELEPHONE (Include Area Code): (207) 555-3322

ZIP CODE: 04022　TELEPHONE (INCLUDE AREA CODE): (207) 555-3322

9. OTHER INSURED'S NAME (Last, First, Middle Initial)

10. IS PATIENT'S CONDITION RELATED TO:

11. INSURED'S POLICY GROUP OR FECA NUMBER:
222-22-ROC

a. OTHER INSURED'S POLICY OR GROUP NUMBER

a. EMPLOYMENT? (CURRENT OR PREVIOUS)
□ YES　☒ NO

a. INSURED'S DATE OF BIRTH MM | DD | YY　SEX
12 | 22 | 65　M □　F ☒

a. OTHER INSURED'S DATE OF BIRTH MM | DD | YY　SEX
| | 　M □　F □

b. AUTO ACCIDENT?　PLACE (State)
□ YES　☒ NO

b. EMPLOYER'S NAME OR SCHOOL NAME
ROCKY CORPORATION

c. EMPLOYER'S NAME OR SCHOOL NAME

c. OTHER ACCIDENT?
☒ YES　□ NO

c. INSURANCE PLAN NAME OR PROGRAM NAME
ROCKY PLAN

d. INSURANCE PLAN NAME OR PROGRAM NAME

10d. RESERVED FOR LOCAL USE

d. IS THERE ANOTHER HEALTH BENEFIT PLAN?
□ YES　☒ NO　If yes, return to and complete item 9 a-d

READ BACK OF FORM BEFORE COMPLETING & SIGNING THIS FORM
12. PATIENT'S OR AUTHORIZED PERSON'S SIGNATURE I authorize the release of any medical or other information necessary to process this claim. I also request payment of government benefits either to myself or to the party who accepts assignment below.

SIGNED　SIGNATURE ON FILE　DATE 01/30/04

13. INSURED'S OR AUTHORIZED PERSON'S SIGNATURE I authorize payment of medical benefits to the undersigned physician or supplier for services described below.

SIGNED　SIGNATURE ON FILE

14. DATE OF CURRENT: ◄ ILLNESS (1st symptom) ◄ INJURY (Accident) ◄ PREGNANCY (LMP)
MM | DD | YY
01 | 30 | 04

15. IF PATIENT HAS HAD SAME OR SIMILAR ILLNESS, GAVE FIRST DATE MM | DD | YY

16. DATES PATIENT UNABLE TO WORK IN CURRENT OCCUPATION
FROM MM | DD | YY　TO MM | DD | YY

17. NAME OF REFERRING PHYSICIAN OR OTHER SOURCE

17a. I.D. NUMBER OF REFERRING PHYSICIAN

18. HOSPITALIZATION DATES RELATED TO CURRENT SERVICES
FROM MM | DD | YY　TO MM | DD | YY

19. RESERVED FOR LOCAL USE
Primary Care Physician

20. OUTSIDE LAB?　$ CHARGES
□ YES　□ NO

21. DIAGNOSIS OR NATURE OF ILLNESS OR INJURY, (RELATE ITEMS 1,2,3, OR 4 TO ITEM 24E BY LINE)
1. | 729 . 5
2. | .
3. | .
4. | .

22. MEDICAID RESUBMISSION CODE　ORIGINAL REF. NO.

23. PRIOR AUTHORIZATION NUMBER

24. A DATE(S) OF SERVICE From MM DD YY To MM DD YY	B Place of Service	C Type of Service	D PROCEDURES, SERVICES, OR SUPPLIES (Explain Unusual Circumstances) CPT/HCPS | MODIFIER	E DIAGNOSIS CODE	F $ CHARGES	G DAYS OR UNITS	H EPSDT Family Plan	I EMG	J COB	K RESERVED FOR LOCAL USE
02 04 04　02 04 04	11	1	99203	1	175 00	1		Y		

25. FEDERAL TAX I.D. NUMBER　SSN EIN
20-2259772　□ ☒

26. PATIENT'S ACCOUNT NO.
MIKMD001　232

27. ACCEPT ASSIGNMENT? (For govt. claims, see back)
☒ YES　□ NO

28. TOTAL CHARGE
$ 175 00

29. AMOUNT PAID
$ 0 00

30. BALANCE DUE
$ 175 00

31. SIGNATURE OF PHYSICIAN OR SUPPLIER INCLUDING DEGREES OR CREDENTIALS (I certify that the statements on the reverse apply to this bill and are made a part thereof.)

SIGNED *Sal Pull*　DATE 2/14/04

32. NAME AND ADDRESS OF FACILITY WHERE SERVICES WERE RENDERED (If other than home or office)

33. PHYSICIAN'S, SUPPLIER'S BILLING NAME, ADDRESS, ZIP CODE & PHONE #
SAL PULL, M.D.
3500 MARKET BLVD., STE 233M
MOUNT, ME 04022 (207) 555-0022

PIN# SPM001　| GRP#

(APPROVED BY AMA COUNCIL ON MEDICAL SERVICE 8/88)　PLEASE PRINT OR TYPE

FORM HCFA-1500　(12-90)
FORM OWCP-1500　FORM RRB-1500

PLEASE
DO NOT
STAPLE
IN THIS
□□□ PICA

SUMMER INSURANCE CO.
70065 SUNNY STREET
SANDY CITY, CO 82963

APPROVED MOB-0938-0008

CLAIM   HMO4

HEALTH INSURANCE CLAIM FORM

PICA □□□

1. MEDICARE MEDICAID CHAMPUS CHAMPVA	GROUP HEALTH PLAN FECA BLK LUNG OTHER	INSURED'S I.D. NUMBER	(FOR PROGRAM IN ITEM 1)
□ (Medicare #) □ (Medicaid #) □ (Sponsor's SSN) □ (VA File #)	☒ (SSN or ID) □ (SSN) □ (ID)	222-22-2222	

2. PATIENT'S NAME (Last, First, Middle Initial)	3. PATIENT'S BIRTH DATE MM	DD	YY SEX	4. INSURED'S NAME (Last, First, Middle Initial)
MORPHINE, MIKE M.	02	12	65 M ☒ F □	MORPHINE, MINDY M.

5. PATIENT'S ADDRESS (No., Street)	6. PATIENT'S RELATIONSHIP TO INSURED	7. INSURED'S ADDRESS (No., Street)
522 MUSHROOM STREET	Self □ Spouse ☒ Child □ Other □	522 MUSHROOM STREET

CITY	STATE	8. PATIENT STATUS	CITY	STATE
MIGRAINE	ME	Single □ Married ☒ Other □	MIGRAINE	ME

ZIP CODE	TELEPHONE (Include Area Code)		ZIP CODE	TELEPHONE (INCLUDE AREA CODE)
04022	(207) 555-3322	Employed ☒ Full-Time Student □ Part-Time Student □	04022	(207) 555-3322

9. OTHER INSURED'S NAME (Last, First, Middle Initial)	10. IS PATIENT'S CONDITION RELATED TO:	11. INSURED'S POLICY GROUP OR FECA NUMBER:
		222-22-ROC

a. OTHER INSURED'S POLICY OR GROUP NUMBER	a. EMPLOYMENT? (CURRENT OR PREVIOUS) □ YES ☒ NO	a. INSURED'S DATE OF BIRTH MM	DD	YY SEX 12	22	65 M □ F ☒
a. OTHER INSURED'S DATE OF BIRTH MM	DD	YY SEX □ M □ F □	b. AUTO ACCIDENT? PLACE (State) □ YES ☒ NO	b. EMPLOYER'S NAME OR SCHOOL NAME ROCKY CORPORATION
c. EMPLOYER'S NAME OR SCHOOL NAME	c. OTHER ACCIDENT? ☒ YES □ NO	c. INSURANCE PLAN NAME OR PROGRAM NAME ROCKY PLAN
d. INSURANCE PLAN NAME OR PROGRAM NAME	10d. RESERVED FOR LOCAL USE	d. IS THERE ANOTHER HEALTH BENEFIT PLAN? □ YES ☒ NO If yes, return to and complete item 9 a-d

READ BACK OF FORM BEFORE COMPLETING & SIGNING THIS FORM

12. PATIENT'S OR AUTHORIZED PERSON'S SIGNATURE I authorize the release of any medical or other information necessary to process this claim. I also request payment of government benefits either to myself or to the party who accepts assignment below.

SIGNED   SIGNATURE ON FILE   DATE   01/30/04

13. INSURED'S OR AUTHORIZED PERSON'S SIGNATURE I authorize payment of medical benefits to the undersigned physician or supplier for services described below.

SIGNED   SIGNATURE ON FILE

14. DATE OF CURRENT: ◄ ILLNESS (1st symptom) INJURY (Accident) ◄ PREGNANCY (LMP) MM	DD	YY 01	30	04	15. IF PATIENT HAS HAD SAME OR SIMILAR ILLNESS, GAVE FIRST DATE MM	DD	YY	16. DATES PATIENT UNABLE TO WORK IN CURRENT OCCUPATION FROM MM	DD	YY TO MM	DD	YY
17. NAME OF REFERRING PHYSICIAN OR OTHER SOURCE Sal Pull, M.D.	17a. I.D. NUMBER OF REFERRING PHYSICIAN 20-2259772	18. HOSPITALIZATION DATES RELATED TO CURRENT SERVICES FROM MM	DD	YY TO MM	DD	YY
19. RESERVED FOR LOCAL USE Referral on File		20. OUTSIDE LAB? □ YES □ NO $ CHARGES

21. DIAGNOSIS OR NATURE OF ILLNESS OR INJURY, (RELATE ITEMS 1,2,3, OR 4 TO ITEM 24E BY LINE)

1. | 729 . 5   3. | ___ . ___
2. | ___ . ___   4. | ___ . ___

22. MEDICAID RESUBMISSION CODE   ORIGINAL REF. NO.

23. PRIOR AUTHORIZATION NUMBER

24.	A. DATE(S) OF SERVICE From To MM DD YY MM DD YY	B. Place of Service	C. Type of Service	D. PROCEDURES, SERVICES, OR SUPPLIES (Explain Unusual Circumstances) CPT/HCPS	MODIFIER	E. DIAGNOSIS CODE	F. $ CHARGES	G. DAYS OR UNITS	H. EPSDT Family Plan	I. EMG	J. COB	K. RESERVED FOR LOCAL USE
	02 04 04 02 04 04	11	1	73550		1	75 00	1				
	02 04 04 02 04 04	11	1	73718		1	1,380 00	1				

25. FEDERAL TAX I.D. NUMBER SSN EIN	26. PATIENT'S ACCOUNT NO.	27. ACCEPT ASSIGNMENT? (For govt. claims, see back)	28. TOTAL CHARGE	29. AMOUNT PAID	30. BALANCE DUE
20-0059770 □ ☒	MIKMD001 232	☒ YES □ NO	$ 1,455 00	$ 0 00	$ 1,455 00

31. SIGNATURE OF PHYSICIAN OR SUPPLIER INCLUDING DEGREES OR CREDENTIALS (I certify that the statements on the reverse apply to this bill and are made a part thereof.) SIGNED *Sally Sample* DATE 2/10/04	32. NAME AND ADDRESS OF FACILITY WHERE SERVICES WERE RENDERED (If other than home or office)	33. PHYSICIAN'S, SUPPLIER'S BILLING NAME, ADDRESS, ZIP CODE & PHONE # SALLY SAMPLE, M.D. 8000 HALLS WAY HUNTERSVILLE, ME 04022 (207) 555-0242 PIN# SAS106 GRP#

(APPROVED BY AMA COUNCIL ON MEDICAL SERVICE 8/88)   PLEASE PRINT OR TYPE

FORM HCFA-1500   (12-90)
FORM OWCP-1500
FORM RRB-1500

SUMMER INSURANCE CO.
70065 SUNNY STREET
SANDY CITY, CO 82963

APPROVED MOB-0938-0008

CLAIM HMO5

HEALTH INSURANCE CLAIM FORM

PLEASE
DO NOT
STAPLE
IN THIS
☐☐☐ PICA

PICA ☐☐☐

1. MEDICARE MEDICAID CHAMPUS CHAMPVA GROUP HEALTH PLAN FECA BLK LUNG OTHER	INSURED'S I.D NUMBER (FOR PROGRAM IN ITEM 1)
☐ (Medicare #) ☐ (Medicaid #) ☐ (Sponsor's SSN) ☐ (VA File #) ☒ (SSN or ID) ☐ (SSN) ☐ (ID)	222-22-2222

2. PATIENT'S NAME (Last, First, Middle Initial)
MORPHINE, MIKE M.

3. PATIENT'S BIRTH DATE
MM 02 | DD 12 | YY 65   SEX   M ☒ F ☐

4. INSURED'S NAME (Last, First, Middle Initial)
MORPHINE, MINDY M.

5. PATIENT'S ADDRESS (No., Street)
522 MUSHROOM STREET

6. PATIENT'S RELATIONSHIP TO INSURED
Self ☐ Spouse ☒ Child ☐ Other ☐

7. INSURED'S ADDRESS (No., Street)
522 MUSHROOM STREET

CITY MIGRAINE   **STATE** ME

8. PATIENT STATUS
Single ☐ Married ☒ Other ☐

CITY MIGRAINE   **STATE** ME

ZIP CODE 04022   **TELEPHONE (Include Area Code)** (207) 555-3322

Employed ☒ Full-Time ☐ Student Part-Time ☐ Student

ZIP CODE 04022   **TELEPHONE (INCLUDE AREA CODE)** (207) 555-3322

9. OTHER INSURED'S NAME (Last, First, Middle Initial)

10. IS PATIENT'S CONDITION RELATED TO:

11. INSURED'S POLICY GROUP OR FECA NUMBER:
222-22-ROC

a. OTHER INSURED'S POLICY OR GROUP NUMBER

a. EMPLOYMENT? (CURRENT OR PREVIOUS)
☐ YES ☒ NO

a. INSURED'S DATE OF BIRTH
MM 12 | DD 22 | YY 65   SEX   M ☐ F ☒

a. OTHER INSURED'S DATE OF BIRTH
MM | DD | YY   SEX   M ☐ F ☐

b. AUTO ACCIDENT?   PLACE (State)
☐ YES ☒ NO

b. EMPLOYER'S NAME OR SCHOOL NAME
ROCKY CORPORATION

c. EMPLOYER'S NAME OR SCHOOL NAME

c. OTHER ACCIDENT?
☒ YES ☐ NO

c. INSURANCE PLAN NAME OR PROGRAM NAME
ROCKY PLAN

d. INSURANCE PLAN NAME OR PROGRAM NAME

10d. RESERVED FOR LOCAL USE

d. IS THERE ANOTHER HEALTH BENEFIT PLAN?
☐ YES ☒ NO   If yes, return to and complete item 9 a-d

READ BACK OF FORM BEFORE COMPLETING & SIGNING THIS FORM
12. PATIENT'S OR AUTHORIZED PERSON'S SIGNATURE I authorize the release of any medical or other information necessary to process this claim. I also request payment of government benefits either to myself or to the party who accepts assignment below.

SIGNED **SIGNATURE ON FILE**   DATE **01/ 30/ 04**

13. INSURED'S OR AUTHORIZED PERSON'S SIGNATURE I authorize payment of medical benefits to the undersigned physician or supplier for services described below.

SIGNED **SIGNATURE ON FILE**

14. DATE OF CURRENT: ◄ ILLNESS (1st symptom) INJURY (Accident) PREGNANCY (LMP)
MM 01 | DD 30 | YY 04

15. IF PATIENT HAS HAD SAME OR SIMILAR ILLNESS, GAVE FIRST DATE MM | DD | YY

16. DATES PATIENT UNABLE TO WORK IN CURRENT OCCUPATION
FROM MM | DD | YY   TO MM | DD | YY

17. NAME OF REFERRING PHYSICIAN OR OTHER SOURCE
Sal Pull, M.D.

17a. I.D. NUMBER OF REFERRING PHYSICIAN
20-2259772

18. HOSPITALIZATION DATES RELATED TO CURRENT SERVICES
FROM MM | DD | YY   TO MM | DD | YY

19. RESERVED FOR LOCAL USE
DME Prescription on File.

20. OUTSIDE LAB? $ CHARGES
☐ YES ☐ NO

21. DIAGNOSIS OR NATURE OF ILLNESS OR INJURY, (RELATE ITEMS 1,2,3, OR 4 TO ITEM 24E BY LINE)
1. 729 . 5
2. ___ . ___
3. ___ . ___
4. ___ . ___

22. MEDICAID RESUBMISSION CODE   ORIGINAL REF. NO.

23. PRIOR AUTHORIZATION NUMBER

24. A. DATE(S) OF SERVICE From MM DD YY To MM DD YY	B. Place of Service	C. Type of Service	D. PROCEDURES, SERVICES, OR SUPPLIES (Explain Unusual Circumstances) CPT/HCPCS MODIFIER	E. DIAGNOSIS CODE	F. $ CHARGES	G. DAYS OR UNITS	H. EPSDT Family Plan	I. EMG	J. COB	K. RESERVED FOR LOCAL USE
02 04 04 02 04 04	99	1	E0114	1	121 00	1				

25. FEDERAL TAX I.D. NUMBER   SSN EIN
20-8859778   ☐ ☒

26. PATIENT'S ACCOUNT NO.
MM555551   232

27. ACCEPT ASSIGNMENT? (For govt. claims, see back)
☒ YES ☐ NO

28. TOTAL CHARGE
$ 264 00

29. AMOUNT PAID
$ 0 00

30. BALANCE DUE
$ 264 00

31. SIGNATURE OF PHYSICIAN OR SUPPLIER INCLUDING DEGREES OR CREDENTIALS (I certify that the statements on the reverse apply to this bill and are made a part thereof.)

SIGNED *Penny Pane*   DATE 02/18/04

32. NAME AND ADDRESS OF FACILITY WHERE SERVICES WERE RENDERED (If other than home or office)

33. PHYSICIAN'S, SUPPLIER'S BILLING NAME, ADDRESS, ZIP CODE & PHONE #
MARVELOUS MEDICAL EQUIPMENT
9 MONEY LANE
MOVE, ME 04022 (207) 555-0409

PIN# MME105 | GRP#

(APPROVED BY AMA COUNCIL ON MEDICAL SERVICE 8/88)

PLEASE PRINT OR TYPE

FORM HCFA-1500 (12-90)
FORM OWCP-1500   FORM RRB-1500

NOTE: The claim scenario for Mike Morphine was recreated, requiring only 5 claims instead of eight. Therefore pages 274 through 276 have been eliminated.

Appendix 21 – 1

[Carrier] Summer Insurance Company
CONTRACT HOLDER: Rocky Company
CONTRACT: January 1, 1998

SMALL GROUP HMO CONTRACT
EFFECTIVE DATE OF

Copayment $15, unless otherwise stated
Emergency Room Copayment $50, credited toward Inpatient admission if admitted within 24 hours
Coinsurance 0% except as stated on the Schedule of Services and Supplies for Prescription Drugs
MAXIMUM LIFETIME BENEFITS Unlimited, **except** as otherwise stated

SCHEDULE OF SERVICES AND SUPPLIES

The services or supplies covered under the contract are subject to all copayments and are determined per calendar year per Member, unless otherwise stated. Maximums apply only to the specific services provided.

SERVICES COPAYMENTS:

HOSPITAL SERVICES:
Inpatient $150 Copayment/day for a maximum of 5 days/admission. Maximum Copayment $1,500/Calendar Year. Unlimited days.
Outpatient $15 Copayment/visit

PRACTITIONER SERVICES RECEIVED AT A HOSPITAL:
Inpatient Visit $0 Copayment
Outpatient Visit $15 Copayment/visit; no Copayment if any other Copayment applies.
Emergency Room $50 Copayment/visit/Member (credited toward Inpatient Admission if Admission occurs within 24 hours)

SURGERY:.
Inpatient $0 Copayment
Outpatient $15 Copayment/visit

HOME HEALTH CARE Unlimited days, if pre-approved; $0 Copayment.
HOSPICE SERVICES Unlimited days, if pre-approved; $0 Copayment.
MATERNITY (PRE-NATAL CARE) $25 Copayment for initial visit only; $0 Copayment thereafter.
MENTAL NERVOUS CONDITIONS AND SUBSTANCE ABUSE:
Outpatient $15 Copayment/visit maximum 20 visits/Calendar Year.
Inpatient $150 Copayment/day for a maximum of 5 days per admission. Maximum Copayment:

$1,500/Calendar Year. Maximum of 30 days inpatient care/Calendar Year. One Inpatient day may be exchanged for two Outpatient visits.

THERAPEUTIC MANIPULATION $15 Copayment/visit; maximum 30 visits/Calendar Year
PODIATRIC $15 Copayment/visit (excludes Routine Foot Care).
PRE-ADMISSION TESTING $15 Copayment/visit.
PRESCRIPTION DRUG 50% Coinsurance [May be substituted by Carrier with $15 Copayment.]
PRIMARY CARE PHYSICIAN $15 Copayment/visit.
OR CARE MANAGER SERVICES (OUTSIDE HOSPITAL)
PRIMARY CARE SERVICES $15 Copayment/visit.
REHABILITATION SERVICES Subject to the Inpatient Hospital Services Copayment above. The Copayment does not apply if Admission is immediately preceded by a Hospital Inpatient Stay.
SECOND SURGICAL OPINION $15 Copayment/visit.
SPECIALIST SERVICES $15 Copayment/visit.
SKILLED NURSING CENTER Unlimited days, if pre-approved; $0 Copayment.
THERAPY SERVICES $15 Copayment/visit.
DIAGNOSTIC SERVICES .
INPATIENT $0 Copayment
OUTPATIENT $15 Copayment/visit

NOTE: No services or supplies will be provided if a Member fails to obtain pre-authorization of care through his or her primary care physician or health center or care manager. Read the Member provisions carefully before obtaining medical care, services or supplies. Refer to the section of this contract called "Non-Covered Services and Supplies" for a list of the services and supplies for which a Member is not eligible for coverage under this contract.

ELIGIBILITY
Eligible Employees
Subject to the Conditions of Eligibility set forth below, and to all of the other conditions of the Contract, all of the Contractholder's Employees who are in an eligible class and who reside in the Service Area will be eligible if
a)]the Employees are Actively at Work, Full-Time Employees, and;
b) the Employees enroll under the Plan.

Conditions of Eligibility
Full-Time Requirement
Except where an Employee is not Actively at Work due to a Health Status Related Factor, and except as stated below, We will not cover an Employee unless the Employee is an Actively at Work, Full-Time Employee.

Enrollment Requirement
We will not cover the Employee until the Employee enrolls and agrees to make the required payments, if any. If the Employee does this within 30 days of the Employee's Eligibility Date, coverage will start on the Employee's Eligibility Date. If the Employee enrolls and agrees to make the required payments, if any:

a) more than 30 days after the Employee's Eligibility Date; or

b) after the Employee previously had coverage which ended because the Employee failed to make a required payment,

We will consider the Employee to be a Late Enrollee. Late Enrollees are subject to this Contract's Pre-Existing Conditions limitation. If an Employee initially waived coverage under this Contract because he or she had coverage under a COBRA continuation provision and the Employee requests coverage under this Contract within 30 days of the date the COBRA continuation ended, We will not consider the Employee to be a Late Enrollee. Coverage will take effect as of the date the COBRA continuation ended.

In addition, an Employee and any Dependents will not be considered a Late Enrollee[s] if the Employee is employed by an employer which offers multiple Health Benefits Plans and the Employee elects a different plan during the open enrollment period.

When Employee Coverage Ends
An Employee's coverage under this Contract will end on the first of the following dates:

a) The date an Employee ceases to be an Actively at Work, Full-Time Employee for any reason. Such reasons include death, retirement, lay-off, leave of absence, and the end of employment.

b) The date an Employee stops being an eligible Employee under this Contract.

c) The date this Contract ends, or is discontinued for a class of Employees to which the Employee belongs.

d) The date for which required payments are not made for the Employee, subject to the

e) The date an Employee moves his or her permanent residence outside the Service Area.

DEPENDENT COVERAGE
Eligible Dependents for Dependent Health Benefits
Except as stated below, an Employee's eligible Dependents are:

a) the Employee's legal spouse;

b) the Employee's unmarried Dependent children who are under age 19; and

c) the Employee's unmarried Dependent children, from age 19 until their 23rd birthday, who are enrolled as full-time students at accredited schools.

Exception: Any dependent who does not reside in the Service Area is not an eligible Dependent. Eligible Dependents will not include any Dependent who is covered by this Contract as an Employee or on active duty in the armed forces of any country.

An Employee's "unmarried Dependent children" include the Employee's legally adopted children, his or her step-children if they depend on the Employee for most of their support and maintenance and children under a court appointed guardianship.

MEMBER PROVISIONS
THE ROLE OF A MEMBER'S PRIMARY CARE PHYSICIAN
A Member's Primary Care Physician provides basic health maintenance services and coordinates a Member's overall health care. Anytime a Member needs medical care, the Member should contact his or her Primary Care Physician and identify himself or herself as a Member of this program. In a Medical Emergency, a Member may go directly to the emergency room. If a Member does, then the Member must call his or her Primary Care Physician or the Care Manager and Member Services within 48 hours. If a Member does not call within 48 hours, We will provide services under this HMO Plan only if We determine that notice was given as soon as was reasonably possible.

THE ROLE OF THE CARE MANAGER. The Care Manager will manage a Member's treatment for a Biologically-based Mental Illness, a Non-Biologically-based Mental Illness, Substance Abuse, or Alcohol Abuse. A Member must contact the Care Manager or the Member's Primary Care Physician when a Member needs treatment for one of these conditions.

IDENTIFICATION CARD
If any Member permits the use of his or her Identification Card by any other person, such card may be retained by Us, and all rights of such Member and his or her Dependents, if any, pursuant to this Contract shall be terminated immediately, subject to the Appeals Procedures.

REFERRAL FORMS
A Member can be referred for Specialist Services by a Member's Primary Care Physician. Except in the case of a Medical Emergency, a Member will not be eligible for any services under this HMO Plan provided by anyone other than a Member's Primary Care Physician (including but not limited to Specialist Services) if a Member has not been referred by his or her Primary Care Physician.

Referrals must be obtained prior to receiving services and supplies from any Practitioner other than the Member's Primary Care Physician.

MEDICAL NECESSITY

Members will receive designated benefits under the Contract only when Medically Necessary and Appropriate. We or the Care Manager may determine whether any benefit provided under the Contract was Medically Necessary and Appropriate, and We have the option to select the appropriate Participating Hospital to render services if hospitalization is necessary. Decisions as to what is Medically Necessary and Appropriate are subject to review by our quality assessment committee or its physician designee.

LIMITATION ON SERVICES

Except in cases of Medical Emergency, services are available only from Participating Providers. We shall have no liability or obligation whatsoever on account of any service or benefit sought or received by a Member from any Physician, Hospital, other Provider or other person, entity, institution or organization unless prior arrangements are made by Us.

COVERED SERVICES & SUPPLIES

Under this HMO Plan, Members are entitled to receive the benefits in the following sections when Medically Necessary and Appropriate, subject to the payment by Members of applicable copayments as stated in the applicable Schedule of Services and Supplies.

(a) **OUTPATIENT SERVICES.** The following services are covered only at the Primary Care Physician's office or Health Center selected by a Member, or elsewhere upon prior written Referral by a Member's Primary Care Physician or Health Center, or the Care Manager:

1. **Office visits** during office hours, and during non-office hours when Medically Necessary.
2. **Home visits** by a Member's Primary Care Physician.
3. **Periodic health examinations** to include:
   a. Well child care from birth including immunizations;
   b. Routine physical examinations, including eye examinations;
   c. Routine gynecologic exams and related services;
   d. Routine ear and hearing examination; and
   e. Routine allergy injections and immunizations (but not if solely for the purpose of travel or as a requirement of a Member's employment).
4. **Diagnostic Services.**
5. **Casts and dressings.**

6. **Ambulance Service** when certified in writing as Medically Necessary by a Member's Primary Care Physician and approved in advance by Us.
7. **Procedures and prescription drugs to enhance fertility,** except where specifically excluded in this Contract.
8. **Prosthetic Devices** when We arrange for them. We cover only the initial fitting and purchase of artificial limbs and eyes, and other prosthetic devices. And they must take the place of a natural part of a Member's body, or be needed due to a functional birth defect in a covered Dependent Child. We do not provide for replacements (unless Medically Necessary and Appropriate), repairs, or wigs. We do not cover dental prosthetics or devices other than as a replacement for natural teeth lost due to Injury, as stated in the Dental Care and Treatment provision of this Contract.
9. **Durable Medical Equipment** when ordered by a Member's Primary Care Physician and arranged through Us.
10. **Prescription Drugs and contraceptives which require a Practitioner's prescription,** and insulin syringes and insulin needles, glucose test strips and lancets, colostomy bags, belts and irrigators when obtained through a Participating Provider. A prescription or refill will not include a prescription or refill that is more than:
    a. the greater of a 30 day supply or 100 unit doses for each prescription or refill; or
    b. the amount usually prescribed by the Member's Participating Provider.
A supply will be considered to be furnished at the time the Prescription Drug is received.]
11. **Nutritional Counseling** for the management of disease entities which have a specific diagnostic criteria that can be verified. The nutritional counseling must be prescribed by a Member's Primary Care Physician and approved in advance by Us.
12. **Dental x-rays** when related to Covered Services.
13. **Oral surgery** in connection with bone fractures, removal of tumors and orthodontogenic cysts, and other surgical procedures, as We approve.
14. **Food and Food Products for Inherited Metabolic Diseases**: We cover charges incurred for the therapeutic treatment of inherited metabolic diseases, including the purchase of medical foods (enteral formula) and low protein modified food products as determined to be medically necessary by a Member's Practitioner. For the purpose of this benefit: "inherited metabolic disease" means a disease caused by an inherited abnormality of body chemistry for which testing is mandated by law; "low protein modified food product" means a food product that is specially formulated to have less than one gram of protein per serving and is intended to be used under the direction of a Practitioner for the dietary treatment of an inherited metabolic disease, but does not include a natural food that is naturally low in protein; and "medical food" means a food that is intended for the

dietary treatment of a disease or condition for which nutritional requirements are established by medical evaluation and is formulated to be consumed or administered enterally under the direction of a Practitioner.

(b) **SPECIALIST DOCTOR BENEFITS.** Services are covered when rendered by a Participating Specialist Doctor at the doctor's office, or Health Center, or any other Participating Facility or a Participating Hospital outpatient department during office or business hours upon prior written referral by a Member's Primary Care Physician.

(c) **INPATIENT HOSPICE, HOSPITAL, REHABILITATION CENTER & SKILLED NURSING CENTER BENEFITS.** The following Services are covered when hospitalized by a Participating Provider upon prior written referral from a Member's Primary Care Physician, only at Participating Hospitals and Participating Providers (or at Non-participating facilities upon prior written authorization by Us); however, Participating Skilled Nursing Center Services and Supplies are limited to those which constitute Skilled Nursing Care and Hospice Services are subject to Our pre-approval:

1. Semi-private room and board accommodations Except as stated below, We provide coverage for Inpatient care for:
  a. a minimum of 72 hours following a modified radical mastectomy; and
  b. a minimum of 48 hours following a simple mastectomy.
Exception: The minimum 72 or 48 hours, as appropriate, of Inpatient care will not be covered if the Member, in consultation with the Participating Provider, determine that a shorter length of stay is medically necessary and appropriate.
As an exception to the Medically Necessary and Appropriate requirement of this Contract, We also provide coverage for the mother and newly born child for:
  a. up to 48 hours of inpatient care in a Participating Hospital following a vaginal delivery; and
  b. a minimum of 96 hours of inpatient care in a Participating Hospital following a cesarean section.
We provide such coverage subject to the following:
  a. the attending Practitioner must determine that inpatient care is medically necessary; or
  b. the mother must request the inpatient care.
[As an alternative to the minimum level of inpatient care described above, the mother may elect to participate in a home care program provided by Us.]
2. Private accommodations will be provided only when approved in advance by Us. If a Member occupies a private room without such certification

Member shall be directly liable to the Hospice, Hospital, Rehabilitation Center or Skilled Nursing Center for the difference between payment by Us to the Hospice, Hospital, Rehabilitation Center or Skilled Nursing Center of the per diem or other agreed upon rate for semiprivate accommodation established between Us and the Participating Hospice, Participating Hospital, Participating Rehabilitation Center or Participating Skilled Nursing Center and the private room rate.
3. General nursing care
4. Use of intensive or special care facilities
5. X-ray examinations including CAT scans but not dental x-rays
6. Use of operating room and related facilities
7. Magnetic resonance imaging "MRI"
8. Drugs, medications, biologicals
9. Cardiography/Encephalography
10. Laboratory testing and services
11. Pre- and post-operative care
12. Special tests
13. Nuclear medicine
14. Therapy Services
15. Oxygen and oxygen therapy
16. Anesthesia and anesthesia services
17. Blood, blood products and blood processing
18. Intravenous injections and solutions
19. Surgical, medical and obstetrical services; We also cover reconstructive breast Surgery, Surgery to restore and achieve symmetry between the two breasts and the cost of prostheses following a mastectomy on one breast or both breasts.
20. Private duty nursing only when approved in advance by Us.
21. The following transplants: Cornea, Kidney, Lung, Liver, Heart and Pancreas.
22. Allogeneic bone marrow transplants.
23. Autologous bone marrow transplants and associated dose intensive chemotherapy: only for treatment of Leukemia, Lymphoma, Neuroblastoma, Aplastic Anemia, Genetic Disorders (SCID and WISCOT Alldrich) and Breast Cancer, when approved in advance by Us, if the Member is participating in a National Cancer Institute sponsored clinical trial. Autologous Bone Marrow Transplant and Associated Dose-Intensive Chemotherapy, but only if performed by institutions approved by the National Cancer Institute, or pursuant to protocols consistent with the guidelines of the American Society of Clinical Oncologists;
24. Peripheral Blood Stem Cell Transplants, but only if performed by institutions approved by the National Cancer Institute, or pursuant to protocols consistent with the guidelines of the American Society of Clinical Oncologists.

(d) **BENEFITS FOR SUBSTANCE ABUSE AND NON-BIOLOGICALLY BASED MENTAL ILLNESSES.** The following Services are covered when rendered by a Participating Provider at Provider's office or at a Participating Substance Abuse Center or Health Center upon prior written referral by a Member's Primary Care Physician or the Care Manager. This section does *not* address coverage for a Biologically-based Mental Illness.

1. **Outpatient.** Members are entitled to receive up to twenty (20) outpatient visits per Calendar Year. Benefits include diagnosis, medical, psychiatric and psychological treatment and medical referral services by a Member's Primary Care Physician or the Care Manager for the abuse of or addiction to drugs and Non-Biologically-based Mental Illnesses. Payment for non-medical ancillary services (such as vocational rehabilitation or employment counseling) is not provided, but information regarding appropriate agencies will be provided if available. Members are additionally eligible, upon referral by a Member's Primary Care Physician or the Care Manager, for up to sixty (60) more outpatient visits by exchanging one or more of the inpatient hospital days described in paragraph 2 below where each exchanged inpatient day provides two outpatient visits.

2. **Inpatient Hospital Care.** Members are entitled to receive up to thirty (30) days of inpatient care benefits for detoxification, medical treatment for medical conditions resulting from the substance abuse, referral services for substance abuse or addiction, and Non-Biologically-based Mental Illnesses. The following services shall be covered under inpatient treatment: (1) lodging and dietary services; (2) physician, psychologist, nurse, certified addictions counselor and trained staff services; (3) diagnostic x-ray; (4) psychiatric, psychological and medical laboratory testing; (5) drugs, medicines, equipment use and supplies.

3. **Chemical Dependency Admissions.** Repeated detoxification treatment for chronic Substance Abuse will not be covered unless in Our sole Discretion it is Determined that Members have been cooperative with an on-going treatment plan developed by a Participating Provider. Failure to comply with treatment shall constitute cause for non-coverage of Substance Abuse services. Court-ordered chemical dependency admissions are not covered unless Medically Necessary and Appropriate and only to the extent of the covered benefit as defined above.

(e) **BENEFITS FOR BIOLOGICALLY-BASED MENTAL ILLNESS OR ALCOHOL ABUSE.** We cover treatment of a Biologically-based Mental Illness or Alcohol Abuse the same way We would for any other illness, if such treatment is prescribed by a Participating Provider upon prior written referral by a Member's Primary Care Physician or the Care Manager. We do not pay for Custodial care, education or training.

(f) **EMERGENCY CARE BENEFITS - WITHIN AND OUTSIDE OUR SERVICE AREA.** The following Services are covered under this HMO Plan without prior written referral by a Member's Primary Care Physician in the event of a Medical Emergency as Determined by Us.

1. A Member's Primary Care Physician is required to provide or arrange for on-call coverage twenty-four (24) hours a day, seven (7) days a week. Unless a delay would be detrimental to a Member's health, Member shall call a Member's Primary Care Physician or Health Center or Us or the Care Manager prior to seeking emergency treatment.

2. We will cover the cost of emergency medical and hospital services performed within or outside our service area without a prior written referral only if:

    a. Our review determines that a Member's symptoms were severe and delay of treatment would have been detrimental to a Member's health, the symptoms occurred suddenly, and Member sought immediate medical attention.

    b. The service rendered is provided as a Covered Service or Supply under this Contract and is not a service or supply which is normally treated on a non-emergency basis; and

    c. We and the Member's Primary Care Physician are notified within 48 hours of the emergency service and/or admission and We are furnished with written proof of the occurrence, nature and extent of the emergency services within 30 days. Member shall be responsible for payment for services received unless We Determine that a Member's failure to do so was reasonable under the circumstances. In no event shall reimbursement be made until We receive proper written proof.

3. In the event Members are hospitalized in a Non-Participating Facility, coverage will only be provided until Members are medically able to travel or to be transported to a Participating Facility. If Members elect to continue treatment with Non-Participating Providers, We shall have no responsibility for payment beyond the date Members are Determined to be medically able to be transported. In the event that transportation is Medically Necessary and Appropriate, We will cover the amount We Determine to be the reasonable and customary cost. Reimbursement may be subject to payment by Members of all Copayments which would have been required had similar benefits been provided upon prior written referral to a Participating Provider.

4. Coverage for emergency services includes only such treatment necessary to treat the Medical Emergency. Any elective procedures performed after Members have been admitted to a Facility as the result of a Medical Emergency shall require prior written referral or Members shall be responsible for payment.

5. The Copayment for an emergency room visit will be credited toward the Hospital Inpatient Copayment if Members are admitted as an Inpatient to the Hospital as a result of the Medical Emergency.

(g) **THERAPY SERVICES.** The following Services are covered when rendered by a Participating Provider upon prior written referral by a Member's Primary Care Physician or the Care Manager.

1. Speech Therapy, Physical Therapy, Occupational Therapy and Cognitive Therapies are covered for non-chronic conditions and acute Illnesses and Injuries upon referral to a Participating Provider by a Member's Primary Care Physician. This benefit consists of treatment for a 60 day period per incident of Illness or Injury, beginning with the first day of treatment, provided that a Member's Primary Care Physician certifies in writing that the treatment will result in a significant improvement of a Member's condition within this time period and treatment is approved in writing by Us.

2. Chelation Therapy, Chemotherapy treatment, Dialysis Treatment, Infusion Therapy, Radiation Therapy, and Respiration Therapy.

(h) **HOME HEALTH SERVICES.** The following Services are covered when rendered by a Participating Provider including but not limited to a Participating Home Health Agency as an alternative to hospitalization and are approved and coordinated in advance by Us upon the prior referral of a Member's Primary Care Physician or the Care Manager.

1. **Skilled nursing services,** provided by or under the supervision of a registered professional nurse.

2. Services of a **home health aide**, under the supervision of a registered professional nurse, or if appropriate, a qualified speech or physical therapist. These benefits are covered only when the primary purpose of the Home Health Services rendered to the Member is skilled in nature.

3. **Medical Social Services** by or under the supervision of a qualified medical or psychiatric social worker, in conjunction with other Home Health Services, if the Primary Care Physician certifies that such services are essential for the effective treatment of a Member's medical condition.

4. **Therapy Services** as set forth above.

5. **Hospice Care** if Members are terminally Ill or terminally Injured with life expectancy of six months or less, as certified by the Member's Primary Care Physician. Services may include home and hospital visits by nurses and social workers; pain management and symptom control; instruction and supervision of family Members, inpatient care; counseling and emotional support; and other Home Health benefits listed above.

Nothing in this section shall require Us to provide Home Health Benefits when in Our Determination the treatment setting is not appropriate, or when there is a more cost effective setting in which to provide Medically Necessary and Appropriate care.

(i) **DENTAL CARE AND TREATMENT.** The following services are covered when rendered by a Participating Practitioner upon prior Referral by a Member's Primary Care Physician. We cover:

1. the diagnosis and treatment of oral tumors and cysts; and

2. the surgical removal of bony impacted teeth.

We also cover treatment of an Injury to natural teeth or the jaw, but only if:

1. the Injury occurs while the Member is covered under any health benefit plan;

2. the Injury was not caused, directly or indirectly by biting or chewing; and

3. all treatment is finished within 6 months of the date of the Injury.

Treatment includes replacing natural teeth lost due to such Injury. But in no event do We cover orthodontic treatment.

For a Member who is severely disabled or who is a Child under age 6, We cover:

a. general anesthesia and Hospitalization for dental services; and

b. dental services rendered by a dentist regardless of where the dental services are provided for a medical condition covered by this Contract which requires Hospitalization or general anesthesia.

(j) **TREATMENT FOR TEMPOROMANDIBULAR JOINT DISORDER (TMJ)** The following services are covered when rendered by a Participating Practitioner upon prior Referral by a Member's Primary Care Physician. We cover services and supplies for the Medically Necessary and Appropriate surgical and non-surgical treatment of TMJ in a Member. However, We do not cover any services or supplies for orthodontia, crowns or bridgework.

(k) **THERAPEUTIC MANIPULATION** The following services are covered when rendered by a Participating Practitioner upon prior Referral by a Member's Primary Care Physician or the Care Manager. We limit what We cover for therapeutic manipulation to 30 visits per Calendar Year. And We cover no more than two modalities per visit. Services and supplies beyond 30 visits are not covered.

NON-COVERED SERVICES AND SUPPLIES
THE FOLLOWING ARE NOT COVERED SERVICES UNDER THIS CONTRACT.

Care or treatment by means of **acupuncture** except when used as a substitute for other forms of anesthesia.

Services for **ambulance** for transportation from a Hospital or other health care Facility, unless Member is being transferred to another Inpatient health care Facility.

Broken Appointments (Charges for)

Blood or blood plasma which is replaced by or for a Member.

Care and/or treatment by a **Christian Science Practitioner**.

Completion of claim forms.

Services or supplies related to **Cosmetic Surgery**, except as otherwise stated in this Contract; complications of Cosmetic Surgery; drugs prescribed for cosmetic purposes. Services related to **custodial** or **domiciliary** care.

Dental care or treatment, including appliances, except as otherwise stated in this Contract.

Care or treatment by means of **dose intensive chemotherapy**, except as otherwise stated in this Contract.

Services or supplies, the primary purpose of which is **educational** providing the Member with any of the following: training in the activities of daily living; instruction in scholastic skills such as reading and writing; preparation for an occupation; or treatment for learning disabilities.

Experimental or Investigational treatments, procedures, hospitalizations, drugs, biological products or medical devices, except as otherwise stated in this Contract.

Extraction of teeth, except for bony impacted teeth.

Services or supplies for or in connection with:

    a. except as otherwise stated in this Contract, exams to determine the need for (or changes of) **eyeglasses** or lenses of any type;

    b. eyeglasses or lenses of any type except initial replacements for loss of the natural lens; or

    c. eye surgery such as radial keratotomy, when the primary purpose is to correct myopia (nearsightedness), hyperopia (farsightedness) or astigmatism (blurring).

Services or supplies provided by one of the following Members of the Employee's **family**: spouse, child, parent, in-law, brother, sister or grandparent.

Services or supplies furnished in connection with any procedures to enhance **fertility** which involve harvesting, storage and / or manipulation of eggs and sperm. This includes, but is not limited to the following: a) procedures: in vitro fertilization; embryo transfer; embryo freezing; and Gamete intra-fallopian Transfer (GIFT) and Zygote Intrafallopian Transfer (ZIFT); and b) drugs and drug therapy: non-FDA approved indications; and non-standard dosages, length of treatment, or cycles of therapy.

Except as otherwise stated in this Contract, services or supplies related to **Hearing aids and hearing examinations** to determine the need for hearing aids or the need to adjust them.

Services or supplies related to **Herbal medicine**.

Services or supplies related to **Hypnotism**.

Services or supplies necessary because the Member engaged, or tried to engage, in an **illegal occupation** or committed or tried to commit an indictable offense in the jurisdiction in which it is committed, or a felony.

Illness or Injury, including a condition which is the result of disease or bodily infirmity, which occurred on the job and which is covered or could have been covered for benefits provided under workers' compensation, employer's liability, occupational disease or similar law;

Local anesthesia charges billed separately if such charges are included in the fee for the Surgery.

Membership costs for health clubs, weight loss clinics and similar programs.

Services and supplies related to **Marriage, career or financial counseling, sex therapy or family therapy, and related services.**

Supplies related to **Methadone** maintenance.

Any **Non-Covered Service or Supply** specifically limited or not covered elsewhere in this Contract, or which is not Medically Necessary and Appropriate.

Non-prescription drugs or supplies, except;

    a. insulin needles and insulin syringes and glucose test strips and lancets;

    b. colostomy bags, belts, and irrigators; and

    c. as stated in this Contract for food and food products for inherited metabolic diseases.

Services provided by a licensed **pastoral counselor** in the course of his or her normal duties as a religious official or practitioner.

Personal convenience or comfort items including, but not limited to, such items as TV's, telephones, first aid kits, exercise equipment, air conditioners, humidifiers, saunas, hot tubs.

Any service provided without prior written Referral by the Member's **Primary Care Physician**, except as specified in this Contract.

In the event of a Medical Emergency, the amount of any charge which is greater than the amount We Determine to be the **reasonable and customary charge**.

Services or supplies related to **rest or convalescent cures**.

Room and board charges for a Member in any Facility for any period of time during which he or she was not physically present overnight in the Facility.

Services or supplies related to **Routine Foot Care, except:**

    a. an open cutting operation to treat weak, strained, flat, unstable or unbalanced feet, metatarsalgia or bunions;

    b. the removal of nail roots; and

    c. treatment or removal of corns, calluses or toenails in conjunction with the treatment of metabolic or peripheral vascular disease.

Self-administered services such as: biofeedback, patient-controlled analgesia on an Outpatient basis, related diagnostic testing, self-care and self-help training.

Services or supplies:

    a. eligible for payment under either federal or state programs (except Medicaid and Medicare). This provision applies whether or not the Member asserts his or her rights to obtain this coverage or payment for these services;

b. for which a charge is not usually made, such as a Practitioner treating a professional or business associate, or services at a public health fair;

c. for which a Member would not have been charged if he or she did not have health care coverage;

d. provided by or in a Government Hospital unless the services are for treatment:

- of a non-service Medical Emergency; or
- by a Veterans' Administration Hospital of a non-service related Illness or Injury;

Sterilization reversal - services and supplies rendered for reversal of sterilization.

Surgery, sex hormones, and related medical, psychological and psychiatric services to change a Member's sex; services and supplies arising from complications of sex transformation.

Telephone consultations.

Transplants, except as otherwise listed in the Contract.

Transportation; travel.

Vision therapy.

Vitamins and dietary supplements.

Services or supplies received as a result of **a war**, declared or undeclared; police actions; services in the armed forces or units auxiliary thereto; or riots or insurrection.

Weight reduction or control, unless there is a diagnosis of morbid obesity; special foods, food supplements, liquid diets, diet plans or any related products.

Wigs, toupees, hair transplants, hair weaving or any drug if such drug is used in connection with baldness.

COORDINATION OF BENEFITS AND SERVICES: OBD rules apply for coordination of benefits

Appendix 21 – 2

Covered Services	MEDICARE		COMMERCIAL						
	Standard	Medi-Medi	AMG	Rocky	CAT	MIPC	CAIT	SBA	RICE
Anesthesia for opening upper femur (01230)	P	P	P	P	P	P	P	P	P
Crutches (E0114)	-	G	G	G	G	G	G	G	G
Emergency department visit, emergency medicine given. (99284)	P	P	P	P	P	P	P	P	G
Emergency Transport, BLS (A0429)	P	P	P	P	P	P	P	P	P
Magnetic resonance lower extremity, without contrast (73718)	P	P	P	P	P	P	P	P	P
New patient, counseling, regular visits (99203)	G	G	G	G	G	G	G	G	G
Outpatient surgery									
Facility charges			P	P	P	P	P	P	P
Physician visits	G	G	G	G	G	G	G	G	G
Surgeon	P	P	G	G	G	G	G	G	G
Assistant surgeon	P	P	G	P	P	G	G	P	G
Anesthesiologist	P	P	P	P	P	P	P	P	P
X-ray technician	P	P	P	P	P	P	P	P	P
Plaster or casting, knee ankle and foot (L2122)	G	G	G	G	G	G	G	G	G
Radiologic examination of femur (73550)	G	G	G	G	G	G	G	G	G
Removal of, foreign body thigh or knee area (27372)	G/P[1]	G/P[1]	G/P[1]	G/P[1]	G/P[1]	G/P[1]	G/P[1]	G/P[1]	G/P[1]

[1]See Outpatient surgery for surgery done on an outpatient basis, see Inpatient Surgery for charges done on an inpatient basis.

Legend: **G = Medical Group Responsibility; P = Plan/HMO Responsibility; G/P = Shared Responsibility; – = Not Covered**

This chart shows a sampling of CPT codes and the party that bears responsibility for covering costs for each procedure under numerous different plans. It is important to check the correct column for the plan being processed to determine if services are covered or not.

Appendix 21 – 3

Rocky Fee Schedule

CPT/HCPCS*	Description	Allowed Amount	Follow-up Days
00400	ANESTHESIA, INTEGUMENTARY SYSTEM, EXTREMITIES	94.23	--
00520	ANESTHESIA FOR CLOSED CHEST PROCEDURES	188.46	--
00534	ANESTHESIA FOR TRANSVENOUS INSERTION	219.87	--
00868	ANESTHESIA FOR RENAL TRANSPLANT	314.10	--
01230	ANESTHESIA FOR UPPER 2/3 OF FEMUR, OPEN	188.46	--
01480	ANESTHESIA, ON BONES OF LOWER LEG, OPEN	94.23	--
15952	EXCISION TROCHANTERIC PRESS ULCER	293.04	90
19125	EXCISION OF BREAST LESION	256.41	30
20205	BIOPSY, MUSCLE DEEP	87.92	15
27372	REMOVAL OF FOREIGN BODY, DEEP, THIGH REGION	190.48	30
27758	OPEN TREATMENT OF TIBIAL SHAFT FRACTURE	36.63	30
27784	OPEN TREATMENT OF PROXIMAL FIBULA	465.21	90
31200	ETHMOIDECTOMY	256.41	90
33217	INSERTION OF A TRANSVENOUS ELECTRODE	347.99	15
36430	TRANSFUSION, BLOOD	14.66	00
39545	IMBRICATION OF DIAPHRAGM FOR EVENTRATION	439.56	90
40808	BIOPSY, VESTIBULE OF MOUTH	25.65	00
47630	BILIARY DUCT STONE EXTRACTION	256.41	45
49560	REPAIR INITIAL INCISIONAL OR VENTRAL HERNIA	421.25	45
61703	SURGERY OF INTRACRANIAL ANEURYSM	476.19	90
62000	ELEVATION OF DEPRESSED SKULL FRACTURE	304.03	90
65800	PARACENTESIS OF ANTERIOR CHAMBER OF EYE	109.89	00
69400	EUSTACHIAN TUBE INFLATION	10.99	00
70250	RADIOLOGIC EXAM, SKULL	85.16	--
73130	RADIOLOGIC EXAM, HAND, MINIMUM 3 VIEWS	76.92	--
73550	RADIOLOGIC EXAM, UPPER LEG	76.92	--
73590	RADIOLOGIC EXAM, LOWER LEG	68.68	--
73718	MRI LEG	1,510.85	--
74250	RADIOLOGIC EXAM, SMALL BOWEL	181.31	--
76092	SCREENING MAMMOGRAPHY, BILATERAL	123.62	--
80048	BASIC METABOLIC PANEL	35.72	--
80053	COMPREHENSIVE METABOLIC PANEL	43.96	--
81000	URINALYSIS	19.23	--
82310	CALCIUM, TOTAL	27.47	--
83540	IRON	43.96	--
85025	BLOOD COUNT, COMPLETE, AUTOMATED	21.98	--
85610	PROTHROMBIN TIME	16.49	--
86901	BLOODTYPING, RH (D)	30.22	--
87040	CULTURE, BACTERIAL; BLOOD	32.97	--
87070	CULTURE, BACTERIAL DEFINITIVE BLOOD	35.72	--
88150	CYTOPATHOLOGY, SLIDES, CERVICAL OR VAGINAL	24.73	--
90782	THERAPEUTIC, INJECTION	80.13	--
97116	GAIT TRAINING	224.35	--
99025	INITIAL (NEW PATIENT) VISIT WHEN STARRED	128.20	--
99201	OFFICE OR OTHER OUTPATIENT VISIT, NEW	208.33	--
99213	ESTABLISHED PATIENT, EXPANDED	288.45	--
99284	EMERGENCY VISIT, DETAILED	801.25	--
99285	EMERGENCY VISIT, COMPREHENSIVE	1,185.85	--
A0429	EMERGENCY TRANSPORT	175.00	--
E0114	CRUTCHES	65.00	--
L2122	PLASTER OR CASTING,KNEE, ANKLE AND FOOT	116.55	--

*CPT codes, descriptions, and two digit numeric modifiers only are copyright 2003 American Medical Association. All Rights Reserved.

22 Coordination of Benefits

In this chapter you will learn:

- To define and explain the purpose of coordination of benefits.
- The order of the benefit determination rules and right of recovery.
- To recognize and investigate potential COB situations involving a claim.
- To compute the correct secondary benefit and benefit reserve.
- To understand the differences between primary and secondary carriers.
- To determine COB benefits as they apply to PPO and HMO plans.

Key words and concepts you will learn in this chapter:

Allowable Expense – Any necessary, reasonable, and customary item of a medical or dental expense, at least partly covered under at least one of the plans.

Claim Determination Period – A period in which COB is determined, usually a calendar year.

Coordination of Benefits (COB) – A process that occurs when two or more group plans provide coverage on the same person so that the insured does not make money from an illness or injury.

Credit Reserve – A cumulative amount within a claim determination period that is derived from the amount of funds that a plan has saved by being the secondary carrier.

EOB – A letter of explanation of benefits from a payor indicating how a member's benefits have been applied.

Insular COB – COB applied separately to medical and dental charges. All savings are kept separately.

Global COB – COB applied to both medical and dental charges combined. All savings are kept intermingled.

Normal Liability (NL) – The amount payable under the secondary plan's provisions without regard to any other coverage.

Order of Benefit Determination Rules (OBD) – Fourteen rules determining the order of payment.

Overinsurance – A situation that occurs when a person is covered under two or more policies and is eligible to collect an accumulation of benefits that actually exceeds the amount charged by the provider.

Primary Plan – The benefit plan that determines and pays its benefits first without regard to the existence of any other coverage.

Secondary Plan – The plan that pays after the primary plan has paid its benefits.

Coordination of benefits (COB) is a process that occurs when two or more plans provide coverage on the same person. Coordination between the two plans is necessary to allow for payment of 100% of the allowable expense but no more. This process was developed in response to a growing problem of overinsurance.

Overinsurance occurs when a person is covered under two or more policies and is eligible to collect an accumulation of benefits that actually exceeds the amount charged by the provider. The purpose of COB is to allow coverage and usually payment of 100% of allowable expenses without the covered member or members "making" money over and above the total costs for care.

In response to the diversity of handling procedures used by various carriers and administrators in coordinating coverages, the National Association of Insurance Commissioners (NAIC) developed a standardized model for COB administration. Most benefit plans follow this model, but it is not mandatory. Therefore, the plan provisions must be checked before processing COB claims, since the handling procedures may vary according to whether or not the NAIC guides are used.

Definitions

To process COB claims correctly, the following definitions must be understood:

Group Plan – a form of coverage with which coordination of benefits is allowed. A plan may include:

- Group, blanket, or franchise insurance policy or plan if not individually underwritten.
- Health maintenance organization or hospital or medical service prepayment policy available through an employer, union, or association.
- Trustee policy or plan, union welfare policy or plan, multiple employer policy or plan, or employee benefit policy or plan.
- Governmental programs (Medicare) or policies or plans required by a statute, except Medicaid or Medi-Cal.
- "No-fault" auto policy or plan. (Applies to some plans only. The plan must specify whether or not this is applicable.)

Primary Plan – the benefit plan that determines and pays its benefits first without regard to the existence of any other coverage.

Secondary Plan – the plan that pays after the primary plan has paid its benefits. The benefits of the secondary plan take into consideration the benefits of the primary plan and may reduce its payment so that only 100% of allowable expenses are paid.

Allowable Expense – any necessary, reasonable, and customary item of a medical or dental expense, at least partly covered under at least one of the plans covering the person for whom a claim is made. Items that are excluded by the secondary plan, such as dental services and vision care services, would not be considered allowable. Conversely, amounts that are limited under the secondary plan would be considered allowable (the entire charge). For example:

- Each plan provides a limit of $35 per visit for outpatient psychiatric care. The psychiatrist charges $50 per visit. Since both plans limit payment to $35 per visit, only $35 would be considered an allowable expense under COB.
- Based on the primary plan's UCR guidelines, the amount allowable for surgery is $1,200. The secondary plan's UCR for the same surgery is $1,000. When coordinating benefits, the secondary plan would allow the greatest amount allowed by at least one of the plans.

Therefore, the allowable amount when coordinating benefits would be $1200. Bear in mind that this amount has nothing to do with how the secondary plan calculates its usual payment. You will see how the two amounts interact later.

Claim Determination Period – usually a calendar year. It does not include any part of a year before the effective date of duplicate coverage under the secondary plan. It does not include any remaining amount during a calendar year occurring after the termination date of the primary plan. As long as the secondary plan is not terminated, COB continues to be performed even though there is no longer multiple coverages.

Normal Liability (NL) – the amount payable under the secondary plan's provisions without regard to any other coverage (what would regularly have been paid if there were no other insurance). This is not necessarily the amount that will actually be paid.

Example: The secondary plan pays 80% of UCR after a $100 deductible. The first claim is paid as follows: (OIS= Other Insurance Payment):

Charge	$200
Deductible	$100
OIS paymt	$160
Secondary plan's NL	$ 80
Secondary plan's actual payment	$ 40

Credit Reserve (CR) (benefit credit, credit savings, etc.) – a cumulative amount within a claim determination period that is derived from the amount of funds that a plan has saved by being the secondary carrier. The credit reserve does not carry over from one calendar year to another. Each year, the balance begins at $0. A running total is kept for each separate determination period (calendar year).

Example: Same benefits as above.

Charge	$200
Deductible	$100
OIS paymt	$100
Secondary plan's NL	$ 80
Secondary plan's Actual payment	$ 40
CR = NL – AP, or $80 - $40 = $40 in savings.	

Insular COB – COB applied separately to medical and dental charges. All savings are kept separately.

Global COB – COB applied to both medical and dental charges combined. All savings are kept intermingled.

EOB – an explanation of benefits letter from a payor indicating how a member's benefits have been applied in response to the submission of a claim for services. The EOB indicates deductibles, coinsurance, amounts, non-allowable amounts, UCR limitations, and other pertinent information. An EOB is required by law to be generated on each claim submission showing the disposition of the claim (i.e., how it was paid, denied, pending for additional information, etc).

Order of Benefit Determination Rules

Before standardized coordination rules were adopted by the benefits industry, a person covered under two policies could collect full benefits from both. Thus, the member could actually make a profit by being sick or injured. Since each plan would prefer to pay as the secondary payor, it became necessary to develop rules to determine when a plan should pay as primary, secondary, and or tertiary.

The 14 rules determining the order of payment are referred to as the **Order of Benefit Determinations (OBD)** and are explained below:

1. The plan without a COB provision will be primary to a plan with a COB provision.
2. When a plan does not have OBD rules, and as a result the plans do not agree on the OBD, the plan without these OBD rules will determine the order of payment.
3. The plan that covers an individual as an employee will be primary to a plan that covers that individual as a dependent.
4. If an individual is an employee under two plans, the primary plan is the one under which the employee has been covered the longest.
5. If an employee is an active employee under one plan and a retiree (or laid off) under another, the active plan will pay as primary.

The parent birthday rule, explained in #6 and #7, affects the OBD for dependent children of parents who are living together and married (not divorced or legally separated).

6. The plan of the parent whose birthday (based on month and day only) occurs first during the calendar year is the primary plan.
7. When both parent's birthdays are the same (based on month and day), the benefits of the plan that covered one parent the longest is the primary plan.

For dependents of legally separated or divorced parents and those whose parents have remarried, the order of benefits determination is based on the following rules:

8. The plan of the parent specified as having legal responsibility for the health care expense of the child is the primary plan.

For dependents of separated parents with no court decree:

9. The plan of the parent with custody is prime.
10. The plan of the step-parent (if any) with whom the child resides is secondary.
11. The plan of the natural parent without custody is tertiary.
12. The step-parent (if any) who does not reside with the child has no legal right to declare dependency. Therefore, no coordination should be performed because the child is probably not an eligible dependent under the plan.
13. For joint custody, with no additional responsibility designation, the plan of the parent whose coverage has been in effect the longest would be the primary payor. However,

this rule may vary by administrator. Some parents pay costs on a 50/50 basis, thereby sharing equally in the health care risk.

14. A few rare plans do not use the birthday rule as previously described. These plans generally use the **gender rule**; which states that the plan covering the male employee is primary, and the plan covering the female employee is secondary.

Right to Receive and Release Information

Certain facts are needed to determine and apply the appropriate COB rules. Therefore, plan representatives have the right to decide which facts are required and to obtain the needed facts from, or give the facts to, any other organization. The plan should get the insured's consent to do this. In addition, each person claiming benefits under a plan must give the facts required to properly process a claim. It is also important to realize that most providers of care do not release any information to a payor without a signed release from the member. Information should be requested or released to others only when absolutely necessary to determine benefits under the plan. The unnecessary request or release of information could be a violation of the right to privacy, which is punishable by law. Therefore, request only what is necessary, and routinely request a written authorization from the member to release information.

Facility of Payment

A payment made under one plan may include amounts that should have been paid by another plan. If it does, there are two options:

1. Payment may be made to the member, with a letter of notification sent to the carrier. In this case, the other carrier would be responsible for recovering payment from the member.
2. The plan may reimburse that amount to the organization or plan that made the initial incorrect payment, thus allowing that payor to recover the overpayment. In such a case, the amount reimbursed to the initial payor will be treated as if it were a benefit paid under the secondary plan. The reimbursing payor will not have to pay that amount again to either the member or the provider of service. The term "payment made" includes providing benefits in the form of services, in which case payment made means reasonable cash value of the benefits provided in the form of services.

Right of Recovery

If the amount of the payments made by the plan is more than it should have paid under the COB provision, the plan may recover the excess from one or more of the following:

- The person or persons it has paid or on behalf of whom it has paid.
- Other insurers/plans.
- Other organizations.

The "amount of the payments made" includes the reasonable cash value of any benefits provided in the form of services.

Miscellaneous Guidelines

Following are some miscellaneous guidelines:

- The difference between the cost of a private hospital room and the cost of a semi-private room is not considered an allowable expense unless the patient's stay in a private room was medically necessary either as generally accepted medical practice or as specifically defined in the plan.
- Items of expense under coverages such as dental care, vision care, prescription drug, or hearing aid programs may be excluded from the definition of allowable expense. A plan that provides only benefits for such items may limit its definition of allowable expense to like items.

This mean that a medical plan may have COB with medical expenses only, and a dental-only plan may limit COB to other dental plans only.

An item of expense covered under the primary plan may be considered an allowable expense under the secondary plan even though that plan does not provide such a benefit. For example:

The primary plan covers routine examinations. The secondary plan excludes routine examinations.

This expense may be considered an allowable expense. This COB rule varies widely from payor to payor. As previously indicated, some payors do not consider excluded expenses as allowable; others do. Therefore, the COB provisions and administrative handling rules must be verified. (Remember that we are talking about the amount considered as an allowable expense under COB, not the amount used to determine the secondary plan's normal liability.)

Health Maintenance Organizations

A **health maintenance organization (HMO)** is a type of prepayment plan in which providers agree to charge members for their services in accordance with a fixed schedule of rates. The HMO member (insured) usually pays a specified co-payment at the time the service is rendered. The patient and the doctor are never involved in having to complete the claim forms for submission to a payor. Instead, the HMO is billed directly, or the HMO pays a monthly retainer fee (capitation) to the physician for membership plus other specified fees.

If the required medical services are available through the HMO but the insured does not go to an HMO provider for the treatment, he or she may be held entirely responsible for all the expenses.

Prepayment plans are included in the definition of the type of policies to which COB provisions apply. However, many HMO's do not have COB provisions, although more are starting to incorporate the COB concept because of the spiraling costs of medical care.

An example of an HMO is Kaiser Permanente. Kaiser provides a prepayment policy for hospital and professional medical services at no cost or at a small fee, as long as the member goes to a Kaiser facility. Subsequently, the HMO provides the member with a "reasonable cost statement," which represents what would have been charged to a non-member. If the HMO does not have the COB provision, the HMO would be considered the primary payor. To coordinate benefits, a request must be made for receipts or statements showing the actual "out-of-pocket" expense. The secondary plan would pay no more than the amount that would be considered the allowable expense. If the HMO does have a COB provision, the regular OBD determination rules should be applied.

Preferred Provider Organizations

As previously covered, **preferred provider organizations (PPOs)** are special arrangements in which members are responsible for expenses based on specific contractual UCR arrangements. Some services may be covered at a higher rate than others, and some may not be covered at all. Usually, COB will apply to PPO claims. The main difference between going to a regular provider is reflected in the patient's liability. That is, if the member goes to a PPO provider, the member is not responsible for any amounts in excess of the PPO contractual UCR amount.

In addition, depending on the payor, the plan, and the PPO, the secondary payor may not be held responsible for any amounts in excess of the contractual PPO amount, even though the secondary payor is not a party to the contract. This handling is based on the premise that if the member is not responsible for anything over the PPO rate, then neither is the secondary plan. Once again, this handling varies.

A PPO EOB usually specifically states the member's responsibility. By referring to the appropriate field on the EOB, the secondary carrier can tell what amount to use to determine the allowable expense.

Anything in excess of the patient's liability amount is not considered allowable.

If the member does not go to a PPO provider, the member is responsible for all the charges including the amounts in excess of the primary plan's UCR. In addition, most plans penalize their members for not going to PPO providers by reducing the plan's payment (i.e., the coinsurance percentage paid by the plan is reduced from 80% to 70%, or even lower.).

Tri-Care

Tri-Care (formerly CHAMPUS) provides a comprehensive program of health care benefits for active duty and retired services personnel, their dependents, and the dependents of deceased military personnel.

Tri-Care is secondary to all other insurance or health policies except Medicaid and Tri-Care supplemental insurance. However, because many services are provided free of charge or with only a minimal fee, many examiners never see a Tri-Care EOB.

Recognizing the Presence of Dual Coverage

The possibility that a claimant may have dual coverage is indicated in the following two examples:
1. The greatest likelihood of dual coverage occurs when the spouse is employed. Claim forms usually request the name of the employee's spouse, and the name and address of the spouse's employer. The claim form defines what is meant by other group insurance and asks the claimant to designate which type of other insurance exists.
2. Even when the claimant states that there is no other coverage, additional inquiries should be made in the following instances:
    - In claims that involve married employees or their dependents, often the spouse also has group coverage on the family.
    - The claim form indicates that the spouse is not employed. Under the policy held by the spouse's previous employer, extended benefits or a provision for the continuation of insurance (COBRA) may be available.
    - The claim is for a dependent child, but the area on the from requesting other insurance information has been left blank.
    - Notations on the hospital bills or claim papers show that some other insurer/plan has paid benefits or that there is other employment within the family.

- The claimant does not assign hospital benefits. This may indicate that the claimant has used other benefits to pay the provider and thus does not want a duplicate payment to be made (to the provider).
- It is known from a group's local sources that a patient is covered under another plan.
- Photocopies of bills are submitted. Usually, the original is submitted, and a copy is kept by the member. The originals may have been submitted to another payor.
- The provider charges for the completion of a claim form, but the submitted form was not received from the provider. The charge may have been for completing a form for another payor.
- Requests for information are received from other policyholders/plans or insurers.
- The occupation of the claimant or spouse of a dependent suggests coverage through a union or some other professional affiliation.
- A hospital or surgeon's bill makes reference to other coverage.
- A bill showing a substantial credit or adjustment to the account.
- The claim submitted is the first maternity bill for the subscriber's spouse. In such a case, the wife may have been regularly employed until her pregnancy, and benefits may be available through the extension of benefits provision of her previous policy.
- The claim is submitted on another carrier's claim form, or an EOB is attached.
- A duplicate coverage inquiry (DCI) is received. This is an industry-approved form designed to establish the existence of other coverage.
- An HMO requests reimbursement for the value of service provided to one of their patients.
- Claims history shows COB payments in the past, but claims are now being paid as primary with no explanation. Or, claims history shows claims paid as secondary and others paid as primary with no explanation.

Pursuit of details pertaining to other coverage can be through a variety of sources. If the claim form indicates that the insured's spouse is employed and includes the name and address of the spouse's employer, contact that employer to determine whether there is other group coverage.

Coordination Of Benefits
Calculation Worksheet

Patient's Name: _____   Year: _____

Payment Calculation:

1. Total allowable amount for this claim is the higher of either the primary plan's allowable amount or the secondary plan's allowable amount.   _____

2. Total primary insurance carrier payment for this claim.   _____

3. Difference between Line 1 and Line 2.   _____

4. Secondary insurance carrier's normal liability for this claim.   _____

5. The lesser of Line 3 or Line 4.
   This is the amount of the secondary insurance carrier actual payment on this claim.   _____

Credit Reserve:

6. Normal liability for this claim (Line 4 above).   _____

7. Actual payment for this claim (line 5 above).   _____

8. Subtract Line 7 from Line 6.   _____

9. Credit reserve on all previous claims for this patient.   _____

10. Total credit reserve (add Line 8 and Line 9).   _____

Instructions:
Place the patient's name and the year that services were rendered in the box on the top of the COB calculation sheet.
1. Enter the total allowable amount on this claim. The total allowable amount is the greater of either the primary plan's allowable amount or the secondary plan's allowable amount.
2. Enter the total amount that other insurance companies have paid on this claim.
3. Subtract line 2 from line 1.
4. Enter the normal liability amount for this insurance company for this claim.
5. Enter the lesser of either Line 3 or Line 4. This is the actual amount of the secondary insurance payor on this claim.

To Calculate Credit Reserve:
6. Enter the normal liability amount for the secondary insurance carrier for this claim.
7. Enter the actual payment for the secondary insurance carrier for this claim.
8. Subtract Line 7 from Line 6. This is the amount of money the secondary carrier has saved by paying secondary on this claim. This amount becomes part of the credit reserve.
9. Enter the credit reserve amount for all previous claims for this patient.
10. Add Line 8 and Line 9. This is the total credit reserve for this patient.

Figure 22 – 1: Coordination of Benefits Calculation Worksheet

If the claim form does not indicate the name and address of the spouse's employer, request the missing information from the subscriber.

Additional sources of information regarding the existence of dual coverage include:

- Files from hospital admissions.
- City directories listing members of a family, their occupations, and places of employment.
- Information cards compiled by the Benefits Office for local employer plans.

COB Worksheet

The COB worksheet is used to help calculate the proper benefits when there is COB between more than one health plan. **Figure 22 – 1** is a sample COB worksheet. To begin, calculate the allowable amount that would be paid on this claim if there was no other insurance. Then,

follow the instructions on the bottom of the COB Calculation Worksheet.

Summary

Coordination of benefits is necessary to ensure that when charges are covered by more than one carrier the total payment does not exceed more than 100% of the bill. These guidelines should be considered whenever there is the possibility of dual coverage or a third party payor. Learn to identify the possible existence of another payor by applying the guidelines and rules that were covered in this chapter.

Assignments

Complete the Questions for Review.
Complete Exercises 22 – 1 and 22 – 2.

Questions for Review

Directions: Answer the following questions without looking back into the material just covered. Write your answers in the space provided.

1. Define COB. _____

_____

2. What is the purpose of COB? _____

_____

3. The _____ is the benefit plan that determines and pays its benefits first without regard to the existence of any other coverage.

4. The _____ is the plan that pays after the primary plan has paid its benefits.

5. What is a PPO? _____

_____

_____

6. What does HMO stand for and describe what an HMO is. _____

_____

_____

_____

7. What is Tri-Care? _____

_____

_____

_____

8. (True or False?) The plan without a COB provision is secondary to a plan with a COB provision. _____

9. Define Global COB. _____
    _____
    _____

10. _____ applies separately to medical and dental charges. All savings are kept separate.

If you were unable to answer any of the questions, refer back to the section and then complete the answers.

Exercise 22 – 1

Directions: Using the following information, complete a COB calculation worksheet.

1. Total submitted expenses = $1,600. Primary carrier, A, considers the allowable amount to be $1,450 and has made a payment of $1,160 on this claim. Secondary carrier, B, considers the allowable amount to be $1,495. Both plans calculate benefits at 80%. Neither carrier has made any previous payments or had any previous allowable amounts.
2. Total submitted expenses = $1,200. Primary carrier, A, considers the allowable amount to be $1,000 and has made a payment of $800 on this claim. Secondary carrier, B, considers the allowable amount to be $1,200. Both plans calculate benefits at 80%. Use previous allowable amounts, payment amounts, and credit reserve amount from Worksheet #1.
3. Total submitted expenses = $1,400. Primary carrier, A, considers the allowable amount to be $1,400 and has made a payment of $1,120 on this claim. Secondary carrier, B, considers the allowable amount to be $1,200. Plan A calculates benefits at 80%. Plan B limits payment to 50% of the allowable amount to a calendar year maximum of $500. $450 has already been paid out. Use previous allowable amounts, payment amounts, and credit reserve amounts from Worksheets #1 and #2.

Exercise 22 – 2 to 22 – 6

Directions: To practice COB claims processing, we will go back to the physicians services and surgery claims and reprocess them using different contracts. Betty Bossy will now be processed with the Ninja plan as primary and the ABC plan as secondary. Danny Dingbat will now be processed with the ABC plan as primary and the XYZ plan as secondary. Patty Patient will now be processed with the XYZ plan as primary, and the Ninja plan as secondary.

Since the primary plan is the one that was previously processed, you do not need to reprocess the claims again, simply use your calculations from the physicians services, and surgery chapters.

Honors Certification™

The Honors Certification™ challenge for this chapter is a written test of the information contained within this chapter. There will also be three COB claims to process. Each incorrect answer will result in a deduction of between 1% and 5% from your grade. You must achieve a score of 85% or higher to pass this test. If you fail the test on your first attempt you may retake the test one additional time. The items included in the second test may be different from those in the first test.

23 Medicare

In this chapter you will learn:

- The purpose of the Social Security Administration's Medicare Department.
- About TEFRA and DEFRA and their relevance to claims processing.
- Medicare eligibility requirements.

Key words and concepts you will learn in this chapter:

Balance Billing – In Medicare, charging patients for more than the Medicare allowance.

Deficit Reduction Act of 1984, (DEFRA) – The Act that amended TEFRA so that spouses, aged 65 years and older, of active employees who are under age 65 can elect their primary coverage, as either Medicare or the private group plan.

Diagnosis Related Group Billing (DRG) – A flat rate payment is made, based on the patient's diagnosis rather than the hospital's itemized billing.

End-Stage Renal Disease (ESRD) – The condition in which a person's kidneys fail to function.

Maintenance of Benefits – A COB provision in many group health plans that allows the person who has Medicare to "maintain" the same group benefits as members who do not have Medicare.

Medicare – The Federal Health Insurance Benefit Plan for the Aged and Disabled.

Medicare Supplements – Separate plans written exclusively for Medicare participants which cover items Medicare does not cover.

Non-Participating Physicians – Physicians who treat Medicare-eligible patients but who decide whether to accept assignment on a case-by-case basis.

Outliers – DRG cases which are atypically expensive (based on the diagnosis) because of complications or an abnormally long confinement.

Part A – The Medicare basic plan or hospital insurance, which covers facility charges for acute inpatient hospital care, skilled nursing, home health care, and hospice care.

Part B – The Medicare medical insurance, which covers doctor's services, outpatient hospital services, home health care, outpatient speech and physical therapy, and durable medical equipment.

Participating Physicians – Providers who have signed an agreement with Medicare to accept the Medicare allowed amount, among other things.

Reasonable Charges – The amounts approved by the Medicare carrier based on what is considered reasonable for the geographic area in which the doctor practices.

Tax Equity and Fiscal Responsibility Act of 1982 TEFRA – A Federal Act that redirected the financial responsibility for medical coverage of active employees age 65 years and older and their spouses aged 65 years and older to Medicare.

Medicare is the Federal Health Insurance Benefit Plan for the Aged and Disabled, Title XVII of Public Law 89-97 of the Social Security Act. This program is for people 65 years of age or older and certain persons who are totally disabled.

Social Security Administration (SSA) offices throughout the United States take applications for Medicare, determine eligibility, and provide general information about the program. The actual processing of the claims is administered by many different insurance companies, usually one or two within each state. Consequently, as an examiner, you will see a diversity in the application or denial of benefits and in the Medicare explanation of benefit (MEOB) forms.

TEFRA/DEFRA

The Tax Equity and Fiscal Responsibility Act of 1982 (TEFRA) – and amendments to it – has redirected the financial responsibility for medical coverage of active employees age 65 years and older and their spouses aged 65 years and older. When this federal program was introduced, it was determined that Medicare would be the primary payor for persons who have reached their 65th birthday, regardless of employment status.

Initially, TEFRA regulations did not apply to spouses over age 65 of active employees who were under 65 years of age. The Deficit Reduction Act of 1984 (DEFRA), effective January 1, 1985, amended TEFRA so that now spouses, age 65 years and older, of active employees who are under age 65 can elect their primary coverage, as either Medicare or the private group plan.

The employers affected by these Acts are those who regularly employ 20 or more workers for each working day in at least 20 weeks of the current or preceding calendar year. Employees of such employers must be offered coverage under the group plan on the same basis as other employees. An election form choosing the primary plan must be completed and signed by each employee who is or becomes affected.

If coverage is chosen under the employer's group plan, the group plan will be the primary payor on all medical services and Medicare will be the secondary payor. If coverage under the group plan is rejected and Medicare is chosen, the employee/spouse by law can be covered only by Medicare. The group plan will not provide secondary coverage.

Employers with fewer than 20 employees are exempt from the TEFRA/DEFRA regulations, and Medicare is the primary carrier for their active employees and spouses age 65 years or older. Medicare is also primary for all retired employees and for active employees and their spouses under age 65 who are totally disabled with conditions other than end-stage renal disease (ESRD).

After it has been determined that the group plan is subject to TEFRA/DEFRA, it becomes necessary to determine the individual's eligibility for Medicare.

Medicare Eligibility

Medicare eligibility is based on three guiding principals:
1. Age.
2. Disability.
3. ESRD.

An individual is eligible for Medicare coverage on the first day of the month in which he or she reaches age 65. Persons born on the first day of the month are eligible on the first day of the month preceding their birth date.
Example:
Birthday: June 15, eligible for Medicare on June 1
Birthday: June 1, eligible for Medicare on May 1

Medicare coverage for totally disabled persons begins on the first of the 25th month from the date approved for Social Security Disability or Railroad Retirement benefits. Those covered include disabled workers of any age, disabled widows between the ages of 50 and 65, disabled beneficiaries age 18 and over who receive Social Security benefits because of disability before age 22, the blind, and railroad retirement annuitants.

End-stage renal disease (ESRD) is the condition in which a person's kidneys fail to function. As a result, the patient needs dialysis treatments (refer to the Physisician's Services chapter for a review of this type of service). Because of the many problems associated with ESRD, patients are considered to be totally disabled, even though some persons with this disease continue to work. As a result, the following special rules apply to ESRD patients.

The employer's group health plan is the primary payor for the first 30 months after a patient (under age 65) with ESRD becomes eligible for Medicare. This 30-month period begins based on the earlier of:
- The month in which a regular course of renal dialysis is initiated.
- The month in which the patient is hospitalized for a kidney transplant.

Medicare is the secondary payor during this 30-month period but will revert to the primary status beginning with the 31st month. As a general rule, all services under a dialysis program are Medicare assigned.

Providers of Service

Providers of services and medical equipment suppliers under Medicare must meet all licensing requirements of the state in which they are located. To be a participating provider under the Medicare program, they must meet additional Medicare requirements before payments can be made for their services. Medicare does not pay for the following care received in non-participating facilities:
- Hospital care.
- Skilled nursing facility.
- Home health agency.
- Hospice.
- Outpatient rehabilitation.
- Dialysis facilities.
- Ambulatory surgical centers.
- Independent physical therapists.
- Independent occupational therapists.
- Clinical laboratories.
- Portable x-ray suppliers.
- Rural health clinics.

The Two Parts of Medicare

The two parts to the Medicare program are A and B. The services covered are as follows:

1. **Part A** is considered the basic plan or hospital insurance, which covers facility charges for acute inpatient hospital care, skilled nursing, home health care, and hospice care.
2. **Part B** is the medical (supplementary, voluntary) insurance, which covers doctor's services, outpatient hospital services, home health care, outpatient speech and physical therapy, and durable medical equipment.

Part A

Eligibility

The two parts of the Medicare program have different eligibility requirements. Part A is automatic upon enrollment for the following:

- All persons age 65 years and over, if entitled to (a) monthly Social Security benefits or (b) pensions under the Railroad Retirement Act.
- All persons who have reached age 65 before 1968, whether or not under the Social Security or Railroad Retirement Programs.
- Workers who reached 65 in 1975, or subsequently, *and* have 20 quarters of Social Security work credits, if female, or 24 quarters of Social Security work credits if male.

All persons age 65 and over who are not otherwise eligible for Part A may enroll by paying the full cost of such coverage, provided that they also enroll in Part B.

Certain exclusions such as members of subversive organizations and aliens who have not been permanent US residents for five years are applicable.

Benefits

As previously indicated, Part A is the hospital insurance portion of Medicare. There is a deductible that is taken from the first admission. If the patient is out of the hospital for at least 60 consecutive days (including the day of discharge), a new benefit period begins and another inpatient deductible would be taken if re-admitted. (This is known as the period of renewal.) For 2003, the Part A deductible is $840 per benefit period.

If a member remains in the hospital for an extended period of time, additional co-payments are required. Medicare deducts the co-pay amount from the billed amount and then pays the amount in excess of the co-pay. The 2002 inpatient hospital co-payments are as follows:

- 1st to 60th day = Deductible only, no additional co-payment.
- 61st to 90th day = $210/day.
- 91st to 150th day = $420. These days are known as the 60-day lifetime reserve. These days do not renew. Once used, they are gone.

For skilled nursing facilities (SNF), there is a separate co-payment schedule and requirement. To be eligible for this benefit, the following conditions must be met:

1. A doctor must certify the necessity of skilled nursing and rehabilitative care on a daily basis. Custodial care is not covered nor is occasional rehabilitative care.
2. The Medicare intermediary must approve the stay.

The 2003 SNF co-payments are as follows:
- 1st to 20th day = No co-payment. Since admission is usually from an acute care facility, during which time the deductible was met, 100% of the allowable is generally paid by Medicare.
- 21st to 100th day = $105 Coinsurance/co-pay per day.

The maximum number of allowable hospital days is 100 per calendar year. These deductibles and co-payments are adjusted upward each calendar year based on inflation.

Psychiatric inpatient hospital care is covered for a maximum of 90 days per lifetime of the member. These days do not renew. The only applicable deductible is the inpatient hospital deductible of $840 for 2003. There are no co-payments. Also, the facility must be a participating Medicare provider for the patient to be covered.

Care at foreign facilities is generally not covered. However, some qualified Canadian or Mexican hospitals may qualify for coverage during emergency situations.

Part time home health care may be covered under the following circumstances:

- The care needed includes intermittent skilled nursing care, physical therapy, or speech therapy.
- The patient is confined to the home.
- A doctor prescribes the care and sets up a home health plan.
- The home health agency is a participating provider.

Hospice care may be covered under the following circumstances:

- A doctor certifies that the patient is terminal.
- The patient chooses to receive care from a hospice instead of standard Medicare benefits (inpatient).
- Care is provided by a Medicare certified hospice program or facility.

Special benefit periods and payments apply to this benefit. If additional clarification is required, refer to a Medicare handbook.

Part A insurance does not cover the following services:

- Replacement fees for the first three pints of blood.
- Personal convenience items.
- Private duty nurses (inpatient).

- Private room difference, unless it is determined to be medically necessary.

Medicare will not cover the following services:
- Full-time nursing care in the home.
- Drugs and biologicals.
- Meals delivered to the home.
- Homemaker services.
- Blood transfusions.

Part B
Part B is the supplementary medical insurance that covers doctors and outpatient hospital services. It is considered a supplemental plan because each participant must pay a stipulated amount each month for the benefits. The monthly premium is adjusted each year based on inflation.

The rules, limits, and maximums under this coverage are subject to change every year. In addition, certain types of services are covered under some circumstances but not under others. Therefore, it is less confusing to have a general idea of the most common benefits and not become overly concerned with the details. Normally, the claims examiner will not be concerned with Medicare except when it is the primary payor. In such circumstances, the Medicare explanation of benefits is needed to process the claim. The following briefly summarizes some of the more common benefits. For more specific rules, refer to a Medicare booklet or carrier.

Benefits
The 2003 yearly deductible is $100, which has a three-month carryover provision. After the deductible has been satisfied, generally 80% of the approved charge is paid. Services covered by Part B of the Medicare program are as follows:
- Medically necessary physician's visits.
- Manual manipulation of the spine for subluxation demonstrated by x-rays.
- Non-routine podiatric care.
- Dental care for surgery of the jaw/related structures and fractures of facial bones.
- Some non-routine optometry surgery.
- Outpatient hospital services.
- Outpatient physical/speech therapy – 2003 maximum, $1,590.
- Independent clinical laboratory/x-ray services.
- Ambulance transportation
- Some durable medical and prosthetic equipment.
- Outpatient treatment of mental illness.
- Home health care.

Doctors' services *not* covered by Part B are as follows:
- Routine physical examinations and related diagnostic, x-ray, and laboratory services (DXL).

- Routine foot care.
- Eye and hearing examinations for eyeglasses or hearing aids.
- Immunizations (exceptions may be pneumococcal and hepatitis B).
- Cosmetic surgery (some exceptions).

Approved or Reasonable Charges

Medicare payments are based on what the law defines as **"reasonable charges,"** which are the amounts approved by the Medicare carrier based on what is considered reasonable for the geographic area in which the doctor practices. Because of the way that the approved amounts are determined and because of high rates of inflation in medical care prices, the approved amounts are often significantly less than the actual charges billed by providers. The charge approved by the carrier is the lowest of either of the following: the charge billed by the provider or the prevailing charge (based on all the customary charges in the locality for each type of service) as determined by Medicare.

Since the participating provider must write off the amounts that are more than the Medicare approved amount, many providers have refused to participate in Medicare. Unfortunately, the member, who is often on a fixed income, and goes to a non-participating provider is then held responsible for a large portion of the billed amount.

Medicare Assignments of Benefits

Medicare assignment of benefits has no involvement as to whom the claims examiner will make payment. A participating provider must agree to accept assignment on all Medicare claims. By doing this, the payment goes directly to the provider for all claims, rather than to the member. In addition, the provider has agreed to accept the amount approved by the Medicare carrier as payment in full for the covered services. The patient is not responsible for any amount over the approved amount. In such a case, the secondary carrier is also not responsible for the amount in excess of the Medicare approved amount.

Physicians Who Accept Medicare Assignment
When a physician agrees to accept Medicare assignment for a bill, Medicare pays the physician directly for that bill. The physician may bill the patient only for any deductibles or coinsurance that Medicare has deducted from the assigned bill. As a result, the total fee that a physician may receive from Medicare and from beneficiaries for an assigned bill is limited by what Medicare deems an appropriate fee for the particular service or procedure (the **"Medicare allowance"**).

To encourage physicians to accept assignment, the Medicare allowance is higher for physicians who agree to accept assignment for all bills for Medicare-eligible persons. These physicians are called **participating physicians**. Thus, participating physicians agree not to practice **balance billing**, that is, charging patients for more than the Medicare allowance.

The phrase "participating physician" can be confusing because physicians who sign these agreements are not the only ones who treat Medicare patients. Physicians who treat Medicare-eligible patients but who decide whether to accept assignment on a case-by-case basis are called **non-participating physicians**. In exchange, for the freedom to make this choice for each patient, non-participating physicians receive only 95% of the reimbursement that participating physicians receive from Medicare. For example, if the Medicare allowance for a procedure is $100 for participating physicians, the allowance for non-participating physicians would be $95. Therefore, if the patient's deductible had been paid, a participating physician would receive $80 from Medicare (80% of $100), and a non-participating physician would receive $76 from Medicare (80% of $95). Although the participating physician is not allowed to charge the Medicare patient more than the $20 coinsurance, the non-participating physician has no such restriction. However, if the non-participating physician agrees to accept assignment for that bill, he or she can bill the patient only $19 ($95 - $76 = $19).

Restrictions on Balance Billing

In Medicare, balance billing is charging or collecting from a Medicare beneficiary an amount over the Medicare approved amount for Medicare covered services and supplies. Beginning on January 1, 1991, the most important Medicare changes took effect. Balance billing by non-participating physicians was strictly limited. (Of course, limits had no effect in states such as Massachusetts, where balance billing is prohibited by law.) In New York, the limits affected only office and home visits, since New York has limits on balance billing for all other services. In addition, participating physicians are not affected, since they were not allowed to balance bill Medicare patients for any services.

In 1993, balance billing was restricted to no more than 15% over what Medicare allows. This restriction is sometimes referred to as **capitation**. Following are some examples of how this rule affects the payment of claims.

Example 1: Provider accepts assignments.

Billed charge	$182	
Allowed amount	$135	
Member pays	$100	to ded = $35 balance
Medicare pays	$ 28	($35 X 80%)
Member pays	$107	(deductible + $35 X 20%)

Example 2: Provider does not accept assignment

Billed charge	$182.00	
Allowed amount	$128.25	($135 X 95%)
Member pays	$100.00	to ded = $28.25 balance
Medicare pays	$ 22.60	($28.25 X 80%)
Member pays	$124.89	

The member payment includes $100 deductible + $5.65 coinsurance ($28.25 X 20%) + $19.24 additional to cover 115% over allowed amount.

COB with Medicare

There are a variety of ways in which group health plans coordinate their payments with Medicare when Medicare is primary and the group plan is secondary. The most common methods in use include the following:
- Non-duplication of Medicare.
- Maintenance of benefits.
- Coordination of benefits.
- Medicare supplemental coverage.

Nonduplication of Medicare

Calculation of benefits under the nonduplication approach is the same as with COB except that allowable expenses are those that are listed as covered expenses under the group plan. To compute benefits under this approach, use the following four guidelines:

1. Regular group benefits are computed. Apply all eligibility requirements, deductibles, limitations, and maximums.
2. If the claim is Medicare assigned, the Medicare-approved amount is used as the base.
   a. Subtract the amount paid by Medicare from the Medicare-approved amount.
   b. Compare the balance with the plan's normal liability (the amount determined in step 1).
      1. If the normal liability amount is equal to or greater than the balance amount, the balance is paid by the plan.
      2. If the normal liability amount is less than the balance, the normal liability amount is paid.
3. If the claim is not Medicare assigned, the base is the lesser of the plan's eligible expense or Medicare's approved amount plus the capitation percentage (balance billing limit).
   a. Subtract the amount paid by Medicare from the plan's approval amount (calculated in step 1).
   b. Compare the balance with the plan's normal liability (the amount determined in step 1).

1. If the normal liability amount is equal to or greater than the balance amount, the balance is paid by the plan.
2. If the normal liability amount is less than the balance, the normal liability amount is paid.

4. The credit reserve is calculated, based on the difference between the plan's liability (calculated in step 1) and the amount actually paid by the plan.

Following are three examples of calculation of benefits using the nonduplication of Medicare benefits approach:

Example 1: Plan benefits: $150 deductible, none paid to date. 80% payable for all expenses, Medicare assigned.

Billed charges
$175.00 Office visit
$165.00 Lab
$ 31.00 Dispensed meds
$371.00

Plan allowed charges
$125.00 Office visit
$150.00 Lab
$ 31.00 Dispensed meds
$306.00

Plan normal liability (NL)
$ 0.00 ($125 to deductible) (OV)
$100.00 ($25 to ded., $125 X 80%) (Lab)
$ 24.80 ($31 X 80%) (Meds)
$124.80

Medicare allowed amounts
$125.00 Office visit
$135.00 Lab
$ 0.00 Dispensed meds
$260.00

Medicare pays
$ 20.00 ($100 to ded., $25 X 80%) (OV)
$108.00 ($135 X 80%) (Lab)
$ 0.00 (Not covered) (Meds)
$128.00

Payment
$260.00 Lesser of plan or Medicare allowed
$128.00 Medicare/primary payor
$152.00 Balance due
$124.80 Plan pays (lessor of NL or balance due)
$ 27.20 Out-of-pocket to patient

Example 2: Same plan benefits as in #1, not Medicare assigned.

Billed charges
$175.00 Office visit
$165.00 Lab
$ 31.00 Dispensed meds
$371.00

Plan allowed charges
$125.00 Office visit
$150.00 Lab
$ 31.00 Dispensed meds
$306.00

Plan normal liability (NL)
$ 0.00 ($125 to deductible) (OV)
$100.00 ($25 to ded., $125 X 80%) (Lab)
$ 24.80 ($31 X 80%) (Meds)
$124.80

Medicare allowed amounts
$118.75 Office visit
$128.25 Lab
$ 0.00 Dispensed meds
$247.00

Medicare balance billable amount (MBBA)
$284.05 ($247 X 115%)

Medicare pays
$ 15.00 ($100 to ded., $18.75 X 80%) (OV)
$102.60 ($128.25 X 80%) (Lab)
$ 0.00 (Not covered) (Meds)
$117.60

Payment
$284.05 Lesser of plan allowed or MBBA
$117.60 Medicare/primary payor
$166.45 Balance due
$124.80 Plan pays (lessor of NL or balance due)
$ 48.85 Out-of-pocket to patient

Maintenance of Benefits

Maintenance of benefits refers to a provision in many group health plans that allows the person who has Medicare to "maintain" the same group benefits as members who do not have Medicare. Benefit credits are not established. To determine the payable benefits under this provision, follow the five procedures indicated below:

1. Compute the regular Basic or Major Medical benefits that would be payable in the absence of Medicare (line-for-line calculation). Apply all eligibility requirements, deductibles, limitations, and contractual maximums.
2. Determine the amount the doctor is allowed to collect (the Medicare allowed amount if the claim is assigned, or the Medicare balance billable amount (MBBA) if the claim is not assigned).

3. Use the lessor of #1 or #2 as the base.
4. Compare the amount paid by Medicare to the base.
5. If the amount paid by Medicare is greater than the base, no payment will be issued by the plan. The patient has received at least the same in benefits as he would have received under the plan.
6. If the base is greater than the amount paid by Medicare, pay the difference. The patient will now have received the amount they would have received if there was no Medicare, up to the amount of the Medicare allowed amount or the balance billing limit.

Example 1: Plan benefits: $150 deductible, none paid to date. 80% payable for all expenses. Medicare assigned.

Billed charges
   $175.00 Office visit
   $165.00 Lab
   $ 31.00 Dispensed meds
   $371.00

Plan allowed charges
   $125.00 Office visit
   $150.00 Lab
   $ 31.00 Dispensed meds
   $306.00

Plan normal liability (NL)
   $ 0.00 ($125 to deductible) (OV)
   $100.00 ($25 to ded., $125 X 80%) (Lab)
   $ 24.80 ($31 X 80%) (Meds)
   $124.80

Medicare allowed amounts
   $125.00 Office visit
   $135.00 Lab
   $ 0.00 Dispensed meds
   $260.00

Medicare pays
   $ 20.00 ($100 to ded., $25 X 80%) (OV)
   $108.00 ($135 X 80%) (Lab)
   $ 0.00 (Not covered) (Meds)
   $128.00
Payment
   $260.00 Lesser of plan allowed or Medicare allowed

Compare:
   $128.00 Medicare/primary payor
   $124.80 Plan NL
Plan pays $0.00 since Medicare has already paid more than the plan's normal liability amount.

   $132.00 Out-of-pocket to patient

Example 2: Same plan benefits as in #1, Not Medicare assigned.

Billed charges
   $175.00 Office visit
   $165.00 Lab
   $ 31.00 Dispensed meds
   $371.00

Plan allowed charges
   $125.00 Office visit
   $150.00 Lab
   $ 31.00 Dispensed meds
   $306.00

Plan normal liability (NL)
   $ 0.00 ($125 to deductible) (OV)
   $100.00 ($25 to ded., $125 X 80%) (Lab)
   $ 24.80 ($31 X 80%) (Meds)
   $124.80

Medicare allowed amounts
   $118.75 Office visit
   $128.25 Lab
   $ 0.00 Dispensed meds
   $247.00

Medicare balance billable amount (MBBA)
   $284.05 ($247 X 115%)

Medicare pays
   $ 15.00 ($100 to ded., $18.75 X 80%) (OV)
   $102.60 ($128.25 X 80%) (Lab)
   $ 0.00 (Not covered) (Meds)
   $117.60

Payment
   $284.05 Lesser of plan allowed or MBBA

Compare:
   $117.60 Medicare/primary payor
   $124.80 Plan NL
   $ 7.20 Amount required to bring patient up to what the plan would normally have paid if there had been no Medicare payment.
   $159.25 Out-of-pocket to patient

Under maintenance of benefits, when a group plan and Medicare are both providing benefits on the same expenses, the total benefits provided should equal what the benefit would have been under the group plan alone as if the member did not have Medicare. However, since most plans exclude any amount for which there would be no charge in the absence of the insurance, the Medicare allowed amount (on assigned claims) or Medicare balance billable amount (on non-assigned claims) must be taken into consideration.

Regular group benefits are provided for charges covered by the group plan but not covered at all by Medicare.

Coordination with Medicare

COB with Medicare is calculated as with any other COB claim. Allowable expenses are based on the amount approved by Medicare on an assigned claim or the amount approved by the plan or Medicare, whichever is greater, on a non-assigned claim. Also, as with other COB claims, allowable expenses are considered those payable in whole or part by one or both plans. Benefit credit reserve is established and used to cover allowable expenses.

Example 1: Plan benefits: $150 deductible, none paid to date. 80% payable for all expenses. Medicare assigned.

Billed charges
   $175.00   Office visit
   $165.00   Lab
   $ 31.00   Dispensed meds
   $371.00

Plan allowed charges
   $125.00   Office visit
   $150.00   Lab
   $ 31.00   Dispensed meds
   $306.00

Plan normal liability (NL)
   $ 0.00   ($125 to deductible) (OV)
   $100.00   ($25 to ded., $125 X 80%) (Lab)
   $ 24.80   ($31 X 80%) (Meds)
   $124.80

Medicare allowed amounts
   $125.00   Office visit
   $135.00   Lab
   $ 0.00   Dispensed meds
   $260.00

Medicare pays
   $ 20.00   ($100 to ded., $25 X 80%) (OV)
   $108.00   ($135 X 80%) (Lab)
   $ 0.00   (Not covered) (Meds)
   $128.00

Payment
   $306.00   Allowable amount (greater of plan's or Medicare's allowable amount)
   $128.00   Medicare payment.
   $178.00   Difference
   $124.80   Plan's normal liability
   $124.80   Lesser of plan's NL or difference (up to the Medicare allowed amounts.)

This is the amount of the secondary insurance carrier payment on this claim.

Credit Reserve:

   $124.80   Plan's NL for this claim.
   -124.80   Actual payment for this claim.
   $ 0.00
   +   0.00   Credit reserve on previous claims
   $ 0.00   Total credit reserve

Example 2: Same plan benefits as in #1, Not Medicare assigned.

Billed charges
   $175.00   Office visit
   $165.00   Lab
   $ 31.00   Dispensed meds
   $371.00

Plan allowed charges
   $125.00   Office visit
   $150.00   Lab
   $ 31.00   Dispensed meds
   $306.00

Plan normal liability (NL)
   $ 0.00   ($125 to deductible) (OV)
   $100.00   ($25 to ded., $125 X 80%) (Lab)
   $ 24.80   ($31 X 80%) (Meds)
   $124.80

Medicare allowed amounts
   $118.75   Office visit
   $128.25   Lab
   $ 0.00   Dispensed meds
   $247.00

Medicare balance billable amount (MBBA)
   $284.05   ($247 X 115%)

Medicare pays
   $ 15.00   ($100 to ded., $18.75 X 80%) (OV)
   $102.60   ($128.25 X 80%) (Lab)
   $ 0.00   (Not covered) (Meds)
   $117.60

Payment
   $306.00   Allowable amount (greater of plan's or Medicare's allowable amount)
   $117.60   Medicare payment.
   $188.40   Difference
   $124.80   Plan's normal liability
   $124.80   Lesser of plan's NL or difference (up to the balance billing limit).

This is the amount of the secondary insurance carrier payment on this claim.

Credit Reserve:

$124.80   Plan's NL for this claim.
-124.80   Actual payment for this claim.
$ 0.00
+   0.00   Credit reserve on previous claims
$ 0.00   Total credit reserve

Example 3: Benefits payable at 85% of PPO schedule. Deductible $150, deductible satisfied. Medicare assigned.

Billed Charges
    $5,000.00   Inpatient Hospital

Plan normal liability (NL)
    $2,125.00   PPO Allowance $2,500 X 85%
    $ 375.00   Patient Liability = 375.00

    $4,000.00   Medicare approved amount
    $3,200.00   Medicare payment ($4,000 X 80%)
    $ 800.00   Patient Medicare liability

In this case the PPO provider has a contractual obligation to provide care on this DRG for $2,500. This is due to a contract between the provider and the PPO. Amounts over $2,500 are not usually collectible.

Until early 1999, the insurance carrier had no liability in this example because Medicare paid more than the normal liability and since the provider is part of the plan network and contractually has to write-off charges over $2,500. Thereby leaving no patient responsibility and no insurance liability.

Since early in 1999 providers have claimed insurance carriers and PPO's are in violation of the Social Security Act anti-kickback clause. The section of the Act basically states that an insurance company or PPO cannot make the provider write-off the Medicare patient responsibility. Therefore, the patient liability is payable by the insurance carrier up to the plans normal liability in the absence of Medicare. Thus, the plan must pay the $800 patient liability on this claim since their normal liability is higher than this amount.

Example 4: Benefits payable at 85% of PPO schedule. Deductible $150, deductible satisfied. Medicare assigned.

Billed Charges
    $5,000.00   Inpatient Hospital
    $1,200.00   Blood transfusions
    $ 200.00   Take home drugs
    $6,400.00

Plan normal liability (NL)
    $2,125.00   PPO Allowance $2,500 X 85% (IP)
    $ 0.00   (drugs included)
    $ 0.00   (blood transfusions included)

    $2,125.00   Plan normal liability

    $4,000.00   Medicare approved amount (IP)
    $ 0.00   Non covered (drugs)
    $ 0.00   Non-covered (blood transfusions)
    $4,000.00   Medicare approved amount

Medicare payment
    $3,200.00   ($4,000 X 80%)
    $2,200.00   Patient Medicare liability

    $5,400.00   Total allowable (Medicare allowed +
                Pt. Liab
    $3,200.00   Medicare Paid
    $2,200.00   Balance

    $2,125.00   Plan normal liability
    $ 75.00   Patient Out of Pocket

Note: Medicare usually calculates the outpatient hospital benefit by first applying the 80% to the total charge less not covered items (personal or take home drugs). Then Medicare applies its schedule of benefits. It is very important to consider the paid amount plus the patient liability as the covered charge so that you do not pay part of the hospital write-off in error.

There are several different Medicare explanation of benefits depending on the payer. Be sure you understand how to read it when coordinating benefits.

Medicare Supplement
Medicare supplements are separate plans written exclusively for Medicare participants. A supplement plan may be written with optional benefits the policyholder wants. Common options are as follows:

- Physicians' services – Covers Part B deductible and 20% coinsurance for reasonable charges. **"Reasonable charges"** means that amounts reduced by Medicare because of prevailing fees are not covered under the plan even though the plan's prevailing fee may be higher than that of Medicare when the bill is assigned. If the bill is not assigned, the plan's UCR or Medicare's UCR is the amount allowable, whichever is greater.
- Hospital services – Covers Part A deductible and may or may not cover the various co-pays not covered by Medicare.
- Nursing care, prescriptions, non-replaced fees on the first three pints of blood – may also be covered.

With the changes in Medicare, supplemental plans have become more flexible. Therefore, the benefits can be complex and comprehensive, or very basic. Read plan provisions carefully to determine which items are covered and which are not. Since the purpose of a Medicare supplement plan is to cover the patient's responsibility, many charges that are covered, are paid at 100%

Estimating Medicare Coverage

Sometimes a member is entitled to Medicare but has not enrolled. In this circumstance, many policies specify that the group plan will estimate what Medicare would have paid if the person had been enrolled properly, or the policy may specify instead that benefits may be reduced only when the member is actually enrolled in Medicare. In this situation, the regular plan benefits will be provided and the Medicare payment will not be estimated.

To estimate the Medicare payment, use the following as a guideline:

Hospital: Part A

1. Provide full benefits toward the Medicare deductible and coinsurance amounts.
2. Provide regular group benefits for services or items covered by the group plan but not covered by Medicare.

Professional: Part B

1. Determine the plan's UCR for the billed charges.
2. The UCR amount is considered the estimated Medicare-approved amount.
3. Multiply 80% of the estimated approved amount (#2). This is your estimated Medicare payment.
4. Once you have estimated Medicare's payment, you can proceed with calculating the coordination of benefits (as shown above)

Diagnosis-Related Group Billing

Effective October 1, 1983, Medicare instituted diagnosis-related group (DRG) payments for inpatient hospital claims. Under **DRG**, a flat rate payment is made, based on the patient's diagnosis rather than the hospital's itemized billing. If the hospital can treat the patient for less, it keeps the savings. If treatment costs more, the hospital must absorb the loss. Neither Medicare nor the patient is responsible for the excess amount.

Exceptions

Provisions have been made for cases atypically expensive (based on the diagnosis) because of complications or an abnormally long confinement. Known as **outliers**, these cases will be reimbursed on an itemized or cost percentage basis rather than DRG. The bill from the hospital must indicate that it is an outlier.

Exclusions

Excluded from DRG are long-term care, children's care, and psychiatric and rehabilitative hospitals. Also excluded are hospitals located in the states of Maryland, Massachusetts, New Jersey, and New York. These states have obtained waivers from DRG. Waivers and exclusions are subject to change, and you should consult your state department of insurance for updated information.

DRG Benefit Payment Calculations

As shown in the following examples, the maximum liability under a plan consists of only the following expenses:

- Those covered by the plan.
- Those that the insured is legally obligated to pay.

Example 1:   Itemized hospital bill exceeds Medicare DRG allowance.

Hospital bill	$8,700
DRG allowance	$7,000
Medicare payment	$6,160
(DRG, $840 ded)	
Patient's responsibility	$ 840
Hospital write-off	$1,700

Although the Medicare DRG allowance is less than the itemized hospital bill, the insured is legally obligated to pay only the $840 Part A deductible. Therefore, exclude the difference between the itemized hospital bill amount and the DRG allowance as not covered, no legal obligation to pay. The plan's benefits would be based on the total charges of $7,000, with the $1,700 reflected as not covered because it exceeds the DRG allowance.

When coding out the claim, different payors may handle the coding differently. However, frequently the actual billed amount for the room and board is used and then the difference between that amount and the actual billed charges is used for the miscellaneous amount.

Example 2: Medicare DRG allowance exceeds itemized billed amount.

Hospital bill	$ 8,700
DRG allowance	$10,000
Medicare payment	$ 9,160
Patient's responsibility	$ 840

Although the Medicare payment exceeds the itemized hospital bill, the insured is legally obligated to pay the $840 Part A deductible. Handling of this type of billing also varies. Check the payor guidelines before processing the claim.

Summary

Medicare is administered through the Health Care Financing Administration. Each year, rules and guidelines for payment and covered charges are established. Claims examiners must stay abreast of the changes in the Medicare system. This can be accomplished by subscribing to the Medicare bulletin that is usually published by the fiscal intermediary for Medicare in the local area. Other agencies conduct seminars in various locations. Contact the fiscal intermediary for these agencies and their locations. By attending seminars, using the Medicare bulletins, and applying the guidelines we have covered in this chapter, claims examiners will establish a consistent approach to processing Medicare claims, which will result in competent and accurate claim decisions.

Assignments

Complete the Questions for Review.
Complete Exercise 23 – 1.

*All Medicare benefits and exclusions are correct as of the date of printing. For updated benefits, contact your local Social Security Administration.

Questions for Review

Directions: Answer the following questions without looking back into the material just covered. Write your answers in the space provided.

1. What is Medicare? _____

_____

2. On what three criteria is Medicare eligibility based?

    1. _____
    2. _____
    3. _____

3. Medicare _____ is considered the basic plan or hospital insurance.

4. Medicare _____ is the medical insurance that covers doctors' services, outpatient services, and so on.

5. What does it mean when a provider accepts assignment of benefits in relation to Medicare? _____

_____

_____

If you were unable to answer any of the questions, refer back to the section and then complete the answers.

Exercise 23 – 1

Directions: Using the attached Medicare EOMB, compute the COB on the claims that are listed on the Medicare EOMB. Be sure to check plan provisions for the type of COB that should be performed.

Honors Certification™

The Honors Certification™ challenge for this chapter is a written test of the information contained within this chapter. Each incorrect answer will result in a deduction of between 1% and 5% from your grade. You must achieve a score of 85% or higher to pass this test. If you fail the test on your first attempt you may retake the test one additional time. The items included in the second test may be different from those in the first test.

EXPLANATION OF MEDICARE BENEFITS

DATE: FEBRUARY 27, 2002
CHECK SEQUENCE NO.: 2AF-01241351-2
PAGE 1 OF 1

BENEFICIARY NAME	SVC FR MO-DY	TO DY-YR	PLACE TYPE	PROCEDURE DESCRIPTION	AMOUNT BILLED	AMOUNT APPROVED	SEE NOTE	DEDUCTIBLE	COINSURANCE	PAYMENT	SECONDARY CARRIER UCR	SECONDARY CARRIER LIABILITY	AMOUNT
HELGA HEARTACHE	02-06	02-06	23	93000	340.00	297.18	56						
	02-06	02-06	23	93545	770.00	699.23	56						
	02-06	02-06	23	85025	40.00	21.21	56						
	02-06	02-06	23	86901	45.00	27.34	56						
	02-06	02-06	23	85610	30.00	19.57	56						
Accepts assignment	CLAIM NOTE			TOTALS	1,225.00	1,064.53	442	100.00	192.91	771.62	846.32	507.79	
BARRY BROKEN	01-26	01-26	23	992885	882.00	699.00	56						
Accepts assignment	CLAIM NOTE			TOTALS	882.00	699.00	442	100.00	119.80	479.20	882.00	433.80	
HELGA HEARTACHE	02-09	02-09	21	33217	245.00	189.46	56						
	02-09	02-09	21	33225	500.00	167.38	56						
	02-09	02-09	21	33240	295.00	295.00							
Accepts assignment	CLAIM NOTE			TOTALS	1,040.00	651.84	442	0.00	130.37	521.47	895.63	716.51	
ALMA ALVAREZ	02-02	02-02	11	99213	330.00	227.56	56						
Does not accept assignment	CLAIM NOTE			TOTALS	330.00	227.56	442	100.00	25.51	102.05	289.44	145.06	
ALMA ALVAREZ	02-02	02-02	11	76092	165.00	127.57	56						
Accepts assignment	CLAIM NOTE			TOTALS	165.00	127.57	442	0.00	25.51	102.06	124.07	105.56	
BARRY BROKEN	01-26	01-26	21	70260-27	70.00	61.12	56						
	01-26	01-26	21	71020-27	55.00	43.21	56						
	01-26	01-26	21	735502-7	80.00	70.88	56						
	01-26	01-26	21	73590-27	100.00	83.83	56						
	01-26	01-26	21	70450-27	325.00	180.67	56						
	01-26	01-26	21	73718-27	770.00	622.39	56						
Accepts assignment	CLAIM NOTE			TOTALS	1,400.00	1,062.10	442	0.00	212.42	849.68	1,203.30	1,082.97	
HELGA HEARTACHE	02-06	02-06	23	99285	1,600.00	1,306.70	56						
	02-06	02-06	23	99285	420.00	383.13	56						
Does not accept assignment	CLAIM NOTE			TOTALS	2,020.00	1,689.83	442	0.00	337.97	1,351.86	1,595.78	1,156.62	
BARRY BROKEN	01-26	01-26	21	21800	560.00	499.99	56						
	01-26	01-26	21	27758	215.00	116.32	56						
	01-26	01-26	21	27784	200.00	159.56	56						
	01-26	01-26	21	62000	150.00	130.99							
Accepts assignment	CLAIM NOTE			TOTALS	1,125.00	906.86	442	0.00	181.37	725.49	975.80	878.22	

56 - Medicare limits payment to this amount.
63 - Medicare considers follow-up care to be an integral part of the surgery with no additional allowance.
92 - An assistant surgeon is not considered medically necessary for this surgery.
442 - Total for these charges.

HELGA HEARTACHE - Ninja
BARRY BROKEN - ABC
ALMA ALVAREZ - XYZ

24 Medicaid

In this chapter you will learn:

- Medicaid eligibility requirements.
- What the HIPD form is and how to use it.

Key words and concepts you will learn in this chapter:

Health Insurance Payment Demand (HIPD) – A bill that lists the health care services paid by the Medicaid program on behalf of a person who has other health care coverage benefits available.
Medicaid – A jointly funded, Federal-State health insurance program for certain low-income and needy people.

Medicaid is not a health insurance program. The Federal Medicaid program was established under Title XIX of the Social Security Act of 1965. **Medicaid** is a jointly funded, Federal-State health insurance program for certain low-income and needy people. It covers children, the aged, blind, and/or disabled, and people who are eligible to receive federally assisted income maintenance payments. The purpose of this program is to provide the needy with access to medical care.

Medicaid is the largest program providing medical and health-related services to America's poorest people. Within broad national guidelines which the Federal government provides, each of the states:

1. Establishes its own eligibility standards;
2. Determines the type, amount, duration, and scope of services;
3. Sets the rate of payment for services; and
4. Administers its own program.

Thus, the Medicaid program varies considerably from State to State.

By law, Medicaid is always secondary to private group health care plans. If Medicaid inadvertently pays primary, it will exercise its right of recovery and seek reimbursement from the private plan. Again, the private plan by law is required to process Medicaid's request for reimbursement and pay back Medicaid the monies it paid the Medicaid provider.

The regulations governing eligibility under the Medicaid program are complex. Individuals may be entitled to coverage due to medical, family, or financial situations. The fact that the individual has private insurance does not preclude him or her from being eligible for Medicaid benefits.

The Medicaid program does not process its own claims. Medicaid contracts with organizations to act as the fiscal intermediary, similar to Medicare. The intermediary processes the claims according to specifications set forth by the Medicaid program.

The rates under Medicaid are based on the results of reimbursement studies conducted by the Department of Health Services. Reimbursement for hospital inpatient services is based on each facility's "reasonable cost" of services as determined from audit cost reports and annual limitations on reimbursable increases in cost.

If the patient is covered by private insurance in addition to Medicaid, the provider may bill the patient's private insurance. There is a 3-year statute of limitations from the date of service for recovering payment. In addition, there is a 3-year subrogation right.

For a claimant's services to be covered under Medicaid, the claimant must be a Medicaid beneficiary and the provider must be an approved Medicaid provider. To be an approved provider, the provider of services must agree to accept Medicaid's determination of approved amounts as binding. This is similar to Medicare's approved amount on assigned claims, the provider is not allowed to bill the patient for any amount not approved by Medicaid. In recent years, many providers have dropped out of the Medicaid program because Medicaid's allowances and payments were extremely low, some even lower than those provided by Medicare.

Health Insurance Payment Demand

The **Health Insurance Payment Demand (HIPD)** is a bill that lists the health care services paid by the Medicaid program on behalf of a person who has indicated that he or she has other health care coverage benefits available. Insurers/plans are to reimburse the Medicaid program for those services to the extent of the plan's available benefits, or the amount paid by Medicaid, whichever is less. If the private plan is not liable for a particular service, the reason for this must be explained on the HIPD, along with indications of what was paid.

The HIPD is a computer-generated list that includes the following:

- The patient's name,
- The policyholder name,
- The policy number,
- The provider,
- The diagnosis,
- The treatment provided,
- The dates of services,
- The charges, and
- Payments previously made by Medicaid on each service.

The HIPD is usually accompanied by a cover letter (see **Figure 24 – 1**). The forms may differ from state to state, but they usually contain similar information.

In addition to the cover letter, the State's Recovery Unit will also supply the HIPD Processing Form, which is used by the payor when responding to an HIPD. It is completed by the carrier and then sent to Medicaid with the state's copy of the HIPD. A sample of the front of this form is shown in **Figure 24 – 2**.

Handling Procedures

When an HIPD is received, the following eight procedures will assist in its handling and in filling out the HIPD processing form.

1. Determine whether or not the patient is eligible under the indicated plan. If not, complete item #3. If the information provided on the HIPD is incomplete and you are unable to identify the member or patient, complete item #4.

2. Determine whether the indicated charges were previously paid under the plan. If so, no payment is due Medicaid. Complete item #2.

3. If no payment has been made for the charges in question and payments were due, calculate the normal plan benefits. Do not request an attending physician's statement because the HIPD constitutes sufficient proof of loss.

4. Usually, a line-by-line comparison is made between the amount paid by Medicaid and the amount payable under the private plan. However, it is also possible to do a total-by-total comparison. To do this, subtract the amounts paid by Medicaid for expenses not covered by the private plan from the total Medicaid payment.

5. Pay the lesser of:
   a. The normal private plan benefit, or
   b. The total Medicaid payment, as adjusted in #4. The payment by the private plan to Medicaid should never exceed the total adjusted Medicaid payment. The draft should be made payable to Health Care Deposit Fund (or the source included on the form).

6. If payment has previously been made, complete item #2. If some or all of the charges are not covered under the terms of the plan, complete item #3 or #4.

7. Send the completed HIPD Processing Form, the state copy of the HIPD, and the benefit draft (if benefits are payable) to the Health Recovery Bureau for your state (or the source included on the form).

8. Retain one copy of the HIPD in the claim file.

After payment has been made to Medicaid, the plan's full liability has been discharged. This is true even if the payment made is less than the payment that would have been made in the absence of Medicaid.

These instructions apply only if the HIPD has been received. If the claims file indicates that the claimant is eligible for Medicaid, but the state has not submitted an HIPD, any charges received should be handled in the usual manner. When processing an HIPD billing, all plan provisions except the timely filing limitations apply.

Check with your supervisor for company procedures on handling HIPDs.

Return Address

Attention: Claims Manager

Warning! Enclosed is confidential information. This information is provided to you so that you may determine the liability of your company or your health insurance carrier to repay the Medicaid program on behalf of the individual listed. This is pursuant to State Code Sections 100XX et sq., 140XX.XX, or 141XX. Any person may be subject to civil or criminal penalties for disclosure, publication, or other use, or for permitting or causing this confidential information to be disclosed, published, or used except as necessary to accomplish the above-mentioned purpose or with specific written permission from the Medicaid beneficiary, personal representative, or guardian (if a minor).

Enclosed are Health Insurance Payment Demands (HIPDs) for claims for health care services paid by the Medicaid program for individuals who indicate that they have health care coverage with your organization.

Payment to the extent of your contractual obligation is now due. Medicaid should be reimbursed for all amounts that it has paid as shown on the following form. When making payment on this claim, please indicate the HIPD number and the patient's Medicaid number on your check. Mark the amount of payment for each service on the state copy and the HIPD. If a service or services are not covered, a complete explanation of the reason for nonpayment should be indicated on the enclosed HIPD Processing Form. The HIPD Processing Form may be reproduced for use within your office.

If you are unable to identify the claimant as an insured policyholder under your plan, mark the HIPD box 4a and return. If you need additional information to locate the claimant or confirm eligibility, list the precise information needed. Additional information that would facilitate future HIPD processing (i.e., Group name, policy #), which is not listed on the HIPD, may be noted under response #4d (Other) on the HIPD Processing Form.

If this HIPD should be sent to another department or location, indicate the appropriate department and the complete address and return the HIPD to us. We will update our files with the proper information.

All policyholders that provide coverage for the claimant listed are indicated under the claimant's name. This information is for use in coordinating benefits with other health insurance carriers.

Thank you for your cooperation. If you have any questions, please write us at the address indicated above.

Sincerely

Jane Doe, Chief
Health Insurance Unit
Recovery Branch

Figure 24 – 1: Sample HIPD Cover Letter

Health Insurance Payment Demand
(HIPD) Processing Form

Please Return State Copy of HIPD to:

Please feel free to write on the HIPD. In addition, complete the appropriate information below and return with the HIPD.

Patient Name (Medicaid Beneficiary): _____   Medicaid #: _____

HIPD Number(s) (From the upper-right-hand corner of the HIPD): _____

HIPD Billing Date(s) (From the upper right corner of the HIPD): _____

☐ 1. The enclosed check(s) for $ _____ represents payment of our liability under this policy. For any charges

    considered ineligible, see Number 3 below.

☐ 2. Charges previously considered (if additional space is needed, please use reverse side).

    Payee _____   Amount $ _____   Date _____

    Address _____   Date(s) of Service _____

    Payee _____   Amount $ _____   Date _____

    Address _____   Date(s) of Service _____

3. Claimant is ineligible due to:

    ☐ a. Claimant's policy is no longer in effect. Termination date: _____

    ☐ b. Claimant was not covered on date of service. Coverage date(s) _____to _____

    ☐ c. Claimant's group was not insured on date of service. Coverage date(s) _____to _____

    If liable carrier is known, provide complete name and address: _____

    ☐ d. Claimant was not a covered dependent on date of service. Explain: _____

    ☐ e. Services are not covered expenses under the policy. Why?

        ☐ Policy does not cover convalescent care.   ☐ Policy covers in-hospital services only.

        ☐ Policy does not cover drugs, vision, etc.   ☐ Other _____

    ☐ f. Maximum benefit of $ _____ per _____ (time period) has been exhausted.

    ☐ g. Charges do not exceed policy deductible. Deductible is $ _____ per _____

    ☐ h. Other reasons (specify) _____

4. This HIPD is being returned or processing is being delayed due to:

    ☐ a. We are unable to identify individual/group as our insured. We need: _____

    ☐ b. Dual coverage is indicated. We need: _____

    ☐ c. Additional information is needed on the following service(s): _____

    ☐ d. Other (specify): _____

Figure 24 – 2: Sample HIPD Processing Form.

Summary

Medicaid guidelines vary from state to state. Medicaid bulletins are produced to assist you in interpreting the rules for coverage and to determine which charges Medicaid covers. These manuals are available to Medicaid providers and are primarily used by billers, however, they may be helpful to the claims examiner. Contact your Medicaid intermediary for copies of the manuals.

Assignments

Complete the Questions for Review.

Questions for Review

Directions: Answer the following questions without looking back into the material just covered. Write your answers in the space provided.

1. What is the purpose of the Medicaid program? _____

   _____

2. (True or False?) By law, Medicaid is always primary to private group health insurance plans. _____

3. In what situation are providers allowed to bill or submit a claim to the Medicaid beneficiary? _____

   _____

4. The _____ is a bill that lists the health care services paid by the Medicaid program on behalf of a person who has indicated that he or she has other health care coverage benefits available.

5. For a claimant's services to be covered under Medicaid, the claimant must be a _____ and the provider must be an _____.

If you were unable to answer any of the questions, refer back to the section and then complete the answers.

Honors Certification™

The Honors Certification™ challenge for this chapter is a written test of the information contained within this chapter. Each incorrect answer will result in a deduction of between 1% and 5% from your grade. You must achieve a score of 85% or higher to pass this test. If you fail the test on your first attempt you may retake the test one additional time. The items included in the second test may be different from those in the first test.

25 Workers' Compensation

In this chapter you will learn:

- To understand eligibility and basic benefits of Workers' Compensation.
- What constitutes a workers' compensation claim.

Key words and concepts you will learn in this chapter:

Company Activities – An injury sustained while attending an activity sponsored by an employer for the purpose of obtaining some business gain or an activity which the company provides remuneration and an injury sustained while in the course of a person's occupation.

Death Benefits – Benefits which compensate the family of a deceased employee for the loss of income which the employee would have provided to the family.

Doctor's First Report of Occupational Injury or Illness (First Report) – The report completed by a doctor upon a Workers' Compensation patient's first visit.

Job Related Injuries – Include any injuries which happen during the performance of work-related duties whether they are in or out of the office.

Lien – A legal document that expresses claim on the property of another for payment of a debt.

Non-Disability Claims – Claims for minor injuries that will not require the patient to be kept from his/her job.

Occupational Illnesses – Any disorders, illnesses, or conditions which arise at work or from exposure to factors at work.

Permanent and Stationary – A term meaning that nothing more can be done and the patient will have the disability for rest of his or her life.

Permanent Disability – When it is determined that the patient will not be able to return to work.

Rehabilitation Benefit. – A benefit that provides for retraining of the employee in a physical ability which will help them to seek future employment (i.e., proper use of a wheelchair, use of the left hand when a person loses their right).

Subjective Findings – Are those that cannot be discerned by anyone other than the patient (i.e., pain, discomfort).

Temporary Disability – Claims for when the patient is not able to perform his or her job requirements until he or she recovers from the injury involved.

Vocational Rehabilitation – Retraining in a different job field when the employee is unable to return to their former position.

Work Hardening – A program wherein an employee is assigned therapy similar to their work in an attempt to strengthen them and build up their endurance toward a full day's work.

Workers' Compensation (WC) – A separate medical and disability reimbursement program which provides 100% coverage for job related injuries, illnesses, and/or conditions arising out of and in the course of employment.

Workers' Compensation (WC) is a separate medical and disability reimbursement program which provides 100% coverage for job related injuries, illnesses, and/or conditions arising out of and in the course of employment. The employer, by law, is responsible for the benefits due an employee for work related injuries and illnesses. WC insurance includes benefits for medical care expenses, disability income, and death benefits.

When a claim is received for treatment of an accident, it is important to obtain a statement of exactly what happened so that you can determine if a claims is covered by WC or by the patient's regular insurance. **Job related injuries** include any injuries which happen during the performance of work-related duties whether they are in or out of the office. **Occupational illnesses** are considered to be any disorders, illnesses, or conditions which arise at work or from exposure to factors at work. Occupational illnesses may be caused by inhaling, directly contacting, absorbing, or ingesting a hazardous agent. Some occupational illnesses may take years to develop, or remain latent for a number of years before flaring up. For this reason, some states have WC laws which cover workers for years after they cease active employment in a field. For example, construction workers who dealt repeatedly with asbestos may develop asbestosis years after exposure.

Federal WC programs cover Washington DC workers, Federal workers, coal miners, (black lung program), longshoremen, and harbor workers. State WC laws covers everyone else. States set up their own guidelines, with the Federal government mandating a minimum level of benefits.

Each state's WC Appeals Board has the sole authority to oversee the rights and benefits of an injured or ill worker. It is through this Appeals Board that an applicant (employee) will file their WC application.

As a general limitation, most health insurance plans specify that the claimant will not be entitled to payment for "bodily injury or disease resulting from and arising out of any employment or occupation for compensation or profit."

Most health insurance plans will investigate and then provide benefits for medical care if they suspect that a claim(s) is work-related. Because the resolution of a WC case usually takes one to two years, private plans are obligated to pay the benefits for which the member is entitled, and then file a lien with the member and the WC Board to recover plan losses when the case is settled.

Once the WC carrier has accepted liability for the claim(s), the plan will discontinue providing benefits for medical care. At that point the claim would be denied on the basis that it is work related.

Employee Activities

The following section contains some general guidelines as to what constitutes an injury or illness as recognized by a WC Board in most states based on the type of activity, not the type of injury.

Company Activities
Company activities can be defined as the following:
1. An injury sustained while attending an activity sponsored by an employer for the purpose of obtaining some business gain. (i.e., company party for morale purposes; sporting activity for which the employee is provided transportation; and/or the company gains advertisement by virtue of having the employee wear a company "athletic shirt").

2. An injury sustained during an activity which the company provides remuneration.
3. An injury sustained while in the course of a person's occupation.

Use of Company Vehicles
Most WC laws provide coverage for an injury sustained while driving or as an authorized passenger in a company vehicle. This is true whether the injury is incurred in the course of the person's occupation, or if the vehicle is provided as a part of the employee's benefits to use to and from work.

The law's interpretation of "in the course of employment" is very different from most layman's interpretation. For instance, someone injured while eating lunch at a company-sponsored event may be considered covered by WC. Therefore, always do an investigation and let the Board handle the final determination.

Business Trips
Most WC laws provide 24-hour coverage for a person who is on a business trip. This coverage is applicable to the entire trip, so long as the person is performing routine activities. Of course, there are always exceptions to this rule.

Company Parking Lot
Most WC laws provide that if an employee is injured in a parking lot which is owned by or maintained by this employer and furnished to the employee free of charge, he/she may be covered under WC. In addition, coverage would extend, in some instances, to an injury sustained by the employee while on neutral ground between the parking lot and the place of employment. An exception would be if such incidents were specifically excluded in the WC law, or if the injuries were sustained from willful or negligent actions on the part of the employee.

Usually, WC is not liable for injuries sustained in a parking lot which is owned by the employer and for which a rental fee is charged for the parking space. In such instances, the employee has a free choice to park elsewhere which would relieve the employer of any and all responsibility.

Occupational Disease
Most of the time, coverage will extend to employees who contract a disease which develops by working within a certain industry. For instance, most states provide compensation for individuals working with asbestos material over a period of years and they then develop asbestosis or silicosis. Likewise, individuals can develop dermatitis from working with certain chemicals, such as those found in the exterminating industry.

Sometimes, a claimant may have an occupational illness which is submitted to the WC Board, and a concurrent non-occupational illness for which he/she may be reimbursed under the plan. In such instances, a separate billing should be completed by the provider indicating those charges which were solely for the treatment of the non-occupational disability.

Types of Claims

WC provides benefits for:

1. Medical expenses, including medical services, hospital treatment, surgery, medications, prosthetics or appliances and durable medical equipment.
2. Temporary disability, allowing payments to continue to the employee even though they are not currently working. Payments are based on the employee's salary and the length of the disability. Payments are usually not taxable as income.
3. Permanent disability, either in the form of weekly or monthly payments, or as a lump sum distribution.
4. Death, to compensate spouses and dependents for the loss of an employee. Some states also provide for a burial benefit to help cover the cost of funeral services.
5. Rehabilitation, to cover rehabilitation services or vocational retraining for permanently disabled workers who are unable to continue in their present position.

There are three types of WC claims. They are non-disability claims, temporary disability claims, and permanent disability claims.

Non-disability Claims

Non-disability claims are for minor injuries that will not require the patient to be kept from his/her job. The patient is able to continue working throughout the extent of the injury. Upon the first visit to the physician the physician should complete a **"Doctor's First Report of Occupational Injury or Illness (First Report)."** This form and a copy of the bill should be submitted to the WC carrier. If you receive a claim with an attached First Report, consult company guidelines regarding whether the claim should be pended for a WC determination, or paid and a lien attached.

Temporary Disability Claims

Temporary disability claims are when the patient is not able to perform his or her job requirements until he or she recovers from the injury involved. When a physician sees a patient in this situation a First Report will be submitted and ongoing reports will be issued every two to three weeks until the patient is discharged to return to work.

Each state has a waiting period before temporary disability becomes effective, usually three to seven days (except in the Virgin Islands where the waiting period is one day). During temporary disability the employee is paid a portion of their salary as a tax-free benefit. Temporary disability ends when the patient is able to return to work, even with limitations or to a different department, or when the patient's condition ceases to improve and the patient is left with a permanent disability. Most health care plans do not have a disability benefit (for either temporary or permanent disability), or death benefits. Therefore, the health claims examiner should not receive a disability claim. If one is received, it should be denied as not a covered benefit.

Permanent Disability Claims

Permanent disability usually commences after temporary disability when it is determined that the patient will not be able to return to work. The physician will prepare a discharge report stating that the patient is **"permanent and stationary."** This means that nothing more can be done and the patient will have the disability for rest of his or her life. The WC Board will review the case and, if determined to be permanent, a compromise and release will be issued. This is a settlement from the insurance carrier for a payment to the injured party.

The amount of the settlement is based upon the age of the disabled worker, the amount of money they were making at the time of the injury, and the severity of the injury. The older an employee is, the higher the disability rating. This is due to the idea that a younger patient has a better chance of finding other employment or of being retrained for another job than an older worker would. Additionally, death benefits and rehabilitation benefits may be provided.

Death Benefits

Death Benefits compensate the family of a deceased employee for the loss of income which the employee would have provided to the family. Some states also provide a burial benefit to assist with the funeral and burial expenses for the employee.

Rehabilitation Benefits

If an employee is found to have a permanent disability, some states allow for a **rehabilitation benefit.** This benefit can be provided to retrain the employee in a physical ability which will help them to seek future employment (i.e., proper use of a wheelchair, use of the left hand when a person loses their right).

Some states participate in a **"work hardening"** program, wherein an employee is assigned therapy similar to their work in an attempt to strengthen them and build up their endurance toward a full day's work. Often employees in such a program will be returned to work on a limited or restricted basis. Physicians, therapists, employers, insurance carriers and all others concerned with the employee's case must keep in constant communication to ensure that the patient is not returned to work either sooner or later than possible.

Many states also allow for **vocational rehabilitation** or retraining in a different job field when the employee is unable to return to their former position. This can include courses in colleges and vocational schools, or –on-the-job training programs. Often employees are paid a weekly allowance (as in the case of temporary disability) while they are attending school and for a limited time after graduation. The time after graduation is to allow them time to locate a job. The employee is then considered to be off temporary disability and have returned to work. Vocational rehabilitation can also include job guidance, resume preparation and placement services.

Patient Records

If a member is being treated for a work related injury, all records relating to the injury and treatment should be kept separate from the patient's regular medical records. Since employers are covering the costs of treatment, privacy guidelines are somewhat different than the normal privacy agreement between the member and provider. In WC cases, the agreement is actually between the provider and the employer not the employee. The employer may request to see records regarding the injury, and these records may be subpoenaed. No information pertaining to the employee's non-work related treatment should be made a part of this file, so that confidentiality between the provider and the member is not breached for non-work related treatments and conditions.

Doctor's First Report

Regardless of the type of claim or benefits, the doctor must file a First Report of Injury (see **Figure 25 – 1**). This form may have a different name, depending on the state, however, nearly all states require the completion of a similar form.

Physicians must make a report of injury, disability or death within a specified time period. This varies from immediately upon knowledge of the incident to within 30 days. Different states set different time limits and different requirements for reporting. There may also be different levels of injury (i.e., injury, disability, death).

This report is considered a legal document and it should be signed in ink by the physician. All information should be typed or printed clearly. The original copy of the form should be sent to the insurance carrier. One copy is retained in the patient's records, and many providers also send a copy to the employer.

If the physician chooses to send a narrative report along with the standard report, the following information should be included:

- A history of the accident, injury or illness,
- Diagnosis,
- Any connection between the primary injury and any subsequent injuries, especially if the interrelating factors between the primary and secondary injuries are not immediately discernable, and
- Subjective and objective findings.

Subjective findings are those that cannot be discerned by anyone other than the patient (i.e., pain, discomfort). The physician should give an opinion as to the extent of pain, description of activities that produce pain and any other findings.

Subsequent Progress Reports

Following the First Report, the physician should follow up with subsequent progress reports (sometimes called supplemental reports) every two or three weeks. Many states have forms for subsequent progress reports, however they may also allow a narrative report to be filed, rather than the completion of the specified form. Subsequent reports should also be sent at the end of a hospitalization, even if the patient is expected to be readmitted later. This report often serves as both a report on the patient's condition, and as a bill.

If the patient's condition changes significantly, a Re-examination Report, or a detailed progress report, should be filed with the insurance carrier.

Physician's Final Report

By obtaining a copy of these reports, a health claims examiner can monitor a patient's progress. Then, if claims are received at a later time, it is easier to determine if subsequent treatment is related to the original WC injury or not. If it is determined to be related to the WC injury, the claim should be denied and the patient should submit the claim to the WC insurance carrier.

The WC carrier will often wait until the physician indicates that the patient's condition is permanent and stationary before finalizing a claim. The physician should then notify the WC carrier that no further treatment is needed (or that no further treatment will significantly alter the patient's condition) and that the patient has been discharged. This is called the Physician's Final Report. Some states require the final report be submitted on a specified form, and some states use the same form for both subsequent and final reports. The Physician's Final Report should indicate that the patient has been discharged, the level of the patient's permanent disability, if any, and the balance due on the patient's account (usually provided as a patient's statement showing services, dates of service, charges, and any payments rendered). Once this information is received, the WC carrier will establish the level of permanent disability, if any, medical and other expenses will be paid, and the case will be closed.

Delay of Adjudication

When a patient is released to work, all benefits have been paid, and the case is closed, the claim is said to have been adjudicated. Often adjudication occurs within two to eight weeks after the physician submits the report stating that the patient has been discharged and is able to return to work.

If the patient suffers a permanent disability, adjudication can take much longer, especially if the amount of permanent disability is protested and a lawsuit ensues. Additional factors which may delay the close of a case include:

1. Confusion or questions on any of the reports submitted by the employer, employee, or physician. This can include conflicting information from one or more parties, or vague or ambiguous terminology (especially by the physician) or illegible items.
2. Omitted information on a report, including incomplete forms, boxes not filled in, or signatures not included.
3. Incorrect billing or questions on the billing provided by the physician.
4. Insufficient progress reports to update the insurance carrier on the status of the patient.

Fraud and Abuse

Unfortunately fraud and abuse occurs frequently in the WC system. Many employees, employers, providers and insurance carriers find it easy to defraud the system and reap significant financial awards.

In the past there has been little deterrent to abusing the system. It was frequently possible to find a doctor who was willing to testify that injuries were more serious than was first thought. Likewise, numerous lawyers stepped in and set up relationships with doctors to produce claims where no actual injury or illness existed. This is especially true when work-related stress became a popular diagnosis for any one of a number of ailments.

While most claims are legitimate, the health claims examiner should recognize what constitutes fraud. Following are some signs of fraud or abuse to look out for.

An injured employee who:
- Cannot clearly describe the pain or injury, or whose description changes each time details of the incident are related,
- Is overly dramatic regarding their injury,
- Complains of an injury which cannot be substantiated by medical evidence. This may include soft tissue injuries which cannot be seen on an x-ray, or a patient who insists there is a serious injury, even when there is medical evidence to the contrary,
- Delays the reporting of an injury, especially an injury that is reported on a Monday when the employee claims it happened on Friday,
- Reports the injury to an attorney or regulatory agency prior to reporting the injury to their employer,
- Changes physicians frequently, or shows up for a first treatment, but seems unhappy with the diagnosis and changes physicians. Patient may be seeking a physician who will grant additional time off or will testify to a greater degree of injury,
- An employee who is a short-term worker, or who was scheduled to terminate employment just after the injury occurred, and
- Has a history of curious or an excessive amount of WC claims.

A medical provider who:
- Orders or performs unnecessary procedures or tests,
- Inflates the severity of the injury to qualify for higher reimbursement (i.e., lists a fracture as open rather than closed, bills for a high complexity exam rather than a moderate complexity exam),
- Charges for services that were never performed, or adds additional procedures onto existing claims,
- Makes multiple referrals to a lab, clinic or hospital and receives a referral fee from these organizations,
- States that an injury exists and needs treatment when no injury is actually present,
- Sends in duplicate billings with information changed (i.e., dates) to make it appear services were performed more than once,
- Files many claims with subjective injuries (i.e., pain, strain, emotional disturbance, inability to perform certain functions), or
- Files claims for several employees of the same company which show similar injuries (i.e., injuries for which reports or x-rays may be duplicated).

An attorney who:
- Pressures an insurer to process and pay immediately.

The above instances suggest signs a health claims examiner should look for. If an examiner suspects fraud, it should be reported to the appropriate authority immediately. If an examiner becomes aware of fraud by any means, the claim file should be noted and the information referred to a supervisor. An examiner can be guilty of fraud if they knew of the fraud and did nothing to prevent it. This is true even if the examiner receives no money from the fraud.

Liens

Since it can take months or even years for a WC claim to be paid by the WC insurance carrier, many insurance carriers will pay these claims, then place a lien to recoup the money when the claim is settled. A **lien** is a legal document that expresses claim on the property of another for payment of a debt (see **Figure 25 – 2**). A lien is completed and submitted to the attorney representing the injured party to be paid upon monetary settlement of the WC claim.

A lien should be sent along with copies of the EOBs. Whenever additional payments are made a copy of the EOB should be submitted to the attorney so that all payments will be included in the lien. All services must be for the care of the injury covered under the WC claim.

Many states have a special lien form for WC purposes. These forms can be obtained through the local Division of Industrial Accidents. (A sample copy of a lien is shown in **Figure 25 – 3**.) The claims examiner should complete the lien form and send copies to the WC appeals board, the patient's attorney, the patient, and the WC insurance carrier. A copy should also be kept for the claims files.

If a lien is not filed, all monies recovered at the close of the case technically belong to the member. It is then the member's responsibility to cover the medical expenses. If any liens are filed, the member must first pay the liens, then pay any other resultant expenses. Therefore if the lawyer files a lien and his fees exhaust most of the money, there will be little or none left for other expenses. If at all possible, members should be persuaded to pay for medical services prior to settlement of the claim.

If a lien is filed, the examiner should have their copy of the lien letter signed by the patient and the member's attorney. This makes the attorney responsible for payment of the physicians bills. If the attorney does not remit the necessary funds from the member's settlement, the attorney must cover the payments for medical services.

A lien should have a specified time limit on it, often a period of one year. If settlement has not been reached by that time, or there are ongoing charges on the member's account relating to the WC injury, an amended lien should be filed. The subsequent lien should state the balance of the patient's account, and should have the word AMENDED stamped across the top or below the Appeals Board Case Number.

The examiner should place all files with liens in a special section and hold them until the cases have been settled. It is illegal to continually bill or harass the member when a lien agreement has been signed. In effect, the lien acknowledges the insurance carrier's agreement to wait for reimbursement until the case has been settled. The examiner should contact the member's attorney at least once every quarter for an update on the case and to determine when settlement is expected to occur. The attorney should also be contacted within two weeks after the date settlement is expected, to find out the results of the case and ask when payment will be received for claims payments.

In some states, the law provides that the insurance carrier will be paid prior to the attorney or member collecting any monies from the settlement. Statues in your state should be checked to protect you. If your state has such a provision, attorney's may not collect their fee and then state that insufficient funds were recovered to cover the outstanding medical expenses. Some states also allow the insurance carrier to bill the member for any funds which were not received from the settlement. Once again, check with the laws of your state to determine if members can be billed or if any amounts not collected should be written off.

Liens are an inexpensive way of insuring that the insurance carrier will be reimbursed for payments made. The cost is much less than suing the member and assures that payment will be received when the dispute between the member and the WC insurance carrier is settled. A lien is a legal document that will be recognized by the court and will provide protection in the event of litigation.

Reversals

Occasionally an accident which was thought to be WC will turn out not to be. This can happen when a patient hides or omits facts regarding when and how the accident occurred. It can also be found that there is a non-industrial, underlying condition which caused the accident. For example, a patient may have epilepsy and suffer a seizure at work. Any injuries directly received on the job site could be considered WC, however, the treatment of the underlying epileptic condition would not be WC.

In some cases the employee may be found to be negligent in their actions, or willfully not abiding by established workplace rules. In such cases, injuries sustained as the result of negligence of the employee may not be considered industrial accidents. For example, if the employee is told they must refrain from wearing hoop earrings, but they chose to anyway, they may be considered liable if the earrings are caught on machinery and ripped from the ear, resulting in an injury.

In such cases, the WC board would deny payment on the claim. All claims for treatment should then be paid by the member's regular insurance carrier. Thus, the claims and subsequent payments would become part of the patient's regular file.

Summary

WC insurance is a separate medical insurance program which covers work-related injuries, disabilities and death. A wide range of activities may be covered under WC laws.

Assignments

Complete the Questions for Review.

STATE OF CALIFORNIA

DOCTOR'S FIRST REPORT OF OCCUPATIONAL INJURY OR ILLNESS

Within 5 days of your initial examination, for every occupational injury or illness, send tow copies of this report to the employer's workers' compensation insurance carrier or the insured employer. Failure to file a timely doctor's report may result in assessment of a civil penalty. In the case of diagnosed or suspected pesticide poisoning, send a copy of the report to Division of Labor Statistics and Research, P.O. Box 420603, San Francisco, CA 94142-0603, and notify your local health officer by telephone within 24 hours.

	PLEASE DO NOT USE THIS COLUMN
1. INSURER NAME AND ADDRESS	Case No.
2. EMPLOYER NAME	
3. Address No. and Street City Zip	Industry
4. Nature of business (e.g., food manufacturing, building construction, retailer of women's clothes.)	County
5. PATIENT NAME (first name, middle initial, last name) 6. Sex ☐ Male ☐ Female 7. Date of Birth Mo. Day Yr.	Age
8. Address: No. and Street City Zip 9. Telephone number ( )	Hazard
10. Occupation (Specific job title) 11. Social Security Number - -	Disease
12. Injured at: No. and Street City County	Hospitalization
13. Date and hour of injury or onset of illness Mo. Day Yr. Hour ___ a.m. ___ p.m. 14. Date last worked Mo. Day Yr.	Occupation
15. Date and hour of first examination or treatment Mo. Day Yr. Hour ___ a.m. ___ p.m. 16. Have you (or your office) previously treated patient? ☐ Yes ☐ No	Return Date/Code

Patient please complete this portion, if able to do so. Otherwise, doctor please complete immediately, inability or failure of a patient to complete this portion shall not affect his/her rights to workers' compensation under the California Labor Code.

17. **DESCRIBE HOW THE ACCIDENT OR EXPOSURE HAPPENED.** (Give specific object, machinery or chemical. Use reverse side if more space is required.)

18. SUBJECTIVE COMPLAINTS (Describe fully. Use reverse side if more space is required.)

19. OBJECTIVE FINDINGS (Use reverse side if more space is required.)
   A. Physical examination

   B. X-ray and laboratory results (State if non or pending.)

20. DIAGNOSIS (if occupational illness specify etiologic agent and duration of exposure.) Chemical or toxic compounds involved? ☐ Yes ☐ No
   ICD-9 Code ___ ___ ___ - ___ ___

21. Are your findings and diagnosis consistent with patient's account of injury or onset of illness? ☐ Yes ☐ No If "no", please explain.

22. Is there any other current condition that will impede or delay patient's recovery? ☐ Yes ☐ No If "yes", please explain.

23. TREATMENT RENDERED (Use reverse side if more space is required.)

24. If further treatment required, specify treatment plan/estimated duration.

25. If hospitalized as inpatient, give hospital name and location   Date admitted Mo. Day Yr.   Estimated stay

26. WORK STATUS -- Is patient able to perform usual work? ☐ Yes ☐ No
   If "no", date when patient can return to: Regular work ___/___/___
         Modified work ___/___/___   Specify restrictions _____

Doctor's Signature _____   CA License Number _____

Doctor Name and Degree (please type) _____   IRS Number _____

Address _____   Telephone Number (___) _____

FORM 5021 (Rev. 4)
1992

Any person who makes or causes to be made any knowingly false or fraudulent material statement or material representation for the purpose of obtaining or denying workers' compensation benefits or payments is guilty of a felony.

Figure 25 - 1: Sample Copy of a Doctor's First Report

TO: Attorney

_____

_____, California

RE: Medical Reports and Insurance Carrier Lien

FOR

I do hereby authorize the above insurance carrier to furnish you, my attorney, with a full report of any records and resultant payments of myself in regard to the accident in which I was involved.

I hereby authorize and direct you, my attorney, to pay directly to said insurance carrier such sums as may be due and owed for payment of medical services rendered me or the provider of services both by reason of this accident and by reason of any other bills that are due, and to withhold such sums from any settlement, judgment or verdict as may be necessary to adequately protect said insurance carrier. And I hereby further give a lien on my case to said insurance carrier against any and all proceeds of any settlement, judgment or verdict which may be paid to you, my attorney, or myself as the result of the injuries for which I have been treated or injuries in connection therewith.

I fully understand that I am directly and fully responsible for reimbursement of any payments for all medical bills submitted for services rendered and that this agreement is made solely for said insurance carriers additional protection and in consideration of its awaiting payment. And I further understand that such payment is not contingent on any settlement, judgment or verdict by which I may eventually recover said fee.

Dated: _____ Patient's Signature: _____

The undersigned being attorney of record for the above patient does hereby agree to observe all the terms of the above and agrees to withhold such sums from any settlement, judgment or verdict as may be necessary to adequately protect said insurance carrier named above.

Dated: _____ Attorney's Signature: _____

Attorney: Please sign, date, and return one copy to our office at once.

Keep one copy for your records.

Figure 25 - 2: Sample Copy of a Lien Letter

WORKERS' COMPENSATION APPEALS BOARD

STATE OF CONFUSION

CASE NO.

NOTICE AND REQUEST FOR ALLOWANCE OF LIEN

_____

LIEN CLAIMANT   ADDRESS

VS.
_____

EMPLOYEE   ADDRESS

_____

EMPLOYER   ADDRESS

_____

INSURANCE CARRIER   ADDRESS

The undersigned hereby requests the Workers' Compensation Appeals Board to determine and allow as a lien the sum of _____

_____ dollars ($_____) against

any amount now due or which may hereafter become payable as compensation to

_____

EMPLOYEE

on account of injury sustained by him/ her on _____.

                                                            DATE

This request and claim for lien is for: (Mark appropriate box)
- ❑ The reasonable expense incurred by or on behalf of said employee for medical treatment to cure or relieve from the effects of said injury; or
- ❑ The reasonable medical expense incurred to prove a contested claim; or
- ❑ The reasonable value of living expenses of said employee or of his dependents, subsequent to the injury, or
- ❑ The reasonable living expenses of the wife or minor children, or both, of said employee, subsequent to the date of injury, where such employee has deserted or is neglecting his family; or
- ❑ The reasonable fee for interpreter's services performed on _____.
                                                                        ▪   DATE
- ❑
- ❑

NOTE: ITEMIZED STATEMENTS MUST BE ATTACHED
The undersigned declares that he delivered or mailed a copy of this lien claim to each of the above-named parties on

_____   _____
ATTORNEY FOR LIEN CLAIMANT   DATE

_____   _____
ADDRESS OF ATTORNEY FOR LIEN CLAIMANT   LIEN CLAIMANT

EMPLOYEE'S CONSENT TO ALLOWANCE OF LIEN

I consent to the requested allowance of a lien against my compensation.

_____   _____
ATTORNEY FOR EMPLOYEE   EMPLOYEE

DEPARTMENT OF INDUSTRIAL RELATIONS
DIVISION OF INDUSTRIAL ACCIDENTS

Figure 25 - 3: Sample Copy of a State Lien Form

Questions for Review

Directions: Answer the following questions without looking back into the material just covered. Write your answer in the space provided.

1. What is Workers' Compensation? _____

   _____

2. What items are likely to cause a delay in adjudication of a case?_____

   _____

3. What do you do if a patient states this is a WC injury but he has nothing from the employer to prove it?

   _____

   _____

4. What is a lien?_____

   _____

5. Why should you file a lien?_____

   _____

6. What signatures should you get on a lien?_____

   _____

7. Define Temporary Disability?_____

   _____

8. Define Permanent Disability?_____

   _____

9. What is a non-disability claim?_____

   _____

10. If an employee is injured while at a company sponsored game, is it considered a WC case?_____

   _____

If you were unable to answer any of the questions, refer back to the section and then fill in the answers.

Honors Certification™

The Honors Certification™ challenge for this chapter is a written test of the information contained within this chapter. Each incorrect answer will result in a deduction of between 1% and 5% from your grade. You must achieve a score of 80% or higher to pass this test. If you fail the test on your first attempt you may retake the test one additional time. The items included in the second test may be different from those in the first test.

26 Adjustments

In this chapter you will learn:

- The various types of adjustments and how to apply them.

Key words and concepts you will learn in this chapter:

Full Credit Adjustment – An adjustment that completely reverses a claim payment.
Partial Credit Adjustment – An adjustment that partially reverses a claim payment.
Statistical Adjustment – An adjustment that changes the claim data but does not increase or decrease the original claim payment.
Supplemental Adjustment – An adjustment that increases the original claim payment.

An **adjustment** is the reprocessing of a claim to correct prior errors. Although the terminology may vary from company to company, the concepts behind each type are basically the same. The four basic types of adjustments are:

1. **Statistical adjustment** – An adjustment that changes the claim data (i.e., procedure coding, type of benefit paid, diagnosis) but does not increase or decrease the original claim payment.
2. **Supplemental adjustment** – An adjustment that increases the original claim payment. A statistical adjustment may also be involved (often but not always), since the original claim coding may have caused the incorrect payment.
3. **Full credit adjustment** – An adjustment that completely reverses a claim payment because the original submission should not have been paid at all.
4. **Partial credit adjustment** – An adjustment that partially reverses a claim payment. The original claim was overpaid.

Statistical Adjustment

A **statistical adjustment** changes claim data but does not increase or decrease the claim payment. As the name implies, this type of adjustment is required to correct historical data only. The original payment is not affected by the corrected data.

The following are some of the more common reasons for requiring a statistical adjustment:

- The claim was processed under an incorrect member identification (ID) number.
- The claim was processed on an incorrect claimant but under the correct ID number.
- The claim payment was issued to an incorrect provider of service. The provider's tax identification number or social security number was input incorrectly, or a totally wrong provider was paid. If the provider paid was in the same medical group, a statistical adjustment may be sufficient. However, if a completely separate and unaffiliated provider was paid, a full-credit adjustment is probably required with a new payment issued to the correct provider.
- The claim was processed under an incorrect group number, but the payment remains the same.
- The claim was erroneously denied; charges should have been applied to the deductible. (no payment will be made even when processed correctly.)
- Charges were applied to the deductible but should have been denied.

Supplemental Adjustment

A **supplemental adjustment** is performed to increase an original claim payment. Often, a supplemental adjustment is required because the original claim was coded incorrectly. Therefore, a statistical adjustment is usually involved, but the changes are such that a payment or an additional payment will result. The following are some of the more common reasons why a supplemental adjustment may be required:

- The original claim was erroneously denied when benefits should have been paid.
- Charges were applied to the deductible in error; benefits should have been paid. This usually occurs when the deductible applies to specific types of expenses, but not to all types.
- Some benefits were paid, but additional benefits should have been paid.
- Late charges are received.
- Corrected billing or other information is received.
- The claims examiner or adjuster applied incorrect benefits.
- The examiner coded the diagnosis or procedure incorrectly, thus, causing an incorrect UCR allowance or other limitation.

Whenever an underpayment is found an adjustment should be pre-formed for the corrected amount. Either a letter or full explanation on the new EOB should be sent to the proper parties.

Full-Credit Adjustment

A **full-credit adjustment** completely reverses the original claim payment. Usually, this type of adjustment is not performed until the original monies paid out have been returned in full to the payor. When an incorrect provider is paid and the money is returned, many companies consider this to be a full-credit adjustment with a subsequent payment remitted to the correct provider. Regardless of whether or not a subsequent corrected payment is issued, the original payment is received back in the claims office and is reversed in the system. Following are some reasons why full-credit adjustments may be required:

- A duplicate claim is received and paid in error.
- The member is not eligible for benefits under the plan.
- Claim benefits are paid incorrectly, or plan limitations are not adhered to.
- An incorrect provider is paid who is unaffiliated with the correct provider of service.

Partial Credit Adjustment

A **partial credit adjustment** partially reverses a claim payment. In this case, part of the original payment is correct and part is incorrect. The common reasons why partial credit adjustments are performed include:

- When a greater payment was made on a claim than what should have been made according to the plan provisions and limitations.
- Because the claims examiner applied benefits incorrectly either through incorrect coding, duplication of payment, inappropriate application of benefits, or some other error.

Collecting Overpayments

Even the best claims examiners may make errors. When this happens, an overpayment of benefits may occur. Under most circumstances, every attempt should be made to recover overpayments when they are discovered. However, there are times when recovery of overpayments are not feasible nor cost-effective. The following are guidelines only and apply to situations in which overpayment recovery should not be attempted:

- The overpayment is under $25.
- The overpayment occurred more than 12 months ago and is under $200.
- The claimant is deceased and the overpayment is under $200.

There are normally three ways to obtain reimbursement of an overpayment.

1. Deduct the overpayment from future benefits of the family member for whom the overpayment occurred. You cannot deduct an overpayment on one family member's claim from benefits due on another family member's claim unless specifically requested by the insured and confirmed in writing. It is not necessary to obtain permission to deduct benefits for the member for whom the overpayment occurred, but advise the claimant of the circumstances of the overpayment and the method that will be used for recoupment.
2. Arrange with the insured for a lump sum payment or establish a payment plan to recoup the overpayment.
3. Obtain reimbursement from a third party, usually another carrier where COB is involved.

Remember that benefits cannot be taken from charges that have been assigned to the provider of services.

When a refund is received or offered, accept or pursue all such refunds, regardless of the amount of overpayment or the time that has elapsed since the overpayment occurred.

Summary

Remember that most adjustments affect the monies that the subscribers, members, or providers receive. This is always a sensitive situation. Therefore, always be sure that an adjustment is necessary and is performed correctly so that a second or third adjustment is not required. Follow the procedures established by the payor for handling adjustments, and give the affected parties adequate notification. Failure to follow such procedures significantly increases the likelihood of subsequent ill will, or legal action. If in doubt, request assistance before making an adjustment.

Assignments

Complete the Questions for Review.

Questions for Review

Directions: Answer the following questions without looking back into the material just covered. Write your answers in the space provided.

1.   List the four basic types of adjustments.

    1.   _____

    2.   _____

    3.   _____

    4.   _____

2.   A _____ adjustment changes claim data but does not increase or decrease a claim payment.

3.   A _____ adjustment is performed to increase an original claim payment.

4.   A _____ adjustment reverses the original claim payment.

5.   A _____ adjustment partially reverses a claim payment.

If you were unable to answer any of the questions, refer back to the section and then complete the answers.

Honors Certification™

The Honors Certification™ challenge for this chapter is a written test of the information contained within this chapter. Each incorrect answer will result in a deduction of between 1% and 5% from your grade. You must achieve a score of 80% or higher to pass this test. If you fail the test on your first attempt you may retake the test one additional time. The items included in the second test may be different from those in the first test.

27 Dental Terminology

In this chapter you will learn:

- To interpret the meaning of dental terms, including prefixes, suffixes, and root words.

Key words and concepts you will learn in this chapter:

Prefix – The beginning portion of a term that modifies the meaning of the root word.
Root Word – Usually found in the center of a term and identifies the organ or body part involved.
Suffix – The ending portion of a term. Suffixes also alter the root word, usually by indicating a state of being.

Additionally this chapter deals with numerous new terms relating to dental terminology.

About 75% of all medical terms are derived from Latin and Greek prefixes, suffixes, and roots. A **prefix** is the portion of the word found at the beginning of a term that modifies the meaning of the root word (i.e., *endo* – meaning within, -dontics meaning teeth = *endo*dontics meaning within the teeth). Prefixes alter the root word by adding a number (bi- two), a direction, (ab- away from), a location (endo- within), or a description (dis- bad).

A **suffix** is the portion of a word found at the end of a term (i.e., gingi- meaning gum, *itis* meaning inflammation = gingiv*itis* meaning inflammation of the gums). Suffixes also alter the root word, usually by indicating a state of being (-itis).

A **root** is usually found in the center of a term and identifies the organ or body part involved.

In dental terminology, and less often in medical terminology, it is possible to combine a prefix and suffix to form a word, even though no root word is involved (as in gingivitis). **Table 27-1** presents a list of prefixes and suffixes used in dental terminology. Health claims examiners should become familiar with the prefixes and suffixes to help accurately process dental claims.

The following is a list of common dental terms and procedures. Health claims examiners should become familiar with these terms to help them accurately bill and process dental claims.

Common Dental Terms and Procedures

Abrasion – Wearing away of the surfaces of the teeth as a result of their use in chewing.
Abscess – A collection of puss in a cavity formed within the tissue of the body.
Absorption – The process of sucking-up, taking in, and assimilating certain substances, such as fluids and other matter, by the skin, mucus membranes, blood vessels, or lymphatics.
Abutment – A tooth used to support or stabilize one end of a prosthetic appliance, such as a dental bridge.
Accretion – An accumulation of foreign matter, such as tartar on the surface of a tooth or decayed matter within the cavity.
Acid-etch – In restorative dentistry, a method of etching the tooth enamel with an acid to provide an adhesion of composite filling material to the tooth's surface.
Acrylic – A synthetic thermoplastic substance resembling clear glass, but lighter in weight, which permits passage of ultraviolet rays and is used in making dental prostheses and temporary artificial eyes.
Acrylic Resins – Plastic restorative materials used in making dentures and crowns and as filling material.
ADA – American Dental Association.
Adaptic – Type of filling (composite); recommended for class I, III, and V restorations.
Adduct – To move toward the center or midline.
Adhesives – In restorative dentistry, a compound used after the acid-etch to provide an adhesion between the composite and the tooth surface.

Adjunctive Treatment – Supplementary and additional therapeutic procedures.

Adjustment – An alteration or modification that may be required on a tooth or a denture (after it has been placed in the mouth). Occlusal adjustment is a form of modification.

Align – To position properly in relation to another object(s).

Alloy – The product of fusing two or more metals; a silver alloy combined with mercury to produce an amalgam for restoration of a destroyed tooth surface.

Alveolalgia – Pain in the alveolus or tooth socket following tooth extraction. It may involve osteitis or dry socket.

Alveolar – Pertaining to an alveolus.

Alveolar Osteitis – A painful condition caused by loss of the blood clot or from an infected socket. Also commonly referred to as "dry socket."

Alveolectomy – Shaping of the dental ridges by removal of prominences of bone and excess soft tissue, usually in preparation for construction of a prosthetic appliance.

Alveolotomy – Incision into a tooth socket.

Alveolus – Bone cavity or a socket in which the root of a tooth is held by the periodontal ligament.

Alveoplasty – Surgical excision or revision of the alveolar process to restore a normal contour. It may range from simple alveolectomy in conjunction with extractions to necessary reconstruction of the ridge in preparation for dentures.

Amalgam – An alloy of mercury with any other metal. The compound of a basal alloy of silver and tin with mercury, used for restoring teeth. Copper and zinc are usually added as modifying metals to the basal alloy.

Amputation (Root) – Excision of the root portion of a tooth. It is usually performed on a multirooted tooth to eliminate a root that cannot be treated.

Analgesia – Reduction or loss of sensitivity to pain without loss of consciousness.

Anesthesia – Loss of sensation.
  Block – Anesthesia produced by injecting an anesthetic solution into the nerve trunks supplying the operative field, called *regional block*, or by infiltrating close to the nerves, called *infiltration block*, or by a wall of anesthetic solution injected about the field, called *field block*. In all these methods, the nerve conduction is blocked, and painful impulses fail to reach the brain.
  General – Loss of sensation with loss of consciousness.
  Infiltration – Anesthesia induced by the injection of the anesthetic solution directly into the tissues that are to be anesthetized.
  Local – Anesthesia limited to the local area.
  Regional – Local anesthesia.

Anesthetics – Drugs that produce loss of feeling or sensation either as local or general anesthesia.

Angle's Classification – A classification of the forms of malocclusion as established by Edward Hartley Angle, an American orthodontist.
  Class I – The normal anteroposterior relationship of the lower jaw to the upper jaw. The mesiobuccal cusp of the maxillary first permanent molar occludes in the buccal groove of the mandibular first permanent molar.
  Class II – The posterior relationship of the lower jaw to the upper jaw. The mesiobuccal cusp of the maxillary first permanent molar occludes mesial to the buccal of the mandibular first permanent molar.
  Class III – The anterial relationship of the lower jaw to the upper jaw with possible subdivision. The mesiobuccal cusp of the maxillary first permanent molar occludes distal to the buccal groove of the mandibular first permanent molar.

Ankyloglossia – Partial or complete fusion of the tongue to the floor of the mouth.

Ankylosis – Fixation or true bony union between bones or a tooth to the jaw; abnormal immobility of a joint.

Anodontia – Failure of tooth formation; congenital absence of teeth.

Antagonist – A tooth in the upper jaw that articulates with a tooth of the lower jaw or visa versa.

Anterior – Situated in front; dentally, referring to the teeth at the front of the mouth (i.e., central incisors, lateral incisors, and first bicuspids).

Anterior Posterior Dysplasia – An abnormal fit of the maxilla and mandible to each other or to the cranial base.

Anteversion – The forward tipping or tilting of the teeth or other surfaces of the oral cavity.

Antibiotic – A drug that inhibits or destroys bacterial growth.

Antiseptic – A pharmaceutical substance that stops or inhibits the growth of microorganisms.

Aperture – An opening.

Apex – The terminal end of a cone; a conical end; the terminal end of a root or tooth.

Apexification – Removal of dental pulp and treatment of the apex with calcium hydroxide resulting in stimulation of growth of the cementum, which promotes apical closure. It is normally performed in a young patient whose apex is incompletely formed. Root canal therapy is usually performed for an older person.

Apical – Pertaining to the apex or conical endings of the roots of the teeth.

Apical Foramen – The opening at the end of a root of a tooth through which the tooth receives its nerve and blood supply.

Apices – Plural form of apex.

Apicoetomy – The excision or resection of the apex of a tooth root, usually following root canal therapy.

Apicostomy – A surgical opening through the mucoperiosteum and alveolar bone for access to the apex of a tooth root.

Aplasis – Lack of origin or development.

Appliance – In dentistry, a device used to replace missing parts, provide function, or perform a therapeutic purpose. Dental prostheses, splints, orthodontic appliances, and obturators are examples of appliances.

> **Craniofacial** – Used to replace and immobilize mandibular or midfacial fractures. Attachments may be external or internal, by means of wires, pins, bars, or headcaps. Holes may be drilled through the craniofacial bones to facilitate placing wires or other attachments.
>
> **Crozat** - A removable orthodontic appliance.
>
> **Fixed** – An appliance attached to the teeth by cement or adhesive materials.
>
> **Fracture** – Device for reduction or fixation of fractures. Pins, screws, and other types of fixation are used in replacing or realigning fractured parts.
>
> **Hawley** – A removable appliance usually made to fit in the palate against the lingual surfaces of the teeth and used as a retainer after the teeth have been aligned. There are numerous forms and uses.

Arch, Dental – The curving structure formed by the crowns of the teeth in their normal position, or by the residual ridge after loss of teeth. The inferior dental arch, or arch of the mandible, is formed by the lower teeth, and the superior dental arch, arch of the maxilla, is formed by the upper teeth.

Arch Retainer – An appliance to prevent collapse of the dental arch.

Arch Wire – In orthodontics, the main wire framework, which is attached to bands and passes around the entire dental arch, on the lingual surface or facial surface or both, and which serves as the frame of attachment for finger springs.

Artificial Teeth – A denture or bridgework composed of two materials – porcelain or plastic. The former is hard, baked vitreous material with specific properties. The latter is less hard, more resilient material with different characteristics and indicated uses.

Attrition – The normal or abnormal loss of teeth structure.

Autogenous Bone Graft – A bone graft obtained from another part of the same person's body to induce new bone formation in a defect.

Axis – A real or imaginary line passing through a body or part, such as the vertical axis of a tooth.

Backing – A piece of metal, usually gold, that backs up an artificial bridge or tooth and to which the tooth is soldered or otherwise attached.

Band – In orthodontics, a metallic attachment that surrounds and is cemented to the tooth, used to anchor archwires to the teeth.

Bar – A connector of two or more parts. It may be used for removable partial dentures, fixed prostheses to provide additional strength, and splinting in treatment of fractures of the teeth and jaws.

Basal Bone – The bone-like tissue of the mandible and maxilla other than the alveolar process.

Base – A protective material, such as cement, placed over the pulpal area of the tooth (pulp not exposed) to reduce irritation and thermal shock of the pulp. In dentures, the part of a denture that replaces the normal contours of the soft tissues and supports the artificial teeth.

Baseplate – A temporary form to represent the base of a denture that is used for making maxillomandibular relation records and for arranging the teeth.

Bell-crowned - Pertaining or referring to a tooth crown that is largest at the occlusal surface and tapers to the gum, usually used on incisors and bicuspids.

Bicuspid- Having two cusps, as in bicuspid teeth, a premolar.

Bifurcate – Fork; divided into two branches; having two roots

Bifurcation – Anatomic area where roots divide into a two-rooted tooth.

Bilateral – Having two sides. Any partial denture having a major connector is said to be bilateral, i.e., one on each side.

Bite, closed – A condition in which the upper teeth close too far over the lower, which usually bite into the roof of the mouth.

Bite Guard – An appliance that covers the occlusal and incisal surfaces of the teeth. It is used to stabilize the teeth or to provide a flat surface for unobstructive movement of the mandible.

Bite, open – A condition in which the upper and lower incisors do not occlude.

Bite Plane – An appliance that covers the palate and is designed to provide resistance to the mandibular incisors where there is contact.

Bite Raising – The process of increasing the distance between the occlusal surfaces of the teeth. It may be accomplished by placing appliances or gold inlays or crowns.

Bite Wing Radiograph – An x-ray showing the crowns of the upper and lower teeth and a portion of the roots and supporting bone.

Bleaching – A technique that restores a discolored tooth to its natural color.

Bone, alveolar – A portion of the alveolar process that surrounds the roots of the teeth; a thin plate of bone to which the periodontal ligament is attached. It is pierced by many small openings that transmit blood, lymph vessels and nerves to the periodontal ligament.

Bracing – Resistance to displacement in a lateral direction.

Bracket – In orthodontics, an attachment that is either welded or soldered to a band (except a molar band), which secures arch wires to bands.

Bridge – A partial denture; bridgework.

> **Fixed** – A bridge that is permanently attached to its abutments.
>
> **Removable** – A denture that may be removed by the wearer.

Removable Fixed – A bridge that may be removed by the dentist (not by the patient) without mutilation of any of its parts.

Bridgework – An appliance made of artificial crowns of teeth to replace missing natural teeth.

Broken Stress Bridge - A fixed bridge that includes a rigid connector at one end and a non-rigid connector, or stress breaker, at the other end.

Bruxism – The unconscious habit of grinding the teeth, often limited to during sleeping or mental or physical concentration or strain.

Buccal – Pertaining to the cheek. The buccal surface of a tooth is a surface next to the cheek.

Buccal Frenum – The string-like tissue that attaches the cheeks to the alveolar ridge in the bicuspid region.

Buccolingual – Pertaining to the cheek and the tongue.

Butterfly – A removable acrylic partial denture for the temporary replacement of front teeth; sometimes referred to as a flipper, provisional partial, or temporary bridge.

Calcification – The act of depositing calcific matter or calcium salts during growth. Bones and teeth become calcified. **Calculus** – A hard calcareous concentration deposited on the surface of the crown or root of a tooth; tartar.

  Salivary – Calcareous deposits in the duct of a salivary gland or on the surface of the teeth, which originate from the salivary secretion.

  Serumal – Calcareous deposits formed about the teeth by exudation from diseased gums.

Canine – The teeth corresponding to the long teeth of a dog, usually referred to as cuspids.

Cantilever – A dental prostheses that has one or more abutments at one end while the other end is unsupported.

Cap – A substance or structure designed to cover the exposed pulp of the tooth.

Capping – The operation of placing a covering over the exposed pulp of a tooth.

  Direct Pulp – A capping that provides a direct contact between the material used and the pulp.

  Indirect Pulp – A capping that applies material to vital or diseased dentin.

Care – The total of diagnostic, preventative, treatment, and restorative services rendered by a licensed dentist.

  Adequate – May denote repair of oral damage and the placing of the mouth in a condition to prevent deterioration. It frequently refers to the substitution of a less costly but satisfactory type of service.

  Comprehensive – All dental services indicated for the restoration and maintenance of oral health.

  Emergency – Any dental services for unexpected and urgent conditions, such as toothache, acute infection, hemorrhage, accidental injury to teeth and supporting structures, and broken dentures.

  Initial – Services required for dental needs existing at the time of enrollment in a planned dental program; frequently called mouth rehabilitation.

  Maintenance – Service required to maintain oral health.

  Minimum – Generally, oral treatment of acute conditions of teeth and gums.

Caries – A molecular depth of bone or teeth, corresponding to ulceration in the soft tissue.

  Of the Teeth – A localized, progressive molecule disintegration of the teeth.

  Inter-proximal – Caries of the surfaces of the teeth in contact with each other.

Cariogenic – Conducive to caries.

Cast – The positive reproduction of the mouth or teeth in plaster or similar material, upon which a prosthetic appliance is constructed.

Cavity Classifications

  Class I – Cavities beginning in structural defects such as pits and fissures.

  Class II – Cavities in proximal surfaces of bicuspids and molars.

  Class III – Cavities in proximal surfaces of cuspids and incisors that do not involve the incisal edge.

  Class IV – Cavities in proximal surfaces of cuspids and incisors involving the incisal angle.

  Class V – Cavities of the gingival third of the labial, buccal, or lingual surfaces of the teeth.

  Class VI – Cavities on the incisal edges and cusp tips of the teeth.

Cavity Liner – A substance that is placed on the walls of the cavity before insertion of a restoration.

Cement – In dentistry, an adhesive filling material used for cementing bridges, crowns, and inlays. It may be used as a temporary filling material.

Acrylic Resin – A type of autopolymerizing acrylic used as a restorative material.

  Copper Phosphate – Zinc phosphate cement to which copper oxide has been added; thought to impart germicidial qualities to the cement created.

  Base – Used for insulation in deep cavity preparation.

  Germicidal – Copper or silver salts added to destroy bacteria.

  Sealer – Used for filling root canals.

  Silicate – Commonly used to fill cavities in the anterior teeth; made of powered kaolin, quartz, lime, and magnesium mixed with liquid phosphoric acid.

  Zinc Phosphate – Commonly used to seal gold inlays and crowns into place on the teeth and as a base under metallic restorations.

  Zinc Oxide Eugenol – A sedative cement used as a temporary filling or a base under restorations, where sedative treatment of the tooth is indicated.

Cementoenamel Junction – The portion of the tooth at which the cementum and the enamel join.

Cementosis – See hypercementosis.

Cementum – The hard calcified tissue that covers the anatomic root of a tooth. It is formed by cementoblast and arranged in layers that cover the root dentin.

Central Ray – The x-ray located in the center of the bundle of x-rays that make up the useful beam.

Cephalometrics – A scientific study of the measurements of the head.

Ceramco – Trade name for a combination of porcelain with metal used in restorations of fixed prosthetics.

Cervical – Pertaining to the neck or cervix of the tooth.

Cervical Anchorage – In orthodontics, a strap of elastic tape with wire hooks that fits around the back of the patient's neck and is used as a force from the outside the mouth to move teeth distally.

Cervical Line – The neck of the tooth; the cementoenamel junction.

Cervicogingival – The space between the gingiva and the enamel of the tooth crowns; the space between the gingiva and the cementum in cases in which the gingiva has receded.

Chamber – An enclosed area.

> **Pulp** – Pulp cavity or space in the coronal position of the tooth containing the pulp.
>
> **Relief** – A recess in a denture to reduce or eliminate pressure from the corresponding area of the mouth.
>
> **Clasp** – The metal part of a partial denture.
>
> **Arm** – The portion of the clasp that extends from the body of the clasp out to the end of the clasp.

Cleft Lip – A congenital cleft or defect in the upper lip, usually due to failure of the median nasal and maxillary process to unite.

Cleft Palate – A congenital defect due to failure of fusion of embryonic facial process, resulting in a fissure through the palate. It may be complete, extending through both hard and soft palates into the nose, or it may be any degree of incomplete or partial cleft.

Cohesive – Uniting together or characterized by cohesion. In dentistry, a property of annealed gold (foil or crystal) that causes separate particles to stick to one another as they are welded when placed in contact with each other by a heavy hand or mallet pressure.

Coil Spring – A small wire spring wrapped around the main arch wire in an orthodontic appliance which is used as a force to pull teeth together or to push them apart.

Cold Cure – Usually relates to denture relining not requiring laboratory service.

Collar – A small part of the root of a denture tooth.

Complete Denture – One that replaces all teeth in an arch.

Composite – A plastic restorative material that blends resin and quartz crystal with a catalyst.

Compressive Strength – The greatest compressive force that can be applied to material before it ruptures.

Concrescence – The union of two teeth, after eruption, by fusion of the cementum surfaces.

Concretion – In dentistry, a deposit on the surface of a tooth. Also a calculus.

Condensation – In dentistry, the packing of a restorative material into the prepared cavity of a tooth.

Condyle – The rounded, knuckle-shaped process of the mandible which forms a joint at the temporal bone.

Condylectomy – Surgical removal of the condyle.

Contact Point – The surface of a tooth that touches the surface of an adjacent tooth.

Coping – A thin metal covering over a prepared tooth which is used as a base for the construction of a crown.

Coronal – Pertaining to the crown of a tooth.

Coronoid – Shaped like the beak of a crown, as the coronoid process of the mandible.

Coronoid Process – The more anterior process on the superior border of the ramus.

Correction of Occlusion – The correction of malocclusion by elimination of disharmony of occlusal contacts. It may be performed by means of many different methods, depending on the degree or severity, from selective spot grinding to gnathologic evaluation with subsequent treatment to correct any disharmonies.

Crest Ridge – The projecting ridge of the alveolar process that surrounds the teeth.

Cross-Bite – Bite in which the jaws may be in normal relationship when closed, but the buccal cusp of the upper molars bite into the buccal cusp of the lower molars.

Crown – Top part of anything; any structure like a crown.

> **Anatomic** – Portion of a tooth covered by enamel.
>
> **Artificial** – A cap of metal, plastic, or porcelain process to cover the portion of the tooth that projects beyond the gum line.
>
> **Clinical** – The portion of the tooth exposed beyond the crest of the gingiva.
>
> **Complete** – The crown that covers the entire clinical crown.
>
> **Of a Tooth** – The part covered with enamel.
>
> **Dowel** – A complete crown that replaces the entire coronal portion of the natural tooth which is retained by a post extending into the root canal.
>
> **Faced** – A metal crown with a tooth-colored material on the labial or buccal surface.
>
> **Full Veneer** – A dental restoration that covers a tooth in its entirety.
>
> **Jacket** – A term generally used to indicate complete veneer crowns that are made entirely of porcelain or acrylic resin.
>
> **Shell** – A metal clasp designed to fit a prepared tooth. It is usually performed and reproduces the natural crown.
>
> **Three-quarter** – A dental restoration that covers all of the exposed tooth to oral environmental except the labial or buccal surface.

Crozat Appliance – A removable orthodontic appliance.

Curettage – Scraping or removal of diseased tissue with a curet.

> **Apical** – Curettement of diseased tissue in the periapical area on the apical portion of the tooth without removal of the root tip.

Gingival – removal of gingival.

Infrabony Pocket – The removal of a soft tissue inflammation located within and around an infrabony defect; debridement and cleaning of the root surface of the pocket.

Root – Removal of accretions on the root's surface providing a more suitable environment for development of healthy tissues.

Sub-gingival – Debridement of the entire pocket and epithelial subjacent connective tissues, performed to eliminate the inflammatory process.

Cusp – An elevation or point on the surface of a tooth, especially on the occlusal surface.

Cuspid – A cuspid or canine tooth with one point or cusp.

Cyst – Sac containing fluid.

DDS – Doctor of Dental Surgery.

Debridement – Removal of diseased or devitalized tissues or foreign materials.

Debris – Soft-formed material loosely attached to the surface of a tooth.

Decalcification – Withdrawal or acid removal of mineral salts of bone or other calcified substance.

Decay – Decomposed structures; caries or other carious lesions of the teeth.

Deciduous – Term used to identify primary teeth.

Def Rate – Similar to the DMF rate but used for primary dentition (baby teeth). Although lower case letters are used, the symbol (d) standing for decayed primary teeth indicated for filling, and the symbol (f) for filled primary teeth, have the same meaning as DMF. The symbol (e) stands for decayed teeth indicated for extraction. Missing teeth are not counted for this rate.

Dens in Dente – A developmental anomaly of a tooth, usually involving the upper lateral incisors. The tooth enamel has the appearance of a tooth within a tooth.

Dental – Pertaining to the teeth.

Dental Floss – Fine string pulled between the teeth to aid in cleaning the space between the teeth.

Dental Hygienist – A person licensed to clean and polish teeth and to instruct in the fundamentals of oral hygiene.

Dental Laboratory Technician – A person trained to prepare dental appliances and restorations for placement in the mouth.

Dental Pulp – The soft tissue that fills the pulp chamber and the root canals of a tooth and is responsible for its vitality. It consists of connective tissue, blood vessels, and nerves.

Dental Senescence – Deterioration of the teeth and associated structures due to the aging process.

Dentate – Having teeth.

Dentifrice – A substance, as a paste or a powder, used in the cleaning of the teeth.

Dentin – The calcified tissue that forms the major part of the tooth. Dentin is related to the bone but differs from it in the absence of included cells.

Dentinogenesis Imperfecta – Hereditary disturbance that affects the development of dentin.

Dentistry – The profession that is concerned with the prevention, diagnosis, and treatment of diseases of the teeth and adjacent tissues, and the restoration of missing dental and oral structures.

Operative – The branch of dentistry concerned with preserving the natural teeth and its supporting structures and with restoring the teeth.

Preventive – The branch of dentistry dealing with prevention of dental diseases by prophylactic and educational methods.

Prosthetic – The phase or branch of dentistry that deals with the replacement of missing teeth or oral tissues by artificial means; also called prosthodontics.

Dentition – The process of teething; the eruption of teeth in the alveolar ridge; the character and arrangement of the teeth.

Deciduous – The 20 teeth which erupt first and are later replaced by the permanent teeth.

Mixed – The compliment of teeth in the jaw after eruption of some of the permanent teeth, before all the deciduous teeth are shed.

Permanent – The 32 teeth that erupt after the deciduous teeth are lost.

Dentulous – Having teeth, as opposed to edentulous, not having teeth.

Denture – The natural or artificial teeth of a person considered as a unit.

Artificial – The complete artificial replacement of either the upper or lower teeth.

Butt – Denture with almost no flange, designed because of full lips, leaving no room for additional thickness of the denture flange.

Duplicate – Usually refers to a second denture that is a copy of the existing denture.

Duplication – Usually refers to a jump case or re-basing of the denture; also known as duplicating or re-material. Re-basing is the replacement of the base of the denture because of deterioration or tissue changes. Duplication can be misleading because occasionally the term is used to mean a spare set. Because of its many uses, it is advisable to ask for an explanation of the service.

Full – Replacement of the complete dental equipment of either jaw.

Immediate Full – Denture constructed to permit some natural teeth to remain in the mouth during its fabrication. When the remaining teeth are removed, the denture is inserted. Hence, the patient is never without teeth of some kind.

Implant – A substructure usually made of cast metal which is implanted over the alveolar ridge and under the soft tissues. Posts extend through the gingival tissues to support a denture. There may also be extensions into the bone for support.

Overlay – Complete denture that fits over one or more retained natural teeth. Ideally, it provides a more comfortable fit and retention because of the attachment to the teeth. It is used in both the upper and lower jaws but is more frequently placed in the mandible. The preparation consists of performing root canal therapy on the remaining teeth and placing a small gold cap or crown. An alternate method is to perform root canal therapy and then cut the tooth off at the level of the alveolar ridge. Attachments are then inserted into the root canal and used to provide support to a denture.

Remote – Denture placed following the healing of an extraction site; may also be the replacement of an existing denture.

Diagnostic Services – Procedures such as x-rays, clinical examinations, biopsies, blood tests, study models, and other vitality tests, which assist the dentist in determining the conditions present and the treatment required.

Die – An exact reproduction in metal of any object or cast.

Inlay – An exact reproduction of a prepared tooth in high-strength dental stone or metal.

Distal – Away from the median line of the face following the curve of the dental arch. The surfaces of the teeth most distant from the median line are called *distal surfaces*.

DMD – Doctor of Dental Medicine.

DMF Rate – For an individual, the number of permanent teeth (or for a group, the average number) that are (d) decayed, (m) missing, or indicated for extractions, and (f) filled. A tooth both filled and decayed is counted only as decayed. The DMF rate is a measure of accumulative effects of caries and a useful means for comparing the lifetime of caries' experience of a group of comparable age.

Dolder Bar - Bar used to connect crowns for stabilization and reduces stress in anterior fixed prosthetics. The bar is attached to the abutments.

Double Lingual Bar – A type of lower partial denture that includes a secondary or auxiliary bar in addition to the lingual bar.

Dowel Post and Pins – Cast metal or manufactured strengthening device placed in a tooth to provide retention for a crown.

Duct – A passage with well-defined walls.

E Clasp – A bar-type clasp that is shaped like the letter "E."

Edentulous – Without teeth.

Elongation – Abnormal elongation of a tooth on a dental x-ray film by improper positioning of the x-ray machine in relation to the x-ray film in the patient's oral cavity.

Embrasure – Space between the sloping proximal surfaces of the teeth. The opening may be toward the cheek (buccal), the lips (labial), or the tongue (lingual).

Enamel – The vitreous covering tissue of the crowns of the teeth, consisting of enamel rods or prisms and a cementing interrod substance.

Rods – The calcified column or prism, with an average diameter of 4mm; extends in a wavy pattern through the entire thickness of the enamel and is generally perpendicular to the surface of the tooth.

Mottled – A defect in the enamel structure of the teeth manifesting as chalky white, yellow-brown, or black discolorations. The enamel may be pitted. The affected areas may vary in size and degree, depending on the severity of the causative factor.

Encirclement – A clasp that extends more than halfway around a tooth to provide a secure attachment.

Endodontics – The branch of dentistry that deals with the diagnosis and treatment of diseases of the dental pulp and periapical tissues.

Endopost – A cast post designed to fit into the treated root canal of a tooth to provide strength and stability.

Epithelium – Membrane that covers a surface or lines the cavity – the layer of cells forming the epidermis of the skin.

Enamel – Ameloblasts that form the dental enamel of the developing tooth.

Gingival – Epithelial covering of the gingival tissue.

Pocket – Cellular structure that lines the gingival or periodontal pockets.

Sulcular – Stratifying squamous epithelium covering the soft tissue walls of the gingival crevice.

Epulis – Solitary tumor-like lesion developing from the periosteum of the maxilla or mandible, appearing clinically as a circumscribed swelling beneath the gum.

Equilibration – Maintenance of the balance as a pressure.

Occlusal – Modification of the occlusal form by grinding for equalizing occlusal stress, producing simultaneous occlusion contact or harmonizing cuspal relations.

Equilibrium – Perfect balance. The condition made possible by complete synchronization and harmony among all vital factors.

Erosion – Wearing away or loss of tooth structure by chemical process without known bacterial action, usually beginning in the enamel at the neck of the tooth.

Eruption – The act of breaking up, appearing, or becoming visible; the appearance of a tooth through the gums.

Esthetics – Harmony of form, color, and arrangement.

Etch and Polish – Removal of portions of enamel, usually performed on primary teeth followed by polishing of the tooth areas.

Ethical – Pertaining to standards of right and wrong.

Ethics – A system of moral principals and ideas of human behavior.

> **Dental** – The principals of professional conduct; duties a dentist owes to self, colleagues, patients, and fellow man.

Exfoliation – A peeling and shedding of a horney layer of skin or tooth.

> **Normal time** – The time at which a primary tooth is expected to become loose and fall out of a child's mouth.

Exodontia, Exodontics – The art and science of extraction of teeth.

Exostoses – Bony outgrowths from the surface of a bone.

Extension of Prevention, Dental – Extending the margins of a cavity preparation to remove incipient carious lesions to areas of the tooth that are either self-cleansing or readily cleansed. Such extensions are to prevent the recurrence of caries at the edges of the restorations.

Extracoronal – The external coronal portion of a natural tooth.

Extraction – Removal of a tooth from the oral cavity.

> **Serial** – Extraction of selected teeth over a period of time.
> **Simple** – Uncomplicated removal of a tooth.
> **Surgical** – Removal by means of surgical methods, usually involving the turning of a flap or removal of bone.

Extraoral – Outside the mouth.

Extrude – To force a tooth out of its normal occlusal position, possibly due to the absence of opposing teeth.

Extrusion – Eruption of a tooth from its socket; movement of the tooth out of the natural occlusal plane.

Eyetooth – A canine tooth of the upper jaw; bicuspid.

Facial – Pertaining to the face; the surface of the tooth or appliance nearest to the lips or cheeks; used synonymously with the words *buccal* and *labial*.

Facing – A manufactured porcelain piece that simulates a natural tooth.

Festoon – Carvings in the base material of an artificial denture, simulating contours of the natural tissues being replaced by the denture.

Fibroblast – Connective tissue cells found in fibrous tissue, fundamental to all healing processes.

Filling – Material used in closing cavities in carious teeth; the process of inserting, condensing, shaping, and finishing a filling.

Finger Spring – A small wire attachment soldered to the main arch wire that acts as a spring force to move teeth into an orthodontic appliance.

Fissure – A groove or cleft; a fault in the enamel of a tooth caused by imperfect union.

Flange – The part of the denture or saddle that extends on the facial or lingual side from the ridgecrest to the periphery.

Flap – Massive tissue partly detached by a knife or blunt instrument in dentistry; the raising of the gingival mucosa from the alveolar bone to access an underlying area. Sometimes a flap procedure is used to remove a broken or retained root. It is frequently required as a result of periodontal disease.

FLC – Full line or finished crown.

Flipper – A provisional partial or temporary bridge.

Fluoridation – The addition of fluoride to the water supply of a community as an aid to the control of dental caries.

Fluoride – A salt of hydrofluoric acid.

Fluoride, topical – The direct application of a solution of fluoride (usually 2% sodium fluoride) to the crowns of the teeth for preventing dental caries; usually carried out at the ages of 3, 7, 10, and 13.

Foramen – A natural opening in a bone or other structure.

> **Apical** – An opening at or near the apex of the root of a tooth, giving passage to the blood vessels and nerve supply in the pulp.
> **Mandibular** – The opening on the medial aspect of the vertical ramus of the lower jaw approximately midway between the mandibular and gonial notches; may be located posterior to the middle of the ramus. It contains inferior alveolar vessels and inferior alveolar nerves.

Foreshortening – Term used in dental radiology denoting the abnormal shortening of a tooth or teeth on a dental x-ray film.

Formocreosal – A solution used in root canal therapy and in treatment of dental pulp.

Fossa – A pit, hollow, or depression.

> **Dental** – A round or angular depression in the surface of a tooth, occurring mostly in the occlusal surfaces of the molar and the lingual surfaces of the incisors.

Frenectomy – Excision of the mucuous membrane attaching the cheeks and lips to the mucuosa of the jawbone; excision of the lingual frenum attaching the tongue to the floor of the mouth and alveolar ridge.

Frenotomy – Division of any frenum, especially for tongue-tie.

Frenum – A fold of integument or mucous membrane that checks or limits the movements of any organ.

> **Labial** – The fold or tissue that connects the lip with the gingiva at a point normally in the midline.
> **Lingual** – The fold of tissue that connects the tongue to the gingiva and the floor of the mouth in the midline.

Full Mouth X-ray – X-ray of the mouth equaling 16 bite wings.

Furcation – The tooth area where roots branch out. Bifurcation relates to two roots. Trifurcation relates to three roots.

Germination – The division of a single tooth germ or bud that produces double or twin crowns on a single tooth.

Gerodontics – Practice of dentistry pertaining to aged patients.

Gigantism – Macrosomia; excessive growth.

Gingiva – The part of the gum that surrounds the tooth and lies close to the crest of the alveolar ridge.

> **Free** – The part of the gingiva about the neck of a tooth that is not closely opposed or attached to the tooth's surfaces.

Gingival – Of or pertaining to the soft tissues of the gum and the tooth.

> **Crevice** – The narrow opening between the circumferential soft tissue of the gum and the tooth.
>
> **Cuff** – The most coronal portion of the gingival tissue immediately surrounding the tooth to where it attaches to the tooth.
>
> **Curettage** – Debridement of a diseased gingival attachment to eliminate edema, inflammation, and pocket formations.
>
> **Margin** – The most coronal portion of the gingiva surrounding the tooth.
>
> **Morphology** – The form, shape, or profile of gingival tissues.
>
> **Papillae** – Extensions or projections of gum tissue between the teeth.
>
> **Stimulation** – Application of frictional activity to the gingival tissue to stimulate circulation and increase keratinization of the surface epithelium.
>
> **Sulcus** – A crevice, group, or pocket in the gingiva; a trough formed by the attachment of the gingiva to the surface of the tooth.

Gingivectomy – The surgical excision from supported gingival tissue to the level where it is attached, creating a new gingival margin, apical and posterior to the old.

Gingivitis – Inflammation of the gingival tissue; may be caused by pressure or contact of dentures, metallic poisoning, faulty restorations, dietary deficiency, herpes virus, hormonal imbalances, malopposed teeth, bacterial invasion, organic malfunction, or pregnancy.

> **Desquamative** – Inflammation of the gingiva but not a pathologic entity; may be associated with a biologic stress.
>
> **Hemorrhagic** – Characterized by bleeding and particularly associated with ascorbic acid deficiency.
>
> **Herpetic** – Inflammation due to the presence of herpes virus.
>
> **Hormonal** – Associated with an endocrine imbalance.
>
> **Necrotizing Ulcerative** – Inflammation with narcosis of the intra-dental papilla, ulceration of the gingival margins, pain, and offensive odor; an acute gingivitis that is sometimes chronic.
>
> **Pregnancy** – Gingival enlargement due to hormonal imbalance during pregnancy.

Gingivoplasty – The procedure by which gingival deformities are reshaped and reduced to create a normal and functional form; surgical contouring of the gingival tissues.

Gingivosis – A degenerative condition of the gingiva and connective tissue of uncertain origin. It is a non-inflammatory disease with many phases: edema of the inter-dental papilla progressing to the marginal and attached gingiva, profuse bleeding progressing to necrosis, recession, and resorption.

Gingivostomatitis – A form of oral inflammatory disease that involves both the gingiva and portions of the remaining oral mucosa. Herpetic gingivostomatitis is caused by invasion of the herpes virus which usually occurs in children.

Glossitis – Inflammation of the tongue.

Gnathology – The science of the masticatory system, including physiology, functional disturbances, and treatment.

Gold – A noble metal used extensively in dentistry, considered superior because of its malleability; may be used in the pure or alloyed state.

Gold Foil – Pure gold rolled into a thin sheet compacted into a cavity. The restoration is built to harmonize with the existing tooth. It is a direct gold filling in contrast to an inlay in which an impression is made and an exact form is made and cemented in. The three types are:

> **Matte** – Not developed by chemical prescription; a non-cohesive form that may be used in combination with cohesive gold.
>
> **Sheet** – Original type, which was 24-karat gold, rolled into thin sheets and then cut; this is a disappearing art.
>
> **Gold Dent** – A combination of matte gold and cohesive made into globules.

Granuloma – A small mass of granulated tissue containing bacterial deposits found on the root of a tooth or in the area of the jaw after the removal of a tooth.

Groove – An elongated depression; the portion of a cast that corresponds to the periphery of the impression.

Gum – The mucous membrane and underlying connective tissue covering the alveolar processes and necks of erupted teeth.

Guttering – Shaping bone to remove dead tissues as a result of osteomyelitis.

Halitosis – Bad breath due to poor oral hygiene, periodontal disease, sinusitis, tonsillitis, or bronchopulmonary disease.

Hard Palate – Approximately two-thirds of the anterior section of the palate composed of relatively hard and unyielding tissue.

Hay Rake – A device used with children which is fixed temporarily to the upper teeth to break undesirable habits such as thumb or lip sucking.

Heel – Denture –The posterior extremities of a denture. It corresponds with the retromolar pad area of a lower denture and the tuberosity area of an upper denture.

Hemisection – Surgical dividing of a tooth to make it easier to remove the ensuing fragments or allow salvage of one part of the tooth that is relatively free of disease. Root canal therapy may be necessary on other roots of the tooth before hemisection is performed.

Herpes – A blister-like elevation appearing in clusters on the skin; an inflammatory skin disease.

>**Labial (Cold Sore)** – Herpes simplex occurring on the lips caused by the herpes virus.

>**Simplex** – A viral infection appearing on the face or genital regions with resulting itching and localized hyperemia. The lesions dry up and form a yellowish crust that normally disappears in 10 to 14 days depending on care.

>**Zoster** – An acute and painful viral disease that affects the cerebral ganglia and posterior nerve roots. Lesions appear on the skin over the infected area. Oral lesions occur on the tongue, soft palate, cheek, and the gingival tissues.

Horseshoe Denture – A partial upper denture from which the palate is omitted. In edentulous cases, a horseshoe denture is termed a *roofless denture.*

Hutchinson's Teeth – Congenitally malformed, peg-shaped incisors with incisal edges narrower than the middle part or notching of the incisal edges. Primary dentition is not affected.

Hygienist – A person trained and licensed by the state to perform dental prophylaxis under the direction of a licensed dentist.

Hypercementosis – Extensive formation of cementum on the roots of the teeth.

Hyperkeratosis – The most common white lesion in the oral cavity. A benign lesion that may be elevated or flat and is in the form of a thickened layer of keratin. It may be associated with a cause such as lip biting, or its cause may be obscure. The lesion usually disappears within two to three months if the cause is eliminated.

Hyperplasia – Excessive growth of normal cells in the normal tissue arrangement of an organ; may have a hereditary or inflammatory cause.

>**Denture** – Enlargement of tissues caused by trauma to the soft tissues from dentures or other injuries.

>**Dilantin** – Caused by the use of dilantin therapy.

Hypocalcification – Reduced calcification; a condition that produces opaque white spots on tooth enamel; a possible hereditary anomaly affecting the dentition, both primary and permanent. The enamel peels off, exposing the dentin and giving a yellow appearance to the teeth.

Hypoplasia – With dental enamel, it is a defective or incomplete development. When it is a hereditary anomaly, a thin layer of hard enamel covers the dentin, giving a brownish appearance to the teeth.

I Clasp – Roach-type clasp shaped like an I.

Immediate Abutment – The metal abutment in a three abutment bridge, with a bridge extending from one cuspid to a second molar with a second bicuspid present.

Immediate Denture – A complete or partial denture made before the natural teeth are extracted. It is inserted at the time the teeth are extracted.

Immediate Surgical Splint – Metal, acrylic resin, or modeling compound fashioned to retain teeth that have been replanted, are unmovable, or have fractured roots; may also be a temporary denture after extraction of teeth. It is an appliance for the protection of a surgical site.

Impacted Tooth – Commonly, any tooth that is positioned or wedged against another tooth, bone, or soft tissue, preventing it from erupting normally.

Impingement – Over-compaction, displacement, or compression. It may be the result of pressure from a unit of a removable prosthesis or traumatization of the periodontal membrane caused by occlusal force on the tooth.

Implants – Dental implants are made of metal or other foreign material and are placed into or on the alveolar bone to provide support.

>**Endosseous** – May be a single metal post inserted into the alveolar bone to support an artificial crown that replaces a missing natural tooth; may also be a metal blade to support one or more artificial crowns or to support a metal crown that would serve as an abutment for a fixed bridge. There are many types and shapes of implants.

>**Sub-periosteal** – Used for support of dentures in which there is sufficient resorption of the alveolar ridge. The gingival tissue is open along the alveolar ridge, and impressions are made. A metal prosthesis is made from this impression and the tissues open again to permit placing the implant that creates an artificial ridge. Extensions from the metal saddle extend above the gingival tissue for denture attachments.

Impressions – A negative reproduction of the teeth or tissues of the mouth. A positive reproduction is made from the impression and is used in the preparation of restorations such as crowns, fixed and removable prosthetics, and appliances. They are also used for diagnostic purposes.

>**Plaginate** – A relationship impression taken in combination of quick-set, plaster, and alginate.

>**Relationship** – Impression taken to establish the relationship of abutment teeth.

Incisal – Pertaining to the cutting edges of incisors and cuspid teeth.

Incisor – A cutting tooth; one of four front teeth of either jaw.

Infrabulge – The formation of the crown that is cervical to the clasp guideline, survey line, or height of contour.

Initial Centric – A centric determination made by the dentist, usually without the use of mechanical aids, which is fairly accurate and commonly used in the final process in establishing true centric.

Inlay – A dental restoration shaped to the form of a cavity and inserted and secured with cement.

Intercusping – A correct occlusion of the cusp of the teeth of one jaw with a corresponding impression in the occlusal surfaces of the teeth in the opposite jaw.

Interdigitation – Enclosure of the posterior teeth; the striking of the cusp of one denture fairly into the occluding surface of the other denture.

Interproximal – Between the proximal surfaces of the adjacent teeth.

Intraoral – Inside or within the mouth.

Ionization – The process of ionizing; use of an electric current to ionize medication within a root canal; used in treatment of sensitive teeth.

Jacket – A term commonly used in reference to an artificial crown composed of fired porcelain or acrylic resin, i.e., porcelain jacket crown, acrylic resin jacket crown.

Jaw – Either the maxilla or the mandible.

Jumpcase – See Denture Duplication.

Labial – Pertaining to the lips. It is the surface of an anterior tooth nearest the lips.

Labial Bar – The metal bar (major connector) used to connect the right and left side of a lower partial denture. It is contoured to the labial tissue anterior to the lower teeth.

Labiolingual – From the lips toward the tongue.

Lamina Dura – The inner bony wall of the tooth socket. It shows up as a fine white line around the root of a tooth in a dental x-ray.

Lateral (Incisor) – An anterior tooth located just distal to the central incisors; the second tooth from the midline.

Ligature Wire – A fine wire used to tie the main arch wire into the bracket of an orthodontic appliance on the bands or the teeth.

Lingual – Pertaining to the tongue; the surface of a tooth or prosthesis next to the tongue.

Lingual Bar – The metal bar (major connector) on the lingual surfaces of the teeth connecting the right and left sides of the lower partial denture. It is contoured to the lingual tissue behind and below the anterior teeth.

Luxation – Detachment of a tooth from its socket as a result of trauma or disease progress; may be partial or complete.

Macrodontia – Abnormally large teeth.

Macrognathia – Abnormally large jaws.

Malalignment – Displacement; not in normal alignment.

Malar Process – The bony extensions of the temporal and maxillary bones that unite with the zygomatic process to form the zygomatic arch; sometimes called the *cheekbone*.

Malocclusion – Any deviation from normal occlusion of the teeth, usually associated with abnormal development and growth of the jaws.

Mandible – The lower jaw.

Mandibular – Pertaining to the mandible.

Marginal Ridge – A ridge or elevation of enamel forming the edge of a surface of a tooth; specifically, one of the mesial or distal borders of the lingual surfaces of anterior teeth and the occlusal surfaces of posterior teeth.

Mastication – Chewing food at the first stage of digestion.

Maxilla – The bone of the skull that supports the upper teeth. Commonly, the term is used to name the upper jaw with its teeth when present, and associated with soft tissues.

Maxillae – The bones of the upper jaw.

Maxillary – Referring to the maxilla or upper arch.

Maxillofacial – Relates to the jaws and the face.

MDS – Master of Dental Science.

Median – The middle; situated or placed in the middle of the body or in the middle of a part of the body.

Megadontism – The condition that results in abnormally large teeth.

Mental Protuberance – A triangular elevation forming the prominence of the chin.

Mesial – The surface of a tooth which, in normal occlusion, is nearest the midline.

Mesioclusion – Occlusion of the teeth in which the mesial buccal cusp of the upper first molar interdigitates between the lower first and second molars.

Mesiodens – Accessory or supernumerary tooth which may be erupted or unerupted and located between the maxillary central incisors.

Mesiodistal – From mesial (the middle) to distal (farthest from).

Mesioversion – In the oral cavity, indicative of a closer than normal position to the median plane or midline of the jaw. When in reference to the maxilla or mandible, the jaw is anterior to its normal position.

Macrodontia – Abnormally small teeth.

Micrognathism – Abnormal smallness of jaws; lack of normal development.

Midline – The imaginary dividing line through the middle of an object or space.

Migration – The movement of a tooth or teeth out of the normal position. It is usually caused by loss of supporting structures.

Milk Teeth – Primary or deciduous teeth (named for their white or milky appearance).

Mineralize – The precipitation of calcium and other salts into an organic matrix to form a hard deposit such as dental calculus.

Mobility – The degree of looseness of a tooth as a result of loss of part or all of the attachments and supportive structures.

Molars – The three teeth in each quadrant that are located distal to the second bicuspids. They are used for grinding.

Morphology – The branch of biology that deals with structure and form. It includes the anatomy, histology, and cytology of the organisms at any stage of its life history.

Mottled Enamel – A dappled condition of the enamel of the teeth caused by ingestion of too high concentrations of fluorides or drugs such as tetracycline during the formative period.

Mucobuccal Fold – The junction between the cheek and the mucuous membrane of the upper or lower jaw.

Mucogingivoplastic Surgery – Procedures designed to correct or modify defects in the morphology and the position of the soft tissues surrounding the teeth.

Mucoperiosteum (Mucoperiosteal Tissue or Periosteum) – A layer of connective tissues that covers the outer surfaces of the bone. Periosteum in the oral cavity is covered with gingival tissue and is significant to periodontics.

Mucositis – Inflammation of the mucous membrane.

Mucous Membrane – The soft tissue covering or lining of the mouth.

Mulberry Molars – Congenitally malformed molars occ The occlusal surfaces are narrow and there is hypoplasia of the enamel.

Multirooted – A tooth with two or more roots.

Nasion – The part of the skull located at the midpoint of the nasofrontal suture at the root of the nose; the junction of the nasal bones with the frontal bone. It is a landmark in clinical prosthetics.

Neutroclusion – Occlusion of the teeth in which the mesiobuccal cusp of the upper first molar interdigitates with the buccal groove of the lower first molar.

Nitrous Oxide – A colorless gas used in dentistry as a general anesthetic with the performance of uncomplicated operations; also called *laughing gas* and *nitrogen monoxide*.

Non-precious Metals – Material developed for use in all types of restorative procedures that are less precious than gold and other precious metals.

Obturator – An appliance designed to fill in a cleft palate defect. It is usually held in place with clasps or splinted to the teeth.

Occlude – To close, specifically so that the cusps of the posterior teeth fit together.

Occlusal – The chewing or masticating surfaces of the bicuspids and molars.

    Balance – Contact relationship of the biting surfaces of the teeth; simultaneous contacts; equilibrium of mastication.

    Equilibration – The process of refining and perfecting the occlusion.

    Film – X-ray exposures made on larger films than those used for the periapical and bite wing exposures. The film is placed in the occlusal plane and held in position by the teeth in occlusion. It is used to augment the other exposures.

    Guard – A removable dental appliance usually constructed of acrylic resin, which covers one or both dental arches to protect the teeth from the damaging effects of bruxism and other occlusal habits.

    Rest – The part of a clasp that lies on the occlusal surface of the tooth.

    Surface – The grinding, chewing, or masticating surface of molars and bicuspids.

Odontalgia – Toothache.

Odontalysis – Examination of the teeth.

Odontectomy – Surgical extraction of a tooth.

Odontexesis – Cleaning of the teeth, including thorough scaling.

Odonthemodia – Treatment of sensitive teeth.

Odontinoid – A tumor composed of tooth substance.

Odontoblast – Connective tissue cells that line the surface of the dental pulp adjacent to the dentin. During the tooth development period, these cells have much to do with the formation of dentin.

Odontoma – An odontogenic tumor composed of enamel, dentin, cementum, and pulp tissue; an anomaly such as dens in dentes or enamel pearl.

Odontomy (Prophylatic Odontomy) – Surgical cutting into a tooth for removal of precarious pits and fissures, with subsequent restoration.

Odontrophia –Imperfect development of the teeth.

Onlay – A cast occlusal restoration that covers the entire incisal or occlusal surface of the tooth, frequently used to restore lost tooth structure and restore vertical dimension.

Opacity – The condition of being impervious to light.

Opaque – Not transparent; not letting light through.

Open Bite – A condition that prevents the anterior mandibular teeth from achieving proper occlusal relationship to the maxilla; more than the correct amount of jaw opening. Cause may be fractures, dislocations, abnormal tongue habits, or genetic or developmental abnormalities.

Operative Dentistry – The branch of dentistry primarily concerned with restoring carious, diseased, or damaged natural teeth to a satisfactory state of health.

Operculum – Cover or lid, such as a tissue over the crown of a tooth.

Oral – Pertaining to the mouth.

    Habit – A frequently repeated practice that may produce injury to the teeth and their attachments, the temporal mandibular musculature, or other structures. Oral habits include bruxism, tongue thrust, lip or cheek biting, and biting on hard objects.

    Hygiene – The laws of health as applied to the mouth.

    Pathology – The study of diseases of hard and soft tissues of the mouth.

    Surgery – The branch of surgery dealing with the operative procedures as related to the teeth and jaws.

Orthodontics – The branch of dentistry concerned with the detection, prevention, and correction of abnormalities in the positioning of the teeth in relationship to the jaws.

Orthodontist – A dentist who has met all the requirements to qualify as a specialist in the practice of orthodontics.

Orthopantomograph Film – An extraoral view of the teeth and associated structures on a single, continuous film. It is similar to a panorex film.

Osseous Tissue – Bone tissue.

Osseous Surgery (Periodontal) – Surgical correction or therapeutic treatment performed to eliminate bone deformities and create a more favorable environment; removal of diseased and defective bone tissue.

Ostectomy – The excision of bone; in periodontics, the excision of bone around the teeth or tooth roots to remove pockets or to provide a physiologic form.

Osteitis – Inflammation of the bone.

Overbite – Vertical overlap of the upper teeth over the lower teeth; overlapping of the mandibular incisors by maxillary incisors.

Overjet – See Overbite.

Overlay – An inlay or splint that fits over the biting or grinding surface of a tooth.

Palatal – Of or pertaining to the roof of the mouth.

Palatal Bone – The bone that forms the posterior portion of the hard palate.

Palate – The roof of the mouth, consisting of a hard anterior part and a soft moveable part. The palatal structures separate the mouth from the nasal cavity.

Palatine – Of or pertaining to the palate.

Palliative Treatment – Treatment that relieves pain or prevents a condition from becoming worse, but does not cure it.

Panoramic – A term applied to any one of several techniques for making an x-ray picture of all the teeth and contiguous structures on a single film.

Panorex – See X-ray.

Pantograph – An instrument used for occlusal tracing as a part of extensive equilibration.

Papilla – A small, nipple-shaped elevation or protuberance.

> **Intradental** – The gingiva filling the intradental spaces between the teeth. It is partly free and partly attached to the gingival tissues.

> **Of Tongue** – Finger-like elevations on the surface of the tongue i.e, taste buds).

Partial Denture – A prosthesis replacing one or more, but not all, natural teeth and associated structures; may be removable or fixed, unilateral, or bilateral.

PCP – Plaque Control Program.

Pedodontics – The specialty of childrens dentistry. It includes training the child to accept dentistry, restoring and maintaining the primary, mixed, and permanent dentitions, applying preventive measures for dental caries and periodontal disease, and preventing, intercepting, and correcting various problems of occlusion.

Peg Laterals – The lateral incisors that are peg-shaped due to a developmental disturbance.

Periapical – The tissues surrounding the apex of a tooth.

Pericoronal – The tissues surrounding the crown of a natural tooth.

Pericoronitis – Inflammation of the tissues over a partially erupted tooth or surrounding the crown of an erupted tooth. It frequently involves an erupting third molar, and there may be infection in the area.

Periodontal Membrane – The fibers between the alveolar bone and the tooth that holds the tooth in its socket; a modified periosteum.

Periodontics – The science of examination, diagnosis, and treatment of diseases affecting the periodontium.

Periodontitis – Inflammation of the periodontium that may cause alterations of the periodontal process. It may be caused by environmental or systematic factors.

Periodontium – Collectively, the tissues that surround and support the tooth.

Periodontoclasia – Condition characterized by inflammation accompanied by degenerative and retrogressive changes in the periodontium.

Periodontosis – Degeneration of the periodontium; a non-inflammatory condition. With resorption of the alveolar bone, loosening and migration of the teeth occur. It is a rare disease, usually occurring in young people.

Periosteum – A layer of connective tissue, which is a tough, fibrous membrane that covers the outer surface of all bone and varies in thickness in the different areas of the bone.

Permanent Teeth – The teeth that replace the primary teeth.

PFC – Porcelain face crown.

Pin Pontic – A pontic with a long pin porcelain facing. Metal pins are embedded in a porcelain facing and extend out of it lingually. The pins fit into a customized cast metal backing that finishes the occlusal surface.

Pinlay (Pinledge) – A thin cast inlay that depends in part on small parallel pins that fit into the prepared tooth for its retention. Pinledge crowns are modified three-quarter crowns gaining retention from cast pins.

Pit – An indentation; a depression.

Pivots – Elevations, usually artificially developed, on the occlusal surface of natural or artificial posterior teeth to induce mandibular rotation. The term may also be used in reference to dowel pins. Pivots may or may not be adjusted.

PJC – Porcelain jacket crown.

Plane – A term used to describe an ideal, flat surface, which intersects solid body and extends in various directions.

> **Axial** – A hypothetical plane that parallels the long axis of an object.

> **Bite** – An appliance that covers the palate and has an incline or flat plane at the anterior border. It provides resistance to the mandibular incisors when there is contact.

Occlusal – A plane established by the occlusal surfaces of the bicuspids and molars of both the upper and lower jaw in opposition. In orthodontics, a line between two points that represents one-half of the incisal overbite and one-half of the cusp height of the posterior molars.

Plaque – An accumulation of bacteria and debris on the tooth's surfaces.

Plastic – In dentistry, the capacity to be moved. A restorative material, i.e., amalgam, cement, gutta-percha, and resin, which is soft at the time of insertion and may be shaped or molded before it hardens or sets.

Plastic Fillings – See restorations.

Pocket – A space between the affected tooth and the diseased epithelium; diseased gingival tissues with resulting discoloration, retraction from the root, bleeding and presence of exudate. Depth of the pocket would be limited by the epithelial attachment at the apex of the root.

POH – Personal oral hygiene.

Polishing – The act of buffing and shining the teeth.

Pontic – The part of a fixed bridge that is suspended between abutments and replaces a missing tooth; an artificial tooth in a removable denture.

Porcelain – A tooth-colored, sand-like material; used for inlays, facings, crowns, pontics, and denture teeth. It fuses at high temperatures to form a hard substance much like enamel in appearance. Dental porcelain is a fuse mixture that is glass like.

Post – In partial denture work, the minor connector that attaches the clasp body to the framework; an upright, metal device that extends into a tube tooth to retain it; in restorative dentistry, a metal projection in crowns to give strength. It may extend into the root of a pulpless tooth, or it may extend through the root into the alveolar bone.

Post and Core – A single cast unit that provides strength and restores lost structure. It is placed into the tooth, followed by the permanent exterior restoration, usually a crown.

Postdam Area – The soft tissues along the junction of the hard and soft palate where pressures can be applied for retention of a denture. Special provision is designed into the denture for the purpose of sealing against the resilient soft tissue in the palate.

Posterior Teeth – All teeth located distal to the cuspids; a tooth having an occlusal surface.

Post-permanent Dentition – Teeth that erupt after the loss of permanent dentition. It is a rare condition and these teeth are usually impacted accessory teeth that erupt following the insertion of dentures.

Pre-deciduous Dentition – Teeth that precede the primary dentition. It is a rare condition in which teeth are present at birth or erupt after birth. They are not fully developed and consist only of enamel or enamel and dentin.

Premolars – Bicuspids.

Primary Stress Bearing Area – The area of the mouth that is suited to withstand heavy stress from wearing dentures.

Primary Teeth – The first teeth to erupt in childhood.

Primate Spaces – In primary dentition, spaces mesial to maxillary cuspids and distal to mandibular cuspids.

Process – In anatomy, a marked prominence or projection of bone. In dentistry, a series of operations that convert a waxed pattern of a dental appliance into a permanent restoration composed of some relatively indestructible material.

　Alveolar – The part of the bone that surrounds and supports the teeth in the maxilla and the mandible.

　Condyloid – The posterior process on the ramus of the mandible that articulates with the mandibular fossa of the temporal bone.

　Coronoid – The anterior part of the upper and ramus of the mandible, to which the temporal muscle is attached.

　Maxillary – The irregular-shaped bone forming one-half of the upper jaw. The upper jaw is made up of two maxillas.

Palatine – One of four shelf-like extensions of the embryonic upper jaw that gives rest to the pre-maxillary palate.

Prognathic - A protrusive relationship of the jaws to the head.

Prognathism – Facial disharmony due to prominence or projection of one or more jaws, occurring most frequently in the mandible.

Prophylactic Odontotomy – The technique of opening and filling structural imperfections of the enamel to prevent dental caries.

Prophylaxis – Prevention of disease by removal of calculus, stains, and other extraneous material from the teeth; cleaning of the teeth by a dentist or dental hygienist.

Prosthesis (plural, prostheses) – An artificial replacement of one or more natural teeth or associated structures; replacement of a part of the body.

Prosthetic – Pertaining to prostheses.

Prosthodontics – The branch of dentistry concerned with restoration and maintenance of function by replacement of natural teeth.

Provisional Splinting – A therapeutic appliance placed to assist with healing, repair, or cure. It may serve as a temporary stabilization for mobile teeth.

Proximal Surface – The surface of a tooth that is next to another tooth; usually, the mesial or distal surface, unless the tooth is rotated.

Pulp – Connective tissues, with nerves and blood vessels which fills the pulp chamber and root canals. "Vitality" of pulp refers to health of the pulp. When there is degeneration or the pulp has been removed, the tooth is termed non-vital.

Pulp Canal – See Root Canal.

Pulp Capping – See Capping.

Pulp Chamber –The space in the coronal portion of the tooth occupied by the pulp.

Pulpectomy – Complete removal of either vital or inflamed pulp from the chamber and the root canal. The term is not appropriate in reference to necrotic pulp tissue.

Pulpotomy – Removal of dental pulp in the coronal portion of the tooth; removal of exposed vital pulp to retain a healthy pulp in the root. It may be partial or complete.

Pyogenic – Pus-producing.

Pyorrhea – Flow of pus from the periodontal wound; an outdated term replaced by "periodontitis" or "periodontal disease."

Quadrant – One-fourth of the two dental arches; one-half of each arch.

Radectomy – Surgical removal of a part of a tooth root.

Radiculalgia – Neuralgia of the nerve roots.

Radicular – Pertaining to the tooth root.

Radiograph – A picture produced on a sensitive surface by a form of radiation other than light; an x-ray or gamma ray photograph. It produces a shadow image.

Ramus – The ascending part of the mandible from the angle to the condyle.

Reattachment – The re-adaptation of the gingival and underlying tissues to the root surface of a tooth.

Rebase – Placement of the denture base material without changing the occlusal relations of the teeth; adding to the denture base to compensate for altered tissues.

Re-calcifiacation – See Re-mineralization.

Reline – Resurface the tissue-borne areas of a denture with new material.

Re-mineralization – The use of calcium hydroxide or similar materials as a treatment prior to placing a temporary restoration.

Remote Denture – See Denture.

Replantation (Re-implantation) – The replacement of natural teeth that have been dislodged or removed, either accidentally or unintentionally; reinsertion of a natural tooth to the alveolar socket.

Resin – A term commonly used to indicate organic substances that may be solid or semi-solid, translucent or transparent. Resins are named according to their chemical composition, physical structure, and means for activation or curing. Examples are acrylic resin, autopolymer resin, synthetic resin, styrene resin, and vinyl resin.

Resorption – Loss of substance. Alveolar resorption is loss of substance or structure; reduction in size or residual alveolar ridges; destruction of bone. Primary tooth roots are reabsorbed as a part of normal shedding.

Rest – An extension of the prosthesis that provides support.

Restoration – Restoring natural or ideal contour and function. The term relates to fillings, inlays, crowns, bridgework, partial and complete dentures, and restoration of contour and function as a result of disease and other factors.

Retained Root – A root or part of a root; remaining soft or hard tissue.

Retainer – An abutment tooth in a fixed bridge that may be in the form of an inlay or a partial or full crown; a removable prosthesis, a clasp, attachment, or device used for fixation or stabilization. In orthodontics, an appliance to maintain the altered position of the teeth and jaws until they stabilize.

Retention – In removable prostheses, a resistance to force or movement. In orthodontics, an appliance used to maintain teeth in the position to which they have been moved for harmonious relationship. The necessary procedure in cavity preparation to prevent loss or displacement of a restoration.

Retrognathism – A disharmony as a result of one or both jaws being posterior to normal facial relationships.

Retrograde Amalgam – Amalgam filling placed into the apex of a tooth root; also called *retrofilm* or *reverse amalgam*. It would normally follow some form of endodontic therapy.

Retroversion – Indicated teeth or associated structures that are posterior to the generally accepted standard.

Ridge Bar – A splint or lingual bar that connects abutments.

Roach Clasp – See Clasp.

Root – The anatomic part of a tooth, normally within the alveolar bone, and attached to it by the periodontal ligament.

Root Amputation – Removal of one or more roots of a multirooted tooth. Also, see Apicoectomy.

Root Canal – The space within the root of the tooth, containing nerves and blood vessels. They connect the pulp chamber with the apex of the root.

Root Canal Therapy – Endodontic therapy; treatment of a tooth having a damaged pulp, or associated with periapical disease. It is normally performed by completely removing the pulp, sterilizing the pulp chamber and root canals, and filling those spaces with a sealing material.

Root Planning – The smoothing of roughened root surfaces by the use of scalers and curets.

Root Resection – Removal of all or part of the tooth root. See Root Amputation.

Rotated Teeth – Teeth rotated out of normal position. The laterals and bicuspids are the most frequently rotated.

Rugae – The irregular ridges in the mucous membrane covering the anterior part of the hard palate.

Saliva – The digestive secretions from the salivary glands into the mouth. It assists in chewing and preparing the food for digestion by moistening the food and lubricating the mouth. It initiates digestion of starches; it aids in excretion of waste products and regulation of water balance.

Sanitary Pontic – A conical-shaped pontic that has been contoured to provide a sanitary environment.

Scale – To remove calculus (tartar) and stains from the teeth with a scaler and other special instruments.

Sealer – A material used to fill the space around the silver or gutta-percha points as part of root canal therapy.

Secondary Dentin – Dentin formed on the inner walls of the pulp cavity after the tooth is fully formed; a protective mechanism whereby the pulp seeks to protect itself from injury. It may be the result of disturbances or irritation and stimulation of the odontoblasts.

Secondary Stress-Bearing Area – An area of the mouth not suited for bearing a major part of the pressure under a denture; a relief area in an upper denture.

Sedative – Drugs or any other means of producing a calming effect.

Semiprecious – Materials developed for dental restorations that have a lesser amount of precious metal.

Semiridge Bridge (Broken Stress Bridge) – A fixed bridge in which one of the connections between the units is composed of a male/female joint that reduces the effect of stress.

Septic Alveolus (Dry Socket) – Pain from breakdown or loss of the blood clot from a tooth socket following extraction.

Shell Crowns – See Crowns.

Shell Teeth – Teeth having a form or dentinogenesis imperfecta; lack of root development and the pulp chambers are wider than normal.

Sialolithiasis – Salivary gland or duct stones.

Sialolithotomy – Incisions of a salivary gland or duct to remove stones.

Silica – One of the three major ingredients in dental porcelain; provides stiffness and hardness.

Sinus – A cavity, a canal or passage, recess or hollow space.

> **Alveolar** –A pathologic cavity in the alveolus connecting with either the oral or nasal cavity.
>
> **Maxillary** – The bony cavity in the body of the maxilla. In dental x-rays, the floor of the sinus may be seen above the alveolar process. Occasionally, the apices of the teeth including the cuspids and posterior teeth may extend into the sinus.

Sinusotomy – Incision into a sinus cavity.

Socket – An alveolus in the alreolar process that holds the roots of a tooth.

Sodium Fluoride – A solution applied topically to the teeth and used in drinking water as a caries preventive agent; also used with kaolin and glycerin as a desensitizing agent for hypersensitive dentin.

Space Maintainer – A fixed removable appliance placed to maintain space created by the premature loss of one or more teeth. It may also be used to create space by moving teeth apart while holding the space open.

Space Obtainer – An appliance used to increase the space between two teeth.

Space Regainer – A fixed removable appliance to move a displaced tooth into proper position; commonly used for the first premature molar.

Splint – An appliance constructed of metal, acrylic resin, or modeling compound, designed to retain teeth in position.

> **Acrylic resin biteguard** – An appliance for immobilizing teeth, eliminating the effect of traumatic oral habits by covering the occlusal and incisal surfaces of the dental arch.
>
> **Cross-arch bar** – A metal bar that united one or more teeth in one side of the arch to teeth on the opposite side; also used to stabilize weakened teeth against lateral forces.
>
> **Fixed** – A fixed prosthesis used for treatment of periodontal disease, designed to prevent adverse occlusal forces and maintenance of good gingival health. It stabilizes and immobilizes the teeth and may also replace missing teeth.
>
> **Gunning's** – A maxillomandibular splint used with maxillofacial surgery.
>
> **Inlay** – A casting to provide retention or support to one or more approximating teeth. This may include two inlays soldered together or a single casting spanning the approximating teeth.
>
> **Intradental** – A splint applied to the teeth on the labial and/or lingual surfaces to provide points for attaching mandibular and/or maxillofacial traction and/or fixation.
>
> **Provisional** – A therapeutic appliance designed to assist in healing, repair, and cure of periodontally involved teeth. It is semifixed and may consist of full crowns to stabilize the teeth during the mandibular movements. Materials used are acrylic resin, metal, and combinations of both.
>
> **Surgical** – A thin acrylic or metal form that fits the contour of the alveolar ridge and is used after surgery. The function is to protect the surgical area during healing.

Splinting – Stabilizing or immobilization of periodontally involved teeth. Splinting may be accomplished with acrylic resin biteguards, orthodontic band splints, wire ligation, provisional splints, and fixed prostheses.

Stannous Acid Fluoride – A more recently developed form of fluoride, applied topically in a single treatment.

Stayplate (Flipper) – An acrylic partial, with or without wire clasps, which replaces one or more teeth; used as a temporary replacement until a more permanent prosthesis is prepared.

Steele's Facing – A pontic having a prefabricated backing combined with an acrylic or porcelain grooved facing.

Stressbreaker – An attachment that is incorporated into a removable partial denture or fixed bridge work to relieve pressure on the abutment teeth.

Study Models – See Diagnostic Casts.

Subgingival Curettage – See Gingival Curettage.

Supernumerary Tooth – A tooth in excess of the regular or normal number.

Supraocclusion – Abnormal overlap of a dental arch or group of teeth over the opposing arch or group of teeth.

Surfaces – Tooth surfaces.

    Buccal – Pertaining to or adjacent to the cheek.

    Distal – Away from the median plane of the face, following the curvature of the dental arch.

    DLG – The distal lingual groove, which normally extends to the occlusal.

    E – The external gingival surface.

    Facial – The same as labial or buccal, external surface or next to the face.

    Incisal – Cutting surface of the anterior teeth.

    Labial – Same as facial, but toward the mouth and lips.

    Lingual – Pertaining to or adjacent to the tongue.

    Mesial –Toward the center of the median line of the dental arch.

    Occlusal – The masticating or grinding surfaces of molars and bicuspids.

    Proximal – The surface nearest the adjacent tooth.

Tartar – See Calculus.

Temporal Bone – The irregular-shaped bone at the side and base of the skull.

Temporomandibular Joint – The joint formed by the condyle for the mandible and the temporal bone.

TMJ Syndrome (Costen's Syndrome) – The symptoms associated with malfunction of the temporomandibular joint, frequently caused by loss of molar support or absence of occlusal balance.

Three-Quarter Crown – See Crowns.

Tinker Bridge – A fixed bridge involving the use of sanitary pontics.

Tissue Bar – A lingual bar connecting crowns for the purpose of stabilizing or reducing stress. They are placed adjacent to the gingival tissues.

Tissue-borne – A partial denture is referred to as a "tissue-borne" when most or all of the masticatory stresses are borne by the soft tissues of the mouth.

Tissue Conditioning – A method of correcting tissue irritation occurring from the wearing of dentures. An impression-type material is placed in the saddle of the denture and, with the denture in place, a displacement of this material indicates any corrections necessary to eliminate distortion from pressure on the tissue. This procedure is more complicated than the usual adjustment.

Tooth-borne – A partial denture is referred to as "tooth-borne" when most or all of the masticatory forces are carried by the abutment teeth.

Traumatogenic Occulsion – A malocclusion that is injurious to the teeth or associated structures; an injury in the periodontal tissues produced by an occlusal pressure.

Treatment Partial Denture – A denture used for a limited time during the transition from normal dentition to complete dentures. It may be the same or similar to a stayplate, thumbplate, splitplate, or butterfly partial, which is also known as a *flipper*. It may be used during a healing period or for esthetics before a permanent denture is constructed.

Trial Baseplate – The temporary foundation used in established maxillomandibular relationship for arrangement of the teeth in a denture, consisting of the baseplate and the occlusal rim.

Trifurcation – The area where roots divide into a tri-rooted tooth.

Truss Bar – The metal piece placed across the edentulous space between two bridge abutments, on which the pontic is constructed.

Tube Tooth – An artificial tooth containing a vertical channel in which a pin or metal post is placed to secure the tooth to a denture base.

Tuberosity – The posterior aspect of the maxillary alveolar process. It may appear as a normal bone carving upward, or it may be in the form of a bridge.

Unerupted Tooth – Tooth that has not broken through the bone or gingival tissue.

Vault – In the oral cavity, the palate or roof of the mouth; a prepared cavity in the bone for placing an implant.

Veneer Crown – See Crowns.

Vertical Dimension – The vertical height of the face with the teeth in occlusion; vertical relationship; the degree of jaw separation when teeth are in contact. This measurement is usually made from the tip of the chin to the base of the nose.

Vestibular Space – Space in the oral cavity bounded by the teeth and gums and externally by the lips and cheeks.

Vestibule – The part of the oral cavity that lies between the teeth and the gingiva or between the residual alveolar ridge and the lips and cheeks.

Vestibuloplasty – Revision of the vestibule; frequently performed to accommodate the placing of dentures.

Vitality – Presence of vital dental pulp in the mouth.

Vitality Test – A test using thermal electrical or mechanical stimuli to determine the vitality of the dental pulp.

X-ray – Roentgen-ray; called x-ray by the discoverer because of its enigmatic character. It has also been named roentgen-ray to honor Dr. Wilhelm C. Roentgen and to identify this form of radiation. The term x-ray is more commonly used.

Bitewing – Both upper and lower teeth shown on one film.

Extraoral – Film held outside the mouth and recording larger areas than is possible with smaller film; used to detect cysts and tumors and used with orthodontic treatment.

Full Mouth – Usually consists of 14 periapical films plus bitewings.

Occlusal – An intraoral film showing the lingual surfaces of the teeth in a portion of the palate.

Panorex – An extraoral film that provides a continuous view of the teeth and associated structures. It is used for orthodontics and for detection of fractures, temporomandibular joint disease, cysts, and tumors. It is also taken with the unit having a swinging arm that moves from one side of the arch to the other.

Periapical – So named because it records the entire tooth including the apex of the root and some of the surrounding bone tissues.

X-ray Film – A shadowy negative that provides a means of diagnostic evaluation.

Summary

We have covered some of the common prefixes, suffixes, terms, and procedures that you will see frequently see when processing dental charges. Familiarize yourself with these; by doing so you will be able to correctly identify dental services and procedures and determine whether the services are a covered dental benefit.

Assignments

Complete the Questions for Review.
Complete Exercises 27 – 1 to 27 – 5.

Questions for Review

Directions: Define the following prefixes, suffixes, and terms without looking back into the material just covered. Write your answers in the space provided.

Prefixes and Suffixes

1. mal- _____

2. pex- _____

3. –itis _____

4. labi - _____

5. arthr- _____

6. –desis _____

7. gloss- _____

8. –antr _____

9. lingu- _____

10. bucc- _____

Terms:

11. Anesthetics_____

_____

12. Plane _____

_____

13. Abrasion _____

_____

14. Abutment _____

_____

15. Pontic _____

_____

16. Rebase _____

_____

17. Bridge _____

18. Bruxism _____

_____

19. Caries _____

_____

20. Plaque _____

_____

21. Impacted Tooth _____

_____

22. Maxilla _____

_____

23. Median _____
_____

24. Onlay _____
_____

25. Splint _____
_____

If you were unable to answer any of the questions, refer back to the section and then complete the answers.

Exercise 27 – 1

Directions: Match each term in each column 1 with the term in column 2 that is closest to its meaning without looking back in the text. Write your answer in the space provided.

	Column 1	Column 2		Column 1	Column 2
_____	1. Calculus	A. Gum	_____	1. fistul-	A. Falling
_____	2. Primary	B. Cleaning	_____	2. –pexy	B. Tongue
_____	3. Cuspid	C. Composite	_____	3. retro-	C. In front of, before
_____	4. Radiograph	D. Top	_____	4. ante-	D. Development
_____	5. Resin	E. Premolar	_____	5. –ectomy	E. A way of
_____	6. Caries	F. Tartar	_____	6. pan-	F. Jaw
_____	7. Bridgework	G. Bad Breath	_____	7. –trophy	G. Duct, tube
_____	8. Bicuspid	H. Groove	_____	8. cid-	H. Surgical removal
_____	9. Pulp Canal	I. Deciduous	_____	9. –ology	I. Half
_____	10. Crown	J. X-Ray	_____	10. lingu-	J. Pipe, tube
_____	11. Prophylaxis	K. Canine	_____	11. gnath-	K. Study of
_____	12. Gingiva	L. Removal	_____	12. top-	L. Suspension, fixation
_____	13. Fissure	M. Cavities	_____	13. doch-	M. All
_____	14. Extraction	N. Root Canal	_____	14. hemi-	N. Backward
_____	15. Halitosis	O. Partial denture	_____	15. –ment	O. Place

If you were unable to answer any of the questions, refer back to the section and then complete the answers.

Exercise 27 – 2

Directions: Define the following prefixes and suffixes without looking back into the text. Write your answer in the space provided.

1. apex- _____
   _____

2. dys- _____
   _____

3. –ostomy _____
   _____

4. infra- _____
   _____

5. –vulse _____
   _____

6. stom- _____
   _____

7. –lysis _____
   _____

8. end- _____
   _____

9. fren- _____
   _____

10. calc- _____
    _____

11. bucc- _____
    _____

12. labi- _____
    _____

13. –itis _____
    _____

14. odont- _____
    _____

15. –plasia _____
    _____

If you were unable to answer any of the questions, refer back to the section and then complete the answers.

Exercise 27 – 3

Directions: Fill in the correct dental term in the space provided without looking back in the text. Write your answer in the space provided.

_____   1. A dental restoration shaped to the form of a cavity and then inserted and secured with cement.

_____   2. Tissues surrounding the apex of a tooth.

_____   3. Doctor of Dental Medicine.

_____   4. A collection of pus in a cavity formed within the tissue of the body.

_____   5. Any deviation from normal occlusion of the teeth, usually associated with abnormal development and growth of the jaws.

_____   6. Pertaining to the mouth.

_____   7. The joint formed by the condyle for the mandible and the temporal bone.

_____   8. The hard, calcified tissue that covers the anatomic root of a tooth. It is formed by cementoblast and arranged in layers that cover the root dentin.

_____   9. Doctor of Dental Surgery.

_____   10. An accumulation of bacteria and debris on the tooth's surfaces.

_____   11. American Dental Association.

_____   12. Complete removal of either vital or inflamed pulp from the chamber and root canal. The term is not appropriate in reference to necrotic pulp tissue.

_____   13. The three teeth in each quadrant that are located distal to the second bicuspids and are used for grinding.

_____   14. The branch of dentistry concerned with restoration and maintenance of function by replacement of natural teeth.

_____   15. The anatomic part of the tooth, normally with the alveolar bone, and attached to it by the periodontal ligament.

If you were unable to answer any of the questions, refer back to the section and then complete the answers.

Exercise 27 – 4

Directions: Define the following terms in the space provided without looking back in the text. Write your answer in the space provided.

1. Crown: _____

   _____

2. Fluoride: _____

   _____

3. Intraoral: _____

   _____

4. Prophylaxis: _____

   _____

5. Bilateral: _____

_____

6. Amalgam: _____

_____

7. Quadrant: _____

_____

8. Space maintainer: _____

_____

9. Endodontics: _____

_____

10. Full-mouth x-ray: _____

_____

11. Partial denture: _____

_____

12. Root canal: _____

_____

13. Overbite: _____

_____

14. Mucous membrane: _____

_____

15. Primary teeth: _____

_____

If you were unable to answer any of the questions, refer back to the section and then complete the answers.

Honors Certification™

The Honors Certification™ challenge for this chapter is a written test of the information contained within this chapter. Each incorrect answer will result in a deduction of between 1% and 5% from your grade. You must achieve a score of 85% or higher to pass this test. If you fail the test on your first attempt you may retake the test one additional time. The items included in the second test may be different from those in the first test

Table 27-1: Dental Prefixes and Suffixes

Prefix/Suffix	Meaning
ab-	away from, not
-al	pertaining to
-algia	pain
alveol-	tooth socket
an-, a	without, not
ante-	in front of, before
antr-	cavity
apic, apex	tip of the root, top
arthr-	joint
auto-	self
bi-	two
benign	mild, not cancerous
bucc-	cheek
calc-	stone
-centesis	punctured
cephal-	head
cervic-	neck
cid-	falling
condyle	knob on the end of a bone
cut-	skin
de-	down from
dent-	teeth
-desis	binding, fixation
doch-	duct, tube
dys-	bad
-ectomy	surgical removal
en-	in
end-	inside, within
esthesia	sensation
ex-	out, from
fistul-	pipe, tube
fistule	pipe, tube
fren-	fold of skin
frenul-	fold of skin
gemin-	twin, double
gen-	originate, produce
gingiv-	gum
gloss-	tongue
gnath-	jaw
grad-	step, stage
gram-	record
hemi-	half
hyper-	above, more than normal, excessive
hypo-	under, beneath, deficient
infra-	beneath, below
inter-	between
intra-	within
-ist	one who practices
-it is	inflammation
labi-	lip
later-	side
lig-	tie
lingu-	tongue

Prefix/Suffix	Meaning
lith-	stone
-lysis	loosening, set free, destruction
macr-, macro-	large
mal-	bad
malign-	bad
mandibul-	lower jaw
maxillo-	upper jaw
menisci-	pad, disc
-ment	a way of
micr-	small
myel-	marrow, spinal cord
neo-	new
occlud, occlus-	close
odont-	tooth
-odyn-	pain
-ologist	a specialist in the study of
-ology	study of
or-	mouth
os-, oss-	bone
ost-, oste-	bone
-osis	any condition
-ostomy	create a new opening/passageway
-otomy	cut into, incision
palat-	roof of mouth
pan-	all
parotid	near the ear
path-	disease
peri-	about, around
-pexy	suspension, fixation
physio-	nature
-plasia	developing, development
plast-	plastic repair
post-	behind, in back of
pre-	in front of, before
pro-	in front of, before
pulp	juicy tissue
quadr-	four
radi-	ray
radic-	root
retro-	backward
sial-	saliva
sinus	hollow space
stom-, stomat-	mouth, opening
sub-	under, beneath, below
temporal	on side of skull
top-	place
trans-	through, across, beyond
traum-	wound, injury
tri-	three
-trophy	development
uni-	one
vestibul-	entrance
-vulse	twitch, pull
zygomatic/malar	cheekbone

28 Anatomy and Physiology of the Mouth

In this chapter you will learn:

- To name the parts of the tooth and its supporting structures.
- To identify the teeth by number and location.
- The difference between primary and permanent teeth.

Key words and concepts you will learn in this chapter:

Alveolar Process – The portion of the mandible or maxilla that contains the tooth socket.

Ankyloglossia – A shortened frenulum of the tongue, preventing proper movement of the tongue.

Cheilitis – Inflammation of the lips.

Cheiloschisis – A deep grove in the lip. It is also known as a harelip or a cleft lip.

Cleft Palate – A deep fissure of the palate. It may involve the soft palate, the hard palate, the lip, or all three.

Complex Cavities – Involve three or more surfaces of a tooth.

Compound Cavities – Involve two surfaces of a tooth.

Cuspids (Canines) – Are located behind the incisors. They are used for tearing and piercing. The normal adult has four, one behind each set of incisors.

Deciduous Teeth (Primary Teeth) – Number to 20 and apply to children. These lettered rather than numbered to avoid confusion with the adult numbering system.

Incisors – Are located at the front of the mouth and have a sharp edge that is used for biting. The normal adult has eight incisors, four on the top and a matching set of four on the bottom.

Gingivitis – Inflammation of the gums. It may include swelling, redness, pain, bleeding, or difficulty in chewing. Possible causes are improper dental hygiene, dentures or dental appliances that fit improperly, or improper occlusion (closure) of the teeth. Occasionally, gingivitis accompanies upper respiratory infections or diseases such as scurvy or metallic poisioning.

Gum (Gingiva) – The firm but soft tissue that surrounds the alveolar process and the mandibular and maxillary bones.

Hard Palate – Along with the soft palate form the roof of the mouth. It is located toward the front and is so named because it is a hard, bony structure. It is formed by portions of the maxillary and palatine bones.

Mandible – The lower jaw that is non-fixed (movable), which allows for not only biting and chewing food, but for speech, vocalization (speech and sound), and opening and closing the mouth.

Maxilla – The upper fixed (non-movable) bone. It is actually made up of two maxillae, which form the skeletal base of most of the upper face, the roof of the mouth, the sides of the nasal cavity and the floor of the orbit (the portion of the skull that contains and protects the eyeball).

Molars (Tricuspids) – Are located behind the premolars and have three cusps.

Mouth – Primarily responsible for the introduction of air, food, and other substances into the body.

Mucus – A liquid containing mucin, leukocytes, inorganic salts, epithelial cells and water.

Oral Cavity (Cavum Oris) – An oval-shaped cavity.

Papillae – Tiny nipple-like protuberances.

Periodontitis – Inflammation of the periodontal tissues. It may be caused by bacteria, calcium deposits, or food particles that collect between the tooth and the gum. If not treated, the infection may spread to the bone, possibly causing loss of teeth. Periodontitis is the primary cause of tooth loss in people over the age of 35 years old.

Periodontosis – Any degenerative disease of the periodontal tissue.

Premolars (Bicuspids) – Are located behind the cuspids and have two (bi-) cusps or grinding protrusions.

Saliva – Consists of salivary amylase and mucus.

Salivary Amylase – An enzyme that helps to break down food molecules.

Sialodentitis – Inflammation of a salivary gland.
Simple Cavities – Involve only one surface of a tooth.
Soft Palate – Along with the hard palate form the roof of the mouth. It is located in the rear portion of the mouth and is composed mostly of muscle.
Stomatitis – Inflammation of the mouth. This can include cold sores, fever blisters, or canker sores.
Taste Buds – Sensory end organs that help carry the sensation of taste to the brain.
Temporomandibular Joint – A sliding joint that hinges the lower and upper jaw together.
Tongue – A muscular organ that lays on the floor of the mouth and continues partway into the pharynx.
Vestibule – The outer, smaller portion surrounded by the lips, cheeks, gums and teeth.

Dentists provide services not only for teeth, but also for their surrounding and supporting structures. Therefore, it is necessary for the Dental Claims Examiner to understand the structure and formation of the entire oral cavity or mouth.

The Oral Cavity

The **oral cavity** (cavum oris) is an oval-shaped cavity (see **Figure 28-1**). Technically, it consists of two parts, the vestibule and the mouth cavity. The **vestibule** is the outer, smaller portion surrounded by the lips, cheeks, gums and teeth. The mouth cavity consists of the area surrounded by the alveolar arches and the teeth. In other words, the vestibule is the area between the teeth and the cheek or the teeth and the lips, and the mouth cavity is everything inside the teeth. The oral cavity stops at the lips in front, the palate on the top, the cheeks on the sides, the tongue on the bottom, and the oropharynx at the back. The oral cavity does not include the nose, the sinuses, the palates, the nasopharynx, or the laryngopharynx.

The **mouth** is primarily responsible for the introduction of air, food, and other substances into the body. It is also used for vocalization and speech. The opening of the mouth is connected to the pharynx and the larynx at the back of the mouth.

The process of digestion is begun immediately when food enters the mouth. The teeth break down the food by chewing. In addition, salivary glands secret saliva, which helps to chemically break down foods and the glands also provides moisture to the mouth.

Saliva and Salivary Glands

Saliva consists of salivary amylase and mucus. **Salivary amylase** is an enzyme that helps to break down food molecules. **Mucus** is a liquid containing mucin, leukocytes, inorganic salts, epithelial cells and water. It is secreted by the mucus membranes and glands that line the mouth. The purpose of mucus is to moisten the food and ease the friction as it passes down the esophagus and into the stomach.

Three main pairs of salivary glands supply saliva to the mouth: the parotids, the submandibulars, and the sublinguals. The parotid gland is located beneath the temporomandibular joint, just in the front of the ear. Saliva is conveyed to the mouth by the parotid duct. The opening of the parotid duct is on the inside of the cheek, across from the second molar; it can be felt with the tongue.

The submandibular glands are located under the mandible, below the bottom molars. The sublingual gland is located below the floor of the mouth. Both the submandibular glands and the sublingual glands secrete saliva through duct openings on the floor of the mouth under the tongue.

The Palates

The hard and soft palates form the roof of the mouth. The **hard palate** is toward the front and is so named because it is a hard, bony structure. It is formed by portions of the maxillary and palatine bones. The **soft palate** is in the rear portion of the mouth and is composed mostly of muscle. The purpose of the soft palate is to prevent foods or liquids from entering the nasal cavity. The opening of the nasal cavity is directly behind the soft palate. The soft palate is aided in this endeavor by the **uvula**, the small muscular projection that is suspended in the center, posterior portion of the mouth.

The Tongue

Although the tongue is generally not treated under dental services, it is helpful to understand its basic function and how it relates to the surrounding structures in the mouth. The **tongue** is a muscular organ that lays on the floor of the mouth and continues partway into the pharynx. The tongue consists of a body and a root. The body of the tongue resides in the mouth, and the root extends down into the pharynx. Its purpose is to assist in the chewing and swallowing of food and the formation of speech and other sounds.

The surface of the tongue is covered with mucus membrane. Mucus membrane also attaches the tongue to the floor of the mouth, the side walls of the pharynx, and the epiglottis. In addition, the tongue is attached by muscles to the mandibular bone in front, the hyoid bone below, the styloid process behind, and the palate (roof of the mouth) above. A fold (frenulum linguae) runs down the center of the tongue. In addition, the **frenulum** is a mucous membrane that connects the tongue to the floor of the mouth. There is also a frenulum of the upper and lower lip, which are mucus membranes connecting the lips to the maxilla and mandible.

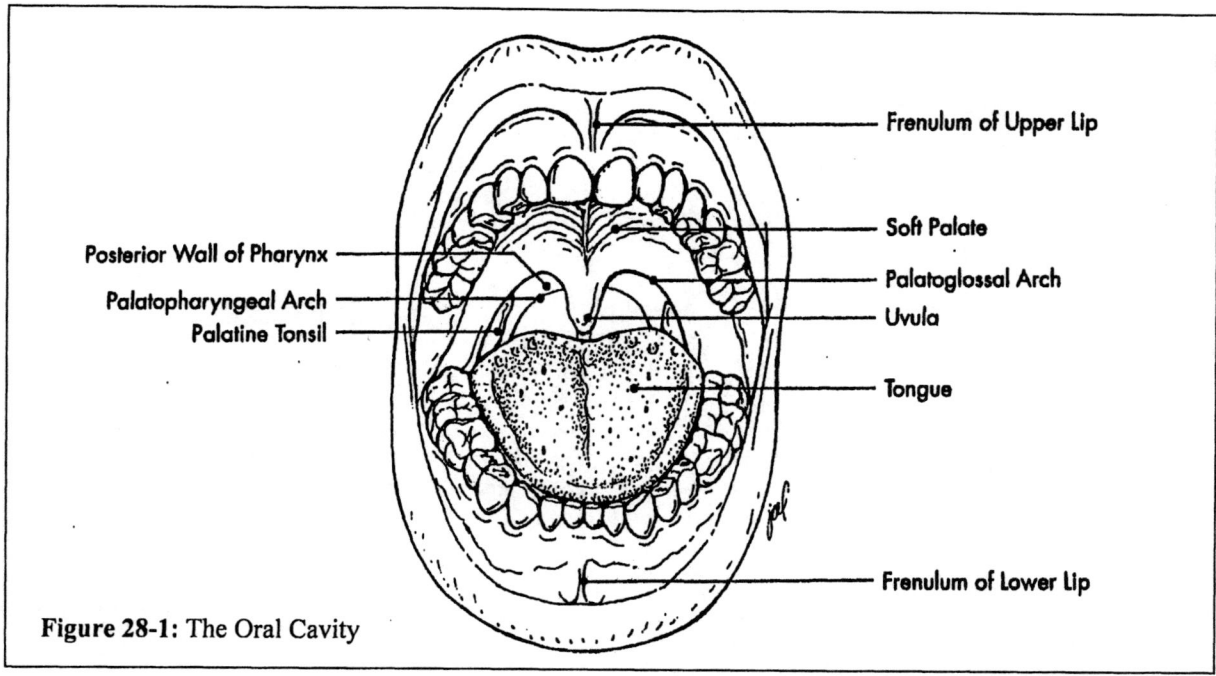

Figure 28-1: The Oral Cavity

Papillae
The surface of the tongue is covered with **papillae** (tiny nipple-like protuberances), which consist of several types:

Filiform papillae are very slender and are situated at the end of the tongue.

Fungiform papillae are broad and flat papillae and resemble a fungus. They are found mostly in the rear central portion of the tongue.

Circumvallate papillae are the large bumps found near the base of the tongue, at the back of the mouth. They are arranged in a V shape.

Gustatory papillae possess a taste bud. They may be either filiform, fungi form, or circumvallate. Not all papillae contain taste buds at any given time.

Taste buds are sensory end organs that help carry the sensation of taste to the brain. They are located on the sides of papillae and on the epiglottis, the soft palate, and portions of the pharynx. When chemical stimuli (such as food) comes in contact with the taste buds, they produce nervous impulses that are carried by means of the lingual and glossopharyngeal nerves to the brain. This produces one of the **four basic taste sensations:** sweet, bitter, sour, and salty.

The lingual nerves carry nerve impulses from the taste buds on the front two-thirds of the tongue. The gloss pharyngeal nerves carry nerve impulses from the posterior one-third of the tongue. The average life span of a taste bud cell is about 10 days. They are constantly dying off and being replaced by new taste bud cells.

The Gums
The **gum,** or **gingiva,** is the firm but soft tissue that surrounds the alveolar process and the mandibular and maxillary bones. It also covers the connecting area between the teeth and bone, thus helping to keep out food particles and bacteria as well as to keep the teeth in place. The gingiva is made up of connective tissue that is covered by mucus membrane.

The **alveolar process** is the portion of the mandible or maxilla that contains the tooth socket. The word *alveolar* comes from the Latin word meaning "small hollow or cavity."

Normal healthy gums are pink, but they may become red, white, or black when injured or diseased.

The Jaw

The jaw consists of two bones. The upper fixed (non-movable) bone is the **maxilla.** It is actually made up of two maxillae, which form the skeletal base of most of the upper face, the roof of the mouth, the sides of the nasal cavity and the floor of the orbit (the portion of the skull that contains and protects the eyeball).

The lower jaw is called the **mandible.** The lower jaw is non-fixed (movable), which allows for not only biting and chewing food, but for speech, vocalization (speech and sound), and opening and closing the mouth. The lower jaw is hinged to the upper jaw by a sliding joint called the **temporomandibular joint.** The temporomandibular joint is the only joint in the skull that is synovial, that is, containing synovia.

Synovia is a colorless liquid that lubricates the joints, bursae, and tendon sheaths; it is secreted from synovial membranes. Synovial joints are prone to irritation and inflammation. They are also associated with arthritis, rheumatic fever, and other connective tissue disorders, emotional states, and malocclusional disorders.

Because of the complexity of the problems and the various forms of treatments (many still experimental), disorders of the temporomandibular joint (more often called temporomandibular joint dysfunction or TMJ) are often regarded as a combined medical and dental problem. For further information regarding this disorder, see the **Temporomandibular Joint Disorder** chapter.

Diseases of the Mouth

Following is a list of the more common diseases of the mouth that may require the services of a dentist:

Gingivitis – Inflammation of the gums. It may include swelling, redness, pain, bleeding, or difficulty in chewing. Possible causes are improper dental hygiene, dentures or dental appliances that fit improperly, or improper **occlusion** (closure) of the teeth. Occasionally, gingivitis accompanies upper respiratory infections or diseases such as scurvy or metallic poisioning.

Periodontitis – Inflammation of the periodontal tissues. It may be caused by bacteria, calcium deposits, or food particles that collect between the tooth and the gum. If not treated, the infection may spread to the bone, possibly causing loss of teeth. Periodontitis is the primary cause of tooth loss in people over the age of 35 years old.

Periodontosis – Any degenerative disease of the periodontal tissue.

The following are also diseases of the mouth. However, since they are generally treated by a medical doctor rather than a dentist, they will be given only brief mention here.

Stomatitis – Inflammation of the mouth. This can include cold sores, fever blisters, or canker sores.

Cheilitis – Inflammation of the lips.

Cheiloschisis – A deep grove in the lip. It is also known as a harelip or a cleft lip.

Cleft palate – A deep fissure of the palate. It may involve the soft palate, the hard palate, the lip, or all three.

Ankyloglossia – A shortened frenulum of the tongue, preventing proper movement of the tongue.

Sialodentitis – Inflammation of a salivary gland.

The Teeth

Humans have four types of teeth: incisors, canines, premolars, and molars (**Figure 28 - 2**). Canines are referred to as cuspids, with premolars called bicuspids and molars tricuspids. The premolars and molars are considered the posterior teeth, and the incisors and canines are anterior teeth.

Incisors are located at the front of the mouth and have a sharp edge that is used for biting. The normal adult has eight incisors, four on the top and a matching set of four on the bottom.

Behind the incisors are the cuspids. **Cuspids** or **canines** are used for tearing and piercing, and the normal adult has four, one behind each set of incisors. Behind the cuspids are the **premolars** (bicuspids), which have two (bi-) cusps or grinding protrusions. Behind those are the **molars** (tricuspids), which have three cusps. The normal adult has eight premolars (two behind each canine) and twelve molars. However, the third molars, or wisdom teeth, may never appear (erupt).

Numbering the Teeth

The normal adult has 32 teeth. Accordingly, these teeth are numbered 1 through 32, beginning with the third molar on the upper-right side of the mouth (see **Figure 28-3**). The upper teeth are the maxillary teeth, numbers 1 through 16. The lower teeth are the mandibular teeth, numbers 17 through 32.

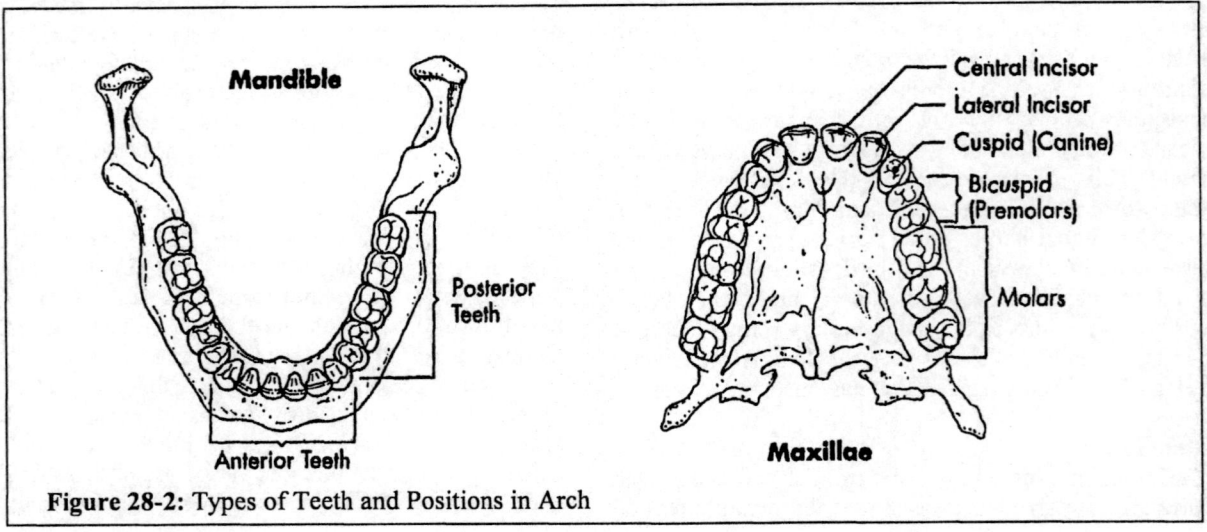

Figure 28-2: Types of Teeth and Positions in Arch

Tooth	Maxillary Teeth	Tooth	Mandibular Teeth
1	Right third molar	17	Left third molar
2	Right second molar	18	Left second molar
3	Right first molar	19	Left first molar
4	Right second premolar	20	Left second premolar
5	Right first premolar	21	Left first premolar
6	Right canine	22	Left canine
7	Right lateral incisor	23	Left lateral incisor
8	Right central incisor	24	Left central incisor
9	Left central incisor	25	Right central incisor
10	Left lateral incisor	26	Right lateral incisor
11	Left canine	27	Right canine
12	Left first premolar	28	Right first premolar
13	Left second premolar	29	Right second premolar
14	Left first molar	30	Right first molar
15	Left second molar	31	Right second molar
16	Left third molar	32	Right third molar

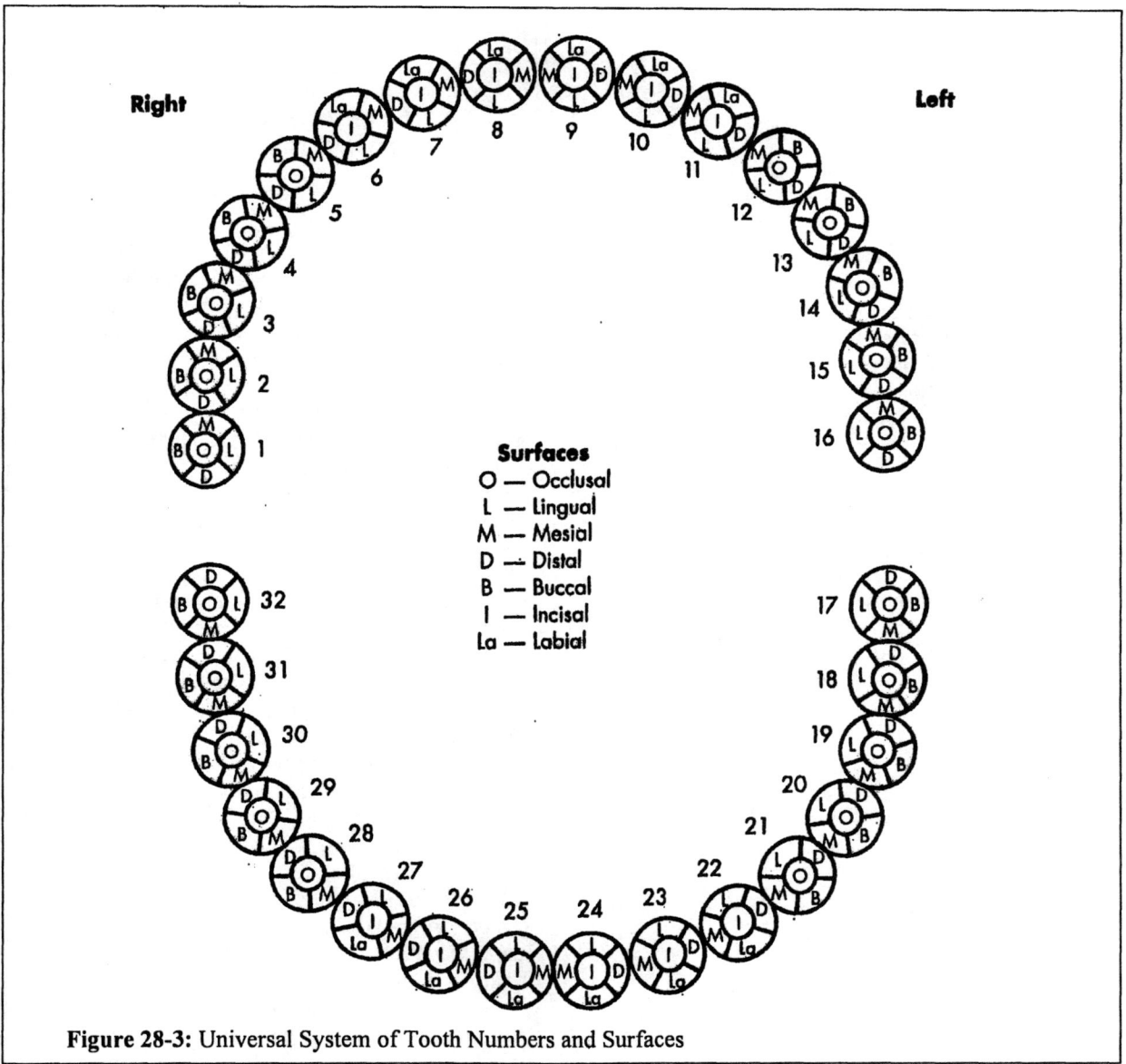

Surfaces
O — Occlusal
L — Lingual
M — Mesial
D — Distal
B — Buccal
I — Incisal
La — Labial

Figure 28-3: Universal System of Tooth Numbers and Surfaces

The primary or **deciduous teeth** number to 20 and apply to children. However, the deciduous teeth are lettered rather than numbered to avoid confusion with the adult numbering system. **Figure 28 - 4** shows the lettering of the primary teeth, beginning on the maxillary right and ending on the mandibular right. Note that there are no premolars or third molars in the deciduous set of teeth.

Tooth	Maxillary Tooth
A	Right second molar
B	Right first molar
C	Right cuspid
D	Right lateral incisor
E	Right central incisor
F	Left central incisor
G	Left lateral incisor
H	Left cuspid
I	Left first molar
J	Left second molar

Tooth	Mandibular Tooth
K	Left second molar
L	Left first molar
M	Left cuspid
N	Left lateral incisor
O	Left central incisor
P	Right central incisor
Q	Right lateral incisor
R	Right cuspid
S	Right first molar
T	Right second molar

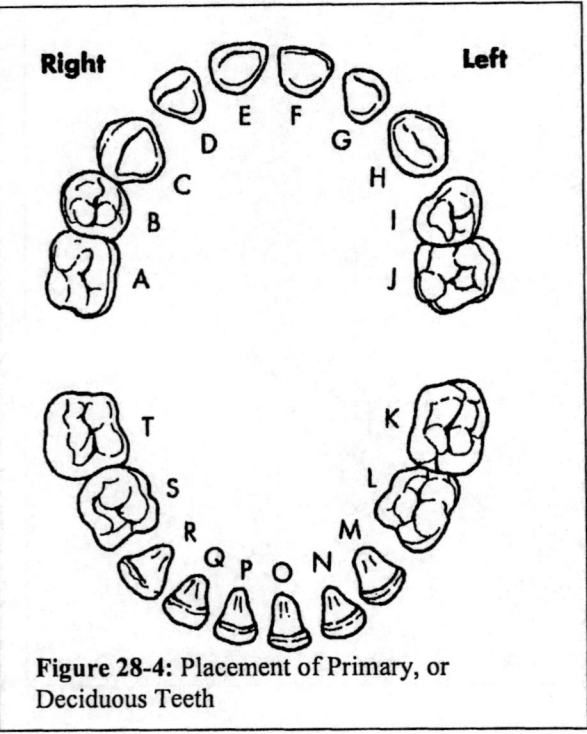

Figure 28-4: Placement of Primary, or Deciduous Teeth

Some dental services are billed according to the section of the mouth that is treated. Most frequently, this involves periodontal (gum) treatment, but it may also apply to the application of sealants. (For more information regarding these procedures, see the **Dental Services and Coding** chapter.)

The mouth may be divided into either quadrants or sextants. A **quadrant** is one quarter of the two dental arches; or one half of each arch. A **sextant** is one third of a dental arch (see **Figures 28 - 5** and **28 - 6**). Quadrants are named and abbreviated in the following manner:

URQ	Upper Right Quadrant
ULQ	Upper Left Quadrant
LRQ	Lower Right Quadrant
LLQ	Lower Left Quadrant

Sextants are named and abbreviated in the following manner:

URS	Upper Right Sextant
UMS	Upper Middle Sextant
ULS	Upper Left Sextant
LRS	Lower Right Sextant
LMS	Lower Middle Sextant
LLS	Lower Left Sextant

The Structure of the Teeth

Each tooth is divided into three parts: the crown, the neck, and the root. The **crown** is the portion of the tooth that shows above the gum. The **neck** is the portion covered by the gum, which links the crown to the root. The **root** is the portion that is embedded in the bone (see **Figure 28 - 7**).

The extreme center of the tooth is called the **pulp cavity**. This cavity contains the tooth nerves, veins, and arteries that allow essential blood flow into the tooth. The **root canal** is the portion of the pulp chamber that carries the blood vessels from the tooth socket to the tooth itself. The **pulp** is made up of connective tissue that contains a network of capillaries. The **capillaries** supply blood nourishment to the tooth. The pulp also contains lymph vessels and nerve fibers. Surrounding the pulp is the **dentin** (sometimes called the ivory), which forms the bulk of the tooth. The **apex** of the tooth is the terminus or end of the root. The root canal connects the pulp chamber with the apex.

In the root and neck of the tooth (the portion below the gum line), the dentin is covered with cementum.

Cementum is a bone-like material. Although hard, it is not in the same category as the enamel or the dentin. The cementum forms a junction with the enamel to seal off the exposed portion of the tooth (the crown). The cementum is actually a part of the periodontium or supporting structure of the tooth, since its main function is neither biting, nor chewing, or tooth nourishment.

In the crown of the tooth (the portion above the gum line), the dentin is covered with enamel, which is smooth and white. This is the hardest substance in the human body.

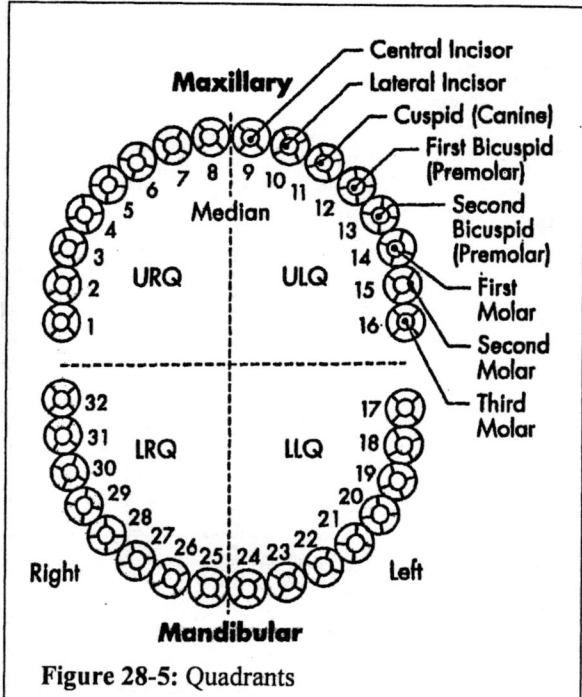

Figure 28-5: Quadrants

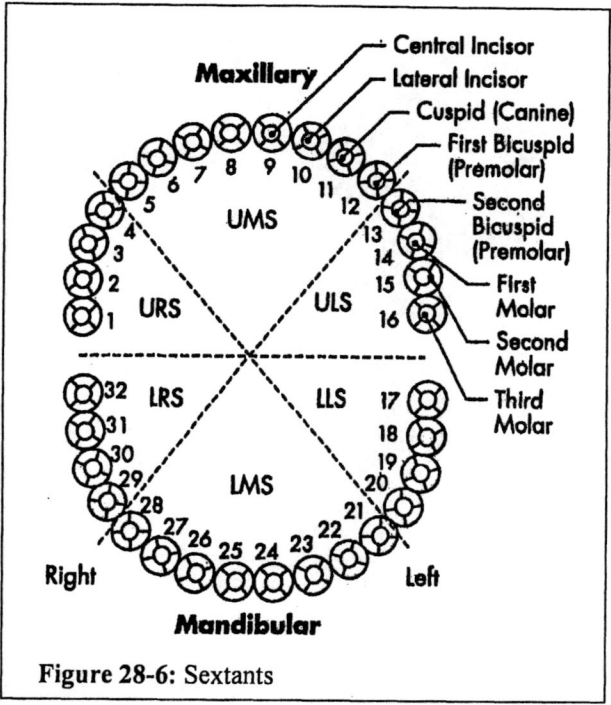

Figure 28-6: Sextants

For functional purposes, the tooth is often classified into two parts: the hard part and the soft part. The **hard part of the tooth** consists of the enamel, the dentin, and the cementum. The main purpose of the hard part is chewing and biting. The **soft part of the tooth** includes the pulp and the periodontal membrane. The periodontal membrane lines each tooth socket and covers the root of the tooth. The entire periodontal membrane acts as a bond between the cementum and the jawbone (mandible or maxilla). The main purpose of the soft part of the tooth is tooth nourishment.

Cementun, dentin, and enamel are composed chiefly of proteins, calcium carbonate, calcium phosphate, and magnesium phosphate. Calcium and phosphorous are constantly being washed away and replaced. For this reason, the human diet must contain enough calcium and phosphorous to ensure the health of the teeth.

Surfaces of the Teeth

Each tooth has five surfaces. These surfaces differ, depending on whether the tooth is a posterior tooth (premolar or molar) or an anterior tooth (incisor or canine).

Surfaces that appear on all teeth are the **lingual** (Li), which is the surface nearest the tongue; the **mesial** (M), which is the surface nearest the midline (an imaginary line drawn between the maxillary centrals and the mandibular centrals); and the **distal** (D), which is the surface farthest away from the midline. Posterior teeth have two additional surfaces consisting of the

buccal (B), which is the surface nearest the cheek, and the **occlusal** (O), which is the biting surface. Anterior teeth also have two additional surfaces consisting of the **labial** (La, L), which is the surface on the anterior teeth nearest the lip, and the **incisal** (I), which is the biting edge or surface (see **Figure 28 - 8**).

The surface names of the primary teeth are the same as for adult teeth. Also, note the tooth surfaces shown in **Figure 28-3**.

Growth and Development of Teeth

All teeth, including permanent teeth, begin their development before birth. Calcification of the deciduous teeth takes place just before and just after birth. That is why it is important that the mother's diet contain high amounts of calcium, phosphorus, and vitamin D. Without these vital nutrients, the teeth remain soft and are prone to decay. Permanent teeth calcify during infancy and childhood, necessitating the need for high amounts of calcium, phosphorus, and vitamin D in children's diets.

As a general rule, teeth erupt from the midline toward the back. The exception is the first molar, which usually erupts third in the deciduous teeth and first or second in the permanent teeth. The deciduous teeth normally erupt by the time a child is two years old. By the time a person reaches 17 to 24 years of age, the full set of permanent teeth is in place. **Table 28-1** shows the order and general time of eruption.

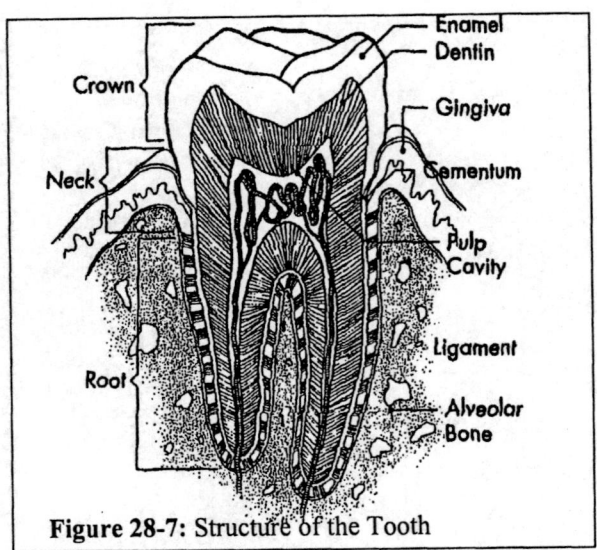

Figure 28-7: Structure of the Tooth

Table 28-1: Eruption of Teeth	
Deciduous Erupts (Months)	
Central incisor	6-8
Lateral incisor	7-12
Canine	16-20
First molar	12-16
Second molar	20-30
Permanent Erupts (Years)	
Central incisor	6-8
Lateral incisor	7-10
Canine	9-13
First premolar	9-12
Second premolar	10-13
First molar	5-7
Second molar	10-13
Third molar (wisdom)	17-23

Diseases of the Teeth

Following is a list of common diseases and conditions of the teeth that may require the services of a dentist:

Bruxism – Grinding of the teeth. It refers to grinding other than chewing and often occurs at night. If it continues, it can cause abnormal wear on the teeth.

Edentulous – Without teeth.

Dentalgia – A toothache or pain in the tooth. It usually indicates another existing condition such as a dental cavity or a periodontal problem.

Dental plaque – A mass of microorganisms that grows on the exposed portions of the teeth and may spread under the gum line. It is the cause of dental caries and periodontal disease. Calcified dental plaque is called **calculus**. Most dental plaque can be removed by brushing and by using dental floss. Calculus may

need to be removed by a dentist or a dental hygienist. Such cleaning of the teeth is called **prophylaxis**.

Dental caries or cavities – Holes or decayed portions of the tooth. They are caused by the progressive decalcification of the tooth. Decalcification begins when the food particles, fluid, or bacteria adhere to the tooth and break down the insoluble calcium salts into soluble salts. The calcium is then washed away and a cavity forms. Proper brushing and use of dental floss can greatly assist in removing food particles and bacteria. Topical application of fluoride while the teeth are still forming (usually prior to age 17 or 18 years) has also proven effective. After a cavity has begun forming, all bacteria must be removed from the hole and the cavity filled. If the cavity is not treated, it may spread into the pulp of the tooth, causing inflammation and abscess. In such a case, root canal treatment may be necessary, or the tooth may need to be extracted. Following are the three categories of cavities:

1. **Simple cavities** – Involve only one surface of a tooth.
2. **Compound cavities** – Involve two surfaces of a tooth.
3. **Complex cavities** – Involve three or more surfaces of a tooth.

Cavities are classified according to the surface(s) of the tooth, the type of surface (smooth or occurring in a pit or fissure), and a numerical grouping. The most common numerical grouping is Black's Classification System, as follows:

Class 1	Caries beginning in structural defects of the teeth, such as fissures or pits.
Class 2	Caries in the proximal surfaces of (the space between) bicuspids and molars.
Class 3	Caries in the proximal surfaces of cuspids and incisors that do not involve removal or restoration of the incisal angle.

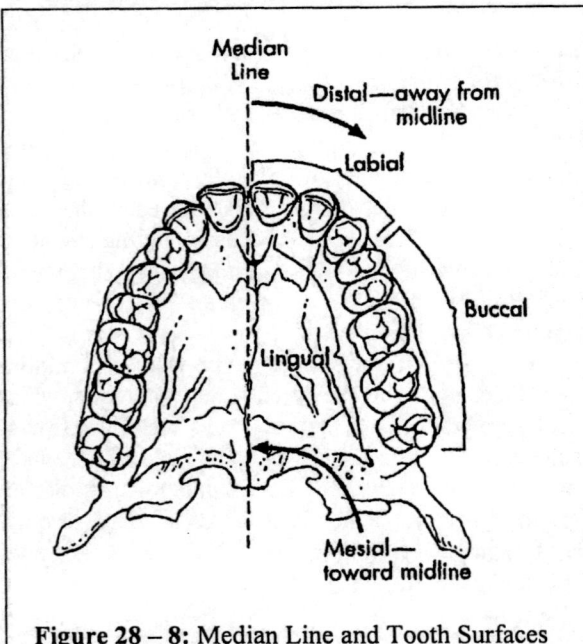

Figure 28 – 8: Median Line and Tooth Surfaces

Class 4 Caries in the proximal surfaces of cuspids and incisors that do require removal or restoration of the incisal angle.

Class 5 Caries in the top third (gingival third, not pit cavities) of the labial, buccal, or lingual surfaces of the teeth.

Class 6 Caries of incisal edges and cusp tips of the teeth.

For further information regarding treatment of cavities, refer to Chapter 28.

the digestive process by chewing and breaking down food particles. Further chemical breakdown of food particles is accomplished by the addition of saliva.

Each tooth consists of a crown, a neck, and a root. The tooth itself is made up of dentin, enamel, pulp, and cementum. Each tooth is numbered, and each surface of the tooth is labeled. This eliminates confusion and helps to pinpoint the exact tooth and area where procedures have been performed.

The most common diseases of the teeth are dental caries or cavities. However, teeth can also fall victim to dentalgia, dental plaque, and bruxism.

Summary

The primary purpose of the mouth is the ingestion of food, the intake of air, and vocalization. The breakdown of food begins as it enters the mouth. The teeth aid in

Assignments

Complete Questions for Review.
Complete Exercises 28 – 1 to 28 – 5.

Questions for Review

Directions: Answer the following questions without looking back into the material just covered. Write your answers in the space provided.

1. What is the primary purpose of the mouth? _____
    _____

2. Are deciduous teeth numbered or lettered? _____
    _____

3. In the permanent tooth numbering system, what tooth is number 1? _____
    _____

4. What is the palate? _____
    _____
    _____

5. What are the seven surfaces of the teeth and their abbreviations?
    1. _____
    2. _____
    3. _____
    4. _____
    5. _____
    6. _____
    7. _____

If you were unable to answer any of the questions, refer back to the section and then complete the answers.

Exercise 28 – 1

Directions: Label the surfaces of the Anterior Tooth and the Posterior Tooth in the boxes provided. The teeth are shown from the inside of the mouth with the midline being to the left.

Anterior Tooth

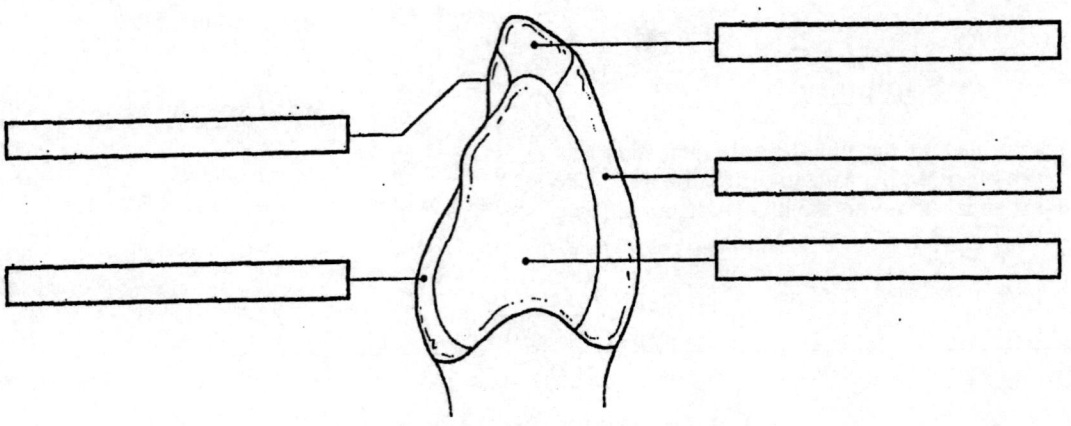

Posterior Tooth

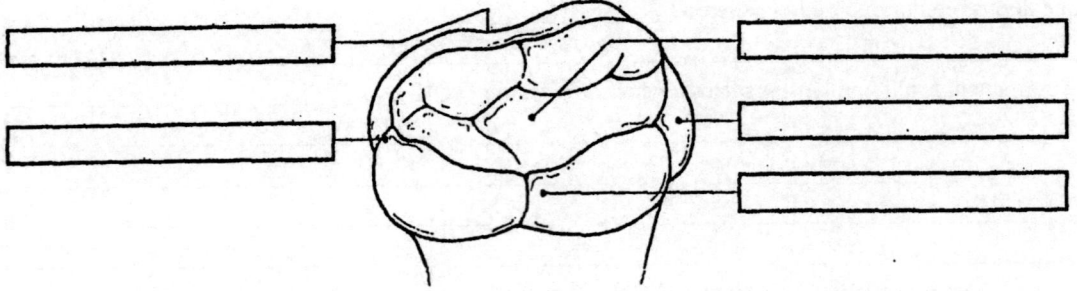

Exercise 28 - 2

Directions: Number the Primary and Permanent Teeth.

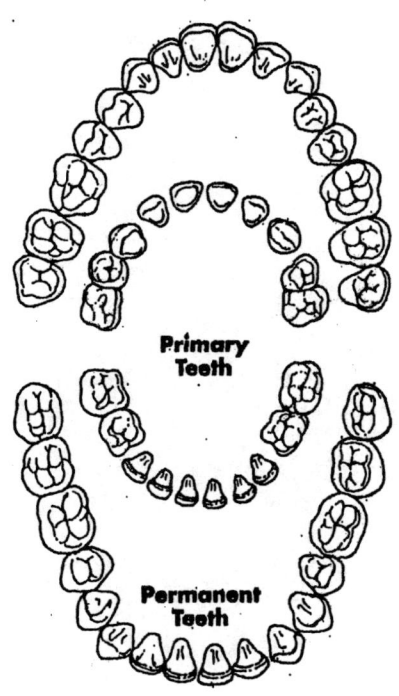

Exercise 28 - 3

Directions: Place the names of the Permanent and Primary Teeth in the boxes provided.

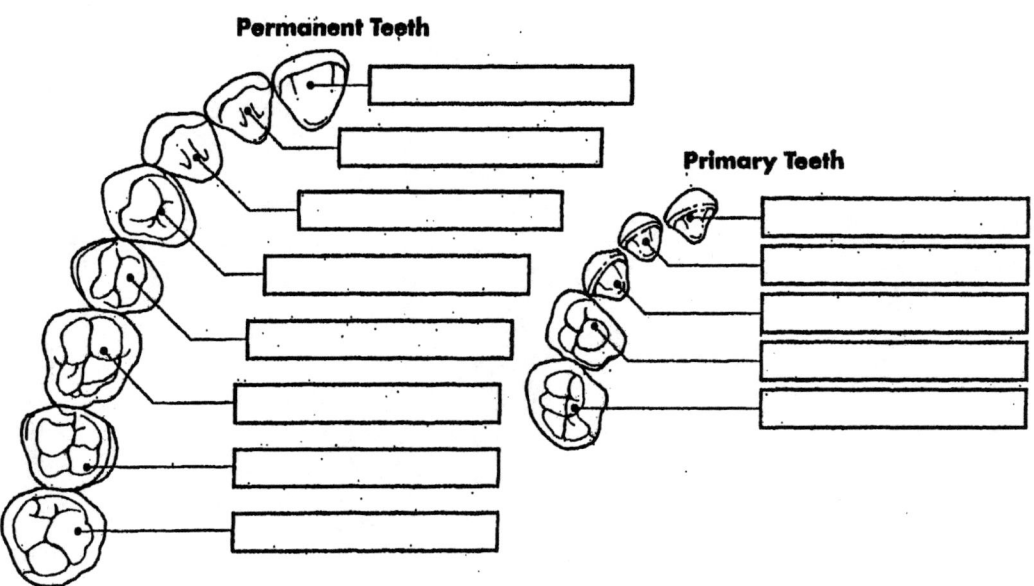

Exercise 28 - 4

Directions: Label the parts of the tooth in the boxes provided.

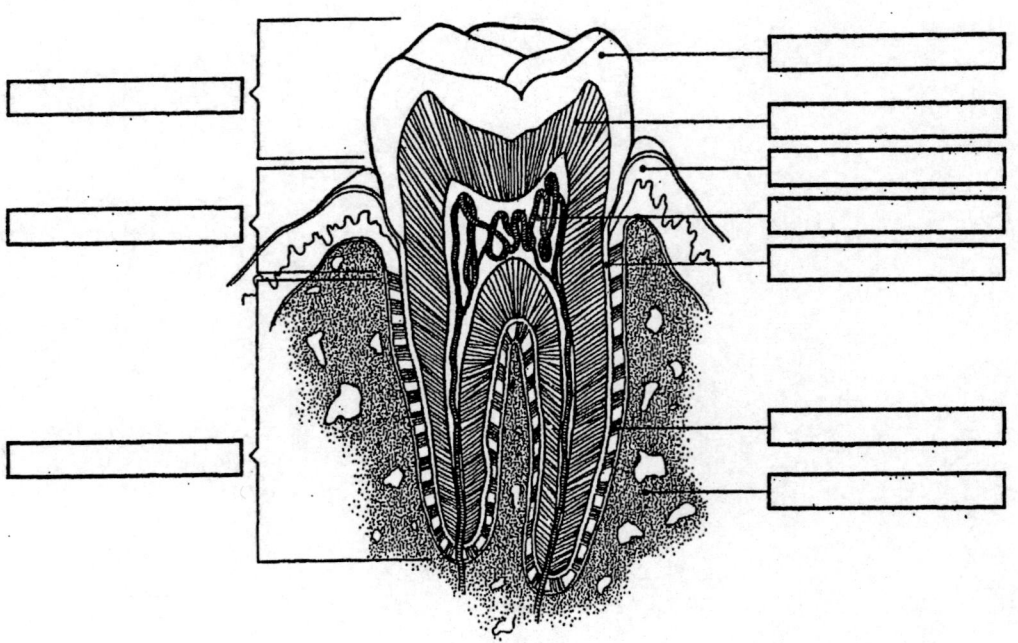

Exercise 28 - 5

Directions: Divide the teeth into Quadrants and Sextants.

Quadrants   **Sextants**

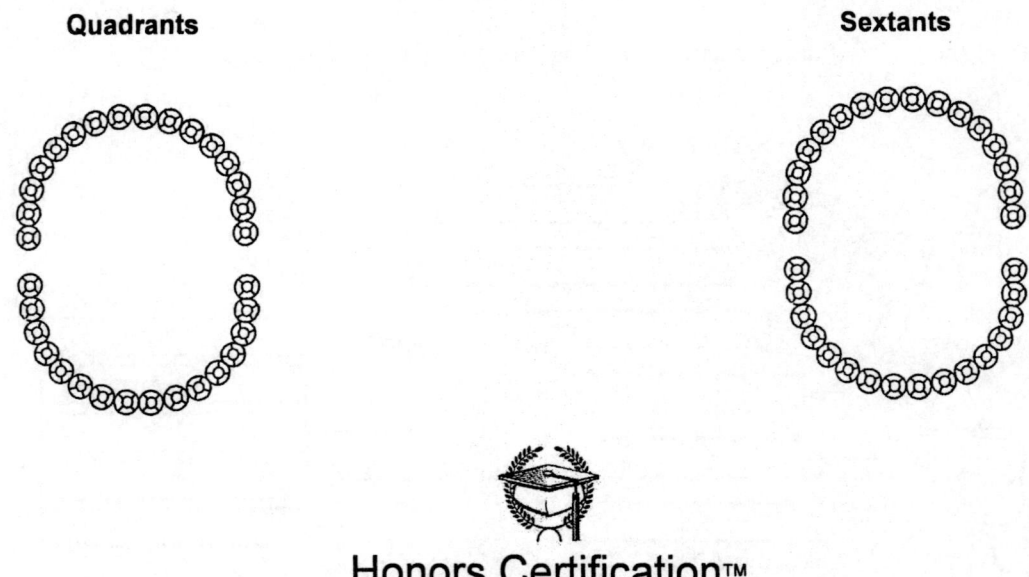

Honors Certification™

The Honors Certification™ challenge for this chapter is a written test of the information contained within this chapter. Each incorrect answer will result in a deduction of between 1% and 5% from your grade. You must achieve a score of 85% or higher to pass this test. If you fail the test on your first attempt you may retake the test one additional time. The items included in the second test may be different from those in the first test.

29 Dental Services and Coding

In this chapter you will learn:

- To identify the different types of dental services performed.
- To identify services that fall within certain ranges to determine the types of services rendered.
- How codes are broken down and when specific codes should be used.

Key words and concepts you will learn in this chapter:

Adjunctive General Services – Miscellaneous services, treatments not listed elsewhere on a dental code listing.

Alveoloplasty – Surgical preparation of a ridge for dentures.

Bitewing X-rays – X-rays that show the relationship of the teeth in two opposing dental arches.

Crown – A covering that is placed on a tooth.

Dentistry – The department of the healing arts that is concerned with the teeth, the oral cavity (mouth) and its associated structures.

Dentists – Doctors who have received a Doctor of Medical Dentistry (DMD) degree.

Diagnostic – Routine services designed to assist in the diagnosis and planning of required treatment.

Diagnostic Casts – Models that duplicate the structure of the mouth.

Diagnostic Photograp – Colored photographs of the oral cavity that are used to show various conditions of the teeth and mouth structures.

Endodontics – Treatment of dental pulp or other internal structures of the teeth.

Extraoral X-rays – Rays taken with the film placed outside the mouth.

Fluoride Treatments – The application of a topical fluoride substance to the teeth.

Impacted Tooth – A tooth that is positioned or wedged against another tooth, bone, or soft tissue and is prevented from erupting normally.

Inlay – A gold alloy or porcelain casting that lies on the occlusal surface of the patient's cusps (the pronounced elevation or edge of the tooth).

Intraoral X-rays – X-rays taken with the film placed inside the mouth.

Occlusal X-rays – X-rays which show the floor of the mouth and the palate.

Onlay – A gold alloy casting that lies on the occlusal surface but covers one or more cusps.

Oral Surgery – Treatment of the internal structures of the mouth limited to the dental structures and surrounding tissues.

Orthodontics – Correction or prevention of poor or misaligned teeth.

Periodontics – Treatment of the tissues surrounding and supporting the teeth.

Preventive – Routine services designed to prevent decay, gum disease, etc., through the care of the dental structures before disease has occurred.

Prophylaxis – The removal of bacterioplaque, calculus, stains, and other potentially harmful materials from the teeth by superficial scaling and polishing.

Prosthodontics, Removable – Replacement of the natural teeth through the use of a removable appliance.

Prosthodontics, Permanent – Replacement of the natural teeth through the use of a permanent appliance.

Restorative – Treatment involving the use of fillings or crowns to save or restore dental structures.

Space Management – The placement of wires or a retainer in the mouth to prevent the wrongful movement of teeth into a space where a tooth has been lost.

Stomatoplasty – Plastic surgery or repair of the mouth.

The terms dentistry and dental are derived from the Latin word *dens*, meaning teeth. **Dentistry** is officially that department of the healing arts that is concerned with the teeth, the oral cavity (mouth), and its associated structures. This includes diagnosis, treatment, restoration, and replacement of missing portions or parts. It also includes surgical procedures performed in and about the inside of the mouth or oral cavity.

Dental Professionals

Dentists are doctors who have received a Doctor of Medical Dentistry (DMD) degree. Other recognized titles and degrees include:

DDS — Doctorate in Dental Surgery (DMD and DDS are graduate degrees)

FACD — Fellow of American College of Dentists

FAGD — Fellow of the Academy of General Dentistry

FICD — Fellow of the International College of Dentists, an English degree with international recognition

MDS — Master of Dental Science

Diplomas are also awarded to dentists who have met the criteria for certification as a specialist in a chosen field. For the purposes of this book, we will use the term dentist to refer to all of the above.

Dental Treatment

In dentistry, the following four pathologic conditions require treatment:

1. Tooth decay.
2. Tissue or periodontal disease.
3. Trauma to teeth (including loss of teeth) or supporting structures.
4. Development diseases such as cysts, tumors, and abscesses.

Services are also performed in dentistry for other than existing pathologic conditions. Some of these services (such as prophylaxis, x-rays, fluoride treatments, and repair of dentures and bridgework) are specifically included as covered dental services under most plans but are usually subject to limitations.

Other services may be performed, not for pathologic conditions but primarily for cosmetic or similar reasons. They may also be elective procedures of the patient or dentist. Although the particular type of category of service that is received might be covered under the plan, benefits are usually not provided for services performed for cosmetic or similar purposes or for elective services. An example would be the placing of the crowns on healthy teeth that require no restoration. In other words, the crowns are placed to improve the appearance of the tooth's color or shape.

Dental Coding

In 1969, the American Dental Association (ADA) created a coding system that also served to categorize dental services. This system also established a uniform nomenclature for all dental services. The ADA listing classifies procedures under certain categories. Services (and thus their codes) are defined based on the type of treatment provided. Following is a list of the 10 ADA categories. Most dental plans separate services into similar classifications.

Diagnostic – Routine services designed to assist in the diagnosis and planning of required treatment.

Preventive – Routine services designed to prevent decay, gum disease, and so on, through the care of the dental structures before disease has occurred.

Restorative – Treatment involving the use of fillings or crowns to save or restore dental structures.

Endodontics – Treatment of dental pulp or other internal structures of the teeth.

Periodontics – Treatment of the tissues surrounding and supporting the teeth.

Prosthodontics, removable – Replacement of the natural teeth through the use of a removable appliance(s).

Prosthodontics, permanent – Replacement of the natural teeth through the use of a permanent appliance(s).

Oral surgery – Treatment of the internal structures of the mouth limited to the dental structures and surrounding tissues.

Orthodontics – Correction or prevention of poor or misaligned teeth.

Adjunctive general services – Miscellaneous services, treatments not listed elsewhere.

It is important to know what type of service is being performed in order to code it properly. Not all plans, insurers, or dental offices code claims according to the ADA code list. Many have developed their own version of the list. However, most of these lists are based on the format of the ADA code list.

The main differences that may often be noted include:

- Dental visits and anesthesia services are given their own section because these services are the most often rendered. Some dental lists also include a section for drugs.

- Many insurance carrier or plan lists omit codes in areas they do not routinely cover. Such areas usually include orthodontic services, fractures, and dislocations.

Regardless of the differences, it is important for the Dental Claims Examiner to become familiar with the types of services since nearly all dental code lists fall under categories similar to the ADA list.

In the following sections we will discuss the treatments covered under each ADA category. It may be helpful to obtain a current ADA Dental Code Listing or a similar listing used in your state, while going through this chapter. Please note that some versions of the ADA Dental Code Listing may or may not have a "D" preceding the code number listed here.

Diagnostic

Diagnostic procedures are those that are necessary to properly determine the most appropriate course of treatment for the patient's condition. The services that usually fall within this category are discussed in the following text.

Clinical Oral Examination

A clinical oral examination is the examination of the mouth by a dentist. Oral examinations are broken into three classifications: initial oral examinations (to indicate the first time a patient is seen), periodic oral examinations (to indicate any examinations other than the first), and emergency oral examinations (to indicate emergency examinations).

Radiographs

Radiographs are x-rays of the mouth and teeth. The first code is for a full mouth set of x-rays (D0210). Following that are intraoral mouth x-rays (D0220-D0240) and extraoral mouth x-rays (D0250-D0260). **Intraoral x-rays** are taken with the film placed inside the mouth. **Extraoral x-rays** are taken with the film placed outside the mouth. **Bitewing x-rays** have separate listings for one film, two films, three films, four films, and each additional film. Bitewing x-rays show the relationship of the teeth in two opposing dental arches.

In addition, **occlusal x-rays** are larger x-rays (2. 5 x 3 inches), which show the floor of the mouth and the palate. An occlusal x-ray shows the lingual (next to the tongue) side of the teeth and a portion of the palate. Its purpose is to aid in locating impacted teeth, bone fractures, cysts, and salivary duct disorders.

In each case, coding is made by the number of films taken. The first film would be coded individually; any additional films taken would be listed under the additional code(s). If a dentist were to take six bitewing x-rays, the appropriate codes would be D0274 for the first four films and 2x D0275 for the additional two films.

In many plans, there are limitations regarding the number of bitewing or other x-rays that may be taken during a given period of time. The plan should always be checked for such limitations. In addition, many plans have a **full-mouth x-ray limitation**. This means that if the dollar amount payable for the total number of x-rays taken exceeds the dollar amount payable for a set of full-mouth x-rays, the allowable amount would be based on the full-mouth x-ray allowance because the dentist could have taken an entire x-ray series to see all tooth structures.

Certain conditions may require posteroanterior and lateral skull and facial bone survey films. These are usually covered only under orthodontic services or TMJ conditions. These films include the following:

- **Posteroanterior and lateral skull and facial bone survey films.** This set of films shows the architecture, size, density, contouring, and positioning of the skull bones. One film shows height and width, and the second shows height and depth. When used together, they provide a nearly three-dimensional picture. Various views can be selected, including the Towne View, the Waters View, and the Basal View. This is usually covered only under orthodontic services or TMJ conditions.

- **Sialography.** This x-ray allows inspection of the salivary glands and ducts. A radiopaque medium (radioactive dye) is injected and enables the x-ray to show any obstructions or blockages (stones) in the salivary glands or ducts. This examination is most often performed by an otorhinolaryngologist (ear, nose, and throat specialist) in a hospital setting. It is usually performed only for a saliva problem or for a suspected cyst or tumor of the salivary glands.

- **Temporomandibular joint film.** The TMJ film allows inspection of the temporomandibular joint and its function. It is usually covered only when TMJ is a covered benefit or when there are orthodontic problems.

- **Panoramic maxilla and mandible film (Panorex).** This is a large x-ray that shows all teeth, the surrounding alveolar bone, the sinuses, and the TMJ all on one film. It helps to show tooth spacing or crowding as well as impacted teeth and jaw fractures. Periodontists use panoramic x-rays to determine the condition of the supporting structures of the teeth. Most plans consider it the same as a full-mouth x-ray and subject to the same guidelines. It is usually covered once every three years.

- **Cephalometric film.** This is an extraoral x-ray done with a cephalometer. The cephalometer is an instrument that holds the patient's head in position while at the same time measuring the bony structure of the head. The cephalometric film provides the greatest dimensional accuracy. It is used in conjunction with orthodontics or TMJ disorders and is usually covered for orthodontic or TMJ conditions.

- **Intraoral x-rays** include periapicals, bitewings, full-mouth series, and occlusal x-rays. **Extraoral x-rays** include Panorex and cephalometrics.

Note: There is also usually a catchall code for any other diagnostic radiographs that have been taken.

Laboratory Tests and Other Services

Occasionally, laboratory tests are needed to help determine a specific disease or patient condition. These tests include the following:

- Complete blood count.
- Urinalysis.
- Hemoglobin.
- Hematocrit.
- Bacteriologic studies for determination of pathologic agents.
- Caries susceptibility tests.
- Histopathologic examination.
- Pulp vitality tests .

Laboratory tests are often covered under medical plans as well as dental plans. Therefore, specific policy guidelines should be consulted to ensure proper payment.

Diagnostic casts and photographs may also need to be taken in order to diagnose the patient's condition. **Diagnostic casts** (models) duplicate the structure of the mouth. They are also called **study models** and **working models**. The only difference between a study model and a working model is how they are used. Study models are studied to assist in determining diagnoses and treatments. They are also used by orthodontists to record and evaluate problems or conditions that need treatment. Working models are used to aid in fabricating restorations, crowns, and fixed and removable prosthetics. Since a working model is an integral part of fabricating restorations, normally no additional allowance is given beyond that for the procedure itself. Diagnostic casts are usually covered only for orthodontic services or TMJ conditions.

Diagnostic photographs are colored photographs of the oral cavity and are used to show various conditions of the teeth and mouth structures. They are also used to show pre- and postoperative conditions. Diagnostic photographs are generally used in conjunction with orthodontic treatment. Many payors do not cover this procedure because they feel it is merely evidence for the dentist's files, not a diagnostic procedure.

Many plans do not cover any laboratory services or casts and photographs under dental services, with the exception of diagnostic casts and photographs, which may be covered if the dental plan covers orthodontic care and treatment. Some services may be covered under the medical plan.

Preventive

Preventive services are designed to assist in preventing the development of diseases of the dental structures. If disease is treated in the early stages, it prevents the disease from spreading to other teeth and structures within the mouth. Dental plans usually cover preventive services because it is less expensive to pay for a small treatment now than for a larger treatment later.

Dental Prophylaxis

Prophylaxis is the removal of bacterioplaque, calculus, stains, and other potentially harmful materials from the teeth by superficial scaling and polishing as a preventive measure for the control of local irritational factors.

The first step involves using a scaler to scrape off the built-up calculus (a whitish-yellow chalky substance, also called plaque) from beneath the gum line, then polishing the teeth with an abrasive mixture (a type of pumice).

There are two ADA codes for prophylaxis: one for adults and one for children. Age 14 years is usually considered to be the dividing line between adults and children. Many dental plans cover a limited number of prophylaxis treatments (generally no more than two per year), and some pay for prophylaxis for children, but not for adults.

Fluoride Treatments

Fluoride treatments are the application of a topical fluoride substance to the teeth. The three types of fluoride are stannous, acid, and sodium. All three types can be obtained in either liquid or gel form. Sodium fluoride is usually applied in four treatments. Acid and stannous fluoride are usually applied in a single treatment. Stannous fluoride is the most commonly used. The only difference in the fluoride treatments is in the chemical make-up of the fluoride compound. Stannous fluoride contains tin, acid fluoride contains acid, and sodium fluoride contains salt.

The enamel surface of the teeth is soft in children and grows harder as the teeth mature. Fluorides help to harden the enamel more quickly, thus helping to prevent cavities. When a child reaches about age 14, the enamel has completely hardened. This is one reason why adults usually get fewer cavities than children. Because fluoride is much less effective after the teeth have matured, most plans cover fluoride treatments only up to a certain age, usually ages 14 to 19. While the teeth are immature, the surface is soft and allows for the absorption of the fluoride. After maturity, this is no longer possible. Therefore, fluoride treatment is not usually covered for adults. For children, one treatment every six months is generally allowable.

Fluoride treatments are coded according to the type of fluoride used and whether or not the treatment includes a prophylaxis.

Other Preventive Services

Occasionally, a dentist provides preventive services other than those already mentioned. These may include dietary planning for the control of dental caries, oral hygiene instruction, and training in preventive dental care. These are considered educational services and thus are generally not covered under most plans.

In addition, a fairly new procedure is the application of **sealants**, which consist of a plastic-like coating that is placed on a healthy tooth to prevent decay. Sealants are coded per quadrant or per tooth. These preventive measures are normally used on children, since the posterior teeth often have fissures (cracks) or pits (holes) during their developmental stage. The application of sealants prevents bacteria, fluids, or food particles from lodging in the fissures or pits, thus preventing cavities. Although the teeth are healthy, the benefits of this type of service are becoming better known and many plans are starting to cover this service.

Note that data indicate that 87% of sealants applied to a tooth are likely to be retained after a period of two years. For this reason, excessive sealant application (more than once every four or five years to the same tooth surface) should be questioned.

Space Management Therapy

Space management is the placement of wires or a retainer (either permanent or temporary) in the mouth to prevent the wrongful movement (known as drifting) of teeth into a space where a tooth has been lost. This type of treatment may be covered for children (usually up to age 18) but usually not for adults. Some of the common names for this appliance are stayplates or flippers.

When a deciduous tooth is lost prematurely, space maintainers not only serve to hold the remaining teeth in place, but also prevent the space from being closed and prevent malocclusion with the opposing teeth. Patients with space maintainers should be examined regularly by a dentist. Adjustment of the maintainers or removal may be required. If a space maintainer is left in place longer than necessary, damage to the teeth can result.

Coding is according to the type (unilateral or bilateral) of maintainer placed and whether or not the appliance is fixed or removable. In many plans, the use of these procedures includes all adjustments and follow-up visits necessary for a specified period of time. Occasionally, it is necessary to re-cement a space maintainer.

Restorative

Restorations are procedures used to restore a natural tooth. They serve two purposes: to restore the dental structure after removal of the diseased portion and to make the tooth appear normal.

Charges/payments for restorations are based on:
- The number of tooth surfaces restored.
- The type of material used in the restoration.

Fillings

Filling restorations include a base, polishing, and local anesthetic. The types of materials used for fillings include:

- **Amalgam** – A silver-colored material composed of a mixture of mercury, silver, tin, copper, and zinc. This is the most durable material but is not aesthetically desirable. It is most appropriate for occlusal surfaces and other surface fillings on posterior teeth. Amalgam is the most inexpensive type of filling material.

- **Composite** – A plastic white material blended with resin and quartz crystal. This is the second most durable material, about 75% as durable as that of amalgam restorations. Composite is not considered appropriate for occlusal surfaces or for other surfaces of posterior teeth because of its reduced strength. Plans normally consider benefits for placement on anterior teeth and labial and incisal surfaces. Composite fillings should be coded as plastic or acrylic fillings.

- **Plastics/acrylics** – Synthetics are not as durable as composites. Many plans either limit or exclude payment for plastics. If used, they are appropriate only on the labial surfaces of the anterior teeth. Although plastic or acrylic restorations match natural teeth and are not complicated to perform, they have a tendency to expand with heat, to shrink during curing, and to discolor. They do not wear well and have a low strength and surface hardness. These restorations are also subject to recurrent decay around the filling.

- **Silicate** – A synthetic porcelain powder (also called synthetic porcelain or silicate cement) composed of silicate, aluminum, and a flux of either sodium or calcium fluoride. Silicate can be mixed to match existing teeth and therefore is used mainly on the anterior teeth. It is less desirable than other fillers because it is brittle, unable to absorb shock, discolors easily, and has a tendency to shrink or dissolve slowly. Silicate restorations generally last less than five years.

- **Gold foil** – A sheet of very thinly pressed gold. Gold restorations are appropriate for cavities covering one, two, or three surfaces. Gold restorations are more time-consuming to perform.

- **Gold and metal alloys** – A combination of one or more different metals. Gold is usually the most desirable fillings because of its resistance to corrosion, ability to be adapted closely to cavity walls, and extreme density (if properly condensed) and because it maintains a high polish and does not dissolve in saliva or other mouth fluids. Gold is generally more expensive than other restorative materials. It also is not as aesthetically appealing, is difficult to manipulate, can be extremely soft (compared with other fillings), and has a high level of thermal conductivity.

Often gold is mixed with other metals to increase strength. When mixed with copper, it becomes stronger, but it tends to corrode and lose its high polish much faster. Platinum and palladium add strength and hardness to gold as well as help to whiten the material. Palladium is a less expensive substitute for platinum. Zinc mixed with gold reduces the melting range and helps the gold to combine with any oxides present.

- Miscellaneous synthetic filling materials – May be known under a variety of trade names.
- Acid etch – A procedure, not a filling material. Because of its use during the cavity-filling procedure, it is often lumped together with filling materials. Acid etch is often referred to as an adhesive because it helps to bond the filling material to the tooth. It provides a far more durable bond than regular composites. Acid etch is generally used with acrylics and with composite resins. However, it is usually used on the labial surfaces of the anterior teeth where the adhesion of filling material is difficult and an aesthetic appearance is desired. The acid etch technique (with composite or acrylic resins) has allowed for restoration of teeth that may not previously have been saved or may have required more extensive work (crowns, inlays, or onlays). Such teeth included fractured teeth, developmental defects, and eroded areas among others.

Amalgam, composite and plastic/acrylic are the most commonly used materials for restorative procedures. **Figure 29 – 1** shows the decay of the tooth and the basic procedure for filling dental cavities, or caries. This is caused by insoluble calcium salts being broken down into soluble salts and being washed away. The breakdown of these salts is caused by bacteria that have attached to the tooth or lodged in a hole or fissure. (For further information on dental cavities, see the **Anatomy and Physiology of the Mouth** chapter.)

To treat the cavity, the dentist must first remove all bacteria and diseased material from the teeth to prevent the bacteria from continuing to grow after the cavity has been filled. The hole is then treated with a cavity liner or varnish. Cavity liners line the outside of the cavity and form a barrier against irritation from the zinc phosphate and silicate cements that are used in the filling material. Cavity liners also reduce the sensitivity of the dentin. Cavity varnishes are applied in several thick layers and help to reduce acid diffusion from the restorative cements into the dentin. They also insulate the pulp from shock due to thermal changes. Finally, the cavity is filled with one of the filling materials previously listed.

Tooth restorations or fillings may involve multiple surfaces. However, only one restoration is generally allowable per tooth.

The following are examples of single restorations (may be multiple surfaces, but only one restoration per tooth):

M	1 surface
MO	2 surfaces
MOL	3 surfaces
MODB	4 surfaces
MODNL	5 surfaces

Examples of multiple restorations:

MOD, B	3 surfaces and 1 surface
MOD-B	3 surfaces and 1 surface
MD	2 single surface restorations
ML, DL	2 single surface restorations if performed on anterior teeth with the exception of teeth #6 and #11; this is because the anterior teeth are so narrow that an M or a D cannot be performed without going into the L surfaces. An ML or DL filling is

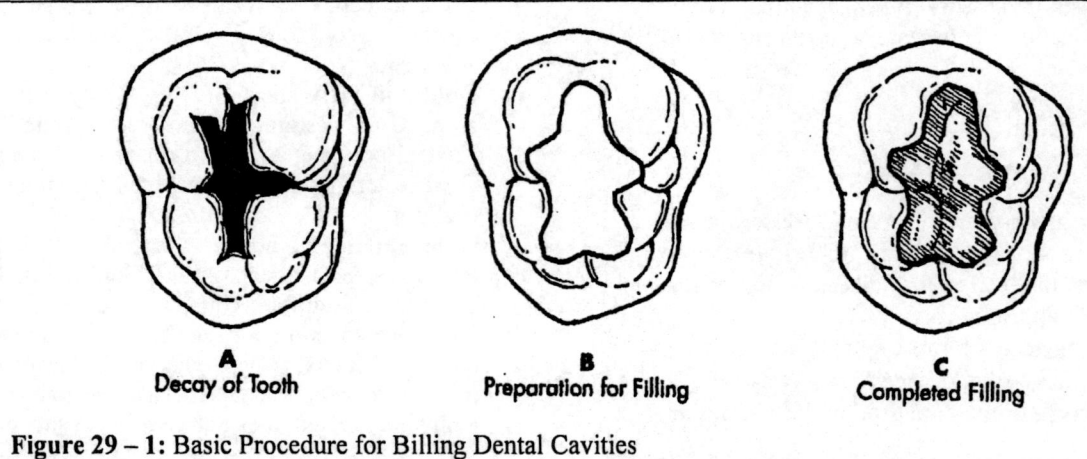

A Decay of Tooth **B** Preparation for Filling **C** Completed Filling

Figure 29 – 1: Basic Procedure for Billing Dental Cavities

really only one surface. In such a case, regardless of how the dentist bills it, only one surface should be allowed.

Coding for tooth restorations is based on the type of filling used, the number of surfaces, and the type of tooth (primary, permanent, anterior, or posterior).

Pin retention is the insertion of a small, thin needle-like pin into the remaining tooth structure to provide extra support for the restoration. Occasionally, a pin retention is done when no restoration was provided. In this case, the pin retention, exclusive of the restoration code, should be used under either the amalgam or acrylic restoration headings.

Inlays and Onlays

An **inlay** is a gold alloy or porcelain casting that lies on the occlusal surface of the patient's cusps (the pronounced elevation or edge of the tooth). An **onlay** is also a gold alloy casting that lies on the occlusal surface but covers one or more cusps. Inlays and onlays are used to restore lost tooth structure and vertical dimension. Vertical dimension (height) allows for proper occlusion with the opposing teeth. One of the main differences between inlays/onlays and fillings is that fillings are performed within the cavity, whereas inlays and onlays are shaped in a mold and then cemented onto the tooth.

Application of an inlay requires two separate visits to the dentist: the first for drilling the cavity and making an impression of the hole to be filled, and the second for cementing the inlay into place after its manufacture. Inlays also require that enough of the tooth be cut away to make an impression of the cavity to be filled.

Inlays have declined in popularity over the last few years. More frequently, a complete crown is provided. As a rule, most plans require that an inlay procedure be referred to a consultant for approval. An inlay can be applied without an onlay, but an onlay cannot be applied without an inlay. Therefore, if you receive a bill for an onlay only, assume that an inlay was also performed and code accordingly.

Crowns

A **crown** is a covering that is placed on a tooth. Crowns are required when a tooth has lost so much of its structure that a filling would not be stable. This means that the disease has progressed to the point where the decay is so large that there is very little, if any, supporting structure to hold a filling.

Crowns can be used strictly for cosmetic purposes. For instance, when a tooth may require treatment and a filling would be appropriate, the patient may prefer a crown to a filling because it appears more natural-looking. Perhaps the tooth in question is off-color or crooked. By applying the crown, the color and the position of the tooth can be improved in addition to treating the disease.

The following are the different types of crowns:
- **Full crowns.** These crowns cover the entire top of the tooth and extend to just below the gum line. A cast preparation is formed and then placed over a tooth on which the four outside surfaces (lingual, facial, mesial, distal axial) have been filed toward each other to form a rounded point. Several full crowns connected together and placed over several adjacent teeth can be used to help to stabilize those teeth.
- **Full veneer crowns.** These crowns are similar to full crowns, but they have a thin layer of acrylic resin or porcelain bonded to the surface of the crown. They replaced nearly the entire tooth and are placed over a "stump" that has been made of the natural tooth.
- **Partial crowns.** Similar to full crowns, partial crowns do not cover all the surfaces of the tooth. The surfaces involved are usually the occlusal or incisal, the lingual, and the proximal. Partial crowns are never done in a series, but are single unit restorations.
- **Partial veneer crowns.** Also called three-quarter veneer crowns, partial veneer crowns do not completely cover the tooth. They are cast metal and cover only that portion of the tooth that needs restoring. Three-quarter crowns also serve as abutments for a fixed bridge.
- **Porcelain-faced crowns.** These crowns have porcelain inlayed or veneered onto the buccal or labial surface.
- **Seven-eights crowns.** These crowns are usually placed on the molars to serve as bridge abutments. Their purpose is to strengthen the tooth to help it withstand the added stress of the bridge.
- **Steel crowns.** These crowns are non-cast (preformed) crowns that are usually made of stainless steel.

Dental plans cover a crown only when less drastic (and less expensive) methods of treatment are not appropriate. That is, if a filling can correct the problem, then a filling, not a crown, would be the appropriate treatment. Remember that the patient or dentist can use whatever treatment is desired. However, the amount allowed would be based on the necessity of services rendered.

There are permanent crowns and temporary crowns. When a crown is required, the dentist makes a model of the mouth (or arch). Then, a match of the surrounding teeth using a color chart is determined. The patient's natural tooth is then filed down until it resembles a spike. A temporary crown is then placed on the diseased tooth while the model is sent to a dental laboratory for casting (some dental offices perform the casting in house). A cast is made from the model from the material ordered by the dentist in a color matching the patient's surrounding teeth. The finished crown is then given to the dentist for application and fitting. The patient usually returns for the "**seating**" (placement) of the finished crown. Normally, the patient has to return to the dentist several times for adjustments to the vertical height of the crown so that it fits comfortably and is in alignment with the surrounding teeth.

The types of permanent crowns are:

- Full cast (gold).
- Three-quarter gold.
- Porcelain veneer (porcelain on the outside and a designated metal frame on the inside, which may be gold, non-precious metal (alloy) or semi-precious metal).

Temporary crowns are usually constructed of stainless steel. The temporary is pre-cast instead of being made specifically for the patient.

As a rule, porcelain crowns are the most expensive. They may be covered only on the anterior teeth. However, since this material has become the most accepted material for crowns, porcelain crowns may be allowed even on posterior teeth. The semi-precious or gold frame is allowable on anterior teeth. At one time, most plans were written with the provision that only gold crowns would be covered on posterior teeth. That was because years ago, gold was the least expensive material. However, now many plans will allow whatever material is the least expensive on the posterior teeth.

Crowns must be prepped and the natural tooth prepared while the patient is covered under the plan. However, many plans allow the actual seating to take place after the coverage has terminated if it is within 30 days of the termination date. The plan provisions must be checked for this exception.

Stainless-steel crowns are usually covered on deciduous teeth; however, regular crowns are not usually allowed on deciduous teeth because they will be lost as the child matures.

If properly prepared, a crown should last a minimum of five years. Therefore, if a replacement is requested on a crown that has been in place for less than five years, a review by a consultant is usually required. If the replacement is necessitated because of poor workmanship by the dentist, the original dentist may be expected to redo the restoration at no extra charge. This approach varies greatly by administrator.

Many plans monitor crowns to see whether more than one crown per arch or quadrant is being performed, since the underlying reason may be cosmetic, not functional. In addition, crowns on teeth that are abutments (teeth used to support or stabilize one end of a prosthesis and lie next to an area of a missing tooth) to dentures are also monitored for necessity.

Crowns are coded according to the type of material used in the crown. This may be a single type of material or a combination of materials.

Other Restorative Services

It may become necessary to re-cement a loosened inlay or crown. The codes for re-cementing are dependent on whether the procedure is for an inlay or a crown.

Medicated or sedative fillings are temporary fillings to help relieve pain. As a rule, they may not be covered. The final restoration only may be the covered expense.

Other restorative services include crown buildup (to build up a crown to match the height of other teeth) and a **labial veneer** (a cosmetic procedure that coats the tooth. This can be done to match the color of other teeth or to whiten the teeth.) The veneer is seldom covered by plans.

Endodontics

Endodontic treatment deals with the diagnosis and treatment of diseases of the internal structures of the teeth, pulp, and periapical tissues. The most common type of endodontic treatment is a root canal procedure. Benefit payments for endodnontic procedures include all x-rays and office visits. Additional charges for these services are denied if billed with endodontic procedures.

Pulp Capping

Another type of endodontic treatment is pulp capping. **Pulp capping** is the placing of a covering over an exposed tooth pulp. Pulp capping is performed only on children, because after a tooth matures, the pulp is occluded and becomes a root instead. Some doctors bill pulp caps consistently on adults. As a rule, the treatment is considered a sedative filling instead of a pulp cap. A dental consultant has to review the x-rays to determine the legitimacy of the billing.

There are two types of pulp caps: direct and indirect. A **direct pulp cap** is directly in contact with the material used (often calcium hydroxide) and the pulp. In an **indirect pulp cap**, the treatment is placed on the vital or diseased dentin and not directly on the pulp.

Recalcification or remineralization is similar to a pulp cap. In this type of treatment, calcium hydroxide or a similar material is placed in the tooth prior to placing a temporary restoration. If this is done on permanent teeth, a consultant should review the x-rays, since it is usually appropriate only on deciduous teeth.

Pulpotomy and **pulpectomy** consist of complete and partial removal, respectively, of the pulp and are appropriate only on deciduous teeth. There are two types of pulpotomies: vital and therapeutic. If the provider does not indicate which type was performed, it is usually safe to assume it was a vital pulpotomy.

Root Canals

A **root canal** is the removal of the entire root pulp, sterilizing of the chamber, and filling of the chamber with sealing material. This is performed when a tooth has an infected or damaged pulp. There are two types of root canal therapies: conventional (traditional) and Sargenti. The Sargenti treatment is done in one seating. The conventional treatment usually takes three treatments. In the conventional treatment, the chamber is sterilized and then allowed to settle before filling. This allows the dentist to be sure that all of the infection is cleared up before the final step – that of placing a crown on the tooth. Today, the conventional style is highly preferred over the Sargenti method, and many consultants will question the appropriateness of the Sargenti when submitted because it is essential that the infection be completely cleared before the crown is placed. After the crown is placed, it cannot be removed without ruining it. It is possible to drill through the top of the crown to reach the canal but this is certainly not desirable.

Table 29 - 1 will assist in identifying whether or not the dentist is billing correctly. If a root canal is performed, all the roots have to be cleaned and filled even if they are not all infected. This is because the infection will inevitably spread and because, as previously stated, once a crown is placed, it is not desirable to have to remove it for any reason. By treating all the roots, this possibility is minimized.

Root canals are coded according to the type of root canal that is performed . If the Sargenti method was used, the code depends on the number of roots involved in the therapy. A conventional root canal is coded according to the type of tooth, anterior, premolar, or molar.

The process of a root canal leaves a cavity in the tooth that must be filled. All root canal codes do not include the final restoration. Therefore, a corresponding restoration should be billed and coded for each root canal performed. In the Sargenti method, the restoration is done on the same day and should be included on the same billing form. In a non-Sargenti method, the restoration is not completed until a subsequent visit and may be billed on a separate claim form.

Apexification

Apexification is performed on the permanent tooth of a young person when the apex of the tooth is incompletely formed. It is a series of treatments, wherein the pulp is removed and the apex is treated with a solution of calcium hydroxide. This procedure stimulates growth of the cementum and helps to form apical closure.

Often apexification is performed prior to root canal therapy. Apexification treatment occurs in a series of visits and can last from six to 18 months.

Table 29 - 1:
Usual Number of Root Canals for Each Tooth

Tooth #	Permanent Tooth Name	# of Canals
1	Upper right 3rd molar	3
2	Upper right 2nd molar	3
3	Upper right 1st molar	3
4	Upper right 2nd bicuspid	1
5	Upper right 1st bicuspid	2
6	Upper right cuspid	1
7	Upper right lateral incisor	1
8	Upper right central incisor	1
9	Upper left central incisor	1
10	Upper left lateral incisor	1
11	Upper left cuspid	1
12	Upper left 1st bicuspid	2
13	Upper left 2nd bicuspid	1
14	Upper left 1st molar	3
15	Upper left 2nd molar	3
16	Upper left 3rd molar	3
17	Lower left 3rd molar	3
18	Lower left 2nd molar	3
19	Lower left 1st molar	3
20	Lower left 1st bicuspid	1
21	Lower left 2nd bicuspid	1
22	Lower left cuspid	1
23	Lower left lateral incisor	1
24	Lower left central incisor	1
25	Lower right central incisor	1
26	Lower right lateral incisor	1
27	Lower right cuspid	1
28	Lower right 1st bicuspid	1
29	Lower right 2nd bicuspid	1
30	Lower right 1st molar	3
31	Lower right 2nd molar	3
32	Lower right 2nd molar	3

Periapical Services

Other types of periapical treatments include:

- **Apical curettage** – Scraping but not excision of the apex.
- **Apicoectomy** – Excision of the apex of a root (usually considered medical, not dental). An apicoectomy is coded depending on whether or not it was performed with other endodontic procedures. The coding method is per root. Therefore, if two or more roots were done, the code (and RVS unit values) should be multiplied accordingly.
- **Endodontic implants** – The placement of an implant through the tooth and into the jaw. It is used to stabilize a loose tooth. Many administrators consider endodontic implants to be experimental; therefore, services are referred to a consultant for review.
- **Retrograde filling** – Amalgam filling placed into the apex of a root. This usually follows an apicoectomy.

- **Root resection** – Cutting off a portion of the root, usually because of disease or decay.

Other Endodontic Procedures

Other endodontic procedures may include:

- **Bleaching of discolored teeth** – A cosmetic procedure to whiten the teeth. As such, it is not covered by most dental plans.
- **Canal preparation and fitting of performed dowel or post** – The drilling of a canal and the inserting of a post or dowel into the canal.
- **Hemisection** – Cutting an organ in half.
- **Surgical procedure for isolation of tooth with a rubber dam** – Use of a thin rubber tissue by the dentist to seal off the tooth from saliva in the mouth. It also protects the patient from dental instruments, assists in the elimination of saliva and other fluids, and helps to keep the gingiva out of the way. Often, payors will not cover this procedure.
- **Recalcification (perforations, root resorption)** – The restoration of calcium salts to the teeth.

Periodontics

Periodontal treatment is the diagnosis and treatment of diseases affecting the periodontium, the tissues that surround and support the teeth. This includes the gingiva, cementum, and periodontal membranes. Periodontal procedures are usually performed by a dentist, periodontist, or oral surgeon. Periodontal treatment is one of the most highly abused areas of dental care. For this reason, many administrators have very stringent periodontal guidelines together with heavy consultant review.

Some periodontal care is considered oral surgery, whereas other treatments are considered strictly dental. To be effective, some periodontal treatments must be used in conjunction with or followed up by other adjunctive treatments. Such in-depth training is best done at the administrator level instead of in this general training guide.

Surgical Services

Surgical services to the periodontium include:

- **Free soft tissue grafts** – Soft tissue grafts that do not involve the use of a pedicle.
- **Gingival curettage** – The intentional surgical removal of the inner soft tissue wall of the gingival pocket. It is usually performed with local anesthetic. Access is through the pocket opening and no flap is performed (see item that follows). Many plans consider gingival curettage to be medically necessary if performed by a licensed provider, but limit treatment to one occurrence per year per quadrant.
- **Gingivectomy** – The surgical removal of diseased gum tissue or gingivoplasty; the surgical correction of the gingival margin or edge.
- **Gingival flap procedure** – The movement of masses of partially detached tissue from one area to an adjacent area – in this case, the gum. The flap is not fully detached so that it retains its own blood supply during transfer. Flap procedures are often used for covering the end of a bone after resection.
- **Mucogingival surgery** – Surgery involving the mucous membranes and the gums.
- **Osseous grafts** – Transplants involving the bone.
- **Osseous surgery** – Surgery involving the bone.
- **Pedicle soft tissue grafts** – Grafts that involve a pedicle. (A pedicle is a narrow, stem-like projection that attaches the graft to a blood or nutrient supply.)
- **Peridontal pulpal procedures** – Surgical procedures that involve the periodontal pulp.
- **Vestibuloplasty** – Surgery involving the vestibule of the mouth.

Gingivectomy or gingivoplasty, mucogingival surgery, and osseous surgery can be used for single tooth procedures, multiple tooth procedures, or full quadrant procedures. Check the tooth numbers on the claim to determine how many teeth were affected by the procedure. Benefits will be allowed according to the number of teeth involved.

Adjunctive Periodontal Services

The following are additional periodontal services:

- **Athletic mouth guard fabrication** – Making of an appliance that fits over the teeth to protect them from harm during rough athletic activity (i.e., football, boxing). This is not usually covered under the plan.
- **Occlusional adjustment** – An adjustment to allow proper occlusion (closing) of the teeth.
- **Scaling** – Thorough removal of calculus and bacterioplaque from the crowns and all root surfaces of the teeth.
- **Root planning** – A more definitive form of scaling to smooth roughened root surfaces (cementum) and to remove deep, heavy plaque. (The ADA describes and codes scaling and root planning as one procedure, since both procedures must be done at the same time).
- **Code D4340** – For scaling and root planning of the entire mouth (more than 12 teeth) during one appointment. This may be performed before or after a routine prophylaxis.

- **Code D4341** – For definitive scaling and planing per quadrant per appointment. The entire mouth should be done. This code should be used with a comprehensive approach to a more complicated or advanced case of periodontal disease.
- **Special periodontal appliances (including occlusal guards)** – Special appliances that may be required to aid in the treatment of periodontal diseases.
- **Splinting** – The attaching together of multiple teeth with wire or some other supportive material. In advanced cases of periodontal disease, the teeth become loosened in their sockets due to the loss of supporting tissue. In an effort to salvage the teeth, multiple teeth may be "splinted" together. This provides a wider base so that if one tooth moves, all teeth must move. To move several teeth requires significantly more pressure than to move a single tooth. Consequently, there is less movement in teeth splintered together.
  There are two types of splinting:
  1. **Intracoronal** (provisional), in which the teeth are wired together.
  2. **Extracoronal**, which is considered a permanent treatment wherein crowns or inlays are placed on the subject teeth and soldered together.
  Many plans limit coverage for splinting, and a consultant review should always be provided.
- **Tooth movement for periodontal purposes** – Allows the teeth to be moved so that the dentist may treat the periodontal tissues underneath.

Description of Case Patterns
Gingivitis and periodontitis are usually classified under a case pattern section that lists the disease and the appropriate treatment under one ADA code.
- Case pattern modifiers (by report) – For use when extenuating circumstances accompany a specific case pattern.

All the following treatments and procedures are included under one code. If treatment is listed or billed separately, all services should be combined under the single code.

Treatment includes: all necessary diagnostic procedures, training in personal preventive dental care, mouth preparation procedures, occlusal adjustment, surgical procedures (involving flap entry and osseous procedures, and complex procedures), routine finishing procedures, and post-treatment evaluation.
- **Type I gingivitis** – Shallow pockets, no bone loss.

- **Type II early periodontis** – Moderate pockets, minor to moderate bone loss, satisfactory topography.
- **Type III moderate periodontitis** – Moderate to deep pockets, moderate to severe bone loss, unsatisfactory topography.
- **Type IV advanced periodontitis** – Deep pockets, severe bone loss, advanced inability patterns (usually cases involving missing teeth and reconstruction).

Other Periodontic Procedures
Preventive periodontal procedures (periodontal prophylaxis) include:
- **Perioprophylaxis (also referred to as a periorecall or periodontal maintenance)** – Performed following the completion of comprehensive periodontal treatment. The patient returns within 12 months (usually at three-month intervals) for post-treatment evaluation and further preventive care. Perioscaling and possibly root planing and polishing of the teeth may be necessary at this time as well as re-instruction in preventive oral hygiene procedures.
- **Unscheduled dressing change** – Used when a dentist other than the treating dentist performs a dressing change.

Prosthodontics

Prosthodontics is the branch of dentistry concerned with restoration and maintenance of function by the artificial replacement of missing natural teeth. It covers the initial preparation and installation of bridges and dentures.

On all claims involving prosthodontics, the examiner needs to determine:
- Which teeth, if any, are congenitally missing.
- The tooth number of any and all teeth being replaced, plus the date of extraction or loss of each tooth.
- Whether any other teeth are missing in the arch and whether they are being replaced.
- For a replacement prosthesis, the date of installation of the prior prosthesis.

Many policies require that the prosthesis replace "natural" teeth. The following are not considered natural teeth:
- Tooth roots, when the condition of the tooth was such prior to the effective date of coverage.
- Congenitally missing teeth.
- Diastema (space between two adjacent teeth)

The following teeth do not require replacement and are usually not covered:

- Third molars that occupy the third molar position.
- Any tooth that is not in functional occlusion, that is, any tooth that is not opposed by another tooth in the opposite arch.

For example, a denture is replacing teeth numbers 14 and 15 teeth. Teeth numbers 18 and 19 (in the opposite arch) are also missing but not being replaced. As number 14 and 15 teeth will not oppose any teeth or prosthesis, their replacement will serve no function and thus, cannot be considered for coverage. The charges for all prosthetics (and therefore the coding and billing) include:

- The initial preparation of the teeth for a prosthetic.
- Study models.
- Fitting of the prosthesis.
- Initial installation of the prosthesis.
- All adjustment required within six months of the installation.

Prosthodontics – Removable

Full and partial dentures and appliances. The following sections explain the types of dentures and give general guidelines concerning them.

Full Dentures

Full dentures are appliances that replace all of the patient's natural teeth. The types of complete (full) dentures are (**see Figure 29 – 2**):

- **Immediate permanent** – Made before all the natural teeth have been extracted. After extractions, it is placed immediately before the healing is complete.
- **Immediate temporary** – Constructed of temporary material; has anterior teeth and posterior biting blocks (not true artificial teeth).
- **Overdentures** – Fabricated to fit over the remaining teeth. Usually, two natural teeth per arch remain in the mouth to provide support. Root canals, posts, copings, and crowns are

performed on the remaining teeth to provide the necessary strength to support the overdenture.

- **Regular permanent** – Made following all extractions and healing of tissues or for replacement of an existing denture.

Full dentures are coded according to the location (upper or lower) and whether they are complete or immediately placed. Full dentures for patients under age 35 and full bridges on patients under age 16 should normally be reviewed by a consultant for appropriateness.

Complete denture codes range from D5110 to D5140. Partial denture codes range from D5211 to D5294. Relines, tissue conditioning, and adjustments six-months after the initial placement of the dentures are usually considered part of the basic denture procedure. Therefore, additional payments are not allowed.

Partial Dentures

Partial dentures are used to replace missing teeth (see **Figure 29 – 3**). For a partial denture to be used, enough structurally sound natural teeth must be available to anchor the partial denture. If the patient has advanced periodontal disease, bone disease, or other conditions, a partial denture may not be able to be used. A partial denture may be either fixed or removable. A fixed partial is usually called a bridge.

The types of removable partial dentures are:

Permanent – Used when only a few, scattered teeth need replacement.

Temporary – Temporary replacement. This is usually not covered except after periodontal work. A consultant review is generally required.

Unilateral partial – Replaces only one tooth. A partial is usually constructed "symmetrically," that is, one or two teeth are being replaced in each quadrant of the arch. When teeth are missing in one quadrant, a fixed bridge is usually used, depending on the circumstances of the missing teeth. If only one tooth is missing in one quadrant, a unilateral partial can be used.

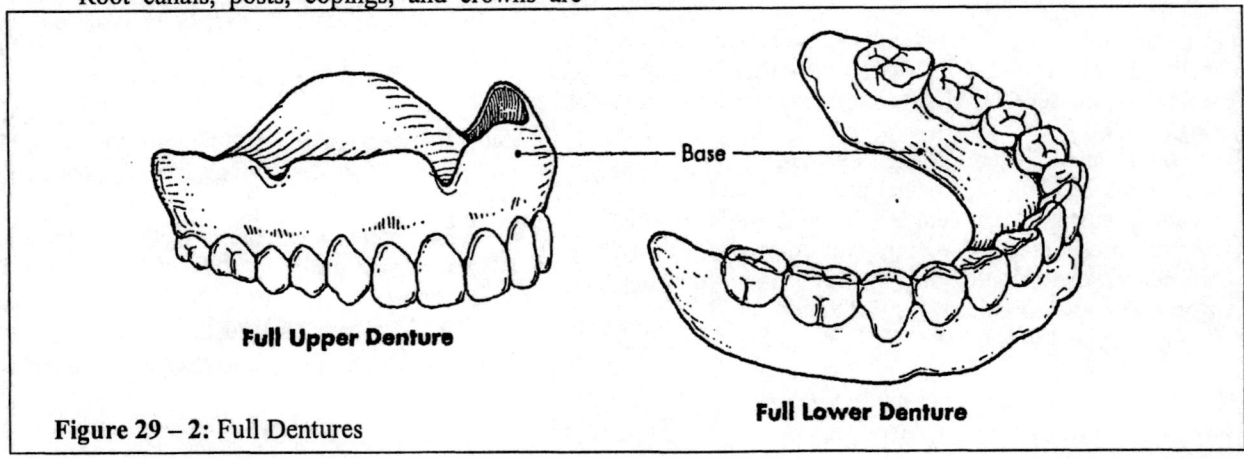

Full Upper Denture

Full Lower Denture

Figure 29 – 2: Full Dentures

The charge for a partial denture include:
- All teeth.
- The base, which is a pink-colored plastic and metal and lies against either the palate or the alveolar ridge (bottom of the mouth).
- Two rests and two clasps.
- All adjustments or relines required during the first six-months following seating

Many dentists routinely itemize their billing for partials showing a separate charge for each tooth, the base, and the clasps and rests. When processing or billing, all these charges should be combined and coded as one appliance. Additional clasps or rests are coded separately. All the teeth are always included, regardless of the number of teeth involved.

A **palatal bar** is the support that runs across the top of the palate (roof of the mouth). A **lingual bar** is the support that runs along the bottom of the mouth. Different codings reflect different materials used in the construction of the partial. Many plans specify that only certain materials, usually non-precious or semi-precious materials, can be used in the construction.

Teeth numbers seven and 10 are often not strong enough to support bridgework or partials. Therefore, care should be taken when approving these teeth for use as abutments. A consultant should review the x-rays and treatment plan prior to approval.

Partial dentures are coded according to the type of denture (complete or partial), their location (upper or lower), the materials (e. g. , acrylic, chrome), and the number of clasps used. The codes most commonly used for partials are D5241 and D5261.

Additional Units for Partial Dentures
Use of these codes and additional allowance may be given if more teeth are being added to an existing partial. Code D5310 is for each additional clasp with rest. Code D5320 is for each additional tooth.

Adjustments to Dentures
Occasionally, a dentist has to adjust dentures because of changes in the mouth (often due to aging or disease).

The codes within the D5410 to D5422 range are used to bill for these types of services.

Repairs to Dentures
Occasionally, it becomes necessary to repair or add to a denture. The code range D5610 through D5690 is used to bill these types of services. These codes are used only when a new denture or partial does not have to be made, when a repair can be made, or when a tooth can just be added on. The codes are as follows:

D5610 Repair broken complete or partial denture – no teeth damaged.

D5620 Repair broken complete or partial denture – replace one broken tooth.

D5630 Replace additional teeth – each tooth (this code should always be used with D5620)

D5640 Replace broken tooth on denture – no other repairs

D5650 Adding tooth to partial denture to replace extracted tooth – each tooth (not involving clasps or abutment tooth)

D5660 Adding tooth to partial denture to replace extracted tooth – each tooth (involving clasps or abutment tooth)

D5670 Reattaching damaged clasp on denture

D5680 Replacing broken clasp with new clasp on denture

D5690 Each additional clasp with rest

Denture Duplication
Denture duplication to replace a lost denture or to make a spare set is usually not a covered expense. Jump or rebase (D7710 and D5720) is the replacement of the base of the denture because of deterioration or tissue changes. Jump or rebase may be covered depending on the circumstances. Since the teeth from the original denture are being reused and only the base material is being remade, the cost is considerably less than the cost of a completely new denture. However, since these three terms are used interchangeably, it is necessary that an explanation be obtained from the provider that clarifies which service is being performed.

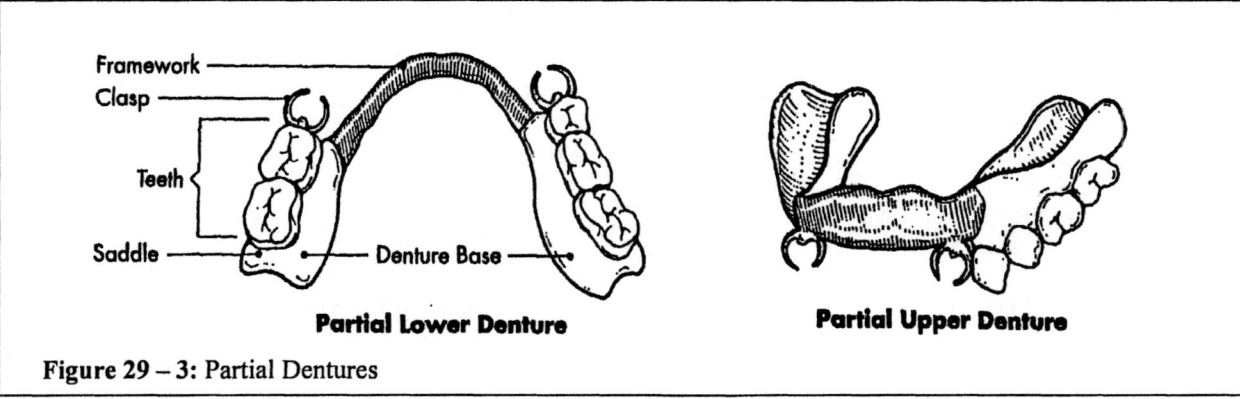

Partial Lower Denture

Partial Upper Denture

Figure 29 – 3: Partial Dentures

Denture Relining

A reline is a soft material placed on top of the base to help prevent tissue damage to the patient's mouth. This makes the partial or denture more comfortable to wear. It is coded according to the type of denture (complete or partial) and where the relining procedure took place (in the office or the laboratory).

Other Prosthetic Services

Temporary dentures are sometimes used until the permanent dentures have been constructed. **Tissue conditioning** is a method of correcting tissue irritation resulting from the wearing of dentures. First, an impression-making type of material is placed in the saddle of the denture. Then, with the denture in place, displacement of this material will indicate any corrections that are necessary to eliminate distortion from pressure on the tissue. Tissue conditioning is more complicated than the typical adjustment.

As previously indicated, an overdenture is considered a full denture, although it is placed "over" two teeth in each arch left for support. Unlike a partial denture in which clasps are used to grab onto the abutment teeth, an overdeunture has two holes left in it to allow it to slide over the two remaining teeth. Overdentures are coded as complete or partial.

Maxillofacial Prosthetics

Many of the following services are not performed frequently and therefore have a BR (By Report) or RNE (Relativity Not Established) unit value. However, they may be covered by some Major Medical plans. As a rule, most plans require that this type of procedure be referred to a consultant for approval. The codes are seldom seen by the claims examiner. For this reason, these procedures will not be discussed in depth. Many of the following prostheses are placed because of damage to the bone or tissues relating to either disease or blunt trauma (i.e., auto accident, being hit by an object). These procedures most often are performed by a dental surgeon or an orthodontist.

Extraoral Prostheses

The following prostheses are actually outside the oral cavity. Please note that these codes include three-month maintenance of the patient and prosthesis.

- **Auricular prosthesis** – A prosthesis in the auricle of the ear.
- **Composite facial prosthesis** – A prosthesis of the facial structure.
- **Facial moulage** – The making of a wax model of the face or a portion of the face or mouth. This is usually done in preparation for the making of a prosthesis.
- **Nasal prosthesis** – A prosthesis of the nasal cavity or nose.
- **Ocular implant** – An implant in the eye.

- **Ocular prosthesis** – A prosthesis of the eye (i.e., a glass eye).
- **Orbital implant** – An implant to the orbit (the bony structure surrounding the eye).
- **Orbital prosthesis** – A prosthesis of the orbit (the bony structure around the eyeball).
- **Prosthetic dressing** – The dressing applied to the injured area before, during, or after the insertion of a prosthesis.
- **Replacement prosthesis** – Replacement or duplicate of an existing prosthesis. Often much of the measuring of the patient and the formation of molds has been done. Therefore, a replacement prosthesis usually costs less than an initial prosthesis.

Intraoral Prostheses

This section is divided into two subheadings, one for acquired defects and one for congenital defects. **Congenital defects** are those that the patient is born with. **Acquired defects** are those that develop after birth. Acquired defects in the field of dentistry are most often the result of disease or blunt trauma.

Acquired Defects

The following are intraoral prosthetics services performed for acquired defects:

- **Refitting of obturator** – The refitting or reforming of an obturator to better-fit changes in the structure of the patient's palate. An **obturator** is an appliance designed to fill in the hole created by a cleft palate defect. It is usually held in place with clasps or splinted to the teeth. Two codes are used to bill for these services: code D5840 if the cleft of the palate was congenitally formed and code D5830 if the cleft is surgically formed.
- **Mandibular resection prosthesis** – A prosthesis to replace bone that was excised (cut out) during a mandibular resection. There are two codes depending on whether the prosthesis is a flange (lower, the part of the denture that extends from the embedded teeth to the border of the denture) or a denture (artificial teeth) prosthesis.

Congenital Defects

The following are intraoral prosthetics services performed for congenital defects:

- **Feeding aid** – A prosthesis used to assist in feeding a person with a congenital defect.
- **Obturator** – A prosthesis to cover the hole created by a cleft palate defect.
- **Palatal lift prosthesis** – A prosthesis that is made to lift the palate.
- **Speech aid** – A prosthesis used to help a person's speech. The two codes for speech

aids depend on whether the prosthesis is for a child or an adult.

- **Superimposed prosthesis** – A prosthesis that is superimposed (placed) over another prosthesis.

Implants

Implant means to transfer or to graft something additional onto or into an existing surface. An implant may consist of a piece of tissue or bone, a pellet of medicine, on a tube or needle containing radioactive material. Coding is either for a single or a complex implant.

- **Subperiosteal implant** – An implant located below the periosteum.
- **Endosseous implant** – An implant in the bone.
- **Endodontic endosseous implant** – An implant through the root and into the bone.

Treatment Prostheses

The following are prostheses that are generally removed after treatment.

- **Docket device** – A device to which something can be anchored or docked during treatment.
- **Fluoride applicator** – A plastic receptacle that is filled with fluoride and then fitted around the teeth, allowing fluoride to be absorbed into the teeth. This is the most common treatment prosthesis used and it often accompanies billings for fluoride treatments.
- **Infant orthopedic appliance** – An appliance to help preserve and restore the skeletal function in infants.
- **Mandibular guide flange** – An implant below the denture line that helps to guide the mandibular bone.
- **Radiation carrier** – A device (usually a tube or needle) that contains a radioactive material.
- **Radiation shield** – A shield that protects a portion of the body from radiation.
- **Splint** – A device that holds a body part rigid or immobile.
- **Trismus appliance** – An appliance to aid in trismus. **Trismus** (often called lockjaw) is a motor disturbance of the trigeminal nerve.

Prosthodontics – Permanent

The bridge or bridgework is usually used in reference to "fixed" or permanent partials. These are bridges that are permanently attached and seated in the patient's mouth. Whereas a partial is usually removed at night, a fixed bridge is never removed unless required by a dentist for repair.

Although there are many different types of bridge, the most common is a three-unit bridge. A three-unit bridge is composed of two abutment teeth and one pontic. An **abutment** is a tooth that is used to support or stabilize one end of a prosthetic appliance. A **pontic** is the part of a bridge that is suspended between abutments and replaces a missing tooth. It is also the artificial tooth in a partial denture. A pontic is the object that is made to look like a natural tooth. Using both definitions just indicated, the normal three-unit bridge (the number of units applies to the number of abutments plus the number of pontics involved in a bridge) is:

Abutment – pontic – abutment

Abutments are normally crowned. This is because either a bridge or a partial causes considerable wear and tear on the abutment teeth. Crowns provide the extra strength and support that is needed. The two most common types of bridges are:

1. **Fixed bridgework** – Made up of pontics (artificial teeth) and abutments (anchors).
2. **Cantilevered bridge** – Composed of one pontic and one abutment. Cantilevered bridges need to be reviewed by a consultant to determine appropriateness of treatment.

A bridge may also have double abutments. Double abutments are sometimes necessary when the abutting tooth is not very strong (such as lateral incisors 7 and 10) or when the bridge is cantilevered. However, some providers consistently bill for double abutments because it significantly increases the cost of the bridge. A bridge is charged and paid for based on the number of units involved. The allowance for an abutment is based on a crown charge, about $800 to $1,200 (depending on the area). The pontic charge tends to run about the same amount. Therefore, a three-unit bridge usually costs $2,400 to $3,000.

If a bridge is covered, the abutments are also automatically covered. If the bridge (replacement of missing teeth) is not covered, the abutment teeth must be evaluated by themselves to see whether they require crowning because of disease. If they are so decayed or diseased that crowning would be appropriate, without regard to a bridge the crowns will be paid for even though the pontic for the missing tooth would not be.

Bridge pontics and crowns (abutments) are coded based on the type of material used in the pontic or crown. Remember that each abutment and each pontic constitute a unit in a bridge. Therefore, a three-unit bridge would be billed as a pontic and two crowns.

Although the crown performed for a bridge is substantially the same as that provided for a stand-alone crown, a different code is used. For instance, D2751 is used for a stand-alone crown, whereas D6791 is used for a bridge crown.

Retainers

A retainer is a device used for maintaining the teeth and jaws in an appropriate position. Retainers are coded according to the number of surfaces (two, three, or more). If there was onlaying of cusps, code D6540 should be used.

Repairs

Occasionally, repairs are needed on fixed prosthodontics. Following is a list of coding repairs:

D6610   Replace broken pin facing with slotted or other facing.

D6620   Replace broken facing where post is intact.

D6630   Replace broken facing where post backing is broken.

D6640   Replace broken facing with acrylic.

D6650   Replace broken pontic.

Other Removable Prosthetic Services

- **Dowel pin** – A metal pin used to stabilize the denture.
- **Replacement bridge** – A duplicate bridge made to replace an existing bridge.
- **Precision attachment** – A specially designed attachment used in fixed and removable prosthetics for attachment to the abutment teeth. It usually consists of a tongue and groove or male/female design.
- **Stress breaker** – A device incorporated into a denture to relieve excess stress on the abutting teeth during chewing.

Oral Surgery

Oral surgery includes the operative procedures related to the teeth and jaws. Technically, surgery to the mouth is split into two sections:

1. **Dental surgery** – For treatment of the teeth and gums, such as extractions.
2. **Oral surgery** – For treatment of the jaw or parts of the mouth other than the teeth and gums, such as treatment of the joints and bones.

A dentist, oral surgeon, or physician, may perform both oral and dental surgery. The type of surgery is defined by the procedure performed, not by the licensure of the person performing the service.

The distinction between oral and dental surgery is important because oral surgery may be covered under the medical portion of the plan, whereas routine extractions are not.

Oral surgery involves cutting into the oral tissues, opening up the area, cutting and removing objects from that area (either teeth or tissues/cysts), and then suturing (sewing) the area. The services that are considered surgical and are therefore usually covered under the medical portion of the plan, include but are not limited to gingival curettage, gingivectomy, gingivoplasty, osseous surgery, gingival or soft tissue grafts, and osseous grafts. Following are some of the more common oral surgeries and exceptions.

Extractions

An extraction normally does not involve any cutting (except in a very superficial manner) or suturing. Therefore, extractions are not usually considered oral surgery. Usually, pincers are used to grab the tooth that is to be removed and the tooth is pulled out. The exception may be for impacted wisdom teeth (third molars).

Extractions include local anesthesia and routine post-operative care.

Surgical Extractions

Surgical extractions include local anesthesia and routine post-operative care.

D7210   The surgical removal of an erupted tooth, which requires elevation of the mucoperiosteal flap and removal of bone or a section of tooth. This is usually not considered to be oral surgery. Therefore, this code is payable under dental, not medical.

D7220   Impaction that requires incision of overlaying soft tissue and the removal of the tooth.

D7230   Impaction that requires incision of overlaying soft tissue, elevation of a flap, and either removal of bone and tooth or sectioning and removal of the tooth.

D7240   Impaction that requires incision of overlaying soft tissue, elevation of a flap, removal of a bone, and sectioning of the tooth for removal.

D7241   Impaction that requires incision of overlaying soft tissue, elevation of a flap, removal of bone, sectioning of the tooth for removal, or that which presents unusual difficulties and circumstances.

An **impacted tooth** is one that is positioned or wedged against another tooth, bone, or soft tissue and is prevented from erupting normally. When this occurs, the gum must be cut and the tooth removed, often by fracturing into smaller pieces. The gum is then sutured closed. The three molars in each quadrant have a tendency to become impacted.

- **Root extraction** – Surgical cutting into the gum and removing the root. This situation may occur when a tooth is extracted and a part of the root breaks off and remains in the gum. This is usually considered a medical procedure.
- **Oroantral fistula closure** – An abnormal opening into the mouth cavity. This code is also used for antral root recovery. Most often, an oroantral fistula occurs when the root of an upper tooth has grown into the nasal cavity. When this tooth is extracted, an unnatural opening occurs between the oral cavity and the nasal cavity. Oroantral fistulas can also

occur as a result of infection; however, it is still most often associated with the extraction of a tooth in which bacteria entered the hole left by the root and infection occurred. If an oroantral fistula occurs more than six weeks after the extraction of the tooth, some plans will cover the expense under medical benefits since the cause is usually bacterial.

Other Surgical Procedures

- **Tooth re-implantation** – Stabilization of accidentally evulsed or displaced tooth or alveolus.
- **Tooth implantation** – Placement of a tooth back into the same socket after it has been knocked-out.
- **Tooth transplantation** – Moving a natural tooth from one location to another. As a rule, implantation is covered but transplantation is not. Of course, it depends on the circumstances and the plan provisions.
- **Surgical exposure** – The cutting of the gum and sometimes the attachment of wires to the crown of the unerupted tooth to assist in the eruption and proper alignment of the tooth. Often, this is done for orthodontic purposes. In such a case, it would be covered only if the plan has orthodontic provisions.

The following codes are considered oral surgery and are usually covered under the medical plan.

D7285   Biopsy of oral tissue (hard)
D7286   Biopsy of oral tissue (soft)
D7290   Surgical re-positioning of teeth

Alveoloplasty

Alveoloplasty is surgical preparation of a ridge for dentures. It is coded per quadrant, either in conjunction with extractions or without. Unless otherwise specified in the contract, alveoloplasties are covered under dental, not medical.

Stomatoplasty

Stomatoplasty is plastic surgery or repair of the mouth. The following codes include revision of soft tissue on ridges, muscle reattachment, tongue, palate, and other oral soft tissues. It is coded per arch as D7340 (uncomplicated) or D7350 (complicated). Complications include ridge extension, soft tissue grafts, and management of hypertrophied and hyperplastic tissue.

Surgical Excision

Surgical excision includes excision of reactive inflammatory lesions, scar tissue, or localized congenital lesions. It is coded as D7410 for a lesion up to 1. 25cm or D7420 for a lesion over 1. 25cm.

Excision pericoronal gingiva is an excision of the gums around the teeth.

Excision of Tumors

Tumors are abnormal (possibly cancerous) growths in the body. The coding for the removal of tumors depends on their size and whether they are benign or malignant.

Removal of Cysts and Neoplasms

A **cyst** is an enclosed pouch that contains fluid, semi-fluid, or solid material. A **neoplasm** is a new tumor or growth. The code depends on the size of the cyst or neoplasm and whether it is **odontogenic** (relating to the origin and formation of the teeth) or non odontogenic. Code D7465 is used for procedures which involve the destruction of lesions by physical methods: electro-surgery, chemotherapy, and cryotherapy.

Excision of Bone Tissue

Removal of exostosis is the removal of a bony growth that arises from either the maxilla or mandible. It often involves the ossification (bone formation) of muscular attachments. An **ostectomy** is the surgical excision of all or part of a bone. A radical resection of mandible with bone graft is coded D7490.

Surgical Incision

An **abscess** is a collection of pus that results in disintegration or displacement of tissues. In such a case, the abscess needs to be opened and drained of pus, then cleansed and sutured closed. Abscesses are coded D7510 if they are intraoral (inside the mouth) and D7520 if they are extraoral (outside the mouth).

Code D7530 is used to bill for the removal of a foreign body, skin, or subcutaneous areolar tissue.

Code D7540 is used to bill for the removal of reaction producing foreign bodies in the musculoskeletal system.

A **sequestrectomy for osteomyelitis** is isolation of a portion of bone due to inflammation. This procedure prevents the inflammation from spreading to the surrounding bone.

Maxillary sinusotomy for removal of tooth fragment or foreign body is the surgical removal of a tooth fragment or foreign body from the maxilla sinuses.

There are some remaining dental codes used for fractures and dislocations. Some administrators will use these codes, but most will use the codes provided in the CPT. Review all the ADA codes until you are familiar with them.

Orthodontic Services

Orthodontics is the branch of dentistry concerned with the detection, prevention, and correction of abnormalities in the positioning of the teeth in relationship to the jaw. The alignment deals with both vertical and horizontal positioning of the teeth.

The principal of orthodontics is that in order for a person to properly chew food, each tooth must have an aligned opposing tooth. This alignment provides for the proper occlusion.

Many plans do not provide orthodontia benefits. Therefore, if teeth are being extracted (it is common for the bicuspids to be extracted to make sufficient room in the mouth for proper tooth alignment) or if teeth are being crowned (to increase vertical dimension and thus provide proper occlusion) for orthodontic purposes, even though the specific services may be covered by the plan, the services would not be covered because of the purpose of the treatment. Some plans may provide orthodontia benefits but only for children, up to a specific age.

Orthodontic treatment is divided into three classifications. The classifications range from the lesser level of misalignment (malocclusion) to the greatest level.

A class I malocclusion is called a **neutroclusion**. This occurs when the upper and lower set of teeth come together normally, but the teeth themselves do not occlude properly (**see Figure 29 – 4**). A class II malocclusions is called a **distoclusion**. This occurs when the maxillary arch protrudes out from the mandibular arch. A class III malocclusion is called a **mesioclusion**. This occurs when the mandibular arch protrudes in front of the maxillary arch.

There are other services in which only very slight guidance is required and the level is not even classified. Coding is based on the classification or the type of guidance being provided.

Preventive Treatment Procedure
Preventive treatment procedures are broken into three classifications: minor treatment for tooth guidance, minor treatment to control harmful habits, and interceptive orthodontic treatment. In each case the coding depends on whether therapy uses a removable or a fixed appliance. Appliances that are necessitated because of harmful habits such as tongue thrust, bruxism (grinding of teeth at night), thumb and lip sucking are usually covered only under orthodontics.

Comprehensive Orthodontic Treatment
Comprehensive orthodontic treatment is broken into two classifications: treatment of the transitional dentition (primary teeth), and treatment of the permanent dentition (permanent teeth). In each case, the coding depends on the degree of malocclusion (misalignment).

D8650   Treatment of the atypical or extended skeletal case

D8750   Post-treatment stabilization

Auto-reposition appliances are used in temporary mandibular joint (TMJ) treatment. Some orthodontic treatment is also done for this reason. TMJ is usually severely limited under most plans, but may be allowed if the plan has orthodontic coverage.

The total case fee is the amount charged by the provider for the entire orthodontic treatment program. This fee should include all diagnostic records, examinations, monthly fees, x-rays, including full-mouth x-rays, cephalometric tracings and photographs, and study models.

Most administrators will pay a portion of the total case fee (called the **banding fee**) upon activation of the orthodontic treatment. The remainder of the total case fee is paid on a monthly basis, and the provider must bill the monthly services charge as treatment is rendered. Some plans have provisions regarding the severity of the malocclusion for orthodontic benefits to be covered. If this is the case, the claim would need to be sent to the dental consultant for review. The average orthodontic case lasts 2 to 3 years.

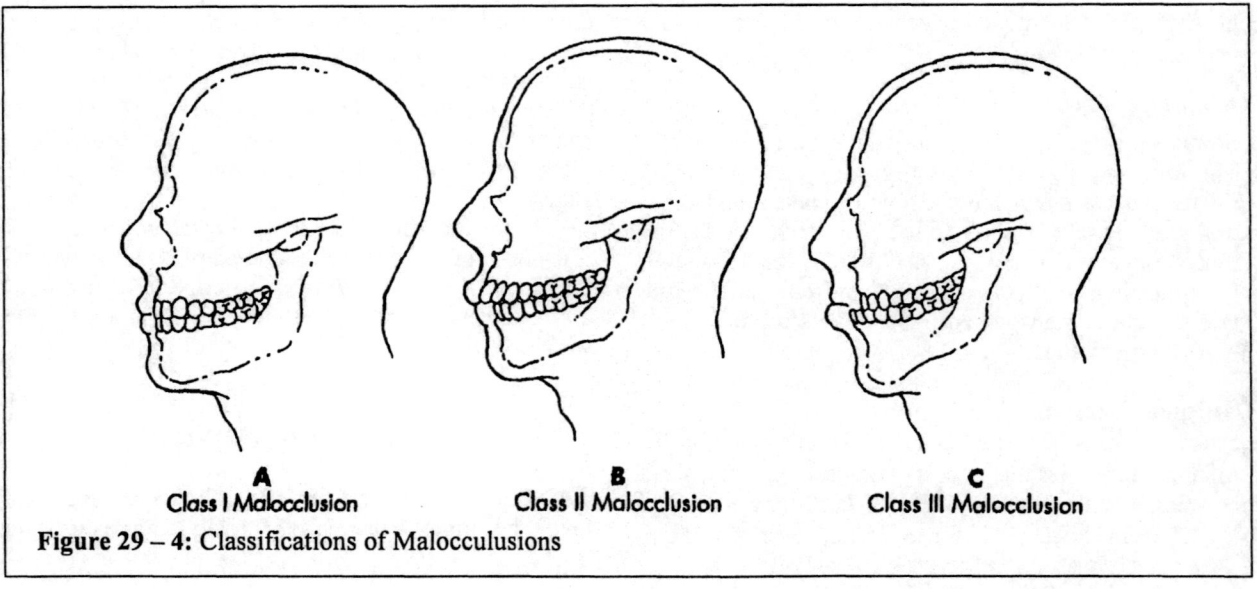

A
Class I Malocclusion

B
Class II Malocclusion

C
Class III Malocclusion

Figure 29 – 4: Classifications of Malocculusions

Adjunctive General Services

A number of miscellaneous services are necessary for the care and treatment of dental conditions. The following will provide a guide for some of the more common ones.

Unclassified Treatment

Palliative treatment is emergency treatment performed to relieve pain or prevent a condition from worsening. It is not a cure for the disease. Palliative treatment is performed on an emergency basis. After treatment, the patient is directed to go to his or her regular doctor during office hours for treatment of the underlying condition causing the pain.

Anesthesia

Code D9210 is used for local anesthesia (not in conjunction with the operative or surgical procedures). If another service is being performed, a local anesthesia is normally combined with the procedure and not allowed separately.

There are numerous types of anesthesia, as evidenced by the following codes:

D9211   Regional block anesthesia.
D9212   Trigeminal division block anesthesia.
D9215   Local anesthesia.
D9220   General anesthesia.
D9230   Analgesia.
D9240   Intravenous sedation.

General anesthesia is usually allowed for limited services. Usually by administration or through plan provisions, it will be allowed only on procedures that are more definitive (such as oral surgery). Many people have an anxiety about going to a dentist. In such cases, the provider may administer general, intravenous (IV) sedation, or "twilight sleep." Twilight sleep is a type of relaxation induced by the patient breathing gas. This may also be referred to as "laughing gas." IV sedation is usually allowed on the same basis as general anesthesia. Commonly, it is nitrous oxide. Many plans handle this on the same basis as a local anesthetic; that is, no additional allowance is provided and it may be combined with other procedures performed.

Professional Consultation

Code D9310 is used for diagnostic service(s) provided by a physician or dentist other than the practitioner providing the treatment. This code is also used for a second opinion. Often, the consulting provider is a specialist.

Professional Visits

These codes are used when a dentist visits a patient at the patient's home, at the hospital, at the office during regularly scheduled hours, or at the office outside of regularly scheduled hours.

Drugs

All drugs are coded as therapeutic drug injections or other drugs or medications.

Miscellaneous Services

These codes are used for services that do not fall into any other category. They are used to denote the application of desensitizing medications, any complications or unusual circumstances, the performance of an occlusion analysis, and the completion of a claim form.

Code D9999 is used for any services or procedures that do not have a code listed in the ADA code listing. It is classified as "unspecified" and usually requires the addition of a medical report describing the procedure.

Summary

Dentistry is officially that department of the healing arts that is concerned with the teeth, the oral (mouth) cavity, and its associated structures. This includes diagnosis, treatment, restoration, and replacement of missing portions or parts. Dentistry also includes surgical procedures performed in and about the inside of the mouth or oral cavity.

There are services in dentistry that are performed for other than existing pathologic conditions. Some of these existing services (such as prophylaxis, x-rays, fluoride treatments, and repair of dentures and bridgework) are specifically included as covered dental services under most plans, but are usually subject to limitations.

Other services are performed, not for a pathologic condition but primarily for cosmetic or similar reasons or at the election of the patient or dentist. Although the particular type or category of service that is received might be covered under the plan, benefits are usually not provided for services that are performed for cosmetic or similar purposes or at the election of the patient or dentist.

In 1969, the American Dental Association (ADA) created a coding system that also served to categorize dental services. This established a uniform nomenclature for all dental services. The ADA list classifies procedures under certain categories. Services (and thus their codes) are defined based on the type of treatment provided. It is important to know what type of service is being performed to code it properly. Familiarity with the different types of dental services and their codes will help to ensure accurate dental coding.

Assignments

Complete the Questions for Review.

Questions for Review

Directions: Answer the following questions without looking back into the material just covered. Write your answers in the space provided.

1. List the 10 ADA classifications of dental services.

    1. _____
    2. _____
    3. _____
    4. _____
    5. _____
    6. _____
    7. _____
    8. _____
    9. _____
    10. _____

2. What are diagnostic procedures? _____
    _____

3. What are preventive procedures? _____
    _____

4. What are cosmetic procedures? _____
    _____

5. What are prosthodontics? _____
    _____

6. What are restorative services? _____
    _____

7. What are endodontic services? _____
    _____

8. What are periodontic services? _____
    _____

9. Under what ADA category do routine fillings fall? _____

10. What are inlays and onlays and under what ADA category do they fall? _____
    _____
    _____

If you were unable to answer any of the questions, refer back to the section and then complete the answers.

Honors Certification™

The Honors Certification™ challenge for this chapter is a written test of the information contained within this chapter. Each incorrect answer will result in a deduction of between 1% and 5% from your grade. You must achieve a score of 85% or higher to pass this test. If you fail the test on your first attempt you may retake the test one additional time. The items included in the second test may be different from those in the first test.

Appendix 29 – 1

Dental Code List
The following list of dental codes is intended to be used for training and reference purposes only, since the particular company or plan guidelines may differ from those started. Please contact the American Dental Association or your State Department of Insurance for any changes or updates on this list. *

ADA Code	Unit Value	CFC	Description of Service
			Diagnostic (1000-0999)
			Clinical Oral Examination
0110	0.7	A	Initial oral examination
0120	0.5	A	Periodic oral examination
0130	0.8	A	Emergency oral examinations
			Radiographs
0210	1.4	A	Intraoral-full mouth series w/bitewings
0220	0.3	A	Intraoral-single, first film
0230	0.2	A	Intraoral-each additional film
0240	0.5	A	Imtraoral-occlusal film each
0250	0.4	A	Extraoral-single, first film
0260	0.3	A	Extraoral-each additional film
0270	0.4	A	Bitewing-single film
0272	0.5	A	Bitewing-two films
0273	0.6	A	Bitewing-three films
0274	0.7	A	Bitewing-four films
0275	0.2	A	Bitewing-each additional film
0290	1.0	A	Posteroanterior and lateral skull and facial bone survey film
0310	1.8	A	Sialography
0321	2.0	A	Temporomandibular joint, film
0330	1.2	A	Panoramic-maxilla and mandible, film
0340	1.2	A	Cephalometric film
0390	BR	A	Diagnostic radiographs (by report)
			Labs and Other Tests
0401	0.6	A	Complete blood count
0402	0.3	A	Urinalysis
0403	0.3	A	Hemoglobin
0404	0.3	A	Hematocrit
0410	0.8	A	Bacteriologic studies for determination of pathologic agents
0420	0.6	A	Caries susceptibility tests
0450	1.2	A	Histopathologic examination
0460	0.5	A	Pulp vitality tests
0470	1.1	A	Diagnostic casts
0471	BR	A	Diagnostic Photographs
0490	BR	A	Miscellaneous tests
			Preventive (1000-1999)
			Dental Prophylaxis
1110	1.0	A	Adults
1120	0.8	A	Children
1201	1.1	A	Topical application of fluoride (including prophylaxis)-children
1210	1.1	A	Topical application of sodium fluoride-4 treatments (excluding prophylaxis)
1211	1.9	A	Topical application of sodium floride-4 (including prophylaxis)

1220	0.3	A	Topical application of stannous fluoride-1treatment-(excluding prophylaxis)
1221	1.1	A	Topical application pf stannous fluoride-1 treatment (including prophylaxis)
1230	0.3	A	Topical application of acid fluoride phosphate – 1 treatment (excluding prophylaxis)
1231	1.1	A	Topical application of acid fluoride phosphate – 1 treatment (including prophylaxis)

Other Preventive Services

1310	BR		Dietary planning for the control of dental carries
1330	BR		Oral hygiene instruction
1340	BR		Training in preventive dental care
1350	0.6	A	Topical application of sealants – per quadrant
1351	0.5	A	Sealant – per tooth

Space Management Therapy

1510	3.8	A	Fixed-unilateral type
1515	5.5	A	Fixed-bilateral type
1520	5.0	A	Removable unilateral type
1525	6.5	A	Removable bilateral type
1550	0.8	A	Recementation of space maintainer

Restorative (2000 – 2999)
Fillings, Inlays Onlays, and Crowns
Amalgam Restorations (Including Polishing)

2110	0.9	B	Amalgam-1 surface, primary
2120	1.2	B	Amalgam-2- surfaces, primary
2130	1.5	B	Amalgam-3 surfaces, primary
2132	1.8	B	Amalgam-4 surfaces, primary
2140	1.1	B	Amalgam-1 surface, permanent
2150	1.4	B	Amalgam-2 surfaces, permanent
2160	1.7	B	Amalgam-3 surfaces, permanent
2161	2.0	B	Amalgam-4 or more surfaces, permanent
2190	0.8	B	Pin retention-exclusive of amalgam

Silicate Restorations

| 2210 | 1.2 | B | Silicate cement per restoration |

Acrylic or Plastic Restorations

2310	1.3	B	Acrylic or plastic or complete resin
2330	1.3	B	Composite resin, anterior teeth-2 surfaces
2331	1.8	B	Composite resin, anterior teeth-2 surfaces
2332	2.3	B	Composite resin, anterior teeth-3 surfaces
2334	0.8	B	Pin retention-exclusive of composite resin
2335	2.5	B	Acrylic or plastic composite resin (involving incisal angle or 4 or more surfaces)
2337	1.9	B	Composite resin with ultra-violet, 1 surface
2338	2.6	B	Composite resin with ultra-violet, 2 surfaces
2339	3.1	B	Composite resin with ultra-violet, 3 surfaces
2340	0.6	B	Acid etch for restorations
2380	1.5	B	Composite resin, posterior, primary-1 surface
2381	2.0	B	Composite resin, posterior, primary-2 surfaces
2382	2.5	B	Composite resin, posterior, primary three surfaces
2385	2.0	B	Composite resin, posterior, permanent-1 surface
2386	2.5	B	Composite resin, posterior, permanent-2 surfaces
2387	3.0	B	Composite, resin posterior, permanent-3 surfaces

Gold Foil Restorations

| 2410 | 5.0 | C | Gold foil-1 surface |
| 2420 | 6.5 | C | Gold foil-2 surfaces |

2430	8.0	C	Gold Foil-3 Surfaces

Gold Inlay Restorations

2510	7.0	C	Inlay-gold, 1 surface
2520	8.5	C	Inlay-gold, 2 surfaces
2530	10.0	C	Inlay-gold, 3 surfaces
2540	2.0	C	Onlay-per tooth (in addition to above)

Porcelain Restorations

2610	3.0	B	Inlay-porcelain

Crowns (single Restorations Only

2710	3.0	C	Plastic (acrylic)
2711	2.5	C	Plastic-prefabricated
2720	11.0	C	Plastic with gold (high and medium noble)
2721	10.5	C	Plastic with nonprecious metal (base metal)
2722	10.7	C	Plastic with semiprecious metal (low noble)
2740	10.8	C	Porcelain
2750	12.0	C	Porcelain with gold (high and medium noble)
2751	11.4	C	Porcelain with non precious metal (base metal)
2752	11.8	C	Porcelain with semiprecious metal (low noble)
2790	11.8	C	Gold (full cast; high and medium noble)
2791	10.6	C	Non precious metal (full cast; low noble)
2792	11.0	C	Semiprecious metal (full cast; base metal)
2810	11.8	C	Gold (3/4 cast; high and medium noble)
2830	2.0	C	Prefabricated stainless steel-primary
2840	1.5	C	Temporary (fractured tooth)
2891	4.5	C	Cast post and core in addition to crown
2892	2.5	C	Prefabricated post and core in addition to crown

Other Restorative Services

2910	0.8	C	Recement inlays
2920	0.8	C	Recement crowns
2940	0.8	B	Fillings (sedative)
2950	2.0	C	Crown buildup-including pins
2960	5.0	B	Labial veneer (laminate)

Endodonic (3000 – 3999)

Pulp Capping

3110	0.6	B	Pulp cap-direct (excluding final restoration)
3120	0.6	B	Pulp cap-indirect (excluding final restoration)
3220	1.2	B	Vital pulpotomy (excluding final restoration)

Root Canal Therapy (Includes Treatment Plan, Clinical Procedures, and Follow-up care)

3310	7.0	B	Anterior (excludes final restoration)
3311	6.5	B	Root canal therap-1 (excluding final restoration), Sargenti
3320	8.5	B	Premolar (excludes final restoration)
3321	8.0	B	Root canal therapy-2 (excluding final resoration), Sargenti
3330	11.0	B	Molar (excludes final restoration)
3331	10.5	B	Root canal therapy-3 (excluding final restoration), Sargenti
3341	11.0	B	Root canal therapy-4 (excluding final restoration), Sarengti
3350	2.2	B	Apexification (treatment may extend over 6 to 18 months)

Periapical Services

3410	8.0	B	Apiceoctomy-performed as separate surgical procedure (per root)

3420	9.0	B	Apicoectpmy-performed in conjunction with endodontic procedure (per root)
3430	3.0	B	Retrograde filling
3440	3.0	B	Apical curettage
3450	4.5	B	Root resection
3460	5.5	B	Endodontic implants

Other Endodontic Procedure

3910	0.8	B	Surgical procedure for isolation of tooth with rubber dam
3920	3.5	B	Hemisection
3940	1.1	B	Recalcification (perforations root resorption)
3950	1.4	B	Canal preparation and fitting of performed dowel or post
3960	BR	B	Bleaching of discolored tooth

Periodontics (4000 – 4999)
Surgical Services (Including Usual Postoperative Services)

4210	6.0	B	Surgical Services (Including Usual Postoperative Services)
4220	2.0	B	Gingivectomy or gingivoplast-per quadrant
4240	6.0	B	Gingival flap procedure
4250	8.3	B	Mucogingival surgery-per quadrant
4260	12.0	B	Osseous surgery (including flap entry and closure) per quadrant
4261	6.5	B	Osseous graft-single (including flap entry, closure, and donor site)
4262	8.5	B	Osseous grafts-multiple sites (including flap entry, and donor site)
4270	6.0	B	Pedicle soft tissue grafts (including donor site)
4271	6.5	B	Free soft tissue grafts (including donor site)
4272	11.5	B	Vestibuloplasty
4280	1.1	B	Periodontal pulpal procedures

Adjunctive Periodontal Services

4320	2.0	B	Provisional splitting-intracoronal
4321	2.2	B	Provisional splitting-extracoronal
4330	1.1	B	Occlusal adjustment (limited)
4332	4.4	B	Occlusal adjustment (complete)
4340	10.0	B	Periodontal scaling and root planning-entire mouth
4341	2.5	B	Periodontal scaling and root planning-per quadrant
4350	8.0	B	Tooth movement for periodontal purposes
4360	8.0	B	Special periodontal appliances (including occlusal guards)
4365	BR	B	Athletic mouthguard fabrication
4370	BR	B	Case pattern modifiers (by report)

Case Pattern Section

4500	BR	Type I Gingivitis – shallow pockets, no bone loss

Treatment
1. All necessary diagnostic procedures
2. Training in personal preventive dental care
3. Mouth preparation procedures
4. Routine finishing procedures
5. Posttreatment evaluation

4600	BR	Type II Early periodontics-moderate pockets, minor to moderate bone loss, satisfactory topography

Treatment
1. All necessary diagnostic procedures
2. Training in personal preventive dental care
3. Mouth preparation procedures
4. Occlusal adjustment (innecessary)
5. Surgical procedures usually involving curettage or gingivectomy

    6.   Routinee fishing procedures
    7.   Posttreatment evaluation

4700	BR		Type III Moderate periodontitis-moderate to deep pockets, moderate to severe bone loss, unsatisfactory topography

Treatment
1.   All necessary diagnostic procedures
2.   Training in personal preventive dental care
3.   Mouth preparation procedures
4.   Occlusal adjustment
5.   Surgical procedures usually involving flap entry and osseous procedures
6.   Routine finishing procedures
7.   Posttreatment evaluation

4800	BR		Type IV Advanced periodontitis – deep pockets, severe bone loss, advanced inability patterns (usually cases missing teeth and reconstruction)

Treatment
1.   All necessary diagnostic procedures
2.   Training in personal preventive dental care
3.   Mouth preparation procedures
4.   Occlusal adjustment
5.   Surgical procedures usually involving complex techniques
6.   Routine fishing procedures
7.   Posttreatment evaluation

Other Periodontic Services

4910	1.4	A	Preventive periodontal (periodontal prophlaxis)
4920	0.7	B	Unscheduled dressing change (by other than treating dentist)

Prosthontics (5000 – 5999)
Complete Dentures (Including Routine Postdelivery Care)

5110	16.5	C	Complete upper
5120	16.5	C	Complete lower
5130	16.5	C	Immediate upper
5140	16.5	C	Immediate lower

Partial Dentures (Including Routine Postdelivery Care)

5211	14.0	C	Upper – excluding clasps, acrylic base
5212	14.0	C	Lower – excluding clasps, acrylic base
5213	18.0	C	Upper – cast chrome base, with acrylic saddles, excluding clasps
5214	18.0	C	Lower – cast chrome base, with acrylic saddles, excluding clasps
5215	18.0	C	Upper – with 2 gold clasps with rests acrylic base
5216	18.0	C	Upper – with 2 chrome clasps with rests, acrylic base
5217	18.0	C	Lower – with 2 gold clasps with rests, acrylic base
5218	18.0	C	Lower – with chrome clasps with rests acrylic base
5230	20.0	C	Lower – with gold lingual bar and 2 clasps, acrylic base
5231	20.0	C	Lower – with chrome lingual bar and 2 clasps, acrylic base
5240	26.0	C	Lower – with gold lingual bar and 2 clasps, cast base
5241	26.0	C	Lower – with chrome lingual bar and 2 clasps, cast base
5250	20.0	C	Upper – with gold palatal bar and 2 clasps, acrylic base
5251	20.0	C	Upper – with chrome palatal bar and 2 clasps, acrylic base
5260	26.0	C	Upper – with gold palatal bar and 2 clasps, cast base
5261	26.0	C	Upper – with chrome palatal bar and 2 clasps, cast base
5280	4.0	C	Removable unilateral partial denture – 1 piece chrome casting, clasp attachments, per unit including pontics.

5281	4.0	C	Removable unilateral partial denture – 1 piece chrome casting, clasps attachments, per unit including pontics
5291	18.4	C	Full cast partial – with 2 gold clasps (upper)
5292	18.4	C	Full cast partial – with 2 chrome clasps (upper)
5293	18.4	C	Full cast partial – with 2 gold clasps (lower)
5294	18.4	C	Full cast partial – with 2 chrome clasps (lower)

Additional Units For Partial Dentures

| 5310 | 1.7 | C | Each clasp with rest |
| 5320 | BR | C | Each tooth |

Adjustments to Dentures

5410	0.8	C	Complete denture
5421	0.8	C	Partial denture (upper)
5422	0.8	C	Partial denture (lower)

Repairs to Dentures

5610	1.7	C	Repair broken or partial denture – no teeth damaged
5620	1.9	C	Repair broken complete or partial denture – replace 1 broken tooth
5630	1.0	C	Replace additional teeth – each tooth
5640	1.7	C	Replace broken tooth on denture – no other repairs
5650	2.2	C	Adding tooth to partial denture to replace extracted tooth – each tooth (not involving clasps or abutment tooth)
5660	3.0	C	Adding tooth to partial denture to replace extracted tooth each tooth (involving clasps to abutment tooth)
5670	1.8	C	Reattaching damaged clasp on denture
5680	2.5	C	Replacing broken clasp with new clasp on denture
5690	1.8	C	Each additional clasp with rest

Denture Duplication

| 5710 | 6.5 | C | Rebase upper or lower complete denture |
| 6720 | 6.5 | C | Rebase upper or lower partial denture |

Denture Relining

5730	4.0	C	Relining upper or lower complete denture (office reline)
5740	4.0	C	Relining upper or lower partial denture (office reline)
5750	5.0	C	Relining upper or lower complete denture (laboratory)
5760	5.0	C	Relining upper or lower partial denture (laboratory)

Other Prosthetic Services

5810	8.0	C	Denture – temporary (complete), upper
5811	8.0	C	Denture – temporary (complete), lower
5820	6.0	C	Denture - temporary (partial-stayplate), upper
5821	6.0	C	Denture – temporary (partial-stayplate), lower
5830	17/0	C	Obturrator for surgically excised palatal tissue
5840	17.0	C	Obturator for deficient velopharyngeal function (cleft plate)
5850	1.6	C	Tissue conditioning
5860	16.5	C	Overdenture complete (by report)
5861	BR	C	Overdenture partial (by report)

Maxillifacial Prosthetics
Extraoral Prostheses (Including 3 Months' Maintenance)

5911	RNE		Facial moulage (sectional)
5912	RNE		Facial moulage (complete)
5913	RNE		Nasal prosthesis
5914	RNE		Auricular prosthesis

5915	RNE		Orbital prosthesis
5916	RNE		Ocular prosthesis
5917	RNE		Composite facial prosthesis
5918	RNE		Replacement prosthesis
5919	RNE		Prosthesis dressing
5920	RNE		Ocular implant
5921	RNE		Orbital implant

Intraoral Prosthesis (Acquired Defects)

5931	RNE		Surgical obuturator
5932	RNE		Post surgical obuturator
5933	RNE		Refitting of obturator
5934	RNE		Mandibular resection (flsnge) prosthesis
5935	RNE		Mandibular resection (denture) prosthesis

Intraoral (congenial Defects)

5951	RNE		Feeding aid
5952	RNE		Pediatric speech aid
5953	RNE		Adult speech aid
5954	RNE		Superimposed prosthesis
5955	RNE		Palatal lift prosthesis
5956	17.0	C	Obturator
5657	RNE		Speech bulb

Implant (Facial, Mandibulaar, Cranial)

5871	RNE		Single implant
5972	RNE		Complex implant
5973	RNE		Subperiosteal implant
5974	RNE		Endosseous implant (in the bone)
5975	5.0	B	Endodontic endosseous pin (through root and into bone)

Treatment Prosthesis

5981	RNE		Splint – per arch
5982	RNE		Surgical stent
5983	RNE		Radiation carrier
5984	RNE		Radiation shield
5985	RNE		Docking device – cone locator
5986	2.8	C	Fluoride applicator – per arch
5987	RNE		Trismus appliance
5988	RNE		Infant orthopedic appliance
5989	RNE		Maxillary inclined plane and/or maxillary occlusal table
5990	RNE		Mandibular guide flange

Prosthesis, Fixed (6000 – 69999)
Fixed Bridges (Each Abutment and Each Pontic Constitute a Unit in a bridge)
Bridge Pontics

6210	11.8	C	Cast gold (high and medium noble
6211	10.6	C	Cast nonprecious metal (base metal
6212	11.0	C	Cast semiprecious low noble)
6220	8.0	C	Slotted facing
6230	10.0	C	Slotted pontic
6235	9.0	C	Pin facing
6340	12.0	C	Porcelain fused to gold (high and medium noble)
6341	11.4	C	Porcelain fused to nonprecious metal (base metal)
6242	11.8	C	Porcelain fused to semiprecious metal (low noble)
6250	11.0	C	Plastic processed to gold (high and medium noble)

| 6251 | 10.5 | C | Plastic processed to nonprecious metal (base metal) |
| 6252 | 10.7 | C | Plastic processed tp semiprecious metal (low noble) |

Retainers

6520	8.5	C	Gold inlay – 2 surfaces
6530	10.0	C	Gold inlay – 3 or more surfaces
6540	2.0	C	Gold inlay – (onlaying cusps)

Repairs

6610	2.5	C	Replace broken pin facing with slotted or other facing
6620	2.5	C	Replace where post is intact
6630	2.5	C	Replace broken facing where post backing is broken
6640	2.5	C	Replace broken facing with acrylic
6650	2.5	C	Replace broken pontic

Crowns

6710	5.5	C	Plastic (acrylic)
6720	11.0	C	Plastic processed to gold (high and medium noble)
6721	10.5	C	Plastic processed to nonprecious metal (base metal)
6722	10.7	C	Plastic processed to semiprecious metal (low noble)
6740	10.8	C	Porcelain
6750	12.0	C	Porcelain fused to gold (high and medium noble)
6751	11.4	C	Porcelain fused to non precious metal (base metal)
6752	11.8	C	Porcelain fused to semiprecious metal (low noble)
6760	10.7	C	Reverse pin facing and metal
6780	11.8	C	Gold (3/4 cast; high and medium noble)
6790	11.8	C	Gold (full cast; high and medium noble)
6791	10.6	C	Nonprecious metal (full cast; base metal)
6792	11.0	C	Semiprecious metal (full cast; low noble)

Other Prosthetic Services

6930	1.5	C	Replacement bridge
6940	2.8	C	Stress breaker
6950	5.8	C	Precision attachment
6960	3.0	C	Dowel pin – metal

Oral Surgery (7000 – 7999)
Extractions (Includes Local Anesthesia and Routine Postoperative Care)

| 7110 | 1.1 | B | Single tooth |
| 7120 | 1.1 | B | Each additional tooth |

Surgical Extractions (Includes Local Anesthesia and Routine Postoperative Care)

7210	2.0	B	Surgical removal of erupted tooth requires elevation of mucoperiosteal flap and removal of bone or section of tooth
7220	2.5	B	Impaction that requires incision of overlaying soft tissue and the removal of the tooth
7230	3.6	B	Impaction that requires incision of overlaying soft tissue, elevation of a flap, removal of bone, and sectioning of the tooth for removal
7240	4,2	B	Impaction that requires incision of overlaying soft tissue, elevation of a flap, removal of bone, and sectioning of the tooth for removal
7241	4.7	B	Impaction that requires incision of overlaying soft tissue, elevation of a flap, removal of bone, sectioning of the tooth for removal or presents unusual difficulties and circumstances
7250	2.0	B	Root recovery (surgical removal of residual root)
7260	8.0	B	Oroantral fistula closure (or antral root recovery)

			Other Surgical Procedures
7270	4.0	B	Tooth reimplantation or stabilization of accidentally evulsed or displaced tooth or alveolus
7271	8.0	B	Tooth implantation
7272	6.0	B	Tooth transplantation
7280	4.5	B	Surgical exposure of impacted tooth for orthodontic reasons including wire attachments when indicated
7281	3.5	B	Surgical exposure of impacted or unruptured tooth aid eruption
7285	3.0	B	Biopsy of oral tissue (hard)
7286	2.2	B	Biopsy of oral tissue (soft)
7290	4.0	B	Surgical repositioning of teeth
			Alveoloplasty (Surgical Preparation of Ridge for Dentures)
7310	2.2	B	Per quadrant in conjunction with extractions
7320	3.2	B	Per quadrant not in conjunction with extractions
			Stomatoplasty (Including Revision of Soft Tissue on Ridges, Muscle Reattachment, Tongue, Palate, and Other Oral Soft Tissues.)
7340	4.0	B	Per arch, uncomplicated
7350	BR	B	Per arch complicated including ridge extension, soft tissue grafts, and management of hypertrophied and hyperplastic tissue
			Surgical Excision (Excision of Reactive Inflamatory Lesions – Scar Tissue or Localized Congenital Lesions)
7410	3.0	B	Radical excision – lesion diameter up to 1.25 cm
7420	6.0	B	Radical Excision – lesion diameter over 1.25 cm
7425	1.7	B	Excision pericoronal gingiva
			Excision of Tumors
7430	3.0	B	Excision of benign tumor – lesion diameter up to 1.25 cm
7431	6.0	B	Excision of benign tumor – lesion diameter over 1.25 cm
7440	4.5	B	Excision of malignant tumor – lesion diameter up to 1.25 cm
7441	7.2	B	Excision of malignant tumor – lesion diameter over 1.25 cm
			Removal of Cysts and Neoplasms
7450	3.0	B	Removal of odontogenic cyst or tumor – up to 1.25 cm in diameter
7451	6.0	B	Removal of odontogenic cyst or tumor – over 125 cm in diameter
7460	3.0	B	Removal of nonodontogenic cyst or tumor – up t 1.25 cm in diameter
7461	6.0	B	Removal of nonodontogenic cyst or tumr – over 1.25 cm in diameter
7465	1.4	B	Destruction of lesions by physical methods; electrosurgery, chemotherapy, cryotherapy
			Excision of Bone Tisue
7470	45	B	ERemoval of exostosis – maxilla or mandible
7480	10.0	B	Partial ostectomy (guttering or saucerizaton0
7490	BR	B	Radical resection of mandible with bone graft
			Surgical Incision
7510	1.5	B	Incision and drainage of abscess – intraoral
7520	2.0	B	Incision and drainage of abscess - extraoral
7530	2.0	B	Removal of Foreign body, skin, or subcutaneous areolar tissue
7540	2.0	B	Removal of reaction-producing foreign bodies, musculoskeletal system
7550	5.0	B	Sequestrecotomy for osteomelitis
7560	8.0	B	Maxillary sinusotomy for removal of tooth fragment or foreign body

Treatment of Fractures (Simple)

7610	42.0	B	Maxilla – open reduction, teeth immobilized (if present)
7620	25.0	B	Maxilla – closed reduction, teeth immobilized (if present)
7630	42.0	B	Mandible – open reduction, teeth immobilized (if present)
7640	25.0	B	Mandible – closed reduction, teeth immobilized (if present)
7650	25.0	B	Malar or zygomatic arch – open reduction
7660	11.1	B	Malar or zygomatic arch – closed reduction
7670	25.0	B	Alveolus – stabilization to teeth, open reduction splinting
7680	53.0	B	Facial bones – complicated reduction with fixation and multiple surgical approaches

Treatment of Fractures (Compound)

7710	42.0	B	Maxilla – open reduction
7720	25.0	B	Maxilla – closed reduction
7730	42.0	B	Mandible – open reduction
7740	25.0	B	Mandible – closed reduction
7750	33.0	B	Malar or zygomatic arch – open reduction
7760	19.4	B	Malar or zygomatic arch – closed reduction
7770	19.4	B	Alveolus – stabilization of teeth – open reduction splinting
7780	53.0	B	Facial bones – complicated reduction with fixation and multiple surgical approaches

Reduction of Dislocation and Management of Other Temporomandibular Joint Dysfunctions

7810	28.0	B	Open reduction of dislocation
7820	5.6	B	Closed reduction of dislocation
7830	5.6	B	Manipulation under anesthesia
7840	4.2	B	Condylectomy
7850	4.2	B	Meniscectomy
7860	2.4	B	Arthrotomy
7870	2.8	B	Arthrocentesis

Other Oral Surgery
Repair of Traumatic Wounds

7910	3.3	B	Stature of recent small wounds up to 5 cm

Complicated suturing (reconstruction requiring delicate handling of tissues, wide undermining for meticulous closure)

7911	5.6	B	Up to 5 cm
7912	8.9	B	Over 5 cm
7920	BR	B	Skin grafts (identify defect covered, location, and type of graft)

Other Repair Procedures

7930	3.3	B	Injection of trigeminal nerve branches for destruction
7931	5.0	B	Avulsion of trigeminal nerve branches
7940	56.0	B	Osteoplasty (for orthognathic deformities)
7941	RNE	B	Osteotomy, ramus, closed
7942	RNE	B	Osteotomy, ramus, open
7943	RNE	B	Osteotomy, ramus open with bone graft
7944	RNE	B	Segmented or subapical per sextant or quadrant
7945	RNE	B	Osteotomy, body of mandible
7946	RNE	B	Maxilla, total (LE Fort I)
7947	RNE	B	Maxilla, segmented
7948	RNE	B	Osteotomy of maxilla or other facial bones for midface hypoplasia or retrusion (Le Fort II and III) without bone graft)
7949	RNE	B	Same as above except with bone graft
7950	BR	B	Osseous, osteoperiosteal, periosteal, or cartilage graft of the mandible – autogenous or nonautogenous

7955	BR	B	Repair of Maxillofacial soft and hard tissue defects
7960	3.3	B	Frenulectomy – separate procedure (frenectomy or frenotomy)
7970	4.4	B	Excision of hyperplastic tissue – per arch
7980	16.0	B	Sialolithotomy
7981	16.7	B	Excision of salivary gland
7982	19.4	B	Sialodochoplasty
7983	16.7	B	Closure of salivary fistula
7990	11.1	B	Emergency tracheotomy
7991	28.0	B	Coronoidectomy
7992	28.0	B	Eminectomy
7993	RNE	B	Alloplastic implant to maxilla and other facial bones
7994	RNE	B	Implant, chin homogous, heterologous, or alloplastic

(Orthodontics 8000 – 8999)
Preventive Treatment Procedure
Minor Treatment for Tooth Guidance

| 8110 | 7.0 | B | Removable appliance therapy |
| 8120 | 8.3 | B | Fixed or cemented appliance therapy |

Minor Treatment to Control Harmful Habits

| 8210 | 4.4 | B | Removable appliance thrapy |
| 8370 | 5.6 | B | Fixed or cemented appliance therapy |

Interceptive Orthodontic Treatment

| 8360 | 7.0 | B | Removable appliance therapy |
| 8370 | 8.3 | B | Fixed appliance therapy |

Comprehensive Orthodontic Treatment
Treatment of the Transitional Dentition

8640	BR		Class I malocclusion
8470	BR		Class II malocclusion
8480	BR		Class III malocclusion

Treatment of the Permanent Dentition

8560	BR		Class I malocclusion
8570	BR		Class II malocclusion
8580	BR		Class III malocclusion
8650	BR		Treatment of the atypical or extended skeletal case
8750	BR		Post-treatment stabilization

Adjunctive General Services (9000-9999)
Unclassified Treatment

| 9110 | 0.8 | B | Palliative (emergency) treatment of dental pain, minor procedures |

Anesthesia

9210	0.4	B	Local anesthesia (not in conjunction with operative or surgical procedures)
9211	0.9	B	Regional block anesthesia
9212	0.9	B	Trigeminal division block anesthesia
9215	0.4	B	Local anesthesia
9220	2.5	B	General anesthesia
9230	0.5	B	Analgesia
9240	1.5	B	Intravenous sedation

			Professional Consultation (Diagnostic Service Provided by Physician or Dentist Other Than Practitioner Providing Treatment)
9310	1.5	B	Consultation-per session
			Professional Visits
9410	1.0	B	House calls
9420	0.9	B	Hospital calls
9430	0.6	B	Office visits-during regularly scheduled office hours (no operative service performed)
9440	1.2	B	Office visit-after regularly scheduled office hours (no operative service performed)
			Drugs
9610	0.6	B	Therapeutic drug injection
9630	0.4	B	Other drugs or medicaments
			Miscellaneous Services
9910	0.6	B	Application of desensitizing medicaments
9930	1.0	B	Complications (postsurgical-unusual circumstances)
9950	11.0	B.	Occlusion analysis (mounted case)
9960	NC		Completion of claim form
9999	BR		Unspecified (by report to be described by statement of attending dentist)

30

Temporomandibular Joint Dysfunction

In this chapter you will learn:

- What temporomandibular joint (TMJ) dysfunction is and possible treatments.
- To recognize and define terms related to the diagnosis and treatment of TMJ.
- Which treatments are accepted and which are not accepted in the treatment of TMJ dysfunction.

Key words and concepts you will learn in this chapter:

Appliance – Any device or brace that includes banding or wiring used to reposition teeth, jaw joint, or lower jaw to restore normal occlusion.

Temporomandibular Joint (TMJ) Dysfunction – A manifestation of an abnormality of the joint where the lower jaw hinges to the upper jaw.

Temporomandibular joint (TMJ) dysfunction is a manifestation of an abnormality of the joint where the lower jaw hinges to the upper jaw (the temporomandibular joint; **see Figure 30 - 1**). This manifestation can result from various conditions: a disease of the bones such as arthritis, an injury to the TMJ joint, a disintegrative wearing down of the joint socket (the hollow area where the lower joint actually fits into the upper jaw), rheumatic fever or other connective tissue disorders, malocclusion, and even anxiety, emotional problems, and stress.

Symptoms of TMJ dysfunction can include tenderness and pain of the TMJ and surrounding areas, muscle spasms, limitation of movement, and clicking or grating sounds during chewing or speaking.

Coverage for TMJ

Because of the variety of causes of TMJ dysfunction, confusion often exists regarding how payment should be handled. If the disorder is caused by arthritis or rheumatic fever, it is due to illness and should fall under medical benefits. If it is caused by anxiety, stress, or emotional problems, it is a psychological problem and should be handled under psychological benefits. If the cause of TMJ dysfunction is malocclusion, it is a dental problem and falls under the dental benefits.

Even under dental benefits, categorizing TMJ dysfunction is confusing because some plans consider it to be a dental problem and some an orthodontic problem. If orthodontic services are not covered, TMJ benefits may then be denied for this reason. Add to all this confusion the knowledge that some dental providers have over-utilized the concept (often a patient has malalignment of the teeth, not TMJ dysfunction) in an effort to make the charges eligible under medical benefits rather than dental. Such an arrangement usually results in greater benefit payments because most medical plans have higher allowances and do not have the typical calendar year maximums that dental plans have.

As a result, most payors have adopted stringent guidelines regarding the payment of TMJ claims. Since treatment of TMJ is a very controversial subject, the following list shows some of the more common handling procedures. This is designed to provide guidance only. Remember that the handling of services vary greatly by payor. Therefore, the examiner needs to be aware of these differences and to recognize that special handling or guidelines may apply. Often, services and supplies must meet the following criteria to be payable:

- They must be recognized by the medical or dental profession as effective and appropriate treatment for TMJ dysfunction and its symptoms.
- They cannot be self-administered by the patient except with guidance by a licensed

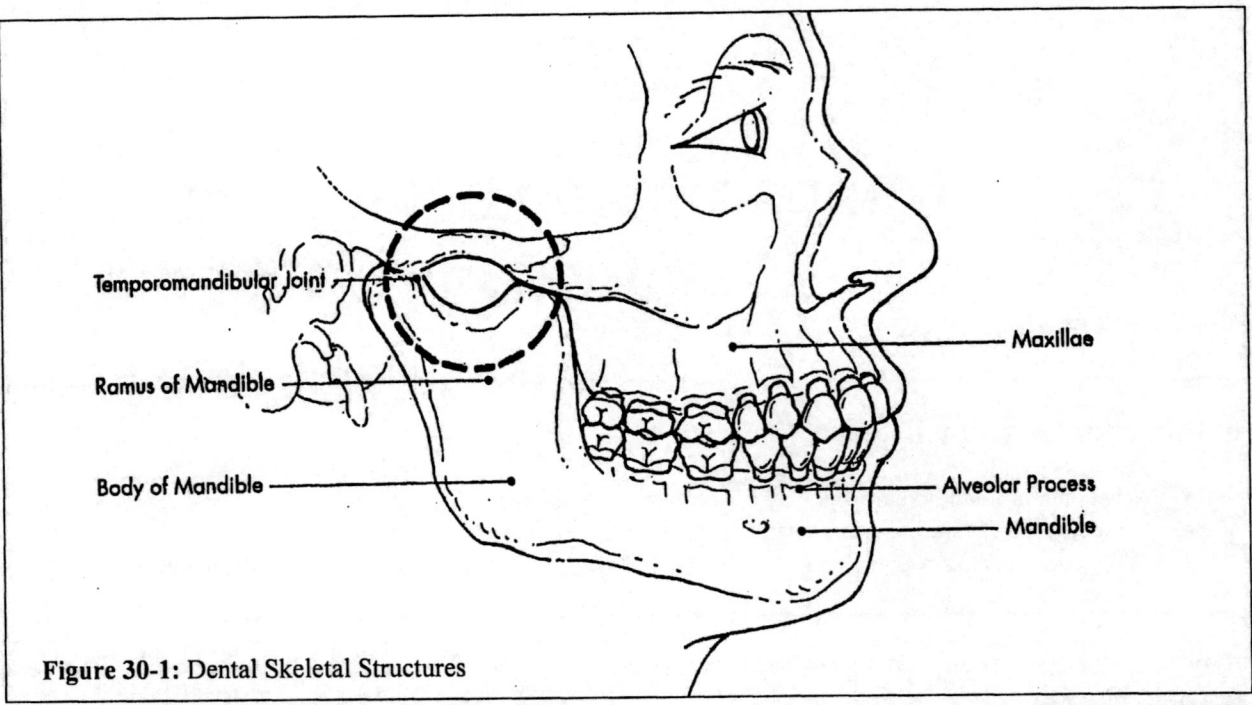

Figure 30-1: Dental Skeletal Structures

physician or dentist. The following guidelines generally apply when processing TMJ claims:

- Services or supplies covered under medical plans when provided or prescribed by a dentist for TMJ dysfunction would be recognized as covered medical expenses if they were provided or prescribed by a physician for treatment of comparable forms if intractable pain not involving TMJ dysfunction.
- Services or supplies covered under dental plans with separate orthodontic benefits are those that are primarily or exclusively used to alter occlusion or reposition the lower jaw.
- Services or supplies not covered under medical plans or dental plans without separate orthodontic benefits are those specifically excluded under the contract or used to alter occlusion or reposition the lower jaw.

In other words, look at the services that have been rendered, not the TMJ diagnosis. For example, if surgery is performed and the surgery would normally be covered under medical benefits for other than a TMJ diagnosis, then the surgery is covered. If onlays or crowns are used to build up the teeth and reduce the malocclusion, these benefits would be covered under dental benefits if onlays or crowns are normally covered for other non-cosmetic reasons.

If the exact cause of the TMJ disorder is proved, the following guidelines are used (often medical or dental review will be necessary before processing the claim):

- If the cause of the disorder is an accident, treatment is covered under both the dental and medical benefits.

- If the cause of the disorder is dental malocclusion (decayed, worn, or missing teeth), services are covered under dental benefits (if there is no exclusion for coverage of worn or missing teeth).
- If the cause of the disorder is congenital malocclusion (hereditary) or developmental (supernumerary teeth, teeth too large for the jaw), the plan should be consulted. If there is an exclusion for congenital or developmental problems, no benefits would be provided. If there is no exclusion, the services would be considered dental.

Some plans eliminate the confusion entirely by excluding TMJ services. In such a case, no benefits would be payable, regardless of the services rendered.

Appliances

An **appliance** is defined as any device or brace that includes banding or wiring used to reposition teeth, jaw joint, or lower jaw to restore normal occlusion. Appliances are often used in restoring normal occlusion to those with TMJ disorders. Examples of appliances include:

- Autorepositioning appliance.
- Bite splint.
- Bite guard.
- Orthopedic appliance.
- Orthodontic appliance.
- Mandibular orthopedic reposition appliance.

Claims Handling

Claims for appliances are usually referred to a dental consultant for review. Referral must include study models and all current x-rays that support the diagnosis.

If the consultant determines that current occlusion/malocclusion contributes to the patient's condition, benefits are usually paid only under orthodontic coverage unless the plan provides special TMJ coverage. If the plan does not have either type of coverage, benefits under medical or dental provisions (without orthodontic) are usually denied for "adjustments, correction, or altering of occlusion, jaw joint by any means, including appliances are excluded under the provisions of this plan." If the consultant determines that occlusion is not contributing to the patient's condition and there is radiographic evidence of degenerative joint changes, an appliance may be recommended and covered as an eligible medical expense. Of course, if the plan specifically disallows TMJ treatment, the services still will not be covered. TMJ handling procedures should always be discussed with your supervisor prior to processing.

Services and Supplies

The following is a list of services and supplies often associated with the treatment of TMJ disorders, their descriptions, and general dental and medical benefit guidelines to be used in the processing of claims for these types of services and supplies. This list is intended as a general guideline only, and specific payor policies should be consulted.

Acupuncture – Insertion of needles into designated areas of the body to relieve or prevent pain. Dental benefits: Allowable only in lieu of general anesthesia for a covered surgical procedure. Acupuncture is covered under the dental plan if medical coverage is not available and is subject to applicable frequency limits. Medical benefits: Allowable only in lieu of general anesthesia for a covered surgical procedure.

Behavior modification and relaxation therapy – Educational training to modify behavior patterns and teach relaxation techniques. Dental benefits: Deny, not usually allowable. Medical benefits: Deny, not for the treatment of a disease or injury.

Biofeedback – Electronic devices used to monitor and control automatic body functions such as blood pressure, respiration. Dental benefits: Deny, not usually allowable. Medical benefits: Apply biofeedback guidelines.

Cranial manipulation – Chiropractic adjustment technique involving manipulation and realignment of skull bones. Dental benefits: Deny, not usually allowable. Medical benefits: Deny, not broadly accepted or recognized as effective or necessary treatment of TMJ.

Diagnostic examinations – Oral examination not including or related to a prophylaxis. Dental benefits: Cover under dental plans if no medical coverage available. Medical benefits: Cover as a medical expense.

Diagnostic x-ray – Dental x-rays, x-ray of the jaw joint. Dental benefits: Cover under dental plans if no medical coverage available; subject to applicable frequency limits. Medical benefits: Cover as a medical expense.

Dry needling – See Acupuncture.

Electrogalvanic nerve stimulation/ stimulators (EGS) – Same as transcutaneous electrical nerve stimulation (TENS) except that a different type of electrical current is used. Refer to discussions on TENS.

Holistic therapy – Hair analysis, fingernail analysis, vitamin therapy. Dental benefits: Deny, usually not listed as a covered expense. Medical benefits: Deny, not broadly accepted or recognized as effective treatment for TMJ.

Injections of muscle relaxants or other drugs – Any prescription item to treat muscle spasms; local anesthesia to relieve pain; and steroids to reduce inflammation. Dental benefits: Cover under dental plan if no medical coverage, unless specifically excluded. Medical benefits: Cover when prescribed or administered by a physician or dentist and not excluded by the plan.

Kinesiographic analysis – Measurement and analysis of muscle movement. Dental benefits: Deny, not necessary. Malfunctioning or spastic muscles can be recognized by direct observation or examination. Medical benefits: Deny, not necessary. Malfunctioning or spastic muscles can be recognized by direct observation or examination.

Mandibular repositioners – Stabilizing appliance to reposition the mandible. Dental benefits: Cover if orthodontic services are covered. Medical benefits: Deny, not covered.

Occlusal equilibration – Corrects minor malocclusion by selective grinding of teeth. This balances the bite and allows the lower jaw to relocate into proper position. Dental benefits: Considered orthodontic treatment; cover only under plans with orthodontic benefits. Medical benefits: Deny. Adjustments, correction, or altering of occlusion by any means including appliances are included as covered expense only under plans that provide orthodontic benefits.

Occlusal rehabilitation – Full-mouth reconstruction using crowns, fixed bridgework, or dentures to restore occlusion and proper relationship between the upper and lower jaw. Dental benefits: Considered orthodontic treatment. Cover only under plans with orthodontic benefits and only for non-cosmetic purposes. Medical benefits: Deny. Adjustments, correction, or altering of occlusion by any means, including appliances, are included as covered expense only under plans that provide orthodontic benefits.

Oral surgery – Any surgical procedure necessary to remove, repair, revise, or reposition the TMJ such as meniscectomy, condylectomy, arthrectomy, high condylar shave, or joint implant. Dental benefits: Cover only when no medical coverage is available and oral surgery is listed as a covered dental expense. Medical benefits: Cover as a medical expense.

Physical therapy – Vapocoolant sprays, moist heat, massage, cold packs, exercise. Dental benefits: Deny, usually not considered a covered expense. Medical benefits: Deny. Physical therapy can be self-administered by the patient with instruction by a physician or dentist. Physical therapy does not require professional administration.

Prescription drugs – Any prescription item to treat muscle spasms. Dental benefits: Cover if benefits are payable for other prescription drugs. Medical benefits: Cover, payable as treatment of a physical condition, not a mental/nervous disorder.

Prosthetic appliances – Fixed or removable appliances (bridges, dentures, space maintainers). Dental benefits: Cover if prosthetic appliances are covered for other conditions. Medical benefits: Deny, not covered.

Splinting – Joining or tying the teeth for stabilization and immobilization or control of bad habits. Dental benefits: Cover if benefits are generally payable for splinting. Medical benefits: Deny, not covered.

Transcutaneous electrical nerve stimulation/stimulators (TENS) – Device used to apply electrical nerve stimulation to relieve TMJ pain. Dental benefits: Deny, usually not considered a covered expense. Medical benefits: Cover charges of a physician or dentist for office visits to administer or supervise TENS therapy for a maximum of one month for intractable pain only (8 to 12 visits, based on 2 to 3 visits per week, are reasonable). If TENS therapy is effective during the 1-month period, purchase or rental may be recommended. Allow benefits by following normal TENS guidelines limiting rental charges up to usual and customary purchase price of TENS unit.

Summary

Temporomandibular joint dysfunction is a manifestation of an abnormality of the TMJ joint. Since the causes of TMJ dysfunction can be many and varied, the treatment can also take a variety of forms. Some treatments fall under coverage for dental services; others are covered as medical services.

Because of the variety of payment options (and the past history of provider abuse in TMJ services), care should be taken to fully understand the terms of the contract and the TMJ policies of the payor.

Assignments

Complete the Questions for Review.

Questions for Review

Directions: Answer the following questions without looking back into the material just covered. Write your answers in the space provided.

1. What is TMJ dysfunction? _____

   _____

   _____

2. Why have some dental providers overutilized the concept of TMJ? _____

   _____

   _____

3. What are the claims handling procedures for TMJ appliances? _____

   _____

   _____

4. What is the description for diagnostic examinations? _____

   _____

   _____

5. Is holistic therapy usually a covered expense for TMJ? _____

   _____

   _____

If you were unable to answer any of the questions, refer back to the section and then complete the answers.

Honors Certification™

The Honors Certification™ challenge for this chapter is a written test of the information contained within this chapter. Each incorrect answer will result in a deduction of between 1% and 5% from your grade. You must achieve a score of 85% or higher to pass this test. If you fail the test on your first attempt you may retake the test one additional time. The items included in the second test may be different from those in the first test.

31 Dental Claim Form

In this chapter you will learn:

- To understand the dental claim form and its proper use.
- To identify the minimum date requirements on a dental claim form.

Key words and concepts you will learn in this chapter:

Dental Claim Form – A form that lists specific information regarding the patient and the services that have been or are going to be performed.

Patient Information Sheet – A form that contains information about the patient and their dental coverage.

There are two basic forms that dental providers use to bill claims. These forms are the American Dental Association (ADA) claim form and the Patient Information Sheet. The **Dental Claim Form** lists specific information regarding the patient and the services that have been or are going to be performed. The **Patient Information Sheet** contains information about the patient and their dental coverage.

The ADA Dental Claim Form

There are several versions of the ADA claim form currently in use; however, there is little difference among each of the versions. (**see Figure 31 - 1 and 31 - 2**). This claim form can be used as a billing statement for services performed, and also for a pretreatment estimate of services to be performed. However, at no time should services already performed be included with those for which the dentist or patient is seeking a pre-treatment estimate.

Following is a list of fields, their descriptions, and uses. The word "Same" as a description indicates that the description of the field is the same as the field name.

Field # Field Name/Description

Following are the numbers, titles and descriptions of the fields found on the ADA Dental Claim form.

1   *Type of transaction.* The appropriate box would be checked depending on whether services have been performed yet or not. Only one box should be checked. Therefore, services previously performed and services to be performed should not be combined on the same form.

2   *Predetermination or preauthorization number.* Enter the number provided by the payer when submitting a claim for services that have been predetermined or preauthorized.

3   *Carrier name and address.* The name and address of the payor to whom this bill is being sent.

Secondary insurance coverage fields
Leave fields 4-11 blank if there is no other coverage.

4   *Other dental or medical coverage?* Indicate yes or no. Fields 5 through 11 should be answered only if the patient has coverage by a second carrier.

5   *Subscriber name.* If the employee or subscriber indicated in 5 is not the patient, list the employee's/subscriber's name here.

6   *Date of birth.* If the employee or subscriber indicated in 5 is not the patient, list the birthdate here.

7   *Gender.* Check the box indicating the gender of the subscriber.

8   *Subscriber identifier (SSN or ID#).* If the employee or subscriber listed in 5 is not the patient, list the social security number here.

9   *Plan/ group number.* Indicate the group numbers of the policies indicated in 5.

ADA. Dental Claim Form

HEADER INFORMATION

1. Type of Transaction (Check all applicable boxes)

☐ Statement of Actual Services – OR – ☐ Request for Predetermination/Preauthorization

☐ EPSDT/Title XIX

2. Predetermination/Preauthorization Number

PRIMARY PAYER INFORMATION

3. Name, Address, City, State, Zip Code

OTHER COVERAGE

4. Other Dental or Medical Coverage? ☐ No (Skip 5-11) ☐ Yes (Complete 5-11)

5. Subscriber Name (Last, First, Middle Initial, Suffix)

6. Date of Birth (MM/DD/CCYY) | **7. Gender** ☐ M ☐ F | **8. Subscriber Identifier (SSN or ID#)**

9. Plan/Group Number | **10. Relationship to Primary Subscriber (Check applicable box)** ☐ Self ☐ Spouse ☐ Dependent ☐ Other

11. Other Carrier Name, Address, City, State, Zip Code

PRIMARY SUBSCRIBER INFORMATION

12. Name (Last, First, Middle Initial, Suffix), Address, City, State, Zip Code

13. Date of Birth (MM/DD/CCYY) | **14. Gender** ☐ M ☐ F | **15. Subscriber Identifier (SSN or ID#)**

16. Plan/Group Number | **17. Employer Name**

PATIENT INFORMATION

18. Relationship to Primary Subscriber (Check applicable box) ☐ Self ☐ Spouse ☐ Dependent Child ☐ Other | **19. Student Status** ☐ FTS ☐ PTS

20. Name (Last, First, Middle Initial, Suffix), Address, City, State, Zip Code

21. Date of Birth (MM/DD/CCYY) | **22. Gender** ☐ M ☐ F | **23. Patient ID/Account # (Assigned by Dentist)**

RECORD OF SERVICES PROVIDED

	24. Procedure Date (MM/DD/CCYY)	25. Area of Oral Cavity	26. Tooth System	27. Tooth Number(s) or Letter(s)	28. Tooth Surface	29. Procedure Code	30. Description	31. Fee
1								
2								
3								
4								
5								
6								
7								
8								
9								
10								

MISSING TEETH INFORMATION

34. (Place an 'X' on each missing tooth)

Permanent: 1 2 3 4 5 6 7 8 9 10 11 12 13 14 15 16 / 32 31 30 29 28 27 26 25 24 23 22 21 20 19 18 17

Primary: A B C D E F G H I J / T S R Q P O N M L K

32. Other Fee(s)

33. Total Fee

35. Remarks

AUTHORIZATIONS

36. I have been informed of the treatment plan and associated fees. I agree to be responsible for all charges for dental services and materials not paid by my dental benefit plan, unless prohibited by law, or the treating dentist or dental practice has a contractual agreement with my plan prohibiting all or a portion of such charges. To the extent permitted by law, I consent to your use and disclosure of my protected health information to carry out payment activities in connection with this claim.

X _____

Patient/Guardian signature   Date

37. I hereby authorize and direct payment of the dental benefits otherwise payable to me, directly to the below named dentist or dental entity.

X _____

Subscriber signature   Date

BILLING DENTIST OR DENTAL ENTITY (Leave blank if dentist or dental entity is not submitting claim on behalf of the patient or insured/subscriber)

48. Name, Address, City, State, Zip Code

49. Provider ID | **50. License Number** | **51. SSN or TIN**

52. Phone Number ( ) –

ANCILLARY CLAIM/TREATMENT INFORMATION

38. Place of Treatment (Check applicable box) ☐ Provider's Office ☐ Hospital ☐ ECF ☐ Other

39. Number of Enclosures (00 to 99) Radiograph(s) Oral Image(s) Model(s)

40. Is Treatment for Orthodontics? ☐ No (Skip 41-42) ☐ Yes (Complete 41-42)

41. Date Appliance Placed (MM/DD/CCYY)

42. Months of Treatment Remaining | **43. Replacement of Prosthesis?** ☐ No ☐ Yes (Complete 44) | **44. Date Prior Placement (MM/DD/CCYY)**

45. Treatment Resulting from (Check applicable box) ☐ Occupational illness/injury ☐ Auto accident ☐ Other accident

46. Date of Accident (MM/DD/CCYY) | **47. Auto Accident State**

TREATING DENTIST AND TREATMENT LOCATION INFORMATION

53. I hereby certify that the procedures as indicated by date are in progress (for procedures that require multiple visits) or have been completed and that the fees submitted are the actual fees I have charged and intend to collect for those procedures.

X _____

Signed (Treating Dentist)   Date

54. Provider ID | **55. License Number**

56. Address, City, State, Zip Code

57. Phone Number ( ) – | **58. Treating Provider Specialty**

Figure 31 – 1: Sample copy of the front of the ADA dental claim form.

General Instructions:

The form is designed so that the Primary Payer's name and address (Item 3) is visible in a standard #10 window envelope. Please fold the form using the 'tick-marks' printed in the left and right margins. The upper-right blank space is provided for insertion of the third-party payer's claim or control number.

a) All data elements are required unless noted to the contrary on the face of the form, or in the Data Element Specific Instructions that follow.

b) When a name and address field is required, the full entity or individual name, address and zip code must be entered (i.e., Items 3, 11, 12, 20 and 48).

c) All dates must include the four-digit year (i.e., Items 6, 13, 21, 24, 36, 37, 41, 44, and 53.

d) If the number of procedures being reported exceeds the number of lines available on one claim form the remaining procedures must be listed on a separate, fully completed claim form. Both claim forms are submitted to the third-party payer.

Data Element Specific Instructions

1. **EPSDT / Title XIX** -- Mark box if patient is covered by state Medicaid's Early and Periodic Screening, Diagnosis and Treatment program for persons under age 21.

2. Enter number provided by the payer when submitting a claim for services that have been predetermined or preauthorized.

4-11. Leave blank if no other coverage.

8. The subscriber's Social Security Number (SSN) or other identifier (ID#) assigned by the payer.

15. The subscriber's Social Security Number (SSN) or other identifier (ID#) assigned by the payer.

16. Subscriber's or employer group's Plan or Policy Number. May also be known as the Certificate Number. [Not the subscriber's identification number.]

19-23. Complete only if the patient is **not** the Primary Subscriber. (i.e., "Self" not checked in Item 18)

19. Check "FTS" if patient is a dependent and full-time student; "PTS" if a part-time student. Otherwise, leave blank.

23. Enter if dentist's office assigns a unique number to identify the patient that is **not** the same as the Subscriber Identifier number assigned by the payer (e.g., Chart #).

25. Designate tooth number or letter when procedure code directly involves a tooth. Use area of the oral cavity code set from ANSI/ADA/ISO Specification No. 3950 'Designation System for Teeth and Areas of the Oral Cavity'.

26. Enter applicable ANSI ASC X12 code list qualifier: Use "JP" when designating teeth using the ADA's Universal/National Tooth Designation System. Use "JO" when using the ANSI/ADA/ISO Specification No. 3950.

27. Designate tooth number when procedure code reported directly involves a tooth. If a range of teeth is being reported use a hyphen ('-') to separate the first and last tooth in the range. Commas are used to separate individual tooth numbers or ranges applicable to the procedure code reported.

28. Designate tooth surface(s) when procedure code reported directly involves one or more tooth surfaces. Enter up to five of the following codes, without spaces: B = Buccal; D = Distal; F = Facial; L = Lingual; M = Mesial; and O = Occlusal.

29. Use appropriate dental procedure code from current version of *Code on Dental Procedures and Nomenclature*.

31. Dentist's full fee for the dental procedure reported.

32. Used when other fees applicable to dental services provided must be recorded. Such fees include state taxes, where applicable, and other fees imposed by regulatory bodies.

33. Total of all fees listed on the claim form.

34. Report missing teeth on each claim submission.

35. Use "Remarks" space for additional information such as 'reports' for '999' codes or multiple supernumerary teeth.

36. <u>Patient Signature:</u> The patient is defined as an individual who has established a professional relationship with the dentist for the delivery of dental health care. For matters relating to communication of information and consent, this term includes the patient's parent, caretaker, guardian, or other individual as appropriate under state law and the circumstances of the case.

37. <u>Subscriber Signature:</u> Necessary when the patient/insured and dentist wish to have benefits paid directly to the provider. This is an authorization of payment. It does not create a contractual relationship between the dentist and the payer.

38. ECF is the acronym for Extended Care Facility (e.g., nursing home).

48-52. Leave blank if dentist or dental entity is **not** submitting claim on behalf of the patient or insured/subscriber.

48. The individual dentist's name or the name of the group practice/corporation responsible for billing and other pertinent information. This may differ from the actual treating dentist's name. This is the information that should appear on any payments or correspondence that will be remitted to the billing dentist.

49. Identifier assigned to Billing Dentist of Dental Entity other than the SSN or TIN. Necessary when assigned by carrier receiving the claim

50. Refers to the license number of the billing dentist. This may differ from that of the treating (rendering) dentist that appears in the treating dentist's signature block.

52. The Internal Revenue Service requires that either the Social Security Number (SSN) or Tax Identification Number (TIN) of the billing dentist or dental entity be supplied **only** if the provider accepts payment directly from the third-party payer.
When the payment is being accepted directly report the: 1) SSN if the billing dentist in unincorporated; 2) Corporation TIN if the billing dentist is incorporated; or 3) Entity TIN when the billing entity is a group practice or clinic.

53. The treating, or rendering, dentist's signature and date the claim form was signed. Dentists should be aware that they have ethical and legal obligations to refund fees for services that are paid in advance but not completed.

56. Full address, including city, state and zip code, where treatment performed by treating (rendering) dentist.

58. Enter the code that indicates the type of dental professional rendering the service from the 'Dental Service Providers' section of the *Healthcare Providers Taxonomy* code list. The current list is posted at: http://www.wpc-edi.com/codes/codes.asp. The available taxonomy codes, as of the first printing of this claim form, follow printed in **boldface**.

122300000X Dentist -- A dentist is a person qualified by a doctorate in dental surgery (D.D.S.) or dental medicine (D.M.D.) licensed by the state to practice dentistry, and practicing within the scope of that license.

Many dentists are general practitioners who handle a wide variety of dental needs. **1223G0001X General Practice**

Other dentists practice in one of nine specialty areas recognized by the American Dental Association:

1223D0001X Dental Public Health	**1223P0221X** Pediatric Dentistry
1223E0200X Endodontics	(Pedodontics)
1223P0106X Oral & Maxillofacial Pathology	**1223P0300X** Periodontics
1223D0008X Oral and Maxillofacial Radiology	**1223P0700X** Prosthodontics
1223S0112X Oral & Maxillofacial Surgery	
1223X0400X Orthodontics	

Figure 31 – 2: Sample copy of the back of the ADA dental claim form.

10   *Relationship to primary subscriber.* Indicate the relationship of the patient to the employee/subscriber listed in field 5.

11   *Other carrier name, address, city, state, zip code.* Indicate the name and address of the carrier indicated in field 5.

Primary subscriber information fields.

12   *Name, address, city, state, zip code.* Enter the name as last name, first name, middle initial, and suffix.

13   *Date of birth.* Enter birthdate as month, date, and year.

14   *Gender.*

15   *Subscriber identifier (SSN or ID#).* Same.

16   *Plan/ group number.* Indicate the group or policy number.

17   *Employer name.* Indicate the full name of the company for which the employee/subscriber works.

Patient information fields.

18   *Relationship to primary subscriber.* Check the appropriate box of self, spouse, child, or other. If other is checked, indicate the relationship of the patient to the employee or insured.

19   *Student status.* If the patient is a full-time student, enter the name of the school and the location (city) of the school.

20   *Patient name, address, city, state, zip code.* Enter the name as last name, first name, middle initial, and suffix.

21   *Date of birth.* Enter birthdate as month, date, and year.

22   *Gender.* Check the box indicating the gender of the patient.

23   *Patient ID/ account #.*

Record of services provided fields.

24   *Procedure dates.* Same.

25   *Area of oral cavity.* Designate tooth number or letter when procedure code directly involves a tooth. Use area of the oral cavity codes set from ANSI/ADA/ISO Specification No 3950 "Designation System for Teeth and Areas of the Oral Cavity".

26   *Tooth system.* Enter applicable

27   *Tooth number(s) or letter number(s).* Enter the tooth or letter number for the treatment described.

28   *Tooth surface.* The surface letter for each surface of the tooth affected by the treatment.

29   *Procedure code.* Enter the ADA procedure code for the service.

30   *Description.* Include all x-rays, prophylaxis, materials used, and so on.

31   *Fee.* Enter the amount billed for the service. Remember to total the fees and place this amount in the "Total fee charged" box at the bottom of the column.

32   *Other fee(s).* Used when other fees applicable to dental services provided must be recorded. Such fees include state taxes, where applicable, and other fees imposed by regulatory bodies.

33   *Total fee.* Total of all fees listed on the claim form.

Note: If the patient made partial payment for the services rendered, the words "Patient paid" should appear at the bottom of the description box and the amount paid should appear at the bottom of the fee column. This payment should then be subtracted from the above fees and the balance due placed in the box labeled "Total fee."

34   *Missing teeth information (Place and "X" on each missing tooth).* Report missing teeth on each claim submission.

35   *Remarks.* Enter any remarks that clarify the services or use of materials in services above. Indicate tooth number or procedure code if necessary for clarification of the procedure being remarked upon. Any additional description needed for fields 24 through 29 can also be added here.

36   *Patient/ guardian signature.* A patient must sign and date this box to authorize the provider (dentist) to release information to the payor.

37   *Subscriber signature.* Necessary when the patient /insured and dentist wish to have benefits paid directly to the provider. This is an authorization of payment. It does not create a contractual relationship between the dentist and the payer.

Ancillary claim or treatment information fields.

38   *Place of treatment.* Check the appropriate box for whether treatment was rendered at an office, a hospital, an Extended Care Facility (ECF), or other.

39   *Number of enclosures (00-99).* Indicate yes or no and the number of radiographs (x-rays) or models enclosed with the claim. These are generally enclosed to allow the claims examiner or review board to determine the necessity of services rendered. Radiographs or models will more often accompany a pretreatment estimate to assist the claims examiner in determining appropriate benefits.

40   *Is treatment for orthodontics?* If your answer is no, skip fields 41-42. If the answer is yes, complete fields 41-42.

41   *Date appliance placed.*

42   *Months of treatment remaining.*

43   *Replacement of prosthesis?* If your answer is no, skip field 44. If your answer is yes, complete field 44.

44   *Date of prior placement. .*
45   *Treatment resulting from?* Check the appropriate box of occupational illness or injury, auto accident, or other accident. If treatment is the result of an auto accident answer fields 46 and 47.
46   *Date of accident.*
47   *Auto accident state.*

Billing dentist or dental entity fields
Leave fields 48-52 blank if dentist or dental entity is not submitting claim on behalf of the patient or insured/subscriber.
48   *Billing dentist or dental entity name, address, city, state, zip code.* Enter the dentist's mailing address. Payments will be sent to this address.
49   *Provider ID.*
50   *License no.* Same.
51   *SSN or TIN.* Enter the dentist's social security number or taxpayer identification number.
52   *Phone number.* Same.
First visit date current series. Enter the date in which this series of treatments began (usually the date of the exam that initiated these treatments).

Treating dentist and treatment location information fields.
53   *Treating dentist's signature and date the claim form was signed.* By signing this form, the dentist indicates that those fees that have a date of service have been performed and that the charges are the actual charges for the services.
54   *Provider ID.* Same.
55   *License number.* Same.
56   *Address, city, state, zip code.* Same.
57   *Phone number.* Same.
58   *Treating provider specialty.* Enter the code that indicates the type of dental professional rendering the service from the "Dental Service Providers" section of the *Health Providers Taxonomy* code list. The current list is posted at: http://www.wpc-edi.com/codes.asp.

At the bottom of the form, there is a space for the dental claims examiner to indicate the maximum allowable amount for the services, the deductible applied to this claim, the coinsurance percentage that the payor is responsible for, the amount the payor is responsible for, and the amount the patient is responsible for. Some payors also use the "For administrative use only" field to list the allowable amount of each service.

As a claims examiner, if you receive a dental claim form, be sure to check whether it is for services that have rendered or if it is a request for a pre-treatment estimate. If the pre-treatment estimate box is checked

and there is no date of when services were rendered, the claim is for a pre-treatment estimate. Be sure not to issue a check for these services. Simply process the claim as you normally would, according to the benefit guidelines, and complete the information at the bottom of the claim form. A copy of the claim form and the EOB should be kept in the patient's file.

Patient Information Sheet

In addition to the ADA Dental Claim Form, a Patient Information Sheet will need to be completed for each patient. These Patient Information Sheets are created by each dentist or medical group. Therefore, the format varies widely from one dental office to another. However, the information contained on the Patient Information Sheet is generally the same.

The dental Patient Information Sheet is different from the medical Patient Information Sheet. Whereas the medical information sheet caries basic identifying information on the patient, the insured, and the carrier, the dental information sheet requests specific information regarding the types and amounts of dental coverages.

The purpose of the **Patient Information Sheet** is to determine the types and amounts of coverage on each individual patient prior to the rendering of services. It also informs the dental office of any procedures that are excluded or limited. This allows the dental office to estimate the coverage that the insurance payor will provide and to inform the patient of the remaining amount that they will be responsible for. Some dental offices require prepayment for services if the amount estimated to be not covered exceeds a specific dollar limit (i.e., $100).

Since the Patient Information Sheet is created by the dental office, it is by no means a determination of the exact benefits that a payor will reimburse. It is merely an estimate to help the dentist and the patient decide the monetary responsibility for the treatment sought.

When a new patient first enters the dental office, they will complete the Patient Information Sheet. However, patient's are often unsure of their dental insurance benefits. Thus, a member of the dental office will often call the claims examiner to confirm coverages.

The information generally found on a Patient Information Sheet is as follows (see **Figure 31 – 3**).
Insured. List the name of the insured.
D O B. List the date of birth for the insured.
S S #. List the social security number for the insured.
Employer. List the employer for the insured.
Group/policy #. List the group or policy number under which the insured is covered.

Patient(s). List the name of the patient for which treatment is planned.

Current date. List the current date.

Treatment date. List the date treatment is planned.

Contact name. List the name of the person who was contacted at the insurance carrier.

Contacted by. List the name of the person who contacted the insurance carrier.

Insurance company name. Same.

Insurance company address. Same.

Telephone number. List the telephone number of the insurance carrier.

Effective date. List the date coverage became effective for the insured.

Current. Indicate whether or not the insurance is current.

Patient Information Sheet

Insured _____ DOB _____

SS # _____ Employer _____

Group/Policy # _____

Patient(s) _____

Current date _____ Treatment date _____

Contact name _____ Contacted by _____

Insurance company name _____

Address: _____

Telephone number _____

Effective date _____ Current _____ Month to month _____

Coverage: Self _____ Spouse _____ Dependents _____

Fee schedule: UCR _____ Ins fee schedule_____ Authorization mandatory?_____

BENEFITS:

Annual/Lifetime maximum? _____ Amount _____ Available balance _____

Preventive _____ Deductible _____

Basic _____ Deductible _____

Major _____Waiting period _____ Deductible _____

Single crowns _____ Sealants _____ Age limit? _____

Replacement of missing teeth prior to coverage _____

Replacement of crowns and bridges _____

Replacement of partials and dentures _____

Prophylaxis _____

Scaling and root planning _____

FMX _____ Panorex _____

Specialist consultation _____

General anesthesia _____

Signature _____

Figure 31 – 2: Patient Information Sheet

Month to month. Indicate whether the insurance is month-to-month, quarterly, or annual premium payments. Most dental coverage is on a month-to-month basis. In such a case, care should be taken that the insured keeps his or her premium payments current throughout the term of the treatment. Otherwise, benefits may cease midway through the treatment process. It may be necessary to contact the payor several times during the course of extended treatment to ensure that coverage is still in place.

Coverage. Check each of the boxes for whom coverage is in force: self, spouse, dependents.

Fee schedule. Check the appropriate box as to whether the payor-allowable amount is determined by a UCR amount or an insurance fee schedule.

Authorization mandatory? Is pre-authorization mandatory for services? If so, at what dollar limit is it necessary to obtain pre-authorization for treatment?

Benefits: The following section is used to determine the benefits available.

Annual or lifetime maximum? Indicate whether there is an annual or a lifetime maximum amount.

Amount. Indicate the amount of the annual or lifetime maximum.

Available balance. Indicate the remaining balance available on the annual or lifetime maximum.

Preventive. Indicate the payor coinsurance percentage for preventive services.

Deductible. Indicate the deductible amount for preventive services.

Basic. Indicate the payor's coinsurance percentage for basic services.

Deductible. Indicate the deductible amount for basic services.

Major. Indicate the payor's coinsurance percentage for major services.

Waiting period. Is there a waiting period before these services come into effect? If so, indicate the amount of the waiting period here (i.e., 3 months, 1 year).

Deductible. Indicate the deductible amount for major services.

Single crowns. Are single crowns covered? If so, are there any limitations regarding materials? A simple notation such as "no gold" will suffice.

Sealants. Indicate whether sealants are covered under the dental plan.

Age limit? If sealants are covered, is there an age limit (i,e., only for children under age 14 can be written "-14" or "under 14")

Replacement of missing teeth prior to coverage. Indicate whether or not the dental plan covers replacement of teeth that were missing prior to the beginning of coverage. Most plans will not cover this service.

Replacement of crowns and bridges. Indicate whether replacement of crowns and bridges are covered under this dental plan. Also, indicate whether there are any limitations to this coverage.

Replacement of partials and dentures. Indicate whether the replacement of partials or dentures are covered under this dental plan. Also indicate whether there are any limitations to this coverage.

Prophy. Indicate any limitations on prophylaxis services. Often, dental plans limit coverage to twice in any 12-month period.

Scaling and root planing. Indicate whether scaling and root planing are covered under this dental plan. Also, indicate whether there are any limitations to this coverage.

FMX. Indicate any limitations on full mouth x-rays. Often, dental plans limit coverage to once every three years.

Panorex. Indicate any limitations on panorex (panoramic x-rays). Often, dental plans limit coverage to once every 3 years, if there is any coverage at all.

Specialist consultation. Indicate whether there is coverage for a specialist if the patient is referred by a dentist. Also, indicate whether the insurance carrier reserves the right to send the patient to a specialist for a consultation on diagnosis or proposed treatment.

General anesthesia. Indicate whether general anesthesia is a covered service under this dental plan. Also, indicate whether there are any limitations to this coverage (i,e., only if the patient is hospitalized).

Signature. Have the employee/insured sign the form at the bottom of the page.

Summary

The two forms used for billing dental services are the ADA Dental Claim Form and the dentist's Patient Information Sheet. The Patient Information Sheet helps the dentist to evaluate the coverage of services before initiating treatment or services. The ADA Dental Claim Form allows the dentist to either request a benefit determination on a proposed treatment plan or to report services already performed and request payment for those services.

Assignments

Complete the Questions for Review.

Questions for Review

Directions: Answer the following questions without looking back into the material just covered. Write your answers in the space provided.

1. What is the purpose of the Patient Information Sheet? _____

   _____

2. On the dental claim form, how would you indicate that the patient had made a partial payment for the services rendered? _____

   _____

3. What does a signature in the "Payment of benefits to provider" box mean? _____

   _____

   _____

4. What does the box "Month to month" denote on the Patient Information Sheet? _____

   _____

   _____

5. What does a dentist's signature on a dental claim form mean? _____

   _____

If you were unable to answer any of the questions, refer back to the section and then complete the answers.

Honors Certification™

The Honors Certification™ challenge for this chapter is a written test of the information contained within this chapter. Each incorrect answer will result in a deduction of between 1% and 5% from your grade. You must achieve a score of 85% or higher to pass this test. If you fail the test on your first attempt you may retake the test one additional time. The items included in the second test may be different from those in the first test.

32 Dental Benefit Structures

In this chapter you will learn:

- To understand general policy guidelines for processing dental claims.
- To understand contract provisions.
- To identify the type of treatment as indicated by the provider.
- To identify contract limitations and exclusions.

Key words and concepts you will learn in this chapter:

Alternative Benefit Provision. – This provision determines the level of care/treatment that can be provided under the plan.

Basic Dental Plan – Pays dental benefits at 100% of either the UCR or a scheduled amount.

Missing and Unreplaced Rule – This rule limits coverage for the replacement of teeth that are lost before the patient was covered by the plan.

Scheduled dental plan – Usually no conversion factors are involved. Instead, each ADA code has a specified dollar amount assigned to it.

The structure of dental plans is similar to the structure of medical plans. The dental portion of a plan is structured as a Basic plan, a scheduled plan, or an integrated/non-integrated comprehensive plan.

Initially, Basic plans were developed to cover the most common illnesses or diseases. This left the patient without coverage for serious or catastrophic illnesses. To alleviate this problem, Major Medical plans were structured to provide coverage against catastrophic illnesses that were left uncovered by the Basic plans. Finally, dental plans and vision plans were added to cover dental and optometry services.

Types of Dental Plans

Like medical plans, dental plans usually have coinsurance, deductibles, and limitations. However, the major difference between medical plans and dental plans is that dental plans encourage (and therefore, usually cover) preventive care. In addition, many dental plans pay a higher amount of coinsurance for diagnostic and preventive services than for other services and may also include an "incentive plan," which encourages participants to make regular visits to their dentist.

Basic Plans

A **Basic dental plan** pays dental benefits at 100% of either the UCR or a scheduled amount. The UCR can be a set amount, or it can be a sliding scale based on when the service was performed and the geographic area of the provider performing the service. The scheduled amount is a set amount based on the procedure code. It is not contingent on a conversion factor nor the location of the provider. As a rule, a Basic dental plan is kept entirely separate from an associated medical plan. That is, if there is a deductible, it is separate from the medical deductible. All dental limitations, exclusions, and maximums are kept separate and unique from the medical provisions. Basic plans are usually easy to process because the exact allowances and procedures are specified in the plan documents.

Scheduled Dental Plans

In a **scheduled dental plan**, usually no conversion factors are involved. Instead, each ADA code has a specified dollar amount assigned to it. This dollar allowance applies to the procedure, regardless of where the provider is located or when the procedure is performed. The scheduled allowance never changes unless a plan change is approved to either lower or raise the allowance. Seldom if ever are only a few procedures adjusted; usually, there is an overall plan adjustment. Many payors consider a Basic plan and a scheduled plan to be the same, and these terms are used interchangeably.

When a scheduled plan is involved, the scheduled allowance is programmed into the computer system so that the examiner simply enters the correct code. For manual claim computation, the examiner would check the schedule listing by code to determine the allowable amount. Deductibles are then subtracted from the scheduled allowances. However, like medical plans, if the scheduled amount exceeds the billed amount, the billed amount is the allowable charge. Generally, scheduled plans allow significantly less than current prevailing charges in most communities.

If a charge is submitted for a procedure that is not listed on the schedule, there are two handling methods:

1. The plan provisions may specify that unlisted procedures are not covered. Consequently, such expenses would be denied as not covered under the plan.
2. Unlisted procedures may be allowable (sometimes based on a consultant review). The amount allowed may be either a specified amount for unlisted procedures or current UCR (or some percentage of current UCR, or the amount billed). The plan provisions must specify which application to use.

Sometimes a Basic dental plan is combined with a scheduled plan, resulting in a scheduled Basic plan. In this case, the variations of the two types of plans will be applied as stipulated by the plan provisions.

Integrated Dental Plans

The ABC contract in the **Contracts** Chapter is an integrated medical-dental plan. What this means is:

- There is only one deductible amount for the plan. Any amount applied to the deductible on a dental claim goes towards satisfaction of the one deductible as does any amount applied on a medical claim. In this case, there is a $100.00 per person deductible, which can include both dental and medical charges.

    Notice that the family limit notated on the dental portion of the card is the same as that notated on the medical portion. This is because, as with the individual deductible, the family deductible limit can consist of both medical and dental charges. The first charges processed are the first charges applied toward satisfaction of both the individual and the family deductibles.

    The easiest way to think of this type of plan is that limits are considered plan limits, not a medical or dental limit.

- As with the deductibles, the same logic applies to coinsurance charges. On an integrated plan, the dental coinsurance percentage is usually the same as the medical coinsurance

percentage, and amounts applied on dental claims apply toward the plan coinsurance limit as do amounts applied on medical claims.

- Dental payments apply toward the plan Lifetime Maximum amount. However, the dental portion of the contract usually has a separate calendar year maximum.
- Benefits are usually based on a UCR basis, with conversion factors, geographic location, and time performed being important.

Nonintegrated Dental Plans

The XYZ contract in the **Contracts** Chapter is a nonintegrated plan. That is, the dental benefits are applied entirely separate from the medical benefits. Each portion of the contract has its own deductible, coinsurance limits, and so on. Only dental charges can be used to satisfy the dental provisions, and only medical charges can be used to satisfy the medical provisions. Therefore, in contrast to an integrated plan, a nonintegrated plan does not have plan limitations; it has dental plan limitations and medical plan limitations with no mixing of the two. Usually, this type of plan uses conversion factors, geographic location, and time performed to determine allowances.

Understanding Dental Contracts

The benefits and structure of a dental contract are set up in much the same way as medical contracts, with the same types of considerations.

Definitions

Before understanding any medical or dental contract, it is important to understand some basic definitions. Following are some of the more common terms and their meanings:

Allowable amount – The maximum amount that a plan will pay for a specific procedure. If the billed amount is less than the allowable amount, then the billed amount is considered the allowable amount. The allowable amount is usually based on a table of charges or a UCR amount.

Carryover deductible provision – Amounts applied to the individual deductible during the last three months of the preceding year are "carried over" and applied to the individual deductible for the following year. The amount will not be applied toward satisfying the family deductible amount.

Child – The offspring of the subscriber or the subscriber's stepchild or legally adopted child.

Coinsurance percentage – The percentage that is applied to the allowable amount after all deductibles and other provisions have been satisfied.

Coinsurance procedures – Procedures for which the payor has agreed to pay benefits, according to the provisions of the plan.

Effective date – The date coverage begins under the plan.

Experimental procedures – Procedures that have been done in laboratory or animal research and have not been approved for use by the general public.

Investigative procedures – Procedures that have been performed on humans, but are not widely accepted by the medical community as proven and effective.

Maximum benefit amount – Fixed dollar amount. The payor will pay up to this amount in a given period of time (usually either a calendar year or a lifetime). After this amount has been reached, no more benefits are paid.

Plan – The contract between the employer and the carrier regarding the benefits and conditions of their agreement for insurance coverage. The plan specifies such things as the deductible, the coinsurance amount, exclusions, any limitations on coverage, and covered and non-covered procedures.

Spouse – The husband or wife as determined by a legally valid marriage between members of the opposite sex. Some plan now recognize "partners" (members of the same sex) as a dependent on the plan.

Subscriber – The insured employee. The insured must be enrolled in the plan at the time that services are rendered to be eligible for benefits. The terms "insured" and "member" are also used.

Usual, customary, and reasonable (UCR) – A process of calculating the usual, customary, or reasonable charges for a given procedure in a given area. The formula takes into account the varying amounts of overhead that prevail in various cities. For example, a prophylaxis in Los Angeles would pay more than the same treatment on the same patient in Long Ridge, South Dakota. This would be due to the increased costs of doing business in Southern California (i.e., higher building costs, higher wage scales for employees, higher insurance costs).

Covered Expenses

In general, benefits are paid for services that are covered by the plan. The date on which services are rendered is considered the date charges were incurred. Benefits are not payable for services that were performed or begun before the commencement of the plan. In addition, most expenses are subject to an allowable amount based on a table of charges or on what is considered UCR for the time and place of the services.

Most dental contracts specifically list the services that are covered and those that are not covered. They also list the conditions (if any) that must be satisfied for treatment to be covered. These conditions can include:

- The person who may provide treatment (i.e., licensed dentist, oral surgeon).
- Coverage of only the least expensive, adequate materials. If other more expensive materials are used, payment will be limited to the allowable amount of the least expensive adequate material.
- Personalized services or special techniques that are covered at the rate of standard techniques.

Deductible

Each insured, if applicable, must meet a deductible amount for covered services before any benefits are paid. Any amounts for services that are not covered under the plan or for charges exceeding amounts covered by the plan are not applied toward the deductible.

Extension of Benefits

As with medical plans, some circumstances allow for an extension of benefits beyond the time when benefits would normally cease or the insured would no longer be eligible for coverage. Extension of benefits can be for the following reasons:

- An insured is totally disabled at the time coverage would normally end.
- An insured is confined in a hospital or skilled nursing facility and is considered totally disabled.

In such cases, benefits normally continue until the insured is no longer totally disabled, the maximum benefits have been paid, coverage commences under another plan, or 12 months have elapsed since the time coverage would have ended.

General Guidelines

Regardless of the method of classification, dental care and treatment provided by most plans is based on the premises covered in the following sections.

Is Treatment Covered or Excluded?

It is not enough to determine whether a disease or injury requires treatment. It must also be determined that specific services, supplies, or treatment received or planned will correct the condition and restore the mouth to form and function. It must then be determined whether these services, supplies, or treatments are covered under the plan.

Covered services are limited to the listed individual services that will correct or eliminate the specific disease or injury in accordance with recognized professional standards of care. Services not listed or specifically excluded, even when such services are necessary to correct or eliminate disease or injury, may not be considered for coverage.

Covered services vary from plan to plan. Examples of services that may fall into this category are periodontal splitting (when specifically excluded), occlusal guards for bruxism (a preventive service not specifically listed), a crown placed on a tooth with only incipient decay (listed service, but service is not appropriate and rendered in accordance with recognized professional standards of care for the degree of decay present).

Is Treatment Appropriate for the Condition?

The proposed treatment should be appropriate in light of the total existing dental condition. Because so much of what happens in the mouth is interrelated, if part of a disease or injury is left untreated or some of the involved teeth are left untreated, the services provided may be rendered ineffective in a short time. Also, certain treatment approaches may be unrealistic when the total condition of the mouth is considered. Examples are (1) the placement of fixed bridgework where the abutment teeth are diseased and untreated and (2) unreasonable efforts to save teeth, especially for older people who are nearly edentulous.

Are Services and Supplies of Acceptable Quality?

Materials as well as services are subject to poor quality. Material failure may result from poor laboratory fabrication or poor installation. Services failure may result from improper diagnosis, inadequate preparation, or poor mechanical skills. Examples of substandard quality are root therapy failure due to incomplete extraction of the root pulp, and denture or bridgework failure due to poor materials and fabrication.

What is the Benefit Level?

One of the major problems in providing benefits for dental services is that in dentistry frequently more than one procedure, material, or technique may be used in accordance with recognized professional standards of care to correct or eliminate a disease or injury. Most dental benefit plans have been designed to provide benefits based on a certain level of care so that each insured person receives the same benefit level consistent with his or her needs.

The intent of dental plans is to provide benefits for covered services based on a level of dental care that is adequate (when determined in accordance with generally accepted professional standards) for treatment of the existing dental condition. This means that for benefits to be payable, the care and treatment must not be below acceptable standards of quality and appropriateness; it also means that benefits will not be payable for care and treatment that exceeds the level that is adequate and necessary.

Expenses for care above the adequate and necessary level are the patient's responsibility unless specifically listed as payable in the plan provisions.

Moreover, benefits for care above this adequate and necessary level will not be provided, regardless of whether they are provided as a result of the member's or dentist's choice or the limited practice of the dentist or whether the services have already been provided. The member or dentist is entirely free in the choice of level of care, but this choice will not affect the benefits payable.

What Treatment Is Required?

Standard dental benefit plans provide benefits for services and supplies that are necessary for the treatment of disease or injury. Following are two examples of some standard wording that may appear in dental plans:

1. "Covered dental expenses are the reasonable charges that a subscriber is required to pay for necessary services received by a covered family member for the treatment of a non- occupational injury."
2. "Covered dental expenses are the usual charges of a dentist that an employee is required to pay for services and supplies that are necessary for treatment of a dental condition, but only to the extent that such charges are reasonable and customary, as herein defined, for services and supplies customarily used for treatment of that condition, and only if rendered in accordance with accepted standards of dental practice."

These definitions are supplemented by additional provisions, exclusions, and limitations, both general and specific. Most plans contain provisions similar to one of the following general exclusions:

- "No insurance is afforded for care, treatment, services, or supplies that are not necessary for the treatment of the injury or disease concerned."
- "Covered dental expenses do not include and no benefits are payable for charges for services or supplies that are not necessary, according to accepted standards of dental practice."

The intent of dental benefit plans is to provide benefits for covered services and supplies that are necessary to eliminate or correct a dental disease or injury to restore the mouth to reasonable form and function. Not only must there be an existing disease or injury present that requires some treatment, but also the specific service received or planned must be required and the disease or injury must be covered under the plan.

Prosthetics

Many policies require that the prosthesis replace "natural" teeth. The following are not considered natural teeth:

- Tooth roots, when the condition of the tooth preexisted the effective date of coverage.
- Congenitally missing teeth.
- Diastema (space between two adjacent teeth in the same arch).

The following teeth do not require replacement and are usually not covered:

- Third molars (wisdom teeth) that occupy the third molar position.
- Any tooth that is not in functional occlusion, that is, not opposed by another tooth in the opposite arch.

Example: a denture is replacing teeth #14 and #15, but teeth #18 and #19 (in the opposite arch) are also missing but are not being replaced. Because teeth #14 and #15 will not oppose teeth or prosthesis, their replacement will serve no function and thus, cannot be considered for coverage.

Initial Installation

Most plans have a plan limitation called the "**Missing and Unreplaced**" rule. This rule limits coverage for the replacement of teeth that are lost before the patient was covered by the plan. If the prosthesis will replace teeth that were missing prior to coverage and teeth lost while insured, benefits usually are provided for the entire prosthesis unless it represents an unusual attempt to gain benefits for teeth missing prior to coverage. If the plan does not have this limitation, benefits are payable (subject to all other policy limitations) for replacement of natural teeth whether or not they were extracted while covered. The way this provision works is:

If a tooth was missing prior to the effective date of coverage, bridgework, regardless of whether it is permanent or removable, will not be eligible for payment consideration under the plan. This would also include payment for crowns on the abutment teeth, unless the condition of those teeth is such that a crown would be appropriate treatment as covered because of an existing disease condition (decay).

For example, suppose that tooth #12 is missing and was extracted before the patient's effective date under the plan. Consequently, if the plan has a Missing and Unreplaced limitation, proceed with the following:

Step 1. Determine whether or not the missing tooth is covered.
a. In this case, bridgework to replace tooth #12 would not be allowable (because the tooth was extracted prior to the effective date of coverage).
b. If the tooth was extracted (or lost) after the effective date of coverage, a replacement for that tooth would be covered. If the replacement of a missing tooth is covered, crowning of the abutment teeth (the natural teeth right next to the space where the tooth is missing) is also automatically covered. X-rays are not required to determine whether or not the abutment teeth are decayed.

Remember that if the missing tooth is covered, the abutment teeth are also covered.

Step 2. Determine whether or not the abutment teeth are covered.
a. If the missing tooth is not covered, then the abutment teeth need to be evaluated on their own merits. That is, are these teeth decayed and in need of restoration themselves? X-rays will be required to evaluate this.
b. If restoration is required, is a filling sufficient or is a crown necessary? As a rule, this determination has to be made by a dental consultant or an experienced claims person. If a crown is required, the abutment restorations are covered even though the missing tooth is not covered.

The following represents how these claims are generally handled. However, such handling procedures vary greatly from administrator to administrator:

- If x-rays do not accompany the claim and no other services reported on the claim would require obtaining x-rays and referral to the consultant, the bridgework should be denied completely as teeth missing prior to coverage. If the claimant or dentist feels that the abutment teeth require crowns for restorative purposes, it is necessary to resubmit for that purpose.
- If x-rays are submitted with the claim or if other procedures would require x-rays and referral to a consultant, ask the consultant whether the abutment teeth would require crowns for restorative reasons. If referral to the consultant is not otherwise required and the examiner can tell that a crown would be required, referral is not required. If crowns would be required, they should be benefited as freestanding crowns, not as abutment.
- If x-rays are submitted with the claim and the consultant determines that crowns are not needed for restorative reasons, the abutments should be denied along with the pontics.

Another common dental plan provision that is often applicable to prosthetics is called an **Alternative Benefit Provision**. This provision determines the level of care/treatment that can be provided under the plan. Although other restorations are also affected by this provision, it is most frequently associated with prosthetics.

There are two basic types of dental programs that provide benefits based on a specific level of treatment:
1. Plans that have an alternate benefit provision.
2. Plans that do not contain an alternate benefit provision.

Note: All plans may not contain the exact wording "alternate benefit provision" or "alternate course treatment." However, the cumulative wording contained in the provisions indicates the applicable type of philosophy.

The terminology "alternate benefit" will be used in the following sections when explaining benefit determinations to members and providers. This terminology has been widely misinterpreted by the dental community to mean that the plan is dictating the course of treatment that must be used. That is not the intent. The member or the dentist can choose any method or materials for treatment. However, payment will be based only on what is determined to be the appropriate level of care.

Alternative Benefit Plans

Usually, an Alternative Benefit Provision (ABP) plan contains wording similar to that indicated in the following:

"Alternate Treatment – If alternate services or supplies may be used to treat a dental condition, covered dental expenses will be limited to the services and supplies that are customarily used nationwide to treat the disease or injury and that are recognized by the profession to be appropriate methods of treatment in accordance with broadly accepted national standards of dental practice, taking into account the family member's total current oral condition."

The "limitations" section may contain examples such as:

"If a cast chrome or acrylic partial denture will restore the dental arch satisfactorily, payment based on the applicable percentage of the reasonable and customary charge for such procedure will be made toward a more elaborate or precision appliance that the patient and dentist may choose to use, and the balance of the cost remains the responsibility of the patient."

The policy may contain a separate section entitled "alternate services," "optional treatment," or "alternate treatment," which details the alternate benefit concept.

The alternate benefit provision has been designed to clearly describe the intent and benefit level of the plans in relation to the various approaches to dental treatment. In combination with the necessary treatment provision, the claims office will have the necessary contractual "tools" to effectively administer the benefits of their dental plans without interfering in the patient/dentist relationship.

If an alternate benefit determination is challenged, detailed and conclusive proof from the dentist that an alternate procedure is inadequate would be required. Since professional dental judgment is necessary in such a challenge, the treatment and results of investigations need to be reviewed by a dental consultant.

Plans Without Alternate Benefit Provision

The benefit level for plans that do not contain an alternate benefit provision are controlled by application of the "necessary treatment" provision as well as the "appropriate" provision. As long as the treatment is not inappropriate in light of existing dental conditions, the service will be considered for coverage without regard to the relative costs of the various treatment methods.

Replacement Provisions

There are normally three provisions in a dental policy, one of which must be satisfied for a replacement prosthesis to qualify for coverage.

1. Additional extractions must occur while the patient is covered under the plan.
2. Five-Year Rule and Unserviceable.
   a. Under the 5-year rule, the former prosthesis must be at least 5 years old and unserviceable. The plan must specify any expectations.
   b. Under some plans, the 5-year rule does not apply to replacement of an unserviceable prosthesis under certain conditions (the plan must specify what the conditions are). If the provision is waived, it is usually because the initial prosthesis was not installed under the current dental expense plan.
   c. "Unserviceable" is fairly constant under all policies. The intent of this requirement is that not only is the existing prosthesis unserviceable, but also it cannot "reasonably" be made serviceable by repair, reline, or replacement of specific parts. "Reasonably" means that the cost of making the prosthesis serviceable versus the cost of replacement makes repair an unreasonable economic choice.
3. Immediate temporary denture and 12-month rule. For a prosthesis to qualify for replacement under this provision, both of the following requirements must be met:
   a. Immediate temporary denture: the existing prosthesis must be constructed of temporary material. Normally, this type of prosthesis is placed until tissue changes have stabilized. The intent of all plans is to provide dentures only once in any 5-year period, so usually a temporary is not covered.
   b. Twelve-month requirement: this requirement applies without exception whether or not the immediate temporary denture was installed before or while insured. No exception is usually made under this requirement for replacement that takes place after 12 months have elapsed. When a temporary denture

exceeds the 12-month limitation, the denture must meet either the additional extraction or 5-year/unserviceable provision to qualify for replacement benefits.

Any denture constructed of temporary material that is being replaced by a permanent denture can be considered "unserviceable" and in need of replacement. All other policy provisions must be met prior to determining benefits.

Office Visits

Office visits are generally eligible for coverage if they are for diagnostic purposes. Therefore, these visits are generally paid only when the office visit is billed alone or when it is billed with x-rays or prophylactic treatment. If an office visit is billed (on the same date of service) with any treatment other than prophylaxis or x-rays, it is usually not a covered benefit but is considered part of the normal service. It is presumed that a diagnosis and a plan of treatment were performed prior to the commencement of services.

Any charges for a follow-up review for treatment that occurs on the same day as the procedure is also considered an integral part of the procedure and should be included in the allowance for the procedure itself.

Care should be taken to ensure that this policy limitation is carried out correctly. A patient should not be penalized for failing to delay treatment for which there was no reason for delay. For example, if a cavity is discovered during a patient's routine 6-month check-up and the dentist fills the cavity at this time, the office visit should be allowable since it was for diagnostic purposes. Remember that if an office visit is billed with a prophylaxis or with x-rays, generally it is for diagnostic purposes.

Occasionally, the word "Consultation" will appear on a claim. A consultation is the same as an office visit, and the same limitations apply.

Cost Containment

Containing the costs that the carrier must pay is taken into consideration when writing a plan. Cost containment can include such provisions as predetermination (pre-authorization), incentive plans, variable coinsurance, and others listed and explained in the following text.

Predetermination

Many dental plans stipulate that expenses over a certain amount are not covered unless an estimate of the cost of services is submitted to the insurance carrier prior to the beginning of treatment. Often, this limit is between $100 and $300. Many dental plans also require predetermination for orthodontics and prosthodontics, regardless of the estimated cost.

If predetermination is not obtained, often the plan will not pay more than the predetermination limit, regardless of the amount that would have been allowable for the services.

Predetermination encourages the insured to take an active part in containing the cost of his or her dental care while giving the insured a basis for determining whether the recommended treatment is appropriate. It also discourages dentists from overcharging or prescribing unnecessary treatment because the complete treatment plan, and the related costs must be submitted prior to the beginning of treatment.

Predetermination is not an authorization to perform the services, but merely a statement of what the plan will pay for the listed services. After the predetermination is received, the decision whether or not to authorize treatment is up to the patient. The patient must determine whether the treatment is worth the cost or whether other treatment may be warranted that would cost less money. The determination of benefits usually has a time limit (generally 90 days) during which it is effective. After that time, a new determination of benefits must be requested.

Eexample: The plan states that predetermination must be obtained for all services over $300 or a limit of $100 is payable. Dental services were charged at a rate of $400. The UCR allowance for the service is $430. The coinsurance is 70%, and all deductibles have been satisfied.

If predetermination was obtained, the plan would pay 70% of $400, or $280. The member would be responsible for $120.

If predetermination was not obtained, the plan would pay only the $100 limit. The member would be responsible for $300.

Incentive Plans

Incentive plans encourage regular dental care, thus, decreasing the possibility that a minor problem will remain untreated until it becomes a major problem. Incentive plans usually work by increasing the coinsurance percentage for each year in which the insured saw a dentist. For example, during the first year of coverage the coinsurance may be paid at 70%. If the insured visited the dentist during that year, during the second year of coverage the coinsurance would be paid at 80%. If the insured visited the dentist the first and second year, the third year coinsurance would be 90% and so on. Usually, failure to visit a dentist (for any reason) during a given year will cause the loss of the increased coinsurance for the following year. In essence, the increased coinsurance is a reward for taking care of one's teeth.

In addition, the incentive programs may be limited by the type of coverage they provide. For example, many incentive programs apply only to preventive services and not to crowns, inlays, onlays, prosthodontics, and orthodontics.

Variable Coinsurance
Some dental plans vary the amount paid for different services. For example, they may pay 85% for preventive services, 65% for fillings and routine dentistry, 60% for prosthodontics services, and 50% for orthodontic services. This type of payment situation encourages the insured to seek treatment for a minor problem before it becomes a major one.

Preventive services can include not only regular diagnostic procedures (bi-annual check-ups), but also prophylaxis and even space maintainers to prevent the drifting of teeth.

Annual Maximums
Dental plans often have an annual maximum rather than a lifetime maximum. Once the "calendar year" limit has been reached, additional services are not covered. Often, dental plan maximums are much lower than major medical maximums. The average dental plan maximum is $1,000, whereas major medical maximums can often be as high as $1,000,000.

There are two exceptions to the annual maximum that are noteworthy:
1. If orthodontic work is covered, there is often a separate lifetime maximum. Some carriers allow only a portion of the lifetime maximum to be paid in any given year. This prevents someone from joining the plan, having expensive orthodontic work done, and then canceling the plan.
2. When dental coverage is integrated with medical coverage, then the dental coverage is often (but not always) considered part of the major medical lifetime maximums. In such a case, annual dental maximums are often eliminated.

Frequency Limitations
Many dental plans limit the frequency of certain treatments. For example, only one routine oral examination and bitewing x-rays may be allowable during a 6-month period. The following are other common frequency limitations:
- Full-mouth x-rays may be allowable only once every 24 to 36 months.
- Prophylaxis may be limited to twice a year.
- The 5-year and unserviceable rule (see previous text under Replacement Provisions) will be in effect for crowns, jackets, gold or cast restorations, bridgework, and dentures.
- Appliances to control harmful habits are usually limited to a single appliance with no allowance made for repair or replacement.

Waiting Period
Many insures include a waiting period within their contract for certain dental services. This reduces the likelihood that payments will be made for preexisting conditions and that the insured will join the plan just to have expensive treatment covered. The waiting period can be anywhere from 3 months to 1 year. Services that may be subject to the waiting period include fixed or removable prosthetics and cast restorations.

Exclusions
It is not uncommon for dental plans to exclude treatment with a high potential for abuse. The following 17 services are generally not covered by dental plans:
1. Cosmetic dentistry or services for comfort or hygiene.
2. Replacement of lost or stolen appliances.
3. Replacement of teeth that were missing before the insured joined the plan.
4. Treatment started before commencement of coverage under the plan.
5. Tooth implants.
6. Orthodontics may be covered by some plans with the payment of additional premiums.
7. Tooth wear. Over time, the surfaces of the teeth may be worn away due to bruxism or normal wear and tear on the teeth.
8. Charges over the allowable amount.
9. Charges covered by a Workers' Compensation plan.
10. Charges for which the insured would not be obligated to pay or for which there would be no charge if the patient were not insured.
11. Charges for treatment received in a U.S. Government hospital or provided by a local, state, or federal government agency.
12. Charges for services that were rendered by a relative (whether by blood or marriage) or by someone who lives in the insured's home.
13. Charges for which a third party is liable or legally responsible.
14. Experimental procedures.
15. Dietary planning or oral hygiene instruction.
16. Wars or acts of God or those for which the underlying cause of the damage was due to nuclear energy.
17. Charges for filling out claim forms.

Some exclusions are listed under the heading "Exclusions" in a contract; however, others may be listed throughout the benefit provisions. It is important to read the contract carefully to determine the proper benefits.

Second Dental Opinion
Questionable services may need to be evaluated by an independent dentist prior to commencement of treatment. The second dentist is usually selected by the plan, and the patient is referred to this dentist.

The first dentist is usually sent a form to fill out, stating the condition and the proposed treatment. This form is then sent to the second dentist or is taken by the patient. The second dentist will complete the examination and provide a report. These reports help

414 *Guide to Health Claims Examining*

the plan to make a determination of the covered expenses and allowable amounts for the services.

Since the second dental opinion is sought by the plan, the responsibility for payment of the consultation rests solely with the plan. The member is not charged for the consultation.

Medical Review

Services that have a high abuse rate are often referred to a dental consultant or a pre-screener prior to payment. The dental consultant determines the necessity of the procedures and makes recommendation for payment.

Before sending a claim to the dental consultant, the claims examiner should gather all of the necessary information for the consultant to make the determination of benefits. These items include the claim, any operative reports, and all x-rays.

Most payors have an itemized list of services that should be sent to the dental consultant before processing. Services on this list can include:

1. Temporomandibular joint procedures or services.
2. By report or relatively not established (RNE) procedures.
3. Multiple fillings (five or more on one claim).
4. Crown restorations, build-ups or posts, or any repairs to crowns.
5. Inlays and onlays.
6. Root canal therapy and apicoectomies.
7. Periodontal services.
8. Prosthodontics (partial dentures and bridges).
9. Multiple extractions (four or more on one claim).
10. Surgical extractions (including impactions).
11. Tests and pathologic exams.
12. Acid etch restorations.
13. Bonding or sealants.
14. Surgical procedures.
15. Palliative treatments.
16. General anesthesia charges.

After review, the claim is returned to the claims examiner with the determination of benefits included. The claims examiner may then adjudicate the claim.

Required Participation

Many dental plans require a high participation rate among the eligible insureds in a plan. For example, a dental plan may require that 95% to 100% of the eligible employees in a company must take the dental plan for it to become effective for the entire group. If the participation level drops below the required percentage, dental coverage for all plan members is suspended.

Other dental plans require the employer to contribute 100% of the cost of the plan for their employees. This nearly ensures that 100% of the employees will enroll in the dental plan since there is no cost for coverage.

Late Enrollment Penalties

Often people delay enrolling in a dental program until they are in need of dental services. This allows them to gain benefits with little or no contribution into the plan. To help discourage this, some plans specify that if an employee enrolls more than 30 days after they are eligible to enroll, many benefits will be limited to 50% of the amounts otherwise payable. In addition, some plans drastically reduce the calendar year maximum during the first year, even as low as $100.

Coordination of Benefits

Most dental plans carry a coordination of benefits clause, which states that benefits will be reduced if the member has other coverage (whether dental or medical) for services. Most plans stipulate that total benefits payable by both plans is not to exceed 100% of the charges.

Major Medical Coverage for Dental Procedures

Some procedures performed on the mouth or teeth are covered under dental plans, but may be covered under Major Medical plans. This holds true even though the services were performed by a dentist or an oral surgeon rather than an MD. These can include the following services:

1. Accidental injury to the teeth (see section on dental accidents).
2. Surgery to remove impacted or unerupted teeth or to remove supernumerary teeth. Major Medical benefits are generally paid in the case of tissue-impacted, partly bone-impacted, or totally bone-impacted teeth.
3. Jawbone surgery.
4. Tumors or cysts within the oral cavity.
5. Nasal, auricular, orbital, or ocular prosthesis.
6. Obturators or repair of the cleft palate.
7. Complex, subperiosteal, or endosseous implants.
8. Lab charges such as urinalysis, hemoglobin, hematocrit, and complete blood count.
9. Repair of fractures of the mandible, maxilla, or facial bones.

If a specific service is covered under the Major Medical portion of the plan, then all related services (such as exams and x-rays) are also covered under the Major Medical plan.

Other services that may or may not be covered under a Major Medical policy include:

1. **Emergency room benefits**. If emergency services are necessary and a dentist is not available, benefits may be allowable under the medical plan.

2. **Hospital and anesthesia benefits**. If hospital confinement is necessary for dental services, some plans allow Major Medical coverage for the hospital expense. Anesthesia expenses are usually covered for services that require hospitalization. Anesthesia charges are not usually covered for outpatient services. Hospital confinement may be necessary because of the severity of the condition or because of underlying factors. For example, if a patient has a history of hemophilia or unstable diabetes, because of the possible complications arising from the surgery, the hospital benefit is usually paid. When hospital benefits are covered under Major Medical, the physician's or dentist's fees are still covered under the dental plan.

3. **Oral-antral fistulas**. Oral-antral fistulas are unnatural openings between the oral and nasal cavities. If the opening occurs as a result of dental treatment (i.e., tooth extraction where the root has penetrated the sinuses), then the services would be considered dental. However, if the opening is treated after a 6-week period, it may be considered a medical expense even though the cause was tooth-related. This occurs because the delayed closure is usually the result of disease or infection. If the fistula is not a result of a dental condition, the cause of the fistula should be indicated (i.e., tumor, disease). In such cases, Major Medical benefits usually cover the services.

4. **Gross misalignment of the jaws**. Often, pretreatment study models and an operative report should be requested to assist in the determination of coverage. If the surgery is a covered expense, it is often covered under both medical and dental plans. The claim usually needs to be referred to a supervisor or a medical review committee for determination of coverage.

5. **Other surgical services**. The following surgeries may be covered under dental or medical benefits, depending on the plan: reduction of fractures to the mandible or maxilla, tumors or cysts of the gums or mouth, alveolectomy (due to a non-dental condition), cleft palate or similar medical condition, and non-dental bone surgery.

6. **Cobalt therapy-related services**. Cobalt or x-ray therapy causes damage to the teeth and tissues of the oral cavity. Dental services that are necessary due to cobalt or x-ray therapy are generally covered as medical.

7. **Prescriptions and injections**. Prescriptions and injections that are generally covered for non-dental services are usually also covered, when prescribed by a dentist or oral surgeon.

Occasionally, an orthodontic appliance (i.e., banding, braces) is used immediately before or after surgery. This appliance is often used as a splint. In this case, the appliance would be covered. However, care must be taken to ensure that the appliance is being used for splinting purposes and not for orthodontic purposes. Appliances used for orthodontic purposes would not be covered unless specifically indicated by the contract.

If a dental service is covered under Major Medical, some payors convert the ADA codes into the appropriate CPT or HCPCS codes and then apply the appropriate UCR conversion. The specific company and plan guidelines vary widely regarding Major Medical coverage for dental services and should be consulted prior to claim processing.

Dental Accidents

Many carriers cover accidental injury to permanent natural teeth under medical benefits. For the injury to qualify as an accident, you should be able to place the exact date, time and place at which the accident occurred. However, damage due to chewing or biting is generally not considered accidental.

Under the provisions of most contracts, the teeth must be permanent natural teeth, which were in place prior to the accident. Often dentures, partials, or "non-natural" teeth are excluded. In this case, if there was damage to the pontic and the adjoining abutment teeth, the abutment teeth would be covered but the pontic would not. However, if the teeth were evulsed (knocked out) as the result of an accident, fixed or removable prosthetics may be covered as "required to alleviate the damage." Likewise, deciduous teeth are often not covered since they are not permanent teeth.

Some plans may restrict payment to "sound" natural teeth. The term "sound" natural teeth defines teeth that are in good condition, without substantial restoration, fractures, cracks, extensive decay, or damage due to periodontal disease. The "good condition" clause applies to the crown of the tooth, and also to the root structure and the supporting structures of the tooth.

If a plan contains the wording "sound natural teeth," the presence of a fracture, large restorations, and other serious conditions may be grounds for denial of services. It may be necessary to obtain pre-accident x-rays of the tooth or teeth to determine whether or not they would be considered "sound."

Temporary Restorations

Occasionally, temporary restorations may be needed during the course of dental treatment. The most common reasons for temporary restorations are:

- When the patient has extensive caries, and several treatments may be required. The dentist removes the decay and inserts a temporary filling to seal the hole. This prevents further decay from taking place.
- When caries are extensive, a temporary filling allows the formation of reparative dentin and

seals the hole from exposure to bacteria. In this case, the temporary restoration may prevent the need for more extensive orthodontic treatment.

• Cavities may need to be sealed during endodontic therapy.

Generally, temporary fillings are not covered. They are considered a necessary part of permanent dental treatment and therefore, are included in the allowable amount of the covered dental expense. Some dental services (i.e., fixed restorations) normally involve several visits to the dentist over a period of time therefore, temporary fillings cover the prepared teeth during the fabrication of the restoration.

X-Rays

X-rays (also called radiographs) are taken because it is impossible to tell the extent of tooth damage by visual examination alone. X-rays are paid as diagnostic procedures, regardless of the licensure of the person performing the x-rays (i.e., dentist, oral surgeon). X-rays are billed individually according to their type and whether they were intraoral or extraoral (inside the mouth or outside the mouth).

Fourteen or more films that are done on the same day are considered a full-mouth x-ray and should be paid at the full-mouth x-ray rate. In addition, any combination of individual x-rays with a combined RVS unit value greater than that of a full-mouth x-ray should be paid at the full-mouth x-ray rate.

Occasionally, the examiner needs to request x-rays of an insured's teeth from the dentist to aid in determining the extent of damage and the amount of benefits that will be covered.

X-rays may be needed to help determine whether the work is cosmetic, to assist in determination of benefits, to aid in determining preexisting conditions, to aid in determining degrees and types of impactions or supernumerary teeth, to locate and identify tumors, cysts, or abscesses of the mouth, to evaluate the need for orthodontic treatment, and to review damage as the result of an accident.

In general, the following situations or services require the requesting of x-rays:

1. By report or RNE procedures (usually).
2. Multiple fillings (usually five or more billed on the same claim).
3. Crown restorations, buildups or posts.
4. Inlays and onlays.
5. Root canal therapy and apicoetomies.
6. Periodontal services.
7. Prosthodontics (partial dentures and bridges).
8. Multiple extractions (usually four or more billed on one claim).
9. Surgical extractions (including impactions).

The claims examiner is not expected to be able to determine the need for services from the x-rays. Reading x-rays requires extensive training and experience. However, the claims examiner can make a cursory examination of the x-rays and try to determine the benefits payable. In reviewing x-rays, claims personnel, as lay persons, can expect only to see where teeth are missing and to identify impacted teeth (but not the degree of impaction), malposed teeth, supernumerary teeth, mixed dentition, extensive caries, existing restorations, some forms of abscesses, and perhaps, evidence of the need for orthodontics. It requires a professional consultant to read and interpret x-rays for other than the most evident condition.

A processor or analyst, on reviewing x-rays, can approve benefits, but a consultant's opinion is required for all denials that require a professional opinion. No person other than a consultant can recommend that benefits be reduced or denied unless the denial is based on plan limitations or exclusions. The following guidelines will assist in the use of x-rays to determine benefits:

• If caries appear on x-rays, benefits should be allowable for restorations (fillings).
• If the caries are deep or extensive, benefits are usually allowable for restorations or crowns.
• If teeth are missing, benefits should be allowable for prosthetics (fixed or removable).
• If there are no teeth (the insured is edentulous), benefits are usually payable for full dentures.
• If several teeth are missing (especially several adjacent teeth), a consultant should review any planned bridgework.
• If there is extensive bone loss, restorative procedures or bridgework near the site of the bone loss should be evaluated by a consultant.
• If treatment is planned and the claims examiner is unable to see the need for treatment, services should be evaluated by the consultant.

Remember that damage or decay is usually more extensive than that shown on an x-ray. For example, treatment or replacement may be recommended for an existing restoration or crown, but the decay may be hidden beneath the restoration or crown on the x-ray (x-rays do not penetrate many crown and filling materials and therefore, show up as dark spots on a radiograph).

Some materials do not show up on x-rays. In this case, a tooth that looks as if it needs treatment may already have been treated. As a general rule, if the sides are rough or irregular, restoration has not been done. Smooth sides usually indicate prior treatment.

X-rays belong to the dentist and should be returned as soon as possible, preferably within one week of receiving them. At no time should x-rays be held longer than two weeks without a letter or call to the dentist to explain the delay and request permission to hold the x-rays for a longer period of time. At all times, x-rays should be handled with care.

Orthodontic X-Rays

If a general dentist makes x-rays to determine the need for orthodontics, the x-rays would generally be covered if orthodontic treatment is not covered. In this case, x-rays are used as a diagnostic tool to determine the need for orthodontic treatment. Policies that exclude orthodontic treatment would exclude all orthodontic services performed after the need for orthodontic services has been established, regardless of whether they were performed by the originating dentist or whether the insured was referred to an orthodontist for continued treatment.

To determine whether an x-ray is for the diagnosis of orthodontic treatment or a part of the orthodontic service, the following guidelines can be used:

- If the date of service for the x-rays is prior to the commencement of orthodontic services, x-rays should be allowable as diagnostic.
- If the date of service for the x-rays is after the commencement of orthodontic services, x-rays should be considered part of the orthodontic services.

Anesthesia

Anesthesia is usually required for most dental services other than x-rays, prophylaxis, and exams. The four types of anesthesia most commonly used for dental services are:

1. Local anesthesia.
2. Intravenous sedation.
3. Analgesia (nitrous oxide, twilight sleep).
4. General anesthesia.

Local anesthesia is the most commonly used anesthesia and is appropriate for most dental procedures. Local anesthesia can be identified as local anesthesia (09210 or 09215), regional block anesthesia (09211), or trigeminal division block anesthesia (09212). The allowances for local anesthesia are included in the allowance for the basic procedure, so no additional payment is provided for this service.

Intravenous sedation (09240) and analgesia (09230) are usually allowable only for surgical extractions or for four or more simple extractions performed during the same visit (intravenous sedation renders the patient semiconscious). Many plans also allow intravenous and analgesic anesthesia for any dental services performed on a patient less than 12 years of age. No permit is required for analgesic or intravenous sedation.

If intravenous sedation or analgesia is performed for other than the previously mentioned services and on a patient above 12 years of age, the allowance for general anesthesia (if any) may be awarded.

Sedative Fillings

Medicated or sedative fillings are considered to be temporary. As a rule, they may not be covered; the final restoration only may be the covered expense. If the medicated or sedative filling is done on the same day as the final restoration, it is usually considered a base and is combined with the charge for the final restoration, since the final should include the base. The combined charge would then be subjected to any UCR limitation based on the coding for the final restoration. If the final restoration is a crown and not a filling, the medicated or sedative filling may be allowable separately. This varies by administrator.

Cosmetic Services

Remember that just because a particular service is cosmetic and "excluded," the cost of the non-cosmetic, less expensive service may be allowable and that amount would be applied toward the cost of the more expensive service. Most plans are subject to the following exclusions:

- Cosmetic services, such as crowns that are not necessary because of disease or injury. This also includes the use of composite fillings on posterior teeth, bleaching of stains from the teeth, using crowns to straighten or align teeth in an arch, and so on.
- Precision attachments are usually excluded from consideration. They tend to be significantly more expensive than conventional clasps with no more usefulness.
- Characterization or personalization of dentures. Dentures can be custom-designed to include such features as staining or selected duplication of gold restorations that were present prior to the need for dentures.

Procedures that are considered wholly cosmetic include labial veneer (laminate) and bleaching of discolored teeth.

Unspecified and By Report Procedures

Unspecified procedures are codes that classify services that are not specifically listed in the section of the ADA code list. There is an individual code for each section of the ADA code list. These codes usually end in 99.

For example:
00999 – unspecified diagnostic procedure
03999 – unspecified endodnotic procedure

By report (BR) or relativity not established (RNE) procedures are procedures for which a unit value has not been assigned. This is usually because a procedure is new or not performed often enough for sufficient data to be collected to establish a unit value.

Generally, the insurer places a dollar limit on unspecified and BR/RNE procedures. Any claims for unspecified or BR/RNE procedures that fall below this dollar limit are allowed as billed. Any claims above this limit need to be sent to the review board to determine benefits. A common dollar amount is $100 to $150.

Summary

Although there can be multiple variations on all types of dental plans, as a rule, dental plans are easy to understand and apply. Missing and Unreplaced,

Predetermination of Benefits, Alternate Course of Treatment and Five-Year Replacement Rule are universal and generally apply to most plans, regardless of whether the plan is basic, scheduled, integrated, or non-integrated. Read the plan provisions to find out how to apply the benefits and what type of plan it is.

Assignments

Complete the Questions for Review.
Read through the dental sections of the ABC and XYZ Contracts to be sure you understand them (see the **Contracts** chapter).

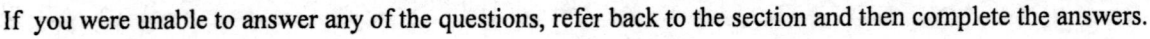 

Questions for Review

Directions: Answer the following questions without looking back into the material just covered. Write your answers in the space provided.

1. (True or False?) On an integrated plan, dental charges can be applied to the medical calendar year deductible.

2. Usually, on a basic plan the fees are not dependent on _____ nor _____

3. What are the four types of anesthesia most commonly used for dental services?

    1. _____

    2. _____

    3. _____

    4. _____

4. On a scheduled plan, an unlisted procedure may be handled in the following two ways:

    1. _____

    2. _____

5. (True or False?) The charges for local anesthesia are included in the allowable amount for the procedure. _____

If you were unable to answer any of the questions, refer back to the section and then complete the answers.

Honors Certification™

The Honors Certification™ challenge for this chapter is a written test of the information contained within this chapter. Each incorrect answer will result in a deduction of between 1% and 5% from your grade. You must achieve a score of 85% or higher to pass this test. If you fail the test on your first attempt you may retake the test one additional time. The items included in the second test may be different from those in the first test.

33 Processing Dental Claims

In this chapter you will learn:

- How to apply dental conversion factors.
- To process dental claims, applying all contractual provisions and limitations.

Key words and concepts you will learn in this chapter:

Claim Payment Worksheet - A form that is equivalent to an explanation of benefits. A copy of this form will be sent to the insured to explain the benefit payment for the claim.

Request for Additional Information Form is used when more information is needed from the provider of services or the patient regarding the services that were performed or the necessity for those services.

When a claim for dental services is received, it is the responsibility of the claims examiner to determine whether the claim received is eligible for payment. This entails several steps including verifying eligibility, determining whether services rendered are covered, and identifying any coverage limitations that may exist. After a preliminary investigation is performed, the processing of the claim can be completed.

Processing of dental claims occur in much the same manner as the processing of medical claims. Basic steps should be followed in each instance for the processing to be properly completed.

The Claim Form

First, determine the following:
1. Was the correct claim form used for the services provided?
2. Has the claim form been properly filled-out?
3. Is all the information complete?
4. Did the patient authorize the release of information?

If the answer to any of the above is no, deny the claim or pend it and request additional information.

Eligibility

Next, determine the eligibility of the patient:
1. At the time of service, was the patient currently enrolled under the plan (check each listed date of service)?
2. If a dependent, is the member within the proper age limit? If not within the proper age limit, is the member a full-time student and within the extended age limit?
3. Is the plan currently in force (i.e., have all premiums been paid)?
4. Have all eligibility requirements set forth in the contract been met?

If the answer to any of the previous questions is no, the claim is automatically denied since the patient was not insured at the time of service.

Other Insurance

Next, determine whether there is other coverage for the services rendered.
1. Does the patient have other insurance that might cover these services?
2. Is the claim related to Workers' Compensation?
3. Is the claim related to an accident? If yes, is there a third party that could be held legally responsible for the payment of the claim?

If the answer to any of the above questions is yes, try to determine the benefits that were paid by the other party.

Provider Authority

1. Who is the provider of service?
2. What is the medical degree of the provider of service? Is this a recognized medical degree for the type of treatment provided?
3. Is the provider's license number included on the form?
4. Is the place of treatment appropriate for the services rendered?

Coverage of Services

One of the most important parts of processing a claim is to determine whether services are covered. Ask yourself the following questions:

1. Are any of the services listed as excluded by the plan?
2. Was prior work done on the tooth that would exclude services?
3. Was there prior damage to the tooth that would exclude services (i.e., is the tooth previously listed as missing)?
4. If there are limitations to the number of times that a service can be provided, has that limitation been met previously?
5. If the service is an office visit, is there an exam, prophylaxis, or x-rays, or was the service in conjunction with a treatment procedure?
6. Does the missing and un-replaced provision apply?
7. Does the 5-year limitation apply for prosthodontics?
8. Does the less than 6-month limitation apply for adjustments to appliances, prosthetics, or dentures?
9. Have calendar year or lifetime maximums already been reached for this patient?

Evaluating the Services

If it is determined that the services are covered, then go to the next step, evaluating the service that was performed:

1. Are tooth numbers consistent with surfaces (anterior and posterior teeth with anterior and posterior surfaces)?
2. Do the services match the codes?
3. Were any services performed on the same day as another service that would disallow one of the other services (i.e., consultation/office visit billed with treatment)?
4. Do any other limitations apply (i.e., for multiple x-rays, full-mouth series)?

5. Does the contract list specific provisions for the services provided (i.e., orthodontic treatment is paid at 50%; second opinions are paid at 100%, and so on)?
6. Is a second opinion required for the services? If so, was a second opinion obtained? If a second opinion was required, but not obtained, what are the ramifications to the processing of the claim (are benefits reduced or denied)?

Processing the Claim

After it has been determined that the claim is correctly filled out, the member is covered, the provider is appropriate, there is no other insurance, and the services are covered, begin processing the claim.

The first step is to determine the allowable amount for the service or procedure. Using the ADA Dental Code List in Appendix 33 - 1, determine the type of service or conversion factor code (CFC). Types of service fall under three categories, and each is listed next to the unit value on the Dental Code list. The three types of services are:

A. Diagnostic and preventive services.
B. All other services excluding gold restorations, crowns, and prosthetics.
C. Gold restorations, crowns, and prosthetics.

Next, determine the appropriate unit value for the service or procedure. The unit value is listed on the Dental Code List next to the codes.

Then, using the first three digits of the provider's zip code, look up the conversion factor in **Appendix 33 - 2**: Dental Prevailing Conversion Factors. Be sure to use the correct conversion factor according to the type of service or conversion factor code.

Multiply the conversion factor by the unit value for the procedure. This will give you the allowable amount. However, remember that if the billed amount is less than the allowable amount, the billed amount is considered to be the allowable amount.

Completing the Claim Payment Worksheet

The **claim payment worksheet** is equivalent to an explanation of benefits. A copy of this form will be sent to the insured to explain the benefit payment for the claim. Therefore, it is important that each section be filled out completely to reduce the likelihood of confusing the insured. The claim payment worksheet is the same for dental benefits as for medical benefits.

The claim payment worksheet used for this book is intended to be an example only. It contains the information in much the same format as other insurance carrier payment forms. The worksheet and the guidelines for completing it are to be used for training and reference purposes only, since the individual company or plan worksheets may differ.

Complete the information regarding the patient and the insured first. This information is contained in the box in the upper left-hand corner of the payment worksheet.

Next, list each code in the first column on the claim payment worksheet. Only codes that are the same should be combined; otherwise, list one service per line, regardless of whether this will mean using more than one claim payment worksheet.

List the date(s) of service in the second column and the amount that the doctor billed in the third column.

Next, skip to the fifth column (Allowable) and enter the allowable amount as figured above. Then, subtract the allowable amount from the billed amount. The resulting figure will be the excluded amount; write this in the fourth column.

Make sure that you also enter a denial reason on the corresponding line in the denial reasons section. Usually, a brief explanation such as "$21.83 Not covered – charge exceeds amount covered by your plan" is sufficient. If the service is not covered, the corresponding code (or description) and an explanation should be listed in the same manner (i.e., $300 Not covered – orthodontic services are not covered by your plan).

If the plan has a basic allowance, the unit value should be multiplied by the basic allowance listed in the contract. For example, if the contract stipulates that the basic allowance for office visits is $7.00 and the service has a unit value of 1.0, the basic allowance is $7.00. Place the basic allowance amount in the sixth column (Basic 100%). Note that if the contract is part of a medical contract, the medical basic allowances do not transfer to the dental plan. If basic allowances are not listed in the dental section, they do not apply.

Subtract the basic allowance from the allowable amount and place the remainder in the seventh column.

After all the charges have been figured individually, add up the totals for each column and place each total at the bottom of each column. Check your totals for accuracy by adding the allowable amount to the excluded amount. The total of these two figures should match the billed amount on the claim. Likewise, the sixth and seventh columns added together should equal the allowable amount.

If the contract allows different percentages depending on the type of service (i.e., diagnostic services pay at 80%, restorative at 75%), then place all services with a similar co-payment amount together in a single column. There is an additional, eighth column to allow for varying percentages.

Figuring the Benefit Payment

Now, begin figuring the actual benefit payment. At the top of each payment column (columns 6 through 8), place the coinsurance percentage amount that applies to the figures in that column.

Next, check the contract for the deductible amount and the beginning financials for any previously paid deductibles.

- Has the deductible for this individual been satisfied?
- Does the deductible combine with the medical plan (the plans are integrated)? If so, has the deductible been satisfied under the medical portion of the contract?
- Has the family deductible been satisfied?
- Is there any carryover deductible from the previous year?

Using the latter questions and information, calculate the deductible that should be applied to this claim. Place the amount of the deductible across from the word deductible in the first column, in which benefits are payable at less than 100% (deductible is not taken from basic benefits). If the deductible remaining is more than the amount of the column, place the amount of the column in the deductible column and carry over any remaining amounts to additional columns with less than a 100% coinsurance amount.

Subtract the deductible amount from the total of the column. This remaining amount is the portion that is subject to coinsurance.

Multiply the amount subject to coinsurance by the insured's portion of the coinsurance amount (the remaining amount needed to reach 100%). For example, if the plan's coinsurance amount is 80%, the insured's responsibility is 20%.

Next ask the following questions:

- What is the maximum coinsurance amount listed in the contract?
- Has the coinsurance limit been met?
- If the individual coinsurance limit has not been met, has the family coinsurance limit been met?

If any coinsurance limits have been met, the coinsurance amount should be adjusted accordingly.

For example, if the individual coinsurance limit is $1,500 and $1,495 has been paid by the individual, then the coinsurance amount is $5. The correct coinsurance amount goes in the next space labeled coinsurance.

Subtract the coinsurance amount from the amount subject to coinsurance. The remaining balance is the amount subject to adjustment; place this amount in the next column.

Then ask:

- If there is other insurance, what amount is paid by the other insurance company?
- Are there any other reasons why there would be an adjustment on this claim?
- If so, what is the proper adjustment amount?

If there is an adjustment, place the amount of the adjustment in the following box labeled "Adjustment (see remarks)," and an explanation should be placed in the remarks box to the left.

Subtract the adjustment amount from the amount subject to adjustment, resulting in the adjustment amount (following box). Add the payment amount from each column and place the resulting payment amount in the box immediately to the right of the words "Payment Amount." This is the amount of the benefits being paid by the insurance carrier.

Note: If any individual or family deductible or coinsurance amounts have been met with this claim, place an asterisk beside the deductible or coinsurance amount and make a notation in the remarks box (i.e., 2004 Family deductible has been met).

Payees

All that is left is to determine to whom to make out the check and to update the financial history. Look back on the claim form. Did the insured authorize payment directly to the provider of services?

- If not, the payee would be the member.
- If so, check the billed amount from the claim and the amount (if any) that the patient/insured has already paid.
- If the difference between the billed amount and the amount the patient or insured paid (balance due) is more than the benefit payment amount and there is a valid authorization of benefits, then the payee would be the provider of services.
- If the difference between the billed amount and the amount the patient or insured paid (balance due) is less than the benefit payment amount and there is a valid authorization of benefits, then the payee would be the provider of services up to the balance due. Any remaining funds would then be paid to the member.

Updating History

Updating the payment history is vitally important to ensure that proper benefit payments are calculated. Each of the previous questions that related to previous payments of deductibles, coinsurance amounts, satisfaction of individual or family limits, and accident benefits will change with the processing of each claim.

On the payment worksheet, the updated history appears in the left-hand corner of the sheet. If claims are processed by computer, the computer usually automatically should handles the updating of the history.

If accident benefits were paid on this claim, add the payment amount of the accident benefits to any previous accident benefit amounts paid on this individual in this calendar year. Place the amount on the first line along with the current year.

Add the amount of the benefits paid to all previous benefits paid. If the plan has a calendar year maximum rather than a lifetime maximum, add the amount of benefits paid to all previous benefits paid during that calendar year. Place the result in the lifetime maximum space on the next line. If the plan has a calendar year maximum, the word "lifetime" should be replaced by the words "calendar year," and the current year should be included.

Add the amount of any deductibles calculated on this claim to any previously paid deductible amounts, and place the result in the deductible space with the current year.

If any of the dates of service on this claim falls within the last 3 months of the calendar year and the contract includes a carryover provision, place the amount of deductible paid on those services on the line labeled carryover deductible, along with the year. If there is more than one date of service and some are in the last 3 months and others are not, the deductible amount should be taken from the amount(s) of the services in the order in which they were received.

For example:

An exam and x-ray were performed on 9/18. Two cavities were found and an appointment was made for filling them on 10/10. The billed amount for the exam and x-ray was $40, and all of it was allowable (the UCR amount was higher than the billed amount). The allowable amount for the filling was $120.

The patient had satisfied $75 of the $150 deductible. The total paid deductible amount would be $75 on this claim. Forty dollars of the deductible would be for the first two services and $35 would be for the two fillings. Therefore, $35 would be considered the carryover deductible amount.

Finally, add the amount listed on the coinsurance line with any previous coinsurance amounts for the calendar year. Place the total, along with the year, on the coinsurance line of the financial history box.

You have now completed payment on this claim.

Dental Form Letters

Occasionally, certain form letters are used during the processing of dental claims. These form letters are the same as those used for medical claims processing, so they have not been duplicated here.

Request for Additional Information

A **Request for Additional Information Form** is used when more information is needed from the provider of services or the patient regarding the services that were performed or the necessity for those services. If there is any question on the claim, especially regarding the services, the patient identification, or other insurance that might be applicable, a request for additional information forms should be completed and mailed out.

Third Party Liability

If the services were performed as the result of a work related situation, The Workers' Compensation carrier should be paying the bill, not the member's insurance carrier. In addition, if the patient was involved in an accident (especially an auto accident), another insurance carrier may be responsible for all or part of the bill. In this case, this would be the insurance carrier of the driver who caused the accident. In an accident that is not auto-related, negligence may be cited as a reason for another carrier to incur responsibility (i.e., the patient fell through a rotted stair at a grocery store and broke his leg).

If any of the latter cases apply, the patient's payor may make payment on the claim; however, the payor usually requires the insured to sign a third party liability statement. In effect, this statement provides that if any monies are paid by a third party on the claim(s), the patient's insurance carrier will receive the money. After the carrier has been reimbursed for all monies paid out then additional monies revert to the patient or the insured.

Authorization to Release Information

Occasionally, no patient or insured signature is on file, nor on the claim that authorizes the release of information to the payor. This authorization must be completed before a claim is sent in.

Often, an insurance carrier has a copy of an authorization to release information on file. This allows the carrier to receive requested claim information without delay.

Handling Fraudulent Dental Claims

Occasionally, dentists and insureds submit fraudulent claims for processing. These fraudulent claims can include the following:
- Claims that have been submitted twice, either to the same insurer or to different insurers.
- Claims that have been submitted for services that were not actually rendered.
- Claims that have been altered to make it appear that services were performed on a different date, or patient.

The various types of fraudulent dental claim situations are as follows:
- Duplicate charges.
- Duplicate services.
- Altering dates of treatment.
- Reporting services that are not on the same as those actually done.
- False information or rationale about diagnosis, treatment, or condition of dentures.
- Submission of incorrect x-rays.

Fraud or mistakes are usually detected during the usual processing or review procedures prior to payment by the following:
1. Review of prior treatment against present treatment.
2. Completion or review of dental charts, checking prior work, existing work, and present or proposed work.
3. Verification of tooth numbers and positions.
4. Verification of dates of services and charges.
5. Checking for date of first visit and age of claimant.
6. Checking for erasures and changes of pen color, and other indications of changes.
7. Reviewing post-treatment x-rays.
8. Evaluating treatment plan by use of x-rays rather than rationale or facts supplied by the dentist. Rationale should be used to supplement x-rays and not as the sole determinant of benefits.
9. Verifying services with claimant.

There are several methods of determining misrepresentation has occurred. Before any steps are taken, the file should be reviewed by the supervisor and the dental consultant.

Post-operative x-rays should be obtained to show satisfactory completion of the work. This is not conclusive evidence one way or the other, since the wrong x-rays can be submitted.

Oral exams by outside dentists are the best method of determining what work has actually been performed. In cases involving large amounts, it may be helpful to request the examining dentist to take x-rays as a record of any discrepancies. It may also be wise to duplicate the pre-operative x-rays before returning them to the attending dentist.

In a few instances, an on-site claim representative may examine the dentist's records. This method should be used judiciously and only for the purpose of verifying dates of treatment and whether duplicate services were rendered.

In all dealings of potential fraud with either claimants or dentists, it is important not to accuse anyone without adequate proof. Mistakes can easily be made in completing a claim form, and every effort should be made to rule this out. The Supervisor or

Administrator should always be advised prior to taking any action.

The rules regarding documentation of the claim file, which were previously discussed in relation to medical claims, apply to dental claims also. Basically, if the information was not written down, the services are deemed not to have happened.

entails several steps, including verifying eligibility, determining whether services rendered are covered, identifying any limitations that may exist on coverage. After all preliminary investigation is complete, the processing of the claim can be completed.

The basic steps just covered should enable you to process claims with the highest degree of accuracy and in the least amount of time.

Summary

When a claim for dental services is received, it is the responsibility of the claims examiner to determine whether the claim received is eligible for payment. This

Assignments

Complete the Questions for Review.
Complete Exercises 33 – 1 to 33 - 6.

Questions for Review

Directions: Answer the following questions without looking back into the material just covered. Write your answers in the space provided.

1.   What is the first thing that the claims examiner should check upon receipt of a claim form?_____

_____

2.   The claim payment worksheet is equivalent to an _____

_____

3.   How do you determine the appropriate unit value for a dental service? _____

_____

4.   How do you determine the allowable amount for a procedure? _____

_____

_____

5.   Why is it important to update the payment history upon completion of the calculation sheet? _____

_____

If you were unable to answer any of the questions, refer back to the section and then complete the answers.

Exercise 33 - 1

Directions: Using the ADA Dental Code List on page **333** and the Dental Conversion Factor chart on page **394**, calculate UCR for the following procedures. Use the conversion factor for zip code **94325**.

Description	Proc.Code	Units	Conv. Factor	Amount
1. Adult prophylaxis				
2. Gold inlay, one surface				
3. Complete upper denture				
4. Composite filling, tooth #28, 2 surfaces				
5. Excise benign tumor, 1.45 cm				
6. Bitewing x-rays, 5 films				
7. Sodium fluoride treatment				
8. Apical curettage				
9. Upper bridge w/2 chromo clasps w/rests, acrylic base				
10. Pulp vitality test				
11. Amalgam filling, primary tooth #F, 3 surfaces				
12. Single x-ray film				
13. Extraction, tooth #21				
14. Oral exam w/2 x-rays				
15. Porcelain metal crown				

Exercise 33 - 2

Directions: Using the ADA Dental Code List on page **333** and the Dental Prevailing Conversion Factor chart on page **394**, calculate UCR for the following procedures. Use the conversion factor for zip code **90020**.

Description	Proc.Code	Units	Conv.Factor	Amount
1. Adult prophylaxis				
2. Gold inlay, one surface				
3. Complete upper denture				
4. Composite filling, tooth #28, 2 surfaces				
5. Excise benign tumor, 1.45 cm				
6. Bitewing x-rays, 5 films				
7. Sodium fluoride treatment				
8. Apical curettage				
9. Upper bridge w/2 chromo clasps w/rests, acrylic base				
10. Pulp vitality test				
11. Amalgam filling, primary tooth #F, 3 surfaces				
12. Single x-ray film				

13. Extraction, tooth #21   _____ ____ _____ _____
14. Oral exam w/2 x-rays   _____ ____ _____ _____
15. Porcelain metal crown   _____ ____ _____ _____

Exercise 33 - 3

Directions: Using the ADA Dental Code List on page **333** and the Dental Prevailing Conversion Factor chart on page **394**, calculate UCR for the following procedures. Use conversion factor for zip code **93504**.

Description	Proc.Code	Units	Conv.Factor	Amount
1. Adult prophylaxis	_____	____	_____	_____
2. Gold inlay, one surface	_____	____	_____	_____
3. Complete upper denture	_____	____	_____	_____
4. Composite filling, tooth #28, 2 surfaces	_____	____	_____	_____
5. Excise benign tumor, 1.45 cm	_____	____	_____	_____
6. Bitewing x-rays, 5 films	_____	____	_____	_____
7. Sodium fluoride treatment	_____	____	_____	_____
8. Apical curettage	_____	____	_____	_____
9. Upper bridge w/2 chromo clasps w/rests, acrylic base	_____	____	_____	_____
10. Pulp vitality test	_____	____	_____	_____
11. Amalgam filling, primary tooth #F, 3 surfaces	_____	____	_____	_____
12. Single x-ray film	_____	____	_____	_____
13. Extraction, tooth #21	_____	____	_____	_____
14. Oral exam w/2 x-rays	_____	____	_____	_____
15. Porcelain metal crown	_____	____	_____	_____

Exercises 29 – 1 to 29 - 4

Directions: Process each of the dental services claims found on the following pages.

Honors Certification™

The Honors Certification™ challenge for this chapter is a written test of the information contained within this chapter. Each incorrect answer will result in a deduction of between 1% and 5% from your grade. You must achieve a score of 85% or higher to pass this test. If you fail the test on your first attempt you may retake the test one additional time. The items included in the second test may be different from those in the first test.

ADA Dental Claim Form

CLAIM DENT1

HEADER INFORMATION

1. Type of Transaction (Check all applicable boxes)

☐ Statement of Actual Services – OR – ☒ Request for Predetermination/Preauthorization

☐ EPSDT/Title XIX

2. Predetermination/Preauthorization Number

PRIMARY PAYER INFORMATION

3. Name, Address, City, State, Zip Code

BALL INSURANCE CARRIERS
3895 BUBBLE BLVD., STE 283
BOXWOOD, CO 85926

OTHER COVERAGE

4. Other Dental or Medical Coverage? ☒ No (Skip 5-11) ☐ Yes (Complete 5-11)

5. Subscriber Name (Last, First, Middle Initial, Suffix)

6. Date of Birth (MM/DD/CCYY)

7. Gender ☐ M ☐ F

8. Subscriber Identifier (SSN or ID#)

9. Plan/Group Number

10. Relationship to Primary Subscriber (Check applicable box) ☐ Self ☐ Spouse ☐ Dependent ☐ Other

11. Other Carrier Name, Address, City, State, Zip Code

PRIMARY SUBSCRIBER INFORMATION

12. Name (Last, First, Middle Initial, Suffix), Address, City, State, Zip Code

MURDOCK, MARIA
9876 MARABAN LANE
MONTROSE, CA 92318

13. Date of Birth (MM/DD/CCYY) 08/23/55

14. Gender ☐ M ☒ F

15. Subscriber Identifier (SSN or ID#) 111-22-3333

16. Plan/Group Number 112233

17. Employer Name XYZ CORPORATION

PATIENT INFORMATION

18. Relationship to Primary Subscriber (Check applicable box) ☐ Self ☐ Spouse ☒ Dependent Child ☐ Other

19. Student Status ☒ FTS ☐ PTS

20. Name (Last, First, Middle Initial, Suffix), Address, City, State, Zip Code

MURDOCK, MAGGIE
9876 MARABAN LANE
MONTROSE, CA 92318

21. Date of Birth (MM/DD/CCYY) 02/16/90

22. Gender ☐ M ☒ F

23. Patient ID/Account # (Assigned by Dentist)

RECORD OF SERVICES PROVIDED

	24. Procedure Date (MM/DD/CCYY)	25. Area of Oral Cavity	26. Tooth System	27. Tooth Number(s) or Letter(s)	28. Tooth Surface	29. Procedure Code	30. Description	31. Fee
1	07/02/03					D0220	1 SINGLE FILM	13 00
2	07/02/03					D0230	1 ADDTL X-RAY	7 00
3	08/13/03			3		D3330	ROOT CANAL TREATMENT	390 00
4	07/02/03					D1120	PROPHYLAXIS	50 00
5								
6								
7								
8								
9								
10								

MISSING TEETH INFORMATION

34. (Place an 'X' on each missing tooth)

Permanent: 1 2 3 4 5 6 7 8 9 10 11 12 13 14 15 16 / 32 31 30 29 28 27 26 25 24 23 22 21 20 19 18 17

Primary: A B C D E F G H I J / T S R Q P O N M L K

32. Other Fee(s)

33. Total Fee 460 00

35. Remarks

AUTHORIZATIONS

36. I have been informed of the treatment plan and associated fees. I agree to be responsible for all charges for dental services and materials not paid by my dental benefit plan, unless prohibited by law, or the treating dentist or dental practice has a contractual agreement with my plan prohibiting all or a portion of such charges. To the extent permitted by law, I consent to your use and disclosure of my protected health information to carry out payment activities in connection with this claim.

X _Maria Murdock_

Patient/Guardian signature   Date

37. I hereby authorize and direct payment of the dental benefits otherwise payable to me, directly to the below named dentist or dental entity.

X _____

Subscriber signature   Date

BILLING DENTIST OR DENTAL ENTITY (Leave blank if dentist or dental entity is not submitting claim on behalf of the patient or insured/subscriber)

48. Name, Address, City, State, Zip Code

MABLE MILLER, DDS
1895 MYRTLE ROAD
MONTROSE, CA 92309

49. Provider ID

50. License Number MM98234789

51. SSN or TIN 95-1234567

52. Phone Number (818) 555 - 1234

ANCILLARY CLAIM/TREATMENT INFORMATION

38. Place of Treatment (Check applicable box) ☒ Provider's Office ☐ Hospital ☐ ECF ☐ Other

39. Number of Enclosures (00 to 99) Radiograph(s) 0 Oral image(s) 0 Model(s) 0

40. Is Treatment for Orthodontics? ☒ No (Skip 41-42) ☐ Yes (Complete 41-42)

41. Date Appliance Placed (MM/DD/CCYY)

42. Months of Treatment Remaining

43. Replacement of Prosthesis? ☒ No ☐ Yes (Complete 44)

44. Date Prior Placement (MM/DD/CCYY)

45. Treatment Resulting from (Check applicable box) ☐ Occupational illness/injury ☐ Auto accident ☐ Other accident

46. Date of Accident (MM/DD/CCYY)

47. Auto Accident State

TREATING DENTIST AND TREATMENT LOCATION INFORMATION

53. I hereby certify that the procedures as indicated by date are in progress (for procedures that require multiple visits) or have been completed and that the fees submitted are the actual fees I have charged and intend to collect for those procedures.

X _Mable Miller_

Signed (Treating Dentist)   Date

54. Provider ID

55. License Number MM98234789

56. Address, City, State, Zip Code

1895 MYRTLE ROAD
MONTROSE, CA 92309

57. Phone Number (818) 555 -1234

58. Treating Provider Specialty

ADA. Dental Claim Form

CLAIM DENT2

HEADER INFORMATION

1. Type of Transaction (Check all applicable boxes)

☐ Statement of Actual Services – OR – ☒ Request for Predetermination/Preauthorization

☐ EPSDT/Title XIX

2. Predetermination/Preauthorization Number

PRIMARY PAYER INFORMATION

3. Name, Address, City, State, Zip Code

BALL INSURANCE CARRIERS
3895 BUBBLE BLVD., STE 283
BOXWOOD, CO 85926

OTHER COVERAGE

4. Other Dental or Medical Coverage? ☒ No (Skip 5-11) ☐ Yes (Complete 5-11)

5. Subscriber Name (Last, First, Middle Initial, Suffix)

6. Date of Birth (MM/DD/CCYY) 7. Gender ☐ M ☐ F 8. Subscriber Identifier (SSN or ID#)

9. Plan/Group Number 10. Relationship to Primary Subscriber (Check applicable box)
☐ Self ☐ Spouse ☐ Dependent ☐ Other

11. Other Carrier Name, Address, City, State, Zip Code

PRIMARY SUBSCRIBER INFORMATION

12. Name (Last, First, Middle Initial, Suffix), Address, City, State, Zip Code

MURDOCK, MARIA
9876 MARABAN LANE
MONTROSE, CA 92318

13. Date of Birth (MM/DD/CCYY) 14. Gender 15. Subscriber Identifier (SSN or ID#)
08/23/55 ☐ M ☒ F 111-22-3333

16. Plan/Group Number 17. Employer Name
112233 XYZ CORPORATION

PATIENT INFORMATION

18. Relationship to Primary Subscriber (Check applicable box)
☐ Self ☐ Spouse ☒ Dependent Child ☐ Other

19. Student Status ☒ FTS ☐ PTS

20. Name (Last, First, Middle Initial, Suffix), Address, City, State, Zip Code

MURDOCK, MAEDEAN
9876 MARABAN LANE
MONTROSE, CA 92318

21. Date of Birth (MM/DD/CCYY) 22. Gender 23. Patient ID/Account # (Assigned by Dentist)
07/21/86 ☐ M ☒ F

RECORD OF SERVICES PROVIDED

	24. Procedure Date (MM/DD/CCYY)	25. Area of Oral Cavity	26. Tooth System	27. Tooth Number(s) or Letter(s)	28. Tooth Surface	29. Procedure Code	30. Description	31. Fee
1	08/28/03					D0274	4 BW X-RAY & EXAM	25 00
2	08/28/03					D0275	3 ADDTL X-RAY	10 00
3	08/28/03					D1120	PROPHY	24 00
4	09/11/03			2	BOL	D2387	COMPOSITE	74 00
5	09/11/03			4	MOD	D2387	COMPOSITE	74 00
6	09/11/03			5	DO	D2386	COMPOSITE	64 00
7	09/06/03			14	BOL	D2387	COMPOSITE	74 00
8	09/06/03			18	BO	D2386	COMPOSITE	64 00
9	09/11/03			31	BO	D2386	COMPOSITE	64 00
10								

MISSING TEETH INFORMATION

34. (Place an 'X' on each missing tooth)

Permanent
1 2 3 4 5 6 7 8 9 10 11 12 13 14 15 16
32 31 30 29 28 27 26 25 24 23 22 21 20 19 18 17

Primary
A B C D E F G H I J
T S R Q P O N M L K

32. Other Fee(s)

33. Total Fee 473 00

35. Remarks

AUTHORIZATIONS

36. I have been informed of the treatment plan and associated fees. I agree to be responsible for all charges for dental services and materials not paid by my dental benefit plan, unless prohibited by law, or the treating dentist or dental practice has a contractual agreement with my plan prohibiting all or a portion of such charges. To the extent permitted by law, I consent to your use and disclosure of my protected health information to carry out payment activities in connection with this claim.

X *Maria Murdock*
Patient/Guardian signature   Date

37. I hereby authorize and direct payment of the dental benefits otherwise payable to me, directly to the below named dentist or dental entity.

X _____
Subscriber signature   Date

BILLING DENTIST OR DENTAL ENTITY (Leave blank if dentist or dental entity is not submitting claim on behalf of the patient or insured/subscriber)

48. Name, Address, City, State, Zip Code

MABLE MILLER, DDS
1895 MYRTLE ROAD
MONTROSE, CA 92309

49. Provider ID 50. License Number 51. SSN or TIN
MM98234789 95-1234567

52. Phone Number (818) 555 - 1234

ANCILLARY CLAIM/TREATMENT INFORMATION

38. Place of Treatment (Check applicable box)
☒ Provider's Office ☐ Hospital ☐ ECF ☐ Other

39. Number of Enclosures (00 to 99)
Radiograph(s) ☐ 0 Oral image(s) ☐ 0 Model(s) ☐ 0

40. Is Treatment for Orthodontics?
☒ No (Skip 41-42) ☐ Yes (Complete 41-42)

41. Date Appliance Placed (MM/DD/CCYY)

42. Months of Treatment Remaining

43. Replacement of Prosthesis? ☒ No ☐ Yes (Complete 44)

44. Date Prior Placement (MM/DD/CCYY)

45. Treatment Resulting from (Check applicable box)
☐ Occupational illness/injury ☐ Auto accident ☐ Other accident

46. Date of Accident (MM/DD/CCYY) 47. Auto Accident State

TREATING DENTIST AND TREATMENT LOCATION INFORMATION

53. I hereby certify that the procedures as indicated by date are in progress (for procedures that require multiple visits) or have been completed and that the fees submitted are the actual fees I have charged and intend to collect for those procedures.

X *Mable Miller*
Signed (Treating Dentist)   Date

54. Provider ID 55. License Number MM98234789

56. Address, City, State, Zip Code
1895 MYRTLE ROAD
MONTROSE, CA 92309

57. Phone Number 818) 555 -1234 58. Treating Provider Specialty

©American Dental Association, 2002
J515 (Same as ADA Dental Claim Form) – J516, J517, J518, J519

ADA Dental Claim Form

CLAIM DENT3

HEADER INFORMATION

1. Type of Transaction (Check all applicable boxes)

[ ] Statement of Actual Services – OR – [X] Request for Predetermination/Preauthorization

[ ] EPSDT/Title XIX

2. Predetermination/Preauthorization Number

PRIMARY PAYER INFORMATION

3. Name, Address, City, State, Zip Code

WINTER INSURANCE CO.
9763 WESTERN WAY
WHITTIER, CO 82963

OTHER COVERAGE

4. Other Dental or Medical Coverage? [X] No (Skip 5-11)   [ ] Yes (Complete 5-11)

5. Subscriber Name (Last, First, Middle Initial, Suffix)

6. Date of Birth (MM/DD/CCYY)	7. Gender [ ]M [ ]F	8. Subscriber Identifier (SSN or ID#)

9. Plan/Group Number

10. Relationship to Primary Subscriber (Check applicable box) [ ] Self [ ] Spouse [ ] Dependent [ ] Other

11. Other Carrier Name, Address, City, State, Zip Code

PRIMARY SUBSCRIBER INFORMATION

12. Name (Last, First, Middle Initial, Suffix), Address, City, State, Zip Code

OWEN, ORVILLE
1000 OSWALD STREET
OJAI, CA 93051

13. Date of Birth (MM/DD/CCYY)	14. Gender	15. Subscriber Identifier (SSN or ID#)
06/03/50	[X]M [ ]F	000-55-0000

16. Plan/Group Number	17. Employer Name
1000001	ABC CORPORATION

PATIENT INFORMATION

18. Relationship to Primary Subscriber (Check applicable box) [ ] Self [ ] Spouse [X] Dependent Child [ ] Other

19. Student Status [X] FTS [ ] PTS

20. Name (Last, First, Middle Initial, Suffix), Address, City, State, Zip Code

OWEN, ODELL
1000 OSWALD STREET
OJAI, CA 93051

21. Date of Birth (MM/DD/CCYY)	22. Gender	23. Patient ID/Account # (Assigned by Dentist)
02/28/95	[X]M [ ]F	

RECORD OF SERVICES PROVIDED

	24. Procedure Date (MM/DD/CCYY)	25. Area of Oral Cavity	26. Tooth System	27. Tooth Number(s) or Letter(s)	28. Tooth Surface	29. Procedure Code	30. Description	31. Fee
1	05/12/03					D0220	1 SINGLE FILM	13 00
2	05/12/03					D0230	4 ADDITIONAL X-RAYS	28 00
3	05/12/03					D4220	1 GINGIVAL CURETTAGE U/R	90 00
4	06/09/03					D1120	PROPHYLAXIS	50 00
5	05/12/03					D0110	COMPLETE ORAL EXAM	30 00
6								
7								
8								
9								
10								

MISSING TEETH INFORMATION

34. (Place an 'X' on each missing tooth)

Permanent: 1 2 3 4 5 6 7 8 9 10 11 12 13 14 15 16 / 32 31 30 29 28 27 26 25 24 23 22 21 20 19 18 17

Primary: A B C D E F G H I J / T S R Q P O N M L K

32. Other Fee(s)

33. Total Fee 211 00

35. Remarks

AUTHORIZATIONS

36. I have been informed of the treatment plan and associated fees. I agree to be responsible for all charges for dental services and materials not paid by my dental benefit plan, unless prohibited by law, or the treating dentist or dental practice has a contractual agreement with my plan prohibiting all or a portion of such charges. To the extent permitted by law, I consent to your use and disclosure of my protected health information to carry out payment activities in connection with this claim.

x *Orville Owen*

Patient/Guardian signature   Date

37. I hereby authorize and direct payment of the dental benefits otherwise payable to me, directly to the below named dentist or dental entity.

x _____

Subscriber signature   Date

BILLING DENTIST OR DENTAL ENTITY (Leave blank if dentist or dental entity is not submitting claim on behalf of the patient or insured/subscriber)

48. Name, Address, City, State, Zip Code

OLIVER O'SHEA, DDS
2711 ORNATE BLVD.
OJAI, CA 93055

49. Provider ID	50. License Number 10001	51. SSN or TIN 95-0000000

52. Phone Number (000) 555 - 0000

©American Dental Association, 2002
J515 (Same as ADA Dental Claim Form) – J516, J517, J518, J519

ANCILLARY CLAIM/TREATMENT INFORMATION

38. Place of Treatment (Check applicable box) [X] Provider's Office [ ] Hospital [ ] ECF [ ] Other

39. Number of Enclosures (00 to 99) Radiograph(s) 0 Oral Image(s) 0 Model(s) 0

40. Is Treatment for Orthodontics? [X] No (Skip 41-42) [ ] Yes (Complete 41-42)

41. Date Appliance Placed (MM/DD/CCYY)

42. Months of Treatment Remaining

43. Replacement of Prosthesis? [X] No [ ] Yes (Complete 44)

44. Date Prior Placement (MM/DD/CCYY)

45. Treatment Resulting from (Check applicable box) [ ] Occupational illness/injury [ ] Auto accident [ ] Other accident

46. Date of Accident (MM/DD/CCYY)

47. Auto Accident State

TREATING DENTIST AND TREATMENT LOCATION INFORMATION

53. I hereby certify that the procedures as indicated by date are in progress (for procedures that require multiple visits) or have been completed and that the fees submitted are the actual fees I have charged and intend to collect for those procedures.

x *Oliver O'Shea*

Signed (Treating Dentist)   Date

54. Provider ID	55. License Number 10001

56. Address, City, State, Zip Code

2711 ORNATE BLVD.
OJAI, CA 93055

57. Phone Number (000) 555 -0000	58. Treating Provider Specialty

ADA Dental Claim Form   CLAIM DENT4

HEADER INFORMATION

1. Type of Transaction (Check all applicable boxes)
   ☐ Statement of Actual Services -- OR -- ☒ Request for Predetermination/Preauthorization
   ☐ EPSDT/Title XIX

2. Predetermination/Preauthorization Number

PRIMARY PAYER INFORMATION

3. Name, Address, City, State, Zip Code

WINTER INSURANCE CO.
9763 WESTERN WAY
WHITTIER, CO 82963

OTHER COVERAGE

4. Other Dental or Medical Coverage? ☒ No (Skip 5-11) ☐ Yes (Complete 5-11)

5. Subscriber Name (Last, First, Middle Initial, Suffix)

6. Date of Birth (MM/DD/CCYY)   7. Gender ☐ M ☐ F   8. Subscriber Identifier (SSN or ID#)

9. Plan/Group Number   10. Relationship to Primary Subscriber (Check applicable box) ☐ Self ☐ Spouse ☐ Dependent ☐ Other

11. Other Carrier Name, Address, City, State, Zip Code

PRIMARY SUBSCRIBER INFORMATION

12. Name (Last, First, Middle Initial, Suffix), Address, City, State, Zip Code

OWEN, ORVILLE
1000 OSWALD STREET
OJAI, CA 93051

13. Date of Birth (MM/DD/CCYY) 06/03/50   14. Gender ☒ M ☐ F   15. Subscriber Identifier (SSN or ID#) 000-55-0000

16. Plan/Group Number 1000001   17. Employer Name ABC CORPORATION

PATIENT INFORMATION

18. Relationship to Primary Subscriber (Check applicable box) ☒ Self ☐ Spouse ☐ Dependent Child ☐ Other   19. Student Status ☐ FTS ☐ PTS

20. Name (Last, First, Middle Initial, Suffix), Address, City, State, Zip Code

OWEN, ORVILLE
1000 OSWALD STREET
OJAI, CA 93051

21. Date of Birth (MM/DD/CCYY) 06/03/50   22. Gender ☒ M ☐ F   23. Patient ID/Account # (Assigned by Dentist)

RECORD OF SERVICES PROVIDED

	24. Procedure Date (MM/DD/CCYY)	25. Area of Oral Cavity	26. Tooth System	27. Tooth Number(s) or Letter(s)	28. Tooth Surface	29. Procedure Code	30. Description	31. Fee
1	04/03/03					D0210	FULL MOUTH X-RAY	45 00
2	07/06/03			17		D7230	EXT.-PART BONE	175 00
3	07/06/03			18	O	D2140	ALLOY	40 00
4	07/20/03					D4341	PERIO ROOT PLANING	38 00
5	07/20/03					D4341	PERIO ROOT PLANING	38 00
6	07/25/03					D4341	PERIO ROOT PLANING	38 00
7	07/25/03					D4341	PERIO ROOT PLANING	38 00
8	08/03/03					D1110	PROPHY	45 00
9								
10								

MISSING TEETH INFORMATION

34. (Place an 'X' on each missing tooth)

Permanent: 1 2 3 4 5 6 7 8 9 10 11 12 13 14 15 16
32 31 30 29 28 27 26 25 24 23 22 21 20 19 18 17

Primary: A B C D E F G H I J
T S R Q P O N M L K

32. Other Fee(s)

33. Total Fee 457 00

35. Remarks

AUTHORIZATIONS

36. I have been informed of the treatment plan and associated fees. I agree to be responsible for all charges for dental services and materials not paid by my dental benefit plan, unless prohibited by law, or the treating dentist or dental practice has a contractual agreement with my plan prohibiting all or a portion of such charges. To the extent permitted by law, I consent to your use and disclosure of my protected health information to carry out payment activities in connection with this claim.

x *Orville Owen*
Patient/Guardian signature   Date

37. I hereby authorize and direct payment of the dental benefits otherwise payable to me, directly to the below named dentist or dental entity.

X
Subscriber signature   Date

BILLING DENTIST OR DENTAL ENTITY (Leave blank if dentist or dental entity is not submitting claim on behalf of the patient or insured/subscriber)

48. Name, Address, City, State, Zip Code

OSCAR ORTIZ, DDS
4444 OLSEN BLVD.
ORANGE, CA 92711

49. Provider ID	50. License Number 13331	51. SSN or TIN 95-3333333

52. Phone Number (000) 555 - 3333

ANCILLARY CLAIM/TREATMENT INFORMATION

38. Place of Treatment (Check applicable box) ☒ Provider's Office ☐ Hospital ☐ ECF ☐ Other

39. Number of Enclosures (00 to 99) Radiograph(s) 0 Oral Image(s) 0 Model(s) 0

40. Is Treatment for Orthodontics? ☒ No (Skip 41-42) ☐ Yes (Complete 41-42)

41. Date Appliance Placed (MM/DD/CCYY)

42. Months of Treatment Remaining   43. Replacement of Prosthesis? ☒ No ☐ Yes (Complete 44)   44. Date Prior Placement (MM/DD/CCYY)

45. Treatment Resulting from (Check applicable box) ☐ Occupational illness/injury ☐ Auto accident ☐ Other accident

46. Date of Accident (MM/DD/CCYY)   47. Auto Accident State

TREATING DENTIST AND TREATMENT LOCATION INFORMATION

53. I hereby certify that the procedures as indicated by date are in progress (for procedures that require multiple visits) or have been completed and that the fees submitted are the actual fees I have charged and intend to collect for those procedures.

X *Oscar Ortiz*
Signed (Treating Dentist)   Date

54. Provider ID   55. License Number 13331

56. Address, City, State, Zip Code

4444 OLSEN BLVD.
ORANGE, CA 92711

57. Phone Number (000) 555 -3333   58. Treating Provider Specialty

©American Dental Association, 2002
J515 (Same as ADA Dental Claim Form) -- J516, J517, J518, J519

Appendix 33 - 1

Dental Prevailing Conversion Factors

The following list of Dental Prevailing Conversion Factors is intended to be used for training and reference purposes only, since the individual company or plan guidelines may differ from those stated. Because all exercise manual claims are within the state of California, only California conversion factor codes are listed.

State: California

Area	Zip Codes	A. Diagnostic And Preventive	B. All Other Excl. Gold Restorations, Crowns, Prosthetics	C. Gold Rest Crowns, Prosthetics
Los Angeles, Long Beach, Code 900	900-918	40.00	41.75	37.35
San Diego, Code 920	920-921	34.00	36.50	33.00
San Bernardino, Riverside, Palm Springs, Code 922	922-925	35.00	36.50	31.75
Orange County, Code 926	926-928	40.00	41.00	35.00
Ventura, Santa Barbara, Code 930	930-931	35.75	38.25	33.50
San Francisco, Oakland, San Jose, Code 940	940-951	40.00	41.25	36.00
Sacramento, Stockton, Code 952	952-953, 956-958	35.75	35.00	30.75
Other California	932-937, 939, 954, 955, 959-966	35.75	35.25	31.00